MUSEUMS AND COMMUNITIES

This book
was published
in cooperation with
the American
Association of
Museums.

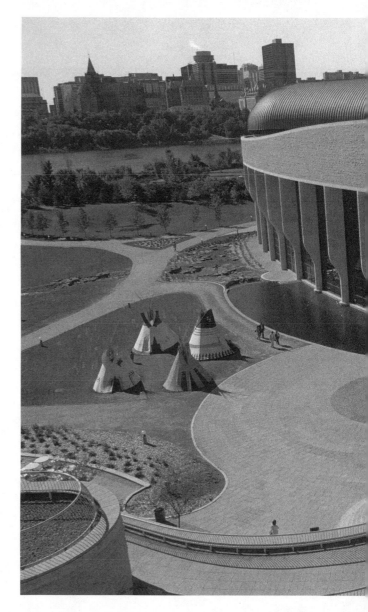

MUSEUMS AND

Edited by

Ivan Karp,

Christine Mullen Kreamer,

and Steven D. Lavine

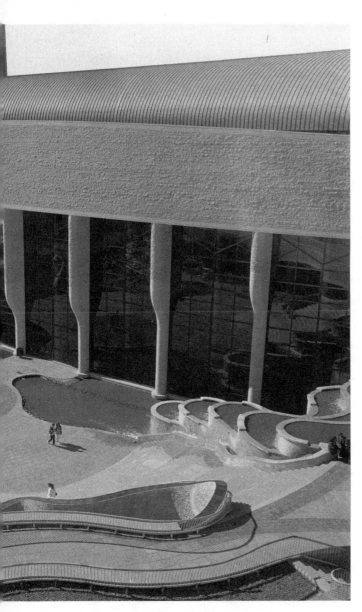

The
Politics
of Public
Culture

Smithsonian
Institution
Press
Washington
and London

COMMUNITIES

Portions of chapter 3 first appeared, in different form, as "The Multicultural Paradigm," reprinted from *High Performance* magazine, 1641 18th Street, Santa Monica, CA 90404, vol. 12, no. 3, Fall 1989, and "Acculturation vs. Frontierization," *Visions* 3, no. 4 (1989), and are reproduced here with permission.

Designed by Linda McKnight.
Edited by Susan Warga.
Production editing by Rebecca Browning.

Library of Congress Cataloging-in-Publication Data
Museums and communities : the politics of public culture / edited by Ivan Karp, Christine Mullen Kreamer, and Steven D. Lavine.
    p.   cm.
   Includes bibliographical references.
   ISBN 1-56098-164-4 (cloth).—ISBN 1-56098-189-x (paper)
   1. Museums—Planning—Congresses. 2. Public relations—Museums—Congresses. 3. Museum techniques—Congresses. I. Karp, Ivan. II. Kreamer, Christine Mullen. III. Lavine, Steven, 1947– .
AM5.M928   1992
069.5—dc20   91-31648

British Library Cataloging-in-Publication Data is available.

Manufactured in the United States of America.

5 4 3 2

96 95 94 93

∞The paper used in this publication meets the minimum requirements of the American National Standard for Permanence of Paper for Printed Library Materials Z39.48-1984.

On the cover and title page: Exterior view of the Grand Hall of the Canadian Museum of Civilization, depicting the melting glaciers at the end of the Ice Age. Photo by Stephen Alsford, courtesy of the Canadian Museum of Civilization.

Contents

Acknowledgements

The essays in this volume were presented at a conference entitled Museums and Communities, held at the International Center of the Smithsonian Institution 21–23 March 1990. Museums and Communities was the second of two conferences on the presentation and interpretation of cultural diversity in museums. Proceedings of the first conference appear in Ivan Karp and Steven D. Lavine, eds., *Exhibiting Cultures: The Poetics and Politics of Museum Display* (Washington, D.C.: Smithsonian Institution Press, 1991). Both conferences were sponsored by the Rockefeller Foundation and, at the Smithsonian, by the International Directorate, the Offices of the Assistant Secretaries for Museums and Research, and the National Museum of Natural History and its Department of Anthropology.

At the Rockefeller Foundation, Alberta Arthurs, director for arts and humanities, encouraged this project from its inception; Ellen Buchwalter, Rose Marie Minore, Carol Bowen, and Tomas Ybarra-Frausto provided patient logistical assistance and advice throughout.

At the Smithsonian Institution, Robert McC. Adams, Francine Berkowitz, David Challinor, Zahava Doering, Tom Freudenheim, Elaine Heumann Gurian, Christine Helms, Robert Hoffmann, John Reinhart, and Ross Simons supported the project. We are grateful to Robert McC. Adams for delivering the opening remarks at the conference. We thank Cheryl LaBerge, director of the Office of Conference Services, Karen Hanson, and Sheri Price for their support throughout the event. Robert Leopold watched over the conference and coordinated the preparation of the manuscript.

Throughout this project we have benefited from the advice of scholars and museum professionals, many of whom participated in planning sessions as well as in the conference. In addition to the authors themselves, these include Maria Acosta-Colon, Donald Cosentino, Zahava Doering, Michael Fischer, Hilde Hein, Mary Jane Hewitt, Corinne Kratz, Hillel Levine, Joanne Malatesta Davidoff, Roger Mandle, Steve Prystupa, Doran Ross, Betsy Quick, Anthony Seeger, Allen Sekula, Jim Sims, Kathy Dwyer Southern, Rowena Stewart, and Michael Watts.

Rebecca Browning, of the Smithsonian Institution Press, guided the preparation of this book, and Susan Warga, more co-editor than copy editor, graciously edited the individual contributions, critiqued drafts of the introductions, and tried to keep us intellectually honest.

Ivan Karp wishes to thank the present and past directors of the National Museum of Natural History, Frank Talbot and Robert Hoffmann, and the present and past chairs of the Department of Anthropology, Donald Ortner and Adrienne Kaeppler, for enabling this project to go forward. He would also like to thank Cory Kratz for commenting on each and every draft of the two introductions he wrote and not sparing him her criticism.

Christine Mullen Kreamer would like to thank her colleagues at the August 1989 Salzburg seminar on Museums and Community for their insights and support for this project. In addition, she would like to thank her husband, Ross G. Kreamer, for his unflagging enthusiasm in this and all other endeavors.

Steven D. Lavine gratefully acknowledges Judy McGinnis of the California Institute of the Arts for her careful attention to this project in the midst of myriad other responsibilities; Alberta Arthurs for her example and encouragement to think through the realistic possibilities of institutional change; and above all his wife, Janet Sternburg, who took time from her own writing and film activities to stimulate, share, and help refine his thinking on this subject, as on so many others.

Introduction: Museums and Communities: The Politics of Public Culture

IVAN KARP

I n 1988 and 1990 the Rockefeller Foundation and the Smithsonian Institution convened two conferences charged with examining how museums exhibit cultures and relate to the multiple communities in which they are situated. This volume is composed of papers from the second conference. In the first conference, published as *Exhibiting Cultures: The Poetics and Politics of Museum Display*,[1] we considered how cultural diversity is collected, exhibited, and managed. Examples ranged from cosmopolitan art museums through world's fairs and folklife festivals. The essays were often cross-cultural, discussing topics such as the assumptions that organize Japanese exhibiting and the decolonization of the museum system in a "new nation," Zimbabwe. Many of the papers were concerned with exhibition contents and their associated politics. In the introduction we described exhibitions as political arenas in which definitions of identity and culture are asserted and contested.

The discussion of the poetics and politics of museum display illustrated how the selection of knowledge and the presentation of ideas and images are enacted within a power system. The sources of power are derived from the capacity of cultural institutions to classify and define peoples and societies. This is the power to represent: to reproduce structures of belief and experience through which cultural differences are understood. *Exhibiting Cultures* showed that this power does not work in the same way for all types of museums. Art museums privilege visual experience, while museums of cultural history and natural history produce exhibitions with more narrative content, and festivals claim to embody experience. These differences are an integral part of the poetics of exhibiting cultures, which was examined in the first volume. The papers related differences in how exhibitions communicate their messages to the political subtexts of the exhibiting process.

Differences among museums are not without their political implications. Communities attempting to gain access to museums connect to different types of museums in distinct ways. Some African American artists, for example, are suspicious of attempts to deconstruct the aesthetic canon. They want a place in art museums, not a world in which art museums no longer assert claims of excellence.[2] Natural-history and ethnographic museums present different problems. African American activists rightly argue that while these museums have not excluded them, they have denigrated African achievements. Here the community demand is not for a place in an accepted scheme, but for revision of the scheme itself.[3]

In *Exhibiting Cultures* we did not devote as much space to the equally political questions of how museums relate to the changing configurations of communities that surround them, ranging from the neighborhood to the nation-state, from groups defined in ethnic and racial terms to social classes. Only one section of that book, containing essays about the exhibition Hispanic Art in the United States: Thirty Contemporary Painters and Sculptors, confronted the question of relations between museums and communities as a major dimension of the politics of cultural institutions.[4] The essays in that section examined the issues that arise when a mainstream institution wishes to exhibit the art of a minority community. The debate over this exhibition raised fundamental questions about who controls the exhibition and collection processes, what happens when works of art from outside mainstream traditions are assimilated to the canon of dominant communities, and, finally, whose interests the multicultural activities of centrally placed museums actually serve.

None of these questions was highlighted in the first conference. The debates showed us, however, that the original title for our second conference, Museums and *Their* Communities, rested on the false assumption that the politics of museums and communities had easy solutions. We wanted to hold a conference on the changing ways museums manage relations with communities, but the act of possession inserted in our original title unconsciously reproduced the acquisitive relationship we challenged in the first volume's section on Hispanic Art in the United States.

The discussions and interventions from the floor at both conferences taught us that while exhibitions and collections were contested, they were not nearly so contested as relationships among diverse museums and diverse communities. Furthermore, the contests that swirl around exhibitions and collections have increasingly become contests over relations between museums and communities. Inspect recent issues of any major museum journal, such as *Museum News*. Its contents include such hot issues as the repatriation of Native American materials, the proper relationship between artists and exhibitors, and the sometimes conflicting responsibilities of boards of trustees to the public and to the mission and mandate of the institution. This is the stuff out of which current museum debates are fashioned.[5]

These debates take their coloration not from the specific activities of museums—"collecting, preserving, studying, interpreting, and exhibiting"[6]—but from the way in which these activities relate to the other institutions and communities that comprise the social order. When people enter museums they do not leave their cultures and identities in the coatroom. Nor do they respond passively to museum displays. They interpret museum exhibitions through their prior experiences and through the culturally learned beliefs, values, and perceptual skills that they gain through membership in multiple communities. What Stephen Weil says of the United States is true for the world: "While American museums may be exempt from taxes, they are in no way exempt from history."[7]

Every society can be seen as a constantly changing mosaic of multiple communities and organizations. Individual identities and experiences never derive entirely from single segments of society—from merely one of the communities out of which the complex and changing social order is made. An individual can in the space of a short time move from emphasizing the part of his or her identity that comes from membership in an ethnic community to highlighting his or her participation in a formal organization such as a professional society and then back to being an ethnic-community member again. We experience these identities not as all-encompassing entities but through specific social events: encounters and social settings where identities are made relevant by the people participating in them. Communities are often thought of as things and given thinglike names such as "the Irish," "the blacks," "the Jews," "the WASPs." But they are actually experienced as encounters in which cultures, identities, and skills are acquired and used. These settings can involve communal groups as small and intimate as the nuclear family or as large and institutional as the convention of a professional society. People form their primary attachments and learn to be members of society in these settings, which can be referred to collectively as the institutions of *civil society*.

Museums and communities make up only a portion of civil society, the complex of social entities in which we act out our lives and through which we fashion our identity. Civil society is a perennial topic in the social sciences and political theory. Periodically a "crisis in civil society" emerges in discourse and thinking about society, generally in periods of social upheaval. The best recent discussions of civil society have been inspired by the way Antonio Gramsci defines the functional differences between civil society and political society. For Gramsci the institutions of political society exercise coercion and control, while civil society creates hegemony through the production of cultural and moral systems that legitimate the existing social order. From this point of view, the cultural parallel to coercion and control is hegemonic relations. If Gramsci were writing in the 1990s, I believe that he would think of civil society both as a site for the production of hegemony, that is, as an intellectual and moral commitment to the way a society is ordered and governed, and as a site for contesting assertions about who has the right to rule and to define the different identities in society. This is how museums are perceived in this volume: as places for defining who people are and how they should act and as places for challenging those definitions.

The key point here is that the institutions of civil society can be thought about separately from the agencies of government specifically charged with social control, such as the police and the courts. Taking the police as an example, one would say that when police act in their capacity as officers of the law, investigating crime, maintaining order, and so on, they are acting as part of political society. When the police form a professional association, they are acting as members of civil society, concerned with promoting the identities and interests of police officers. While some museums in the United States may be part of local, state, or national governments, they are not part of political society; they remain agents of civil society.

Civil society includes such diverse forms of organization as families, voluntary associations, ethnic groups and associations, educational organizations, and professional societies. These are the social apparatuses responsible for providing the arenas and contexts in which people define, debate, and contest their identities and produce and reproduce their living circumstances, their beliefs and values, and ultimately their social order.[8]

Economic activities, social life, and cultural affairs are all constructed within civil society. The movements of persons from one identity and/or institution to another connect these forms of organization and their practices. Institutional identities often overlap. Our talk continually makes connections among the institutions of civil society. Someone comes not just from a family but from an "old English family" or an "Orthodox Jewish family." A person is not simply a lawyer but a "Harvard lawyer" or a "feminist lawyer." Art can be called "mainstream," "black," "Chinese," "modernist," or "primitive." The last characterization, for example, suggests (among other things) that the artist making the object lacks formal training in an institution of civil society known as an art school or academy.[9]

Sociologists, anthropologists, and observers of society from the time of Alexis de Tocqueville, Karl Marx, and Max Weber to the present have argued that the strength and resilience of a social order resides in the capacity of civil society to aid in shaping the direction of change. Civil society is the crucible in which citizenship is forged. As integral parts of civil society, museums often justify their existence on the grounds that they play a major role in expressing, understanding, developing, and preserving the objects, values, and knowledge that civil society values and on which it depends. Arguments about the social significance of museums assert that museums can provide services that other institutions cannot. As repositories of knowledge, value, and taste, museums educate, refine, or produce social commitments beyond those that can be produced in ordinary educational and civic institutions. For example, museums are sometimes held up as the antidote to the failure of families to engage in moral education—or so the argument goes. Underlying this line of thinking is the assertion that museums play a unique role in civil society.[10]

There is another side to civil society. It is not merely the benign agent of social reproduction and education. Its institutions can either support or resist definitions imposed by the more coercive organs of the state. Furthermore, elements of civil society need not fit amiably with one another. Class, ethnic, and racial conflict can be as characteristic of civil society as harmonious social reproduction. Commu-

nities are as often thought of as being separate and unequal as they are
tolerated and respected in civil society. Henry Ford, for example, set
up the Ford English School in Dearborn, Michigan,

> and compelled his foreign employees to attend it before and after
> work two days a week. . . . The first thing [they] learned in the Ford
> school was how to say, "I am a good American." Later the students
> acted out a pantomime which admirably symbolized the spirit of the
> enterprise. In this performance a great melting pot (labeled as such)
> occupied the middle of the stage. A long column of immigrant stu-
> dents descended into the pot from backstage, clad in outlandish garb
> and flaunting signs proclaiming their fatherlands. Simultaneously
> from either side of the pot another stream of men emerged, each
> prosperously dressed in identical suits of clothes and each carrying a
> little American flag.[11]

This is surely an image of civil society that asserts the value of some
communities over others and strives to define the direction of cultural
change. More than a mosaic of communities and institutions, civil
society is a stage, an arena in which values are asserted and attempts at
legitimation made and contested.

If civil society is a stage, then it has a script that the actors follow
or at least use as a basis for improvising their performances. This
script contains the social ideas of a society, the set of beliefs, assumptions, and feelings in terms of which people judge one another and
which they sometimes use to guide their actions. Social ideas often set
up hierarchies of moral values in which communities and institutions
are interpreted. Social ideas embody notions people have about their
differences and similarities, and these are organized in terms of which
is good and which bad, which superior and which inferior. As significant elements in civil society, museums articulate social ideas. They
define relations with communities whether they intend to or not. The
processes of making meaning and of negotiating and debating identity—localized in institutions such as museums—provide the unwrit-
ten, ever-changing constitution of civil society. The social ideas of civil
society are articulated and experienced through striving for consensus
and struggling against the imposition of identity. Museums are one of
a number of settings for these conflicting but simultaneously operating
processes, which make social ideas understandable, but not always
legitimate.

The very nature of museums as repositories for knowledge and
objects of value and visual interest makes them key institutions in the

production of social ideas in many nations. Museum collections and activities are intimately tied to ideas about art, science, taste, and heritage. Hence they are bound up with assertions about what is central or peripheral, valued or useless, known or to be discovered, essential to identity or marginal. The history of debates about identity and the mosaic of communities that could or should constitute civil society is the central issue to which the presentations and discussions in the Museums and Communities conference returned. Conference participants considered how museums could accommodate multiple communities in their programs and why this process is critical to the production of a civil society that accommodates diversity.

The essays in this volume are divided into three parts. Part 1, "On Civil Society and Social Identity," inquires into how people make and experience identity in civil society and how identity is manifested in forms of public culture ranging from museums in India to festivals in Minnesota. The essays argue that the making of identity and its manifestations are really just two ways of looking at one process. The present moment in North American and European museums, which is characterized by experiments with museum-community relations, is described in part 2, "Audience, Ownership, and Authority: Designing Relations Between Museums and Communities." This moment emerges out of a specific historical context in the United States and, we suspect, elsewhere. Part 3 of this volume, "Defining Communities Through Exhibiting and Collecting," shows that the interrogation of cultural diversity is not a new concern for museums, and that the process of asserting and questioning can be seen most clearly by looking at the multiple ways the same objects are made to stand for different identities; for example, at different places and at different times the same object can be a piece of art, a sign of a culture's place in an evolutionary hierarchy, a sign of heritage, or a mark of oppression. The essays examine how identity is asserted in exhibitions, how such assertions change over time and are affected by specific relations among museums and communities, and finally how the audience itself can assert its own identity as part of its experience of exhibitions.

Most of the essays in the volume concern cases from the United States. U.S. museum history shares many features in common with that of other industrialized nations. But what happens over the long term in Europe is often compressed in the United States. As a result, the historical changes and circumstances that have produced the current concern about the relationship between museums and communities can be seen in sharper outline here than elsewhere. No one has outlined the cultural history of American museums better than Neil Harris, the master of museum historiography. He provides a historical scheme that describes how this moment emerged. Harris depicts extraordinary transformations in museums' attitudes toward their audiences in the twentieth century.[12] These changes are visible in many ways—for example, museums that were content to do a survey of audience demographics now sponsor in-depth focus groups that elicit visitors' responses to and feelings about exhibitions.

Harris also demonstrates the degree to which the perceptions of museums have changed along with the institutions themselves. In the 1950s, Harris tells us, cultural historians wrote histories of museums that were "self-confident and optimistic." "Almost any institution that managed to survive . . . was admired, a tribute to sacrificing founders bent on combining the democratic genius with obvious needs for enlightenment, recreation, standardization, or reform."[13] The triumphalist history they told was a story of American modernization, a narrative of how cultural institutions helped to create the new forms of persons needed in industrial society.

Current writing on museums takes a more critical approach. Left-wing points of view hold that cultural institutions such as museums can be perceived as instruments of the elite that are used to assert class-based claims to interpret and control "high" culture. At the same time, attempts to democratize them and open them up have been critiqued from the right because these processes are thought to promote values that degrade the great works contained in museums.[14]

One factor that helped museums resist change has been what Harris describes as "a professional reluctance to see how museums were linked functionally with other units concerned with market share." This attitude operated primarily at the ideological level of self-definition, as Harris has shown elsewhere.[15] Actually, museums have always looked over their shoulders, albeit reluctantly, and been influenced by competing institutions of public culture, ranging from the world's fair to the department store and, more recently, the theme park. While this is not a line of influence that Harris traces, one could also add that museums have had their own influences on more commercial ventures: witness the way in which "total resort hotels" have been designed to attract clients by mimicking the cultural authority of the museum.[16]

Interestingly enough, the degradation argument, now perceived as a critique from the radical right outside of museums, was an attitude that flourished inside museums before World War I. Harris describes this earlier time as a period of "authoritarian condescension" in museums, when upper classes presumed to speak for others. This was a period in which museum authorities "acknowledged the values of popularity, but not its priority."

In the 1920s and 1930s museums became more interested in diverse audiences and sought to design environments better able to educate them. No one raised questions about how collections were made, about how they reinforced elite taste and standards, or about the claims to knowledge embodied by the curator or asserted through the authority of the exhibition. Harris refers to this time as the period of "authoritarian experimentalism."[17]

Increasing concern over commercial and financial considerations had produced by the 1960s another phase of museum history, which occured primarily in art museums. This was a period in which museums underwent a vast expansion, using market surveys to help them capture as large a share of the public's attention (and money) as possible. Harris sees museums as "absorbed by issues of reputation and promotion and [as a result] making some better accommodation to multicultural constituencies" that in general are poorly represented in museum staffs, collections, and exhibitions. I would add that the blockbuster art exhibition, which draws as large a public as possible into the museum (but usually for only that one time) is also characteristic of what Harris aptly terms "an age of populist deference," his third phase of museum history. As art museums go, so goes the museum world. Few major museums of any genre—natural history, cultural history, or science and technology—feel able to survive without public attention.

The impetus for museums to change their attitudes has often been economic, with members of the museum community arguing that their survival was at stake. The means of change have been social; major redefinitions of the audience were undertaken, and museums increasingly asserted that they were essential components of the social order. American art museums often justified their existence in the nineteenth century on the grounds that they exposed the urban working classes to objects that embodied "civilized" values. The result, museums claimed, was to make better citizens out of working men and women.[18]

But the claims museums make inevitably put them in a vulnerable position. Museums assert that they can compensate for the failures of other cultural institutions, such as schools, to perform the work of social reproduction. These assertions define the museum as one of the central institutions of civil society; they also make museums answerable for how well they educate and represent the citizens who compose society. In other words, the very roles that museums desire to play in civil society leave them open to accusations that they are responsible for features of the social order such as pervasive discrimination and injustice. As definitions of inclusion and exclusion become more negotiable, museums are asked to explain their history of exclusion, and to fashion inclusive ways of going about their work.

This brings us to what Harris identifies as the current phase of museum history. He points out that "deference was one thing, power another." Now, he argues, we live in an age of "existential scrutiny, one in which the institution stands in an unprecedented and often troublesome relationship to its previous sense of mission." For Harris this is a period in which cultural deconstruction dominates the museum playing field, as elsewhere. "Throughout our entire culture the canons of taste and the assumptions of scholarship have been challenged and challenged from within. There is no reason to believe that museums can be immune from this any more than universities, libraries, or medical schools."[19]

Perhaps. Harris seems to me too confident about the end of museum history and too sure about how the contests will conclude. History does not necessarily proceed in a straight line. Nor are all claims to authority necessarily bad. Furthermore, the challenges to authority made on behalf of communities can be surprising, even disturbing, and come at museums from unexpected directions. The secretary of the Smithsonian Institution was recently "startled," according to the newspapers, when he was asked while giving testimony to the Senate to justify the National Museum of American Art's revisionist exhibition The West as America, which treated portraits of frontier experience as ideological tracts.[20] In this instance an establishment attempt to set the historical record straight (as that museum saw it) was challenged by elected representatives of the American citizenry.

An acute moral dilemma is raised by the acknowledgement that museums have responsibilities to communities. What happens when one community makes a request that will inevitably oppress another community? Who actually speaks for a community? Are all demands equally valid? If not, what procedure should be set in place to adjudicate among them?[21]

The Smithsonian experience provides just a single instance of what is becoming a major issue for museums: how to manage the increasingly political relations between museums and communities. Repatriation is yet another case where communities are taking an intense interest in how museums conduct their affairs. Nor is this just a domestic issue in the United States. Museums with collections derived from overseas will soon have to justify their retention of the collections and their exhibition of them. Natural-history museums may be no more exempt than art museums. Biological type specimens are usually found in museums in the capital cities of wealthy, industrialized countries. Yet they are equally valuable to the scientific and museum communities of the states or countries in which they were acquired.

Harris is more than correct to assert that the relations between museums and audiences have also taken on more overtly political overtones, and that these relations take the form of questioning the claims to truth and beauty made by museums and their staff. The new relationship is not simply one in which museums make assertions and members of the audience challenge them. Claims to authority are countered by parallel claims made by different museum constituencies. A good example involves the fall 1990 meeting of the Smithsonian Institution Council, during which they considered problems of cultural diversity. On the very day that the council was meeting in the National Museum of Natural History, tours of the museum's exhibitions were being conducted by antievolutionist religious groups, who were enacting in the exhibit halls of the museum a diversity different from the kind the council was considering in another wing of the same building. But the claim to possess authoritative knowledge was no less apparent.

Political contests have the peculiar tendency of overflowing the boundaries that are designed to contain them. It is one thing for museums to try to broaden their audiences, and another for the public to claim the museum. The museum world tends to think of art museums as the site of controversy, but museums such as the National Museum of Natural History have had their moments as well. The claims made on the museum by different publics are instructive. Religious groups resist the assertions of science in the natural-history halls, while racial and minority groups resist the assertions about culture made in the anthropology halls.

The Smithsonian Institution has its apparatus for generating inclusion: it conducts audience surveys and has an outreach program, and the education departments of its museums schedule many community events. In spite of these efforts, different segments of the public demand more. Presently they claim the right to assert their communities' point of view in the essential activities of the museums. Stephen Weil is right: museums are not exempt from history, and the communities that have been eliminated from museums or denigrated by them now insist that museums rectify their errors—errors that can be viewed in out-of-date exhibit halls.

This is a historic moment, not a unique one. It is a time in which audiences are claiming their rights as diverse communities. The current period of "existential scrutiny" described by Neil Harris is as much a response of the museumgoing public to changing museum practice as museum practice has been a response to policy changes within museums. The nature of what museums do, and their claims to a particular status in civil society, only create the possibility for the situation they now confront. Changes in civil and political society outside museums often provide the actual impetus for community requests and demands to museums. It cannot be accidental that in the United States communities are asking museums to accommodate themselves to cultural diversity at the same time as the courts are reducing the scope of affirmative action programs. Changes in political society are channeling the battle for equal opportunity into the cultural sphere of civil society.

Suddenly, communities that have not previously been thought about as communities have sprung uninvited into museum deliberations. National museums may have to answer even to communities in other nations. These newly emergent communities raise questions that museums often do not have the experience to answer. Many of the essays in this volume ask the fundamental questions of how museum experience becomes a community issue, and how museums accommodate communities. The museum experience is supposed to be intensely private and personally transforming. Communities are the setting in which the skills for appreciating museums are acquired, but museums' audiences belong to many communities, often simultaneously. Part of the politics of museum-community relations involves the politics of asserting and legitimating claims to identity. People speak on behalf of collectivities about an experience that they also think of as essentially private and individual.

The best way to think about the changing relations between museums and communities is to think about how the *audience,* a passive entity, becomes the *community,* an active agent. This is a process in which self-appointed or delegated representatives of a community contest a museum's perspective by articulating a community point of view. This is not so new a phenomenon. Thomas Crow's important study *Painters and Public Life in Eighteenth-Century Paris* describes how the early salons became scenes of contestation, where different actors fought over who was to represent the public. At the same time as contemporaries described the audience as being composed of individual fragments, the audience also was assigned unitary opinions and a single will. Crow sees this paradox as part of a political contest:

> We can . . . arrive at empirical knowledge concerning the salon *audience* because an audience is by definition an additive phenomenon [that is, it can be counted]. . . . But what transforms an audience into a public, that is, a commonality with a legitimate role to play in justifying artistic practice and setting value on the products of that practice? The public . . . is a representation of the *significant* totality [of the audience] by and for someone. A public appears, with a shape and a will, via the various claims made to represent it; and when sufficient members of an audience come to believe in one or another of these representations, the public can become an important art-historical actor.[22]

A community can be one form of what Crow here calls a "public," a "commonality" for which someone presumes to speak. Many of the essays in this volume describe contests between communities and museums over who is to speak on behalf of and to the commonality. Speaking for and speaking to are often combined, since the right to speak often depends on the creation of community consciousness and a sense of identity and mission. This is the only way in which a public can become an actor.

Some of the most telling accounts in this volume describe claims to the right to speak on behalf of a community. Jack Kugelmass's penetrating account in part 3 of American Jewish tours to former Nazi concentration camps in Poland shows that there are major differences between individual visits and organized tours. The tours are controlled by people who serve as guides and interpreters. In this guise they act out the political meanings of the visit to the camps, interpret the past and contemporary Poland to the tourists, and attempt to fashion a consistent sense of identity and opinion in their clients. They seek to be the representatives of a public as much as the critics of the salon did in the eighteenth-century context described by Crow.

This involves a process of paring down multiple voices and complex identities into relatively clear identities and messages. It often involves challenges to accepted and sanctioned interpretations and wisdom, and often impassioned claims, counterclaims, and denials about who has the right to articulate a point of view. Vera Zolberg's account in part 1 of "contentious communities" of artists and museums, for example, describes the disputes between museums and artists about how to interpret the art displayed in museums.

No paper describes this political process better than Fath Davis Ruffins's history in part 3 of African American preservation efforts. She tells a complex story of resistance to hegemonic interpretations of African American life, the desire to tell an insider's story, competing claims over who has the right to represent African American experience, and finally, the development of a professional cadre of interpreters among curators and museum professionals. What Ruffins describes is a movement from outsider status vis-à-vis the museum to insider status within museums. It has had the consequence of putting former outsiders in the position of resisting the claims of other members of African American communities to speak on behalf of "the community." The political contests over who has the right to speak for whom are an inevitable result of the emergence of new communities that make claims on museums. This is how publics are created.

The acknowledgement by museums of the existence of publics entails the idea that these entities should be asked about their own opinions and interests and about the effects of exhibitions on their sense of who they are. Inevitably we will discover that audiences have multiple opinions and multiple identities. As a result, the audience becomes not a single commonality but many commonalities, called communities. The process Crow describes for eighteenth-century Paris has its parallels with Harris's history of museums in twentieth-century America. On one side are the museums, who query their audience about its beliefs, opinions, and desires; on the other side is the changing mosaic of communities, which seek to influence and control how museums act, what they examine, what they represent, and how they represent it.

This political process takes place in civil society. For communities, the struggle over identity is vital to their existence: they often feel that they live or die to the degree that they are accorded or denied social space. But museums are learning that members of communities are active agents. They can resist museum definitions of space and even redefine spaces in subversive ways.[23] Because museums are drawn into the process of according or denying identity to communities, they become embroiled in communities' struggles for public recognition. The intensity of these debates in museums are directly related to their prominence in civil society. As privileged agents of civil society, museums have a fundamental obligation to take sides in the struggle over identity (and indeed cannot avoid it). In fact, this struggle is essential to the life of civil society. The essays in this volume recognize the situation of museums and seek to interpret and explain the role of museums in civil society at the same time as they also seek to describe how museums are currently experimenting with models for living in civil society.

NOTES

1. See Ivan Karp and Steven D. Lavine, eds., *Exhibiting Cultures: The Poetics and Politics of Museum Display* (Washington, D.C.: Smithsonian Institution Press, 1991).

2. Patricia Failing, "Black Artists Today: A Case of Exclusion," *ARTnews,* Mar. 1989, 124–31.

3. This issue has recently crystallized around literature on the Egyptian roots of African and Western civilizations. For a summary of the current positions on this debate, see Joyce Mercer, "Nile Valley Scholars Bring New Light and Controversy to African Studies," *Issues in Higher Education* 7, no. 26 (1991), 1, 12–16.

4. See the following essays in Karp and Lavine, *Exhibiting Cultures:* Carol Duncan, "Art Museums and the Ritual of Citizenship"; Jane Livingston and John Beardsley, "The Poetics and Politics of Hispanic Art: A New Perspective"; and Tomas Ybarra-Frausto, "The Chicano Movement/The Movement of Chicano Art."

5. Museum professionals reading this passage may experience *déjà vu*. We have indeed been here before. In 1971 Stephen Weil delivered an address to the annual meeting of the Western Museums Association in which he described "the multiple crises in our museums." He examined three crises, involving money, power, and identity. The fiscal crisis is obvious and perennial. Crises of power crystallized in struggles among trustees, staff, artists, and communities. Crises of identity had to do not only with the future shape of the museum and its role as a definer of culture, but with the museum as an arena in which "forces contend to determine museum identity." Reflecting on his analyses in 1983, Weil saw himself as having been too caught up in current debate and too "millenarian." In 1992 it is possible that he would think that the 1970s have come around once again, for it now appears that his 1971 address needs little revision today. See Stephen E. Weil, *Beauty and the Beast: On Museums, Art, the Law, and the Market* (Washington, D.C.: Smithsonian Institution Press, 1983).

6. This list of museum goals is taken from Joseph Veatch Noble, "Museum Manifesto," *Museum News* 48, no. 8 (1970), 16–20. It is cited in Weil, *Beauty and the Beast,* 71.

7. See Weil, *Beauty and the Beast,* 3.

8. See Antonio Gramsci, *Selections from the Prison Notebooks of Antonio Gramsci,* ed. and trans. Quinton Hoare and Geoffrey Nowell Smith (New York: International Publishers, 1971). For an excellent discussion of how different authors' use of the concept of civil society compares to Gramsci's formulation, see Norberto Bobbio, "Gramsci and the Conception of Civil Society," in Chantal Mouffe, ed., *Gramsci and Marxist Theory* (London: Routledge and Kegan Paul, 1971).

9. See Ivan Karp, "High and Low Revisited," *American Art 5*, no. 3 (1991), 2–7, where I describe how producers of "low" art tend to be divided into two categories: the popular, savvy artist versus the naive, unconscious amateur. This is a way of distinguishing between commercial art and so-called folk or primitive art. It creates a false opposition between trained artists and spontaneous artists. The result is that so-called folk and primitive artists are presented as if they had not painstakingly acquired their skills or as if they had no predecessors.

10. See the fall 1990 issue of *New Perspectives Quarterly,* "The Stupidification of America," in which conservatives, liberals, and radicals debate the causes of the declining standards of American education. This is just the sort of debate in which museums increasingly insert themselves, and in terms of which they justify their existence. This line of reasoning has unexpected consequences. Museum professionals are uncertain whether museums should be repositories of objects or conduits of information. The very claims that museums increasingly make open them up to this sort of debate.

11. John Higham, *Strangers in the Land* (New York: Atheneum, 1973), 244, 247–48.

12. Neil Harris, "Polling for Opinion," *Museum News,* Sept./Oct. 1990, 46–53.

13. Ibid., 97.

14. For left-wing critiques, see, for example, Carol Duncan and Alan Wallach, "The Universal Survey Museum," *Art History* 3, no. 4 (1980), 448–69, and Lawrence Lavine, *Highbrow/Lowbrow: The Emergence of Cultural Hierarchy in America* (Cambridge, Mass.: Harvard University Press, 1988). For the critical right-wing position, see the arts writing found in such neoconservative journals as *The New Criterion.*

15. Neil Harris, *Cultural Excursions: Marketing Appetites and Cultural Tastes in Modern America* (Chicago: University of Chicago Press, 1990).

16. Ivan Karp and Corinne Kratz, "The Fate of Tippoo's Tiger: A Critical Account of Ethnographic Display" (Los Angeles: Getty Center for the History of Art and the Humanities, 1991).

17. Harris, "Polling for Opinion."

18. See Lavine, *Highbrow/Lowbrow* for a spirited account of how elites appropriated culture from the lower classes in nineteenth-century America. Stephen Weil points out that although the Metropolitan Museum of Art was started to make reproductions of European and classical art available to New York's working class, it was closed on Sunday "out of deference for the religious sensibilities of members of its board" (Weil, *Beauty and the Beast,* 4).

19. Harris, "Polling for Opinion."

20. "View of West Raises Hackles in Congress" read the headline in the *Philadelphia Inquirer* (16 June 1991).

21. These are not hypothetical questions. Each of them is raised by the current debate over the repatriation of Native American materials. There are cases in which two competing tribal groups have claimed the same objects. There are instances in which requests have been made in the name of religious sensibilities to exclude people from access to collections on the grounds of gender. All of these raise painful moral dilemmas and also produce situations that could conceivably engender resistance to lawful and morally correct requests from Native American communities. Civil society is never wholly coherent, and responsible persons are often forced to take difficult stands.

22. Thomas Crow, *Painting and Public Life in Eighteenth-Century Paris* (New Haven: Yale University Press, 1985), 5.

23. The best account of "everyday forms of resistance" is James Scott, *Weapons of the Weak: Everyday Forms of Peasant Resistance* (New Haven: Yale University Press, 1985).

PART I

On Civil Society and Social Identity

IVAN KARP

This部分... his part of the volume takes a broad perspective on museum-community relations. The essays in this section examine how identity is manifested and experienced in public culture, which includes settings such as museums and fairs. The examples include commercial expositions in India, minority museums in the United States, community festivals in Minnesota, and art museums in New York City. People come to these events and places to be edified, educated, and entertained, but these settings are also sites for the play of identity. Art, history, and ethnography displays, even natural-history exhibitions, are all involved in defining the identities of communities—or in denying them identity. Every one of these museum events and places are part of public culture, which can be shown to take on a large part of the responsibility of defining civil society.[1]

Public culture provides some relatively formal settings for definitions and experiences of identities, but public culture is only one forum in which people experience who they are. There are others. Identities are made and experienced in settings that differ from the social spaces of public culture in multiple ways. These other settings can include the intimacy of the family or the sacred quality of religious worship. No matter where or when identities are defined, they are acted out in ways that often contradict official definitions of a social group's identity. The way people perform their social roles shows more about how they feel about their identity than does the content of the roles themselves. And the way people perform their roles and express their individual feelings demonstrates that more than one identity enters into their actions. People know themselves to have more identities than they are allowed in a single setting, and these identities often overlap and even contradict one another.

The essays in part 1 discuss four aspects of the process of identity formation as these emerge in museum-community relations: (1) identities are defined by the content and form of public-culture events such as exhibitions and performances; (2) identities are subjectively experienced by people participating in public culture, often in ways conditioned by their other identities and experiences; (3) expressions of identities can contain multiple and contradictory assertions—that is, there can be more than one message in a single expression or performance of identity—and the same is true for the experience of identities; and (4) identities are rarely, if ever, pure and uncontaminated by other identities, because they are usually fabricated from a mix of elements.

There are many types of identities other than community identities, but this is a book devoted to museums and communities. Nonetheless, community identities cannot be discussed without first considering identity in general and the relationship between community identities and personal identities in particular. Even museum settings relate personal and community identities: consider Thomas Crow's analysis of how "the public" came to be defined in eighteenth-century Paris (discussed in the introduction to this volume). As Crow argues, the experience of visiting an exhibition and judging its materials is often intensely personal. But museum professionals or cultural activists who try to explain and account for the ways audiences experience and respond to exhibitions usually invoke collective entities: "She's Latino"; "He's middle-class"; "They're children." We believe that communities exist within us in some way, and that their values affect our perceptions and structure our own personal values. Hence, the individual experience of viewing a museum exhibition is also organized by memberships in (that is, identification with) communities.

This belief results at least in part from the ways personal identities and community identities interact. Personal identities are complex entities that are fashioned from community identities as well as other identities and experiences. Similarly, community identities emerge out of personal identities. There cannot be a community if there are no individuals who think of themselves as members of it. What Benedict Anderson says about nations, that they are *imagined* communities, is true of all communities.[2] In order for communities to exist in time and space, they must be imagined and represented by individuals as significant components of their identities.

Identities are not easily known or clearly experienced phenomena. Personhood, Meyer Fortes observes, poses problems that individuals have to solve.[3] These include formulating answers to the questions of how we know ourselves to be the persons we are supposed to be and how we display our personhood. These are questions frequently asked in the literature on personhood in anthropology and philosophy. They arise out of the distinction that is commonly made between the person (the socially defined aspect of the self) and the individual (the uniquely experienced side of the self). Thus personhood is a Janus-faced phenomenon. Individuals strive to be persons, attempting to fulfill expectations they have come to hold of what it is to play a role or be a member of a community. Ideals are often invoked in this process, and museums are clearly places where representations of such ideals are displayed. These ideals communicate messages about how persons should be defined; they set up models for behavior or display modes of being that are to be avoided.

In many cultural displays, ideals about the person are often asserted tacitly, derived from implicit contrasts between the viewers and makers of exhibitions, on the one hand, and the persons and cultures displayed in the exhibitions, on the other.[4] We might call this the ideological aspect of identity making. However, people think of themselves as being more than the sum total of their social roles and personhood. They also define themselves in terms of "those particular contingencies which make each of us 'I' rather than a copy or replica of somebody else."[5] This is the subjective aspect of identity. The person and the individual are always simultaneously cooperating and at war with each other. There is a parallel here with museum displays, which are one of the sites in which identities are made: here museums and communities simultaneously cooperate and do battle.

All of this (and more) enters into that element of museum-community relations that revolves around the play of identity. Museumgoers usually come to exhibitions with expectations about what they will find in museums; often they are disappointed at not finding their expectations realized or infuriated at seeing what they had hoped would be omitted.

Exhibition makers have parallel problems. They too have identities; these include their professional standing and commitments they have to serve the community. Exhibitions portray their makers' sense of how the world is defined. This sense is not unrelated to the role museums play as archives of knowledge and objects. Responsible museum personnel identify with the professional and curatorial obligations associated with this museum role, and seek to portray the social world in terms that honor their sense of purpose and identity. Yet they are also members of communities, and bring to their world personal and communal histories that often relate to and interact with the histories of the communities that compose the constituency of their museums. This complex situation creates a postmodern problem for museums. First, they must fashion exhibitions that can present multiple perspectives on the world. Then they must ensure that those perspectives respect but also are critical of not only museums' own worldview but also the worldview of the people whose lives, culture, knowledge, and objects they are exhibiting. This will require exhibitions that encompass all aspects of cultural experience, both the typical (a culture or community's ideas of what it is to be a person, to be a member of that culture or community) and the unique (what it is to be an individual in that culture or community and have experiences that are different from another's).[6]

The essays collected in this section all address these central issues of identity formation. Some focus on personhood and identity, some on exhibitions, and some on both. Appadurai and Breckenridge's essay shows how colonial displays in Indian museums are interpreted by postcolonial Indian audiences in ways that go far beyond the images presented in the exhibitions themselves. While colonial messages and postcolonial interpretations engage and contradict each other, the multiplicity of identities that are asserted and experienced in museum exhibitions are affected by a set of interpretive processes that derive less from museums themselves than from other aspects of public culture in India today.

Appadurai and Breckenridge argue that public culture is changing rapidly in India. It is becoming a site for the production of a national culture that is particularly important for a society in which the other institutions of civil society, such as schools, are often in direct competition with the state. Aspects of public culture in postcolonial India such as television, films, advertising, commercial expositions, and tourism developed not sequentially but simultaneously, and in a world in which physical distance is rarely any longer a barrier to inter-action among different ethnic and national groups. As a result, an aesthetic of viewing has emerged that is at once transnational and In-dian. Appadurai and Breckenridge argue that the Indian public ap-plies this aesthetic, rather than different sets of interpretive skills, to these different forms of public culture.[7] Consequently the distinction between "serious" and "popular" culture that we in Europe and North America tend to make is not particularly relevant for Indian audi-ences' experience of museum exhibitions.[8] In a sense Appadurai and Breckenridge's vision of the Indian public is George MacDonald's nightmare vision of the North American future—one in which the public cannot distinguish between the educational messages created by exhibition makers and the trivializations of culture perpetrated by the popular media in the name of commercialization (see his essay in part 2). Yet there are differences, for Appadurai and Breckenridge be-lieve that what is important in India is the very way in which the var-ious forms of public culture affect one another and the way they combine local, national, and transnational elements. The result of these conflicting and contradictory identities and histories is a truly hybrid cultural formation. But the existence of this hybrid should not be shocking, for all cultural formations are hybrid. Appadurai and Breckenridge's achievement is to show the historical contexts and pat-terns of mixing that make Indian public culture what it is today.

Edmund Barry Gaither's essay also examines the multiple nature of identities in museums. His is a passionate plea to acknowledge the role museums can play in the reconstruction of civil society. But he as-serts that we must also acknowledge the complex nature of peoples' identities and, by implication, the histories of their communities. Gai-ther rejects simple distinctions between assimilation and separatism; for example, people have the capacity to be both African American and American at the same time. The problem is not how people choose identities, but the checkered history of how those identities have been manifested in civil society and exhibited in museums.

James Baldwin elegantly describes how African Americans have subjectively experienced the public denial of their identity (which Gai-ther calls "silences") in a way that illuminates the suspicion many Afri-can Americans and other minority peoples feel toward museums:

It is a very grave matter to be forced to imitate a people for whom you know—which is the price of your performance and survival—you do not exist. It is hard to imitate a people whose existence appears, mainly, to be made tolerable by their bottomless gratitude that they are not, thank heaven, you.[9]

The silences do more than simply deny African American existence. In exhibitions that celebrate cultural achievement, the very fact that the achievements of people of color are ignored introduces implicit messages about their worth. A hierarchy of cultures is erected, in which those worth examining are separated from those that deserve to be ignored. Racial imagery and ethnocentrism can be communicated by what is not exhibited as well as by what is. Large, historically important museums, such as the universal survey art museums, now have to face the consequences of their history of silence. Communities are often no longer content to remain passive recipients of museum activities. At the very least they demand to be included in the celebration of cultural achievements.

Hierarchical assertions of cultural differences tell a story that has a disturbing history with contemporary ramifications for all museums, even those that do not have older exhibit halls badly needing revision. African American and other ethnic museums have had to engage in tasks that involve more than simply filling in the silences of other museums' exhibitions and educational activities. As Fath Davis Ruffins's essay in part 3 on African American preservation activities demonstrates, these museums have been involved in combating racist imagery and in reconstructing self-identities and knowledge about heritage and achievements that have become attenuated in many communities. Gaither supports John Kinard's call for the museum to act as an agent of redemption in society (see Ruffins's essay). But Gaither believes that not only minority communities will be redeemed by minority museums. The challenges minority museums present to larger, more well established museums will inevitably result in those museums changing the stories they tell and reaching out to wider audiences. They will not only fill in the silences about major segments of American civil society and world cultures; they will also correct the messages they deliver. Let us hope so. A major reason for Gaither's optimism is that he believes minority museums will create a new cadre of museumgoers who will demand more from the older museums. As the composition of museums' constituencies changes, so will the nature of museums' participation in civil society. Gaither's hopes also rest upon his belief in the capacity of people to make the effort to identify with what they see in museums—if they are given the chance to do so and if the exhibition provides support and encouragement. This identification will be only the beginning; curiosity and a desire for knowledge will follow, and museums are the natural entities for satisfying these desires, thus producing more knowledgeable citizens.

Gaither advocates a positive role for museums in society. He envisions museums as crucibles for forging citizens who see themselves as part of civil society, as important members of a valid social order. Museums have the responsibility to compensate for the failure of other institutions, such as schools, to show members of minority groups their stake in society. Museums can play this role because they are spaces for the play of identities, and the multiple nature of those identities can be made part of museums' exhibitions and programs. For Gaither, museums that serve communities with multiple identities, such as African American museums, are now important locations for innovative practices that will show the way for mainstream museums to expand their constituencies and reform their exhibiting and educational programs.

Guillermo Gómez-Peña defines identities in a way that goes beyond thinking about them as multiple and complex. Assertions about identity may attempt analytically to disentangle and separate out components of a particular community's identity and try to show how people shift from one identity to another, but this interpretation ignores the perspective from the margins. The making of identities is as intrinsically "syncretic, diverse, and complex as the fractured realities we are trying to define." Gómez-Peña writes from the border, that is, from the point of view of people who continuously melt down, merge, and amalgamate seemingly incommensurate senses of identity and points of view. He calls for the acknowledgement of a new "world topography," which implies a way of seeing that acknowledges that the margins are actually the center, that the center is continually shifting, and that it is the task of the artist to bring out the hybrid and dynamic nature of these fractured realities.

Gómez-Peña appears to be taking a postmodern position—to be arguing that the goal of the artist should be not to reproduce the dominant aesthetic but to resist it, and to celebrate the particular stories through which people make spaces in a world that seems determined to organize everything for them.[10] Yet Gómez-Peña denies any affinity with postmodernism: "Postmodernism is a crumbled conceptual architecture, and we are tired of walking among someone else's ruins."

He desires to replace postmodernist critique with "experimental techniques and . . . practices to intervene directly in the world." This is a political position that recognizes that today's margin may be tomorrow's center, and that to be at the center is to reproduce the structure of hegemony. His are subtle but penetrating observations. Gómez-Peña acknowledges that power is always a danger and can be fought only with politics. All hegemonic assertions, which are embedded in definitions of the canon and criteria of taste, must be fought with "creative appropriation, expropriation, and subversion of dominant cultural forms."

Assertions of cultural centrality are also assertions of hegemony for Gómez-Peña. The claim that any artist is centered in his or her culture, often made about Latino and African American artists, is a hegemonic claim that seeks to prevent the search for new content and for an art that is against "monoculturalism." Such claims implicitly define a canon against which other works of art or forms of culture will be judged. The result is that the hierarchical structure of evaluations set up by dominant cultures is reproduced in minority and subordinate cultures. Gómez-Peña counsels resistance. "To step outside one's culture equals to walk outside of the law," he says, "but it also means to maintain one's dignity outside the law." This is an ideal, not a possibility. What Gómez-Peña envisions is a stance that does not blindly accept the world as being defined by the tenets of any single culture. Such dominating practices have no place on the border.

For museums, this implies that exhibitions that claim to present true and authentic pictures of peoples and their cultures—that attempt to define what is essentially African or American or English or Mexican—are hegemonic practices that reproduce the values and privileges of the center. Gómez-Peña denies all claims to the privileged possession of any experience, whether it be ethnic, racial, or artistic.

Gómez-Peña counters Gaither's call for reconstruction with a demand for perpetual deconstruction. He is leery of the way in which claims to cultural authenticity (that is, being a source for the correct cultural traditions) can also be strategies of oppression. What should museums do, for example, with the assertion that Native American religious traditions require that women not be allowed to touch tribal objects in museums? This has already happened. If museums have no right to assert a dominant perspective vis-à-vis minorities, what rights do they have to assert any perspective about anyone? Gómez-Peña's answer, with which I agree, is that neither museums nor communities should have special interpretive privileges. Rather, they must be mutually responsible. Museum practices should be reviewed continually and judged in terms of multiple perspectives. Just as museums have the obligation to examine the consequences of their own exhibiting and educational practices, so communities have the responsibility to see that exhibitions about themselves are more than celebratory.

All types of museums have responsibilities to communities. These matters are not just the special preserve of cultural-history or ethnic and minority museums. Art and science museums have the same obligations as the others. Science museums, for example, usually define themselves as possessing privileged access to verifiable truths. But science is as partial a perspective on the world as any other. Like any other body of knowledge, it can be used in a hegemonic fashion.[11] Even the seemingly innocent and uncriticizable demand that natural-history museums play a major role in advocating environmental concerns should be critically evaluated, for far too often in the history of the environmental movement, unconfirmed facts and the selection of issues that are mostly white and middle-class concerns get presented as the outcome of "scientific research." This is yet another situation in which Western points of view assume a falsely universal significance. Sadly, these points of view can become the justification for doing a great deal of harm to the rural poor and the native peoples of the Third World. For example, a recent exhibition on the highland gorilla and its status as an endangered species, which toured the major natural-history museums of the United States, uncritically reproduced some of the most offensive racial stereotypes about the sexuality of Africans. Yet not a single public protest was made by any responsible scientific institution, nor was there any mention of the racial imagery and attitudes in the reviews of the exhibition.[12] If museum professionals take up Gómez-Peña's challenge, the cultural assumptions they will have to confront critically include their own. They too will have to walk outside their cultures and the law, with dignity.

Gómez-Peña's essay raises questions about multiple perspectives, the hybrid nature of expression, and politics that are addressed in more detail in the remaining two essays in this section. Robert Lavenda and Vera Zolberg both consider a number of issues directly related to how identities are defined in exhibitions and how these definitions are experienced by the different parties in the exhibiting process. These issues include how perspectives define different voices, even when people have more than one perspective and claim more than one voice at the same time; the ambivalence that is present in communities about the role of the museum or festival as a certifier of culture; and questions of control as a primary political issue. This last issue is one that museums and communities must continuously manage and renegotiate, and it is a central concern of parts 2 and 3 of this book. Part 2 contains case studies of exhibitions that allow power to be shared by museums and communities, and part 3 uses a historical perspective to look at exhibiting contexts as sites for contestation between museum and community or even community and community.

Robert Lavenda's essay, "Festivals and the Creation of Public Culture: Whose Voice(s)?" questions cherished assumptions held by the general public and the museum community about the nature of communities. Lavenda examines community festivals in Minnesota, a state where the local festival is a flourishing enterprise. Festivals are generally held to be special events in which everyday cares and social differences are put aside and people interact as part of the larger community to which they belong.[13] Yet the communities that Lavenda examines are like all communities in the world: they are internally divided and made up of segments that have overlapping but sometimes different interests.

Lavenda describes festivals from many types of communities in Minnesota, from the smallest rural town to the large urban celebrations of St. Paul. His account shows that these festivals have a major shared problem that must be managed anew each and every year. While the festivals assert that they are the expression of a unified, inclusive community, they actually must find ways to deny or mask community diversity and patterns of exclusion. The forms of diversity that these community festivals manage vary according to the type of community; for example, rural towns are divided between farmers and merchants, the older, established members of the community and the unemployed or underemployed young, and sometimes between male and female. Though small-town festivals explicitly undertake the promotion of a communitywide identity, in practice they often reinforce social divisions. By contrast, St. Paul's long-established and nationally famous urban festival is a successful combination of celebration of bourgeois achievement and ritualized mockery of social pretensions. In Lavenda's description of the St. Paul Winter Carnival's events we can see a familiar phenomenon: the assertion of a common community of high and low that is achieved by the denial of social claims. This is an element missing in the formal organization of the small-town festivals. It may be that in small towns social relations are too intimate and face-to-face for the community even to imagine its differences in festivals. But even there multiple voices are manifested and different points of view expressed at the same time as their existence is denied.

In St. Paul issues of gender and class intrude on the organization
of festival performances. Vulcans, the anonymous pranksters who
mock the pretensions of the festival's royal court, also act out a carni-
valized denial of bourgeois standards of sexuality. But their playful ac-
costing of women is no longer acceptable in a society in which
violence against women has become a public issue. The wives of the
princes of the royal court are now included in the public ceremonies
as well, but Lavenda shows that the liberal assertions of gender com-
plementarity serve only to emphasize the actual gender inequality.
Wives make brief appearances that only demonstrate their irrelevance
to the celebration of individual male achievement that is at the heart
of the festival's public ceremonies.

Class differences and conflict intervene in all the festivals Lavenda discusses, but in the St. Paul case the class-based control of the
festival extends far beyond the control in the other Minnesota festivals described in the essay. The urban nature of the St. Paul milieu enables the organizers to have far less contact with lower-class audiences
than is possible in small towns. The St. Paul elite do not need to keep
their own activities secret, and the vast expenditures required for their
participation provide an effective barrier against lower-class groups
penetrating their events.

But this creates a problem. After all, the St. Paul Winter Carnival
is a *community* festival. How is community participation maintained
at the same time that segments of the community are excluded? This
has become a gender issue as well as a class issue. As St. Paul becomes
more diverse, it may become a racial and ethnic issue as well. Lavenda
examines how this problem is managed in all the Minnesota festivals
by describing how voices are defined and experienced.

The voices Lavenda discusses have both official and unofficial
sides. The festivals are defined by official voices, but even those voices
can express doubt, as in the halfhearted attempts to give wives a significant role. In St. Paul the institutionalized mockery of the Vulcans
provides an official setting for unofficial attitudes to be voiced; here,
too, doubt and uncertainty creep in about how different segments of
the community have been defined and treated.

Sometimes people do begin to voice the ways in which their subjective experiences can contradict dominant voices or official definitions of cultures. This is now happening in some of the festivals
Lavenda mentions and in some museums. People know how they are
defined and often find means of resisting definitions. The result is that
voices and definitions become multiple and contradictory, but not ar-

bitrary. In some contexts people's responses are as hybrid as Gómez-Peña's concept of the border as a site for the production of culture would suggest. In other contexts conflict becomes an overt problem in relations between communities and cultural institutions.

Overt conflict between museums and a specific type of community, namely artists, is the theme of Vera Zolberg's essay. Zolberg describes relations between museums and a set of individuals, artists, who only occasionally come together to form a community. When they do, however, they often perceive themselves as being in opposition to the art museums whose job it is to exhibit them. Art museums also have complex senses of their mission and identity. Just as artists aspire to recognition and reputation, so do art museums. There are few directors of art museums who do not define their legacy as a distinguished collection. One major issue for artists and museums is the degree to which an art museum should define itself as an agent for the local artistic community. The more cosmopolitan the art museum, the more involved it becomes in the history of modern and contemporary art, which is usually represented as a history of artistic production in Paris and New York.

Zolberg's essay describes how artists in other major cities, including Washington and Chicago, have reacted against the history of art as it has been defined by critics and museums. They also seek to resist the silences in terms of which they are defined. It may be that artists' most important experience in the process of defining themselves as a community is their interest in asserting their local existence in the art world.

Zolberg observes that "artists tend not to form durable communities." When they do so it is usually because they have a temporary sense of shared identity as a group that is resisting a definition of art and defining new modes of expression. Zolberg cites the dadaist tradition of flouting bourgeois conventions as a significant theme in contemporary arts and observes that this pits many artists against art museums, which have patrons who possess bourgeois taste and often assert bourgeois moral standards.

Even more important, however, is the tendency of many contemporary artists to subvert the categories of high and low cultural expression on which museums rely to construct an artistic canon. This conflict can be observed in the reactions to the Museum of Modern Art's massive but ambivalent attempt to exhibit the high and low distinction in modern art (the 1990 exhibition High and Low: Modern Art and Popular Culture). MOMA was attacked from both the artistic right and left; on the one hand, it was condemned for abandoning its role as guardian of aesthetic standards, and on the other it was condemned for castrating the best and most outrageous in popular arts in its exhibition. The curators' nervousness was manifested in the opening pages of the catalogue, which made multiple references to the religious quality of high art.[14]

Zolberg argues that museums do not like to deal with artists as a community, but attempt to interact with them as individuals. This is a classic response to community demands on cultural institutions. Institutions assert that these issues can be dealt with only on a case-by-case basis. Hence they deny the legitimacy of claims made by people who act as spokespersons for communities. I am not making a judgment here; I am describing a strategy. As this essay pointed out earlier, claims to speak on behalf of a community can also involve denying the interests of segments of that community. But the insistence that the issues are individual and not the community's also denies the claimed interests of the community. The cases discussed in this volume are political contests; hence it should not be surprising that the means of conducting business is political.

A major contribution of Zolberg's essay is to show how assertions or denials of identities in museum-community relations are political processes. Museums are certifiers of taste and definers of cultures. As such, they are intimately involved in the task of defining identities and setting up schemes that classify and relate cultural identities. The way that museums are inserted in civil society and their power to produce cultural values make them an integral part of the processes by which cultures are placed into hierarchies that define them as superior or inferior to one another.

This need not be the fate of museums. They are also repositories of knowledge and objects; some do represent the range of human creativity. Even though the collections museums make are not comprehensive (how could they be?), they can strive to contain and exhibit the range of human communities, capacities, and artistic achievement. This task involves not just seeking out objects and cultural materials that are representative or stylistically central. It also involves engaging in dialogue with people who stand apart from their communities or who form different communities, and it involves seeking out objects and knowledge that can be used to deny essentializing assertions of identity. Most of all, however, the tasks of museums involve questioning their own claims about identity and engaging in serious and systematic dialogue with other points of view.

NOTES

1. *Public culture* is a term coined to describe forms of popular culture and more formal institutions such as museums. See Arjun Appadurai and Carol Breckenridge, "Why Public Culture?" *Public Culture* 1, no. 1 (1988), 5–9. (In the introduction to part 2 of this volume Steven Lavine refers to the literature on civic culture. This debate has nothing to do with the writings about public culture.)

2. See Benedict Anderson's *Imagined Communities: Reflections on the Origin and Spread of Nationalism* (London: Verso, 1983).

3. Meyer Fortes, *Religion, Morality, and the Person: Essays on Tallensi Religion,* ed. Jack Goody (Cambridge: Cambridge University Press, 1987), 122–23. Fortes's is the most relevant work on the relation between the person and the individual. Amelie Rorty's excellent collection of essays on the concept of personhood (*The Identities of Persons* [Berkeley: University of California Press, 1976]) covers the history of the philosophical debate over these matters.

4. See Ivan Karp, "Other Cultures in Museum Perspective," in Ivan Karp and Steven D. Lavine, eds., *Exhibiting Cultures: The Poetics and Politics of Museum Display* (Washington, D.C.: Smithsonian Institution Press, 1991), and Tony Bennett, "The Exhibitionary Complex," *New Formations* 4 (1988), 73–102.

5. Richard Rorty, *Contingency, Irony, and Solidarity* (Cambridge: Cambridge University Press, 1989), 25.

6. This raises the question of how to define authority. This is discussed in parts 2 and 3 of this volume, and extensively in the proceedings of the previous conference, published as Ivan Karp and Steven D. Lavine, eds., *Exhibiting Cultures: The Poetics and Politics of Museum Display* (Washington, D.C.: Smithsonian Institution Press, 1991). Multiple parties, each claiming authority, compete to control the content of exhibitions. Museums experiment with sharing power and means of distributing authority. Yet how authority is manifested in museums has not been investigated. In "The Fate of Tippoo's Tiger: A Critical Account of Ethnographic Display" (Los Angeles: Getty Center for the History of Art and the Humanities, 1991), Ivan Karp and Corinne Kratz begin to unpack museum assertions of authority by distinguishing between "ethnographic authority," which is exhibition-specific, and "cultural authority," which relates to the implicit claims museums make about their role in civil society.

7. A major difference between Appadurai and Breckenridge's argument and this introduction is that they believe that the subjective museum experience is far more collective in India than in the United States, while I have argued that the viewing experience tends to be inherently private. I think Appadurai and Breckenridge are focusing more on the shared criteria in terms of which

exhibitions are viewed rather than the actual act of viewing, which is what I believe is a private experience. But there are cultural differences between India and some Western settings. In the West art museums in particular invoke the sacred qualities of the church, while in India far more interaction is apparent in museum visits. But even in the West there are certain kinds of visits where the audience is inherently interactive. The hierarchically organized tour is one such kind of visit, and certainly parent-child visits are occasions for teaching and interaction. My point is that even interaction is only an approximate way of expressing an interior experience: viewing. There is always a space between what we experience and how we express it.

8. See Ivan Karp, "High and Low Revisited," *American Art 5*, no. 3 (1991), 2–7.

9. Cited in *Black Arts,* no. 136 (1991), 9. No reference provided.

10. See Lyotard's famous definition of the postmodern as "incredulity toward metanarratives" (Jean-François Lyotard, *The PostModern Condition* [Manchester: Manchester University Press, 1984], xxiv).

11. See the recent critical evaluations of natural science by Sandra Harding in *The Science Question in Feminism* (Ithaca: Cornell University Press, 1986), and by Donna Haraway in *Primate Visions* (London: Routledge, Chapman, and Hall, 1987). David Hull's recent study of the history of theory in biology (*Science As Process* [Chicago: University of Chicago Press, 1988]) shows how fundamentally politicized and personalized debates in classificatory biology have become.

12. The National Museum of Natural History was concerned enough to pull the most offensive picture, a blurry photograph of an African child that made him look like a monster. See *Gorilla: Struggle for Survival in the Virungas,* photographs by Michael Nichols and essay by George B. Schaller, ed. Nan Richardson (New York: Aperture, 1989), 44–45.

13. For a discussion of the problems inherent in this view and the politics of festivals in general, see part 4 of Karp and Lavine, eds., *Exhibiting Cultures,* and Karp's introductory essay in that section.

14. These reactions and assertions are discussed in Karp, "High and Low Revisited."

CHAPTER I

Museums Are Good to Think: Heritage on View in India

ARJUN APPADURAI AND CAROL A.
BRECKENRIDGE

One of the striking facts about complex societies such as India is that they have not surrendered learning principally to the formal institutions of schooling. In this type of complex society, urban groups tend to monopolize postsecondary schooling and the upper middle class tends to control the colleges and universities. In such societies, therefore, learning is more often tied to practical apprenticeship and informal socialization. Also, and not coincidentally, these are societies in which history and heritage are not yet parts of a bygone past that is institutionalized in history books and museums. Rather, heritage is a live component of the human environment and thus a critical part of the learning process. These observations are particularly worth noting since societies such as India are often criticized for having created educational institutions where learning does not thrive and where credentialism has become a mechanical mode for selection in an extremely difficult economic context. Informal means of learning in societies such as India are not, therefore, mere ethnographic curiosities. They are real cultural resources that (properly understood and used) may well relieve the many artificial pressures placed upon the formal educational structure. Museums are an emergent component of this world of informal education, and what we learn about museums in India will tell us much of value about learning, seeing, and objects, which in turn should encourage creative and critical approaches to museums (and informal learning arrangements in general) elsewhere.

Museums in India look simultaneously in two directions. They are a part of a transnational order of cultural forms that has emerged in the last two centuries and now unites much of the world, especially its urban areas.[1] Museums also belong to the alternative forms of modern life and thought that are emerging in nations and societies throughout the world. These alternative forms tend to be associated with media, leisure, and spectacle, are often associated with self-conscious national approaches to heritage, and are tied up with transnational ideologies of development, citizenship, and cosmopolitanism. Conducting an investigation of museums, therefore, entails being sensitive to a shared transnational idiom for the handling of heritage while simultaneously being aware that this heritage can take very different national forms.

MUSEUMS AND HERITAGE

Although there is a growing literature (largely by scholars outside the museum world) that concentrates on museums, collecting, objects, and heritage, these discussions do not generally extend to museums in India. Our concern is to build on a few recent efforts in this direction as well as some earlier ones,[2] so that comparative evidence from non-Western, postcolonial societies can be brought into the mainstream of theory and method in this area.

In anthropology, there is a renewed interest in objects, consumption, and collection more generally.[3] What emerges from the literature on this topic is that objects in collections create a complex dialogue between the classificatory concerns of connoisseurs and the self-reflective politics of communities; that the presence of objects in museums represents one stage in the objects' cultural biographies;[4] and that such classified objects can be critical parts of the "marketing of heritage."[5] Here we are reminded that objects' meanings have always reflected a negotiated settlement between longstanding cultural significations and more volatile group interests and objectives.

A related set of discussions explicitly links museums to material culture in a consciously historical way.[6] We are reminded that archaeological and ethnographical collections emerged out of a specific set of political and pedagogical aims in the history of anthropology;[7] that collections and exhibitions cannot be divorced from the larger cultural contexts of philanthropy and ethnic or national identity formation; that anthropologists and "natives" are increasingly engaged in a dialogue out of which cultural identity emerges; and that museums contribute to the larger process by which popular culture is formed. As far as India is concerned, museums seem less a product of philanthropy and more a product of the conscious agenda of India's British rulers, which led them to excavate, classify, catalogue, and display India's artifactual past to itself. This difference affects the ethos of Indian museums today, and also affects the cultural dynamics of viewing and learning.

Another relevant body of literature emphasizes the relationship between museums and their publics as well as their educational mission.[8] For the most part, these studies lack a sense of the historical and cultural specificity of the different publics that museums serve. While the public sphere has been most richly discussed in terms of the last three hundred years in Europe,[9] there are now a host of non-Western nations that are elaborating their public spheres—not necessarily ones that emerge in relation to civil society, but often ones that are the result of state policies in tandem with consumerist interests. Thus, there is a tendency in these discussions for the idea of "the public" to become tacitly universalized (though some of these studies are concerned with sociological variations within visitor populations). What is needed is the identification of a specific historical and cultural public, one which does not so much *respond* to museums but is rather *created,* in part, through museums and other related institutions. In India, museums need not worry so much about finding their publics as about making them.

There is, of course, a vast body of literature that is about art in relation to museums. This literature is not very relevant to the Indian situation because, except for a small minority in India and for a very short period of its history, and in very few museums there, art in the current Western sense is not a meaningful category. Art continues to struggle to find a (bourgeois) landscape it can be comfortable in.[10] In place of art, other categories for objects dominate, such as handicraft, technology, history, and heritage. Of these, the one on which we focus is the category of heritage.

History becomes heritage in various ways.[11] Artifacts become appropriated by particular historical agendas, by particular ideologies of preservation, by specific versions of public history, and by particular values about exhibition, design, and display. Tony Bennett's concept of "the exhibitionary complex"[12] and Donna Haraway's argument that natural history has the effect of naturalizing particular histories[13] both remind us that museums are deeply located *in* cultural history, on the one hand, and are therefore also critical places for the politics *of* history, on the other. Ideologies of preservation might frequently conceal implications for transformation.[14] For example, the effort to present vignettes of life from other societies often involves the decontextualization of objects from their everyday contexts, with the unintended result of creating aesthetic and stylistic effects that do not fit the original context. In other cases, objects that were parts of living dramas of warfare, exchange, or marriage become mechanical indicators of culture or custom. In yet other cases, the politics of cultural patrimony and political conquest are concealed in the technical language of ethnographic signage. All of these examples reveal a tension between the dynamic contexts from which objects were originally derived and the static tendencies inherent to museum environments. This is a valuable tension to bear in mind as we explore the context of museums in India, where the politics of heritage is often intense, even violent.

Among anthropologists, folklorists, and historians, there has recently been a spate of writing about the politics of heritage.[15] Much of this work suggests (in some cases using non-Euro-American examples) that the appropriation of the past by actors in the present is subject to a variety of dynamics. These range from the problems associated with ethnicity and social identity, nostalgia, and the search for "museumized" authenticity, to the tension between the interests states have in fixing local identities and the pressures localities exert in seeking to transform such identities. The result is a number of contradictory pressures, some toward fixing and stabilizing group identities through museums (and the potential of their artifacts to be used to emblematize existing or emergent group identities), and others that attempt to free and destabilize these identities through different ways of displaying and viewing objects.

This body of literature is a reminder that heritage is increasingly a profoundly political issue and one in which localities and states are often at odds, and that museums and their collections are in the midst of this particular storm. Focusing on the politics of heritage in India brings out the place of Indian museums in these politics, and problematizes the cultural modes of viewing, traveling, experiencing, and learning in which heritage is negotiated.

THE CULTURAL AND CONCEPTUAL BACKGROUND

The public sphere in contemporary India, as in the rest of the world, has emerged as part of the political, intellectual, and commercial interests of its middle classes. In India in the last century, this public sphere has involved new forms of democratic politics, new modes of communication and transport, and new ways in which class, caste, and livelihood are articulated. We are concerned with one dimension of this evolving public sphere, which we call public culture. By public culture we mean a new cosmopolitan arena that is a "zone of contestation."[16] In this zone, private and state interests, low and high cultural media, and different classes and groups formulate, represent, and debate what culture is (and should be). Public culture is articulated and revealed in an interactive set of cosmopolitan experiences and structures, of which museums and exhibitions are a crucial part.

On the surface, museums as modern institutions have only a short history and appear to emerge largely out of the colonial period:

> The museums started under British rule had been intended mainly for the preservation of the vestiges of a dying past, and only subsidiarily as a preparation for the future. Museums were the last haven of refuge for interesting architectural fragments, sculptures and inscriptions which saved them from the hands of an ignorant and indifferent public or from unscrupulous contractors who would have burned them to lime, sunk them into foundations or melted them down. Into the museums the products of the declining indigenous industries were accumulated, in the vain hope that they might serve as models for the inspiration of artisans and the public. Mineralogical, botanical, zoological and ethnological collections were likewise started, though rarely developed systematically: often they did not grow beyond sets of hunting trophies.[17]

As a consequence, until recently most museums in India have been moribund and have not been a vibrant part of the public cultural life of its people. One early analysis of this "failure" of museums in India comes from Hermann Goetz. The factors he identifies as reasons for this failure include the fragmentary nature of many collections, the failure of industrial art to inspire capitalist production, and the lack of response to natural-history collections by a public "still living in the world of myths."[18]

The ambiguous place of museums in India is partly a result of longstanding cultural and historical factors: first, India still has a living past found especially in its sacred places and spaces, so there is little need for "artificial" conservation of the Indian heritage; second, the separation of sacred objects (whether of art, history, or religion) from the objects of everyday life had not really occurred; and third, the separation of human beings from the overall biological, zoological, and cosmological environment in which they lead their ordinary lives had barely began.

More recently, museums have begun to play a more vigorous role in Indian public life. In part this is because of a renewed concern with education as one element of social and economic development; in part because private commercial enterprises have begun to use an exhibition format for displaying their wares; and in part because museums have become plugged into a circuit of travel, tourism, pilgrimage, and leisure that has its own distinctive history and value in Indian society.

Here it may be useful to make a historical contrast. Museums in Europe and the United States have been linked to department stores through a common genealogy in the great nineteenth-century world's fairs. But in the last century, a separation of art and science and of festivity and commerce has taken place in these societies, with the objects and activities in each category fairly sharply distinguished in terms of audience, curatorial expertise, and visual ideology. In India, such a specialization and separation is not a part of either the past or the present.

This is not to say that there are not department and chain stores in contemporary India. There are, and they are clearly distinguishable from public festivities as well as from permanent exhibits in museums. Rather, there is a gray zone where display, retailing, and festivity shade into one another. It is precisely because of this gray zone that museums have taken on fresh life: objects in India seem to flow constantly through the membranes that separate commerce, pageantry, and display. The two major forms that characterize the public world of special objects in contemporary India are the exhibition-cum-sale and the ethnic-national festival. The exhibition-cum-sale is a major mode of retailing textiles, ready-to-wear clothing, books, and home appliances. These merchandising spectacles (which recall the fairs of medieval Europe) are transient, low-overhead, mobile modes for transporting, displaying, and selling a variety of goods. In them, in contrast to department stores, ordinary consumers have a chance to combine gazing, longing, and buying. This combination of activities, which is at the core of the informal schooling of the modern Indian consumer, is bracketed between two other, more permanent poles.

One pole is the modern museum—whether of art, craft, science, or archaeology—in which the Indian viewer's visual literacy is harnessed to explicitly cultural and nationalist purposes. The other pole is the newly emergent, Western-style department store, where gazing and viewing also go on but buying is the normative goal. In our usage, *gazing* implies an open-ended visual and sensory engagement tied up with fantasy and desire for the objects on display, while *viewing* implies a more narrowly framed, signage-guided visual orientation.

Framing these three display forms and contributing most actively to the regeneration of the museum experience is the festival form, especially as it has been harnessed by the Indian state in its effort to define national, regional, and ethnic identity. Such festivals are on the increase throughout the world[19] and everywhere represent ongoing debates concerning emergent group identities and group artifacts.

In India, the museum-oriented Festival of India, first constructed in 1985 as a vehicle for the cultural display of India in foreign nations and cities, quickly became indigenized into a massive internal festival called Apna Utsav (Our Festival), which began in 1986 and now has an elaborate national and regional administrative structure. Part of a vast state-sponsored network for local and interregional displays of art, craft, folklore, and clothing, these spectacles of ethnicity are also influencing the cultural literacy and visual curiosity of ordinary Indians in a manner that gives further support to the reinvigoration of museums, on the one hand, and the vitality of exhibition-cum-sales, on the other. What is thus emerging in India, and seems to be a relatively specialized cultural complex, is a world of objects and experiences that ties together visual pleasure, ethnic and national display, and consumer appetite. Museums, marginal in the eyes of the wider Indian public in the last century, have taken on a new role in the last decade as part of this emergent constellation of phenomena.

This constellation, which may be called the "exhibition complex" (museum-festival-sale), is further energized by new technologies of leisure, information, and movement in contemporary India. Cinema and television (and the landscapes and stars that they display), packaged pilgrimages and tours (which take thousands of ordinary Indians outside their normal locales as part of "vacation" experiences), and the growing spectacularization of political and sports events (especially through television) all conduce to a new cosmopolitan receptivity to the museum, which would otherwise have become a dusty relic of colonial rule. It is these new contexts of public culture that are now transforming the Indian museum experience.

The photographs in this essay constitute a narrative parallel to the text. They provide a representative visual sample of the archive of visual experiences that Indian visitors bring to museums. They are meant to convey the points of contact between different segments of Indian visual reality, which range from film and television images to mythic and political scenarios, and constitute the "interocular field" within which the museum experience operates and to which we refer in the conclusion.

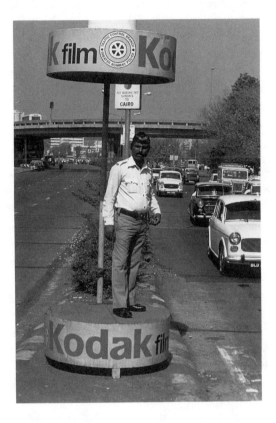

Fig. 1-1. The visual promise of Kodak film frames the disciplinary gaze of a traffic policeman. Bombay, 1989. Photo by the authors.

Museums in India have to be seen in tandem with exhibitions of several sorts, and as parts of a larger cosmopolitan world of leisure, recreation, and self-education for wide sectors of the Indian population. Nothing of this emergent cosmopolitanism can be grasped without also understanding the impact that modern modes of communication have had on Indian public life. Print media, especially newspapers and magazines, have a history going back over a century in India (as in the West) but the last decade has seen an explosion of magazines and newspapers (both in English and in the vernacular languages), which suggests both a quantum leap in Indian readers' thirst for news, views, and opinion and the eagerness of cultural producers to satisfy this thirst profitably. Film (both documentary and commercial) has a history in India that clearly parallels its history in the West, and remains today the dominant medium through which large numbers of Indians expend time and money allotted to entertainment. Television and its sister technology, video recordings, have entered India in a big way and constitute a new threat to the cultural hegemony of cinema, while at the same time they extend the reach of cinematic forms to the smaller towns and poorer citizens of India.

Though Indian television programming is controlled by the state (just as radio programming is), it already has a very large component of privately produced soap operas, docudramas, and other forms of televised entertainment. This is, of course, in addition to a fairly large amount of state-sponsored and state-controlled programming, which ranges from news programs (which are still largely state-controlled) to live sports programs, "cultural performances," and informational programs on everything from birth control to new farming techniques. In general, though a number of the most popular serials on Indian television are variations of the Hindi film formula, many television programs have a historical, cultural, or documentary dimension. In television above all, it is the Indian heritage that is turned into spectacle. The most striking examples of this process are the three most popular television series of the last few years: *Buniyaad,* which concerned the trials and tribulations of the partition of India as experienced by a large Punjabi extended family, and the television serializations of the two great Indian epics, the *Ramayana* and the *Mahabharata,* for the weekly broadcast of which the whole television-watching audience of India apparently dropped everything. Thus, museums are part of a generalized, mass-media-provoked preoccupation with heritage and with a richly visual approach to spectacles.

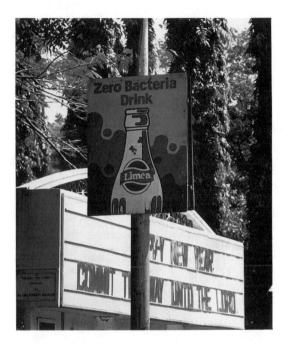

Fig. 1-2. The discourses of health, leisure, and thirst form a consumption vignette. Madras, 1989. Photo by the authors.

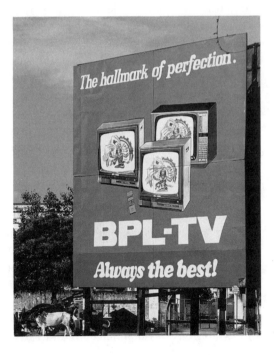

Fig. 1-3. Classical images underwrite the mechanical excitement of television and lend archaism to the space of the billboard. Madras, 1989. Photo by the authors.

MUSEUMS AND PUBLIC CULTURE

In countries such as India, the challenge of training skilled teachers, the rudimentary resources available for primary and secondary education, and the bureaucratization and politicization of higher education all mean that education outside formal settings has continued to be crucial to the formation of the modern citizen. Such education—which involves learning the habits, values, and skills of the contemporary world—happens through a variety of processes and frameworks, including those of the family, the workplace, friendship networks, leisure activities, and media exposure. Museums and the exhibition complex in general form an increasingly important part of this nonformal educational process, the logic of which has been insufficiently studied, especially outside the West.

Museums are also a very complex part of the story of Western expansion since the sixteenth century, although they are now part of the cultural apparatus of most emergent nations. Museums have complex roots in such phenomena as cabinets of curiosities, collections of regalia, and dioramas of public spectacle.[20] Today, museums reflect complex mixtures of state and private motivation and patronage, and tricky transnational problems of ownership, identity, and the politics of heritage. Thus museums, which frequently represent national identities both at home and abroad, are also nodes of transnational representation and repositories for subnational flows of objects and images. Museums, in concert with media and travel, serve as ways in which national and international publics learn about themselves and others.

Museums provide an interesting contrast with travel, for in museums people travel short distances in order to experience cultural, geographical, and temporal distance, whereas contemporary tourists often travel great distances in short spaces of time to experience "otherness" in a more intense and dramatic manner. But both are organized ways to explore the worlds and things of the "other." In the public cultures of nations such as India, both museums and tourism have an important domestic dimension, since they provide ways in which national populations can conceptualize their own diversity and reflect (in an objectified way) on their diverse cultural practices and histories. Such reflexivity, of course, has its roots in the colonial experience, during which Indians were subject to a thoroughgoing classification, museumification, and aestheticization in the museums, fairs, and exhibitions of the nineteenth and early twentieth centuries.[21] Finally, both museums and travel in India today would be hard to imagine apart from a fairly elaborate media infrastructure, as has been suggested already.

The media are relevant to museums and exhibitions in specific ways. For example, verbal literacy affects the ways in which people who come to museums and exhibitions are able to understand the objects (and signage) that are at the center of them. Thus, the issue of the ability to read is critical. Media are also important in the form of advertising, particularly through billboards, newspaper advertisements, and television coverage, which in many cases inform people about exhibitions (especially those associated with national and regional cultural representations). Literacy (both verbal and visual) is also relevant to the ways in which pamphlets, photographs, and posters associated with museums are read by various publics as they travel through different regions, visit various sites, and purchase inexpensive printed publicity materials associated with museums, monuments, and religious centers. Exposure to the media affects as well the ways in which particular groups and individuals frame their readings of particular sites and objects, since media exposure often provides the master narratives within which the mininarratives of particular exhibitions and museums are interpreted. Thus, for example, the National Museum in Delhi and its various counterparts in the other major cities of India offer specific narratives of the colonial, precolonial, and postcolonial periods (for example, the classification of the tribal as "primitive").

Viewers do not come to these museums as cultural blanks. They come as persons who have seen movies with nationalist themes, television serials with nationalist and mythological narratives and images, and newspapers and magazines that also construct and visualize the heroes and grand events of Indian history and mythology.

In addition, it is important to reiterate that the museum experience is part and parcel of learning to be cosmopolitan and "modern." This learning process has a consumption (as well as a media) dimension. Whether for city dwellers or for villagers, the experience of visiting museums is always implicitly connected to the consumption of leisure and pleasure. As regimented as many groups visiting Indian museums may seem, visits to museums and exhibitions are part of the pleasures of seeing, and visual pleasure has a very deep and special logic in the Indian context. In the annual traveling commercial exhibition known as the Ideal Home Exhibition, for example, the mastery of modern modes of domestic technology and lifestyle is the key to the exhibition experience, even for those who do not actually buy anything.

There is a complex dialectic among the experiences that Indians have in ethnic-national museums (that is, museums where national heritage and ethnic identity are key concerns), in art museums, and in commercial exhibitions. In each case, they are being educated in different forms of cultural literacy: in the first case, they are being educated in the objectified narratives of nationality and ethnicity; in the second case, in the experience of cosmopolitan aesthetics; and in the third case, in the habits and values of the modern, high-tech householder. These three forms of cultural literacy play a central role in the construction of the modern Indian, who is drawn into the visual and auditory narratives of modern citizenship by his or her experiences in museums and exhibitions. The outstanding question is, how does the museum and exhibition experience help create such cultural literacy?

A major theoretical cue comes from what has been called "reception theory,"[22] a body of ideas developed largely out of postwar German neo-Marxism, but now modified by interaction with reader-response theory and associated approaches to problems of audience analysis in mass-media studies. From this rather diffuse and developing body of theory, four hypotheses can be suggested as especially relevant to those postcolonial societies outside the Euro-American axis, such as India, in which nationalism, consumerism, and leisure have become simultaneous features of contemporary life for important segments of the population. We see these hypotheses as particularly applicable to societies such as India, since in them the connoisseurship of "art" as a distinct category is relatively undeveloped, the visiting of museums is not sharply separated from other forms of leisure and learning, and the idea of expert documentation and credentials in the interpretation of objects has not displaced the sense that viewer groups are entitled to formulate their own interpretations.

The first hypothesis is that sacralized objects and spaces generate specialized modes of viewing and interaction, which are likely to be rooted in historically deeper modalities of seeing as a cultural practice. In the Indian case, there is a considerable literature showing that the mutual gaze (*darsan*) of sacred persons or objects and their audiences creates bonds of intimacy and allegiance that transcend the specifics of what is displayed or narrativized in any given context.[23] The faculty of sight creates special bonds between seer and seen. Museum viewing

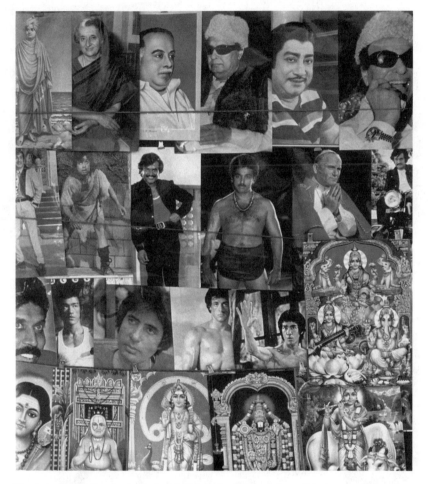

Fig. 1-4. A street hawker's gendered anthology of cinematic, political, and religious images of stardom. Madras, 1989. Photo by the authors.

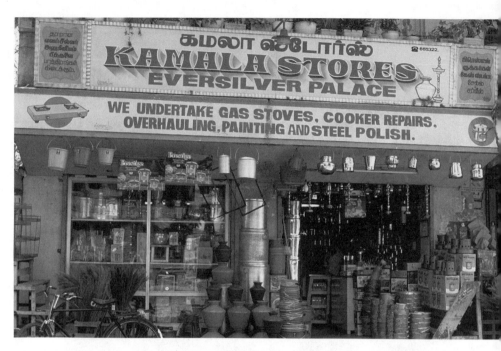

Fig. 1-5. Old tech and new gloss in the world of the kitchen. Madras, 1989. Photo by the authors.

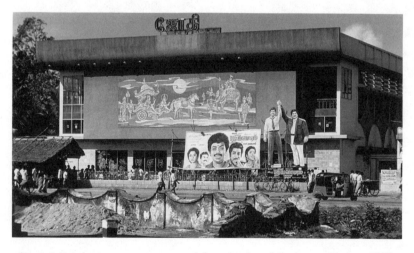

Fig. 1-6. Epic horizons, superstars, and the seduction of the theater. Madras, 1989. Photo by the authors.

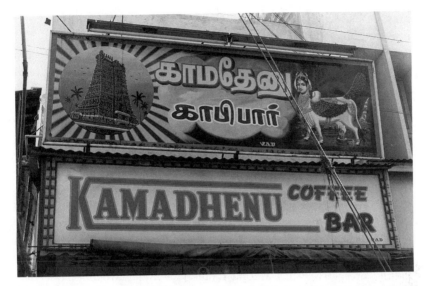

Fig. 1-7. Coffee and the wish-fulfilling cow in a mythic Hindu landscape. Madurai, 1989. Photo by the authors.

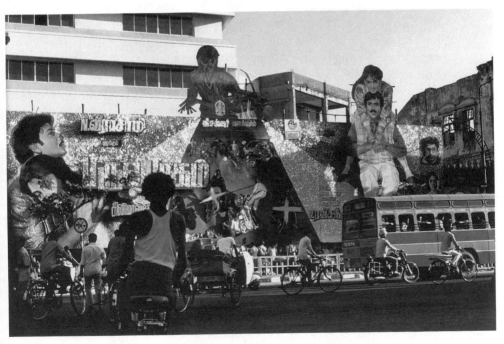

Fig. 1-8. Cinematic superdramas frame the microtraffic of the street. Madras, 1989. Photo by the authors.

may be expected, therefore, to display some transformation of this longstanding cultural convention.

The second is that the reception of specialized sites and spaces is a profoundly communal experience, and the objects and landscapes of museums are viewed by "communities of interpretation"[24] in which the isolated viewer or connoisseur is a virtually absent type. Thus, in any museum or exhibition in India (with the possible exception of certain museums devoted to "modern" art) the lonely and private gaze that we can often observe at places such as the Museum of Modern Art in New York is absent. Viewing and interpretation are profoundly communal acts.

The third hypothesis is that viewers are not likely to be passive and empty receivers of the cultural information contained in exhibitions and museums. Rather, as in all societies, they come with complex ideas of what is likely to be seen, and share this knowledge in highly interactive ways among themselves and with those few "experts" who are cast in the role of explainers. Thus museums and exhibitions are frequently characterized not by silent observation and internal reflection, but by a good deal of dialogue and interaction among the viewers, as well as between them and whoever is playing the role of guide. Here the museum experience is not only visual and interactional, it is also profoundly dialogic; that is to say, it is an experience in which cultural literacy emerges out of dialogues in which knowledge, taste, and response are publicly negotiated among persons with very diverse backgrounds and expertise. In many cases, the near-absence in Indian museums of docents and the underdevelopment of the idea that exhibited objects need to be explained (either by signage or by guides or docents) create a much wider space for discourse and negotiation among viewers: viewers are left free to assimilate new objects and arrangements into their own prior repertoires of knowledge, taste, and fantasy. Such freedom characterizes a great many Indian museums, even those in which there is a strong effort to determine viewer interpretations, but is true only of smaller, less intensively curated, less well funded museums in the contemporary United States and Europe. There is thus a profound tension between the museum or exhibition as a site of defamiliarization, where things are made to look strange, and the viewer-dominated process of dialogue and interpretation, which familiarizes cosmopolitan forms and narratives into larger master narratives from other arenas of public life, such as travel, sport, and cinema. Thus, the museum experience has to be understood as a dialogic moment in a larger process of creating cultural literacy, in which other media-influenced narratives play a massive role.

Fourth, the responses of viewers, gazers, and buyers vary significantly, along at least two axes: (1) the type of exhibition or museum to which they are exposed, and (2) personal characteristics, such as the class, ethnic group, and age group to which they belong. These differences create significant variations within a larger common structure that is predictable from the previous three theoretical assumptions. Since the study of reception is in a general way not highly developed and is especially poorly developed for the study of readerships outside Europe and the United States (and even less so for reception in contexts such as museums), further examination of the exhibition complex could make a significant contribution to more general methodological debates.

Much of the structure, organization, taxonomy, and signage strategy of Indian museums is colonial in origin. Thus while the *contexts* of current museum viewing may require new applications of reception theory, the *texts* contained in many museums (that is, the collections and their associated signage) require the analysis of colonial modes of knowledge and classification.

CONCLUSIONS

Like many other phenomena of the contemporary world, museums in contemporary India have both internal and external logics. As far as the rest of the world is concerned, there is no denying that museums constitute part of an "exhibitionary complex"[25] in which spectacle, discipline, and state power become interlinked with questions of entertainment, education, and control. It is also true that museums everywhere seem to be increasingly caught up with mass-media experiences.[26] Finally, museums everywhere seem to be booming as the "heritage industry"[27] takes off.

In India, each of these global impulses has crosscut a particular colonial and postcolonial trajectory in which new visual formations link heritage politics to spectacle, tourism, and entertainment. In making this link, it seems that older Indian modes of seeing and viewing are being gradually transformed and spectacularized. While the investigation of the museum experience in India is only in its infancy, we would like to suggest that it will need to focus especially on the deep interdependence of various sites and modes of seeing, including those involved in television, cinema, sport, and tourism. Each of these sites and modes offers new settings for the development of a contemporary public gaze in Indian life. The gaze of Indian viewers in museums is certainly caught up in what we would call this interocular field (the allusion here, of course, is to intertextuality, as the concept is used by the Russian literary theorist Mikhail Bakhtin). This interocular field is structured so that each site or setting for the disciplining of the public gaze is to some degree affected by viewers' experiences of the other sites. This interweaving of ocular experiences, which also subsumes the substantive transfer of meanings, scripts, and symbols from one site to another in surprising ways, is the critical feature of the cultural field within which museum viewing in contemporary India needs to be located. Our effort in this paper has been to argue for the importance of such an interocular approach to museums in India, and perhaps everywhere else in the contemporary world where museums are enjoying a fresh, postcolonial revival.

NOTES

1. See, for example, Arjun Appadurai, "The Global Ethnoscape: Notes and Queries for a Transnational Anthropology," in R. G. Fox, ed., *Recapturing Anthropology: Working in the Present* (Santa Fe, N.M.: School of American Research, 1991).

2. For a more recent work, see Carol A. Breckenridge, "The Aesthetics and Politics of Colonial Collecting: India at World Fairs," *Comparative Studies in Society and History* 31, no. 2 (1989), 195–216. Earlier efforts include Ray Desmond, *The India Museum, 1801–1879* (London: Her Majesty's Stationery Office, 1982); Hermann Goetz, "The Baroda Museum and Picture Gallery," *Museum* 7, no. 1 (1954), 15–19; and Grace Morley, "Museums in India," *Museum* 18, no. 4 (1965), 220–50.

3. Arjun Appadurai, ed., *The Social Life of Things: Commodities in Cultural Perspective* (Cambridge: Cambridge University Press, 1986); Burton Benedict, ed., *The Anthropology of World's Fairs: San Francisco's Panama Pacific International Exposition of 1915* (Berkely: Scolar, 1983); James Clifford, *The Predicament of Culture: Twentieth-Century Ethnography, Literature, and Art* (Cambridge, Mass.: Harvard University Press, 1988); Virginia R. Dominguez, "The Marketing of Heritage," *American Ethnologist* 13, no. 3 (1986), 546–55; Nelson H. H. Graburn, ed., *Ethnic and Tourist Arts: Cultural Expressions from the Fourth World* (Berkeley: University of California Press, 1976).

4. Igor Kopytoff, "The Cultural Biography of Things: Commoditization as Process," in Arjun Appadurai, ed., *The Social Life of Things: Commodities in Cultural Perspective* (Cambridge: Cambridge University Press, 1986).

5. Dominguez, "The Marketing of Heritage."

6. Michael Ames, *Museums, the Public, and Anthropology: A Study in the Anthropology of Anthropology* (Vancouver: University of British Columbia Press, 1986); Douglas Cole, *Captured Heritage: The Scramble for Northwest Coast Artifacts* (Vancouver: Douglas and McIntyre, 1985); Neil Harris, "Museums, Merchandising, and Popular Taste: The Struggle for Influence," in Ian M. G. Quimby, ed., *Material Culture and the Study of American Life* (New York: Norton, 1978); Masatoshi Konishi, "The Museum and Japanese Studies," *Current Anthropology* 28, no. 4 (1987), S96–S101; Mark P. Leone, Parker B. Potter, Jr., and Paul A. Shackel, "Toward a Critical Archaeology," *Current Anthropology* 28, no. 3 (1987), 283–302; Ian M. G. Quimby, ed., *Material Culture and the Study of American Life* (New York: Norton, 1978); George W. Stocking, Jr., *Objects and Others: Essays on Museums and Material Culture*, History of Anthropology, vol. 3 (Madison: University of Wisconsin Press, 1985).

7. Leone, Potter, and Shackel, "Toward a Critical Archaeology."

8. W. S. Hendon, F. Costa, and R. A. Rosenberg, "The General Public and the Art Museum: Case Studies of Visitors to Several Institutions Identify Characteristics of Their Publics," *American Journal of Economics and Sociology* 48, no. 2 (1989), 231–43; Kenneth Hudson, *Museums of Influence* (Cambridge: Cambridge University Press, 1987); Leone, Potter, and Shackel, "Toward a Critical Archaeology"; Michael H. Frisch and Dwight Pitchaithley, "Audience Expectations as Resource and Challenge: Ellis Island as Case Study," in Jo Blatti, ed., *Past Meets Present: Essays about Historic Interpretation and Public Audiences* (Washington, D.C.: Smithsonian Institution Press, 1987); Elliot W. Eisner and Stephen M. Dobbs, "Museum Education in Twenty American Art Museums," *Museum News* 65, no. 2 (1986), 42–49; Danielle Rice, "On the Ethics of Museum Education," *Museum News* 65, no. 5 (1987), 13–19; Sheldon Annis, "The Museum as Staging Ground for Symbolic Action," *Museum* 38, no. 3 (1986), 168–71.

9. Jürgen Habermas, *The Structural Transformation of the Public Sphere: An Inquiry into a Category of Bourgeois Society*, trans. Thomas Burger with the assistance of Frederick Lawrence (Cambridge, Mass.: MIT Press, 1989).

10. Cf. Pierre Bourdieu, *Distinction: A Social Critique of the Judgement of Taste,* trans. Richard Nice (Cambridge, Mass.: Harvard University Press, 1984).

11. Robert Lumley, ed., *The Museum Time-Machine: Putting Cultures on Display* (New York: Routledge, 1988); Jo Blatti, ed., *Past Meets Present:*

Essays about Historic Interpretation and Public Audiences (Washington, D.C.: Smithsonian Institution Press, 1987); Robert Hewison, *The Heritage Industry: Britain in a Climate of Decline* (London: Methuen, 1987); Donald Horne, *The Great Museum: The Re-Presentation of History* (London: Pluto, 1984).

12. Tony Bennett, "The Exhibitionary Complex," *New Formations* 4 (1988), 73–102.

13. Donna Haraway, "Teddy Bear Patriarchy: Taxidermy in the Garden of Eden, 1908–1936," *Social Text* 11 (Winter 1984–85), 20–64.

14. See Blatti, *Past Meets Present,* especially the following essays therein: Michael J. Ettema, "History Museums and the Culture of Materialism"; Jane Greengold, "What Might Have Been and What Has Been—Fictional Public Art about the Real Past"; and Michael Wallace, The Politics of Public History."

15. Shelly Errington, "Fragile Traditions and Contested Meaning," *Public Culture* 1, no. 2 (1989), 49–59; Richard Handler, *Nationalism and the Politics of Culture in Quebec* (Madison: University of Wisconsin Press, 1988); Michael Herzfeld, *Ours Once More: Folklore, Ideology, and the Making of Modern Greece* (Austin: University of Texas Press, 1982); Eric Hobsbawm and Terence Ranger, eds., *The Invention of Tradition* (Cambridge: Cambridge University Press, 1983); Richard Johnson et al., eds., *Making Histories: Studies in History-Writing and Politics* (London: Hutchinson, 1982) William W. Kelly, "Rationalization and Nostalgia: Cultural Dynamics of New Middle Class Japan," *American Ethnologist* 13, no. 4 (1986), 603–18; Jocelyn S. Linnekin, "Defining Tradition: Variations on the Hawaiian Identity," *American Ethnologist* 10, no. 2 (1983), 241–52; David Whisnant, *All That Is Native & Fine: The Politics of Culture in an American Region* (Chapel Hill: University of North Carolina Press, 1983).

16. Arjun Appadurai and Carol A. Breckenridge, "Why Public Culture?" *Public Culture* 1, no. 1 (1988), 5–9.

17. Goetz, "The Baroda Museum and Picture Gallery," 15.

18. Ibid.

19. For example, see Handler, *Nationalism and the Politics of Culture in Quebec.*

20. See Richard Altick, *The Shows of London* (Cambridge, Mass.: Harvard University Press, 1978) for descriptions of these dioramas in the development of museums in England.

21. Breckenridge, "The Aesthetics and Politics of Colonial Collecting."

22. For example, Jane Feuer, "Reading *Dynasty:* Television and Reception Theory," *South Atlantic Quarterly* 88, no. 2 (1989), 443–60.

23. For example, Diana L. Eck, *Darshan: Seeing the Divine Image in India,* 2d ed. (Chambersburg, Penn.: Anima, 1985); J. Gonda, *Eye and Gaze in the Veda* (Amsterdam: North Holland, 1969).

24. Stanley Fish, *Is There a Text in This Class? The Authority of Interpretive Communities* (Cambridge, Mass.: Harvard University Press, 1980).

25. Bennett, "The Exhibitionary Complex."

26. Lumley, *The Museum Time-Machine.*

27. Hewison, *The Heritage Industry.*

CHAPTER 2

"Hey! That's Mine": Thoughts on Pluralism and American Museums

EDMUND BARRY GAITHER

I n reflecting on the American experience, the authors of *Museums for a New Century* note that a "major force of change we believe to have implications for museums is our society's evolving sense of its own pluralism."[1] This view grows from two important observations: the recognition that many cultural groupings that previously have been rendered invisible in our population no longer accept that status, and the fact that recent immigration from other parts of the Western Hemisphere as well as more distant areas has altered the makeup of many communities—large and small, urban and semirural. African American people, whose numbers exceed thirty million, have become a meaningful political force able to wield considerable muscle and influence in many urban areas. Atlanta and other large cities easily demonstrate this truth. In all probability, African Americans and Hispanics will constitute one-fifth of the whole population of the United States by the year 2000. By that point, the Asian population will have risen from four million to eight million. To put it differently, minorities will be a much greater percentage of the population. Currently a full one-quarter of the annual growth of the U.S. population is the result of immigration, and the vast majority of these immigrants are both nonwhite and non-European.[2] The traditional dominance within the United States by whites of European ancestry will inevitably give way as a more pluralistic view of who is American takes firmer root.

There are clear consequences deriving from these demographic changes. As more formerly invisible social groups exercise political expression, public support by virtue of our tax laws will have to become more accountable to and reflective of a broader segment of the public. The story these institutions tell of the history of our nation and its arts and sciences will have to be richer and more inclusive, which also means that it will have the potential to be both truer and more provocative.

Among the institutions that will be most affected are schools. All of us have come to think of schools, along with homes and religious institutions, as constituting the bedrock of society. Yet by almost all accounts, many urban schools are more mire than rock, more quick-sand than stone. As you would expect from the demographics cited earlier, the majority of students at many public schools are now "mi-nority," and other school populations are significantly more mixed than at any other point in our history. Overwhelmed by the scope of society's extra educational expectations, the schools need the cultural and educational benefits that museums offer. They need the profound and intimate understanding of different cultures that is fundamental to museum programming. They need the alternative approaches to edu-cation that museums—with their authentic objects—present. And they need the highly specialized types of encounters between people and their physical and cultural environment that museums provide. These encounters foster appreciation of the myriad accrued meanings of things, meanings which constitute the fabric that holds a community together. Without such a knitting-together of our social fabric, we will become a still more fractured, fragmented, and violent society.

I believe that we must embrace a fresh understanding of the American experience. We must reject models of American experience that express—directly or indirectly—a concept of *either/or*. We must not tolerate thinking in which folk are *either* African American *or* American. Lurking behind such concepts are constructs such as *sep-aratist/integrationist*, *we/they*, and *ours/theirs*. Instead, we must honor the comprehensive character of American experience. We must assert its inclusiveness and embrace the reality that folk can be simul-taneously African American and American. We belong inseparably both to ourselves and to the whole. We are our own community while also being part of the larger community.

What does all of this mean for museums? Two implications stand out with immediate and perfect clarity. First, museums must serve an ever-broader public in ever-bolder ways. And second, museums must honor America's diversity without paternalism and condescension. To the extent that museums effectively address these broad objectives, they will move closer toward fully satisfying their mandate as institutions that receive public support. It must be noted here that I believe there exists an implied contract between museums, as tax-exempt entities, and the public, which directly or indirectly supports them. Museums have obligations as both educational and social institutions to participate in and contribute toward the restoration of wholeness in the communities of our country. They ought to increase understanding within and between cultural groups in the matrix of lives in which we exist. They ought to help give substance, correction, and reality to the often incomplete and distorted stories we hear about art and social history. They should not dodge the controversy that often arises from the reappraisal of our common and overlapping pasts. If our museums cannot muster the courage to tackle these considerations in ways appropriate to their various missions and scales, then concern must be raised for how they justify the receipt of support from the public. The United States' social health is too important to go unaddressed by any significant sector of its institutions.

How can museums have an impact on such concerns? Of course, there is a straightforward answer to this question. And as is almost always the case, that simple answer belies the complexity and the bedeviling multiplicity of dimensions of this problem. The straightforward answer is that museums can more accurately and more sensitively balance the programs they offer so that those programs not only would delight and educate but also would enhance understanding of humanistic and pluralistic values. Again I quote from *Museums for a New Century:* "When it comes to preserving cultural pluralism, museums have an important role to play. They represent cultural diversity in their collections and their exhibitions. The museum community— within its own institutional makeup—exemplifies our cultural pluralism. . . . But museums are in an uncomfortably contradictory situation in that their celebration of pluralism does not always extend to their internal hierarchies. Their staffs and boards generally do not represent the full diversity of our society."[3] This comment helps us see more clearly both what resources we already have and what areas badly need change.

After their reference to cultural pluralism within the institutional makeup of the museum community in the quotation immediately above, the authors of *Museums for a New Century* make the following observation: "Institutions dedicated to fostering and preserving particular ethnic heritages will be increasingly important in helping Americans understand their historical experience from different perspectives."[4] This is a key thought because it points to the role museums can play in reshaping their communities.

The American cultural arena is a vital and competitive place. In it, cultural expressions from all corners bump into and influence one another. Out of the resulting cacophony, new forms and ideas are born. Criticisms, interpretations, reassessments of values, claims, and counterclaims abound, and out of the muck come impressions of who we are as a people. Museums are important contributors to this dynamic process because they are institutional sponsors of discussions relevant to their disciplines and cultures. Museums that commit themselves to the criticism and fostering of specific cultural heritages— African American, Hispanic, Native American, Asian—have a unique role to play in such settings since they are at the center of the discussion of their own traditions. Unlike general museums, these institutions treat their cultural heritage neither as a short-term focus nor as an aspect of a larger story. Their heritage is their primary subject matter. The presentation of their own cultural traditions is the foundation on which their identity rests.

The existence of museums dedicated to specific cultural heritages does not diminish the need for other museums to share in the work of increasing knowledge and understanding. Instead, all museums become partners in the larger enterprise of education. Certainly, the complexity of a large American city is better reflected in a complementary network of many museums, each with its own primary and secondary foci, and all of which, in the aggregate, represent a fuller picture of the community's historical, cultural, and scientific life. Within this museum network, many and varied educational and exhibition opportunities exist for all partners. Large, medium-sized, and small museums can all enjoy reciprocal relationships with one another, underpinned by mutual respect.

I now wish to turn my attention toward the unique role in American society that can be played by culturally specific museums (also known as minority museums), couching my discussion in terms of African American museums, with which I have had two decades of experience. I believe that the general principles to be derived from the following discussion are by and large valid for Hispanics and other cultural groups in the United States that have been largely ignored or devalued in the telling of our national story.

Museums committed to specific heritages become the institutional buttresses of those traditions because they have unique features. Most often, they enjoy an intimate relationship with real communities of people, which are themselves extensions of those cultures. Because most African American museums were established after 1960, they are still at the outset of their development and are therefore freer to evolve new or different institutional forms. Free from historical association with discrimination and prejudice, these museums are able to provide a forum for the discussion of cultural issues and for the development of criticism without becoming bogged down in racism, which often attends European American museums' engagement of controversial issues.

The close relationship between African American museums and their communities permits the museums to validate the communities' experiences. For this reason, the museums' programs often have a familiarity and a truthfulness that cause the communities to feel a strong bond of kinship with the institutions. Using both conventional and new program formats, these museums provide exciting models for forging community-museum marriages.

For example, when John Kinard became the director of the Anacostia Museum—then the Anacostia Neighborhood Museum—he brought with him a deep love for African American people, a profound understanding of African American communities, and a sense that an African American museum ought to be the product of a dialogue with its immediate neighbors. Drawing on a background in social organization and valuation formation via theology, he did not look first to the museum field for guidance and sanction of his subject matter. Instead, he talked to people and discovered their concerns and issues. He framed an informed and constructive response to their reality and thereby helped teach them to see and understand their own situation more clearly. His now-famous 1969–70 exhibition The Rat: Man's Invited Affliction was a pioneering and audacious act that brought new meaning and relevance to exhibition: by exploring the impact of these rodents on poor city dwellers, what is a tragedy in urban neighborhoods was made a subject for examination in the museum. Kinard's boldness and the quality of the dialogue that he and his staff were able to sustain with the Anacostia community made the Anacostia Neighborhood Museum a worldwide model and a prototype for something new—a neighborhood museum. The museum was an experience that enfranchised a community of people and enabled them to talk about their lives and to take greater responsibility for the reconstruction of themselves and their children. The experience also provided an opportunity for the museum to teach conventional history, whether about Anacostia or about other places, more effectively.

Museums are collecting institutions. In amassing the objects and artifacts that will be the basis of their interpretations, museums also signal which materials they regard as important. In the process, they convey to their publics a sense of direction regarding cultural, scientific, and historical interests. The Rhode Island Black Heritage Society and the Afro-American Historical and Cultural Museum in Philadelphia, both of which (at different times) have been under the direction of Rowena Stewart, have set a high standard and offer excellent examples of how to weave a closer relationship between a museum and its community through the activity of collection. Their model demands closer attention. For example, Stewart and her associates have developed and published a five-step approach for collecting African American documents and artifacts.[5] The model is usable by any museum and is instructive for all. Their approach is rooted in a "people orientation" rather than an object search. The artifact holders, or "keepers of the tradition," are central: they provide not only the objects but also the initial interpretation of those objects. These keepers are for the most part ordinary people who may not have thought that the treasures they own were of the slightest interest for anyone beyond their immediate family and friends. They may even be folks who have not themselves placed much value on the evidence of their own personal and familial heritage.

Here are the five steps that are used by Stewart's museum in collecting African American materials. For openers, she or an appropriate member of her staff goes to visit a person who has been identified as an informal historian of the family or group whose material is of interest. Much time is spent, over many visits, becoming acquainted with the keeper and allowing the keeper to become knowledgeable about the museum. This portion of the process is concluded at the point when the keeper has fully accepted the credibility of the museum and feels that it is playing a vital and correct role vis-à-vis the keeper's understanding of his or her own heritage. In the next stage, the keeper's help is enlisted in interpreting the objects, photographs, or documents to others who are close to and interested in the material. This may be done by arranging a small gathering of the keeper and his or her friends and family, and the event may take place in the museum. At this point, the keeper is the primary interpreter of artifacts that are personal extensions of that person's life and times. Following this event, the museum introduces a professional historian into the mix, who launches the work of more fully explaining and interpreting the larger matrix into which the objects fit. The historian also commences an assessment of the implications of the materials for a general discussion of African American experience and their place in that discussion. Next, attention turns to the preparation of what will become the exhibition or presentation of the materials. This aspect of the work is called giving the materials back to the community. It provides the occasion for the keepers and their peers and associates to share the materials with the community at large and to share their own experiences with other keepers. The final dimension of the process is the education plan and the publications that record the materials and their complete interpretation. This phase of the work may involve the use of the original keeper as a docent speaking to the public about his or her materials as well as those of others. Almost always it will also involve the release of a catalogue, which pulls together the contributions of all parties who were active agents in the collection, interpretation, and ultimate display of the new acquisitions. Significantly, this approach underscores the trust that can be built between a museum and its community. It brings to the museum an advocate whose relationship is predicted on the ennoblement of a shared heritage. Both the advocate and the museum are empowered by their teamwork and its product.

The issues that concern African American museums are not unrelated to larger, more general themes that draw attention in the international world of ideas, such as modernism, deconstructionism, and other thrusts in the arena of contemporary criticism. Because this is so, the critical, social-historical, and art-historical contributions of African American museums are urgently needed in mainstream discussions of such themes. Toward this end, the exhibition Contemporary African Artists: Changing Traditions, which debuted at the Studio Museum in Harlem in 1990, is noteworthy. Africa and its peoples have a strong historical and cultural relationship to black Americans. African cultures in all of their manifestations everywhere are perceived as part of the symbolic and actual legacy of black people in America. Thus it is especially appropriate that an African American museum should take the step of bringing critical definition to issues raised by contemporary African artists, who are redefining their historical relationship to their own cultures and influencing the international vocabulary of contemporary art. Participation in this kind of discussion is part of a continuing and full-time commitment of the African American museum toward understanding the growth and development of the visual arts and traditions of black people worldwide.

Knowing one's community means knowing its strengths and its weaknesses. Serving one's community means designing programs that are tailored to its needs and that anticipate its future requirements and demands. For small to moderate-sized museums, there exists a clear opportunity to develop programs and educational activities that respond very directly to community concerns and issues. For example, in the case of my own institution, the Museum of the National Center of Afro-American Artists, we have created several programs that were immediately inspired by observed needs in our primary public. A popular program called Father and Son Sharing was designed as a means of helping heal the sometimes strained male relationships that exist in separated families. Our program was focused around a newly commissioned public statue of an African American man reading to his son. John Wilson, the sculptor, is a Boston African American artist with a long history of working with father-son themes. Over the course of the ten-session program, the fathers and sons who participated visited the studio of the artist, created a portfolio of drawings and poems, and visited the foundry to observe how sculptures are cast in bronze. The program concluded with a public exhibition and reception for the participants' families and friends.

We are presently conducting an educational program based on the decorative appliqué traditions of the old African kingdom of Dahomey (the present-day Republic of Benin). In this program, teenage mothers draw on Dahomean textile traditions to create quilted blankets for their infants. Beyond the lessons in cultural history and the direct encounter with the art of Dahomey, these young women also gain social and family skills that will help them reconstruct their lives in more fruitful ways.

Being situated in a region with a large Caribbean population, we became concerned with helping the students we serve to better understand the cultural and social forces that created the Caribbean and that still inform its visual and performing arts. A quick examination of the materials available in the region's schools and from other cultural institutions in the Boston area revealed that no one had effectively addressed the cultural and social history of this region, which is so close to us and from which we have received such a large number of immigrants. With support from the Massachusetts Council for the Arts and Humanities we spent two years developing a series of three presentations that focus on the Caribbean and are accompanied by a substantial publication in four parts. Our Caribbean program, which began in 1969, is divided into parts based on language groups: French/Creole, English, and Spanish. Each subprogram is anchored by a widely recognized art-producing activity or festival from which we have acquired appropriate artworks. Through this series, we are able to provide an in-depth study of cultural traditions that are immediately influential in the lives of our primary community. We believe that such activities are important vehicles for fostering the marriage of a community and its museum(s).

The several examples I have mentioned above show the excitement that "minority" museums bring to the museum field. Without disregarding the professional standards demanded by the stewardship of collections, these institutions are increasingly able to introduce fresh ideas and suggest how museums may become more socially responsible and responsive. Through their programs, African American and Hispanic museums, among others, are developing new and growing audiences. Audiences who previously felt intimidated or alienated by museums now increasingly enjoy the remarkable educational and entertainment opportunities museums offer. Such new visitors are destined to become shared audiences as other museums also broaden their exhibition and educational offerings in response to the demands of American pluralism. When museums in the Unites States tell a more accurate and integrated story, more Americans from all cultural groups will feel ownership in them, and will say, "Hey! That's mine."

NOTES

1. American Association of Museums, Commission on Museums for a New Century, *Museums for a New Century* (Washington, D.C.: American Association of Museums, 1984), 24.

2. Ibid.

3. Ibid., 25.

4. Ibid.

5. Rowena Stewart, "Bringing Private Black Histories to the Public," in Janet W. Solinger, ed., *Museums and Universities: New Paths for Continuing Education* (New York: Macmillan, 1990).

CHAPTER 3

The Other Vanguard

GUILLERMO GÓMEZ-PEÑA

The notion of border culture and the role of the border artist/intellectual have changed dramatically in the past five years; from the strong regionalism of the mid-eighties to a new *ex centris* internationalism in the late 1980s, we are trying to find our role and place in the new decade.

I hope that the following texts, which were written over a period of five years, reflect some of the changes in the way Latinos perceive identity, community, national culture, and art along the United States–Mexico border.

1986: THE CONFLICTS AND CULTURE OF THE BORDERLANDS

This text was written in 1986, and functioned as a kind of border art manifesto.

Few places in the world reflect so vividly the contradictions of two worlds in permanent conflict as does the Mexico–United States border. The contrasts are infinite: mariachis and surfers, secondhand buses and digital helicopters, tropical whorehouses and video discotheques, Catholic saints and monsters from outer space, and shanty houses and steel skyscrapers.

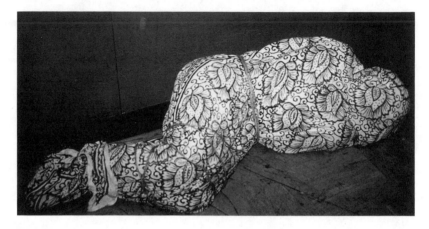

Fig. 3-1. *The Loneliness of the Immigrant*, by Guillermo Gómez-Peña. Two-day performance in a public elevator, Los Angeles, 1979. Photo courtesy of *The Broken Line/La Linea Quebrada*.

The border region is filled with paradoxes that in a very graphic way illustrate the tense relations between Latin America and Anglo America, between the North and the South, between the conqueror and the conquered. "Crossing the border" is taking an instantaneous leap from the past into the future, from a partially industrialized society to an information-based society, and occasionally from a bad dream to a nightmare.

From the border we observe the clash of waves of the two Americas—Contadora against the White House, Atahualpa Yupanqui against Michael Jackson, Sandino against Rambo—and the synthesis is a third reality. It is punk mariachi. It is postmodern flamenco, Spanglish poetry, video corrido. As border citizens, our great challenge is to invent new languages capable of articulating our incredible circumstances.

Who are we exactly? The offspring of the synthesis or the victims of the fragmentation? The victims of a double colonialism (Europe and the United States) or the bearers of a new vision in gestation? What the hell are we? De-Mexicanized Mexicans, pre-Chicanos, cholo-punks, Mexamericans, or something that still has no name? And our Anglo-Saxon colleagues who sympathize with us, who are they? Transplanted ex-gringos, South-Americanized North Americans, Americans in the largest sense of the word, or simply brothers and sisters of vision?

Educators, artists, activists, and journalists are dealing with a project of redefinition, which conceives of the border not only as the limits of the two countries, but as a cardinal intersection of many realities. In this sense, the border is not an abyss that will have to save us from threatening otherness, but a place where the so-called otherness yields, becomes us, and therefore becomes comprehensible.

1987: MEXICO BECOMES THE SPEAKING SUBJECT—AN INVENTORY OF BORDER ART

A. neo-rascuache, post-rascuache, political kitsch, involuntary post-modernity, multimedia altars, sound altars to *Saint Frida* (Kahlo), *Saint Roque* (Dalton), *Border Brujo, Superbarrio, Supermojado, Su-*

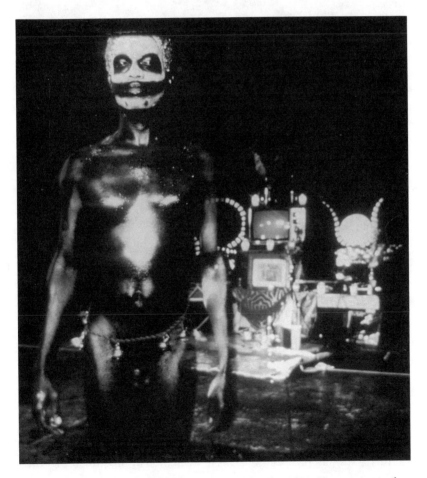

Fig. 3-2. *Europa*, by Poyesis Genética Troupe. Los Angeles, 1981. Photo courtesy of *The Broken Line/La Linea Quebrada.*

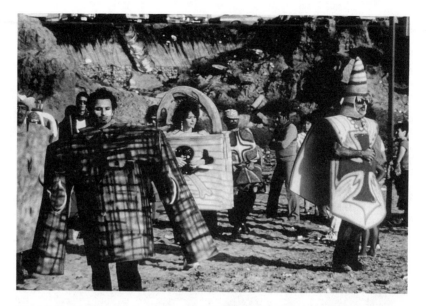

Fig. 3-3. *End of the Line*, by Border Arts Workshop. Binational performance at the United States–Mexico border, 1986. Photo courtesy of *The Broken Line/La Linea Quebrada.*

perviviente, and other social wrestlers who are into linguistics, politics, and shamanism.

B. neon temples, paper flowers floating in pesticide, velvet paintings depicting leaders of the political opposition, scenes of dangerous California freeways, K Mart signs, corpses displayed in a gallery, the skeleton of *Chicanosaurus,* the infrared mask of a border patrol, red light, cumbia Rock, disco salsa, radioactive piñatas, dead roses, Brazilian punk, Oaxacan nostalgia, contaminated sperm, oil spills into Mexico, ashes, albino male prostitutes, Spanglish poetry, caló franflé, graffitijuana per omnia saecula speculorum, con safos.

1989: THE MULTICULTURAL PARADIGM

The United States suffers from a severe case of amnesia. In its obsessive quest to "construct the future," it tends to forget or erase the past. Fortunately, the so-called disenfranchised groups who don't feel part of this national project have been meticulously documenting their histories. Latinos, African Americans, Asians, women, gays, experimental artists, and nonaligned intellectuals have used inventive languages to record the other history from a multicentric perspective.

"Our art functions both as collective memory and alternative chronicle," says the San Francisco–based Chicana artist and theoretician Amalia Mesa-Bains. In this sense, multicultural art, if nurtured, can become a powerful tool to recapture the desired historical self. The great paradox is that without this historical self, no meaningful future can ever be constructed.

Métier is being redefined. In Latin America, the artist has multiple roles. He/she is not just an imagemaker or a marginal genius, but a social thinker/educator/counterjournalist/civilian diplomat/human-rights observer. His/her activities take place in the center of society and not in specialized corners.

So-called minority artists in the United States have also been forced to develop multidimensional roles. In the absence of enough institutions that are responsive to our needs, we have become a *sui generis* tribe of community organizers, media interventionists, and

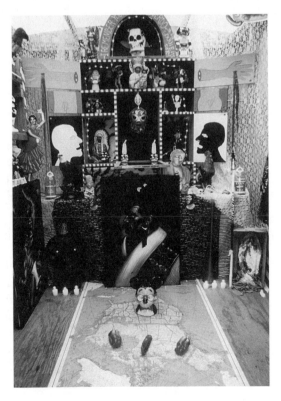

Fig. 3-4. *Tijuana-Niagara,* by Guillermo Gómez-Peña in collaboration with Emily Hicks. Installation at the United States–Canada border, 1988. Photo by Biff Hendricks, courtesy of *The Broken Line/La Linea Quebrada.*

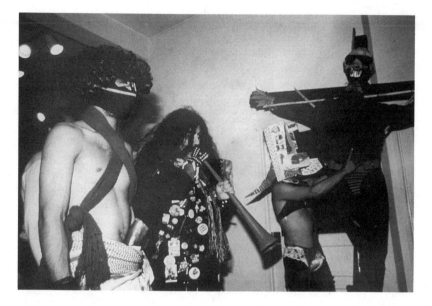

Fig. 3-5. *Pedos Bilingües*, performance by Guillermo Gómez-Peña, Hugo Sánchez, and Gerardo Navarro. San Diego, 1988. Photo by Isaac Artenstein, courtesy of *The Broken Line/La Linea Quebrada*.

alternative chroniclers. And the images, texts, and performances we produce are an integral part of these activities.

These models are much more pertinent to our times than those of the established art world.

Unlike modernist times, today's avant-garde has multiple fronts, or, as *High Performance* magazine editor Steven Durland has stated, "the avant-garde is no longer in the front but in the margins." To be avant-garde in the late 1980s means to contribute to the decentralization of art. To be avant-garde means to be able to cross the border, to go back and forth between art and politically significant territory, be it race relations, immigration, ecology, homelessness, AIDS, or violence toward disenfranchised communities and Third World countries. To be avant-garde means to perform and exhibit in both artistic and nonartistic contexts: to operate in the world, not just the art world.

According to Border Arts Workshop member Emily Hicks, "nothing is intrinsically marginal. Margins are constantly shifting. What today is marginal tomorrow becomes hegemonic, and vice versa."

In order to articulate our present crisis as multicultural artists, we need to constantly invent and reinvent languages. These languages have to be as syncretic, diverse, and complex as the fractured realities we are trying to define.

Postmodernism is a crumbled conceptual architecture, and we are tired of walking among someone else's ruins.

Border artists use experimental techniques and performance-derived practices to intervene directly in the world. The permanent condition of political emergency and cultural vulnerability we live in leaves us no other choice. If our actions are not daring, inventive, and unexpected, they won't make a difference, and border reality, with its overwhelming dynamics, will supersede us instantly.

In this sense, the experimental nature of border art is informed more by political and cultural strategies than by postmodernist theory.

Like artists operating in other politically sensitive parts of the world, border artists understand that formal experimentation is only worthwhile in relation to more important tasks such as the need to generate a binational dialogue, the need to create cultural spaces for others, and the need to redefine the asymmetrical relations between the North and the South and among the various ethnic groups that converge in the border spiral. Confronted with these priorities, the hyperspecialized concerns of the art world appear to be secondary.

1989: THE BORDER IS . . .

This piece was written before the fall of the Berlin wall and after a gathering of Latin American and U.S. Latino performance artists in Philadelphia.

Border culture is a polysemous term.

To step outside of one's culture equals to walk outside of the law.

Border culture means boicot, complot, ilegalidad, clandestinidad, contrabando, transgresión, desobediencia binacional; en otras palabras, to smuggle dangerous poetry and utopian visions from one culture to another, desde allá, hasta acá.

But it also means to maintain one's dignity outside the law.

But it also means hybrid art forms for new contents in gestation: spray mural, techno-altar, poetry in tongues, audio graffiti, punkarachi, video corrido, anti-bolero, anti-todo: migra (border patrol), art world, police, monocultura; en otras palabras y tierras, an art against

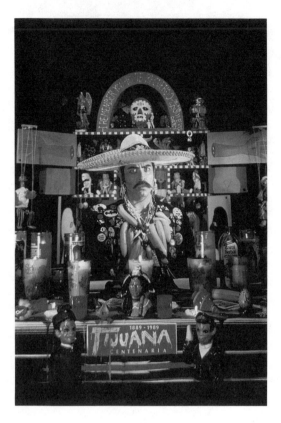

Fig. 3-6. *Border Brujo*, still from film by Isaac Artenstein and Guillermo Gómez-Peña, 1989. Photo by Max Aguilera-Hellweg, courtesy of *The Broken Line/La Linea Quebrada*.

the monolingües, tapados, nacionalistas, ex-teticistas en extinción, per omnia saecula speculorum . . .

But it also means to be fluent in English, Spanish, Spanglish, and Ingleñol, 'cause Spanglish is the language of border diplomacy.

But it also means transcultural friendship and collaboration among races, sexes, and generations.

But it also means to practice creative appropriation, expropriation, and subversion of dominant cultural forms.

But it also means a new cartography; a brand-new map to host the new project; the democratization of the East; the socialization of the West; the Third-Worldization of the North and the First-Worldization of the South.

But it also means a multiplicity of voices away from the center; different geocultural relations among more culturally akin regions:

Tepito–San Diejuana, San Pancho–Nuyorico, Miami–Quebec, San Antonio–Berlin, your home town and mine, digamos, a new internationalism *ex centris*.

But it also means regresar y volver a partir: to return and depart once again, 'cause border culture is a Sisyphean experience and to arrive is just an illusion.

But it also means a new terminology for new, multihybrid identities and métiers constantly metamorphosing: sudaca, not Hispanic; Chicarican, not Latino; mestizaje, not miscegenation; social thinker, not bohemian; accionista, not performer; intercultural, not postmodern.

But it also means to develop new models to interpret the world-in-crisis, the only world we know.

But it also means to push the borders of countries and languages or, better said, to find new languages to express the fluctuating borders.

But it also means experimenting with the fringes between art and society, legalidad and illegality, English and Español, male and female, North and South, self and other; and subverting these relationships.

But it also means to speak from the crevasse, desde acá, desde en medio. The border is the juncture, not the edge, and monoculturalism has been expelled to the margins.

But it also means glasnost, not government censorship, for censorship is the opposite of border culture.

But it also means to analyze critically all that lies on the current table of debate: multiculturalism, the Latino "boom," "ethnic art," controversial art, even border culture.

But it also means to question and transgress border culture. What today is powerful and necessary, tomorrow is arcane and ridiculous; what today is border culture, tomorrow is institutional art, not vice versa.

But it also means to escape the current co-optation of border culture.

But it also means to look at the past and the future at the same time. 1492 was the beginning of a genocidal era. 1992 will mark the beginning of a new era: America post-Colombina, Arteamerica sin fronteras. Soon, a new internationalism will have to gravitate around the spinal cord of this continent—not Europe, not just the North, not just white, not only you, compañero del otro lado de la frontera, el lenguaje y el océano.

I JANUARY 1990: A MESSAGE FROM THE UNITED STATES–MEXICO BORDER TO THE EUROPEAN BORDER ARTISTS COMMUNITY

This text and the accompanying image were created by Guillermo Gómez-Peña and Robert Sanchez. In different forms, it has been presented at the Meeting of the Worlds Festival in Finland, recreated in Barcelona under the title Five Hundred Years of Genocide *at the invitation of the Joan Miró Foundation, and published in* Shift *magazine. The two columns of text are meant either to be read by two persons speaking at the same time or to be broadcast on separate tracks simultaneously.*

(Warning: by the time this piece is exhibited, published, or broadcast in your country, the information will very likely be outdated.)

Dear fellow citizen of the End-of-the-Century Society:
    We approach the last decade of the twentieth century submerged in total perplexity as we witness, from the United States–Mexico border region, structural changes in the world topography.

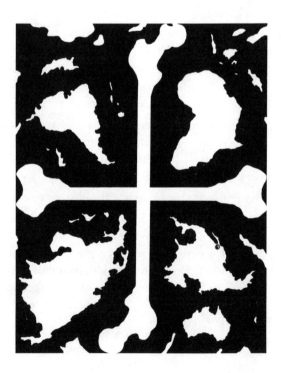

Fig. 3-7. *A Message from the U.S.–Mexico Border*, collaborative conceptual public mural project by Robert Sanchez with Guillermo Gómez-Peña. Joensuu, Finland, 1990. Reproduced with the permission of the artists.

We can't help but feel like uninvited actors in a disnarrative science-fiction film with the following plot:

THE COLD WAR ENDS AS THE U.S. DRUG WAR BEGINS. THE SOUTH REPLACES THE EAST AS THE NEW THREATENING OTHERNESS. RUSSIA IMPLEMENTS PERESTROIKA AND GLASNOST. A NEW ERA OF EAST-WEST RELATIONS BEGINS. THE CHINESE STATE CARRIES OUT THE MASSACRE OF TIANANMEN SQUARE. THE BERLIN WALL IS ABOLISHED EXACTLY WHEN THE UNITED STATES BEGINS TO MILITARIZE ITS BORDER WITH MEXICO. HUNGARY, POLAND, BULGARIA, AND CZECHOSLOVAKIA EXPERIENCE AN INSTANTANEOUS, RELATIVELY PACIFIC TRANSITION TOWARD "DEMOCRACY." THE SALVADOREAN CIVIL WAR REACHES A STALEMATE. ROMANIAN DICTATOR NICOLAE CEAUŞESCU FALLS WHILE CHILEAN DICTATOR PINOCHET LOSES THE AWAITED FIRST ELECTION SINCE THE FALL OF PRESIDENT ALLENDE. CENTRAL AMERICA AND MEXICO MOVE TO THE RIGHT. AND TO THE OUTRAGE OF THE INTERNATIONAL COMMUNITY, THE UNITED STATES INVADES PANAMA.

The birth pains of the new millennium are overwhelming. We don't know what will happen next. The amount, complexity, and intensity of the changes surpass our capability to digest them and codify them adequately.

For the moment, as much as we can aspire to is recognizing collectively that (1) drastically different relationships between East and West and therefore between North and South are being developed; (2) the centers of power are irreversibly shifting; (3) a new international society is being born; and (4) a new culture will have to emerge from its foundation.

In the United States there is a movement toward tolerance and reform that is equivalent to glasnost and that is mistakenly called multiculturalism; there are aggressive government sectors devoted to its destruction.

As border artists, we wonder what our role will be in this whole process. Should we be chroniclers, activists, philosophers, or diplomats? And what kind of art must we make to contribute to a world dialogue?

For the moment, as Europe prepares for the grand opening of its borders, we are preparing ourselves for another major project: the grand redefinition of 1992. We won't be celebrating the "discovery of America" or the "encounter of cultures." We will be attending a funeral for all the victims of five hundred years of genocide of our indigenous cultures.

CHAPTER 4

Festivals and the Creation of Public Culture: Whose Voice(s)?

ROBERT H. LAVENDA

I t's a Saturday evening in mid-July. The temperature is still in the high eighties, and it's humid. Pea-pack at the Green Giant plant has just ended; corn-pack starts on Monday. The smell of the insecticide sprayed in the afternoon to kill mosquitoes hangs over the park. The queen pageant has just ended, the park lights are on, a band is playing mid-sixties favorites from the back of a flatbed truck parked on the edge of the picnic area. In the pavilion, men in feed caps are pouring foaming pitchers and glasses of 3.2 beer from a trailer with twelve taps and an endless supply of kegs. Over a thousand people are jammed between the band and the beer, dancing, drinking, eating bratwurst, meeting friends, running into people they grew up with but haven't seen in years. More people, mostly college-age and just beyond, are downtown, crowding the sidewalk and spilling into the intersection between the town's two main bars. The atmosphere is festive; it is exciting to be in the midst of this crowd of people so obviously enjoying themselves. It is the forty-ninth annual Kolacky Days, in Montgomery, Minnesota, a small town south of Minneapolis and St. Paul. On the face of it, this is the stereotypic small-town festival—people celebrating themselves and their community in an "authentic" and traditional way, or at least emerging spontaneously from their homes for a communitywide expression of fellowship.

As one of the few moments in the annual cycle when it is claimed that a community publicly celebrates itself, civic or community festivals play a central role in the creation of public culture in Minnesota towns and cities. From queen pageant to parade, community barbecue and food stands to street dance, municipalities create a momentary, if recurrent, popular architectonics, a symbology of local significance, a public presentation of the community to itself and to outsiders. A public culture emerges.

Yet the public culture that Minnesota festivals produce does not simply emerge out of the collective unconscious of a single-voiced, organic community.[1] The voices of most of the people out for a good time on a Saturday night in a small Minnesota town do not influence the design of the festival; rather, as I will show, it is carefully constructed by the local middle class. An exercise in impression management, a Minnesota community festival is the more or less self-aware celebration of the values of its middle-class organizers, made in the name of the community as a whole. The appropriation of "our community" by these organizers in small towns is generally (but not always) accepted by other segments of the local population who share their vision of a harmonious community of mutually supportive equals. The tension between this ideal and the daily experiences of uninvolved individuals who are linked by fragile, contingent social ties in the town engenders the characteristic earnest and nonironic official voice of the small-town festival.

Out of the relatively large number of festivals that I have studied, I will draw on data from several small-town festivals during the period from 1981 to 1987, the Hutchinson Jaycees Water Carnival in 1987, and the 1990 St. Paul Winter Carnival. These festivals are points along a continuum, ranging from uncontested monologue (and absence of irony) to dialogue and open contestation of organizers' voices.

The small towns that I have studied, although certainly different from one another in many respects, have certain structural commonalities that are reflected in and condition the shape of their festivals. First, they are small—650 to 3,500 people. Second, they are farm service towns: feed stores, implement dealers, an auto parts store, one or two banks, gas stations, bars, schools, two grocery stores, one or two lawyers, two or more churches, a motel or two, one or two hardware stores, clinic or hospital, one or two dentists, a bakery, floral and gift shop, etc. There are usually a nursing home or retirement home and some government offices. Third, class differences are muted, although not absent.[2] Most of the people in the town depend on the surrounding farm areas, and many are small-business or professional families. There are people who work as custodians, wage laborers in agricultural or light industrial plants, truck drivers, service station attendants, construction workers, and the like. There is a core of teachers at the schools, who are ordinarily set apart from the main social patterns of the town. There is an identifiable group of retired persons, many former farmers who now live in town, and there is a group of young people, mostly males, who are marginal to the community for essentially economic reasons. Given the sheer weight of their numbers, it is not surprising that the principal voice heard in these communities is that of the business and professional community. The other groups, in part because their livelihoods depend on the health of the business and professional community, tend to go along with that voice, or at least not to contest its claim that it speaks for the entire community.

Festivals in these towns are organized by the businesspeople, with some assistance from those elements of the professional community that are most closely aligned with them—lawyers and dentists. As they design the festival they think both of their own interests and of what they imagine to be the interests of the portion of the population that is not like them. They are concerned with "family issues" and with providing events for the young children of the community. It is important to remember that in a small Minnesota town, especially during the summer, there is very little of a public, community nature for anyone to do. Children in particular are home with no publicly organized activities to occupy them: school is not in session and the high school athletic teams are not competing, which affects not only the children but also the adults who follow the teams. This is changing a bit. The influence of the video store is increasing in small towns, and one festival organizer told me that the proliferation of summer sports camps, cheerleader camps, and so forth has made it difficult to schedule the events of her festival, since so many people have children in these activities now.

The festival text that emerges is one that attempts to provide activities for families in the community, that will bring the community together and former residents back, and will "give something back" to the community. The typical festival takes place over a weekend, with events beginning Friday afternoon or evening and concluding Sunday afternoon or early evening. Table 4-1 presents in frequency order the events to be found at a sample of fifty-four Minnesota small-town

TABLE 4-I
Small-Town Festival Events in Order of Frequency

Event	Percentage of festivals with this event	Event	Percentage of festivals with this event
Parade	81.5	Other children's events	24.1
Dances	79.6	Food provided mostly by local vendors	24.1
Food provided by local organization	74.1	Ethnic food	24.1
Beer garden	74.1	Other water events	22.2
Children's contests	62.9	Ethnic concert	20.4
Art/craft fair	62.9	Fishing contest	18.5
Queen pageant	59.3	Farm-related events	18.5
Other contests	59.3	Ethnic dancing	18.5
Kiddie parade	57.4	Food provided by about half local and half outside	16.7
Concert	55.6		
Food provided by local individuals	40.7	Boat races	14.8
Flea market	40.7	Junior king and queen contest	12.9
Barbecue	37.0	Children's story hour	13.0
Firemen's water fight	35.2	Ethnic religious service	11.1
Events for senior citizens	35.2	Waterski show	9.3
Carnival	35.2	Other ethnic events	5.5
Food provided by outsiders	33.3	Food provided mostly by outside vendors	5.5
Ecumenical church service	33.3	Swimming races	3.7
Kiddie carnival	29.6		
Senior king and queen	27.8	Sample size = 54	
Crazy days	27.8	One festival = 1.85 percent	

festivals. The core of the Minnesota small-town festival is a parade, events for children, one or more dances (usually in the street), a beer garden, a queen pageant, several contests, an arts and crafts fair, and food provided by local organizations—Lions, Minnesota Women of Today, church youth groups, the hockey boosters, etc. While there are differences in attendance patterns at these events, by age and sex, many people from the town attend these events, which create an undemanding sense of belonging to the community.

A former student of mine writes about her town's festival:

> In . . . every summer in the first week of July we have our celebration. And I believe every year the *same* thing happens, there is a kiddie parade early in the week, the Jaycees put on a Turkey BBQ, there is a river raft race on the Rum River, all of the "carnies" begin milling around town much to the dismay of every young girl's mother and of course it all ends with a parade followed by every citizen in the whole town heading down to the carnival afterwards. Every year, everybody says the same thing afterwards, "It's just not the same as it used to be," but nevertheless you see those same people there year after year doing the same things year after year. The same bands, the same old cars, the same floats and of course the same old fire truck going by and squirting whoever they see that they know.
>
> During this time *everyone* comes home, and of course, all new gossip starts circulating: who got married, who had a baby, and who passed away. You see people you haven't seen in months and spend the whole night trying to catch up on all that has happened. And every year I wonder why I come back for the same old celebration— yet I do![3]

I have argued elsewhere for the community-creating qualities of small-town festivals,[4] and those qualities are certainly there. Still, organization of the festival, since it takes several months of meetings and coordinated effort, creates a special sense of solidarity among the organizers, who always plan some sort of social event for themselves after the festival is over. In small towns, however, differences that divide people tend to be expressed in terms of individualities rather than in class terms (for example, I'm not interested in an auto swap meet, and you're not interested in the crafts show). There are few events that are dramatically class-marked and exclusive. First, to some degree there *is* an overlap of interests among the banker, grocery store manager, auto parts dealer, and construction worker—they all fish and hunt, they all follow sports, etc. Thus, some events of a typical small-town festival will naturally appeal to many residents of different backgrounds. Second, a small town cannot survive with serious internal rifts, and most residents share a commitment to the ideology of community and cooperation that is not entirely illusory. Many of these people do in fact believe in community and will attend events that seem to them to build community. Because many festival events are undemanding, it is easy for a wide range of people to attend and enjoy them and come away with the feeling that they are part of an organic, harmonious community.

Nevertheless, the festival is the product of the work and world-view of a powerful segment of the community, and the dominant voice heard is theirs. Strikingly absent in small-town festivals, for example, is the voice of the rural people on whom the town depends. In town after town, the community festival ignores or actively excludes farmers and events of interest to them. That is, farmers may attend the events of the town festival, but they do not attend as farmers. Indeed, in some festivals, they cannot even attend: primary events are scheduled for seven o'clock in the evening, which in rural Minnesota is milking time. When farmers pointed this out to the organizers of one festival, the organizers apologized, averring that the festival was for everyone. But they still have not changed the time of those events.[5] Similarly, there are no small-town festivals that provide activities for adolescents, the group that is perhaps most economically marginal in the town: the queen pageant involves only a relatively small number of young women, and the young men are completely excluded. And even in festivals that propose to celebrate ethnicity, it is ordinarily the ethnic heritage of the dominant group that is accented.[6]

Sometimes the tie between the organizers and their festival's ethnic theme is tenuous and paradoxical. Montevideo, Minnesota, was named by its sturdy Scandinavian founders after the capital of Uruguay, and is now its sister city. The town celebrates this unusual tie every year at Fiesta Days, highlighted by the presence of the Uruguayan ambassador or a high-ranking deputy. A wreath is laid at the foot of the statue of José Artigas (a gift of the people of Montevideo, Uruguay, in the 1940s), the queen and her princesses wear Spanish-inspired lacy dresses with mantillas and combs, and there are a few other general Spanish-style touches to the festival and the city's architecture. But the town's Mexican or Mexican American migrant-labor pool is not represented in the festival at all. Festivals, even in small towns, are not untouched by the divisions and disagreements of everyday life. While the divisions between the "us" of the organizers and the "them" of the other groups within the community may be blurred, they are never absent, and a festival script that asserts community may be interpreted by other participants as denying their membership in that community.

Once the festival begins, it takes on a life of its own, out of the control of its organizers; as Paul Ricoeur notes, "In the same way that a text is detached from its author, an action is detached from its agent and develops consequences of its own. . . . [O]ur deeds escape us and have effects which we did not intend."[7] The festival, both text and action, becomes public property, creating a public culture. And the inability to control what happens once the festival begins is a loophole that lies at the center of this public culture. This loophole affects all the groups that meet in the festival, not just the organizers. The outsiders who now buy tours to small-town Minnesota festivals may find the performance quaint, pretentious, soaked in small-town tradition, or embarrassingly naive, but the organizers are equally free to find the outsiders' performance boorish, unpleasant, friendly, or cynical. Rural people may find the festival performance exclusionary, and young people may similarly find that they have no place in the festival; by extension, both groups may see this as symbolic of their place in the structure of things in the town. The organizers and their adherents, seeing the withdrawnness of the rural people, or what they interpret as the insolence of the young, may decide that the farmers are unsophisticated and the young incorrigible, and act accordingly.

The disagreements that are muted within small-town festivals can become increasingly audible in the festivals put on in larger towns. This is the case in Hutchinson, Minnesota, a city of some 9,200 people in the central part of the state. Its festival, the Jaycees Water Carnival, began in 1942, and is held annually over three days in June. The festival is a project of a civic organization, the Jaycees, that exists for reasons unconnected to festivals. That is, men in Hutchinson do not join the Jaycees because they want to work on the festival. They see the Jaycees as an organization with business and social importance. It is nevertheless the case that the Water Carnival has become the single most important project of the Jaycees, and working on the Water Carnival follows from membership. This is an important point: the Jaycee organizers, unlike organizers of festivals in other, smaller towns, are not "festival people," and this fact shapes both the festival and the community response to it.[8]

For one thing, the Jaycees are essentially an age grade: until very recently, men were required to leave the organization at age thirty-five. As a result, the long-term, continuous commitment to the festival by its organizers, a phenomenon found in towns where the organizing body is either festival-specific or not restricted by age, is absent in Hutchinson. This presents the Jaycees with two structural problems. First, members who may not be interested in the festival have to organize it. Second, as soon as someone has become good at organizing part of the festival, he leaves the organization. One solution that the members have developed is to organize the festival according to "the books." These are a set of loose-leaf notebooks, one for each aspect of the festival, which each committee chairman receives from his predecessor and passes on to his successor. Each includes a timeline and all of the details about the organization of the event. A committee chair has only to follow the book to do the job. And this is what most of them do most of the time. The option of canceling the festival is not one that seems open to them. They feel strongly that "the town would rise up in arms" if the festival was ever canceled. As a result, the dead hand of tradition rests heavily on them.

In Hutchinson there are two separate, official programs that result from the organizers' planning: one is open to the public, and the other is hidden from the public and open only to Jaycees and their wives. The events of the Water Carnival, especially given the size of the town, are rather limited compared with most small-town festivals. There is a queen competition, unusually divided into two parts, with the pageant on Friday night and the coronation on Sunday night. There are races (a two-mile one and a ten-kilometer one), three children's events (Big Wheel races, a parade, and a junior royalty coronation), a square-dance demonstration, the Queen's Ball, a fly-in breakfast organized by the Civil Air Patrol at the county airfield, a large parade, powerboat races, mud volleyball, a traveling carnival and midway, a pork chop dinner at the airfield put on by the Civil Air Patrol, and fireworks. A tennis tournament and men's and junior girls' softball tournaments are held concurrently, but are not official, Jaycees-run events. Most of the food concessions are provided by the carnival, which is located away from the main part of the town but near the park at which the powerboat races and mud volleyball are held. Such classic small-town festival events as a beer garden, street dance, firemen's water fight, arts and crafts fair, and various other contests are not held. There is beer sold by the Jaycees near the boat race and mud volleyball area, but the location is out of the way, poorly marked, not publicized before the festival, and seems to be frequented mainly by Jaycees.

Unknown to the general public are the events of what I call the festival within the festival. At the local motel that serves as the Water Carnival headquarters there is a hospitality room, open to all Jaycees at any time during the festival and well stocked with cold beverages and food of various kinds. An appreciation party, a semiformal cocktail party at the home of a wealthy business or professional man, dinner at the country club, a "royal buffet" (held for queens, princesses, and their chaperones from other communities who have come for the parade), and a large concluding party called Afterglow are, from the point of view of the Jaycees, the major events of the festival, and their reward for raising the money and putting on the festival. About one-quarter of the $31,000 budget goes to this festival within the festival. These events help to create the private culture of the Jaycees—one based on privilege, and the justification of both their way of life and their entitlement to it. While very few people we spoke with in the city know much about the details of these parties, there is certainly a general consensus that the Jaycees are "cliquey" and do not want any input from the rest of the town. In this they are correct. A former Water Carnival commodore (the head of the festival organization) told me that were other organizations to get involved, there would be conflicts over who was running the festival. Hence it was better that only one organization run it.

It is interesting to note, however, that out of all the festivals I have studied, including the St. Paul Winter Carnival, this was the only festival in which there was ambivalence about our project on the part of the organizers, and in which we were excluded from some events and made to feel uncomfortable at others. This is not, I think, accidental. Some of the Jaycees see their parties, and their festival within the festival, as private, and did not want to be the subject of observation by a group of college students and their professor. Some seemed worried about our "blowing their cover," as it were, and revealing the extent to which the Water Carnival could be interpreted as a justification for Jaycee parties. Some seemed unwilling to consider the contradiction between their private parties and the public festival, which they may sense (and even profit from), but which they cannot fully control or justify. By contrast, the commodore of the 1987 festival, who was a high-ranking member of the Jaycees, and the vice commodore were most hospitable and very supportive of the research. They, too, have their own agendas for the future of the festival and the Jaycees: diversification of membership in both the Jaycees and the festival organizing group, the inclusion of more events, and the incorporation of more of the city's civic organizations.

The explicit ideology expressed by the Jaycees is that they put on the Water Carnival to develop community pride and togetherness. They are doing something for the community. The Water Carnival is a way that they can be of service to the people of the area. Yet at least half of the men in the Jaycees had moved to Hutchinson within the last three to ten years from elsewhere (several more had moved back after several years' absence), and joined the Jaycees "to meet other men their age who have similar interests." There is a major structural feature of life in Hutchinson that the Jaycees cannot control: many Jaycees members are newcomers who find themselves in this city at this moment for career reasons. They are alienated from the community by their youth, occupation, and relative wealth, and by the way they set themselves apart as the organizers of a public celebration of a community in which they themselves are relative newcomers. Hutchinson is unusual in that the main employer in the city is 3M, which produces a great deal of its videotape at its Hutchinson plant. Over two thousand people work at 3M, some of whom are executives or managers, some of whom (although not many) join the Jaycees. Hutchinson is also an important banking center for that region of the state, and there are three large banks in the city. The young bankers are very active in the Jaycees and the festival. There are several prominent people in the city who work in the Twin Cities, some fifty miles away, and some who have moved to Hutchinson from the Twin Cities. People in town regularly talk about shopping in the malls in the western suburbs of Minneapolis or attending other events in the Twin Cities metropolitan area.

At the same time, most of the employees at 3M are wage laborers, most from the city and smaller cities in the area, though some are farm wives. There are other relatively large employers in Hutchinson, and they too employ wage laborers, assemblers, semiskilled workers, etc. The class divisions that are downplayed in small towns are much clearer in Hutchinson: the man who is in a public position in the festival may be a man who has power over your future. He may be the man who denied you a loan or began foreclosure proceedings against your uncle's farm, wears an elegant suit, went to college, and belongs to the country club.[9]

The standard community-festival ideology—that the organizing body is open to anyone in the community who wants to participate—is not entirely absent in Hutchinson. To be sure, except for certain peripheral events such as the tennis and softball tournaments, organizers must be Jaycees, but Jaycees membership is theoretically open to all men under the age of thirty-five. Nevertheless, the issue of social class is not far from the surface. The commodore complained that although the Jaycees are open to all men of the correct age who wished to join, they had been having a great deal of trouble getting working-class and lower-middle-class members. He was of the opinion that this was in part because the only place the Jaycees could find to meet was the country club, and many potential working-class or lower-middle-class members did not feel comfortable in those surroundings. He added that some of the Jaycees liked it that way, though he did not; one of his goals was to find another place for the Jaycees to meet because he felt it necessary for the organization to diversify. There still exists an egalitarian ethos in Hutchinson: the idea that it should be possible for any man in town to join the Jaycees works against the idea that the Jaycees are (or ought to be) an elite organization. This may contribute to the discomfort many Jaycees seem to feel with the privileges they grant themselves during the festival.

To summarize, a nonrandom group of men in the community, the Jaycees, who are young businessmen, bankers, insurance agents, owners or managers of businesses, lawyers, or dentists, are the people behind the festival. They have taken it upon themselves to speak for the community, as do all festival organizers, and to present an event that becomes the public expression of the community, both to itself and to outsiders who are only in the community during the festival. The Jaycees do not share this work with other civic organizations, nor do they share the credit. This is resented in Hutchinson. A surprising number of people on the street, going about their regular business, informed us that they would attend only the parade, that they didn't feel that the other events were for them. Some even suggested that the entire festival was really an event for the Jaycees.

The festival as it is practiced reflects both the Jaycees' relative unfamiliarity with Hutchinson as well as the characteristics of the social fraction to which they belong. It could even be argued that, counter to the ideological statements made by the members, the festival is designed in such a way as to separate the Jaycees from the rest of the community, bringing the two groups together only for certain specific events. Indeed, the ways in which the groups come together are carefully orchestrated. The queen coronation, for example, becomes an occasion for the community to thank the Jaycees for all they have done for Hutchinson. The coronation is held in front of a backdrop representing the statue of an Indian that is the official symbol of the city. The winner is called Miss Hutchinson, and is supposed to represent the city at other festivals that she will attend. In her white evening gown, she receives from the tuxedo-clad commodore a diamond cocktail ring representing her position. Her first and last acts during her year as queen (and her only opportunities to speak during the coronation ceremony itself) consist of tearful speeches thanking the Jaycees. Here, then, the community—in the form of its "official" representative—grants the Jaycees the recognition they believe they deserve, assures them that their efforts have not been in vain, and proclaims that their view of the city, the festival, and their relationships to both are satisfying and appropriate. As I noted earlier, many people in the community do not share this understanding. But those people do not pay forty or fifteen dollars per couple for reserved seats, nor three dollars for seats in the back, to attend the queen pageant.

In terms of the organization of events, the Hutchinson Water Carnival presents a public culture emphasizing division rather than solidarity. For example, although the traveling carnival, which attracts children and adolescents from a wide variety of backgrounds, was in action on Friday, the major event of the day was the queen pageant, an expensive event that attracted 625 people, many fashionably dressed. On Saturday, all but one of the public events attracted both Jaycees and others. Several of the forty-three entrants in the ten-kilometer run were Jaycees. All but one of the Jaycees were married and many had children, and the Kiddie Day events were of interest to them. Indeed, my students observed that many of the people in the crowds at the children's events were Jaycees. The one event that was not of interest to the Jaycees was the square-dance demonstration, and it was scheduled to overlap with an important Jaycee cocktail party. The Queen's Ball was another event that attracted far more Jaycees than anyone else: the candidates and the outgoing queen and princesses were in formal gowns, and those Jaycees who were most involved with the Water Carnival were in tuxedos. This is a far cry from the small-town street dance, where dress is blue jeans, shorts, and various kinds of appropriate shirts and tops.

The one "populist" day was Sunday, which for most people started at one o'clock in the afternoon, when the parade began. The parade was followed by the powerboat races and the mud volleyball tournament, and then later in the evening by the coronation and fireworks. The parade drew a very large crowd—there were nearly 16,000 people lining the route.[10] Particularly striking was the number of reunions and parties being held on lawns along the residential blocks of the parade route. Here were people's private celebrations, carried out in counterpoint to the official communal ideology of the festival. All festivals provide, at the very least, a focal point for scheduling reunions and family get-togethers. They are a justification for sociability within preexisting, private spheres of social interaction. However, most small-town festivals also provide the opportunity for an experience of communality through a meal open to and convenient for everyone in town, where the private pleasures of friends and family are extended and complemented by the public expression of community membership made possible by festival-provided commensality. The absence of such a meal in Hutchinson reinforced the distinction between the Jaycees and the rest of the community, who had to make private picnics on their own lawns or in the parks.

This same pattern was continued in the other events on Sunday, the powerboat races and the mud volleyball tournament. Over 1,700 people attended the three events scheduled soon after the parade (this includes those counted in the area near the traveling carnival). Many had brought lawn chairs and coolers with food and beverages, but there was no food for sale. Once again, the emphasis was on individual clusters of people independently seeking entertainment. The irony is that the Jaycees were intensifying *their* own sense of community, rewarding *themselves* for a job well done, and establishing and reestablishing *their* own communal ties. It is scarcely surprising that following the fireworks should come the Afterglow for the Jaycees.

Thus, in Hutchinson, the festival organizers are rather dramatically alienated from and alienating to those segments of the city that are not their own. Their control over the festival is obvious and resented, and it is not countered by any outlet for the disaffected. In contrast, the small-town festival organizers are not so strikingly alienated from the people for whom the festival is organized. Their control is hidden, and as a result, opposition or disaffection is diffuse, with no clear target.

A striking contrasting case can be found in the St. Paul Winter Carnival. St. Paul, the capital of Minnesota, has a population of about 270,000, and is part of the Twin Cities metropolitan area of more than two million people. The St. Paul Winter Carnival was celebrated irregularly in its early history, beginning first in 1886 and being held off and on until 1946, since when it has been held annually. It is a large and elaborate undertaking that extends over twelve days, boasting a full-time staff of four and a legion of over sixteen hundred volunteers. Several key features of the Hutchinson Jaycees Water Carnival are even more highly developed in the St. Paul Winter Carnival. All are related to the fact that class divisions in St. Paul are well established, multiply determined, and clear-cut. The egalitarian ethos that still has the power to make some Hutchinson Jaycees uncomfortable has become little more than a slogan for many in St. Paul. This accentuates the prominence of certain features of the festival that have a lower profile in Hutchinson.

The St. Paul Winter Carnival operates on two levels, that of performance and that of administration and organization. The St. Paul Winter Carnival Association is the body that is responsible for the official program of the event. Composed of a board of directors, a festival cabinet, an executive director, and a three-member professional staff, it handles thematic coordination, fundraising, publicity, and the scheduling of official Winter Carnival events. This is a year-round job, and much of it is behind the scenes.

For most residents of St. Paul, however, the distinctive features of Winter Carnival are the Royal Family and the Vulcans, two uniformed groups who enact the fifty-year-old festival legend during the last ten days of Winter Carnival[11] and who then travel all over Minnesota and beyond during the rest of the year. The Royal Family is composed of twenty-one members: King Boreas (the king of winter, and the ruler of Winter Carnival); his brothers, the Princes of the Winds (North, South, East, and West); the Queen of the Snows; the four Wind Princesses; the Prime Minister; the Captain of the Guard; and the nine King's Guards. The Royal Family makes over 150 appearances during

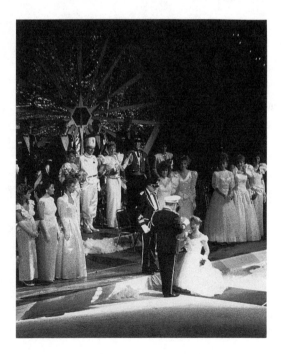

Fig. 4-1. The new Queen of the Snows kneels before King Boreas to receive her crown. Photo by the author.

the ten days, some public, some at Winter Carnival functions, and many at hospitals, schools, nursing homes, and other care facilities.

Opposing these rather stodgy guardians of winter and social order are the eight Vulcans and Vulcanus Rex, the fire king. The Vulcans dress in red running suits and capes, crested hoods, and ski goggles, and smear greasepaint on their cheeks and chins. Formerly renowned in St. Paul for their traditional practice of kissing women and smudging them with their greasepaint—the sooty symbol of the increasing power of the forces of warmth—the Vulcans now are permitted only to rub their faces against the cheeks of consenting women. The Vulcans are completely anonymous, both to the public and to one another: during the festival, they refer to one another by their "Vulcan names," such as the Prince of Ashes, Grand Duke Fertilious, or Baron Sparkus (also known as Sparky). The Vulcans are the most carnivalesque feature of Winter Carnival. They lodge together during the ten days they are active in the festival, ride around the city in an antique fire truck, make fun of the Royal Family, and engage in mock battles with them. Safe in their anonymity, the Vulcans, representing warmth and disorder, deconstruct the stuffed-shirt pomposity of the Royal

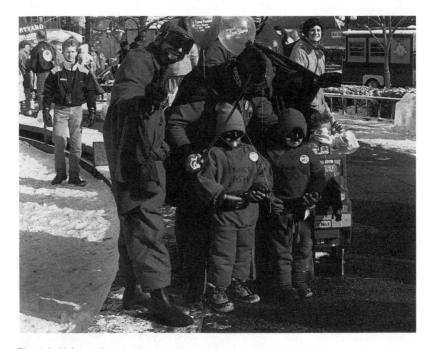

Fig. 4-2. Vulcanis Rex (with a sword) and a member of the Vulcan Krewe pose with two winners of the Kiddie Parade, Vulcans-in-Training. Photo by the author.

Family and, by extension, the order they represent. At the end of every Winter Carnival, they make one final attack on the Royal Family and win. Winter has been defeated. The Vulcans are the popular favorites, universally recognized and cheered around the city. Two of my students had a chance to ride with the 1990 Vulcan Krewe on their fire truck for a few hours as they traveled to schools, nursing homes, hospitals, restaurants, and department stores. They reported that wherever in St. Paul they were—and they went through many of the city's neighborhoods—people honked their horns and waved, made the V-for-Vulcan sign, and shouted "Hail the Vulc!" As with everything carnivalesque, however, the Vulcans are not just safely domesticated figures of fun; they can be frightening and potentially dangerous. At night, leaping off the truck, capes flying, the powerful smell of alcohol enveloping them, running after women to smudge them even if the women object, they exude a whiff of the chaos that lies at the heart of carnivalesque disorder.

The uniformed groups are not officially part of the Winter Carnival Association. Each uniformed segment has its own alumni association, a fraternal order dedicated to choosing (sometimes) and supporting (always) the annual incumbent(s) of the role. So there are four wind organizations, the Order of the Royal Guard, the Star of Boreas, the Queens, the Churchill Club (for former Prime Ministers), and—the most powerful, wealthiest, and best organized of all—Fire and Brimstone, for former Vulcans. There is also a women's division, which is the backbone of Winter Carnival and seems to be composed largely of wives of members of the uniformed groups, especially Fire and Brimstone. Each fraternal order has its own uniforms for different occasions, and produces emblems in the forms of buttons, embroidered patches, pins, and so on: some to sell, some to distribute to other uniformed groups or to the public, and some with which to adorn themselves. These groups are active throughout the year but the level of their social activities increases around the time of Winter Carnival. Many of the events they sponsor, dinners especially, are officially open to anyone who wants to attend and is willing to buy tickets. These dinners are expensive: several informants remarked that it could cost around a thousand dollars per couple to attend all of them. For example, the October fundraiser, called the Snow Ball, costs one hundred dollars per person. About five hundred people attend. The dinner that precedes the royal coronation, which features the introduction and investiture of the new male members of the Royal Family and the coronation of the new Queen of the Snows and the new princesses, costs fifty dollars per person. Slightly over a thousand people attended in 1990.

The jewelry, furs, clothing, hair styles, cars, deep tans, and so on that are on display at these events signal clearly that Winter Carnival is organized and performed by an elite. It takes money and position to be part of the core of Winter Carnival. All the members of the uniformed groups must be able to be absent from their jobs for ten days during the festival, and must have the freedom afterwards to make appearances on evenings and weekends (King Boreas and the Queen of the Snows now make over four hundred appearances a year). The King's Guards are men in their mid- to late twenties who can afford the $1,500 in uniforms, pins, lodging, food, and entertainment it will cost for the year. Vulcans are older and better established; it costs about $3,000 for a year on the Krewe. Vulcanus Rex, usually in his forties or early fifties, will normally spend about $15,000. The Prime Minister, usually a man in his early to mid-thirties, normally spends about $10,000. The Princes of the Winds are usually in their forties, and well-known and successful businessmen; they are chosen by their wind organizations. It costs at least $10,000 to be a Prince of the Wind. Boreas must be a man at the height of an executive career, in his late forties or early fifties, who is prepared to make an investment of upwards of $40,000. Frequently, the corporations for which these men work contribute to their support, sometimes substantially.[12]

During Winter Carnival, the major players, including the chairman of the board and the president of the festival cabinet, chaperones for the queen and princesses, and all the uniformed characters, take up residence in three hotels in downtown St. Paul. One of these, the stately St. Paul Hotel, becomes the de facto center of the festival within the festival. As in Hutchinson, the St. Paul elite regularly congratulates itself for its festival activities, although it does so in a rather more spectacular style. The festival within the festival, which is concealed and almost furtive in Hutchinson, is openly, elaborately, vigorously, and joyously celebrated in St. Paul. As the doorman of the St. Paul Hotel remarked, "Those people know how to party."

For the people most deeply involved, the two weeks of Winter Carnival are a time of intense social activity and like a rite of intensification. Those in a given year's performance wing are in at least a liminoid period, approaching and perhaps reaching the truly liminal.[13] They are separated physically, emotionally, mentally, and in attire and activity from their everyday lives. They live what appears to most of them later to have been a dream of remarkable power and

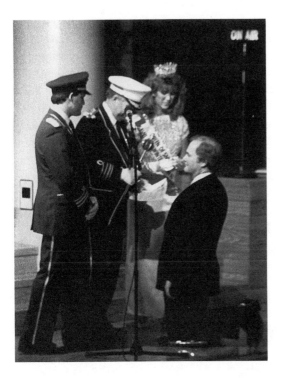

Fig. 4-3. King Boreas (center), his Prime Minister, and the Queen of the Snows knight a worthy subject, tenor Vern Sutton. Photo by the author.

affect. For those who put on the festival, there are parties, meetings, events to attend and direct, and more parties. Those who are members of the fraternal organizations seem to be involved in a round of parties and events that never stops. A former Vulcan reviewed his schedule for one of the weeks with me. Every night was taken up with some Winter Carnival–related social activity: the Seventh Street Parade, a traditional Vulcan event that involves drinking in every bar along a street famous for the number of its bars; the reunion of Fire and Brimstone at the hotel to initiate and swear in the new Krewe the night before the Vulcan Coming-Out (an event for which my informant checked into the hotel to avoid the temptation to drive home and risk a DWI arrest); the reunion of his Krewe (this event with wives); the get-together that his Krewe always has with their successors; the Vulcan Conclave; a party for the parade street directors (he was the director for parades); the West Wind dinner; and the Torchlight Parade and Vulcan Victory Dance. While this man's schedule may have been a bit more crowded than most, my students and I saw the same faces at many of the social events associated with Winter Carnival that we were able to attend (which were by no means all of them).

This festival within the festival at Winter Carnival reflects, perhaps, the intensity of the experiences of the people who have performed in Winter Carnival. They have certainly created a social world that they find compelling and satisfying, and that extends beyond the specifics of Winter Carnival. In this, they are similar to the West Indians who celebrate Carnival in Notting Hill, discussed by Abner Cohen: "The two-day event is the culmination of months of preparation by various artistic groups, which over the years have become permanent cliques of friends, interacting in primary relationships that are not necessarily connected with the carnival."[14] The Winter Carnival people patronize one another's businesses. They vacation with one another. They marry one another. They have their own language of address and reference, their own kinship system (for example, the Princes of the Winds are brothers to Boreas, and men who have had the same Vulcan name in different years have been heard to refer to each other as "brother"), and even a lengthy formal protocol manual. Indeed, the president of the festival cabinet, a senior vice president at the St. Paul Companies, told me his response to friends who were asking why anthropologists were studying Winter Carnival: "We've created a culture here, with tribal differences and so on, and that's something anthropologists study."

The public performance itself, however, plays with symbols of domination and appropriation. The stress on the quintessential hierarchical figures of royalty provides one field for the expression of these symbols. The Royal Family dress in elaborate costumes that proclaim and catalogue hierarchy—the princes as an Oriental potentate, a Mexican charro, a wealthy cowboy complete with leather coat, silver buckle, and snakeskin boots, and a vaguely Tartarlike lord; the Prime Minister and King Boreas in the kind of military uniforms worn by modern European royalty, the king with his scepter, the queen and princesses in formal attire with crowns, and the King's Guards in military uniforms with braid. The language of subjects and rulers, of "our right royal city," the knightings of worthy people[15] into the service of Boreas, the medals bestowed, the buttons distributed, the Captain of the Guard with his sword, and the guards themselves, who march in rhythmic step into every public setting, all provide an overwhelming image of political domination. The Landmark Center, the old federal courts building in St. Paul, now beautifully restored and a symbol of the city, becomes the King's Castle, and in the three-story atrium a dais is erected with two thrones (one for King Boreas and one for the Queen of the Snows). The Grande Day and Torchlight parades are the most popular Winter Carnival events in those years when an ice palace is not constructed. These parades are filled with floats carrying not just the Royal Family, but also members of the different fraternal orders. Most St. Paulites know that the members of the uniformed groups are wealthy, and they see that almost all the players are male and all are white. Here is an elite with very clear criteria for membership. Their festival performance suggests that they *deserve* this position, and they are not shy about advertising and celebrating the rightness of their dominion.

The Royal Family, in particular, has appropriated the right to speak for St. Paul. In speech after speech, King Boreas talks about the pleasure and honor of representing Winter Carnival *and the city of St. Paul.* In the promotional material, too, the same conflation is made. When the Royal Family travels to Winnipeg, Manitoba; Austin, Texas; Bradenton, Florida; Memphis, Tennessee; or to small towns around the state, its members see themselves, and are referred to by their hosts, as representing not just the St. Paul Winter Carnival but St. Paul. This, in the context of present-day St. Paul, is problematic. The community ethos of St. Paul is one of pluralism, or at least involves an ideology of multiple communities and distinct neighborhoods. The celebration of domination and the claim of representativeness are contradicted by both the official ideology of the city and the everyday experience of its citizens. There are people who are aware of this contradiction; many of them belong to groups that do not see themselves in Winter Carnival. They, and others, reject or ignore details of Winter Carnival that are most important to the insiders. For example, the attendance by the general public at the coronation has been declining over the last few years. In 1990 there were fewer people in the free-admission balcony seats than there were on the main floor tables, which cost fifty dollars per person. Instead, the general public concentrated on those events that were urban entertainments—the snow-sculpture and ice-carving contests, the firebird and Russian Orthodox chapel created by the visiting Soviet ice carvers, and the parades.

But much less resentment was expressed to us by excluded citizens in St. Paul than we encountered in Hutchinson. In part, I believe, this is because the Vulcans represent an ironic counter to the Royal Family. The ordinary people of St. Paul can support the Vulcans, cheering them on as they poke fun at the Royal Family and sow a little disorder. It does not seem to matter that the Vulcans hardly differ from the Royal Family in background: white, male, wealthy, and on the way up (perhaps the sole difference is that the only Jews in Winter Carnival have been Vulcans). For the moment, the Vulcans represent the counterforce to the overly orderly world of King Boreas.[16] The resentment that people might feel toward the festival's organizers is deflected, although not erased, by the Vulcans. It is also true that the show that is put on in St. Paul is better than the show put on in Hutchinson, and for obvious reasons. The entire budget for the Hutchinson Water Carnival is the budget for one Winter Carnival *parade* in St. Paul. The scale of the organizations is hardly comparable; for example, the organizers of the St. Paul Winter Carnival arranged to bring in ice carvers from the Soviet Union in 1990 and from China in 1989. The St. Paul Winter Carnival also offers a wider range of events for different constituencies: from ski and snowshoe races and hockey tournaments to concerts, parades, dances, children's events, senior citizens' events, and a fun fair with midway, music, craft sales, concessions, displays, and more.

Nevertheless, as in Hutchinson and the small towns, the organizers of Winter Carnival do not speak with one voice. The executive director, a remarkable man named Bob Carter, as centrally located in Winter Carnival as it is possible to be, is keenly aware of many of the contradictions within Winter Carnival, and is working on strategies to do something about them without alienating the core of Winter Carnival people who have devoted an enormous amount of time and money to the festival and who have built their social lives around it. For example, following the 1990 coronation, he decided that the next year the princesses would no longer kneel in front of their princes to receive their crowns. He is also working to change the image of the Queen of the Snows from that of a virginal daughter of the community to that of a prominent St. Paul businesswoman, the female equivalent of King Boreas. Carter is aware that some people believe that Winter Carnival is just a fraternity party for rich white businessmen, and he is hoping to change that image by decentralizing the carnival: moving events into St. Paul's neighborhoods and inviting representatives of ethnic and racial groups to develop their own events under the carnival rubric. He is not alone in his assessment of Winter Carnival, but he does not represent the only voice within the carnival. There are many who like Winter Carnival just as it is, and some would quit if the festival changed much at all. Carter himself recognizes the multiple interpretations of Winter Carnival. He pointed out, in regard to his proposal to make the Queen of the Snows a prominent businesswoman, that for every woman who felt it was about time to make this change, there was at least one who swore that if it happened, she would never support Winter Carnival again.

The future of Winter Carnival is not, of course, something that the organizers alone will decide. It will also be shaped by the wider economic, political, and cultural changes that are going on in the community, and by the contested interpretations of these changes.

For example, changes in the economic base of St. Paul brought about by corporate restructuring and consolidation are affecting Winter Carnival. In contradistinction to both the small-town festivals and the Hutchinson Water Carnival, many, perhaps most, of the people who organize and perform in Winter Carnival are St. Paul natives. Growing up in the tradition, sometimes with fathers or grandfathers who had been part of Winter Carnival, many St. Paulites have come to see Winter Carnival as an important resource for their own social and business activities. But the changes in the economic structure of St. Paul have had an effect on Winter Carnival. Many formerly independent businesses have become part of larger corporations, and some of the larger corporations have moved their headquarters to Minneapolis, or have moved large segments of their workforces out of state. Of the three great St. Paul breweries that had been of signal importance to the festival over the years, Hamm's is gone, and both the Stroh's and Schmidt breweries have been taken over by larger beer conglomerates. In fact, during Winter Carnival this year, the city of St. Paul had to begin seriously to consider ways of keeping the Stroh's and Schmidt breweries from closing. The other side of the economic transformation is the development of "corporate suburbs," made up in large measure of people who have been transferred into the St. Paul area. While these people are expected to become involved civically, such localized civic activities as Winter Carnival may not be as attractive as national activities such as the United Way, the American Heart Association, and so on, membership in which is portable. Here is another challenge that Winter Carnival must face, and the strategies put in place now for attracting volunteers will shape the future of the festival.

The attempt to bring other groups and neighborhoods into the carnival itself is interpretable in several ways. On the one hand, it can be seen as a long-overdue recognition that Winter Carnival must, work actively to be inclusive, rather than exclusive, and that its claim to represent all of St. Paul rings hollow without the participation of other constituencies. But it can also be seen as conveying a kind of second-class citizenship on people who cannot afford to become part of the core of Winter Carnival people. It highlights the difficulty that Winter Carnival is having in finding people who can be seen as representative of these multiply-voiced communities in St. Paul. It can also be interpreted as an attempt to extend middle-class control outward into ethnic and working-class communities,[17] incorporating groups that already have their own festivals. But in diversifying the makeup of Winter Carnival, more volunteers are made available, and Winter Carnival must also respond to the changes in the corporate volunteer pool.

The growing litigiousness of American society has caused the Winter Carnival organizers to cancel, rethink, or replace several traditional, classic participatory Winter Carnival events, ranging from the ice palace (insurance companies would not write liability insurance except at an almost impossibly high cost; engineers and architects refused to "inspect" the construction, although they would "observe" it) and toboggan runs to ice slides for children. The effect of the loss or scaling-back of these events is felt in the declining public participation in Winter Carnival, which has been replaced with increased spectatorship.

There have also been attempts since the late 1970s to control carnivalesque disorder by limiting what the Vulcans can do. There is a clear ambiguity in the figure of the Vulcan, who represents freedom and challenges the domination of the "rulers" by attacking women. The simultaneous impact of the women's movement and the rise of litigiousness have led the Vulcans to feel beleaguered, and have forced them to "clean up their act." They have modified many of their traditional practices: for example, they no longer kiss and smudge all women they see; many of their traditional pranks that used to be directed toward the Royal Family are now directed from the outgoing to the incoming Krewe; and they are trying to shift public attention to their civic activities. But the public still expects the Vulcans to be as the public remembers them. Winter Carnival is sedimented in people's memories and in the history of St. Paul; the weight of that performance tradition also serves to control the performers. People would be disappointed if the Vulcans became too tame, however politically correct or legally prudent that might be. At the same time many members of Fire and Brimstone oppose the women's movement, decry the litigiousness of modern American society, and resent the changes that have been implemented or suggested. Some Vulcans on the street push at the edges of the changes, for example smearing women even if they protest.

The women's movement has also had an effect on the coronation ritual of the Royal Family. Formerly, the wives of the Princes of the Winds and Boreas were never even mentioned, let alone introduced during this ceremony. Today, members of the uniformed groups in Winter Carnival now formally recognize the contributions of wives to their husbands' role activities. In 1990, the wives of both the outgoing and incoming princes and kings even appeared on stage with their husbands. Let me take a moment to describe these scenes. Each outgoing fortyish prince and his twenty-two- or twenty-three-year-old princess came forward from the royal grouping at the back of the stage to receive recognition from the crowd. The prince's wife was then introduced and came onstage, joining her husband and his princess. She received a bouquet of roses from her husband, kissed him, and then leaned across him to embrace the princess. Together, all three, husband in the middle, acknowledged the cheers of the crowd. The incoming prince was then introduced and, with his wife, climbed the steps to the end of the runway, some twenty feet or more from the front of the stage. Husband and wife walked together about a third of the way to the stage, where they stopped and kissed. She returned to the steps and disappeared into the darkness. Her husband, the prince, continued forward to the stage, where a line of twenty young women, the contestants in the Queen of the Snows competition, waited. Moments later, he received his princess, who knelt before him to receive her crown from his hands.

To an anthropological observer, this ceremony looked like either a ritual of acceptance by a first wife of her husband's new wife in a polygynous society or, alternatively, the public bestowal of a subservient second (or "trophy") wife with at least the tacit approval of the senior wife. I do not want to suggest that the organizers wished to achieve this problematic, tension-producing, awkward outcome; far from it. I do wish to point out, however, in traditional anthropological terms, how their good-faith attempts at change can produce unexpected results, and how the serious pursuit of change in women's roles is bound to affect the structure of Winter Carnival at levels the organizers might not have anticipated. The modified coronation ceremony was, after all, designed to reflect positively the contemporary, egalitarian model of husband-wife relations, and to recognize explicitly the wife's contribution. Yet it had quite the opposite effect, throwing into sharp relief the conflicts, especially in the marriages of successful men, between their duty to their wives and their attraction to an image of themselves as having earned the right to appear in public with beauti-

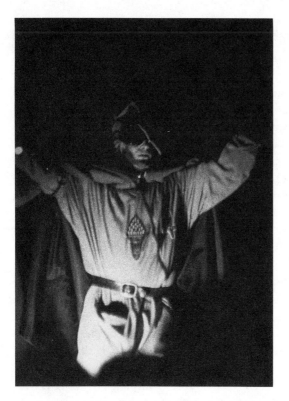

Fig. 4-4. The moment of Vulcan triumph: King Boreas is overturned, and the Vulcans rule. Photo by the author.

ful young women on their arms. The conflict was certainly present in the performance, and was obvious to more observers than just the anthropologist.

In conclusion, the public culture created by community festivals is a contested and contestable culture, a field of both political and cultural forces, constituted by events satisfying different tastes and subject to the play of varying interests. But festivals as public events par excellence are accented by the communities in which they are found. The social ties in Minnesota communities are fragile and contingent. In small towns, these ties must be nurtured and protected, for divisiveness is a danger to the community's survival as a more or less coherent entity. The people who remain earnestly support the communitarian ideology, avoiding the corrosive irony of carnival.[18] This ideology is plausible and necessary because the town is small. A midsized town such as Hutchinson is sufficiently diverse and divided that the communitarian ideology is both implausible and less vital for the life of the city. But this leads to a split in the city that the festival makes plain. In a large city such as St. Paul, a monolithic communitarian ethos is both implausible and unachievable, and the festival's potential for making visible and "thinkable" the sharp divisions within the city is shaped and colored by the presence of the Vulcans. The Vulcans do not deny the divisions, they incarnate them. But the dialogue is formalized in play—there are antagonisms, but nobody gets hurt. Beyond that, Boreas and the Vulcans appear to form a necessary combination. Neither makes sense without the other, and the outcome of their struggle creates the image of a playing field that is truly level. After all, even though the Vulcans triumph at the end of Winter Carnival, by the next January Boreas is back on his throne and the Vulcans must break out once again. Abner Cohen points out that "carnivals are irreducible cultural forms, but, like all other cultural forms, are seldom free of political significance. They range in their political functions from the maintenance of the established order, serving as 'rituals of rebellion', to the articulation of protest, resistance and violence against that order. The same carnival may vary in its politics over time."[19] I wish to suggest that they may speak with and to more than one voice at the same time and that, indeed, this loophole is the dialogic potential at the heart of public culture.

NOTES

This paper is based on research that I began in the summer of 1981, when I began directing the St. Cloud State University field school in cultural anthropology. Field schools in the summers of 1983, 1985, and 1987 provided much additional data, as did the winter 1990 field school at the St. Paul Winter Carnival. Intensive research at seven festivals during the summer of 1984 was made possible by an NEH summer stipend. My thanks go to the many students who have worked with me on these field schools. Great thanks are also particularly due to the organizers of and participants in the eighteen festivals I have studied. We have valued their generous hospitality and openness. In the past, community members who have read my work on their festivals have told me that it seemed right to them. In this essay, my voice joins, but sometimes contends with, theirs. In various stages of this research, I have been much influenced by discussions with Don Handelman and James Fernandez. The present essay has benefited much from discussions I have had with Richard Flores and Jack Kugelmass. Ivan Karp has been of signal importance to the development of this work, both generally and specifically. My greatest intellectual debt is, as always, to Emily Schultz, whose incisiveness and insight strengthened both fieldwork and writing.

1. My claims here are limited solely to the eighteen Minnesota festivals about which I have direct knowledge. Nevertheless, it is clear from the literature that this assertion is true for many other festivals in the United States. See especially Frederick Errington, "Reflexivity Deflected: The Festival of Nations as an American Cultural Performance," *American Ethnologist* 14, no. 4 (1987), 654–67; Beverly Stoeltje, "Cultural Queens: Modernization and Representation" (paper presented at the 1987 annual meeting of the Association for the Study of Play, Montreal); Richard M. Swiderski, *Voices: An Anthropologist's Dialogue with an Italian-American Festival* (London, Ontario: Centre for Social and Humanistic Studies, University of Western Ontario, 1986); and W. Lloyd Warner, *The Living and the Dead: A Study of the Symbolic Life of Americans* (New Haven: Yale University Press, 1959).

2. In their 1966 study of Benson, Minnesota, a county seat of some 4,000 people, Martindale and Hanson list the following self-reported occupational categories: farmer, 5; laborer, 9; white-collar worker, 5; professional, 25; businessman, 18; other, 15; total, 77. Even if the "other" category is not included in the middle class, nearly two-thirds of the sample is still in the same basic social category. Benson's own planning report from 1961 categorizes sixty percent of all male employees as proprietors, officials, managers, foremen, and craftsmen (Don Martindale and R. Galen Hanson, *Small Town and the Nation: The Conflict of Local and Translocal Forces* [Westport, Conn.: Greenwood, 1969], 70, 94–95).

3. Lynn Brink, course essay for Honors 310 Folklore, St. Cloud State University, St. Cloud, Minn., 1988.

4. Robert H. Lavenda, "Family and Corporation: Two Styles of Celebration in Central Minnesota," in Frank E. Manning, ed., *The Celebration of Society: Perspectives on Contemporary Cultural Performance* (Bowling Green, Ohio: Bowling Green University Popular Press, 1983), and "Community Festivals, Paradox, and the Manipulation of Uncertainty," *Play and Culture* 4, no. 2 (1991), 153–68; Robert H. Lavenda et al., "Festivals and the Organization of Meaning: An Introduction to Community Festivals in Minnesota," in Brian Sutton-Smith and Diana Kelly-Byrne, eds., *The Masks of Play* (West Point, N.Y.: Leisure Press, 1984).

5. The county fairs are the alternative festival for farmers, who are sometimes quite explicit on this point.

6. In my experience, festivals with ethnic names in Minnesota are no different from festivals with product names, or geographic-feature names. Kolacky Days is not much different from Turkey Days, and both are quite similar to Waterama.

7. Paul Ricoeur, *Hermeneutics and Human Sciences: Essays on Language, Action, and Interpretation,* ed. and trans. John B. Thompson (Cambridge: Cambridge University Press, 1981).

8. There are many other towns in which the Chamber of Commerce, Lions Club, or similar service club organizes the festival. My observation is that the people in these organizations who run festivals are much more interested in them than are the Hutchinson Jaycees, who seem to put on the Water Carnival because they are supposed to. These organizations are not age grades, and members who enjoy putting on festivals can continue to work in the organization for many years.

9. This is not to suggest that bankers in small towns do not deny loans or foreclose on farm mortgages. They do. But on the one hand, they are much closer to many of their clients, and frequently have multiplex social connections to them. On the other hand, small-town bankers do make loans to people to whom bankers less enmeshed in a community would deny loans. Small-town banks sometimes get into financial trouble because their loan officers find it very difficult to say no or to foreclose.

10. This count is accurate for the crowd at the moment the first units passed each block. Two students counted the entire parade route, staying even with the flags. The remaining eight students each took a detailed demographic count on half of the blocks along the parade route. Their totals are very close to half the total of the first, general count.

11. Winter Carnival is officially twelve days long, beginning on a Wednesday, but the new Royal Family is inaugurated two days later, on Friday night. The new Vulcan Krewe "comes out" early the following Saturday morning.

12. For Boreas and Vulcanus Rex, the major expenses tend to be formal dinners for their supporters, which they underwrite. There are also the expenses associated with travel. Boreas is expected to pay for some of the expenses of his court, especially the Queen of the Snows, when they are on the road. He also invests in commemorative medals, coins, certificates, three uniforms, and so on.

13. A student in the field school remarked to me that, earlier in the project, after having read Turner, Manning, and others on the concepts of liminal and liminoid, she hadn't believed that either really existed in contemporary urban society. Then she spent a night with the queen's chaperone in the St. Paul Hotel and the next day with the Royal Family. "Now I know it exists," she told me.

14. Abner Cohen, "Drama and Politics in the Development of a London Carnival," *Man* 15, no. 1 (1980), 66.

15. Even anthropologists, who become Royal Researchers.

16. This same irony is found in the Marx Brothers' masterwork, *Duck Soup.* If we accept as convincing Ivan Karp's argument about the film ("Good Marx

for the Anthropologist: Structure and Anti-structure in 'Duck Soup,'" in W. Arens and Susan Montague, eds., *The American Dimension* [Sherman Oaks, Calif.: Alfred, 1981]), viewers identify with the Marx Brothers in their assault on the etiquette of public occasions and hierarchy, and as a result, the viewers' own private and inchoate experience of those structures is given form, legitimated, and transformed. At the time the film was made, in 1933, the Marx Brothers were immensely wealthy and famous, living in Hollywood, and a long way from the characters they played on screen.

17. John Fiske, *Understanding Popular Culture* (Boston: Unwin Hyman, 1989), 70–81.

18. Robert H. Lavenda, "Not Carnival But Fellowship: Communitas and Community in Minnesota Festivals," paper presented at the annual meeting of the American Anthropological Association, Washington, D.C., 1988.

19. Cohen, "Drama and Politics," 83.

CHAPTER 5

Art Museums and Living Artists: Contentious Communities

VERA L. ZOLBERG

You may wonder why in this book, I have left the artist until last. The reason is simple. In the art game he is the least important player. I am speaking, of course, of the living artist, who . . . is considered by most dealers to be a risky investment who has to be subsidized by the profits made out of dead artists.   ROBERT WRAIGHT (1965)

The museum and the living artist, so poignantly interdependent, must keep a wary distance. This means strain and altercation, but that is the natural order of things, a check and balance.

WALTER D. BANNARD (1975)

No one caught on to artists like Rothko faster than Alfred Barr and Dorothy Miller. . . . Without them, I would never have survived. I would have starved, and the artists along with me. They were always helping and showed all my painters at the museum. You're not going to see that happening today. Museums have relinquished their responsibility to keep up with what's going on.

BETTY PARSONS (1984)

The love-hate affair of artists and art museums has been a recurrent theme of literature, history, and sociological writings virtually since public art museums came into being.[1] No one doubts their interdependence, but the quality of their relationship depends upon whether the artists are living or dead; whether artists and museums face each other directly or through the mediation of dealers or collectors; whence comes the support on which both rely; the size and complexity of the museum; and the condition of the art world in which they find themselves.[2] They interact as suitors, duelists, petitioners and, sometimes, confederates. Although their relationship has undergone many changes, it seems appropriate to characterize it as one of fretful symbiosis.

Although American art museums are much admired throughout the world for their accomplishments in disseminating culture to a broad public,[3] they tend to exclude artists themselves from authoritative positions in aesthetic decisionmaking. This is an anomaly that has been little examined and calls for consideration. It is my contention that although museums of modern art have many occasions to deal with artists, they have rarely viewed living artists as forming a *community* toward which they have particular obligations. By the same token, except under certain conditions, artists tend not to form durable communities. Despite the prevalence of the theme, surprisingly little serious research has been devoted to their relationship, perhaps because those of us who study museums have had other important intellectual priorities that have dominated the research agenda, leaving artists to be studied in other contexts.[4]

This essay considers the relationship of art museums and living artists in order to highlight the bases of both their incompatibilities and their commonalities. Typically, once tensions between museums and artists have become public, strategies similar to those adopted in other conflicts are likely: forced or voluntary resignations, administrative restructuring, and/or mutual recognition of grievances. Whatever the resolution, further conflict is probable because of the structural conditions in which artists and art museums exist, and the divergence of their personal, institutional, and aesthetic goals.

It would be oversimplifying to characterize this relationship only as an us-against-them phenomenon. Rather, the degree of tension is reinforced by cultural and institutional traditions, and by demands based on professional and material interests. As the more powerful agent, art museums play a major role in constructing the artists' communities that they confront. Far from viewing their often vexed relationship as a permanent barrier to mutual understanding, I point to innovative methods that some museums have used in order to overcome it, drawing examples from large, well-established institutions and more recently created, smaller, less well established ones. The conflicts and compromises are inextricably intertwined with how art is defined, which is itself linked with how the character of communities of artists is changing today.

SOURCES OF TENSION IN THE ARTIST–ART MUSEUM RELATIONSHIP

Asymmetry of Need

As public institutions, American art museums are expected to provide services to their communities of visitors and members. They frequently confront conflicting demands, in particular in balancing the resources they provide to public education as opposed to the conservation efforts, exhibitions, and lavish catalogues preferred by many major donors. The other main source of contention concerns the art of living artists that they select for their collections. Although the especially contentious occasions are the ones that become widely known, it should be remembered that many art museums depend for their existence on old works by artists of the past. When they do collect or display new works, American museums are likely to receive them as gifts, or purchase them from dealers or other intermediaries rather than from artists directly. Their contacts with living artists are often fraught with tension because of the paradoxical nature of the relationship between the museum as an institution and the art that constitutes it. If they exclude contemporary artworks they are treated as conservative and timorous; if they welcome certain works but not others they may be accused of favoritism, of promoting artists whose works are collected by some of their donors or are found attractive by the politicians who control public funding; when they reject works that challenge conventional norms, they may be denounced for censorship and for violating creative freedom.

While the museum needs artworks, only some kinds of museums need the *creators* of the works. As the art historian Francis Haskell has pointed out, museums have two kinds of historical ancestors: the European academies, which acquired their art collections from works submitted by artists who competed for entry, and the collections of religious or secular rulers, which served as repositories of exemplary artworks. The collecting of exemplary works continued even after church and royal patronage weakened and these collections came under public control. Only with the creation in 1818 of the Musée du Luxembourg for *living* French artists did creators gain the chance of seeing their works in a permanent and prestigious institution.[5] But as in the academies and princely collections, once the works had been purchased they were no longer the artists' own to do with as they would. They belonged to the institution and/or to the state, which could decide whether to display or conceal them.

If anything, it would appear that living artists create problems that museums prefer to do without, such as importuning staff to acquire certain works or objecting to a work's placement in the museum. Museums deal with artists directly only when they have to, and on their own terms. Among these terms is that the artist must support the museum in upholding the aesthetic ideology of the autonomous artwork.[6] It is no wonder, therefore, that claims to different subject matter (especially when it is political), genres, and art forms threaten the established genre boundaries of art museums.

Beyond aesthetics, artworks in market societies (not very differently from other things) tend to be treated as commodities. Indeed, it is within that logic that artists create: they make art to order (by commission for an individual, firm, institution, or government), or to meet contractual obligations to their dealers, who act as go-betweens representing the artists' works to a largely anonymous market. On the whole, what happens to the works once these transactions are completed concerns others, not the artist. Although in the domain of commerce (advertising or commercial films, for example) the commoditization of art is taken for granted, when it comes to the fine arts a certain ambiguity pervades the relationship between artists and their works. In most European countries artists retain a continuing nonpropertied interest in their works even after they have consigned them to others. This *droit moral* stipulates that the artists or their heirs have the right to stop works from being mishandled or subjected to ridicule, for example being hung upside down or displayed in demeaning conditions. Aspects of the idea of *droit moral* are coming to be adopted in certain American states as well.[7] However, in the United States in general even museum-quality fine art and its creators are dealt with in a businesslike manner, which tends to exclude moral right from considerations of material right.[8] This highlights the opposition between the interests of museums and those of artists. This businesslike approach to art implicitly supports the conception of the artist as an alienated outsider to society, an idea that has pervaded the way in which artists view themselves in relation to the art market and to museums.[9]

Not only is it rare in the United States for artists to have direct access even to museums that collect works by living artists, but it is normal for their contacts to be mediated by collectors or dealers. This mediation is dictated both by custom and, practically speaking, by law. For whereas in other countries, even where an art market exists, artists themselves may be encouraged to donate or sell their works to museums,[10] in the United States the opposite tends to be the case. American tax laws have encouraged collectors to donate works to museums by granting them generous tax deductions, but artists are permitted to claim only the "literal cost of materials in any gifts of their works they might make to charitable institutions."[11] One result of this fiscal discrimination is that it has become extremely rare for artists to donate their own works to museums.[12] Most artists have little expectation or ambition of ever having their works enter a museum collection. Only for artists who identify themselves as actors in the arena of art history is access to the art museum an issue. This poses a particular problem for avant-garde artists, who have a vital interest in having their works in museums but who consciously strive to innovate rather than merely produce saleable works.[13] The result is that comparatively unknown artists must come as petitioners for entry to the relatively few institutions that might accept them, which forces them to deal from a position of weakness that points up the inherent asymmetry in the relationship.

This context clearly suggests that the artist confronts the art museum as an individual. But what about artists as a community? Framing the relationship in this way is problematic and suggests that a prior question must be asked: whether a community of artists is actually capable of existing, and if so, what its nature is.

What Is a Community of Artists?

The concept of community encompasses a set of meanings, only some of which may be appropriate to artists today. Ordinarily *community* refers to a social group whose members reside in a specific locality; they may share some aspects of governance, and often they claim a common cultural and historical heritage. Geographic contiguity, however, is not a necessary feature for designating a group a community, since group members may live far apart yet share similar characteristics or concerns. Moreover, a community's ties may be largely symbolic. Nevertheless, while shared interests may constitute the minimal features that define a group of artists as a community, when artists also are located in close proximity to one another they are more visible and sometimes more effective in gaining their professional ends than they would be acting as individuals. The sine qua non of a community of artists is their commitment to working, preferably full time, as professional artists.[14] Artists or aspirants to careers in the arts tend to locate themselves in a metropolis to which other artists are drawn, and congregate in neighborhoods that enhance access to materials and services and provide large work spaces along with proximity to dealers, patrons, and collectors.[15] However, other features commonly associated with communities, such as ethnicity or religion, are generally absent or less salient. Because of their shared professional needs artists may become engaged in concerted action vis-à-vis government agencies in order to improve their material situation.[16] Ironically, despite the preference of artists for living in low-rent districts, their very presence seems to invite the gentrification whose rent increases inevitably drive out all but the most successful ones.[17] Real estate market pressures are among the forces that tend to scatter artists.

The Case of the New York Abstract Expressionists

The abstract expressionists constitute the prototype for a modern community of artists, its possibilities, and its probable limits. They resided for the most part in or near Greenwich Village during the period from the 1940s to the 1960s, but they were more than a geographic entity. As Charles Kadushin has suggested, the New York School functioned not only as a community, but as a "movement circle." As such, they took up arms against certain established principles, creating a sense of embattlement that supported the bonding among its members typical of a social movement. They shared an affinity for the European modernist tradition, knowledge of which they elaborated through their participation in intellectual discussions. In this they benefited from the companionship of sympathetic critics and dealers. Together they founded the "club" in which they developed a discourse about the styles they pioneered, and which facilitated their unity.[18]

The regularity of their meetings and the articulateness of their supporters made them an ideal community for open-minded art world members to deal with. Moreover, the artists' emergence at a period of American dominance on the world stage following the Second World War, along with the temporary demise of European cultural vitality, lent them a prominence that previous American artistic communities such as the Eight, the Ashcan School, or the American Scene painters had lacked.[19] It converged with the period in the history of the Museum of Modern Art when it had attained a degree of respectability as a serious institution, yet still embodied the spirit of adventure of its origins. The museum's Alfred H. Barr, Jr., and Dorothy Miller became two of the most important advocates for the abstract expressionist movement.[20]

This seemingly idyllic community, which combined location with common aesthetic aims, shared interests, and companionship, did not—and perhaps could not—last. Eventually, its core group became an "establishment" in relation to other artists, tending to exclude still newer artistic ideas.[21] In part the community was eroded by success: as is often the case, artists who had achieved great prominence moved away from the city. But it is not merely their dispersion that accounts for the decline of the community. Nor does their dispersion alone explain why successive waves of artists espousing newer styles did not form similarly cohesive communities. An important difference that Diana Crane observes is that later artists were more likely to meet through the mediation of dealers and critics; at times even commonalities in their stylistic outlooks were "discovered" or constructed by those mediators. She notes that "[a]s the number of artists working in New York increased, the character of the artistic milieu shifted from a tightly knit counterculture to a set of relatively transient, interlocking subcultures. . . . The major New York museums became increasingly conservative in their selection of new artworks."[22]

Abstract art presents more difficulty for most viewers than do the visually more accessible works of pop art and photorealism that succeeded abstract expressionism, and so it may seem inexplicable to call museums conservative for acquiring works in these later styles more slowly than they had done with abstract expressionist works. But as radical as the appearance of abstract expressionism was, the movement gained acceptance by being interpreted within what had become a legitimate intellectual framework of modernism: the definition of the autonomous fine-art work in terms of formalist and/or psychological discourses, to the exclusion of social and political content.[23] Many of the new styles after abstract expressionism (minimalism was the major exception) subverted this aesthetic paradigm by violating genre boundaries between fine art and commercial forms (pop, photorealism, pattern) or appearing to be throwbacks to preabstraction (figurativism, certain forms of neo-expressionism). Their emergence coincided with declines in museum attendance,[24] unprecedented labor contention among museum staff, and lagging budgetary expenditures for acquisition of artworks. Though works in the later styles were fairly frequently exhibited, they were more likely to be shown in large group shows than in small ones, and rarely individually. Treated as temporary crowd pleasers, works in the new styles entered permanent collections in New York museums more slowly than had the abstract expressionist works. As a result, artists (or their dealers) were increasingly obliged to seek other outlets and means of existence: regional museums for recognition; corporations for commissions or sales; teaching positions to make a living.[25]

Despite the favorable conditions that made the New York School of abstract expressionists possible, their actual artworks represent considerable stylistic diversity. That they became a community had as much to do with the social circle that they constructed, and the common discourse that they and their advocates developed, as with the art itself. But their success as a community could not survive the development of new support structures, chief among them the art market, that began to define the conditions within which artists now operate. In the context of these structures, as I will show next, the artist tends to be treated as an isolated actor rather than as part of a durable artistic community.

Individualists Despite Themselves?

Although both historically and more recently groups of avant-garde artists have often acted for a time as artistic communities, these communities have tended to be fragile. One reason for this is that artists are at the mercy of market forces, which tend to turn them into competitors rather than enhance companionship. The museum's treatment of individual artists is congruent both with the structure of the art market and with the cultural tradition of the artist. The idea for the social type or role of the artist as individual genius originated as early as the Renaissance, converged with the rise of bourgeois individualism, and is structurally supported by the development of modern capitalism. The art market did not by itself create this role, but its forces contribute to the continuing cultural construction of that Romantic image, which has been incorporated into the ideas guiding museums and their patronage.[26]

On the whole, museums do not deal with communities of artists, but with individual artists. This stance is clearly formulated in the credo of Juliana R. Force, the Whitney Museum's cofounder and first director. Asserting that the museum's primary concern was "the work of living artists," she specified that the Whitney was not in search of "schools" but of "individual artists."[27] Even the existence of the ab-

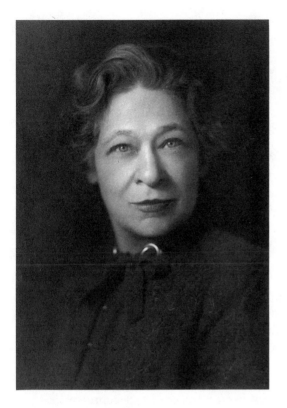

Fig. 5-1. Juliana Force, circa 1940. Whitney Museum of American Art, Library Archives, New York.

stract expressionists' strong, relatively durable community, with their remarkable success in achieving entry into the canon, does not mean that their works entered museum collections as a group; rather, they did so one work or one artist at a time.[28]

What happens, then, when artists act as a community in which they emphasize their social distinctiveness over their aesthetic contribution? In recent years the involvement of certain artists in social activism has tended to blur the boundaries between the social and aesthetic contents of their works. On occasion artists have reacted to crisis situations by producing artworks in which their social demands are as prominent as their aesthetic concerns. Artists are also insisting upon the legitimacy of "marginal" or "marginalized" artists, for example members of racial or ethnic minorities, women, and AIDS victims.[29] For the most part they have met with strong opposition from art world participants who define the aesthetic canon as necessarily apart from political content or social criticism. The latter warn that giving in to social demands for the inclusion in the museum of hitherto unrecognized groups of artists risks subverting the art museum's rai-

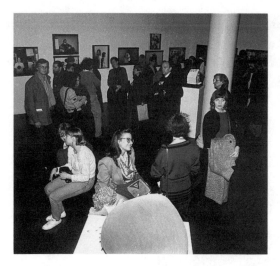

Fig. 5-2. Opening reception of the 1989 exhibition Until That Last Breath: Women with Aids, New Museum of Contemporary Art. Photo by Catherine McGann, courtesy of the New Museum of Contemporary Art.

son d'être as an institution bound by its charter to provide its public with exemplary art in which an aesthetic for its own sake dominates.[30]

In light of extraordinary aesthetic changes in this century, it is clear that the attack on the idea of the museum as the home of a universal, transcendent aesthetic is not a passing phenomenon. It is necessary, therefore, to look at the historical and structural connections that militate in favor of the recurrence of such controversies.

ARTISTS AND ART IN MUSEUMS

Lost in History

It is sometimes forgotten that artists themselves have played a major role in the founding and running of American art museums. This is especially true of those museums that began as art schools modeled on the European academy, such as the Art Institute of Chicago. Organized in 1869 by a group of artists as the Chicago Academy of Design, this school became the venue in which the artists successfully taught, exhibited, and sold art. But the enterprise was unexpectedly brought to ruin by the great fire of 1871. In response to the disaster these entrepreneurial artists raised needed capital by enlisting the support of wealthy laymen. In exchange for the then fairly substantial fee of one hundred dollars each, the new members received drawing lessons and entry to art exhibitions, but were not entitled to authority in the academy's management. The aims of the two groups, however, turned out to be incompatible. For while the artists wanted to put on exhibitions primarily to sell their own works, the businessmen wanted to use them to show and perhaps sell works from their own collections. Once the number of lay members had increased sufficiently, they were able to reorganize the academy, transforming themselves into a board of trustees. In the process, they discovered previously undisclosed debts incurred under artist governance. The trustees resigned in a body and founded a new association to achieve some of the academy's aims "but unencumbered by financial obligations and artists."[31] From having been activists and insiders, artists were made dependents and outsiders.

Although both artists and trustees continued to share a commitment to creating a great museum for the sake of art, thus enhancing their city's standing, in certain other respects their interests diverged. As art collectors, the trustees wished the Art Institute to show great works of the past or from other countries and civilizations. Particularly as their own and the museum's holdings increased, they tried to make the museum serve as an exemplar for educational ends, as an inspiration for artists, and as an uplifting institution for the public. Even though the trustees accorded the founding artists a certain privileged standing within the museum's circles (for example, allowing some of them to rent studio space on the museum's premises for a time), they largely excluded them from decisionmaking. Instead, as the museum's collection of European art expanded, local artists were increasingly left out. Partly in response to their pleas, the Art Institute of Chicago instituted annual or biennial exhibitions in which the artists could compete for space. Eventually it established a rental and sales gallery, primarily for their works. This gallery served the dual purpose of supplementing the city's meager store of commercial dealerships willing to market local artworks, and of providing a museum-related activity for the wives and daughters of trustees, who volunteered to staff it. Still, these were ancillary and marginalized projects. Governance of the collections was kept in the hands of male trustee-collectors, with professional artists as their employees: teachers in the art school, advisers on collecting and exhibitions, and lecturers to the museum members.[32]

The case of the Art Institute of Chicago suggests reasons for the recurrent division between artists and museums around the broad issues of how art is to be selected for temporary display and how to determine its fitness to enter a museum's permanent collection. During most of the nineteenth century American artists agreed with museum officials that European art had much to teach them. Many of them sought to study in the academies and schools of Paris, Munich, and other European centers. Eventually some came to be influenced by European aesthetic innovators. But whereas nineteenth-century European stylistic revolutionaries challenged the aesthetic canon of Old Master works and academic styles, subject matter, genres, and hierarchies of values, they did not challenge the privileged standing of the artwork itself, nor did they immediately reject the agencies of official recognition. Instead, many of them, such as Cézanne and Henri Rousseau, continued for some time to submit their paintings to academic salon juries, as had realists and impressionists.[33] Most artists continued to adhere to the idea of the autonomous artwork belonging to a realm of meaning of its own rather than being a moral narrative. By creating new discourses and aesthetic criteria based on formal analysis that would encompass both new abstract styles and recently recognized "primitive" art, they achieved the triumph of the modern. The triumph was short-lived: soon it was challenged by several art movements and tendencies, with serious consequences for art museums.

Art After the Tradition of the New

Criteria of aesthetic quality for contemporary artworks conform to no fixed objective canon, but depend upon a competitive process of negotiated meanings in which artists and their public (including critics, dealers, and collectors) are involved.[34] This makes it understandable that the more actively an art museum shows contemporary works, the more controversial its choices become. Indeed, with art that often deliberately intends to contest conventional genre boundaries altogether, traditional enfranchisement mechanisms are questioned. Such challenges are not really new, of course; beginning with the impudent provocations of Marcel Duchamp and other dadaists, the idea of the artwork as a unique object, created *de novo* by a single genius, is no longer taken for granted. Dadaists and some of their surrealist successors deliberately used found objects or ready-mades, collaborated in making artworks so that no single artist could be associated with them (*cadavres exquis*), pioneered new forms such as performances and constructions, and introduced aleatory processes, either playful or political, sometimes both at the same time. Often acting as a community (perhaps *gang* would be a better term), by ridiculing the successive stylistic innovations that had become the characteristic pattern of artistic practice, such artists challenged the very legitimacy of art museums.

The dadaist tradition, carried on to the present, highlights one aspect of the problematic nature of art itself. Its antiaesthetic and its implied political and social critiques are pervaded by an anarchic zaniness and fantasy that have influenced many artists, especially since the 1960s. At a time when a pile of bricks is displayed in a museum, music is composed for performance underwater, and the boundaries between popular and fine art have become fluid, conventional understandings of what art is are strained. In these circumstances, how are museums to evaluate art?

While many artists eliminated recognizable imagery altogether, some took this freedom as a rationale for interjecting new, previously rejected themes of a critical or political kind. These themes constitute a contrary challenge to the idea of the aesthetic purity of the autonomous artwork. Modeling themselves on such forerunners as the socially committed artists of the Mexican mural movement or—more directly—New Deal artists in the United States, they use both words and pictures to convey their messages. Debates that were thought to have been laid to rest with the triumph of modernism have been reopened, and have become an important element in the process by which art museums and artists confront each other.

HOW ART MUSEUMS DEAL WITH ARTISTS

Debates over style and genre boundaries intersect with persistent tensions between local artists' communities, which want representation in "their own" museums (where some may teach or work in museum-sponsored programs), and the preference of most art museums for works by "cosmopolitan" artists. Museums with aspirations to a national (let alone international) reputation sometimes view local artists as provincial nuisances.[35] Considering that New York City has been the unquestioned art center of the United States, it may seem surprising that this derogatory view of local artists was once the case there as well. The dominance of New York artists on the world scene from the 1950s to the 1970s should not blind us to the past, when American artists in general were considered to be distinctly provincial,[36] nor to the possibility that in a world in which transnational corporations support art, American artists may again come to be viewed as provincials.

Surface appearances, such as the proliferation of museums or the explosion of auction prices, indicate that the art world is a growth industry in which there is room for many artists to make successful careers. But, as Diana Crane shows, appearances may be deceptive. In spite of the expansion of every aspect of the American art world since World War II, art museums now acquire works in new styles at a slower pace than they did when abstract expressionism was new—which was a time when the number of modern-art museums was expanding and when the post–World War II government subsidy programs began.[37]

Although art museums continue to be confronted by communities of local artists who seek recognition for their paintings and sculpture, they also deal with artists whose work transgresses the boundaries between art and life, art and politics, and fine art and commercial design. As some of the following cases suggest, when aesthetic considerations come into conflict with the moral beliefs of influential sectors of the public and their representatives—when larger institutional, civic, and aesthetic aims seem to be at stake—the interests of artists often take second place.

The Corcoran Gallery of Art

The controversy centering on the Corcoran Gallery's decision in 1989 to cancel an exhibition of photographs by the late Robert Mapplethorpe that included some sexually explicit and homoerotic images is revelatory of both the tensions endemic to the relationship between modern-art museums and artists in the United States, and the complex, many-layered character of this relationship. But the momentous issue of the freedom of artistic expression from overt and covert censorship tends to overshadow the material concerns that artists face, concerns that make them extremely vulnerable to threats against their creative freedom. It must not be forgotten that American artists depend for their livelihood on an art market, for symbolic recognition on foundations or the state, and for access to a broader public on museums. The combination of market, state, foundation, and museum constitutes the support structure that may permit an artist to subsist in comfort and dignity, and possibly to achieve fame. The crisis at the Corcoran Gallery needs to be seen in that context.

Even before the Mapplethorpe show, Washington artists were dependent on and often resentful of the Corcoran, not primarily because of the gallery per se, but because it represented the deficiencies in the opportunity structure of the local art market. As Florence Rubenfeld has pointed out, Washington is a mecca for tourists, who visit its numerous museums, but it provides living artists with relatively few opportunities to exhibit their work, especially since the middle of the 1970s, when the Corcoran's Washington Room was closed. (The Corcoran had been the principal museum in which the color-field school, championed by Clement Greenberg, had been exhibited.) Since then, Washington artists have had to depend chiefly upon commercial galleries. But in comparison with New York City, artists in Washington (and, indeed, in most American cities) suffer from being "local" artists in places that are relatively poorly endowed as art centers. Artists are already hampered by the District of Columbia's lack of studio space, and because the pool of potential art collectors is small local dealers have tended to move to New York City, either drawing their artists along or jettisoning them for a stable of New York–based artists.[38]

By the 1980s the tensions between the Corcoran and Washington artists had turned into open conflict. Angered by what they took to be an insulting remark by a museum official, a group of artists began to view the only museum in that area open to regional living artists as their adversary.[39] Attempts by the museum to mollify them by inviting them to serve on an advisory panel produced the no doubt unanticipated result that some of the artists formed the Coalition of Washington Artists in 1981. As such, they demanded that the museum extend them greater recognition by including Washington artists in more exhibitions. As the controversy escalated so did their demands: representation on the board of trustees and its decisionmaking committees, honoraria for allowing their works to be exhibited, and a pledge that the museum set aside special funds to purchase works by Washington artists. In the wake of this contention, a curator and the director resigned, and city funding that the museum had hoped to obtain was diverted to other ends. Under a new director (formerly of the Brooklyn Museum), a dialogue with the Coalition was opened. It concluded with a promise that the artists would be consulted on major curatorial appointments and exhibitions, but their other demands were not met.[40]

These disputes, which had revolved around the classic sociological conflict of locals versus cosmopolitans, were dwarfed by the Mapplethorpe controversy, the implications of which concern the entire nation and go beyond art per se into the realm of freedom of speech, rights to privacy, and competing conceptions of morality. It leads us to question the boundaries separating fine art from fashion photography, the distinction between legitimate erotic expression and pornography, the status of pornography itself as a genre appropriate for art museums, and the degree to which government officials or representatives appointed or elected by a heterogeneous public have the right to make decisions that privilege the preferences of one set of constituencies over another.

The Brooklyn Museum

One of the country's oldest art museums (dating back to the 1820s, though in its present building only since the turn of the century), the Brooklyn Museum has prided itself not only on its excellent collections, but on innovative approaches to art and public-education activities. Because in the Brooklyn Museum (unlike many other art museums) collections and education are not mutually exclusive, it is difficult to separate the museum's relationship to artists from its general community orientation. In 1971 the retiring director noted that the museum had successfully adapted to changes in its sources of patronage: with the departure of many upper-income families from Brooklyn and their replacement by low-income minorities (many of them African American and Puerto Rican families) who usually are not thought to be museumgoers, the museum's attendance nevertheless tripled, with a substantial proportion of the audience being individuals of blue-collar origin. He implied that this unusual success came from playing the museum's strong suit: its permanent collection of ancient Egyptian, Mexican, and African arts.[41]

With respect to artists, the museum has tried to reconcile two frequently incompatible aims: on the one hand, as befits a venerable institution, to maintain standards of quality and stay in touch with national and international trends; on the other, to play an active role in the life of the community. Beginning in 1968 it organized exhibitions of young or less well known artists in its Community Gallery, a space used to create opportunities "*for community artists of all ability levels to have access to museum space.*" As an autonomous unit, its works were chosen not by the museum's curators, but by a separate advisory committee whose members, many of them artists, came from diverse neighborhoods of Brooklyn.[42]

In 1985 the museum launched a new program, a series of exhibitions by contemporary Brooklyn artists under the heading Working in Brooklyn. Beside displaying works, many of them by artists who had not yet found dealer representation, the museum also organized sessions for these artists to meet the public, so that they could convey their artistic intentions. More recently the museum has invited a num-

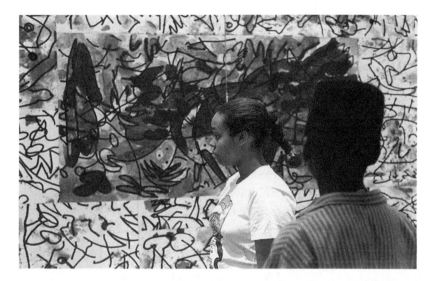

Fig. 5-3. Children looking at a work by Espada at the show Hispanic Art in the United States: Thirty Contemporary Painters and Sculptors. Brooklyn Museum, 1989. Photo courtesy of the Brooklyn Museum.

ber of artists to set up installations of their works, using constructions, media, sound, and "castaways."[43]

By creative deployment of its strong permanent collection and its openness not only to beginning and semiprofessional artists but also to better-known artists who live or have lived in Brooklyn (an increasing number, given real estate costs in Manhattan), the Brooklyn Museum obtains support from its communities of artists. It shows works by American and foreign artists, and exhibitions that originate in museums elsewhere in the United States and abroad, thus maintaining its cosmopolitan character. When it comes to controversial artwork, the Brooklyn Museum has been judiciously daring. It exhibited the early feminist work *The Dinner Party* by Judy Chicago in 1981, when it was still relatively unusual for an established museum to give space to works in which aesthetic and political statements are so inextricably intertwined. Thus far the Brooklyn Museum has tended to avoid more public disputes, in part, perhaps, because it is somewhat farther away from the art core of Manhattan. Still, it has recently been accused of subordinating the aesthetic project to "a UNESCO-type approach to art" in the form of a large traveling exhibition of works by Hispanic painters and sculptors in the United States.[44] Other critics, however, consider it "an institution where new ideas and contemporary art seem welcome, and where there is a sense that the fresh and unexpected are possible."[45]

It would be easy to dismiss these innovations as devices for segregating the museum's social obligations from the business of "separat[ing] the artistically worthy from the artistically unworthy."[46] But this would be adopting an extraordinarily narrow conception of the multifunctional institutions that American art museums have tried to be. Each museum decides for itself how much attention it will give to each of the constituencies in its purview, according to its means, congruent with its traditions, and within the changing circumstances of financial constraints and public wishes. In this light, the Brooklyn Museum has been able to take risks that have met with considerable success.

The Whitney Museum of American Art

Dedicated to the art of Americans, Gertrude Vanderbilt Whitney's collection of six hundred works gave a clear message of her commitment at a time when American artists enjoyed little patronage. With her associate, Juliana Force, as director, she designed her museum explictly for "gaining for the art of this country the prestige which

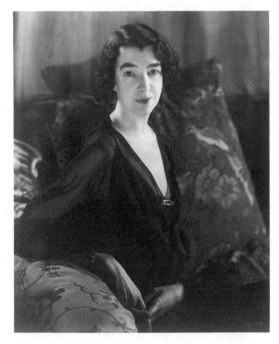

Fig. 5-4. Edward Steichen, *Portrait of Gertrude Vanderbilt Whitney*, 1937. Photograph. 15 5/8 x 13 7/16 inches. Collection of Whitney Museum of American Art. Gift of the family of Edith and Lloyd Goodrich 89.7. Photo by Geoffrey Clements, courtesy of the Whitney Museum of American Art.

heretofore the public has devoted too exclusively to the art of foreign countries and of the past."[47] In recent years the museum has continued to be bound by this idea, but has gone beyond Whitney's own preference for figurative art. Instead it has plunged wholeheartedly into the aesthetic turmoil of the contemporary. In large measure this shift stemmed from the policies of Lloyd Goodrich, director of the museum from 1958 to 1968. Goodrich shared Whitney's taste and commitment, contributing with his scholarly writing to the valorization of a number of American painters, such as Winslow Homer, Thomas Eakins, and Edward Hopper. Beyond that, however, he was instrumental in reorienting the museum from its status as a private preserve to its new mission as a public institution that acquired abstract works by such artists as Mark Rothko and Willem de Kooning.[48]

Goodrich wrote that he believed the museum's job was to "maintain standards," but not by narrowing choices to a particular school. "The museum, after all, is not a dealer or an artists' society. It is an institution devoted to showing, collecting and publicizing the best in art."[49] Aside from indicating that each style, whether pop, hard-edge, or various forms of abstraction, could be evaluated according to its own criteria of excellence, Goodrich (perhaps no differently from most other critics) did not specify what those criteria might be. This became increasingly problematic after his retirement, as the museum's annual (biennial beginning in 1972) exhibitions enlarged their coverage of the range of existing styles and art forms.

The Whitney is the only New York modern-art museum that provides something akin to a salon for artists: the biennial. By now a rather venerable institution in its own right, it began in 1932 as an annual survey of contemporary American art.[50] Although widely imitated, the Whitney's exhibition continues to be considered the most visible and important of such shows. The exhibition's format and rationale have changed since 1972, when it became the enlarged biennial. In particular, grants from the Ford Foundation and the National Endowment for the Humanities permitted it to embrace a more national scope by sending staff members to visit art studios, cooperative galleries, and collectors in cities throughout the country. Thereafter, instead of merely surveying art, the Whitney redefined the biennial as an "opportunity to make a critical statement on aspects of contemporary art." The resultant show was equally provocative because it excluded works by artists who were already represented by commercial galleries or who had had one-person shows in New York or previous Whitney exhibitions. The rationale for this change was twofold: first,

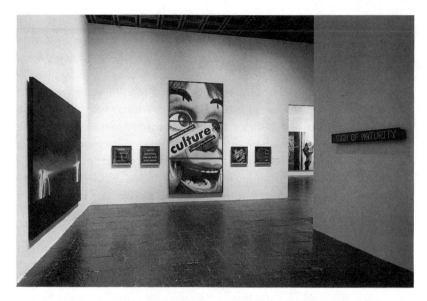

Fig. 5-5. Installation view of the 1985 biennial exhibition (21 March –2 June 1985) at the Whitney Museum of American Art, New York. Photo by Geoffrey Clements, courtesy of the Whitney Museum of American Art.

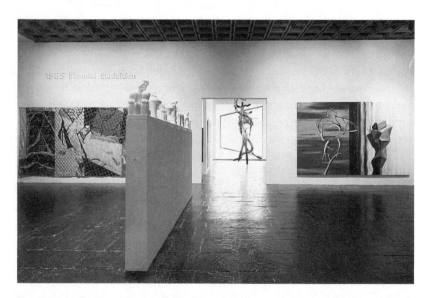

Fig. 5-6. Installation view of the 1985 biennial exhibition (21 March –2 June 1985) at the Whitney Museum of American Art, New York. Photo by Geoffrey Clements, courtesy of the Whitney Museum of American Art.

it would acknowledge the growing importance of other art centers throughout the country, and second, it would rely on "the increasing ability of commercial galleries in New York to present the current work of established artists."[51]

Its centrality and visibility have made the Whitney a lightning rod for either delight or anger, more often the latter—for example, for excluding well-known artists or for featuring them, or for catering to trendiness to the neglect of solid, less flamboyant artworks; it was castigated for the 1985 biennial specifically because of its "juvenile exaltations of an East Village disco."[52] It is assailed for catering to fads and fashions and to influential dealers, and for neglecting art-historical depth, but rarely for neglecting artists. After all, Gertrude Vanderbilt Whitney's allegiance to her circle through her "studio building" on Eighth Street and as collector and patron is legendary. Lloyd Goodrich was equally committed to sustaining American artists, having helped to administer the Public Works of Art Project under the New Deal. Long after, in a 1964 speech, he suggested that artists should be paid for showing in museums and for reproductions of their works, and should receive a percentage of admission charges.[53] This stand is very much in the tradition of New Deal artists' unions, and converges with the position of the local Washington artists in their dispute with the Corcoran, as I have indicated above. In fact, however, except in a limited way in its biennials and its program of seminars with artists, the Whitney does not seem to have many direct dealings with artists. In the months before the biennial, curators receive hundreds of slide sets directly from artists aspiring to have their works shown. On the whole, however, the bulk of artists selected are professionals whose dealers act for them. The sympathy for artists that led its founders to create the museum in the first place does not extend to giving them a formal role in decisionmaking processes. In certain respects the Whitney serves as both model and antimodel for the New Museum of Contemporary Art.

The New Museum of Contemporary Art

The most recently established of the museums examined here, the New Museum is the creation of Marcia Tucker, who had been dismissed from a curatorship at the Whitney Museum in 1976. It embraces a radically different conception of what a modern-art museum should be. Tucker has said that she had found the Whitney's probable direction of change incompatible with her commitment to art and the art community. She believes that the museum's allegiance should be to artists rather than to dealers, to controversial rather than to "sanitized" art, to the risky rather than the fashionable. Unlike more established art museums, such as the Museum of Modern Art or the Whitney, the New Museum early eschewed the dominance of modern aestheticism in favor of an aesthetics that either fully incorporates political and social critique or revels in the interplay of the social with the idea of the autonomy of the artwork. It welcomes art based on narrative and ideology, performance art, ephemeral works, unknown or neglected artists, and conceptual art. Although most of the works it exhibits or purchases are by individuals, the New Museum has frequently included works by dual or collective creative teams.[54]

The New Museum is also unconventional in that it acquires many works from its regular exhibitions, yet also acts as a gallery in that its collection is considered semipermanent rather than immobile. After ten years virtually everything is reviewed and offered for sale to other public institutions or individuals.[55] The funds raised by the sales are used to acquire new works, in order to emphasize innovation and freshness rather than what the museum considers enslavement to a permanent collection.[56]

As an institution oriented to experimentation, the New Museum sees itself as uniquely suited to probe the limits of art and the possible role of artists themselves in redefining it. Rather than act as an arbiter of taste, the New Museum wishes to help interpret the qualities and meanings of new art.[57] Accordingly, it shows works by minority artists who deliberately challenge art history (Robert Colescott), politi-

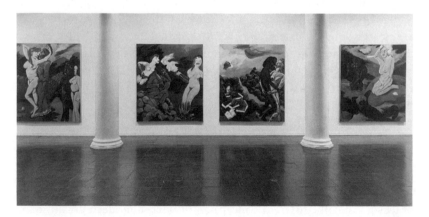

Fig. 5-7. Installation view of Robert Colescott: A Retrospective, 1989 exhibition at the New Museum of Contemporary Art. Photo by Fred Scruton, courtesy of the New Museum of Contemporary Art.

cal artists who challenge regimes, art collecting, and the "art industry" (Hans Haacke), and "amateur" artists (such as those in the show Until That Last Breath: Women with AIDS).[58]

Organizationally, the museum's most innovative program concerning the role of artists was to invite twenty-four artists from around the country to serve as an advisory panel in 1984. Charged with debating the museum's future, the panel, now stabilized at twenty members, meets to be informed about previous activities and proposals for new ones. In reportedly long and heated discussions, they evaluate and offer suggestions for future developments. The panel includes both collectives of artists as well as individuals. Artists serve three-year terms, and may also be consulted separately throughout the year. This does not mean that the museum is an artist-run organization, but rather that it acknowledges that living artists are important to it in many ways. Significantly, not only are artists viewed as providers of the works shown, but they are recognized as composing a significant part of the museum's public. It is estimated that about one-half of the museum's members are artists.[59]

Although its SoHo location tended to give it a New York flavor, the New Museum has become increasingly oriented to a broader regional and international range of artworks and exhibitions.[60] Its global reach has been enhanced by the engagement of curators from other countries, who have extended and diversified the museum's networks of artists beyond the United States and Western Europe to Eastern Europe, Australia, and elsewhere. This makes it clear that the

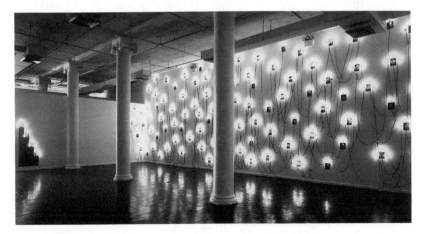

Fig. 5-8. Installation view of the 1988–89 exhibition Christian Boltanski: Lessons of Darkness. Photo courtesy of the New Museum of Contemporary Art.

New Museum conceives of the "community of artists" not as being bound to one locality, but as encompassing a world community.

CONCLUSIONS

I began by contending that the art museum and the artist make an odd couple. Mutually interdependent, they tend to interact at one or more removes rather than through direct contact. Even though tensions between them may be unavoidable because of their conflicting interests, and even though in the final analysis museums are dominant, it is nevertheless clear, on the basis of some of the experiences I have cited, that they are not ineluctably fated to enmity. From the artists' standpoint, their own communities tend to be more durable when their aesthetic commitments are buttressed by extra-aesthetic interests and traditions, such as gender, ethnic or racial identity, geographic location, and professional needs. With the changes in aesthetic conceptions in the 1980s, these concerns are gaining legitimacy. The profusion of styles, art forms, and genres that coexist with little consensus about quality is changing the face of museums as well. What is equally clear is that museums are not all the same.

Museums that previously held artists at arm's length have begun promising experiments in new forms of participation. The persistent or recurrent aesthetic, political, and moral issues they face reveal not only their conflicts but also their common interests. Although it may be easier for small, relatively informal museums to develop close ties with artists, even large institutions, as I have shown, have overcome some of the barriers that artists resent by developing innovative programs. The creation of new institutions that challenge their elders to expand the horizons of art by including new artists and art forms is increasingly being taken as an opportunity rather than a threat.

As I have tried to show, many of the problems that museums of contemporary art face today are not new at all, but are of long standing and recurrent. These issues include the role of commercial dealers, on the one hand, and the role of artists in authoritative positions in art museums, on the other. To provide some international context for these issues, consider a debate among museum directors reported in 1975. On the occasion of a meeting of the American Association of Museums, participants in an international panel discussed the ethical problems involved in selecting works for museum collections, a sensitive task in light of museums' role in legitimating art. Assertions by some that dealers had too much influence on museums were denied by most of the American museum directors, and many of the Europeans, too, expressed special horror at the claim, though not necessarily for the same reason.[61] The keeper of exhibitions and education at the Tate Gallery argued that ideas of quality came not from dealers but artists, who were the true validators of art. This was a view with which most of the participants concurred. Considering their alacrity in attributing to artists a special ability to judge art, it is somewhat surprising that these directors, both European and American, did not envisage assigning such a role to them within the museum itself. When asked if artists could participate in the restricted "subculture of social rituals that validates and proselytizes on its own behalf," they avoided any answer at all. As reported by Hilton Kramer, they seemed as reluctant to trust artists to speak for the museum as they were to trust the lay public.[62]

The idea that artists might have a role in selecting contemporary art was thought to place artists in too influential a position and involve them in conflicts of interest. The fact that many trustees and curators are also collectors does not seem to raise similar concerns. Yet if trustees make gifts of artworks to museums, they might conceivably have something to gain materially from their acceptance. Even though the tax benefits of the past have been reduced, donors still receive some fiscal advantages. Moreover, when their donations include works by artists whose other works they collect, the value of works by the same artists that they retain in their collection is likely to increase. If artists were encouraged to offer their own works, the honor of having works accepted by a museum would go directly to the artist rather than to the collector.[63]

Although the incompatibility of artists and art museums is what gains the most notoriety, the recent attacks upon art institutions and artists by political actors should have revealed to both of them that they share interests and a common fate. It should not take a crisis for art museums and artists to cooperate in standing up to maintain the American cultural matrix of vital institutions that took a century and a half or more to construct, often in the face of scorn and negative prejudgment. Despite the disproportionate influence art museums have in their relation to artists, they need each other. In a spirit of mutual respect, together they may be able to change the ethos of paternalism and the corresponding dependency that have tended to pervade their relationship. This ethos is at odds with that of a democratic society. Its persistence implicitly denies the possibility of assuming good will on both sides. When museums treat artists as responsible adults, and artists recognize that museum professionals are not inherently corrupt, timorous, or in some way their enemies, both art museums and artists benefit. In the face of structural barriers and traditional practices that militate against it, this understanding is not easy to achieve.

NOTES

1. The ambivalence that artists experience toward museums is highlighted in studies carried out both in Europe and in the United States. See Bernard Rosenberg and Norris Fliegel, *The Vanguard Artist: Portrait and Self-Portrait* (New York: Quadrangle, 1965); Sophy Burnham, *The Art Crowd* (New York: David McKay, 1973); Dore Ashton, *The New York School: A Cultural Reckoning* (New York: Viking, 1973); Neil Harris, *The Artist in American Society: The Formative Years, 1790–1860* (New York: George Braziller, 1966); and Deborah Ericson, *In the Stockholm Art World* (Stockholm: Department of Anthropology, University of Stockholm, 1988).

2. The concept of *art world* was formulated and elaborated by Howard S. Becker in his book *Art Worlds* (Berkeley: University of California Press, 1982). It encompasses the collectively developed activities of artists and others who work in one of the specialized domains of the arts. A rough division of labor characterizes their roles: producers, distributors, consumers.

3. Some observers believe that art museums could do much more in this field. See Vera L. Zolberg, "American Art Museums: Sanctuary or Free-for-All?" *Social Forces* 63, no. 2 (1984), 377–92.

4. We have delineated the ways in which collectors seek symbolic and material gains from having their works in prestigious public institutions (Burnham, *The Art Crowd,* and Vera L. Zolberg, "Tensions of Mission in American Art Museums," in Paul J. DiMaggio, ed., *Nonprofit Enterprise in the Arts: Studies in Mission and Constraint* [New York: Oxford University Press, 1986]); evaluated the degree to which museums expand the art public through educational programs (César Graña, "The Private Lives of Public Museums: Can Art Be Democratic?" in *Fact and Symbol: Essays in the Sociology of Art and Literature* [New York: Oxford University Press, 1971]; Paul DiMaggio and Michael Useem, "Social Class and Arts Consumption: The Origins and Consequences of Class Differences in Exposure to the Arts in America," in *Theory and Society* 5 [1978], 141–61; and Zolberg, "American Art Museums"); traced the development of professionalism in museum-related occupations (curators and education specialists) and university disciplines (art historians and aestheticians) and the consequences of their intersection; and evaluated the importance of art museums to their cities as tourist attractions, and to the nation as a means of increasing its world standing (Michael Useem, "Government

Patronage of Science and Art in America," in Richard A. Peterson, ed., *The Production of Culture* [Beverly Hills: Sage, 1976]).

5. Francis Haskell, "The Artist and the Museum," *New York Review of Books,* 3 Dec. 1987, 39.

6. In general, except for extremely well established artists whose works are embraced by art museums under nearly any terms, if artists are concerned with the verdict of posterity, they are obliged to depend on their heirs. It is their executors, widows, or descendants who have to make a case for acceptance into museums of works by dead artists. Along with collectors or dealers, and with the support of art critics or historians acting as advocates, they confront, compete, or collaborate to persuade the "gatekeepers" who determine whether their works are socially recognized as having high aesthetic value. See Gladys Engel Lang and Kurt Lang, "Recognition and Renown: The Survival of Artistic Reputation," *American Journal of Sociology* 94, no. 2 (1988), 79–109.

7. Kenneth P. Norwick and Jerry Simon Chasen with Henry R. Kaufman, *The Rights of Authors and Artists* (New York: Bantam, 1984); Jody A. van den Heuvel, "Moral Rights for Artists: The Development of a Federal Policy," *Journal of Arts Management and Law* 19, no. 3 (1989), 8–58.

8. For example, in its 1988 annual report, the American Association of Museums stated that it had "actively sought protection for museums' interests" in the Visual Artists Rights Act. This proposed legislation, which combines both nonproperty and property aspects, is designed "to provide copyright protection for works of art without copyright notice and allow artists to claim damages for works subject to unauthorized 'alteration' or 'mutilation' " (reported in *Museum News* 68, no. 1 [1989], 8). The vicissitudes of the bill are recounted and analyzed in van den Heuvel, "Moral Rights for Artists." No doubt this stance is quite appropriate to the AAM's mandate to support the interests of museums vis-à-vis other forces. It is unfortunate when these "other forces" are taken to include artists.

9. Rosenberg and Fliegel, *The Vanguard Artist;* Harris, *The Artist in American Society;* Raymonde Moulin, *The French Art Market,* tr. Arthur Goldhammer (New Brunswick, N.J.: Rutgers University Press, 1987).

10. Ericson, *In the Stockholm Art World,* 5.

11. Karl E. Meyer, *The Art Museum: Power, Money, Ethics* (New York: Morrow, 1979), 259.

12. When they do so, it is assumed that they are trying to achieve the canonicity that entry into art museums, as Arthur Danto puts it, enfranchises (Arthur C. Danto, *The Philosophical Disenfranchisement of Art* [New York: Columbia University Press, 1986]). Louise Nevelson's donation of more than twenty-five sculptures and collages to a number of art museums in the United States and Europe made headlines. "The gifts are highly unusual in that major

artists have rarely donated such a large portion of their estates during their lifetimes" (Douglas C. McGill, "Louise Nevelson Giving 25 Works to Museums," *New York Times,* 18 Mar. 1985). Museum administrators are driven to despair by the results of the overhaul of tax laws, which no longer provide a major incentive to donors to contribute works to museums.

13. These are not the majority of all artists, to be sure, as Diana Crane has pointed out (in *The Transformation of the Avant-Garde: The New York Art World, 1940–1985* [Chicago: University of Chicago Press, 1987], 20–21).

14. Since artists' incomes are notoriously low, many who aspire to full-time work as artists are obliged to work as well at other occupations. These range from teaching art to any job they can find. Charles Simpson's study of SoHo (*SoHo: The Artist in the City* [Chicago: University of Chicago Press, 1981]) indicates that a number of artists use their craft skills installing electricity and plumbing in order to convert industrial spaces into habitable lofts, not only for themselves but also for others in barter or for remuneration.

15. Hall Winslow, *Artists in Metropolis: An Exploration for Planners* (Brooklyn: Planning Dept., School of Architecture, Pratt Institute, 1964); James Heilbrun, "The Distribution of Arts Activity Among U.S. Metropolitan Areas" (paper presented at the Fifth International Conference on Cultural Economics, Ottawa, Ontario, September 1988).

16. Simpson, *SoHo: The Artist in the City.*

17. Sharon Zukin, *Loft Living: Culture and Capital in Urban Change* (New Brunswick, N.J.: Rutgers University Press, 1989), but for a different perspective see James R. Hudson, "An Alternative to Succession in an Artistic Community," paper presented at the annual meeting of the Eastern Sociological Society, spring 1988.

18. Charles Kadushin, "Networks and Circles in the Production of Culture," in Richard A. Peterson, ed., *The Production of Culture* (Beverly Hills: Sage, 1976), 117–18.

19. Crane, *The Transformation of the Avant-Garde;* Ashton, *The New York School;* Serge Guilbaut, *How New York Stole the Idea of Modern Art: Abstract Expressionism, Freedom, and the Cold War,* tr. Arthur Goldhammer (Chicago: University of Chicago Press, 1983).

20. Betty Parsons, quoted in Alan Jones and Laura de Coppet, *The Art Dealers: The Powers Behind the Scene Tell How the Art World Really Works* (New York: Clarkson N. Potter, 1984).

21. Kadushin, "Networks and Circles in the Production of Culture."

22. Crane, *The Transformation of the Avant-Garde,* 137.

23. One of the few exceptions is the set of elegies created by Robert Motherwell in the 1940s and 1950s and dedicated to the ordeal of republican Spain. But aside from the titles, these works are expressly abstract in imagery.

24. This was the case between 1969 and 1980 for the Brooklyn Museum, the Jewish Museum, and the Metropolitan Museum of Art, according to Crane. Her figures show, however, that attendance at the Museum of Modern Art and the Whitney actually increased (Crane, *The Transformation of the Avant-Garde,* 150).

25. Ibid. Although Crane largely excludes them from consideration, it is important to note the rise of specifically antidealer, antimuseum art forms: conceptual art, performance, and site-specific works (frequently created in inaccessible locations). See Vera L. Zolberg, *Constructing a Sociology of the Arts* (New York: Cambridge University Press, 1990).

26. For a fuller development of how the persona of the artist came to be constructed, see Zolberg, *Constructing a Sociology of the Arts.*

27. Whitney Museum of American Art, *Catalogue of the Collection* (New York: Whitney Museum, 1931), 9–11.

28. In *The Transformation of the Avant-Garde,* Crane reports that the Museum of Modern Art purchased its first Pollock in 1943 and by 1953 had accumulated works by twelve of the painters. It was not until 1983 that the museum finally held works by every member of the original abstract expressionist group.

29. Russell Lynes, *Good Old Modern: An Intimate Portrait of the Museum of Modern Art* (New York: Atheneum, 1973); Burnham, *The Art Crowd;* New Museum of Contemporary Art, "On View at the New Museum, 24 February–16 April, 1989" (pamphlet describing events and exhibitions at the museum).

30. Hilton Kramer, "Brooklyn Museum Hispanic Show: A UNESCO-Type Approach to Art," *New York Observer,* 3–10 July 1989, 1. "Marginal" or "marginalized" in this case refers to the artists' exclusion from established, institutionalized domains that control what is claimed to be the "legitimate" discourse of value in the arts.

31. Helen Lefkowitz Horowitz, *Culture and the City: Cultural Philanthropy in Chicago from the 1880s to 1917* (Lexington: University Press of Kentucky, 1976), 38. See also Vera L. Zolberg, "The Art Institute of Chicago: The Sociology of A Cultural Organization," Ph.D. diss., University of Chicago, 1974.

32. Zolberg, "The Art Institute of Chicago." This is not to say that trustees usually, let alone always, governed badly or chose foolishly. In fact, at the Art Institute, on many occasions the trustees were more prescient and venturesome in their acquisitions than were professional staff members or artists in their school. It was trustees who insisted upon purchasing works of Odilon Redon and permitted the Armory Show works to be shown at the museum, against the will of the professional director.

33. Harrison C. White and Cynthia A. White, *Canvases and Careers: Institutional Change in the French Painting World* (New York: John Wiley and Sons, 1965).

34. Becker, *Art Worlds;* Zolberg, *Constructing a Sociology of the Arts.*

35. Chicago is typical of this phenomenon. With the expansion from the 1920s on of the permanent collection of Old Masters, European modernists, and American works from outside of the Midwest, local Chicago artists came to feel excluded from the Art Institute. Many felt similarly excluded in the 1960s and after from Chicago's Museum of Contemporary Art (Zolberg, "The Art Institute of Chicago"). Partly in reaction, local artists organized movements (the Hairy Who, the Chicago Imagists) and disdained museum exhibitions. Although this gave a number of Chicago artists a national reputation, which then reflected positively back on the museum, the tension between local artists and museums persists.

36. Guilbaut, *How New York Stole the Idea of Modern Art;* Harris, *The Artist in American Society.*

37. Crane's study (*The Transformation of the Avant-Garde*) is revelatory as far as it goes. But she takes for granted that political or social art is permanently marginal to the art world of the museum / gallery / market. By excluding or minimizing its presence in her analysis, she has produced an elegant and parsimonious interpretation of the complex developments in the post–World War II American art world. Yet without considering artists who included social and political concerns in their work, the study of art movements and artists' communities is inherently impoverished.

38. Florence Rubenfeld, "Washington Artists Pressure Corcoran," *New Art Examiner* 12, no. 1 (1984), 41–43.

39. According to a report on the incident, a curator is supposed to have characterized the Washington art scene as one in which "nothing is going on." She later denied having made this statement (Rubenfeld, "Washington Artists Pressure Corcoran," 42).

40. Ibid.

41. Brooklyn Museum, *The Brooklyn Museum Annual, 1970/71* (New York: Brooklyn Museum, 1971), 13–16.

42. Brooklyn Museum, *The Brooklyn Museum Annual Report, 1981/1982* (New York: Brooklyn Museum, 1982), 61 (my emphasis).

43. Brooklyn Museum, "Site-Specific Installations by 10 Brooklyn Artists to Go on View at the Brooklyn Museum," news release, April 1990.

44. Kramer, "Brooklyn Museum Hispanic Show," 1.

45. Michael Brenson, "Are Major Museums Slighting Today's Art?" *New York Times,* 23 Dec. 1984.

46. Kramer, "Brooklyn Museum Hispanic Show."

47. Whitney Museum of American Art, *Catalogue of the Collection*, 8.

48. Douglas C. McGill, "Lloyd Goodrich, Art Expert, Dies: Ex-Director of Whitney Museum," *New York Times*, 28 Mar. 1987.

49. Whitney Museum of American Art, *Whitney Review*, 1964–65, 17.

50. Unlike the nineteenth-century French salon, which was juried and awarded prizes, the Whitney invited artists to exhibit in its annual shows, but gave no prizes. Its annual surveys had alternated sculpture one year (sometimes with watercolors and drawings) with paintings the next (*Whitney Review*, 1971–72, 5).

51. *Whitney Review*, 1974–75, 7.

52. Danto found the 1987 biennial "distressing" though understandable, since it "has succeeded in mirroring the times. The problem this year is not with the Whitney but with the world of art. What it shows is what, alas, alas, alas, there is" (Arthur C. Danto, "The Whitney Biennial," *The Nation*, 16 May 1987, 660).

53. McGill, "Lloyd Goodrich, Art Expert, Dies."

54. Having begun with little material support, the New Museum now has a staff of thirty, supported by ten or fifteen volunteers, to carry on its operations. Informed as to its selections and programs, its trustees have been generally supportive of the frequently unconventional ideas proposed. Budgets, salaries, and other issues are worked out by an inner structure of participatory project teams. The original plan had intended that all staff members would receive the same pay, but this has given way to a more differentiated pattern of remuneration as the museum has grown.

55. Robert Storr, "The New Museum: An Interview with Marcia Tucker," *Vantage Point* 6, no. 1 (1984), 2.

56. Stuart Greenspan, "The New Museum Raises $250,000 with Annual Auction of Outré Art," *New York Observer*, 15 May 1989, 12.

57. Storr, "The New Museum: An Interview with Marcia Tucker."

58. New Museum of Contemporary Art, "On View at the New Museum." The works by women with AIDS were elicited by Ann Meredith, a professional photographer from California. She acted as a catalyst in encouraging a group of women patients to express their emotions in a group of touching artworks that were displayed as part of the show.

59. Interview with the director of public affairs, New Museum of Contemporary Art, January 1990.

60. The exhibition Christian Boltanski: Lessons of Darkness (9 Dec. 1988–12 Feb. 1989) encompasses "several series of works using rephotographed snapshots and the interplay of light and shadow to evoke collective memories of

childhood and death. Much of the exhibition space was completely darkened with the sole illumination provided by tiny lights, candles and clamp-on lamps incorporated in the works. One gallery was devoted to [a] series based on a 1931 photograph of the graduating high school class of a Jewish school in Vienna. This series . . . reflects Boltanski's attempt to come to terms with his Jewish heritage and the horror of the Holocaust." This description is from the New Museum of Contemporary Art's booklet *1989 Twelfth Anniversary* (1989).

61. One of them scoffed at the idea of collusion as the kind of conspiracy that "is a peculiarly American phenomenon that derives from your tradition of muckracking journalism." From a different perspective, the director of the Stedelijk Museum in Amsterdam noted "that dealers were absolutely essential to the operation of any museum specializing in contemporary art, and no one suggested that these dealers were disinterested parties." More worrisome to the director of the Kunsthalle in Hamburg was that the "destabilizing" of art has threatened to stop museums from serving as the "stabilizing institution[s]" that he considered them to be. Only Pontus Hulten, then the director of the Centre Georges Pompidou, took the position that one should accept the idea that museums validate art, "but not for eternity, only for a very short time." Hilton Kramer, "Museum Chiefs Debate Modern-Art 'Conspiracy,' " *New York Times,* 26 June 1975.

62. Ibid.

63. Museum officials might hesitate to deal with artists directly on the grounds that, should it be necessary to refuse works offered, this might cause artists embarrassment and pain. But the same problem arises when a donor offers an unsuitable work. Since curators have faced this problem in the past, they know that they are not obliged to accept everything they are offered. Most museums have devolved this decisionmaking function to committees that have much experience with tactful refusal (Zolberg, "The Art Institute of Chicago").

PART 2

Audience, Ownership, and Authority: Designing Relations between Museums and Communities

STEVEN D. LAVINE

Many museums have taken up the challenge of responding to their various constituencies and relating to them more inventively; many have even begun to reimagine who those constituencies might be. Museums often try to accomplish these goals by appointing one or more trustees from groups the museum has newly targeted as part of its constituency, or by adding staff, usually in lower-level and outreach positions, from underrepresented groups. These efforts result most often in occasional exhibitions and special festival programs centered around themes designed to appeal to certain target groups. Museums hope that these efforts, along with their outreach programs, will win new audiences for their regular work. These developments increasingly are accompanied by a good deal of institutional worrying and conversation—seminars, guest speakers, workshops, community advisory committees—about the relation of these new enterprises to the institution's historical mission.

These changes, however major they may feel from within an institution, have thus far been modest. Large-scale social and demographic changes in industrial societies generally and the United States specifically will inevitably mean that museums will be asked to alter their programming to accommodate more diverse constituencies. In the past, cosmopolitan and municipal museums have worked from the assumption that taste and expertise justified the right of trustees, curators, and museum scholars to present what they believed their audiences should know. Often this expertise was laboriously acquired and contributed to scholarship and education. Yet the definition of what should be included in museums is now under attack, as are the canons and presumptions of many other disciplines. Perhaps the most fundamental challenge disputes the value of "scientific" and "scholarly" museum displays by those who argue that feelings about the past, particular groups' mythological constructions, and models for the future are more important than so-called factual accounts. This is a debate that will not soon be resolved. But it should be incontestable that even science is organized by cultural and political agendas that shape the body of facts examined and define the phenomena either ignored or given privileged places in museums.[1]

Further institutional change is inevitable. Since the civil rights and war protest movements of the 1960s and 1970s, every institution—cultural, educational, and governmental—that is seen to hold power has been open to question. The stance of benign neutrality has lost credibility. In the case of museums, this means that exhibitions will be "subjected to searching examinations for social, cultural, political, or sexual commitments."[2] As the demographics of the U.S. population continue to shift and we move toward being a society in which the majority of the population will belong to minority groups, we can expect these external pressures to grow. At the same time, current scholarship in the arts (as in every discipline of the humanities and social sciences) is attending to the subterfuges of power. Canons that justified inclusion and exclusion are being exploded. Institutions are being interrogated about their ways of retaining and dispersing power. An ever-greater self-consciousness can be anticipated among museum practitioners as they go about their business in disciplines and institutions that rest on no settled grounds. It is to be hoped that pressures from the outside will merge with changed attitudes from within to produce a mutually tenable redefinition of museum practice.

At present, the most promising innovations in museums' relationships with communities are coming not from the largest, oldest, and best-funded institutions but rather from institutions once viewed as marginal: children's museums, in which interactivity is necessitated by the age of the clientele and the educational goals of the institutions; history museums, in which the extraordinary efflorescence of social

history has combined with the relative unavailability of materials relating to nonwhites, women, and the poor to require new research,
collecting, and exhibition techniques; and ethnic and community-
based museums, many of which emerged in tandem with the civil
rights movement and have always considered their obligations to
community to lie at the heart of their missions. That the richer, cosmopolitan museums have been slower to act is partially the product of
the particularly hierarchical background out of which art collecting,
connoisseurship, and science emerge and partially related to the complexity attendant on such institutions' mandate to serve not only local
but national and international audiences.[3]

For larger museums, audience research has emerged as an important mechanism for achieving community input while maintaining
current patterns of organizational control. Through questionnaires,
interviews, and focus groups, curators and educators are able to gain
some purchase on who is learning what in their institutions. In her essay "The Communicative Circle: Museums as Communities," Constance Perin draws on a "limited ethnography of the communicative
circle" in the Smithsonian Institution's National Museum of Natural
History. She argues that in the traditional model of exhibition making, museum professionals draw on their collections when they initiate conversations with audiences and structure those conversations
with a syntax of objects. Audiences are expected to listen and learn.
Since there is rarely a way for exhibition makers to hear what audiences have to say, they must imagine the way viewers receive and respond to the exhibition, and the communicative circle breaks down.
Given the diverse "repertoires of prior knowledge, semantic systems,
and interpretive frames" that audiences bring, it is patently false, and
certainly patronizing, to assume a unitary public.

Stories of the disjunction between curators' assumptions and actual audience response are commonplace in every museum. Given the
diversity of audiences and the variety of reasons for visiting museums,
it can be tempting to withdraw to a position of skepticism and relative
helplessness: if it is not feasible to address audiences in all their bewil-
dering diversity, what alternative is there but for the curator and designer to make their best guesses about what audiences understand
and desire, or (in an older mode) what they should know and
appreciate?

Perin suggests that recognizing the different interpretive resources audience members bring with them—resources that are different from and more important than personal characteristics such as

socioeconomic background—provides a way to bridge the chasm between those who make exhibitions and those who visit them. By opening the process of exhibition development to include audiences, information on how audiences use these resources to understand their visit, and information on how they may use that understanding to shape meaning in other parts of their lives, it may be possible for exhibition makers to better understand how their own "repertoires of scientific paradigms, canons, and didactic aims" are likely to be understood. Done sensitively, this may lead to reformulations affecting not only the packaging or "spectacle" of exhibitions, but also their content. Thus, for example, an appreciation of how audiences employ the concept of tribe may lead to an exhibition on the problematics of this concept itself. Indeed, one development might well be that the multivocality of audience response will encourage the creation of multivocal exhibitions that actually reflect the state of scholarly debate in a way that monovocal exhibitions cannot.

A second key theme in Perin's paper is what she calls the principle of conservation: people "will add new information if they can conserve what they already know alongside it; or, if they can assimilate the new information gradually, they will allow it to replace previous understandings." This principle, broadly applied, might lead to exhibitions in which objects are included that resonate with the previous life experiences of visitors and in which themes are foregrounded that likewise resonate with the lives of visitors. The principle of conservation may have particular relevance to the effort to invest new audiences in museums. Thus, an awareness, derived from audience research, of various communities and the repertoires of interpretive resources they are likely to bring to museums could lead to fundamental, curator-driven renovations of museum practice. Current patterns of institutional and curatorial authority would be retained; only the definition of the competence and knowledge of curators and of the goals of exhibiting would evolve.

The installation of Gallery 33 at the Birmingham Museum and Art Gallery, described in Jane Peirson Jones's essay, reveals the potential for renewal when community needs and demands converge with a curator's educated guidance. Peirson Jones's mandate in reinstalling the museum's ethnography collection—which is, as she describes it, a colonial construction—was to respond to the complexities of contemporary community relations, taking into account the issues of cultural diversity that arise in a city such as Birmingham (whose population is

now twenty-five percent black and ethnic minority) and reflecting issues of public interest rather than a "traditional academic format."
Jones's mandate placed her in a complex situation. She was required
to mediate among the expectations of disparate communities in Birmingham, including longtime residents, members of different classes,
museum and municipal administrators, other curators, and the newly
arrived (in relative terms) communities whose cultural heritages were
to be part of the exhibition. The result was an exhibition entitled A
Meeting Ground of Cultures, designed to "encourage visitors to examine assumptions they make about their own and other people's
cultures."

Peirson Jones assembled an advisory group whose members were
chosen not as representatives of other communities but for their specific expertise (a community worker, a journalist, an anthropologist,
etc.). They acted as liaisons to communities. As she describes it, community involvement was significant but clearly within the boundaries
of the role of consultant; the authority remained with the museum
professionals, in a continuation of their more or less traditional role.

Gallery 33 emphasizes human experiences shared cross-cultur-
ally, thereby subordinating cultural and social differences. One might
view this as an appropriate civic policy for forging a larger community out of smaller communities, all of which have their own different
(and perhaps unavoidably conflicting) interests. On the other hand,
one might argue that this emphasis emerges out of the interests of the
dominant fraction of the population and is more acceptable to them.
The dominant group need have no fear that their distinctive characteristics and perspectives will be ignored, whereas subordinate elements of the population are alternately encouraged and pressured to
adapt and assimilate.[4] It is dangerously easy to appear to celebrate
shared experiences while actually selecting exhibiting themes that implicitly support claims to superiority by the dominant culture. To develop a genuinely cross-cultural exhibition practice will require
museum professionals to interrogate the history and inbuilt assumptions of their institutions and to reflect with patient self-consciousness
on their own exhibiting styles. John Kuo Wei Tchen's consideration of
the Chinatown History Museum, included in this section, offers a
good example of such institutional self-examination. Encouraging the
mutual recognition of cultural differences is a major challenge for museums. Exhibitions that represent one group as different and exotic
are common. Exhibitions that are cross-cultural encounters for more

than one group are rare. Yet such encounters have a tremendous potential to inform people about themselves, by setting their culture and
history side by side with others'.

Birmingham's Gallery 33 demonstrates one way in which the
concerns of current scholarship and of specific communities can be
brought together. The exhibition utilizes interactive videodisc technology to allow the visitor to follow the histories of four collectors—
four persons who have some connection with the objects in the museum's inventory. This focus on the collector is indebted to current anthropological concerns with unveiling and analyzing the specific
historical circumstances under which bodies of thought (and museum
collections) come into existence.[5] Yet this device of focusing on the
collectors also raises the question of the relevance of scholarly concerns to other segments of the local community. As Peirson Jones
notes, Afro-Caribbean commentators pointed out that an interest in
collectors is primarily a Western preoccupation. Peirson Jones herself
was concerned to display a phase of British history now virtually
obliterated in the school system: the nineteenth-century colonial and
imperial period. In a sense the history of the objects in this museum
stands for the history of Britain in general and Birmingham in particular. Peirson Jones's implicit position is that Birmingham is a multicultural society without any historical sense of how it came to be so.
The self-consciousness of this aspect of the exhibition may have been
addressed as a challenge to the white community to recognize the
other communities in Birmingham, rather than to those communities
themselves.

Large social questions, on the order of "Why are we living here?"
are likely to place exhibition makers in a difficult position. Many
communities would prefer celebrating their distant past to examining
their present circumstances. If exhibition makers are simple facilitators, they still have to decide which version of the past to articulate. If
they take an active view of their role as mediators, then they are likely
to present material and views other than those provided by the community that created the objects they may wish to exhibit. A solution
to this problem will be found only if exhibitions turn from monologue
to conversation. This is a difficult endeavor; no exhibition described
in this section fully succeeds in this task.

Gallery 33, in its emphasis on cross-cultural commonalities,
raises the crucial and increasingly pressing issue of civic culture. If we
take museum work seriously, we must believe that decisions such as
those Peirson Jones had to make influence visitors' views of them-

selves and their community. Among social scientists, there is little agreement about what produces a crisis in which civil society fractures along ethnic lines. In many nations of the world, and particularly in the United States, there is now acrimonious debate about how much diversity should be encouraged as a matter of policy. Under these uncertain circumstances, should museums, as publicly supported institutions, encourage the celebration and retention of difference, or should they be working to create shared cultures? If museums respond to the concerns of particular communities, should they have any further obligation to a larger civic whole?

In his recent study *The American Kaleidoscope: Race, Ethnicity, and the Civic Culture,* Lawrence H. Fuchs argues that the United States has a virtually unique record of ethnic and racial accommodation.[6] Fuchs maintains that the very act of organizing to maintain ethnic differences and to seek redress from social and governmental agencies leads ethnic and racial groups to modify their positions and adopt conciliatory stances vis-à-vis the larger society. He suggests that political and social participation eventually leads to partial assimilation.[7] Fuchs traces this pattern in wave after wave of immigration, and though he carefully details the variety of tactics used by various groups and the variety of responses by state and national legislatures, he finds that the pattern holds true.

Fuchs's comprehensive account has as background the civic-culture debate of the 1960s. The argument about civic culture ran as follows: civic culture is an ideal realized in only a few societies, notably Britain and the United States, in which communities moderate their demands on society in order to achieve their goals. The larger society tolerates cultural differences, and all members of the polity desire to participate but remain willing to delegate authority. The civic culture is based on political activism combined with the willingness to delegate responsibility to governmental officials. The civic culture of the United States and Great Britain has "a form of partisanship which is dynamic yet contained within overarching norms of a common civic unity."[8] Civic culture is characterized by political activity combined with "involvement" and "rationality" and is opposed to "passivity, traditionality, and commitment to parochial values."[9] Fuchs argues that political participation by ethnic and racial groups produces a changing set of attitudes that presumably moves from parochial values to more universal ones.

If Fuchs's argument is correct, the expression of cultural difference and the polemics of ethnic and cultural separatism are fundamental to civic culture in the United States. In this view, limiting or denying that expression will only impede participation in civic culture with (perhaps) the unintended side effect of making the maintenance of group difference the only alternative. A comparable viewpoint lies behind many mainstream and minority museums' arguments for opening up museums to diverse communities. It is one of the articulations of the role of the museum in civil society Ivan Karp described in the introduction to part 1. This position is not without pitfalls. Substantial reservations can be raised about civic-culture arguments, including Fuchs's account of American social history. There is evidence to suggest that even for the United States and Great Britain, the segments of society that are willing to moderate their demands are those who are generally better off. Those who have the least to gain from remaining part of the process do not feel any great hope or see the benefits from compromise and coalition.[10]

The argument for civic culture is also limited by its partial vision of Western history. Corrigan and Sayer's *The Great Arch* demonstrates that cultural organs such as museums were potent instruments of social control and cultural coercion over the course of British history. The civic culture, from this point of view, is an instrument of hegemony and a means of supporting the class position of elites.[11] Civic culture may be imposed upon the subordinate groups rather than be produced by their willing participation in society. It can benefit the few while helping to control the many.

Finally, the concept of civic culture may depend on a characterization of other cultures as "traditional," a way of thinking that is itself part of our colonial inheritance. If some people are particularistic and others accommodating, then it is "obvious" that the more particularistic group should change in the direction of the more modern other. Implicit criteria defined in terms of universal standards are set up to measure some peoples and find them wanting. Exhibiting practices of the sort examined in part 3 of this book manifest this attitude.

With all its limitations, why, then, invoke the concept of civic culture? First, the concept is implicit in the way that many museums think of their civic responsibilities and in the way that they think about diversity in the civil society of which they are a part. Second, a notion of civic culture, for all the dangers it entails, provides a useful model for some forms of museum-community interaction. In its most elementary form, civic culture suggests that museums and communities should be engaged in activities that constitute a conversation. The problem for museums is that the habits of the past can easily turn dialogues into monologues. While the model of civic culture may set up two unequal conversational parties, all the experiments in museum practice considered in this section attempt to resist this tendency.

For national institutions such as the Canadian Museum of Civilization, the problem of civic culture and civil society looms even larger than for municipal institutions. The community the Canadian Museum of Civilization serves is, according to the museum's director, George MacDonald, a society recognized by the Canadian constitution to be "bilingual but multicultural." Moreover, the mandate extends further, for as a national museum, the Canadian Museum of Civilization is an agent in the community of nations, and therefore has transnational responsibilities and, practically speaking, an international tourist audience.

For the Canadian Museum of Civilization, Native American groups are a prime concern. Native Americans have actively participated in creating exhibitions that represent their cultures. For MacDonald, real involvement means involvement with the concerns of the people being represented in the museum. In the case of Native Americans, these concerns include land claims, cultural renewal, and the repatriation of objects currently in museum collections. Controversial as these issues are, the Canadian Museum of Civilization has indeed addressed them. A particular challenge in this arena is to acknowledge that within any given group, there are internal disagreements and competing views and interpretations. How are museums to recognize and represent these divergent points of view within groups? Museum officials, accustomed to speaking authoritatively, must recognize that their choice of whom to hire and whom to listen to retains for them the cultural power to cast the terms of discourse about people and history. Even when museums consult representatives of minority cultures or bring them onto their staffs, they still must consider how and on what basis their selections of such representatives have been made. The risk of suppressing many voices by delegating to one representative of a community the authority to tell that community's stories should be clear. In a significant degree, it is problematic in the same way as is allowing the traditional curatorial class—drawn primarily from among white, middle- or upper-class, college-educated males—to speak for all the minority cultures represented in the museum. Once again, a solution is likely to be found only in an adequate process of dialogue, one that can transform the voice of authority on which museums have traditionally relied into the voice of a pluralistic society. The emergent compound identities (Chinese Canadian,

Ukrainian Canadian, and others, not to mention those south of the
border, such as African American and Jewish American) that are
spawned by such pluralism require not only that museums embrace
cultural particularities as a fact but also that they explore the ways
cultural differences engage and alter one another. Through such an investigation, museums can transcend the limitations of the civic-culture model. Instead of "them" becoming more like "us," the
conversation promises accommodation and change on all sides.

MacDonald devotes considerable attention to the implications
for the museum of the information age. He postulates that museum
collections are important chiefly for the information they contain.
The Canadian Museum of Civilization attempts to make this information available to all by using computer-based technologies to "customize museum experience to the interests and learning styles of diverse
visitor groups" (a strategy that Jane Peirson Jones, working on a far
more modest scale, also uses). At the opposite extreme, computer
technologies make it possible for the museum presentation to approach the level of spectacle more commonly found in the entertainment and leisure industry. MacDonald does not shy away from the
enormous challenge—recognized by museum officials but rarely so
openly aired—of balancing the demand for spectacle against the sub-
tlety required to achieve educational goals for widely varying groups
of visitors. MacDonald, along with several other authors in this volume, classifies visitors in part in terms of the amount of time and concentration they are likely to devote to the exhibitions they encounter.
The spectacular element of the museum is designed to capture the attention of what are often called "streakers," people who usually move
through the museum very quickly; in addition to providing them with
information they can carry away and add to their preexisting store of
information, museum personnel hope that these streakers' interest
will be stimulated and that they will want to spend somewhat more
time in the future going into greater depth on topics that interest
them. Spectacle, however, runs the risk of having to depend on shallow, deracinated images. One is led to ponder the issue of the authentic object in an age of virtuality.

Classifications that define categories of visitors by the length of
their visits, like all such simple classifications, represent visitors as an
audience that passively consumes a product. Against this simplifying
grid, one wants to set others that acknowledge visitors in Perin's
terms, as members of specific interpretive communities. A restored
complexity would consider what various publics see, how they pro-

cess the information in exhibitions, and what criteria they find important. For a large national museum that serves a broad range of visitors, this process may seem to involve an almost infinite regress that detracts from the job of attracting visitors enticed by the pricey lures of the commercial media. The task of recognizing and responding to the diversity represented in museum audiences may require smaller institutions rooted in specific communities.

The Brooklyn Children's Museum is an institution defined in significant ways by its local community. Like many museums in urban centers, it has seen its original community change over time. In this case, a middle-class European immigrant population moved away and was replaced by mainly Caribbean (West Indian and Haitian) and African American families. With that change has come a major shift in economic resources, social and educational needs, and cultural predispositions. Mindy Duitz, the current director, tells the inspirational story of a museum searching its soul to discover the strengths and obligations of its new situation.

The Children's Museum, as Duitz observes, had always been "conceived as experience-oriented" and focused on "participatory exhibitions," and so in the long run change could be evolutionary. As so often happens, the change was occasioned first by external and economic factors, as the number of visitors dropped (in part because the museum was located in what had come to be seen as a dangerous neighborhood) and local legislators made it clear they wanted to see a commitment to the local neighborhood. Those measures led to tension within the museum, which in turn led to a formal planning process eventuating in a new mission statement and a commonly shared sense of purpose.

The mission statement, as Duitz describes it, turns on the relationship of the self to the community, the environment, and the past and future. It is a usefully suggestive universalizing and particularizing grid. The stages of childhood development provide the universalizing dimension; the needs of specific communities provide the particular. Hence, for example, an early-childhood area provides programs in parenting, recognizing the needs of teen parents and single parents. After-school programs acknowledge the latchkey problem among members of their audience by providing social and educational activities for third to sixth graders. Similarly, an exhibition on dreams, Night Journeys, deals with phenomena that are both intensely personal and yet presumably universal, and provides a thought-provoking cross-cultural perspective. The museum's mission statement, with its grid—which identifies audiences, and establishes programs that lead to exhibitions and exhibitions that lead to programs—may be suggestive for other types of museums as well. Too often a commitment to community is seen as fundamentally opposed to a commitment to collections and scholarship, and the effort to serve one community as replacing service and responsiveness to another. The Brooklyn Children's Museum continues to see itself as serving New York City and the metropolitan area, even as it has made a formal commitment to its local community. It is clear that for institutions to keep track of their souls, their historical missions, it will be useful to think through the interrelationship of past practices and commitments to current needs and demands.

At the same time, the Children's Museum story underlines the likely ramifications of new community commitments for every aspect of institutional operations, from staff (where the need to find employees who could feel comfortable in a surrounding community perceived as dangerous led to recruitment from such nontraditional sources as the theater and social-service fields) to public affairs (volunteer groups and special events) and from public programs (reflecting new community interests and stressing badly needed after-school activities) to collections (the purchase of Afro-Caribbean materials). Each of these changes spawns others: internships, new collaborations, new exhibitions. The process of change also generates new internal tensions. When broader societal tensions were brought into the Children's Museum, staff training on racism and stereotyping became necessary and was instituted. The end result of these multiple, overlapping changes will almost certainly involve a reallocation of time, staff, and funding.

Duitz does not focus on the process of exhibition development, preferring to stress the museum's participatory activities; indeed, it is Kids Crew—the expanded program for unaccompanied children— that she nominates as the museum's legacy to its future, that is, something participatory. But it is telling that in formulating curricula and exhibitions the museum maintains its dual universalizing and particularizing mode. The museum staff works with teachers and students to formulate curricula, thereby insuring an adequate fit with the universalizing force of school curricula and presumptions about childhood development. Visitors are involved in formative evaluation, allowing the museum staff to check these general schemata against visitor experience. Both subject specialists and visitor focus groups are drawn on in the development process. Community does not replace subject-area expertise; indeed, Duitz's examples make the case that there is no reason for one to supplant the other.

If we imagine a spectrum from curator-driven to community-driven institutions, the Brooklyn Children's Museum remains very much at the curator-driven end. While the museum was being pushed by external pressures from legislators and by the problems it was having attracting staff and audience, the museum's transformation was clearly director- and curator-driven. Indeed, the first step was to look to the staff, both to those already there and to those newly hired. Too often, the addition of trustees is seen as the first step; in the case of the Brooklyn Children's Museum, that part of the development is still incomplete. The staff initiated the change and, significantly, Duitz gives no indication of community input to that process. Indeed, even Kids Crew, which appears to be a cornerstone project for the new museum, appears to be staff-driven, deriving ultimately from staff concerns about how to serve unaccompanied students. In the Brooklyn Children's Museum case, with staff competence defined so as to include deep knowledge of the community, apparent conflicts between institutional authority and community concern and involvement largely disappear.

The Chinatown History Museum, as described by its co-founder, John Kuo Wei Tchen, is devoted to the effort to "document, reconstruct, and reclaim" the history of a particular local ethnic community. Central to its work, however, is interconnectedness and the possibilities of broader civic and national participation. Their labors begin in personal memory and heritage, but the projects' leaders are concerned to bring that memory up against a broader historical discourse, which clarifies "why and how life has become the way it is." In the process, they combine professional responsibility to their discipline with a sense of obligation to the community studied; they do not believe that one necessarily excludes the other. For example, they hope to overcome the overvaluation of the local which so often follows from social history, thereby contributing to the new synthesis for which many historians have called. At the same time, they hope to help Chinatown residents, whose history is their main object, to escape the limits of nostalgia and gain the "more integrative and inclusive community history [that] can help to counter the sense of marginalization and disempowerment."

Many museum officials and curators (along with others exerting cultural authority) have expressed reservations about what they see as both a disregard for objective truth and a movement toward cultural separatism implicit in African American, Asian American, and other ethnic-group-specific institutions. The Chinatown History Museum offers a paradigm that might counter those fears. The valorization of a community's experiences—as in the museum's exhibitions on laundry and garment workers, which have their roots in the life histories of older members of the community that were collected by the staff and volunteers of the Chinatown History Museum—creates an exhibition and programming environment resonant with their personal experiences, one that allows visitors from the community to identify actively with the production of history. But this valorization is only a first step, allowing visitors to think about differences and continuities in the present. No longer required to defend a past forgotten or undervalued by the larger society, the museum is able to achieve "more critical, distanced insights" that "challenge simple nostalgia." From this more critical understanding comes a reshaping of identity.

This dynamic project—at once historical and moral/social—is possible because the Chinatown History Museum rejects any kind of ethnic essentialism. Its work stands firmly on the conviction that individual and collective identities are always complex and shifting. Within the Chinatown community, there are differences between a bachelor laundry worker and an import/export merchant with a family. Further, both participate in not only the history of New York but also that of the United States, each of which calls forth and shapes other and overlapping senses of identity.

Accomplishing these ends requires the creation of a new sort of museum, described by Tchen as "a cultural free space for open discussion." Into this space are invited Chinese New Yorkers, other residents of the city's Lower East Side, tourists, and scholars and other cultural producers—in short, representatives of the varying groups who have defined the experience and perception of Chinatown. With each, there is a process of discussion dependent on a kind of respectful listening that has not generally characterized the curator in larger, cosmopolitan institutions. This listening characterizes the creation of exhibitions; equally, it becomes part of the exhibitions themselves. Interactive installations jog the memories of visitors and create the means for them to leave behind data, which will then become evidence for future exhibitions. Part of what is at stake here is a reorientation of museums, to make them information sources as much as object repositories. For all their fundamental differences, the Birmingham Museum's Gallery 33, the Canadian Museum of Civilization, the Brooklyn Children's Museum, and the Chinatown History Museum all share this vision. The work of the Chinatown History Museum cannot take place without a more fully implemented and respectful conversation. In this approach, what Tchen calls "surface definitiveness"—that authoritative single voice that is so common a feature in all kinds of museums—is sacrificed. What is gained is "a learning environment in which personal history and testimony unfold and are infused by historical context and scholarship."

The other exhibitions described above are likewise concerned with engaging visitors in conversations. This involves a process of sharing with visitors the exhibition-making process or the collection process or the selection process. An opening is created for more equal conversation and interchange, even though no institutional power is given up in any formal sense—curators and other museum professionals will still make all the decisions. Tchen even speaks of wanting "the seams" of research to show and the process of constructing, exhibiting, and interpreting a community to be exposed. Tchen, like Duitz, insists that all museum work assumes a conversation among the different parties; without it, one could not know how to design exhibitions. The Birmingham exhibition seeks to show that its process of acquiring collections is an artifact of the same history that brought diverse communities to the city. In the Canadian Museum of Civilization this conversation exists in a somewhat truncated form, perhaps because of the national and international ambitions of the museum and all they imply about the need for spectacle and the desire to serve a greater variety of visitors.

The "cultural free space" of the Chinatown History Museum, like the renewal of the Brooklyn Children's Museum and the continuing development of Gallery 33, requires that virtually every aspect of museum work and structure be reconsidered: archives, staff job roles, the allocation of organizational resources. This final step is key. The Chinatown History Museum has, according to Tchen, found itself overwhelmed with the new responsibilities it has taken on. Traditional collection-driven institutions, especially ones with a large number of artifacts to care for and display, have evolved structures to support that process. If active exchanges with communities are to become part of an institution's work, it will not happen by adding these activities at the margins, but by fundamentally reorganizing—with all that means, financially and organizationally. Indeed, it will also require funding agencies to rethink their programs, so as to recognize process as part and parcel of product. But this change is not likely to happen quickly—indeed, Tchen cites several projects that have been held up or limited by conventional funding patterns.

The Chinatown History Museum, for all the evident depth of its involvement in and commitment to New York's Chinatown, retained for its professional staff the right to make final decisions. The CARA project (Chicano Art: Resistance and Affirmation), organized by the Wight Art Gallery at the University of California, Los Angeles, represents a more radical revision in conventional museum practice. The Wight Art Gallery, whose goal was to mount an interpretive exhibition of the Chicano art movement despite the fact that the gallery had no special expertise in this area, created a potentially cumbersome apparatus including an advisory council of forty to fifty scholars, artists, and administrators; smaller working groups, including nine regional committees; a three-member national executive committee; a five-member national selection committee; a three-member editorial board; five task forces; and a design team. In the process, the Wight Art Gallery limited its own authority over the exhibition, casting itself as facilitator and financial manager.

So extensive was the process that it became, in significant measure, a goal in itself, equal to and perhaps more important than the exhibition. The challenge, as Alicia González and Edith Tonelli indicate, was to create a process through which an exhibition of artworks from a living culture might reflect the spirit and values of the culture itself. González and Tonelli summarize the goals of the project, as defined by its Chicano advisors, as self-representation, the inclusion of multiple voices, and adherence to a Chicano spirit, aesthetic, and values. The goals of the museum professionals were the accommodation of partners without the abandonment of expertise, the maintenance of a coherent exhibition concept focusing on art without discounting social context, and communication with a culturally diverse, largely non-Chicano audience. González and Tonelli's essay does not provide new formulations in response to these challenges. Rather, these issues seem to have pressed back onto the exhibition development process itself, including the selection of work to be included. From the experience, Tonelli concludes that it is essential for museum professionals to "look at our jobs as including this kind of risk-taking and confrontation" if they ever hope to "accomplish the goals we often profess to have concerning the representation and participation of a diverse and multicultural citizenry." Writing as a social scientist, Gonzáles argues that the process of defining themes and selecting work requires as part of its methodology an ongoing self-reflection. Surely no recent exhibition has gone so far in placing the rights and powers of the participants in question. Each had to be negotiated and renegotiated every step of the way.

Can and should collaborations along the lines of CARA be encouraged elsewhere? The process added to the length and cost of organizing the exhibition. Curatorial authority was broadly shared, but the Wight Art Gallery remained the responsible and liable financial agent, which can only have created internal institutional stress. Did a "better" exhibition result than if a single curator, or a curator with consultants, had organized the show? It is impossible to say. But certainly a different exhibition emerged, one which constructed a new pattern of involvement and ownership among artist, audience, and museum. If museums are to play an active role in reflecting and even shaping emergent identities, an expanded process of exhibition making—imagined as dialogue, conversation, argument, or ownership—may well emerge as crucial. Indeed, just as the full analysis of a contemporary blockbuster exhibition requires consideration of promotion and shop sales alongside the exhibition proper, so, in the future, it may become essential to consider the exhibition and its process as one extended cultural act or artifact.

None of the exhibitions thus far considered takes the final step of transferring all aspects of exhibition-making authority to a community or its representatives. The development of African American and Latino museums over the past several decades provides evidence that this process can work. Often, assistance and even sponsorship has come from institutions with quite different histories, as, for example, the Anacostia Museum's emergence under the Smithsonian Institution's umbrella, and the Metropolitan Museum of Art's involvement with El Museo del Barrio. These newer museums have evolved over time and now define their relation to communities in a broad variety of ways. Some have remained local museums, rooted in their immediate communities; others have cast their ambitions more broadly. Still others try to balance these purposes. The Anacostia Museum, for example, now sees itself as a regional institution, encompassing the African American communities of the upper South. The administrators and curators of these museums, as professionals, share goals, values, and aspirations that may not completely correspond with the aspirations of the communities they serve. Most of these museums were begun at a more hopeful moment in American history, as a direct outgrowth of the civil rights movement, but the ecomuseum project undertaken by the Ak-Chin Indians of Arizona manifests this process in the present. Nancy Fuller, part of the team of Smithsonian consultants who worked with the Ak-Chin, describes the museum as resulting from at least three separate impetuses: the increased sense of agency stemming from the development of agriculture on tribal lands and the settlement of their water rights claims; the ecomuseum movement, which developed out of the political and intellectual turmoil of late-1960s France; and the lifetime-learning movement that grew up during the same period. It is significant that each stimulus reflects the development of power through action, rather than the discovery of power or the turning-over of power from previously existing institutions.

In Fuller's account, the Ak-Chin Indian Community's ecomuseum grew out of the Ak-Chin concern that rapid economic development was placing long-sustained cultural traditions in jeopardy. The tribal council reasoned that a museum and archive might help produce in a younger generation pride in community achievements. At first trusting to outside guidance, the council, drawing on some basic audience research, discovered the need for a more participatory environment than a traditional museum would provide. The council developed a museum development plan modeled on their water settlement strategies—a remarkable instance of the application of discovery of agency in one field to another.

The depth of involvement that followed obviated one problem that is encountered by many community museums built on the model of mainstream museums: the tendency to become small treasure houses that enshrine the history and accomplishments of only one portion of the community, with the result that there is limited community involvement. The Ak-Chin project exemplifies an alternative strategy wherein "real-life experiences of exploration, experimentation, and questioning" become the basis of the institution. It is this commitment that Fuller finds inscribed in the ecomuseum concept. Ecomuseums are designed to respond to a specific area's problems through an array of museumlike and educational activities; each museum would therefore look different, joined to the others by only a shared "participatory approach and a goal to be a catalyst for change."

Training becomes a central component in the ecomuseum concept—the building-up of expertise within a given community. The statements of the Ak-Chin themselves poignantly reveal how the process of making a museum in a community turns members of the community into witnesses to the community's aspirations and difficulties in managing change—difficulties all communities experience. The staff are moving toward a role described by John Berger and Jean Mohr as "clerk-recorder of the community."[12] The museum becomes not so much a collection of objects as an assemblage of objects and documentation. On the surface this makes them no different from any other museum; objects and some sort of documentation are part of all museum collections. The combination of objects, records, and oral histories is commonly found in ethnographic collections. What is important here is not that the museum will come to look much like other museums, but that the work of cultural documentation is an organic process that is part of how a changing community defines itself. Here, the Ak-Chin museum, based explicitly on the ecomuseum idea, draws close to the somewhat more traditional but still community-centered efforts described by Peirson Jones, Duitz, Tchen, and González and Tonelli. The difference is that the impetus derives from the community itself. This is not a process without tensions. As the staff finish training they will begin to bring in perspectives derived from outside the community. As a result, they will inevitably have goals that conflict with those held by some members of the community. Nor does the community itself speak with a single voice; no community does. If the museum works, however, the conversations continue.

Taken together, the array of museums described in this section raises fundamental issues about community, authority, and exhibition development. The exhibition of the Birmingham Museum's Gallery 33 that Jane Peirson Jones describes offers an integrative social view developed jointly by a curator and consultants with limited community dialogue. The explicit assumption there is that commonalities join us across difference; it appears that the underlying assumption is that participation in civil society requires a set of shared understandings, which in turn create a meeting ground of cultures. In contrast, exhibitions such as CARA or the products of the Chinatown History Museum, developed with a significantly greater amount of advice and counsel from community members outside the museum, assume that if we are joined it is through the contestation and confrontation of ideas. Exhibitions can present the internal and differential experiences of various groups (CARA), and may even trace how heritage interacts with external history (Chinatown History Museum). Decisions about commonality and difference have, in turn, profound present-day social implications. As a society, we are debating how much difference is tolerable and desirable. Given the influence of museums as valorizing agencies, whatever view is presented is (at least at this historical moment) of consequence. Even if the influence of museum exhibitions is less than we like to imagine, museums can expect to find themselves challenged, whichever direction they take. There is no way to avoid challenges, and not to treat them seriously will simply render museums irrelevant. Rather, museums are summoned to treat challenges not so much as problems to be surmounted, but as invitations to engage in conversations with the shifting publics who compose their most important constituencies.

NOTES

1. Sandra Harding, *The Science Question in Feminism* (Ithaca, N.Y.: Cornell University Press, 1982).

2. Neil Harris, *Cultural Excursions: Marketing Appetites and Cultural Tastes in Modern America* (Chicago: University of Chicago Press, 1990), 85.

3. See the discussion of these issues in the introduction to part 1.

4. See the discussion of this issue in Ivan Karp, "Other Cultures in Museum Perspective," in Ivan Karp and Steven D. Lavine, eds., *Exhibiting Cultures: The Poetics and Politics of Museum Display* (Washington, D.C.: Smithsonian Institution Press, 1991), 373–86.

5. George W. Stocking, Jr., ed., *Objects and Others: Essays on Museums and Material Culture* (Madison: University of Wisconsin Press, 1985); James Clifford and George E. Marcus, *Writing Culture: The Poetics and Politics of Ethnography* (Berkeley: University of California Press, 1986); Ivan Karp and Steven D. Lavine, eds., *Exhibiting Cultures: The Poetics and Politics of Museum Display* (Washington, D.C.: Smithsonian Institution Press, 1991); Ivan Karp and Corinne Kratz, "Tippoo's Tiger: A Critical Account of Ethnographic Display" (Los Angeles: Getty Center for the History of Art and the Humanities, 1991).

6. Lawrence H. Fuchs, *The American Kaleidoscope: Race, Ethnicity, and the Civic Culture* (Middletown, Conn.: Wesleyan University Press, 1990).

7. Ibid., 1–6.

8. See Gabriel A. Almond, "The Intellectual History of the Civic Culture Concept," in Gabriel A. Almond and Sidney Verba, eds., *The Civic Culture Revisited: An Analytic Study* (Boston: Little, Brown, 1980), 17. This volume contains an excellent overview of the concept as well as telling critical essays.

9. Almond, "The Intellectual History of the Civic Culture Concept," 24–25.

10. See Carol Pateman's "The Civic Culture: A Philosophical Critique," in Gabriel A. Almond and Sidney Verba, eds., *The Civic Culture Revisited* (Boston: Little, Brown, 1980), for a fuller exposition of these criticisms.

11. Philip Corrigan and Derek Sayer, *The Great Arch: State Formation, Cultural Revolution* (Oxford: Basil Blackwell, 1985).

12. John Berger and Jean Mohr, *A Fortunate Man: The Story of a Country Doctor* (New York: Pantheon, 1981).

CHAPTER 6

Change and Challenge: Museums in the Information Society

GEORGE F. MACDONALD

I t is easy to imagine that museums, focused as most are on matters of the past, are timeless institutions standing apart from the processes of change operating on the present—observing and recording, but not participating in, nor affected by, change. The history of museums itself contradicts this. We may remember, for instance, that museums were not always accessible to the general public—not until the democratizing trend of the last century. Museums *are* products of their social context, and it is proper that they should be so. It is, however, dangerous to assume that a place is guaranteed for museums in the society of the future. If we accept that their purpose is to be of service to society, then it is vital they be responsive to their social environment in order to remain relevant to changing social needs and goals.

The current direction of change has been characterized as taking us toward an information society. There are many forces for change operating today, but one of the most resonant is the rapid development of information, communication, and media technologies, which are infiltrating all aspects of our lives: public, professional, domestic, educational, and even recreational. A colleague of mine[1] recently noted that the movement toward democracy in the former Warsaw Pact nations owes less to Thomas Jefferson than to Ted Turner—that is, less to democratic principles than to the access television provides to information about events going on in other countries.

The transition from industrial age to information age necessitates a review of museum philosophies and practices, and a reevaluation of how well museums are serving their communities. For a national museum such as the Canadian Museum of Civilization, the "community" is a multicultural society, a nation of nations—not unlike the United States in origin, but never subjected to the same pressure to be a melting pot. The Canadian constitution recognizes the country to be bilingual but multicultural. It is the responsibility of Canada's national museum of human history to reflect this multicultural character; and, by extension, to be concerned with all the peoples of the world, since they are part of us and we part of them. The collections of the Canadian Museum of Civilization (hereafter CMC) cover over 350 specific cultural groups, of which almost one hundred are our native peoples. We see it as a museum not just for the Canadian nation, but for the global village. Canada is often described as a cultural mosaic, but I like to think that a hologram is a more appropriate image for such postcolonial societies; Europe is moving toward the same model.

The consequence of the above is that CMC's audience comprises not merely the whole Canadian population, but also foreign visitors to Canada's capital and people around the world who have a need for knowledge about Canadian history and culture. This may seem obvious. But if we do not remain consciously aware of the character of our community, we may fail to perceive some of our obligations— particularly the implications concerning outreach.

Part of the reevaluation of museums currently under way entails reconsideration of their fundamental role or mission. Insofar as this takes the form of defining some idealized model for the concept of museum, the effort is misdirected. Diversity is one of the great strengths of the museum world—it is for museums, as in evolution generally, a survival mechanism—and to try to fit all museums into one mold is counterproductive. No single museum can respond to all social needs with equal effectiveness; for this reason alone we must have a variety of museums and museum styles, serving different purposes or tackling challenges from different approaches. This does not invalidate a role review, since that process gives the opportunity to reexamine what we are doing and how we are doing it, and to point to necessary adjustments.

Today's reigning paradigm is of an educational role for museums, if we define *education* in broad enough terms. But consensus will thereafter begin to trip up over the value-laden connotations of the term. For me, it has connotations of prerequisites, classroom discipline, lectures to a passive audience, exams, and so on. Such features, in the context of democratization, are almost wholly inappropriate to museums. I prefer to think in terms of learning rather than education, as the former implies a process directed by the recipient of knowledge, with the museum as facilitator rather than authoritative imposer of "facts."

The premise underlying this essay is that all museums are, at the most fundamental level, concerned with information: its generation, its perpetuation, its organization, and its dissemination. Implicit in this premise is the idea that museums' principal resource—their collections of material remnants of the past—are of value, and are worth preserving, primarily for the information embodied in them. The information may be intellectual, aesthetic, sensory, or emotional in nature (or more likely some combination), depending on the object and its associations. The same value is also applicable to the newer, nonmaterial resource collections museums are building, such as oral histories, photographs, audiovisual materials, replicas, and reenacted processes.

It is beyond this level of being information institutions that different museums begin to go their separate ways. For one thing, while original artifacts are inherently objective arbiters of our understanding of the past, *how* we understand them is inescapably subjective.[2] This is true of the names we give them, the importance we ascribe to them, the ways in which we relate them to other objects (such as through classification systems, or in the context of period rooms, for instance), or anything that falls under the heading of "interpretation." Another way in which museums differ is in what they *do* with their information or, to resort to current jargon, how they *package* information. Education and entertainment may be viewed as two forms of packaging.

At the risk of overgeneralizing, museums of the industrial age could not achieve their full potential because their society—dominated by male, middle-class values—expected of them that they would validate the material-wealth-based foundations of social status (by their emphasis on collecting and displaying valuable objects), celebrate the concept of progress as defined by an industrialized society, and commemorate the domination of certain civilized cultures over supposedly primitive ones (by relegating the power objects of the latter to the status of captured trophies). But the shifts in values, attitudes, and

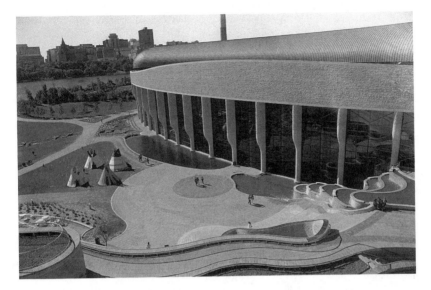

Fig. 6-1. By breaking free of cultural paradigms of architectural style, and by speaking of the historical landscape (here the Grand Hall, depicting the melting glaciers at the end of the Ice Age), Douglas Cardinal's creation is appropriate for the global village in which all peoples seek their common heritage. Photo by Stephen Alsford, courtesy of the Canadian Museum of Civilization.

perceptions that accompany the technological transition from industrial to information society can make it possible for museums to achieve their full potential as places for learning in and about a world in which the globetrotting mass media, international tourism, migration, and instant satellite links between cultures are sculpting a new global awareness and helping give shape to what Marshall McLuhan characterized as the global village. Aspects of this new global awareness include a greater sensitivity to environmental issues that affect all nations; a growing preoccupation with social justice; and a fuller appreciation of the increasingly culturally pluralistic character of Western society, and the ramifications of this in terms of cultural values. These issues themselves present challenges to which museums need to respond and are, indeed, beginning to respond.

In a multicultural society, the problem facing a national museum such as CMC is to reflect an identity that has national validity, yet is relevant to individual ethnic groups. Museums are often perceived as preserving for posterity that which society considers to be of value; if museums don't represent all elements of society, they run the risk of alienating those groups. At the same time, ethnic groups feel the need to participate in the process of portraying and interpreting their cultures.

Overall, people seek from human-history museums some understanding of their society in terms of its historical development and of their own place within that society. Ideally, museums should encourage and assist their users to develop the skills to make their own interpretations of history using museums' information resources. What precisely they will do with the interpretations they may acquire is difficult to predict, and it is arguable whether this is really any business of museums. But CMC's hope is that through acquiring an understanding of other cultures, people will come to appreciate the inner logic of social systems that are different from their own, and will develop an appreciation and respect for them that will combat prejudices. Mutual appreciation and cooperation among the cultural groups that make up Canadian society is seen as the necessary foundation for Canada to remain a single nation.

Museums alone cannot create a sense of cultural identity. The media and the entertainment industry have much more impact here. But what museums particularly offer is an object base—the collection of the real, material remains of the past—as a sort of yardstick that people could use (if they were taught the skills) to evaluate cultural mythologies.

In sum, the importance of museums to the future development of society lies not merely in their role as repositories of information. It is also in how they *use* that information to create understanding; or, perhaps more significantly, how they help their audiences to exploit the information resources in the quest for knowledge.

THE MUSEUM AUDIENCE

Although Canada's national museum of human history has long been in existence, in one form or another, the prospect of a new site and a new, custom-designed building provided the welcome opportunity for my staff and me to review every aspect of operations and consider how to bring the museum up to date and in line with the needs of its community. One thing that became apparent during the project was that the rapid pace of social change creates the need for ongoing review and adjustment. Early conceptual outlines for organizational structure, operations, programs, and facility requirements were unprepared for the developments of the 1980s. It was only after we were well into the design phase that the need became apparent for theatrical facilities associated with the galleries themselves, for a fiber-optic-based telecommunication network, and for television production studios. Fortunately, these needs could be accommodated. Without these facilities we could not expect to achieve our vision of being an interactive museum that could serve both on-site visitors and electronic users at a distance.

Since the community for a national museum is extensive, one of our chief concerns was to differentiate the various components of that community. Museums have tended to view their audiences as homogeneous groups, and to provide services and programs on a single level. This approach has been reinforced by visitor studies, which consistently characterize the typical museum visitor as a middle-class WASP (white Anglo-Saxon Protestant) with an above-average income and education. Perhaps a self-fulfilling prophecy is at work here. It is really only in the context of the social changes I have already outlined, as well as in the face of economic pressures, that museums have recognized their restricted audience appeal as a problem. This failing of mainstream museums is one reason why we are seeing growing numbers of specialized museums designed for specific audiences, such as children, indigenous peoples, and specific ethnic communities.

One of the challenges of the future is to utilize computer-based technologies in imaginative ways to customize museum experiences to the interests and learning styles of diverse visitor groups. We have scarcely begun to experience the impact of culturally interactive software—that is, software that allows members of one culture to learn another cultural grammar. By "cultural grammar" I mean the hidden rules that drive the social systems and aesthetics (right down to things such as sports, music, and cuisine) that characterize each culture. Anthropologists have spent almost a century defining social and cultural grammars that can now be programmed into interactive software, in a variety of formats from games to full roleplaying. One such program, used in CMC's Children's Museum, encourages the user to become an Inuit hunter and to make life-and-death decisions for the community, such as how many animals to harvest each season without endangering the herd on which community survival depends. This kind of cultural literacy—familiarity with cultures other than one's own—is a way of promoting intercultural understanding, and should be addressed very seriously by cultural-history museums.

In the last couple of years the issue of whether museums should be quality-driven or market-driven has become something of a battle-

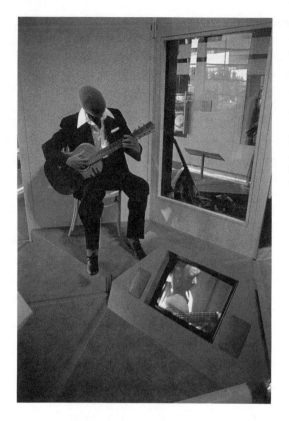

Fig. 6-2. The teaching of cultural grammars through exhibits will require emphasis on visual literacy, to break across barriers of verbal language, and on communication with the senses as much as with the intellect. Photo by Stephen Alsford, courtesy of the Canadian Museum of Civilization.

ground.[3] This is unfortunate, particularly since it is the nature of such conflicts to cause opposing sides to become entrenched, their arguments polarized. It is as though museums must be either one thing or another. One of the greatest challenges facing museums today is to reconcile these two elements of our reality. I hope all of us in museums place the highest value on quality in packaging our information products for public consumption. As responsible educators, we must be dedicated to the highest quality achievable, even though quality is hard to define operationally because it is to a large extent a product of the recipient's experience.[4] And this quest for quality need not be incompatible with marketing techniques; certainly part of the solution should be to try to create in the marketplace a demand for what museums produce best. But there is, at the same time, a certain responsibility to try to maximize the audience that museums' messages reach, not least because, as pragmatists, we must recognize that our funding—upon which achieving quality partly depends—derives, directly or indirectly, from our audiences; we must therefore be aware of and responsive to the requirements of those audiences. No museum, however high the quality of its information products, can be considered successful if it fails to make those products relevant to what concerns the society in which it exists.

So at CMC, market segmentation was an important part of planning the design of exhibitions, programs, and facilities for the new museum. It was a question of trying to accommodate better the informational, social, and personal needs of the existing user community, as well as to attract nontraditional audiences. Audience segmentation is a very complex affair. There seems no end of ways in which the public can be broken down—the ideal being to address the specific needs of every individual. All such breakdowns, like any classification system, involve some generalization and some subjectivity. Far more audience research is required before museums can properly appreciate the characteristics and, particularly, the needs of their existing publics, as well as a far greater effort at sharing the results of research among museums.

In the task of market segmentation we were helped by Dr. Robert Kelly of the University of British Columbia, who has long been involved in the socio-anthropological study of museum visitors.[5] He suggested that there are three fundamental kinds of needs visitors have: intellectual, sacred, and social. Intellectual needs—the need to know and understand—have been the principal, explicit target of museums. Sacred needs are tied to the role of museums as pilgrimage sites, where visitors are linked with their ancestral past, as well as to rites of passages conferring social status—museum visiting being a traditional indicator of cultural good taste. Sacred needs are already catered to by museums, but we could do with more research to help us understand the nature of these needs and how museums might design their facilities or exhibitions to provide more meaningful experiences in this area—including enhancing the ritualistic qualities of some experiences. Social needs, like sacred needs, relate to "being seen" in museums, as well as being able to socialize there. The facilities that are now commonly built into major new museums (CMC included)— lobbies, salons, shops, theaters, restaurants—may seem subsidiary to a museum's principal functions, but do serve a real public need. It is also very healthy for museums to be perceived by the public as institutions operating in the center of social life, rather than out on the periphery. (We should make note of the trend in some Third World countries to prefer the name "cultural center" for institutions we in the

West characterize as museums.) Rental of museum facilities to community or private groups, and events such as receptions and exhibition openings, as well as the existence of "friends of the museum" and volunteer associations, also answer these social needs.

At CMC we are responding to intellectual needs by readying the museum to operate on three levels. We differentiated among what we call streakers, strollers, and students, in terms of the degree of detail of information sought by visitors. Streakers spend relatively little time in the exhibitions, and will not make side trips into subgalleries, nor are they inclined to read labels. Such visitors receive messages in an impressionistic fashion. One of the reasons we built life-size environmental reconstructions in our Grand Hall and History Hall was so that streakers might obtain a holistic sense of the cultures represented there, one that we hope will communicate some of the main themes of the exhibitions. We have yet to undertake evaluation to determine the educational effectiveness of this.

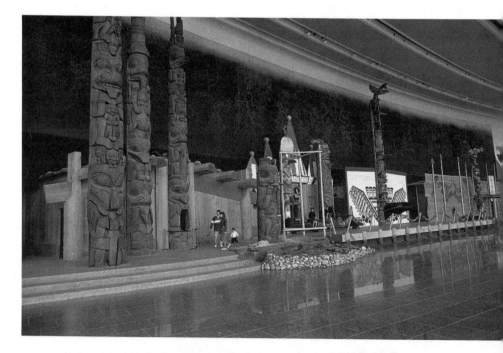

Fig. 6-3. The exhibition of a Pacific Coast Indian village in the Grand Hall, by simulating various elements of the historical environment, seeks to make an impression on visitors through their senses and their emotions. Photo by Stephen Alsford, courtesy of the Canadian Museum of Civilization.

For strollers—who more closely approximate the traditional museum visitor, prepared to spend more time in the museum—it has been important to provide additional information, such as labels, gallery guides, and audiovisual presentations, depending on the appropriateness of each medium for any particular exhibit. Strollers often want more information on specific topics (though their inquiries are still likely to be, for the most part, casual and often impromptu), so we provide a degree of depth to the exhibits, as well as supplementary exhibits off the main circulation route.

Our third category—students—includes people (not necessarily enrolled in some formal course of study) who come to the museum with strong interests in particular areas. The level of knowledge they seek cannot be adequately accommodated through the main exhibitions alone. Although we have yet to put in place the facilities to serve them, the forms these will take include: study collections in secondary areas of galleries; gallery-based electronic information kiosks that allow querying of museum data banks, including a pictorial database with a complete visual inventory of the museum's artifactual collections—in effect permitting typological displays that can be configured to each student's special interest; and a multimedia library accessible to public use.

Crosscutting the streaker/stroller/student categorization are others. Age, for example: we felt it desirable to provide exhibitions specifically aimed at the interests and learning capabilities of children, and so established the Children's Museum within CMC. Visitor demand outstripped available space there on several occasions during our opening year; fortunately we still have fifty percent of the allocated space to develop. To bring us in closer contact with the needs of this audience, we have established an advisory committee of children aged eight to fourteen to help staff evaluate programs and exhibitions, and steer the future course of the museum. Seniors are not so easily provided for; while they will become an increasingly important audience as the baby-boom generation ages, their particular needs have not yet been studied in detail. Here, too, I see the urgency for more research to determine how museums can better meet their needs.

Another way in which we segmented our audience was by expectation. For instance, tourists tend to seek an experience that packages its informational content in an entertaining form; some are more interested in heritage, others may prefer shopping, movies, restaurants. As organized groups, tourists also have the need for an experience that meets a predetermined schedule; this seems particularly true of Japanese tourists (a increasingly important audience), whose visits are often timed to the minute. A potential audience not often appreciated is business visitors to the city, who like to mix relaxation and sightseeing in their evenings, as well as the opportunity to purchase souvenirs for the family. When we are talking about expectations, it is no less important to be aware of the effects that the media, the entertainment industry, and new information technologies are having on the public. Regrettably, it is not museums that establish public expectations on how information is packaged and communicated; we are obliged to play a reactive role here, or risk being ignored by a leisure-seeking public.

One of the keys to audience development is to provide for as much diversity of experience and as much flexibility in programming as is possible, not least because predicting the future is, at best, a guessing game. In this age of rapid change we must not box ourselves in. Although at CMC we have placed large, relatively permanent exhibition structures in the Grand Hall and the History Hall, we have made space in both areas for changing exhibitions. Because those galleries include live interpretation, performances, and audiovisual elements, they can easily be reprogrammed. Another major gallery, our First Peoples Hall, has yet to be developed, but we have moved away from our initial idea of large, permanent structures and toward the idea of flexible spaces for changing exhibitions. In addition, we have devoted one whole level of galleries entirely to temporary exhibitions. In terms of flexibility and programmability, we have also found that our lobby areas have provided a good deal of scope for mounting small and short-lived exhibitions or for serving as demonstration areas.

The important thing is to make the museum's information resources accessible for exploration, but without overloading visitors with information. Layering the information permits each visitor to probe to whatever level meets his or her specific needs. Interactive technologies and hypermedia (programs in which access to information is not linear or hierarchical) appearing on the market provide a previously unavailable opportunity for museums to enable visitors to take greater control of the learning process, but museums have to be prepared to develop applications specific to their audience's needs. (Much work is, in fact, already underway in this area, but again more has to be done to share the results among museums.) Audio tours on cassette or by infrared transmission also provide a vehicle for offering interpretive information at different levels of detail, or geared to specific interests. We are presently developing these for our galleries. New computer-based technologies now emerging promise greater potential for future customizing of tours to individual needs: for example, the digital transmission of information from individual exhibits into a Walkman-type device would allow visitors to explore museums without following the preset route that corresponds to the narrative of an audio cassette. I should also mention films as an important vehicle for communicating context; information-intensive and holistic, they can be experienced at a variety of levels, if guidance is provided. This is an area we are hoping to develop at CMC in association with Imax Systems, a maker of giant-screen films that are shown on either rectangular (Imax) or dome-shaped (Omnimax) screens.

At the same time, we must not forget the importance of takeaway materials; for most visitors, the best a museum can really hope to do is spark an interest that will encourage return visits and/or further investigation of a topic elsewhere. The museum shop plays a central role in such dissemination. At CMC we have established a secondary shop adjacent to our library and specializing in information products; it will increasingly make available our own resources, such as videotapes, laser-disc-based collections catalogues, and copies of archival materials.

All these factors must be provided for in modern museums if they wish to maximize their audiences. At this point in time, a museum cannot be customized to meet perfectly the personal mix of interests, behaviors, learning styles, physical needs, etc., of every individual. But the greater the *range* of experiences and opportunities available, the wider the audience a museum can hope to attract, and the greater the number of visitors who are likely to leave the building stimulated, satisfied, and informed. The pressure on publicly funded museums to generate a larger percentage of their revenues directly from their public is leading them to become more concerned with the perceived quality of their services, and to add services targeted at the more affluent segment of their audience.

Bob Kelly's studies have also been important in differentiating between traditional museum visitors and a new audience that has been growing out of the development of the information society. Information and expertise—especially technological expertise—are becoming increasingly valued and increasingly a foundation of social status, in place of material wealth. The features of this new visitor group that are important for museums include its inclination to reject traditional, low-tech, interpretive technologies that employ academic jargon with which they have no familiarity; its preference for new information technologies, with which many people feel comfortable and in control, and which allow them to query more; its greater interest in behind-the-scenes technical operations; and its demand for non-collections-based facilities and services, such as lounges, restaurants, and film presentations.

The challenge for museums is to be relevant to this new social elite, or else face being defined out of its list of leisure activities. The future is likely to see a more competitive economic environment for museums, partly because the number of recreational institutions generally, museums included, is increasing at the same time as population growth is facing a downturn, and partly as changing lifestyles and work habits reduce the amount of shared leisure time available to families, resulting in greater value placed on meaningful use of leisure time.

THE COMPETITIVE ENVIRONMENT

From almost the beginning of the project to design the new Canadian Museum of Civilization, our staff were busy looking at other new museums and institutions outside the museum world in order to analyze their successes and failings and to seek inspiration. It was also essential to examine how, in general, the public spends its leisure time.[6]

Although we looked at a wide range of institutions around the world, I shall deal here only with open-air museums and theme parks. We commissioned a detailed study of Canadian open-air museums,[7] as well as looking at leading examples elsewhere. At that time—back in the early 1980s—there was still debate over whether these institutions were really museums at all! There were two principal things we absorbed from open-air museums. One was the concept of contextualization: the effectiveness of reconstructing a historical environment in which each object is given meaning from its contextual relationship to other objects. This type of display technique operates on various informational levels; it also allows visitors to enter into the exhibitions, a participatory style (at a simple level) that makes for a more emotional, and consequently more memorable, experience. The other lesson was the use of live interpretation, whether as a way of customizing replies to visitor questions or as a way of communicating processes and ideas via dramatization and demonstrations. One ramification of this is the need to build "living history" collections of objects—originals or replicas—that can be used in such programming. We are engaged in such a task at CMC. But there is lacking a philosophical rationalization of the natures of, and relationship between, the collections of touchables and untouchables in museums. It is unfortunate that the term *living history* has now become a marketing catchword, overused and abused, promising things museums cannot deliver.[8]

The influence of open-air museums is certainly seen in our History Hall, where we have adopted a modified streetscape approach, and in the Pacific Coast Indian village in our Grand Hall. An indoor setting inevitably imposes constraints on total environmental reconstruction, but it is possible to improve upon existing indoor streetscape exhibitions, as well as to obtain the same benefit as outdoor museums of establishing a more intimate bond between visitor and exhibits. Live costumed interpretation and audiovisual effects—such as the projection of weather effects onto the vaults above our streetscapes, or the rear-screen projection of animated scenes viewed through building windows—can enhance the environmental setting of the exhibit structures, in terms of both plausibility and interpretive effectiveness. Most indoor museum streetscapes have neglected to provide that animation element.

At CMC we have gone so far as to employ a small but full-time troupe of professional actors from various ethnic and linguistic backgrounds. During the first year of operation, they experimented with interpretive theater by mounting almost a dozen set-piece, scheduled playlets, varying from fifteen to thirty minutes in length. Most were written to provide supportive interpretation of specific exhibits, and are presented in the context of those exhibits. This theatrical use added another complication to the design of the exhibits. While the vignettes have proven popular with visitors, it has not always been easy to acquire a ready audience in the off-peak season, and some audience members do not want to stay in one place for half an hour—the museum ritual is a mobile one. Although there is a certain audience-cast intimacy and even interaction in some performances, theatrical interpretation still leaves the audience in a largely passive role. There is certainly a place for this in museums, but our next thrust is to supplement it with visitor-responsive, one-on-one interpretation in first-person mode.

Critics have charged that CMC's content is overloaded with "simulations." They are thinking particularly of the use of interpretive theater in the context of the environmental reconstructions (which

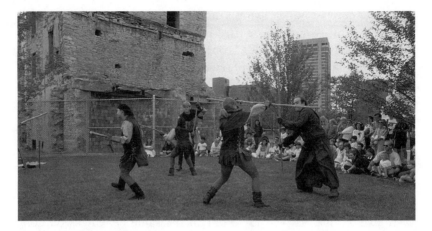

Fig. 6-4. The adaptation, for children, of a sixteenth-century folk play about Robin Hood is used to provide a lighthearted examination of sexual stereotyping—for Robin and his Merry Men are all played by women! Photo by Stephen Alsford, courtesy of the Canadian Museum of Civilization.

incorporate replicas as well as original artifacts), and of the Omnimax presentations of the docudrama coproduced by CMC: *The First Emperor of China*. One reason we selected that film technology for the museum was because of its ability to help viewers suspend disbelief and imagine themselves witnessing—almost participating in—actual events, rather than screened replays. The intent is not to deceive, but to create a more intimate and more powerful experience that leaves a greater impression on the viewer's memory.

Despite connotations of imitation or fakery associated with the term *simulation,* I find it hard to be disturbed by the charge. After all, the term derives from the Latin word meaning "similar," which—notwithstanding museums' warranted concerns for authenticity—is the best we can realistically hope to achieve with *any* exhibition or interpretive program. What our critics fail to remember is that all knowledge of the past is a *reconstruction,* tying together isolated hard facts by the use of hypothesis. What is this if not simulation? On the other hand, despite the incredible current popularity (all around the world) of traveling exhibits of robotic dinosaurs—which is one hundred percent simulation—we should not ignore the fact that people have a special, if inexplicable, experience when looking at real, original artifacts. Museums need a finer understanding of the appropriate balance of real and replicated objects in an exhibition.

Despite some criticism CMC has received, I do feel that our

design approaches have been validated by the findings of a Gallup survey of visitors. By quite a large margin, the favorite exhibitions were identified as the History Hall (23%) and the Grand Hall (22%), with the Imax/Omnimax theater ranking third (13%). Exhibitions using traditional, passive display styles (which remain the most appropriate for some subjects) were the least popular. The Imax/Omnimax theater has proven the biggest success of our commercial facilities, and has confirmed the existing theory that, with a local population of half a million, it is possible to keep a good film showing at a profit for about six months. The weakness of Imax at the moment is the lack of films with human-history themes; there is a need for museums to collaborate in ensuring that new films are made that fit their mandates. At CMC we also feel that a film in isolation is less effective than if it is part of a larger programming package. At the same time as we ran *The First Emperor of China,* an exhibition of props (museum-quality replicas) used in the film was being shown, along with a major exhibition on Chinese Canadian culture and a series of performances and demonstrations by Chinese community groups. We hope to pursue this model of mutually reinforcing programming more in the future.

A careful study of Disney theme parks was made early on in our building project. This fact (which we have never sought to hide), combined with our own nontraditional exhibition styles, has led critics to level the charge that CMC is Disneyland North. Probably this notion has done more to draw visitors than turn them away. Like it or not, theme parks *are* part of our competitive environment in North America.[9] In the Orlando, Florida, region there are now sixteen theme parks! On average you would find that leading American parks draw about a million visitors a year. Only a handful of museums—even if we limit the survey to large urban centers—can make that claim. The newest trend, movie studio theme parks, combines two powerful elements of popular culture, and promises to be the biggest draw yet.

The quality of content of theme-park presentation leaves much to be desired. This alone makes it all the more important that museums become able to compete with them for public attention. To a large extent it is the *way* they present their content that makes them so popular: they use entertainment forms, new technologies, and multisensory experiences. Theme parks tend to have high presentation standards, but low standards when it comes to information content; as a generalization, one could suggest the reverse to be true of museums.

Another important attribute of theme parks is their detailed attention to the physical and psychological needs of their guests, all aimed at ensuring a visit that leaves only good memories and a desire to return. The challenge, for larger museums at least, is to be prepared to adopt techniques and technologies employed outside the museum world, while ensuring that the content they communicate adheres to the highest standards of quality. If we are simply prepared to learn, I believe we can combat the growing public need for escapism and show them that fact can be more interesting than fiction.

A similar approach might be taken to the rest of the competitive environment. To take the example of television: We may love it, we may hate it. But it has commandeered too prominent a role in the lives of our citizenry to ignore it or its effects on the tastes, behaviors, and expectations of the public. This is especially true of the younger generation. In 1988, as part of the process of designing CMC's Children's Museum, we held a seminar with the creators of Sesame Street in order to obtain a better understanding of the effects of television on children. Among the points that were brought out against TV at that meeting were that it can be addictive, causing children to neglect other activities or family and social relationships, and that it encourages a spectatorship attitude, inhibiting active or creative play. These two factors can slow down language development, which requires conversation; because visuals fill in much of the meaning, TV narrative is often inadequately explicit and does not do a good job of teaching language structure, vocabulary, or verbal reasoning. Also, TV gives children access to all sorts of experiences and issues with which they are not equipped to deal; above all, it exposes them to violence at an age when they are trying to suppress their own aggressive behaviors. The rapidly paced, image-based events call for an emotional rather than intellectual response, encouraging an unreflective style in viewers. Finally, stereotypes are rampant in many TV programs; also, that which is *not* shown (e.g., minority cultures) may consequently be peripheralized by children in real life.

There are some good things to be said about television, however. Compared to verbal narration, images are more memorable and motion retains attention better. Spatial awareness and visual skills (e.g., drawing) can be improved. Children can be exposed to new experiences outside the realm of everyday life, thus broadening their horizons. It is a good tool for showing processes. Juxtapositions of images can emphasize differences or similarities that might not normally be perceived. It can be good for dissecting activities (for example, through slow motion) and so can help teach physical skills. Children who understand what is involved in making a television program—editing, special effects, and so forth—might be better equipped to evaluate what they view; for this reason CMC has given some consideration to creating a simple television studio in the Children's Museum.

Again, it is a question of differentiating the medium and the message; as McLuhan pointed out, though, this can never be done entirely. All methods of communication have their drawbacks, but many of television's relate more to the programming than the technology. We must distinguish between commercial broadcast television, which has largely succumbed to a purely market-driven approach, and educational television and other specialty services. We cannot expect to divert audiences en masse from TV to museums, but if we could create a specialty service, or at least contribute much more programming to educational television, the potential exists to take museums to a much wider audience. This is a project in which museums need to combine their resources to make an impact.

Television is creating an audience more familiar with the use of visual information than textual information, with consequences for museums' interpretive technologies. While it is right to be concerned about television's adverse impact on verbal literacy, we must accept—particularly in a multicultural world, where language embodies cultural biases from which we need to free ourselves—that visual literacy is an important skill that should be fostered. Museums need to develop further their communications skills, and particularly to determine which types of ideas are best conveyed visually and which verbally. At the same time, museums could help combat the subversive effects of television by introducing children to the technology and the techniques, and allowing children to control them. Already a number of museums have established television studios for this educational purpose. Media literacy is increasingly found as a compulsory subject in school curricula, and there is a role here for museums, too.

Television is an outreach tool that has been around for a while, a harbinger of the information age. Newer developments such as VCRs, VSAT dishes (small satellite earth stations that can serve as the foundation for information networks), high-resolution imagery, pay-per-view programs, interactive television, and videophones are beginning to make it possible to customize and personalize the TV experience, and perhaps will encourage moves in the direction of quality rather than quantity programming. Home computers, linked with developing communication channels, offer another route for electronic out-reach. Technology has often been accused of controlling our lives, but it also presents the potential for empowerment. This means being able to select the information to which we are exposed; being able to take the initiative in charting one's own educational course; being able to *query* information resources, not merely receive information pas-sively; and being able to contribute information and perspective to the body of understanding. In theory this means a greater democratization of the process of interpretation, as individuals and communities could decide for themselves what information is important in interpreting a subject. Museums must be prepared to meet people's new expectations about what they can learn and do with their leisure time and to steer the novice learner in the right direction.

CULTURAL CROSSROADS

If empowerment means participation, it also implies the right to par-ticipation by all elements of the community. A multicultural society is emerging hand in hand with the information society. The current ethnic consciousness in what was formerly the Soviet Union, the ef-forts to create a more open European Community by 1992, the cul-tural effects of immigration in the English-speaking world—all these, in one way or another, reflect the apparently conflicting needs to build a global society in which all peoples can participate while preserving specific cultural heritages and identities.

My own country is presently facing a crisis along these lines, attempting to create a vision of a Canadian identity that accommo-dates the distinct cultural entities falling under the national umbrella. A fundamental issue today is whether nationhood remains a viable concept at all. It is in this area that a national museum of human history has a possibly crucial role to play, as a forum for discussion and exchange of understandings. If museums are to play a useful and relevant role in a multicultural society, they must be institutions that represent the viewpoints of all of their constituents. These viewpoints may often be at odds with one another; but if we can accept the notion that no interpretation is truly definitive, that all are subjective, it will be easier to develop a tolerance for ambiguity and dissonance.

CMC has installed, as an integral part of its building, an intel-ligent network able to accommodate the widest range of communica-tion technologies, including telephones, television, and computers.[10]

This is presently used to serve the in-house information needs of the staff and the public, but we are looking toward its future use for electronic outreach. The hope is to create a network of museums and other cultural institutions interested in sharing information resources and programming via satellite—not merely in Canada, but internationally. A number of nationally based museum networks are already beginning to form for this purpose, such as the European Museums Network, which hopes to have its first field trial at Expo 92 in Seville, and the North American network that has grown out of the Jason Project.[11] In the longer term, the network envisaged by CMC could become an "information utility," into which every computer-equipped home could plug, as one plugs an appliance into an electrical wall socket. It will be vital to avoid using such a network merely to reinforce, through a one-way communication flow, a concept of national identity that, in Canada, is already technologically mediated. The challenge will be to give free access to communication technology, to empower the community—to use the network for interactive exchange of information, a conversation that could itself contribute to the formation of a communally based consciousness of identity.

A national museum like my own faces considerable challenge in representing its entire community, especially in a country so strongly multicultural as Canada. We have made efforts, although there is much more to do, in trying to get the component communities involved. Native West Coast peoples have participated in creating the Grand Hall villagescape, and have expressed great satisfaction at their culture receiving pride of place in the museum. Each group has "adopted" the particular house representing its culture. Native peoples are helping provide interpretive programming for the houses. As we develop the First Peoples Hall I expect that such participation will increase in scale and quality, and that the end product will be not only a source of revitalizing pride for them, but also a forum through which they can communicate and converse with other Canadians. Of course, this commitment is a two-way street. Native peoples (Indian and Inuit) expect CMC to become involved in their concerns. This includes everything from their language and cultural-revival programs to land claims; CMC can and does provide a forum for these issues. They also expect more fruitful dialogue than has taken place in the past on the question of display of sacred objects, such as masks, and the return of objects such as medicine bundles, treaty wampum belts, and ancestral remains. My staff is involved in many such conversations at the moment and good progress is being made. We are now working with native communities to return major segments of CMC's collections to their museums.

Our Chinese Canadian exhibition (Beyond the Golden Mountain: Chinese Cultural Traditions in Canada, which ran from 1989 to 1991) was also successful in kindling the enthusiasm of that community and encouraging them to participate by supplying artifacts and information and providing live programming that, again, permitted a meeting of cultures. Fortunately, we already had on staff a Chinese Canadian curator to guide the development of the exhibition. But the whole issue of bringing onto the staff more representatives of minority cultures, and of finding mechanisms for consultation with the many communities, is one that we have to address more in the immediate future. Only through a process of dialogue—an exchange of understandings between museum staff and communities, and between members of different communities—can museums produce interpretation that avoids the pitfalls of the "voice of authority" on which they have traditionally relied, and instead becomes the voice of the pluralistic society.

What we have achieved since our opening in June 1989 is to signal our intent to be a museum for all Canadians, not just those of European heritage and perspective. Practicalities of space make it

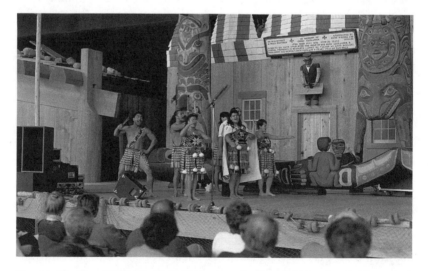

Fig. 6-5. The Grand Hall provides a dramatic setting for cultural performances, such as this by the (Maori) Kahurangi Dance Theatre. Photo by Stephen Alsford, courtesy of the Canadian Museum of Civilization.

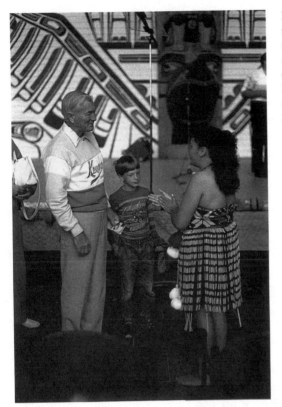

Fig. 6-6. After the performance come opportunities for representatives of different cultures to meet and exchange understandings. Photo by Stephen Alsford, courtesy of the Canadian Museum of Civilization.

impossible for us to represent every culture simultaneously, but our Chinese Canadian exhibition was replaced by one on the Ukrainian community in Canada, and that gallery will be used to showcase a different community each year. This is being supplemented by smaller, more temporary exhibitions, by films, and by live performances, reflecting both Canadian ethnic communities and the homelands of immigrants to Canada. In our first year we will have shown something from Chinese, Japanese, Filipino, Ukrainian, Jewish, Mexican, Argentinian, Korean, Maori, (East) Indian, and several African cultures, to name only some, and not to mention the many native Canadian cultures presented. It is perhaps in the area of live programming that CMC has been most successful, with well over a thousand performances in its first year by groups and individuals brought from across the country and around the world.

The first years of operation were for us both stressful and exciting. Successes, failures, rewards, disappointments—we have had all these. Although we have yet to undertake formal evaluation of the educational effectiveness of our exhibitions and programs, we have nonetheless learned much about what does work and what doesn't. CMC is, in many ways, experimental and will remain in that mode for some while. All museums have to be prepared to experiment—to succeed and to fail—in order to meet the challenge of the future. CMC has been planned to be a museum that should meet the needs of audiences of the global village. I hope it will be both a national museum and an international museum, since I think that best reflects the needs and character of the Canadian people themselves.

NOTES

1. Peter Sterling, director of the Indianapolis Children's Museum, in a presentation to the Greater Pittsburgh Museum Council symposium "Energizing the Museum Experience—Entertainment with Scholarship," 6 March 1990, Oakland, California.

2. This is an increasingly popular theme in museological writings. See, for example, Chris Miller-Marti, "Local History Museums and the Creation of the Past," *Muse* 5, no. 2 (1987), 36–39; Robert Sullivan, "The Museum as Moral Artifact," *Moral Education Forum* 10, nos. 3–4 (1985), 2–18; Brian Durrans, "The Future of the Other: Changing Cultures on Display in Ethnographic Museums," in Robert Lumley, ed., *The Museum Time-Machine* (London: Routledge, 1988).

3. See, for example, Cuyler Young, "Value Driven, Market Oriented," *Rotunda* 19, no. 1 (1986), 6–7; Roy Strong, "Scholar or Salesman? The Curator of the Future," *Muse* 6, no. 2 (1988), 16–20, and the reply by Terry Fenton in the same issue (27–30); Peter Ames, "A Challenge to Modern Museum Management: Reconciling Mission and Market," *Museum Studies Journal* 3, no. 2 (1988), 10–14.

4. Marjorie Halpin, "Quality and the Post-Modern Museum," paper presented at the Canadian Museums Association Trainers Workshop, Ottawa, August 1987.

5. Robert Kelly's works include "International Tourism: Pilgrimage in the Technological Age," in Chin Tiong Tan, William Lazer, and V. H. Kirpalani, eds., *Emerging International Strategic Frontiers: Proceedings of the American Marketing Association's International Marketing Conference*, Singapore, 16–18 June 1986, and "Museums as Status Symbols II: Attaining a State of Having Been," in R. Belk, ed., *Advances in Nonprofit Marketing*, vol. 2 (Greenwich: JAI Press, 1987). Kelly's work for CMC is embodied in the "Tourism Master Plan" (1988), an unpublished document.

6. The results of this study of the competitive environment are reported at more length in George MacDonald and Stephen Alsford, *A Museum for the Global Village: The Canadian Museum of Civilization* (Hull: Canadian Museum of Civilization, 1989), 38–56.

7. Stephen Alsford, "The Looking-Glass World: A Study of Reconstructed-Community Museums in Canada" (Ottawa: National Museum of Man, 1984).

8. On this, see John Fortier, "The Dilemmas of Living History," in *Proceedings of the Annual Meeting [ALHFAM], June 21–25, 1987* (Washington, D.C.: Association for Living Historical Farms and Agricultural Museums, 1989).

9. George F. MacDonald, "The Future of Museums in the Global Village," *Museum* 155 (1987), 212–13; George F. MacDonald, "Epcot Centre in Museological Perspective," *Muse* 6, no. 1 (April 1988), 27–31; MacDonald and Alsford, *A Museum for the Global Village*, 51–55.

10. For further information, see Ian and Lis Angus, "The Canadian Museum of Civilization: The Most Intelligent Building," *Telemanagement* 66 (June 1989), 4–6; MacDonald and Alsford, *A Museum for the Global Village*, 220–223.

11. The Jason Project is an underwater exploration project involving the Woods Hole Oceanographic Institution in Massachusetts and the Museum Satellite Network, an association of American and Canadian museums that are equipped to receive satellite signals. Using the same robotic submersible that was used to discover the *Titanic,* underwater wrecks in the Mediterranean and the Great Lakes were explored and live pictures beamed back to the museums, where they were made available to public audiences (mostly student groups) who could ask questions via satellite of a team of experts conducting the exploration.

CHAPTER 7

The Communicative Circle: Museums as Communities

CONSTANCE PERIN

M useums and their audiences are no longer taking their relationship for granted. They are reconsidering it in every dimension—intellectual, cultural, educational, political, and aesthetic. Museum professionals are themselves rethinking disciplinary canons and exhibition methods, while citizens, critics, anthropologists, and historians are becoming more involved in the choice and interpretation of exhibition topics.[1] Paralleling this ferment, empirical studies of museum visitors as well as those who do not visit museums have begun to appear.[2] In order to bring together the concerns of museum professionals, scholars, and critics, on the one hand, with the expectations and experiences of museum audiences, on the other, I examine the workings of the communicative circle that links them as exhibition makers and viewers.

The museum-audience relationship is more complicated than current conventions suggest—an inevitable conclusion, perhaps, from a cultural anthropologist, who is always, in Clifford Geertz's phrase, a "professional complicator" of received knowledge. To simplify these complications, this paper offers a cultural theory of representation and reception to guide the reassessment of both research in cultural studies and practice in museums. To develop and ground this theory, I carried out a limited ethnography of the communicative circle at the

Smithsonian Institution's National Museum of Natural History in Washington, D.C. These data illustrate how, once we acknowledge the cultural processes at work, we might begin to ask and eventually to answer new questions about museums' relationships to their audiences. Far from definitive, the theory opens new grounds on which to think about the processes of exhibition making and viewing, in all their variety and contexts.

Drawing on discourse theory, semantics, and the anthropology of knowledge, this theory describes the operations of an ideal communicative circle for museums, in which exhibition makers and viewers cooperate in achieving mutual understanding. Understanding does not necessarily entail agreement: it may lead not only to audience ratification and appropriation of the exhibition makers' perspectives, but also to audience resistance and reinterpretation as well. Acknowledging the existence of two-way communication between exhibitions and viewers changes conventional conceptions of the exhibition development process. Currently, museum professionals, drawing on their collections, initiate conversations with audiences and activate the communicative circle. Exhibition makers structure their turns in the conversation with a syntax of objects. Audiences "hear" the messages exhibitions convey, but what audiences say during their own turns can today only be assumed. Talking only to and among themselves, audiences find that their turns in the museum's communicative circle rarely if ever come up.

It is here that the circle breaks apart. As they shape their messages exhibition makers have assumed that they have little choice but to imagine viewers' reception and responses. But there is no guarantee that viewers will interpret exhibitions as their makers intend: exhibitions' messages are as much constructed by audiences' interpretations as by curators' and designers' intentions. Instead, if exhibition developers' ideas about the importance and significance of a collection—concepts both simple and sophisticated—were to take into account the various ways in which audiences already understand, misunderstand, and see the pertinences of those concepts, they would enlarge the chance of successful collaboration between themselves and their audiences. This theory proposes that by considering representation and reception as cultural processes, this rupture in the communicative circle might be repaired.

I asked curators, educators, and administrators to discuss with me their approaches to representing their collections, and I sat in on a meeting of an exhibition development team. Subsequently, a first draft of this paper was the point of departure for a workshop discussion with about twenty members of the Smithsonian Institution's professional staff—curators, educators, designers, audience advocates, and administrators from several museums on the Mall. That discussion was recorded, with permission, and its contents are reflected throughout this paper (without attribution to particular speakers). Throughout, the expectations, models, experiences, and perspectives that I associate with museum professionals are drawn from their own discourse. And, to include the wider professional discourse of historians, anthropologists, and critics, I also refer to relevant published work.

In parallel, engaging in discussions with visitors to the National Museum of Natural History (NMNH), I listened for the frames of reference they bring to their reception of exhibitions' messages and through which they understand and interpret them. I heard adult visitors talk about their viewing experiences by randomly inviting them to join tape-recorded discussion groups held over coffee and by listening to people who were willing to talk about what they were looking at.[3] I joined a Highlight Tour of the NMNH led by an experienced docent. Off the Mall, I recorded a discussion with adults about museumgoing and other subjects, and later I draw on direct quotations from these discussions as well as on visitor comments recorded in other studies.

As they construct exhibitions museum professionals assume one-way communication and an unmediated relationship between sending and receiving. Their model of the museum-audience relationship assumes that if they knew how exhibitions make their "impact" on audiences, it would then be possible to develop techniques to assure that their intentions will be received just as they hope they will. But this model not only implies audience research projects of a scope and on a scale that are well beyond museums' means; it also underestimates the significance of an exhibition's "impact" after the visit ends. The relationship between exhibitions and what audiences carry away is not linear, but rather is complexly mediated by myriad factors, not least of which are audiences' repertoires of prior knowledge, semantic systems, and interpretive frames. To reduce these to their lowest common denominators (in concert with much of the mass media) not only stereotypes, patronizes, and impoverishes, but also assumes a unitary public.

Instead, recognizing the inherent difficulty of acknowledging audience pluralism, I shift the question from audience impact to that of the integrity of the exhibition development process itself. This process should include rationales for choosing exhibition rhetorics and techniques intended to stimulate, enlighten, and inform museum visitors in ways that other media cannot replicate. The theory of representation and reception I present here and the practices it implies can of course only partially transform museums' monologic stance toward their publics; to acknowledge a plurality of audience voices in museums' communicative circles, many kinds of strategies are needed.

By concentrating on adult audiences, I complicate a second model through which the audience-exhibition relationship is currently understood, namely the teacher-student relationship. At the extreme, some curators regard an exhibition as a direct translation of their semester lectures to undergraduates. Students tend to represent a relatively homogeneous age and socioeconomic group. Adults, by contrast, have experienced more varied life contexts and situations, which condition their viewing experiences and interpretations. Moreover, students are more likely not only to experience museums as extensions of classrooms but subsequently to talk about their museum visits in more or less structured situations with peers and teachers.

As differently as adults' museum experiences may be situated, we know little about them, however. We can speculate that adults' viewing experiences are less likely to be structured ahead of time; nor is there any institutionalized interest afterward in the immediate or long-term intellectual, affective, or cognitive consequences of these experiences. In the days and weeks after a visit, adults may or may not refer to their museum experiences as they carry on their everyday lives. Although it stands to reason that they continue to integrate them—with their reading, in conversation, and at the movies, for example—we just don't know much about the longer-term "impacts" of museums on adult visitors.

There is a third prevalent image of visitors' experiences. At the Smithsonian, at any rate, audiences are perceived as being either "streakers," who "roller-skate" through exhibitions, "strollers," who take more time to engage the exhibitions, and "readers," who spend even more time absorbing exhibitions and their texts. By grounding their exhibition strategies in audiences' time investments, curators and designers hope to "grab" and "hook" streakers and convert them into strollers, and lure strollers into becoming readers. This temporal model of exhibition viewing controls important beliefs and expectations in the exhibition development process. Even streakers and "whiskers" should "get something" out of their brief encounter, museum professionals aver. In explicit reference to the journalistic styles of newspapers and television, they prefer exhibitions that are structured to resemble familiar media. If the "headlines" are right, they believe, more visitors will be motivated to move to the next "layer" of exhibition details, and thereby learn more. Exhibition makers discuss these as "ten-second points" and "sixty-second points," for example.

Such expectations define a continuum anchored by two poles that I call spectacle and cabinet. Spectacles that emphasize large scale and dramatic portrayals are believed to draw viewers into the deeper "layers" of elaboration that offer detailed evidence and explanations of patterns. In offering a "quick read," which is believed to appeal to streakers, spectacles require curators to condense their concepts into "basic underlying messages." Curators may then feel themselves limited to communicating only the most general concepts, which may not do justice either to the collection or to visitors' curiosities. This temporal model of reception processes may exacerbate rather than reduce the political and creative tensions between curators and designers inherent in the exhibition development process.[4]

Besides those impact, academic, and temporal models, here are others I distill from the ways that museum professionals express their conceptions of the relationship between exhibitions and audiences:

Active learning. Active-learning models emphasize physical interaction with computer screens and keyboards, levers, buttons, and other such sensory interfaces, which involve visitors by giving them some control over their viewing. These techniques recognize an increasingly wide range of learning styles (such as nonlinear, affective, and experiential). Children's learning is stressed.

Market. In a market model, museum professionals view the audience as "consumers" whose "needs," "attitudes," or "preferences" are to be satisfied by exhibition producers, or conversely as consumers whose tastes and preferences are to be shaped by producers' choices. Preferences for one exhibition over another can be measured by attendance; an exhibition is successful to the degree it is popular; an indicator of audience absorption of information is length of visit (again drawing on a temporal model). Such quantitative measures are the chief, perhaps only, indicators of audience responses. The market model, with its production-consumption terms, puts a competitive frame around exhibition making—exhibitions are in competition not only with other leisure and educational attractions, but also with other exhibitions. That frame defines showmanship and salesmanship as signifi-

cant principles of design, administrative decisions, and funding opportunities. During the exhibition development process, entertainment
values are in tension with educational values, and museum professionals sometimes characterize their choices as being on a continuum
between "glitz" and "pure information."

Rhetorical. This model for reaching audiences combines curatorial
charisma with the theatrics of design. Dedicated to their subjects and
engrossed in their complexities and mysteries, curators are indefatig-
able champions of enlightenment; exhibitions translate their passion
for persuading, converting, and proselytizing on behalf of their specialties and the excitements of scholarship. Just as enthusiastically,
designers strive to achieve visually dramatic exhibitions. During the
development process, curators and designers continually negotiate the
priority of content and form. Curators may nevertheless regard their
exhibition-making activities ambivalently: their honor, reputation,
and membership in the curatorial community, inside and outside their
discipline and museum, depend far more on their specialist research
and publications than on communicating with lay audiences. Much of
the work of educators and administrators, who are perforce concerned with audiences, is structured by that ambivalence. Pushing
charisma to its limits, audience studies and a team approach to exhibition development are sometimes eschewed; in this model, curators
alone should be the composers and orchestrators of messages that they
"intuit" will appeal to audiences.

Aesthetic. In this model, gaze, not voice, is the chief mediator of the
relationship between viewer and exhibition, the formal and aesthetic
qualities of which are seen as being valuable and compelling in themselves apart from the content. In tension with didactic and rhetorical
models, the aesthetic model raises questions that preoccupy professional discourses.

MUSEUMS AS COMMUNITIES

There are of course circles within the communicative circle. Museums
are constituted by internal professional communities of curators, designers, educators, and administrators, who are one another's audiences for ideas, perspectives, and interests, even as they also rely on
peers in their professions. Professional communities are themselves

interpretive communities that construe and construct the knowledge of their special fields. Museums' internal sociology, politics, and cultural structures significantly affect the nature of exhibition makers' conversations with audiences.

But because the dynamics of this inner circle tend not to be acknowledged as affecting its interpretive work and its representations, "the museum" tends to be conceived as a single, corporate agent. That totalizing illusion has given rise to the legalistic if not adversarial notion of audience "advocates"—museum professionals who represent the concerns and interests of various publics. There is no denying that museums—that is, the communities that fund and work in them—have more often limited than widened their circles. Considering now how to listen to audience voices requires that we understand more about how curators, designers, educators, and administrators talk among themselves and how their discourse is affected by bringing others into it.

These professional communities can, understandably, be threatened by what they see as challenges to their expertise and their social and institutional authority, as well as by challenges to their preconceptions of audiences. In practice, however, this theory of representation and reception, as I will illustrate, is intended to broaden rather than narrow their freedom to express a wider scope of intellectual and disciplinary concerns and to maintain balance between exhibition content and display technique.

Visitors, too, belong to communities, which, from a communicative perspective, are more significantly defined as interpretive communities rather than as ethnic communities or age or interest groups, for example. When visitors are viewed as members of the communicative circle, it is more telling to identify them by the frames of reference that filter their viewing experiences than by socioeconomic criteria. Their relative opportunities to discuss their museum experiences during a visit are also significant differentiae: the kinds of work that visitors do to assimilate and situate their museum experiences depend on social contexts, as does any learning experience. Yet, as I have said, we know little about how visitors process their reception either on-site or later, alone or in discussions.

In the case of the Smithsonian, for example, a communicative perspective would consider the differences among the social contexts of visitors in terms of those who are: participating in Smithsonian Associate activities; in a group led by a docent; on a Highlight Tour; in school groups led by teachers; in family groups; in groups of peers (older or younger adults, adolescents or children); in pairs; or alone.

A couple looking at an exhibition on Minnesota history at the National Museum of American History were recollecting memories of a visit they had made to family members about ten years before. A museum educator who overheard them reflected to me, "If you looked at them, you wouldn't know what they were doing. I imagine that this happens many times, but it was the first I'd seen. The exhibit designer would probably be upset, because that was not the experience he had the intention of creating." Similarly, this educator recollected, a study of visitors to an outdoor science museum found that mothers do most of the talking in family groupings; they refer to objects as a way of talking about values and family history, rather than talking about the objects per se. The theory of representation and reception that I present here redefines such work of interpretive communities as invaluable consequences of museum visits, rather than as evidence of exhibition makers' failure.

At the Portland (Oregon) Museum of Art, where the Rasmussen Collection of Northwest Coast pieces is being reinstalled, James Clifford reports that many prominent Tlingit elders were brought in to interpret particular objects and to "say how they thought about these objects." Until then, he and many of the curators had been "very much focused on the objects themselves."

> I guess we were expecting the elders to explicate them in some sort of detailed way: this is how this object functioned, it was made by so-and-so, this is what its power is in terms of the clan, in terms of our traditions—whatever. But, in fact, the objects were not the subject of much direct commentary by the elders, who had their own agenda for the meeting. Not that the objects were unimportant; they were important. But they served essentially as kind of aides-mémoire for the telling of rather elaborate stories and the singing of many songs. . . . And in some sense the physical objects, at least as I saw it, were left at the margin. What really took center stage were stories and songs. And these stories suggested by the objects are very powerful stories.[5]

Aides-mémoire abound at the Smithsonian: a visitor looking at a case in the Native Americans hall said, "I had forgotten how tiny the beads were. My father had several pieces and he always told me, 'Don't touch.' "

When audiences "read beyond" exhibitions, as it were, rather than reading them directly, they are drawing on various ways of ratifying and appropriating exhibitions' messages. The Japanese "art of citation," a convention whereby objects intentionally refer audiences to collective myths to remind them that they belong to the same interpretive community, is a cultural process with distinctively American parallels.[6]

After outlining the sociolinguistic dimensions of the communicative circle, I illustrate how to gain access to the cultural resources that populate audiences' ordering systems and provide evidence of what, in this instance, I found there. All together, my approach aims to give both curators and exhibition designers access to a theoretically grounded body of information about audiences' conceptual receptivities. Knowing more about these receptivities puts museum professionals in a better position to make principled choices throughout their representation processes.

A CULTURAL THEORY OF REPRESENTATION AND RECEPTION

The Communicative Circle

The central issue for the communicative circle is audiences' conceptual receptivities to exhibitions, no matter whether audiences assimilate or contest exhibitions' contents. Exhibition contents and rhetorics that activate relevant resources and repertoires stand a better chance of inviting audiences' involvement in interpretation.

In exhibition making, as in speaking, I suggest, the audience understanding that curators and designers seek "comes to fruition only in the response":

> In the actual life of speech, every concrete act of understanding is active; it assimilates the word to be understood into its own conceptual system filled with specific objects and emotional expressions, and is indissolubly merged with the response, with a motivated agreement or disagreement. To some extent, primacy belongs to the response, as the activating principle: it creates the ground for understanding, it prepares the ground for an active and engaged understanding. Understanding comes to fruition only in the response. . . . Understanding and response are dialectically merged and mutually condition each other; one is impossible without the other.[7]

In choosing among various ways of conveying their ideas, speakers and exhibition makers draw on their expectations of and beliefs about what their audiences are likely to "assimilate in their conceptual systems." For communication to occur, audiences must collaborate with them. Indeed, sociolinguists suggest that the audience should be considered a "coauthor" in that the resources it draws on equally define what it understands.[8] Audiences are as creative and constructivist in receiving exhibitions' messages as curators and designers are in composing them.

Their previous knowledge or curiosity about a particular subject is only one aspect of audiences' "ground for understanding." Their ordering systems fill out the rest—the frames of reference through which they situate, contextualize, translate, evaluate, and interpret what they see and experience. The museum context, almost by definition, presents audiences with artifacts and information that fall outside of the demands of their daily routines and relationships, yet their responses are grounded in many of the same assumptions, worldviews, knowledge, and associations through which they make sense of the world.

The relationship between exhibitions of ethnographic artifacts and viewers is considered by Michael Baxandall as a "field of exhibition" occupied by the original makers of objects on display, by exhibition designers, who label and situate these objects vis-à-vis one another in the present, and by the viewer, who, upon reading labels and viewing objects, occupies a "space in which [he] will act by his own lights to his own ends."[9] The exhibitor should help to enlarge that mental space, thereby putting viewers to work at making their own connections:

> To offer a pregnant cultural fact and let the viewer work at it is surely both more tactful and stimulating than explicit interpretation. Sufficient interpretation lies in the selection of the fact. This can be made even more wholesome by incorporating a concept, indeed a word, from the culture that produced the object. The systematic incompatibility of another culture's concept with one's own culture not only makes the viewer work, but reminds him of cultural difference.[10]

But in so "reminding," we must be prepared to ask what the difference signifies. The varieties of viewers' memories suggest that they find many ways of filling up that "mental space" between themselves and objects and labels. How viewers understand their own culture and their experiences will shape their interpretations of any difference. In a society of many audiences, we should expect a multiplicity of frames of reference to which viewers will assimilate and ratify the significances of objects and of differences in cultures. As things stand, however, exhibition makers display the "tendency to reduce the process of reception to that of production" by believing, as do many mass-media producers, that their messages are "automatically realized in [viewers'] consciousness."[11]

The interpretive resources that visitors bring to the circle are the focus of this theory of representation and reception, rather than visitors' characteristics (such as socioeconomic status, frequency of museumgoing, etc.) Nor are visitors' preferences, attitudes, or opinions as significant as the systems of meanings and symbols constructing them and through which visitors coauthor exhibitions. These cultural resources constitute the substance of audience reception processes.

Constructing Representation and Reception

Most of the work of any communicative circle consists of clarifying ambiguities and the misunderstandings they give rise to. That is, despite positivist assumptions, language systems are only imperfectly literal: they depend on symbols and semantic domains having invisible, unspoken associations and implications, which all participants in a circle may not share or which some may interpret differently. Communication succeeds because all work at cooperating to make meanings, references, and implications clearer, just as they may agree to leave ambiguous that which is intended to be evocative and open to many interpretations.

Not everything requires such work, of course, or we would be immobilized—there are sufficient social agreements about most interpretations and categories to lighten the workload. The point is, as I have said, that audiences' reception is as creative and constructivist a process as representation. The messages audiences receive from exhibitions emerge from this dialogue; exhibitions are therefore dynamic products of a communicative circle, not static objects with unvarying significances.

Audiences are quintessential bricoleurs. As they craft meanings and reconstruct knowledge they employ repertoires of collective and personal symbols and experience. This interpretive work makes use of many cultural operations, such as categorization, explanation, evaluation, and description. Exhibition makers have drawn on their own repertoires as well—theirs may or may not be commensurate with the audience's.

My hope is that once brought into the circle, audience repertoires would then suggest to exhibition makers how *their* repertoires—of scientific paradigms, canons, and didactic aims—will be received. It is here that the exhibition development process opens up more scope for curators' concerns. Do they want to build upon audience repertoires by showing how new information fits into them? Do they want to play on them by elaborating their implications and possibilities? Do they want to contradict or correct current repertoires by showing how and why they do not hold? Do they find audience repertoires to be imaginative, informative, and corrective to their own?

At a time when museum professionals are becoming more conscious than ever before of acknowledging the social derivations of the stories they construct about their collections, they are left with little choice but to imagine audiences' reconstructions of their tellings. Curators want to "wake people up," "grab them," and be sure that "information will stick."

> [T]he quality of an exhibit's relationship with its audience resides in telling a story. . . . Even if the museum does not offer a story, the audience will provide one of its own devising. So we need to understand the stories these people are likely to come up with and guide them down a path with a story that we want to tell, too.[12]

But it is through the cultural resources that visitors bring with them that they shape their own stories and condition their reception of others'. In this theory, those stories consist of the semantic systems through which Americans understand, for example, concepts such as "evolution," "history," "race," "the future," "tribes," and so on, as I soon illustrate.

Indirect Communication

As varied as audiences are in this plural world, how can exhibition makers gauge the consonance between their intentions and audience reception? The concept of indirection, as developed in sociolinguistics, may be helpful.[13] Indirection is a characteristic, intentional or unintentional, of the speaker's message that influences the kind of work audiences do in interpreting and making sense of it. When indirection is intentional, speakers hope and expect audiences will go to work on the ambiguity and derive many meanings. When unintentional, audiences may miss the message or they may receive multiple, unintended messages.

Curators and designers, therefore, have less control over their communicative intentions than they believe themselves to have. No matter how clear their representations, clarity only partially accounts for their reception. For example, a study of visitor perspectives on a Smithsonian exhibition about tropical rainforests reports that the exhibition's central message was perceived as clear by some and not by others. Visitors' spontaneous comments suggest that some thought the film was especially good; that the exhibition allowed visitors to understand the seriousness of the topic while presenting it in an informative, attractive manner; that it was extremely comprehensive, giving all sides of the issue; and that it made it easy for ordinary Americans to understand how rainforests affect their everyday lives. Other comments indicate communicative inadequacy. One viewer said that although she understood the message that the rainforests are disappearing, she didn't think uninformed people would get the message. Others felt that the exhibition needed to explain more, that it was confusing and not as focused as they had hoped, or that they had to read between the lines to get the message from the exhibition.[14] Knowing the differences between the frames of reference of viewers who arrived at these contrary evaluations might suggest alternative rhetorical and didactic strategies.

Although the concept of indirection may seem only to suggest that exhibition makers are unable to target messages, it is pivotal to developing principled strategies for considering audiences' interests and receptivities. Those receptivities do not, I want to emphasize, represent the lowest common denominator of viewers' capacities to entertain new or complex information, nor are they majority preferences, attitudes, or opinions. The variety of audiences' frames of reference instead should suggest to exhibition developers a wider range of conceptual "hooks" than they may otherwise be aware of.

The seeming infeasibility of hearing audience voices in the inner circle of curators, designers, educators, and administrators leads to the contrary practices presently dominating exhibition making, in which those museum professionals themselves speak for audiences. In so doing, they rely on myths about the audience for guidance. These may not be entirely ungrounded myths—they may reflect widespread professional observations and personal viewing experiences—but as suggested earlier, the process of reception may be equated to that of production when museum staff believe that messages are automatically realized exactly as sent. Exhibition designers may believe, for example, that "strong visuals will tie it all together" and thereby assure communicative success.

Curators and designers by and large act as audience ventriloquists in the communicative circle today, and aside from its political and marketing implications, in terms of the representation process itself ventriloquism inhibits curators' and designers' imaginations. Myths inscribe boundaries around their imaginations: "People expect . . ." "They won't understand it if it's presented this way . . ." Exhibition makers are no less bricoleurs of semantic and symbolic systems in their "dialogue with the materials and means of execution."[15] The frames of reference of audiences, not exhibition makers' projections, should be the sources of their representations.

Acknowledging the property of indirection disabuses exhibition makers of the assumption that the clarity of their intentions equals the clarity of audiences' reception. Because indirection defines exhibition makers' relationship to audiences as one of interpretive indeterminacy, it frees them to imagine a wider variety of stories and vehicles that may resonate with audiences' resources.[16]

Audience Reception: Cultural Resources and Cultural Forms

Audience reception processes are both substantive and formal. I call these substantive processes *cultural resources:* repertoires of frames of reference that are constituted by systems of meanings, ideals, myths, beliefs, and prior understandings. Audiences employ these in responding to exhibitions as well as in interpreting experience and exploring the world generally. *Cultural forms* are the ordering architectures that Americans use in transmitting and assimilating new or ambiguous information and experience. Most familiar, perhaps, are narrative structures, timelines, and maps; what exhibition makers term "layering"—providing information at different levels of detail and complexity—is another cultural form. Language systems provide still others, such as metaphor, paradox, and irony, with which people transform and assimilate new, ambiguous, or contradictory information. These cultural forms also have content, of course, just as the repertoires of cultural resources have form; both are aspects of cultural processes that I only arbitrarily divide.

Together, cultural resources and forms constitute the *structure* of audience voices, to which, this model suggests, exhibition makers would listen throughout the development process, using them as probes and prompts to their representational decisions. These voices become questions with which exhibition makers interrogate themselves about exhibition contents and forms. By so opening the hermetic seal on their discourse and acknowledging others' discourses in the communicative circle, the integrity and quality of the exhibition-making process may be assured; for their part, audiences' museum experiences may carry more intellectual and affective weight.

Attention to cultural forms seems to take precedence over that paid to cultural resources when exhibition makers are deciding about how best to "grab" audience attention. Their discourse seems to privilege disciplinary constructs and storytelling forms and display techniques over the cultural resources audiences may draw on. Yet communication may depend more on acknowledging those resources. The Smithsonian study of the tropical rainforests exhibition, mentioned earlier, compares visitors who had and had not been reading or hearing about rainforests in other media. When exhibitions provide "information that reinforces an individual's prior exposure to or commitment to a topic," the study concludes, they are likely to accomplish their educational goals, as well as acquainting newcomers with the issues.[17] The more familiarity visitors have with its topic, the greater an exhibition's influence. When there is familiarity, the grounds of understanding have already been seeded.

More important for this model of reception, when asked "What do you think is the future of tropical rainforests?" museum visitors who said they didn't know or had no opinion divided this way: 21 percent of those who had seen the exhibition but had had no prior exposure to the topic via other media; 11.3 percent of those who had not seen the exhibition but who were otherwise informed; and 5.2 percent of those who had already been aware of rainforest issues and had also seen the exhibition.[18] That is, visitors who had been unfamiliar with the topic before visiting the exhibition were more likely to come away without being able to restate the exhibition's message or to articulate their own opinions than those who had previously been familiar with the topic. In terms of cultural resources, however, the question depends entirely on shared understandings of the concept of the future, which is itself a semantic and cultural domain. Perhaps those who came away from the exhibition without an opinion about rainforests' future may not have found that the exhibition resonated with their frames of reference for thinking about the future. Alternatively, it is possible that thinking about the world's future, as compared to their personal futures, was an unfamiliar or unexercised cultural process for those having no opinion.

Other findings of that study suggest that exhibition developers might profitably recognize still other conceptual grounds on which audiences cooperate. To the question "How do you think [these issues] affect your everyday life?" about 26 percent who had only seen the exhibition and had had no prior exposure to the topic said "not much," compared to about 14 percent who were informed both previously and by the exhibition. Twenty-one percent of the first group had no opinion on this question or said they didn't know, compared to only 6.2 percent of the second group.[19] This suggests another cultural question: through what substantive frames of reference and by what formal processes do Americans associate global and macro issues with local and personal issues? In the workshop discussion with Smithsonian staff, one person commented that in studying audiences' understandings of Africa, one museum not only held discussions with African Americans within the museum, but approached others randomly on the street. The responses revealed both expected and surprising images. Older people spoke of "missionaries," younger people of "apartheid." They also revealed a "romantic" image of Africa as "everything I would ever want"—less as a nationalistic image than as fantasy and yearning.

To gain access to audience reception processes, I held two types of discussions with adult museum visitors. With the three groups that met over coffee in a museum restaurant, I stimulated a general discussion of their responses to the Native Americans hall in the National Museum of Natural History, which they had been visiting when invited to join the discussion. I began with a single question: "What have you seen that confirms what you already know and what have you seen that surprised you?" My priority was to let the discussion take its own course; I hoped that the visitors would stimulate one another's spontaneous talk, and my interpolations had the same intent. Off the Mall, with adults living in the Boston metropolitan area, I inquired about museumgoing as an activity and asked specific questions relating to conceptual issues that curators and educators concerned with Native Americans had expressed to me.

The next two sections present my annotations of excerpts from the four discussion groups.[20] I also draw on briefer conversations held with visitors in other parts of the NMNH. The first section, "Representation Systematics: Cultural Resources of Audiences," suggests some of the substantive frames of reference I see being expressed in these texts. The second section, "Reception Systematics: Cultural Forms in Exhibition Viewing," similarly identifies some of the formal ordering processes I find.

What we might ordinarily consider to be audience positions, preferences, attitudes, or opinions, I instead consider as semantic domains and ordering processes with which viewers participate in the communicative circle. Rather than being taken as positions, they are to be seen as pointers to some of the grounds of audiences' "active and engaged understanding." Nor are they presented as findings, but as plausible guides to the semantic domains and ordering forms that visitors may employ.

Not only does it go without saying that my annotations are open to alternative readings, but in fact, that is my point. I hope professionals in the communicative circle will draw out their significance, the better to design exhibitions that engage in a dialogue with them. Following my thematic annotation, I have chosen to reproduce excerpts of these conversations as recorded, with only minor editing. They are not always easy to read; but to make them easier would negate the very idea of the communicative circle that I want to convey. As it stands, museum professionals are less practiced in listening than in speaking. Indeed, as I carried out this ethnography, many were astonished: "You're actually *listening* to visitors?" Even at second hand, these excerpts may close some of that distance by letting readers practice the work of pondering and interpreting audiences' turns in the communicative circle.

A word is in order about audience misinformation, plain ignorance, and inanities—these appear throughout the discussions side by side with acute observations, unsatisfied curiosity, and insightful criticism. I am proposing that we should take these, no matter how seemingly off the mark, as being seeds from which audience reception may grow if cultivated during the representation process. Their cultivation can take many forms—exhibitions may be developed to confirm, disrupt, contradict, enhance, or disappoint them—but, one way or another, I intend that exhibition makers would regard them as resources with which audiences co-author exhibitions.

Similarly, curators' and designers' beliefs and observations about audience orientations also should be explored during the exhibition development process. These influence their representational strategies. For example, one curator believes that "people come to museums to get away from current events and issues, not to learn more about them." Another believes that when most Americans think about Native Americans, they envisage a single, prototypical Plains Indian outfitted in "fur, feathers, and fringe."

REPRESENTATION SYSTEMATICS: CULTURAL RESOURCES OF AUDIENCES   The understandings with which visitors interpret their museum experiences I annotate just before the texts they refer to. These understandings are the cultural resources that I propose curators and designers should take into account during the exhibition development process.

Native Americans. A Canadian couple and a Southern couple (CW, CM, SW, SM) discussed their impressions of Native Americans in Coffee Group A.

• The mass media stereotype North American Indians
  CW/I didn't know anything about Indians except what I learned through my husband. I'm English, we just learned about cowboys and Indians.

  CM/Movies in particular have given the wrong picture of the Indian and his lifestyle. They depict the Indian as wild, bloodthirsty person who's on a rampage all the time. But basically what they're doing is defending their land. . . . Many were farmers and fishermen. There were warlike tribes—predators if you want a better word—they preyed on other tribes. But the Huron tribe that I'm familiar with were farmers. They grew corn and maize and gourds. . . . We didn't do them any favors by bringing them smallpox.

• Assimilation works differently for different groups
• Enforced dependency has untoward consequences
When you think about other American groups, say black Americans or African peoples, how are they different from Native Americans?
  SM/I don't know. The original African natives were brought over here against their will. They were emancipated and set free to go wherever they wanted to go. But the Indian has never had that choice. He's put on a reservation and just left there. . . . While [African Americans] played a very important part in our history, they probably got a better deal when they were emancipated where they were absorbed into our society. Whereas with the Indians we just put them on reservations. Like any ethnic group, they could make some contribution to our culture.

  CM/Any ethnic or cultural group will certainly band together. You have your Orientals coming over and running all your 7-Eleven stores right now. They stay together in their own churches and meeting halls, but at the same time they're integrated with the general populace.

CW/Indians are less integrated than any others.

SM/They're put on reservations, and then they use the reservation as a crutch. They've been there generation after generation, and as I say, it's like a crutch.

• The past relates to the present
Do you think museums should show their current situation? All agreed that it is an "excellent idea" to depict their current situation.

• Individual behaviors have social sources
  CM/I think they have been taken advantage of in the past. Now a lot of them are taking advantage of that—saying we're going to live on your bounty. A lot of them don't want to help themselves. Live on a reservation, government providing schools for them, and they just won't bother to learn.

• Sympathy and understanding mix with bewilderment toward Native Americans' current situation
• Imposed and voluntary segregation have different consequences
I asked whether they thought that Indians are like other ethnic groups who may keep to themselves.

  SM/I always thought Indians would have been much better off if they'd been merged into our society. Instead of putting them into an enclosure, set aside land for them, even though it may preserve some of the culture.

  CM/But others are free to come and go. In Canada, if an Indian leaves the reservation, they lose the bounty. If an Indian girl leaves, she loses any advantage.

  CM/In northern Ontario there's a frontier town with fifty whites and five hundred Indians, and the Indians were just treated like dirt. Part of the Greentree radar line—an end of the road—not a reservation. In a town store, there's a big round table in the middle of the room, and if four or five whites were sitting there and you walked in, it didn't matter if they knew you, they'd make room for you. But the Indians had to stay on the perimeter.

  SM/Same as one hundred years ago when they put them on reservations. Nothing's changed.

  CW/Maybe they should take them off reservations and help them to learn.

SM/Exhibit I saw yesterday, I forget where. Maybe over at American History. Had a whole entire section of a part of our history where American Japanese were put into camps in World War II. And we devoted an entire section to just that. And here you have the American Indians in a camp and they're still there. . . . If we'd continued to keep them there I doubt that as a group they would have contributed very much to society. Indians being isolated on reservations haven't contributed as much to society as they would have.

CM/On their own land to start with. You're right that they're using the reservation as a crutch. And yet I think they have native spokesmen who seem to be very, very intelligent people. They speak well and have a lot of information and they know how to put it across. They fall right back into the reservation. I don't understand why.

CW/That needs research. It's a fascinating subject.

- Local ties and enclaves can remain strong for generations
- Not all Americans move around a lot

I told them about islanders and mountain peoples who also seem to have trouble leaving, how they can't adjust to being away and return, and sometimes have high rates of alcoholism (for example, European American natives of Martha's Vineyard). I asked whether these observations relate to their own experiences.

CW/That's like the area of London I come from. My father, mother, sisters, and brothers are still there. I'm the only one to have left. I've become a tourist in my own country now. We never left our little neighborhood. My sister doesn't even just take a short bus ride and go shopping in the West End. It's pretty general there.

SW/My mother's family—both our families have stayed in the same area.

SM/I have a brother who's been all over the world, so it's open to them.

SW/My mother had three brothers, and all family members have been in the same community since she was four years old. The grandchildren have moved out. Her brother came back from a nearby town in his retirement. It's her home, her property.

SM/People know your father, grandfather, and maybe your great-grandfather. It's unlike some states where it's very transient. People tend to stay in the area. That's our home.

- Scale of settlement makes a difference to assimilation
- Social support and personal development are related

CM/When [Indians] do come out, they're pretty well accepted one hundred percent. In this town, they were the majority and dependent on white people for their livelihood. If they come to Toronto with its two million people, they just disappear.

CW/They become just like other ethnic groups who've integrated into the city.

CM/One of our supervisors is a full-blooded Indian, and he made the move off the reservation. He's one of our better-liked supervisors.

CW/Need to give them the opportunity to find out if they want to take that step forward.

Humans and animals. Members of two coffee groups discussed ideas about the human-animal relationship.

• What are "appropriate bridges" between humans and animals?
Wanting to hear visitors discuss the differences they define between humans and other animals, I asked why they thought humans and mammals are exhibited in the same building. Coffee Group B discussed this question (W1 = Wyoming woman, CW = Chicago woman, CM = Chicago man).

CM/I remember an exhibit at the Franklin Institute very well. It described humans as animals that used tools. [That's an] appropriate bridge between humans and mammals.

• Humans tend to deny their natural history
W1/A lot of people don't think we're animals, that we're a different species of something.

• Humans and animals are in symbiotic relationships
I asked Coffee Group C the same question (TW = Texas woman, TM = Texas man, W = woman, V = Dutch woman).

W/That would be more lifelike. Eskimos hunted seals, Indians hunted bears and elks.

• History and evolution are not the same, nor are nature and culture
V/The first time I came I went to the American History museum to see Indians and was very surprised that they were not there. I think they're in the wrong museum.

W/In New York, you have the American Indian museum.

V/Coming here in 1985, I wanted to see about American history. They belong to American history, not to natural history, according to my view. I found it very odd.

- Systems of exchange structure history

    W/I suggest that you should show the trade route all the way from Alaska way down to the tip of South America two thousand years before Christ, where they found jewelry from South America and found fish hooks from the north. They traced the whole route down and there was regular trading up and down the entire coast, and I think that would be interesting to show, how these things moved. If you go to Mesa Verde, which was two thousand years before Christ, they were very intelligent people. They built chimneys with no sketches and absolutely perfect ellipses. They are fantastic. It was quite a civilization all the way down. I suggest that ought to be shown, how the Indians did work with each other through trade.

Tribes. Several groups shared with me their thoughts on the concept of "tribe."

- Size and interaction define "tribe"

I asked Coffee Group B, "How do you define a tribe?"

    CM/More a collection of people, a group of people who hang out together.

So there are tribes today?

    CM/Sure. Families—a lot of Catholics are tribes—they have large families. I think it's just a group.

- Ecology and tribal practices are related

    CW/Indian tribes, groups with very specific customs and ceremonies that separate them from all other tribes. The first thing that came to my mind was geologically—I mean geographically different areas. They created different tribes. I don't know if the geography was there first or the tribes.

    W2/Mores, what they wear, different areas. They look different. Religion, beliefs.

- "Primitive" implies simple

I asked the Boston-area group first to say what they thought of as the opposite of *primitive,* and then what *tribe* means to them (W=woman, M=man, MM=man). Not having recently visited the NMNH, their references are more general.

    M/Complex—complex structure, complex design, complexity of the mind that is brought to bear to create [an] object.

    F/Sophisticated, in terms of fanciness—plain versus fancy.

    MM/Modern in the sense of economics or industrialization. Primitive could be anywhere in place and time, but it's not something we associate with modern industrial society.

How do you think about primitive peoples?

M/They would create art differently, at different levels. Unlayered, less conscious, less deliberate. Just there and comes out. Represents something that person who created it might not be able to put any words around.

• "Tribes" suggests distance, in space, time, and experience

How do you define *tribes?*

M/Locally focused, common purpose, organized somehow. Common traditions, language, culture, art.

W/ *Tribe* itself sounds to me like a primitive word. I conjured up an image that's not necessarily what you think. . . . Antique word to me.

M/Middle East—I think about tribes of Abraham in Jordan.

W/My association with the word is more primitive, residual of primitiveness.

M/I think local, not worldly, not expansion.

M/It's a traditional, lay term. If [there's a] tribe in [the] modern world, [it] would probably go back long way. I think of tribes of common groups within cities, in [a] barrio, [for example].

• Social difference and social aggression are related, if not reciprocal

W/Defensiveness, when I think about it some more. Boundaries. Defense, even aggression.

M/Hostility toward rest of the world.

W/Could be.

M/Whatever's outside that locale.

• Cultural membership is limited to/transcends locality and propinquity

What do you think about American Indian tribes?

M/Locally or regionally bounded.

By what?

M/Other tribes, and then as white men came in, then by white man's definition.

MM/Modern organizations that are still in isolation from rest of society, tribal organizations, reservations, independently functioning economy.

M/Extending ideas of boundaries particularly in last century or century and a half as white man has taken physical control that it's become . . . much more a mental construct . . . than it is a physical affiliation that may not have a physical counterpart.

- Cultures can be decimated
- Tribal membership today is conceptual

W/Adding *American Indian* to *tribe* is almost an oxymoron. That the tribalness and what I was associating to it—all those feelings got watered down because of [the] overwhelming nature of the culture that's come in. I think of American Indian tribes as remnants and residues of the kind of strength I would associate with the tribe itself. Only a tribe in mind and not a tribe in fact.

- Maintaining ethnic distinctions requires cultural work

I asked what differences they see between American Indian tribes.

W/Same things that make differences between Americans from different European or Asian or South American cultures after a few generations. It's sort of a residue of cultural memory as anything. Some tribes—I really have very little experience—you're getting the perceptions of someone who's lived on the East Coast and knows no tribe. But I don't imagine that the distinctions are very alive unless there have been conscious efforts over the generations to maintain these. I think it would take that kind of conscious effort.

- Cultural practices constitute the static "core" of a tribe
- Change is exogenous

M/It may have to do with resources available to them. Some tribes are coherent and prospering and others have fragmented and drifted apart and maybe all they have left is some residential consciousness, like other ethnic groups in the country. Other tribes have growing enterprises and are intact.

You think of them as once being a coherent entity and self-contained, I commented. Do you they think they stayed the same?

MM/[They had] a large variety of things . . . in place for a long time over generations. Stories and lore are embellished from one generation to next, but are extended where there's some core set of truths passed on from one generation to the next. There may be some calamitous event—an earthquake or something that may jolt that passing of lore in some way, but it takes some calamitous event. Otherwise it's just extended and embellished.

W/I have almost the opposite sense. I imagine that tribes would have changed, especially nomadic and wandering tribes would have changed and evolved the same way other cultures would over time, especially as they moved around. [Some] tribes would have changed after large-scale encounter with white men and at that point we get the culture that's defending itself against the outside. Whatever's left in this frozen residue of tribal identity.

In order to learn how these cultural resources might influence exhibition development ideas, at the workshop with Smithsonian staff I chose one example from those reported and asked, "If you considered the notion that tribes are associated with 'distancing,' how might you conceptualize an exhibit designed to narrow down that distance?" The discussion raised several points. One was that Americans' understandings of "tribes" depend on their experiences—those from Arizona and those from Cambridge, for example, will have different conceptions. Another issue was whether curators should present to the public a "metaunderstanding" of the difficulties associated with the term itself. One person asked, "Does a visitor from Delaware think differently about American Indian and African tribes? There seem to be two ways to go: to extend the concept of tribe, or to start the exhibit with the problematic of tribe." For another curator, the concept of tribe raises a "potent question. The exhibit might begin with a big sign, What Is a Tribe? Because tribe is an administrative, not an indigenous, category, the exhibit would have to be situated in the colonial experience. The term *tribe* has been used to create Africans."

This imaginative discussion illustrates ways in which audience resources might aerate the exhibition development process. One person on the staff commented that while this process can be a "rich experience" for the professional participants, it often tends to be "self-referential." Another person suggested that we may often be "making exhibits for other museum people, not for visitors."

The workshop suggested the need for research on other crosscutting questions. For example, a systematic study of Smithsonian visitors' understandings of evolution found that while most accept the notion of animal evolution, only sixty percent believe that the concept applies also to humans. Such data raise the initial question of whether or not to confront this issue—and that of creationism, with which it resonates—and, if so, then to work out how this confrontation might influence the design of the exhibition as a whole. This question led to the point that just as visitors might be puzzled over how to define "natural history," so are museum staff. One suggestion was that exhibitions could make their point not by asserting consensus, but by bringing out the multiplicity of perspectives.

RECEPTION SYSTEMATICS: CULTURAL FORMS IN EXHIBITION VIEW-ING   The social authority of museums provides the basic architecture for visitors' ordering processes—not necessarily undeservedly, to be sure. But the issues of how exhibition topics have been selected and how the stories told about their objects have been written are, in general, unlikely to be brought to audiences' attention, nor, in the past, have these activities been seen as belonging in the communicative circle.

The Smithsonian is for many the pinnacle of authority. One visitor said, "We're very impressed with the Balboa museum in San Diego, but that's like comparing a Model T with a Rolls Royce." The Smithsonian staff finds that visitors' awe inhibits comments: Smithsonian exhibitions, especially of technology, are assumed to be the best, beyond criticism, beyond questioning, the last word. The wider context of Washington, a national shrine for many tourists, makes the Smithsonian another temple. Another comment: "We're here for a couple of days, and will spend one or two days of museuming. The museums in Chicago are wonderful, they're right there, but you just don't go. When you go to the Smithsonian, you feel you've been to *the* museum."

During a Highlight Tour of the NMNH, organized as a quick overview, the docent's discourse about a variety of objects emphasized magnitudes—the biggest, most costly, most prestigious—thus reinforcing the "Rolls Royce" aura. Such social meanings condition audience receptivities—and their vulnerabilities, which exhibition makers may want to take into special account. Nevertheless, critical faculties are far from absent, especially with respect to cultural and historical exhibitions, as these comments from two visitors attest:

> The Indian exhibits are meager—there's not enough information available. I'm familiar with a group of Maine Indians. Information could be shared about why they've become depleted. It's important for everyone to know. I know Indians personally. The presentation is historical, but I want to see Native Americans as they are today. There was a mass annihilation to do away with an entire culture—how strong they are to have survived!
> The exhibits should have added something on the present state

of Indians. Are they being mainstreamed? They're very poor on reservations. The reasons for their alcoholism has never been established. Eskimos and Aleuts became alcoholics when the English brought them rum. May have genetic problem with alcohol. We passed out smallpox to eradicate Eastern Indians. It's a bad history. Maybe we'll go forward and not do this to a new group.

These are some cultural forms of viewing and interpreting that I see in the texts:

• Resistance to assimilating the unfamiliar
As they viewed a diorama of a West African initiation ritual in the Africa hall, I asked an older white couple what they thought was going on and if it made them think of events in their own lives. The woman replied, "We wouldn't want to be there—it's scary. There's nothing similar in our experience." Although the shock—and the "scare"—of the unfamiliar is a prime source of resistance to novelty and ambiguity, exhibition makers' didactic optimism may underestimate it:

> Cross-cultural exhibitions present such stark contrasts between what we know and what we need to know that the challenge of reorganizing our knowledge becomes an aspect of exhibition experience. This challenge may be experienced in its strongest form in cross-cultural exhibits, but it should be raised by any exhibition. . . . Audiences are left with two choices: either they define their experience of the exhibition to fit with their existing categories of knowledge, or they reorganize their categories to fit better with their experience. Ideally, it is the shock of nonrecognition that enables the audience to choose the latter alternative. The challenge for exhibition makers is to provide within exhibitions the contexts and resources that enable audiences to choose to reorganize their knowledge.[21]

But the chief resource people bring to that choice is conservation. They will add new information if they can conserve what they already know alongside it; or, if they can assimilate the new information gradually, they will allow it to replace previous understandings. Even though museum audiences visit in the first place because they are receptive to new information and experiences, they are at the same time likely to resist whatever asks them to rearrange familiar and comfortable semantic and symbolic systems.[22] Moreover, the "shock of nonrecognition" can be so great as to leave people unreceptive to new information, which, in denying it entry into their schemata, they may call "boring" and "uninteresting." Another possible result is that people simply do not get the message, as documented in the study of the tropical rainforests exhibition, where the percentage of those who left the exhibition without an opinion was four times greater among those without prior knowledge of the issue than among those who were previously acquainted with the issue.[23]

• Resonance with familiar subjects heightens interest
Visitors may be drawn into exhibitions because they resonate with the visitors' current interests:

> I've never seen a Native American Indian exhibit anywhere. And as we were going through I saw—I'm reading the book *Alaska* by Michener—and I saw stuff about Eskimos, and I said, "Barry, we have to come back because everything that I'm reading about now is here." I'm really interested to go back and see them.

A visitor from Damascus was drawn to the diorama showing Indians making jewelry—he was himself a jeweler and was satisfied that the process as it was portrayed was authentic. When asked about his museum visit, he said he came to see objects, as neither photographs nor films can replace them.

• The scale of museums influences reception strategies
A Dutch visitor said, "You have to pick little pieces" out of the whole range of exhibitions and then return to them. A man who is employed in Cambridge but comes often to Washington on business and "works in visits to the Smithsonian" between appointments said, "I always know exactly what I want to see" there. Visitors who are not selective are "overwhelmed":

> It's hard to remember everything we've seen. It's our first visit—very, very enjoyable. Love it. Too much to absorb. Can't remember this stuff. Can't even remember how many columns there are around the Lincoln Memorial, although I must have heard it two or three times—they represent the number of states in the union at the time. We've been so overwhelmed by the whole thing. . . . Our three kids gave us this gift of a trip to D.C. for our fortieth anniversary. They gave us a list of things to see. This is our first free day—we've been on tours.
>
> We just got here today, we've been walking in and out of different halls. It's kind of hard to keep track.

• Personalizing and identifying
Speaking of art exhibitions, one man said, "I personalize things at the museum. I try to imagine the person's intent." Visitors often commented that in touring Washington, they concentrated on sites that relate to their hometown or state—for example, visitors from Illinois made sure they saw the Lincoln Memorial and Lincoln memorabilia. Identifying her husband as "half Cherokee," a woman in the Native Americans hall remarked jokingly, "It's our first visit, and we just happened to start here."

• Stories of material and cultural minutiae
One visitor, who has visited reservations in the West and who "was impressed with the Indian presentations [at the NMNH] of the ways of life of different tribes in different areas," said, "I just want to know where they got the beads. How did they make little, tiny beads? Where did the beads come from?" Another wanted to know why Indians apparently didn't mine silver but took the roundabout way of melting down Mexican silver coins. And another woman wanted to know when Indians started to weave cotton cloth. One man commented, "Tools interest me the most. Like fishing hooks, what you take for granted. The spears, arrows—the tools they had to make to survive. That really interests me."

• The past relates to both present and future
To a deliberately vague question about how the experience of coming to museums fits with the rest of your life, a man replied:

> Asking about coming to museums—its reputation [is the reason]. Here, people really care about what they're doing. What you've done here—nobody's ever asked my opinion in a museum [this was said with gratitude and wonder]. I think museums are a kind of road map of where we came from and where we might be going. Kind of learn from our mistakes and plot a course for our future. One suggestion: at the end of the museum, when you're ready to leave, show the most popular ideas of what we'll look like years from now. There might be five leading theories, and you'd show all five, not just one. Most popular theories of what we might look like, how we'll evolve in hundreds of thousands of years. So when you leave it kind of completes that book, beginning, middle, and end.

This suggests an expectation that stories will be structured by connections among past, present, and future for a sense of "completeness."

Do Americans seek in the present a route to the past—to whatever is remote from their experience? They appear to use the familiar to get a better purchase on the less familiar, which similarly constructs their concern, perhaps anxiety, about the future. I asked that man, "What museums have you seen that show the present?" He responded, "Only ones I've seen are Disney World. They have that process of showing where we are today, where we were, where we're going."

In the Western Civilization hall, a man said, "I'm impressed by mummies' coffins—the first time I've seen them." When I asked him, "What do you make of mummies?" he said that he was "amazed at their ability to preserve human remains. We can't do that today."

• Alternative theories are expected
In asking for "five leading theories," the visitor quoted above assumes that scientists disagree.

• Exhibitions in different museums relate to one another
To repeat an earlier excerpt from a discussion about American Indians:

> Exhibit I saw yesterday, I forget where. Maybe over at American History. Had a whole entire section of a part of our history where American Japanese were put into camps in World War II. And we devoted an entire section to just that. And here you have the American Indians in a camp and they're still there.

In his two days on the Mall, this visitor was synthesizing and interpreting connections between exhibits.

CONCLUSIONS: IMPLICATIONS FOR RESEARCH AND PRACTICE

Word-of-mouth recommendation was the "single predominant factor that influenced attendance"—this was one of the major findings of the Smithsonian study "Visitor Perspectives on Tropical Rainforests." Of those who had only seen the tropical rainforests exhibition and had no prior awareness of the issues, about sixty-one percent had heard about it from others, as did forty-seven percent of those who were already aware of the issues before seeing the exhibition.[24] The communicative circle extends well beyond museums' precincts.

The recommendations of teachers account for some of that sixty-one percent, though the report does not intimate who else in visitors' circles had said, "See it." "Don't miss it." "It's wonderful." But that is exactly what museums' professional communities hope will happen for every exhibition, permanent or temporary. They especially hope for publicity that will bring in first-time visitors. It comes as no surprise by now that I would speculate, first, that visitors spread the word to the interpretive communities to which they belong to the degree that they find an exhibition somehow relevant and salient to their frames of reference, experience, prior knowledge, beliefs, or myths, and second, that such recognition and acknowledgement have made their assimilation of new knowledge pleasurable, further stimulated or satisfied their curiosity, and deepened the meanings they live by.

The J. Paul Getty Museum and the Getty Center for Education in the Arts have recently published their pioneering study of the perceptions of visitors (and nonvisitors) to eleven art museums in as many cities, conducted over two years. The study is based on a focus-group methodology, whereby eight to twelve people, chosen from a targeted population and paid for their participation, are led in a discussion by a trained moderator who follows a prepared guide. Staff from each museum listened to and observed their discussions from behind a one-way glass partition (with the participants' knowledge). One of the study's aims was to help art museums to "understand themselves better from the perspectives of their visitors."[25] Repeat visitors, the study finds, tend to come in order to reinforce what they already know and like, while nonvisitors, among other reasons, do not come because they perceive themselves to lack enough knowledge to appreciate the works. For both first-time and repeat visitors, the study concludes, "The more visitors know about a particular object and its background, the greater their connection with it."[26] Translating this into my terms, I suggest that the more that exhibitions resonate with the cultural resources—not only specific information—visitors bring with them, the greater the possibility of connection.

I see several themes with implications for research and practice:

Overwhelming Scale and Scope

The Getty study's methods are themselves suggestive about ways of reducing the confusions and overload of museum visits. After an initial discussion had been held, both visitors and nonvisitors visited the museum in their city "with an assignment to see specific galleries identified by the staff" and to keep a diary of that visit. They then met to discuss their actual experiences and how they compared to their expectations. The study found that "the experiences of most first-time visitors exceed their expectations."[27] Although the study doesn't tease out the influence of the assignment and the diary, its other data suggest that all visitors might welcome staff recommendations or other ways of bringing the museum experience down to a manageable scale. One visitor commented, "I probably wouldn't have done so much thinking about what I was doing if I hadn't been taking notes and taking part in this thing here. I think the whole thing opened my eyes to another way of looking at things."[28]

Finding ways not to feel overwhelmed by museums' variety of exhibits and their size is a general issue. "Orientation is a problem at all eleven museums," the report concludes. "Introductory information on how to organize the visit, what to see, and how the museum is arranged is needed."[29] Moreover, the lack of information with which to situate the works of art was a common complaint: "The perceived lack of information is frustrating; it detracts from the museum experience."[30] It was even more of an issue for non-Western art collections at several museums: "Explanations of cultural symbols and beliefs are needed to define their meaning and significance."[31]

To diminish the often-expressed sense of "so much to take in, so little time" and the burden of information overload, smaller-scale exhibitions—even those developed for specialists—might have wide appeal and provide a more satisfying sense of involvement.

Making Connections Among Exhibitions

The reference one visitor made to the Japanese-relocation exhibition at the National Museum of American History while discussing Native Americans reveals an internal dimension of the communicative circle—how people talk to themselves about what they have seen—as does the comment of the Dutch visitor for whom American Indians belong in the National Museum of American History rather than in the National Museum of Natural History. Building on this process of interreference and synthesis could be an important consideration for exhibition makers hoping to maximize the force of their messages, especially at large museums or complexes of museums such as the Smithsonian.

To make transparent some of the connections between the secular spaces of everyday concerns and the sacred precincts of exhibition halls, and in order to intrigue and stimulate, museums might consider a "relevance and salience" curator, educator, or committee, whose work would consist of constructing relationships among the museum's exhibitions (permanent and temporary) and topical concerns—political issues, social trends, hobbies, the seasons, weather phenomena, etc. A bulletin board, banners, or a television monitor at the entrance might flag various exhibitions for their relevance.

To capitalize further on the power of synthesis and intertextuality, self-guides might encourage visitors to follow related themes through different exhibitions and halls, and in the case of museum complexes, though different museums. The themes might be technological, aesthetic, ethnographic, etc.

Deconstructing Authoritative Paradigms

If museums present a number of alternative theories, as one visitor suggested, they are asking visitors to do more interpretive work than usual. If exhibitions are increasingly to be developed around contested concepts and interpretations, audience reflection becomes an even more important part of the museum experience. Perhaps the communicative circle might be realized in actuality in regularly scheduled informal discussions with docents and curators or in "talk-back boards," where visitors can express themselves.[32] The willingness of visitors who were strangers to one another to sit down together over coffee to discuss with me and with one another their museum experiences stands as evidence of the untapped vitality of the communicative circle.[33]

Such spontaneous expression could be a source of hypotheses testing the operations of information assimilation. How does talking with others about viewing experiences affect that process? Do the frames of reference people use account for differences in assimilation? An art museum visitor commented, "Every gallery that I've gone into, I've wished that there was more explanation, discussion, something there that I could use to understand what it is, what's going on here."[34]

Moreover, if museums that have been socially constructed as repositories of authoritative paradigms begin to offer multiple perspectives, that move challenges cultural expectations. Audiences may then need special supports to experience and interpret them. In her studies of middle-class women's book groups, Elizabeth Long finds that although the groups rely on critics' tastes to legitimate their choice of genres and books and "tend to deprecate their own adverse reactions to books the critics praise" as well as to exclude books they enjoyed but that critics do not recommend, "groups appear to be less constrained by cultural authority when they discuss books than when they select them."

> Members talk about books with deep engagement, but very differently from experts or professionals, and they sometimes interpret characters and evaluate novels with marked disregard for learned opinion. . . . [Given the nonacademic context] the groups usually truncate the process of making a case for any given interpretation of a book. But on the other hand, the discussants are willing to entertain a variety of readings. Not only can they be persuaded that other views are possible, but they enjoy a multivocal response to the same text.[35]

Museum staff could anticipate audiences' proclivities to welcome alternative interpretations.

Although this cultural theory of representation and reception is obviously relevant to issues of exhibition evaluation and criticism, the process of developing exhibitions is its subject. Exhibitions once conceived and built are symbols of that process, which, as much as any total effect, should also be open to evaluation and critique. After-the-fact evaluations may offer useful lessons for the next project, but the economics and technology of large-scale installations obviate the possibility of major editing and revision. The theory suggests instead how the resources of interpretive communities might be incorporated heuristically into the dialogues of professional communities during the development process itself. These moves should *precede* tests of audience responses (and those of potential funders) to exhibition mockups—such testing is presently one of the most prevalent vehicles for audience participation in the communicative circle.

An even longer research agenda is implicit in all that has been said, of course. Two issues in particular deserve attention. First, museum professionals who are designated audience advocates walk a fine line in the exhibition development process. The evidence of audience concerns they bring to the process should do as much to inform the rhetoric of spectacles as to inform the elaborations of cabinets. In practice, however, advocates develop evidence that seems to influence spectacles more than cabinets. When the requirements of spectacles override curators' interests in conveying complex content, the tension among museum professionals is exacerbated. Studies of visitors' semantic domains (for example, "tribe," "evolution," "race," "gender," etc.) could provide exhibition developers with insights into visitors' cultural resources and with fresh points of departure for presenting cabinet-level details. Those should be coupled with studies of different strategies for bringing these audience understandings into the development process. Finally, that greater emphasis on spectacle may be based on unexamined assumptions about the nature of adult learning experiences, about which research from many perspectives is sorely needed.

Those assumptions raise a second, more general question for the humanities. By virtue of their age alone, adults bring larger stores of information, experience, and memory to the cognitive, affective, and interpretive dimensions of museum visits. One research question for cultural studies is the extent to which museum visits (compared to other leisure activities) activate the integration and synthesis of adults' lives. People living in a society that compartmentalizes and institutionalizes lived experience—dividing it into work, family, politics, and religion, for example—depend on cultural institutions for their opportunities to achieve coherence, growth, and an evolving sense of identity. Museums are singularly important stimuli for human synthesis. This theory of representation and reception is offered in hopes of helping them to be even more effective by acknowledging the stratigraphy of meanings their visitors bring with them. By enhancing the integrity of the exhibition development process, all members of museums' communicative circles stand a better chance of speaking and being heard.

NOTES

For urging this work on, I'm grateful to Ivan Karp, and for financial, field, and intellectual support, to Zahava D. Doering, director, and the staff of the Institutional Studies Office of the Smithsonian Institution. To all at the Smithsonian who talked with me—curators, designers, educators, and visitors—my thanks.

1. For example, with its March 1989 (vol. 41, no. 1) issue, *American Quarterly* initiated a new department devoted to "the critical assessment of museum exhibitions in the American Studies field" (141). See also Gary Kulik and James Sims, "Clarion Call for Criticism," *Museum News* 68, no. 6 (1989), 52–55; Michael M. J. Fischer, "Museums and Festivals: Notes on the Poetics and Politics of Representation Conference," *Cultural Anthropology* 4, no. 2 (1989), 204–21; and Ivan Karp and Steven D. Lavine, eds., *Exhibiting Cultures: The Poetics and Politics of Museum Display* (Washington, D.C.: Smithsonian Institution Press, 1991).

2. C. L. Fronville and Z. D. Doering, "Visitor Perspectives on Tropical Rainforests: A Report Based on the 1988 *Tropical Rainforests: A Disappearing Treasure Information Study*" (Washington, D.C.: Office of Institutional Studies, Smithsonian Institution, 1989); "Insights: Museums, Visitors, Attitudes, Expectations—A Focus Group Experiment" (Los Angeles: The Getty Center for Education in the Arts and the J. Paul Getty Museum, 1991).

3. I am grateful to Janet Pawlukiewicz of the National Museum of Natural History Office of Education for field support. In the Native Americans hall primarily, wearing Smithsonian badges and identifying ourselves as "being with the Smithsonian," we approached visitors randomly, asking, "Would you like to sit down over a cup of coffee and discuss your visit to the Smithsonian?" We set up a flip chart in front of a display representing an African initiation ritual and asked visitors as they went by to tell us what they saw in the case. More people refused to engage than did. The most responsive person was a man who identified himself as West African; he provided a gloss on the ritual (for example, he suggested that it couldn't have been important because women were present). We abandoned the flip chart, thinking that it inhibited interaction.

We also sat on benches in the Native Americans hall, in the Western Civilization exhibition, and in front of the elevators on the second floor, inviting people to join us for a few minutes and talk about what they had been seeing in the museum. One curator joined me in the Native Americans hall, where we asked a couple of visitors to talk about a particular case. We gave everybody who talked with us an NMNH button with the slogan Very Informative Person.

Because of many refusals ("just got here," "not enough time") and the unpredictable volume of visitors, these methods were very time-intensive for a small yield, but they should not discourage on-site, in-depth, and informal discussions with visitors. I would try another method next time: At the entrance, I would, in effect, establish a contract upon visitors' arrival, asking them, "Would you let me accompany you and talk to me about the exhibitions you're looking at?" Or as visitors were preparing to leave, "Would you join a small discussion group to talk about your visit?" The three coffee groups met for about an hour in the Associates' Restaurant, which would have been perfect except for the level of background noise on the tape. A room in the Learning Center, with coffee available, would probably be optimal. Participants in the discussion groups all thoroughly enjoyed it, felt honored, welcomed a chance to sit down, and as can be seen in the transcripts, talked easily with one another.

4. See William H. Honan, "Say Goodbye to the Stuffed Elephants," *New York Times Magazine,* 14 Jan. 1990, 35–38, for a case study of these tensions at the Field Museum of Natural History in Chicago.

5. James Clifford, interviewed by Brian Wallis in "The Global Issue: A Symposium," *Art in America* 77, no. 7 (1989), 152–53.

6. Masao Yamaguchi, "The Poetics of Exhibition in Japanese Culture," in Ivan Karp and Steven D. Lavine, eds., *Exhibiting Cultures: The Poetics and Politics of Museum Display* (Washington, D.C.: Smithsonian Institution Press, 1991).

7. Mikhail Bakhtin, quoted in Alessandro Duranti, "The Audience as Coauthor: An Introduction," *Text* 6, no. 3 (1986), 241.

8. Duranti, "The Audience as Co-author."

9. Michael Baxandall, "Exhibiting Intention: Some Preconditions of the Visual Display of Culturally Purposeful Objects," in Ivan Karp and Steven D. Lavine, eds., *Exhibiting Cultures: The Poetics and Politics of Museum Display* (Washington, D.C.: Smithsonian Institution Press, 1991), 39.

10. Ibid., 41.

11. Elizabeth Traube, "Secrets of Success in Postmodern Society," *Cultural Anthropology* 4, no. 3 (1989), 275.

12. Kulik and Sims, "Clarion Call for Criticism," 55.

13. Donald Brenneis, "Shared Territory: Audience Indirection and Meaning," *Text* 6, no. 3 (1986), 339–47.

14. Fronville and Doering, "Visitor Perspectives," 47–48.

15. Claude Lévi-Strauss, *The Savage Mind* (Chicago: University of Chicago Press, 1966), 29.

16. Recent attempts to unify discourse and cognitive theory (for example, Jonathan Potter and Margaret Wetherell, *Discourse and Social Psychology: Beyond Attitudes and Behaviour* [London: Sage, 1987]) suggest that exhibition makers' stereotypes and prototypes of audiences are themselves limiting. Discourse perspectives reveal flaws in cognitivists' inside-the-head versions of categorization processes. Cognitive understandings of categories of thought (for example, frames of reference, interpretations, beliefs) are based on three premises: that people exaggerate differences between categories and play down the differences within them; that people work from prototypes, typifications, or paradigms to create fuzzy sets whose members are both like and unlike the prototype; and that people work from preformed and enduring categories.

Alternatively, discourse studies find that such categories are social and constructed, not individual and permanent: different situations occasion different mobilizations of shared interpretive repertoires. Moreover, when people's experience threatens a prejudice, they will make exceptions and particularize.

Consistency and variability seem, then, to work together. Cognitivists deal with variability, however, by adopting a coding scheme that reduces the variations and internal contradictions, while discourse theory suggests that categories are not nested or hierarchical, but instead are grouped into collections ready for use in interpreting and assimilating different life experiences. Their different uses account for the variability.

In the communicative system of museums, where exhibitions and viewers exchange information and experience, variability suggests that there are likely to be many different ways to activate the conceptual and categorical resources viewers bring to their interpretive practices. Exhibition makers could make reference to a variety of such repertoires, rather than those their stereotypes suggest, to help assure that viewers will receive new information or correct their misapprehensions or become more curious.

17. Fronville and Doering, "Visitor Perspectives," vii.

18. Ibid., 15 (table 3.3).

19. Ibid., 16 (table 3.4).

20. The transcripts of these discussions reproduce the sequence of conversational turns, but the excerpts here may not, in order to aggregate texts on the same or related topics. The complete transcripts are on file in the Smithsonian Institution's Office of Institutional Studies and are available there for perusal.

21. Ivan Karp, "Culture and Representation," in Ivan Karp and Steven D. Lavine, eds., *Exhibiting Cultures: The Poetics and Politics of Museum Display* (Washington, D.C.: Smithsonian Institution Press, 1991), 22–23.

22. Constance Perin, "The Reception of New, Unusual and Difficult Art," in *The Prinzhorn Collection: Selected Work from the Prinzhorn Collection of the Art of the Mentally Ill* (Urbana and Champaign: University of Illinois, 1984), and *Belonging in America: Reading Between the Lines* (Madison: University of Wisconsin Press, 1988).

23. Fronville and Doering, "Visitor Perspectives," 16.

24. Ibid., 11.

25. "Insights: Museums, Visitors, Attitudes, Expectations," 1.

26. Ibid., 21.

27. Ibid., 16.

28. Ibid., 19.

29. Ibid., 18.

30. Ibid., 22.

31. Ibid., 23.

32. Elaine Heumann Gurian, "Noodling Around with Exhibition Opportunities," in Ivan Karp and Steven D. Lavine, eds., *Exhibiting Cultures: The Poetics and Politics of Museum Display* (Washington, D.C.: Smithsonian Institution Press, 1991).

33. Some who were unwilling to join a group or even to talk in the halls left the impression that they perceived the interaction as pedagogical: in the

Smithsonian context, they feared that they were going to be "quizzed," as it were.

34. "Insights: Museums, Visitors, Attitudes, Expectations," 41.

35. Elizabeth Long, "Women, Reading, and Cultural Authority: Some Implications of the Audience Perspective in Cultural Studies," *American Quarterly* 38, no. 4 (1986), 602–3. This growing literature about the cultural resources of a middle-class population that is also likely to frequent museums is a singularly important point of comparison with museums' communicative circles. A historian of books and readers suggests that "by focusing on social process—that is, on what people do with texts and objects rather than on those texts and objects themselves—we should begin to see that people do not ingest mass culture whole but often remake it into something they can use" (Cathy N. Davidson, "Towards a History of Books and Readers," *American Quarterly* 40, no. 1 [1988], 12).

CHAPTER 8

The Colonial Legacy and the Community: The Gallery 33 Project

JANE PEIRSON JONES

This essay focuses on the issues of community and interpretation that have arisen during the development of a new permanent anthropology exhibition that opened in 1990 in the Birmingham Museum and Art Gallery. The essay outlines the exhibition concept, describes its development process, and considers some of the responses to it. The exhibition is called Gallery 33: A Meeting Ground of Cultures. It uses a portion of the museum's ethnography collection, which had been in storage for nearly thirty years. Thus the opening of Gallery 33 in 1990 marked a new beginning for one division of the city of Birmingham's multidisciplinary museum service, which was founded in 1885.

The Birmingham ethnography collection, which was formed in the first thirty years of the twentieth century, was put together by museum patrons who were part of the colonial process. They were either colonial administrators or missionaries on active service abroad, or they were wealthy local industrialists who exported metal goods around the world (the slogan "made in Birmingham" became a catchphrase throughout the British Empire). The far-off societies those people visited are now independent nations, and the Birmingham they knew is radically different. Birmingham is no longer a metal-manufacturing center but is looking to services and cultural industries for its economic regeneration. The city's population base has changed: twenty-five percent of the population comes from black and ethnic minority backgrounds, and is largely derived from postwar immigration from former colonial territories.

In 1985 I was asked to develop a new anthropology exhibition that would put on public display the city's collection. The director of the museum, Michael Diamond, set out four objectives for the exhibition: it should be unique in concept as well as in quality of material; it should take account of multicultural issues specific to Birmingham; it should be designed to take account of the multidisciplinary potential of the museum service; and it should deal with public-interest issues rather than follow a traditional academic format.[1]

The process of interpreting this brief using the existing collection, which is itself a colonial construction, poses the question of how a museum exhibition that must use artifacts collected in earlier times can contribute to an understanding of the late-twentieth-century world. Subsidiary questions follow: Can a display of this kind meet the expectations of the many different communities of museum visitors? How should a centrally placed museum service reflect the city's diverse, multiethnic history and culture? The exploration of these questions (often intuitively, sometimes explicitly) has led me to examine the multiple meanings that ethnographic artifacts hold, and has necessitated facing up to a number of issues about interpretation and representation.

The result is the exhibition called Gallery 33. With its mission statement, "a meeting ground of cultures—an exhibition about the way people live: beliefs, values, customs, and art from around the world," the exhibition aims to encourage visitors to examine assumptions they make about their own and other people's cultures. It explores anthropological themes at a popular level, using a cross-cultural approach. It integrates artifacts from contemporary minority and majority cultures in Birmingham with the historic museum collection.

BIRMINGHAM MUSEUM

The Birmingham Museums and Art Gallery is a large public multidisciplinary museum service. The main building, the Museum and Art Gallery, is a Victorian temple of culture that opened in 1885 "to extend the knowledge, refine the taste, instruct the judgement and

strengthen the faculty of those who are engaged in Birmingham industries."[2] It is located in the civic and financial section of the city. There
is a staff of about two hundred, one-third of whom are women. Of the
small number of black and ethnic minority staff, few occupy positions
of authority. The museum service has a further eight sites in the city:
five historic houses, a medieval ruin, the Nature Centre, and the
Museum of Science and Industry. There are extensive educational
programs based on these sites, but there is no off-site community
outreach.

About 550,000 people visit the Museum and Art Gallery each
year. 30,000 come in organized school groups. Currently about eight
percent of visitors come from outside the Birmingham region, but this
figure is expected to change after 1991 with the opening of the new
convention center, which is at the heart of the city's plan to make
business tourism a focus of its economic regeneration. A visitor survey
in 1984 indicated that the majority of visitors are relatively well-off
and well educated. Skilled and semiskilled workers are underrepresented, and so are visitors from the inner-city area, where forty-three
percent of the population live in households whose heads were born in
the New Commonwealth or Pakistan.[3] Principal sources of migration
are, in descending order, India, the Caribbean (principally Jamaica),
Africa, Pakistan, Bangladesh, and Ireland.[4] These data are based on
the 1981 population census and provide a surrogate rather than a
direct measure of the size and composition of the local black and
ethnic minority communities. The Chinese community is probably
growing at the fastest rate. To generalize, there are twenty-six different ethnic minority groups, and about twenty-four languages are spoken by city residents. The communities are culturally rich and varied,
and correspondingly the community issues are complex. There is no
single pattern of cultural expression or consumption.

I worked with an advisory group on the multicultural implications of the Gallery 33 project. There were eight advisors, who had
complementary experience and a shared interest in the presentation of
cultural history in museums. They included a community worker, a
journalist, a photographer, an anthropologist, a curator, a librarian,
and two educators. Being both black and white, they were invited not
as representatives of particular interests but as individuals who had
specific, relevant experience and who were prepared to work together
within the museum's existing institutional framework.

The advisors were invited to comment on the design brief, to
advise on the choice of display topics and education programs, and to

create links to the communities and to specialists. The consultant designers were reluctant to design for a committee, so the mandate given to the advisors specified that their role was to provide advice to me. In turn I formed a liaison with the designers. The designers and the advisors occasionally came together to discuss a particular agenda item, and they usually met informally for lunch after advisory group meetings. There were four staff members at these meetings, two from the curatorial team and two from the educational team. For the staff it was a learning process, not only about the development of Gallery 33 but also about outside perceptions of the Museum and Art Gallery as a whole.

The advisory group questioned the content of the exhibition at all levels. They examined the use of positive and negative images and whether the exhibits confronted or reinforced cultural stereotypes. They looked at the balance among cultural groups represented and paid special attention to the needs of people with disabilities. The advisors also made individual contributions to the project at different stages. Three of them were closely involved in reviewing the exhibition script, and one assisted with the choice and acquisition of Hindu and Sikh artifacts. One facilitated a sponsorship deal; another undertook a photographic commission; yet another carried out research for the exhibition.

The advisory group met four times during the design development phase to review concepts and content. One meeting focused on educational programming. Three further meetings examined the content of specific exhibits and reviewed the exhibition script. The final meeting took place three months before the gallery opened. This took the form of a seminar, and each advisor invited five people from his or her own professional networks so that a total of about forty people from a wide range of cultural and educational venues from Birmingham and beyond attended. Following a formal presentation on the aims and objectives of the project, the advisors spoke positively about their involvement. The gallery was enthusiastically received, and lively discussion followed on a number of representation issues (particularly focusing on the use of language and imagery in the exhibition). Without exception, all the topics raised at the seminar had been previously discussed in the advisory group. This indicated that the group had worked through an appropriate agenda even though not every issue under discussion had been resolved nor had consensus been reached in certain areas. Many recommendations of the advisory group were followed; however, decisions ultimately had to be made by the curator and the designers. It is clear that those decisions were made from a position of greater awareness than they would have been had the advisory group not existed.

It is difficult to quantify the impact the advisory group undoubtedly had on both the concept and the physical look of the gallery. The group possessed creative synergy, and the project benefited from the expertise and access to new networks that individual advisors brought with them. They saw their role as one of raising and debating issues, not of rubber-stamping decisions made elsewhere. They individually gave me support in dealing with the inevitable difficulties encountered when working in the equal-opportunities field. The existence of the advisory group certainly added validity to the project in political and professional circles. This was a challenging and rewarding experience, and I would not hesitate to work this way again on any kind of interpretive project.

GALLERY 33 PROJECT

From the start I had several specific goals. First, I wanted to incorporate current thinking on the way cultural anthropology should be presented in museums, drawing on the experience gained in the South Pacific and in North America, where the growing politicization of ethnic minority peoples has been most keenly expressed. Second, I wanted to involve visitors by offering a strong hands-on component, as well as including a multisensory experience as a stimulus to intellectual interaction with the concepts. Third, I wanted the distinctive conceptual approach to be reinforced by a design that would create a space very different from any other part of the museum.[5] The consultant designers, Morag Bremner and Mick Orr, achieved this using a high-tech design and a color scheme and logo inspired by the mural art of Ndebele women from South Africa.

Around the perimeter of the 2,500-square-foot gallery a series of cased exhibits explore popular, visitor-friendly topics such as "Eating and Drinking," "Music," and "Masks." A central cased exhibit called "Societies" is more theoretical and explores the nature of human society in seven sections, each headed up by a leading question, for example "Why Is Ethnic Identity Important?" "How Did You Gain Your Position in Society?" and "What Shapes the Roles of Women and Men?"

Each topic or question is illustrated by a wide range of photo-

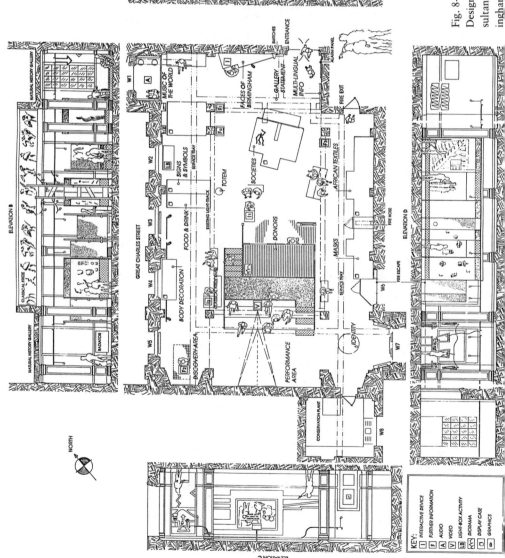

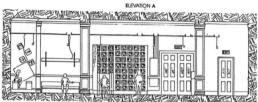

Fig. 8-1. The floorplan of the Gallery 33 exhibition. Designed by Morag Brenner and Orr Design Consultants Ltd. Reproduced by permission of Birmingham City Museum and Art Gallery.

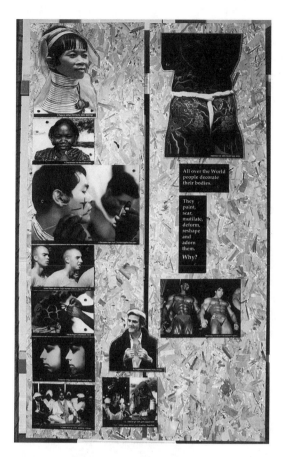

Fig. 8-2. "The Decorated Body" photomontage in Gallery 33. Photo by John Cope, courtesy of Birmingham City Museum and Art Gallery.

graphs and artifacts. Objects and images from Britain are mixed with those from "foreign" cultures and cover a long span of time, from the archaeologically known past to the present day. Exhibits have been chosen from the museum's art and local-history collections, thus breaching the traditional (and racist) divide that exists in many museums between ethnographic material (often linked with natural-history collections), on the one hand, and Western art and material culture, on the other. For example, the section on "The Decorated Body" has thirty-five references, which include Italian plastic surgery, ancient Egyptian face painting, British Sikh turbans, Japanese, Maori, and British tattoos, African hairstyling, and modern cosmetics.

Museums are places where "things" are usually classified and separated. Gallery 33 declassifies and mixes—the familiar with the unfamiliar, the past with the present, and the majority with the minor-

ity. I hope that the discordance created by these unfamiliar juxtapositions will attract the visitors' attention and challenge their sense of
order, their sense of the "other," and thus their sense of themselves.

Hands-on features include a signs-and-symbols game, discovery
boxes, and a mask exhibit in which visitors can experience transformation by trying on hand-held replica masks. Four information stands
will enable visitors to explore for themselves topics such as language
and minority rights. A twenty-foot-high metal totem pole will carry
children's work and visitors' comments, thus reflecting the identities
and opinions of visitors to Gallery 33.

About twenty percent of the exhibition space has been given over
to a performance area, which has seating for thirty people and is fully
equipped with audiovisual equipment. This space can be used for a
wide range of teaching activities, workshops, and performances, and
there is a continuously running audiovisual introduction to the gallery.
The aim here is to integrate oral, intellectual, and performance aspects
of culture into the static artifact exhibition and to promote intercultural understanding through person-to-person contact. I hope that
a wide variety of ethnic minority and other social groups will come in

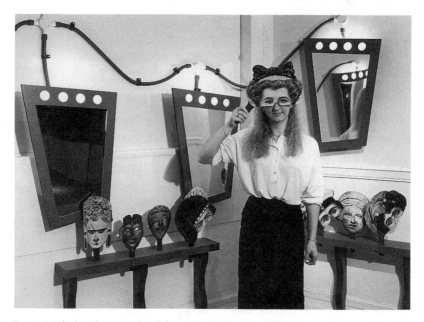

Fig. 8-3. The hands-on mask exhibit in the "Identity" section of Gallery 33. Photo by
John Cope, courtesy of Birmingham City Museum and Art Gallery.

to use this space in ways they determine for themselves—in ways facilitated, rather than prescribed, by museum staff. The performance area is a venue in which cultural diversity can be expressed and celebrated. Adventurous programming in this area will be a key element in making Gallery 33 a true meeting ground of cultures.

Plans are being made to put together a program of events that will explore cultural diversity and give prominence to groups of people who do not normally visit the museum.[6] The idea is to develop a dialogue among visitors and to present different perspectives on issues raised by Gallery 33 directly or indirectly. A number of speakers at the conference on which this volume is based called for programs that move away from the so-called icons of diversity (festivals, food, music, and dance) to address the discord and conflicts implicit in the multicultural experience. It should be possible to do this. However, effective programs must start with the realization that the targeted audience often desires to see these icons of diversity displayed in museums. Experience suggests that displays focusing on discord and social conflict will not necessarily be the chosen goal of a community's museum program. Curators need to be flexible enough to respond to the aspirations of different community groups and move with them through an examination of issues.

There is one diorama in the exhibition, called "The Collectors." It is set in the 1920s and features Ida Wench, who was a missionary in the Solomon Islands; Percy Amaury Talbot, an officer in the colonial service in Nigeria; and Arthur Wilkins, a private collector in Australia. Models of the three of them are located on the veranda of Arthur Wilkins's house. Through the windows a lavish arrangement of artifacts can be seen, reminiscent of Wilkins's display in his house in Sydney. The exhibit is designed to be nostalgic and emotive. The associated label text raises questions about the collectors' motives and their selection criteria.

This diorama is reinforced by an interactive video exhibit called "Collectors in the South Pacific." It profiles four people who collected artifacts from the Solomon Islands. They are Ida Wench and Arthur Wilkins, who were active in the 1920s; a fictional American tourist; and Lawrence Foanaota, the current director of the Solomon Islands National Museum. Using a touchscreen, visitors can access their choice of video sequences, still images, and commentaries. They can explore the individual experiences of the four collectors or they can track any of four artifacts. The exhibit reveals different interpretations of and alternative responses to museum artifacts; a commentator

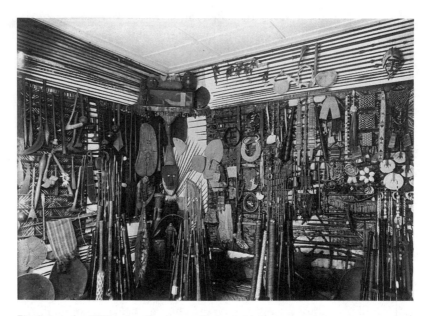

Fig. 8-4. Arthur Wilkins's collection on display in his house in Sydney, Australia, circa 1922. Department of Archaeology and Ethnography Historical File NH24' 30. Reproduced by permission of Birmingham City Museum and Art Gallery.

raises related issues about mission activity, patrimony, the role of museums, and economic development, and poses questions to the visitor.

The second interactive exhibit, called "Archives," is a picture bank of one hundred and seventeen images of objects in the collection, each with an optional one-hundred-word caption. Images can be called up in any of twenty-two categories—under collector name, geographical location, or topic. Visitors can browse through the visually rich images at their own speed and following their own interests.

Interactive video has proven to be an excellent medium in which to present different perspectives because it is possible to convey contrasting points of view, personality, and mood quickly and effectively. Visitors can choose their own pathway and make their own decisions about what line of inquiry to pursue.[7] The interactive video exhibits were externally financed by grant aid and sponsorship from the English Tourist Board, the Calouste Gulbenkian Foundation, the Friends of Birmingham Museum and Art Gallery, and Central Independent TV. Further money has been awarded by the Calouste Gulbenkian

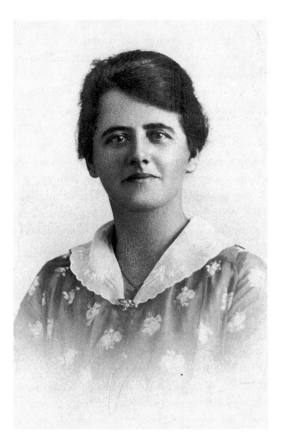

Fig. 8-5. Ida Clara Wench, missionary, circa 1910. Photo from the Melanesian Mission Archives, courtesy of Birmingham City Museum and Art Gallery.

Foundation to carry out a visitor evaluation program, which will provide useful data for the design of other exhibits.

THE COLLECTORS

Why have we chosen to focus attention on the collectors? People are intrigued by how ethnographic material is acquired by museums. Exhibitions have sometimes failed to address this question because it is a story curators often do not feel comfortable with. However, the story of the objects in our collection is a fascinating one, and in telling it we find the key to the puzzle of how to relate ethnographic collections to present-day concerns.

In the past, anthropology displays have focused on the indigenous cultural context of an artifact, thus leading to the cultural voyeurism of traditional display approaches. But once in the museum, artifacts also have a second cultural context relating to their collection history and museum identity. In this additional, acquired context the artifact in the museum ceases to be a cultural fossil in an estranged environment, rather becoming an artifact defined by the dynamic social processes in its acquired domicile. In regard to this second context, studies of the process of acquisition, the rationale of the collection, and the way the collection has been used in the museum reveal an additional set of meanings that deepen and broaden the interpretive potential of the artifact. A few examples taken from the Birmingham collection will demonstrate how the examination of an artifact's history reveals the values and motivations of the collectors, places British colonial history on the agenda, and exposes the anthropological museum as a colonial construction.

Nick Stanley has shown that the missionary Ida Wench assembled her collection by gift, purchase, and commission. In order that her schoolgirls should have money for church collections and to teach them the "spirit of giving," Wench encouraged them to make craft items, especially bags, which she purchased at a penny each. The money was eventually sent on to a mission school in China.[8] Back in England her collection, including these craft items, was put into missionary exhibitions. In this way her collection was used to promote and raise money for the missionary cause by marking racial difference.[9]

A rare Fijian female ancestor figure in the Birmingham Museum not only has its intrinsic Fijian value but also reflects the social status and wealth of its collector, Herbert Chamberlain. It is one of a large number of artifacts collected by Chamberlain when he spent two months in Fiji while buying a copra plantation in 1877. A member of a leading Birmingham industrial family, Herbert was a younger brother of Joseph Chamberlain, who later became colonial secretary. Nicholas Thomas has shown how the practice of collecting among the colonial elite in Fiji at that time was influenced by the ideological standpoint and political goals of the governor, Sir Arthur Gordon. Artifacts that were produced by Fijians became elements of British colonial practice with altered meanings and social effects.[10]

It is possible to see the museum process at work in the correspondence beginning in 1927 between Arthur Wilkins in Sydney and Donald Payler, the keeper of natural history of the museum in Birmingham. Payler urged Wilkins to list and identify his eclectic

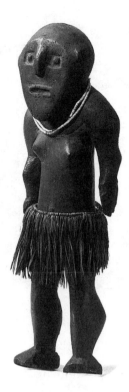

Fig. 8-6. Fijian ancestor figure collected by Herbert Chamberlain in 1877. Department of Archaeology and Ethnography accession no. 1918A17.24. Photo by David Bailey, courtesy of Birmingham City Museum and Art Gallery.

collection of curios before it was shipped to Birmingham. Once in the museum, Payler separated and classified the collection and set out an ordered display "showing one example of each type placing them near together for comparison." In a letter to Wilkins dated 23 January 1931, Payler describes how he had included "with the specimens a number of illustrations of natives, customs etc. with descriptive matter, in order to give a sort of living interest to the exhibits." Wilkins's "curios" became museum "specimens" that, according to a review in the *Birmingham Gazette* dated 5 April 1931, "vividly depict the quaint customs and the ingenuity of the natives of the South Pacific area."

Percy Amaury Talbot, the distinguished ethnographer and African colonial administrator, recognized that as the latter, he was an agent of destruction of indigenous culture. He carried out his ethnographic work for two reasons: "first for the pleasure of it and secondly because primitive races the world over are changing so rapidly that it seemed well to place on record the story of a people most of whom were untouched by white influence on my arrival among them in 1907."[11] Talbot and his wife, Dorothy, collected with equal vigor representative samples of artifacts, head measurements, and plants.

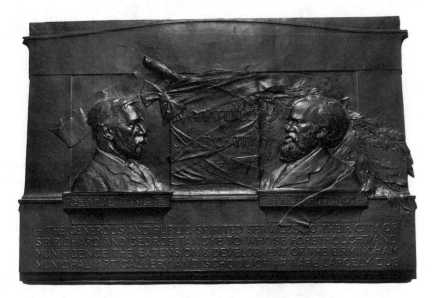

Fig. 8-7. Bronze plaque of George and Sir Richard Tangye in the museum entrance hall. Photo by David Bailey, courtesy of Birmingham City Museum and Art Gallery.

However, by virtue of his administrative position, his collecting activities took place in the context of unequal relationships. "On first entering one of the compounds with the idea of purchasing typical examples of pottery etc the women rushed in a state of panic to hide their treasures but no sooner did they understand that we wished to take away nothing that they did not wish to sell and at a price for which they were willing to exchange than we were almost mobbed by would-be sellers."[12]

Sir Richard Tangye was a museum patron of a different kind. In 1880 he and his brother George gave £10,000 toward the cost of building the Museum and Art Gallery. Their wealth came from the manufacture and export of equipment and tools, including hydraulic jacks and steam engines—the heavy machinery that built the infrastructure of empire. A bronze plaque in the museum entrance hall commemorates the Tangye brothers, and the adjacent foundation stone bears the legend "By the Gains of Industry we promote Art." Not only is Tangye's patronage part of the colonial process, but also the Australian Aboriginal artifacts collected on one of his visits to company offices in Australia can be seen as part of a complex system of redistribution of cultural and economic resources.

In presenting these examples I do not wish to undervalue the indigenous contexts of anthropological artifacts—which would be an extreme form of cultural appropriation. Rather, I wish to demonstrate that the historical dimension gives an artifact a new role, a new identity. The artifact ceases to be a relic of an exotic past, or a work of art, or simply a piece of loot. Instead it becomes symbolic of complex colonial and postcolonial relationships, and can inform our understanding of the present-day world.

THE COLONIAL LEGACY

When we were editing the labels for the installation on the collectors, one of our teachers advised me that the term *British Empire* would be unfamiliar to Birmingham schoolchildren. If this assessment is correct, it demonstrates how knowledge of the colonial past has been suppressed and how postwar immigration to Britain has been systematically decontextualized. This is also evidenced by the current debate about future immigration from Hong Kong in the playing out of what Douglas Hurd, then home secretary, called "the last chapter of British colonial history."

Paul Gilroy, in his review of the Hayward Gallery exhibition of black art called The Other Story, pointed out that to be black and British was thought by some to be an impossibly compound identity. In his view, the challenge facing black English people today is to strive to integrate the different dimensions of their hybrid cultural heritage more effectively. In doing so they may discover that their story is not "the other story," as the Hayward show suggested, but the story of England in the modern world.[13] Ethnographic artifacts are a resource with which to explore hybrid cultural heritages, and they represent a point in time when the stories converge.

The final piece in the Gallery 33 jigsaw is the exhibit at the entrance of the exhibition: a photomontage of the people of Birmingham commissioned from a local photographer, Vanley Burke. It is captioned with the word *welcome* in twenty-six different languages, and the associated label text raises some questions about the nature of the multicultural city. The original plan was to support the photomontage with an interactive video that would explore the development of Birmingham's industries and its world markets and would profile the experiences of migrants to and from Birmingham. As it turned out, funds were not available to develop this exhibit. However, this concept would be interesting to explore, and it would make a valuable

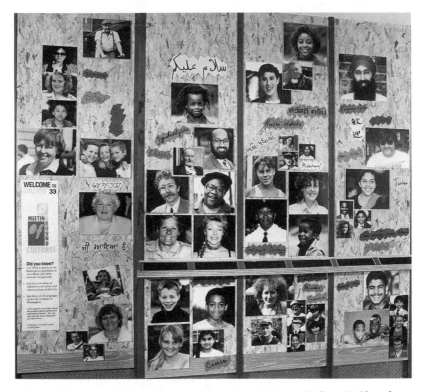

Fig. 8-8. "Words of Welcome" photomontage at the entrance to Gallery 33. Photo by John Cope, courtesy of Birmingham City Museum and Art Gallery.

exhibit at other museum venues in Birmingham, such as the recently acquired branch museum Soho House, the home of the eighteenth-century manufacturer Matthew Boulton, located in Handsworth, now one of the principal areas of black and ethnic minority settlement.

THE RESPONSE

If Gallery 33 is to be a venue for discussion of issues about cultural identity and cultural representation, then it follows that questions about the nature of the exhibition itself and the wider role of the museum will feature on the agenda. Therefore, part of the exhibition has been set aside to accommodate and display visitors' comments. In this way the process of consultation and dialogue started by the advisory group is being continued. A full-scale visitor evaluation was carried out in 1991. At this stage, the general tone of both the professional responses and the visitors' comments recorded in the gallery is positive and enthusiastic.[14] Discussion and comments received to date focus on a number of key issues. For example, the high-tech visual presentation and the dominance of metals in the exhibition design have been questioned. These are partly a designer signature, and the response is largely a matter of personal taste. However, the use of metal supports and finishes can be seen as an ironic reflection on the source of Birmingham's wealth and patronage, which was based on worldwide trade in metals.

The "Collectors" diorama and interactive video have been well received. However, Afro-Caribbean commentators have pointed out that interest in collectors is primarily a Eurocentric preoccupation. The recent debate over the Into the Heart of Africa exhibition at the Royal Ontario Museum in Toronto, which questioned the motives of the messages conveyed about the colonial context in which the collection was formed, shows how controversial such an approach can be.[15] The labels in the "Collectors" diorama have been further examined with the advisors in the light of this controversy. The exercise revealed how crucial and difficult it is to convey explicit, rather than implicit, critiques in labels and supporting information.

Pilot work by Susan Werner on school use of the interactive video indicates that the video does raise issues about Britain's colonial past and perceptions of "otherness." She studied five school groups, aged seven, ten, and twelve, from both multicultural and white catchment areas. Her study revealed that many children have little knowledge of Britain's colonial past—without which they cannot expect to understand present-day Britain. The focus on the Solomon Islands provides a neutral territory in which to explore concepts of race and "otherness" because the absence of Solomon Islanders in Birmingham removes it from the multicultural reality of the classroom and playground. When asked to make a collection of artifacts representing their cultural identities, white children had difficulty in defining their identity, while black children had no difficulty in defining themselves, bringing to school artifact signifiers of their cultural identity and their "difference" from their classmates. The visit to Gallery 33 gave black children a sense of parity and validated aspects of their daily cultural experience. On the other hand, the visit challenged the ethnocentrism of those coming from monocultural backgrounds and encouraged them to view themselves in a broader context.[16]

Gallery 33 provides a resource to develop what is called in Britain "antiracist" or "race-equality" education (trying to change negative attitudes) in addition to and distinct from "multicultural" education (celebrating difference). Work in the gallery raises many new questions about teaching cultural diversity in a museum context. Further work is going on with museum staff, teachers, and pupils to develop teacher materials and to promote examples of good practice related to the gallery.

Antiracist materials are being incorporated into museum events, which are an integral part of the gallery. The first events program sponsored by the gallery, called Family Festivals, has focused on the religious calendar and is growing both in its own confidence and in its popularity with the public. Performers and audiences have been drawn from different communities centering on schools or cultural organizations. Celebrations of Greek Orthodox Christmas, Chinese New Year, and Ramadan, for example, have brought in children as performers who, with their parents and friends, are first-time visitors. The atmosphere is relaxed and celebratory, and performers report feeling a sense of belonging.

The language used in the exhibition provokes different responses. While some people have celebrated its brevity and strength and the way it speaks directly to the visitor, others have questioned the use of specific words and phrases. It was to be predicted that the language used in Gallery 33 would be contested; the writing of the labels has revealed to me how curators customarily use different language conventions to describe the "other." There is a need for a new vocabulary before objects can be treated equally. We can improve upon and develop this aspect of the exhibition in the future.

The question of creating new stereotypes has arisen with reference to photograph and artifact selection. The job of creating an exhibition involves a severe editing process. For example, in this exhibition about world cultures there are only a hundred photographs and 350 objects representing just over a hundred different cultural groups. However, at the same time a museum display is a very prestigious phenomenon. These two factors conspire to create a situation in which every image or artifact used in an exhibition is automatically in danger of becoming a stereotype. I see no way around this problem, except to be aware of the issue when making selections—to know why particular choices were made and to be explicit about who made them. This problem was frequently addressed in the advisory group meetings and will become a key issue for future discussion.

In their different ways, both museum policymakers and black and ethnic minority commentators have at times voiced the expectation that Gallery 33 should focus on the heritages of local black and ethnic minority groups. Gallery 33 resisted this temptation, for this would have effectively marginalized the black and ethnic minority presence within the museum service, confining it to the anthropology gallery, which would then have become on a par with festivals, marketplaces, and temples as one of the acceptable places in which to express cultural diversity.[17] On the other hand, by using a worldwide approach, Gallery 33 leaves other museum departments free to focus on black and ethnic minority history and art as appropriate. This fully integrated approach will ensure that black and ethnic minority people see something of themselves in all parts of the museum service.

Never before has an exhibition in Birmingham been subject to so much discussion and debate even before it opened. Nevertheless, some skepticism has been expressed about the open agenda and invitation to dialogue that are conveyed by the direct, open-ended questions individual exhibits ask viewers to consider. How much scope is there for long-term participation and influence by communities? Can the museum provide the resources necessary to sustain the commitment to dialogue? What are the implications of this for the museum as a whole? These are the questions currently being asked by black arts activists, who have now shifted their interest from specific projects such as Gallery 33 to concerns about the cultural politics of the museum institution as a whole. This, and a voiced realization among colleagues that Gallery 33 represents a challenge to some current practices, have combined with other factors for change to lead to the formation of a staff study group that will examine multicultural issues in many areas of operation. This group will make recommendations on areas where policy needs to be reviewed and the kind of forum in which the review should take place.

THE PROCESS

The Gallery 33 project is an experiment in refiguring the relationship between the museum and its visitors, and has demanded a different approach at every stage of development. Curators, graphic designers, conservators, photographers, and educators have all been required to work in unfamiliar ways to address new concepts or new technical processes. This management of change is a complex and challenging process. There is a high degree of inertia and inbuilt conservatism within organizations. Change is perceived as risky and requires external validation.

Experience suggests that there are several additional key factors. There is the necessity to confront both personal and institutional racism. Curators are trained both to be authorities and to exercise authority, and sometimes find it hard to move away from these positions when they find themselves working on unfamiliar terrain. It takes time to develop trusting relationships with new contacts and colleagues, to learn to value different thinking, and to be receptive to alternative perspectives. There is ambivalence about sharing power. It is good to be the person who tells the story, and there is a reluctance to relinquish that position. All these problems are intensified by the conventional leadership models prevalent in organizations that favor direction rather than facilitation.

A continuing commitment to addressing such issues at both institutional and personal levels is an important part of realizing the full potential of Gallery 33. There is no blueprint, and the process is as important as the resolution. The opening of Gallery 33 has implications across the museum service. This is reflected in the way critics ask about its relationship to broader museum philosophy on black and ethnic minority arts and in the way museum staff are talking about the issues raised. The process of creating the exhibition has been something of a personal journey for those most closely involved in it. The institution itself now can learn from the process. The experience gained from this and other museum initiatives needs to be evaluated, consolidated, and incorporated into policy and practice.

In conclusion, what does Gallery 33 achieve? Gallery 33 re-presents the museum's ethnography collection and reflects the heritages of local ethnic minority communities. At the same time it is an exhibition about cultural diversity. But the focus on collectors and collecting achieves several additional goals: deconstructing colonialism, recontextualizing twentieth-century migrations, and integrating the histories of white Britons and ethnic minorities. In doing so, Gallery 33 moves forward and becomes more than an essay in cultural diversity: it begins to inform and challenge all of Birmingham's communities.

NOTES

1. Michael Diamond, "Ethnography Display Brief" (Birmingham: Birmingham Museum and Art Gallery, 1985).

2. Arts Gallery Purchase Committee minutes, April 1881, quoted in Stuart Davies, *By the Gains of Industry: Birmingham Museums and Art Gallery, 1885–1985* (Birmingham: Birmingham Museum and Art Gallery, 1985), 23.

3. Linda Bauer and David Heald, "Birmingham Museum Visitor Survey Report" (Birmingham: Birmingham Museum and Art Gallery, 1984).

4. Birmingham Inner City Partnership, "Inner City Profile, 1983" (Birmingham: Birmingham Inner City Partnership, 1983).

5. Jane E. Peirson Jones, "Initial Design Brief" (Birmingham: Birmingham Museum and Art Gallery, 1987).

6. Blacks and ethnic minorities currently make up about seven percent of visitors to the Museum and Art Gallery. See J. Henderson, "Complete Visitor Survey Results" (Birmingham: Birmingham Museum and Art Gallery, 1990).

7. Jane E. Peirson Jones, "Interactive Video and the Gallery 33 Project," *Museum Development* (June 1990), 10–16.

8. Ida Wench, "Southern Cross Log," Melanesian Mission, March 1921, 36.

9. Nick Stanley, "The Unstable Object: Reviewing the Status of Ethnographic Artefacts," *Journal of Design History* 2, nos. 2–3 (1989), 107–22.

10. Nicholas Thomas, "Material Culture and Colonial Power: Ethnological Collecting and the Establishment of Colonial Rule in Fiji," *Man* 24, no. 1 (1989), 41–56.

11. Percy Amaury Talbot, *In the Shadow of the Bush: A Story of the Ekoi of Southern Nigeria* (London: Heinemann, 1912), foreword.

12. Ibid., 219.

13. Paul Gilroy, "This Island Race," *New Statesman and Society* (2 Feb. 1990), 30–32.

14. Full results of this evaluation are discussed in Jane E. Peirson Jones, "Gallery 33: Objectives and Responses," *Museums Journal* 92, no. 1 (1992), 32–33. For reviews of Gallery 33 see Barbara Tilson, "Totems and Taboos," *New Statesman and Society* 4, no. 146 (1991), 26–27, and Anandi Ramamurthy, "Multiculturalism Incarnate," *Museums Journal* 92, no. 1 (1992), 33.

15. Jeanne Cannizzo, *Into the Heart of Africa* (Toronto: Royal Ontario Museum, 1989).

16. Susan Werner, "Report on the Findings of a Pilot Study of Schools' Use of the Interactive Video 'Collectors in the South Pacific' in Gallery 33, Birmingham Museum and Art Gallery," in "The Use of Ethnographical Collections in the Representation of Cultural Diversity in Local Authority Museums in the 1990s" (M. Soc. Sci. thesis, University of Birmingham, 1990).

17. Ivan Karp, "Identity: Personal, Cultural and Social," paper presented at the Salzburg Seminar on Museums and Their Communities, Salzburg, Austria, 1989.

CHAPTER 9

The Soul of a Museum: Commitment to Community at the Brooklyn Children's Museum

MINDY DUITZ

I will be exploring the subject of museums and their communities through a case study of the Brooklyn Children's Museum, focusing particularly on the years from 1984 to 1989. What is important about our story is the analysis of what it means to commit an institution thoroughly to serving nontraditional museum audiences—in particular, how this decision affects both the internal operation of the museum and its relationship to the outside world.

What is possible—and imperative—for the Brooklyn Children's Museum is not going to be possible or appropriate for every institution. However, it is critical that all museums realize that serving their communities does not mean just a seasonal program or an annual exhibition in the "community gallery." It is an ongoing activity that requires clear policy and sufficient resources. It is also a reflection of an institution's mission and its vision of its role as a public educational institution.

Museums are well aware of the increasing pressure on them to become more responsive to changing populations. Yet the fear inherent in change and in sharing power prevents most institutions from exploring the full range of possibilities. At the Children's Museum, embracing this challenge has brought renewal and direction to the museum's future, and our experience can perhaps serve as a model for others.

Following a brief summary of the museum's history, I will outline in detail the planning stages and the institutional changes that resulted in new programs that now define our relationship to the immediate community. (Given the many possible definitions of the word *community*, let me state that for the purposes of this essay it means the residents of the neighborhood surrounding the museum.)

THE HISTORY OF THE BROOKLYN CHILDREN'S MUSEUM

The Brooklyn Children's Museum was the world's first museum for children and has stood for more than ninety years in its original location since opening in December 1899. It was founded as an alternative to traditional museums, and it revolutionized museumgoing. The museum was conceived as experience-oriented rather than object-oriented, and it developed participatory exhibitions along with special techniques for teaching with museum objects. Although committed to collecting, the museum's primary focus was helping its young audience to understand themselves and the world in which they live. The museum's unique commitment to its audience and its belief in learning through firsthand experience have remained constant throughout its history. At the same time, this philosophy also encouraged experimentation while remaining faithful to the institution's original mission.

Throughout its history the museum has been at times more successful and at other times less successful in fulfilling its mandate to meet the needs of its visitors. In particular, the demographic changes that have occurred in our part of Brooklyn, as in many inner-city neighborhoods, over the past thirty years have forced a thorough reexamination of the museum's mission, contents, facility, and future.

The Children's Museum is in Crown Heights, a neighborhood formerly dominated by white middle-class immigrants (Jewish, Italian, Irish) and known for its luxurious brownstones and open spaces. Located a mile from the Brooklyn Museum and the Brooklyn Botanic Garden, the area was a haven for families looking for refuge within New York City. Two Victorian mansions in Brower Park (formerly Bedford Park) housed the original Children's Museum.

Beginning in the 1950s, the population of Crown Heights began to change, and the neighborhood, whose residents currently total

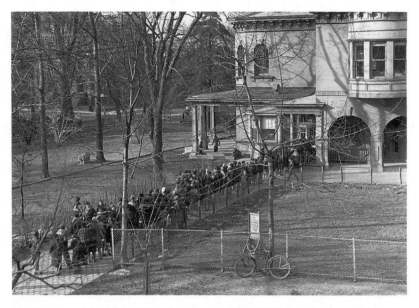

Fig. 9-1. One of the original Victorian mansions (Smith Building) that housed the museum, circa 1936. Photo courtesy of the Brooklyn Children's Museum.

about 120,000, is now home to mainly Caribbean (West Indian and Haitian) and African American families. One of the largest Hasidic communities in the United States also calls Crown Heights home, having settled there after World War II.

Current demographic information on the museum's community indicates that unemployment rates in the area (ranging between twelve and seventeen percent) are among the highest in the city, and single-parent families make up sixty-one percent of the households. More than half the households earn less than ten thousand dollars per year, and thirty-four percent have publicly supported incomes. Twenty thousand school-age children live in Crown Heights and attend public schools that rank academically among the poorest in the city.

In 1967, the old museum buildings were torn down because of serious deterioration, and a new facility was planned, to be constructed with city funds. This was a critical time for the institution. Debate on whether to move the museum to a more economically stable and accessible location was heated and protracted. Community residents organized a sit-in in the mayor's office to demand that "their museum" be rebuilt on its existing site.

At this point it is important to explain the museum's relationship to New York City. Like many of the city's cultural institutions, the Children's Museum operates in a private-public partnership with the city. It is a wholly independent, private, nonprofit corporation and receives major operating funds as well as capital support from the city's annual budget. Therefore, it is no surprise that when the mayor decided to support the community's position, the museum's leadership elected to remain in Crown Heights.

This decision had an enormous impact on the museum. Its staff had to operate a citywide institution with an international and national reputation in a neighborhood that had come to be perceived as dangerous. Furthermore, the museum was situated far from public transportation and had no provision for parking. All of this has significantly affected the growth and operation of the institution, and has been at once a serious disadvantage and the greatest opportunity.

While the new museum building was under construction and its collections were in storage, a temporary facility known as Muse opened in 1968 to continue to provide public service. Muse emerged as the first storefront museum in New York State. Its programming reflected the needs of area residents, integrating the performing arts and social and civic issues into a program of arts and sciences. When the Children's Museum moved into its new home in 1974, Muse was incorporated as a separate entity, New Muse, by a local board of trustees. It operated until 1988, when the institution folded because of funding and management difficulties.

The new building (which did not open until May 1977 because of problems with the New York City building code) is a unique underground structure featuring a turn-of-the-century subway kiosk as the entrance, and a "stream" running the length of the "people tube": a neon-lit enclosure connecting four levels of exhibit space. Designed by Hardy, Holzman Pfeiffer, the dramatic structure was filled with technological exhibits. The museum's extensive natural-science and cultural collections were not much in evidence. In the desire for innovation, the museum seemed momentarily to have forgotten its past as well as the recent success of its programming at Muse.

In addition, the museum's planners neglected to deal with issues stemming from the changes in the community. By putting the building underground (to conserve energy and preserve the rooftop as outdoor space), the museum lost its physical presence in an architecturally distinctive neighborhood. Essentially, people no longer knew it was there; those looking for it had difficulty finding it. The architects also

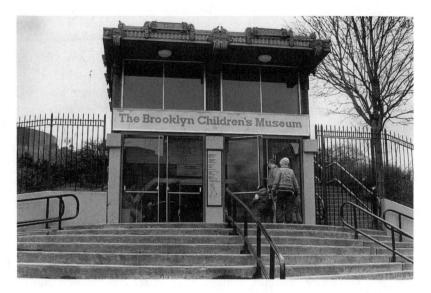

Fig. 9-2. Entrance to the museum's new building through the original 59th Street trolley kiosk. Photo by Rodney K. Hurley, courtesy of the Brooklyn Children's Museum.

created an extraordinary geography around the building and on top, not realizing the security and vandalism problems that would result. Moats and bridges and all sorts of things to climb on and hang from—especially when they are hidden from sight—are magnets for neighborhood kids.

During the 1970s visitation suffered as crime rose in the area. Staff were counseled to leave as early as possible and in groups. The museum was never open in the evening, and was closed on certain holidays to avoid crowds. A sense of belonging to the community was not in evidence.

THE MUSEUM'S NEW MISSION: INCREASED COMMUNITY INITIATIVES

When I became the director of the museum in 1984, I met with local legislators to begin to develop a relationship with them and learn about their perceptions of the institution. They made it clear that they were interested in the museum's future hiring decisions and in our sensitivity to the community. Internally, museum staff were torn between wanting to care for and serve neighborhood kids and blaming "management" when behavior problems arose. Both inside and out-side the museum, the issue of the museum's relationship with its com-munity needed attention.

The museum was clearly ripe for change and a new direction. Following the departure of some entrenched staff and board members, the museum was ready to enter into a formal planning process. We began in 1986 with a review of our mission statement, and completed strategic plans for every department by 1987.

The museum's newly adopted mission statement reads as follows:

> The Brooklyn Children's Museum provides interactive and enter-taining experiences in an environment designed for children and their families. It presents exhibitions and other programs which draw upon issues relevant to the interests of its visitors. These ex-hibits and programs encourage visitors to develop an understanding and respect for themselves, their cultural heritage and their environ-ment, and the heritage and environment of others. The Museum has a commitment to collecting and preserving objects that support its educational functions. The Museum serves families in the greater New York City metropolitan area and reflects the diversity of that community.

By involving all board and staff members in the process of developing the mission statement, we achieved a consensus as to its meaning. In the expanded mission statement (which includes a more detailed dis-cussion of the mission as well as a conceptual framework for all programs), the three major areas of focus are the *self* (its physical, emotional, and intellectual aspects), the *community* (which extends from the immediate family to the world community), and the *earth* (the natural environment). The museum's aim is to examine the inter-dependency among these areas in relationship to the present, the past, and the future, with the point of departure always based in the present and all exploration beginning with the self. Core exhibitions are being planned based on each of the three concept areas; research is just beginning on the topic of the community. The expanded mission state-ment also includes policy decisions regarding the immediate commu-nity, such as "The Brooklyn Children's Museum is committed to al-lowing unaccompanied children to visit the Museum" and "The Museum provides training opportunities ranging from high school and college internships, to adolescent and adult volunteer oppor-tunities for all members of the community. The Museum will strive to broaden the base of cultural diversity in the museum profession by providing these opportunities, including collaboration with other professional institutions."

What emerged was a formal commitment to serving the local community while continuing to serve New York City and the metropolitan area. This responsibility was too large to be met by relying on informal relationships between caring instructors and visitors or on occasional programs. Rather, an institutional mandate was put in place to assure that the financial and staff resources needed to support this commitment would be available. This meant having a board, leadership, and staff committed to searching the soul of the museum. All aspects of the institution were to be reassessed based on the overall goal of increasing the number of community initiatives.

Staff

We began by looking internally, at the board and the staff. The museum's personnel represent a microcosm of the city. More than fifty-five percent of the staff at all levels are people of color, including four of nine department heads. As compared to most museum staffs, the staff of the Children's Museum is exemplary in its balance. At the same time, this balance carries with it all the complications and difficulties present in the broader society. For example, it meant that during the planning stage, when we listed the opportunities and threats facing the museum, racism appeared as both an external and internal issue. Indeed, many people were uncomfortable looking at the word written on a chart. But uncomfortable as it is, the complex phenomenon of racism is present in many ways at the Children's Museum. Internally, for example, it means that the hiring and firing of staff has an added dimension. European American, Latino, and Asian American staff commuting to Crown Heights are sometimes viewed as outsiders who are taking jobs from local residents.

The importance of working on recruitment and internal staff problems before proceeding with related community initiatives was clear. We determined that it was essential to seek out staff who were interested in working in a minority community and to work with existing staff about their mixed feelings toward one another and toward our audience. Training now includes lectures and written information about the ethnic backgrounds of the museum's visitors, and discussions to try to counteract prevailing stereotypes. Job listings were targeted to attract minority candidates, and contacts with placement services were developed to recruit staff from nontraditional sources such as the theater and social-service fields, thus broadening both our reach and the pool of talent we could draw upon. Hiring from the community became a priority.

It was also determined that the museum's unique situation demanded a commitment to increasing cultural diversity in the museum profession by establishing a major training program. The training of museum staff takes many forms. Almost all weekend and part-time staff are high school and college students who are carefully supervised and trained in a variety of areas: public relations, clerical work, and programs and exhibitions. Every summer ten youngsters come to the museum as part of the city's Summer Youth Employment Program, which includes a career day and an orientation to the world of work. Many of these summer participants stay with us throughout the year in paid part-time positions. We are beginning to form a corps of talented new professionals ready to enter the museum field or work in related fields.

To help us cope with a growing audience and an ever-increasing number of visiting schoolchildren, in 1988 we also started a professional museum education training program. In its third year, the program includes three groups of interns annually, and is attracting graduate students definitely interested in museum work as well as those exploring the possibility. In addition to helping us reach more people and providing role models for visitors, these interns and part-time staff provide an unexpected benefit to the museum: they bring energy and enthusiasm that inspires and rejuvenates the permanent staff.

In looking at the board of directors, we recognized the need for more diverse representation. (Currently, the board is thirty percent black [African American and Caribbean] and forty-five percent women.) We are particularly interested in recruiting board members from among those in prominent positions in the business community, which has proven to be very difficult since the obvious candidates are few and in great demand. Another complication lies in achieving a balance between the desire for local representation and the pressing need for a well-connected board. Through board training (which includes professional workshops and museum orientation sessions) combined with the museum's increasing reputation for excellence, we hope to attract more qualified candidates and expand minority representation on the board within the next two years. In 1990 the museum applied to the Minority Board Placement Project of the New York City United Way, and two excellent potential candidates have already been referred to the museum's nominating committee.

Public Affairs

The Children's Museum also entered into many dialogues with the outside world—particularly the world of politics. The museum had not previously pursued the support of the area's elected officials (city, state, and federal), and as a result was not receiving full financial support. An even greater problem was that the museum and its programs were not well known by these legislators. This became apparent in a rather dramatic way following the firing of a public relations assistant in 1986. The disgruntled employee proceeded to mount a campaign to "save the Brooklyn Children's Museum," charging that we had secret plans to move out of the community, discriminated against local schoolchildren, had racist personnel practices, etc. His extraordinary persistence lasted for over six months and included picketing, leaflets, and radio and press coverage.

Had we been better situated with local community leaders and politicians, we would not have had to spend so many hours defending and explaining ourselves. In the end, however, we made many new friends. Most of the officials we spoke with comforted us with tales of

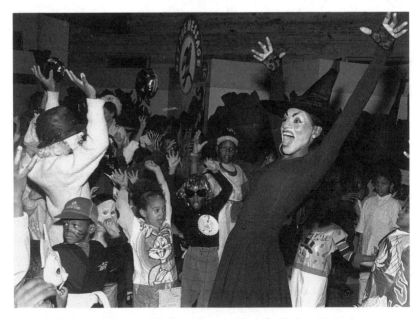

Fig. 9-3. The museum's annual Halloween party. Photo by Rodney K. Hurley, courtesy of the Brooklyn Children's Museum.

their own irate employees or constituents. Funding from government sources has increased, and involvement with the local community board, parks department, and youth services committees has put us in a leadership position. Activists who years earlier had fought to keep the museum in the community are now reinvolved as volunteers and contribute financial support to programs for local kids.

The museum's volunteer corps also reflects its location and community. Volunteers are mostly senior citizens and young people who have spare time and also find a welcome and a refuge in the museum. We are as committed to training our volunteers as we are to training staff. Given the museum's relatively small size, we have the opportunity to get to know volunteers and can provide them with work that is of personal interest to them. They are, of course, a major source of good public relations.

Public affairs staff and volunteers are now a visible presence throughout Brooklyn at festivals and business events. More important, the museum has become a center for community activities. Recently, and for the first time ever, the museum's theater was the site of

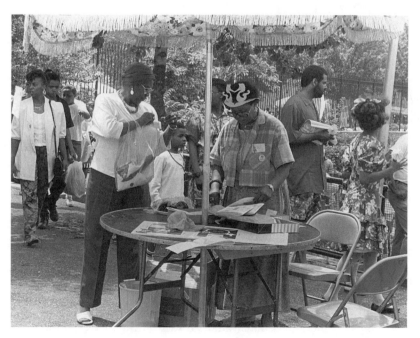

Fig. 9-4. Volunteers at the museum's annual June Balloooon family arts festival. Photo by Rodney K. Hurley, courtesy of the Brooklyn Children's Museum.

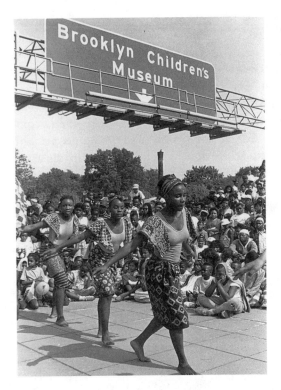

Fig. 9-5. Performing for capacity crowds at June Balloooon. Photo by Rodney K. Hurley, courtesy of the Brooklyn Children's Museum.

a local wedding! In addition, the museum is now open at night for special events, such as the popular Halloween Monster Mash. Outdoor workshops and programs include a Friday-evening summer performance series in our rooftop theater. June Balloooon, an annual family arts festival begun to reestablish the museum's presence in the community, attracted thirty-five thousand people in 1991. In order to include community residents at important events, such as our ninetieth-anniversary gala, we have sought underwriting to permit us to offer a range of affordable ticket prices.

In 1989 our public affairs and education department began a collaboration with the Crown Heights/East Flatbush Parent Advocacy Center of the Center for Law and Social Justice of Medgar Evers College (City University of New York). A series of forums delving into issues affecting families in the community began in February of that year. Subjects included educational survival in the black community, safety, and child care. The collaboration is an outgrowth of our work with neighborhood kids, and represents a growing recognition of the museum's importance as a community resource.

In August 1991 Crown Heights became the focus of nationwide media attention following the death of a Caribbean American child struck by a car driven by a Hasidic man and the retaliatory attack that killed a young Hasidic scholar. Days and weeks of racial violence ensued, involving many young people. The Brooklyn Children's Museum was well positioned to serve as a resource for youngsters struggling to understand the violence surrounding them. City and community leaders met in the museum to develop strategies to address the immediate crisis. The press discovered the museum as a place where the two conflicting communities regularly came together. Museum staff implemented programming, including collaborative work with local agencies, to address longstanding issues highlighted by these tragedies: racism, isolation, anger, and fear. The importance of the museum's mission has never been more obvious.

PROGRAMS AT THE BROOKLYN CHILDREN'S MUSEUM

Program decisions are based on the interests and needs of our audience, which are determined through a variety of research and evaluation techniques. The museum reaches 175,000 people annually. Over sixty percent of our audience comes from Brooklyn (twenty percent from the immediate neighborhood), and the remaining forty percent from the other boroughs, the greater metropolitan area, and visiting tourists. Most of our visitors are working-class and middle-class families, equally divided between white and black. (The museum serves very small Hispanic and Asian audiences.) On any given day a cross section of people from local communities and families from throughout the metropolitan area come together at the museum. For many children (and parents), a visit to the Brooklyn Children's Museum is their first exposure to the world of museums.

Being a museum with multiple and overlapping audiences that range from neighborhood residents to international visitors means meeting the needs of all those audiences. We believe exhibitions and public programs must be of the highest quality, and equally interesting to parents as well as to children. Programs designed to meet the needs of special audiences reflect the museum's commitment to serving a diverse constituency, as it is defined in our expanded mission statement.

In keeping with this commitment, the museum has allocated the time, staff, and funding necessary to carry it out. It has taken several years and many small steps to accomplish what we envisioned in the area of community programming, and we are really just at the beginning. Below I outline some of our program initiatives to date.

Public Programs

Throughout the year the museum provides an enormous array of public programs, including performances, workshops, special events, and films. Community interests, as well as those of our broader audience, are always taken into consideration in planning these activities. During Black History Month we invite guests from a wide range of professions to speak to museum visitors about their lives and achievements; winter holiday celebrations explore many cultures; and dance companies present a wide range of styles, from classical to Caribbean, and we include local performance groups whenever possible.

In conjunction with our early-childhood area—a gallery developed to meet the needs of a rapidly growing audience of very young children—we are planning to develop a series of programs on parenting. Our goal is to provide resources and information to teen parents, single parents, and visiting families. This program will involve collaboration with local service organizations. For example, a special program serving homeless parents with small children who live in shelters was organized in 1990 in collaboration with the New York City Department of Cultural Affairs and the city's Human Resources Administration. This project was funded with both city and corporate dollars.

School Programs

In 1987 the Aaron Diamond Foundation approached the museum and suggested we develop a special classroom curriculum in order to teach natural science to disadvantaged children. The result of that project, Evi"dents", is now available to local schools. The curriculum teaches children about the properties of living things by focusing on food chains, eating, and particularly on teeth. The foundation has funded an award-winning exhibition on the same subject, which opened in the spring of 1990. Full evaluation of the school program and the exhibition has helped assess the success of our approach and materials. The exhibition based on this project is of interest to all our visitors, but grew out of a need for effective science education in schools such as those in Crown Heights.

With funding from the New York State Council on the Arts, the museum developed another curriculum, entitled Night Journeys, that is about sleep and dreams. It is currently being implemented in two school districts: the museum's home district and another in Brooklyn that represents an Asian and European American community. A major exhibition exploring the physiological, personal, and cross-cultural experiences of this universal subject opened in the fall of 1990. Night Journeys includes a section entitled "Home Is Where I Sleep," exploring children's first cultural and personal experiences of home.

It is from the background research we are conducting for this exhibition that we hope to begin to refine the focus of the core exhibitions on the concepts of the self and the community. As with previous exhibitions, we anticipate working with teachers and students in formulating curricula on these topics, involving visitors in evaluations that will help shape the exhibitions, and working with advisory groups of subject specialists and visitor focus groups in the development process. Where our present collections do not adequately cover aspects of the exhibitions, we will seek the necessary objects. Current plans, for example, call for acquisition of material to augment our small Caribbean collection so that it will better reflect community interests.

After-School Programming

One of our main objectives was to increase after-school visitation. We particularly wanted to address the problems that sometimes arose when unaccompanied children came to the museum. With funding from the New York State Council on the Arts, a pilot latchkey program was begun in 1986 in collaboration with the local school district. It was extremely efficient and effective for us to link up with an existing after-school program, as the museum then did not have to recruit youngsters directly. Bus transportation was provided, and a special curriculum was designed, along with a workbook to be used at home or at the after-school center. Over 650 third through sixth graders participated in these visits, which introduced the museum to them as a place of individualized learning. The curriculum also recognized the need for social activity after school. Its informal approach to teaching included one-to-one contact and cooperative activities. At the end of the year, all participants and their families were invited to a special exhibition of student work. After several years of refinement, the Afterschool Adventures program now reaches twelve hundred children from three school districts and other after-school programs. We anticipate doubling that number within the next few years.

Above, I mentioned the museum's problem surrounding the issue of unaccompanied visitors. The Children's Museum is the only museum in New York City, and one of the few in the country, that welcomes children visiting without adult supervision. This has been a longstanding tradition, but has not been without its difficulties. Although caring instructors have always inspired individual youngsters, there was never an institutional commitment to these unaccompanied children. Security staff were extremely hostile because of frequent discipline problems. Young children came with even younger children in their charge. Other visitors were often intimidated by the behavior of these unsupervised children.

It was time for a clear policy on the question of whether children should be allowed to visit without adults, and if so, how they should be accommodated. A task force was organized, consisting of security, program, public relations, and administrative staff. After many long months of discussion, it was determined that it was important and in keeping with the museum's mission that we continue the practice of admitting unaccompanied youngsters, and we decided to set up a formal program. However, a set of rules and conditions needed to be imposed. The program required full-time staff; children needed their parents' permission to register; hours of attendance needed to be limited; and a full series of ongoing programs had to be developed to meet the interests and needs of these repeat visitors. When we had established all of these, Kids Crew was born.

The public relations concerns associated with Kids Crew were enormous. We did not want to be wrongly perceived as kicking the neighborhood out of the museum. Many possible techniques of publicizing the program were discussed, such as notifying local leaders and politicians, distributing flyers, speaking to community groups, etc. We finally decided to begin in a very low-key way by talking to the kids themselves. In the spring of 1988, one of our instructors, a neighborhood resident herself, was installed in the reception area with a box of file cards and pencils. She greeted every youngster and proceeded to explain about the great new program that would be starting up soon. Names and addresses were collected, and "Kids Crew kids," as they are now known, were thrilled with her attention. A small grant from Citibank enabled us to hire a full-time Kids Crew intern in the summer of 1988, who continued to expand on this informal phase by

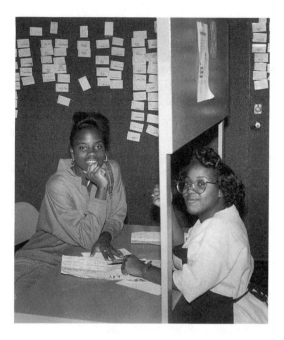

Fig. 9-6. The Kids Crew desk. Photo courtesy of the Brooklyn Children's Museum.

formally registering participants. By the end of that summer over two hundred kids were registered. At the close of the first year there were five hundred, and by the summer of 1991 the number had grown to twelve hundred.

Using interns, instructors, and part-time staff, the Kids Crew desk was in operation, but programming was not yet in place. Funds for a full-time staff person were sorely needed. We went to yet another public source, the New York City Youth Bureau, with the results of the privately funded pilot phase and in 1989 received a grant to staff the program. An after-school coordinator with experience in community youth work is now in charge. Funding has been raised to develop intensive museum curricula relating to our exhibitions, the children's library, and the greenhouse. Kids Crew members are beginning to conduct their own programs, such as a biweekly dance class.

To join Kids Crew, children are required to register via a consent form signed by a parent or guardian. Members are welcome every day after school from three until five o'clock, and on weekends and holidays from twelve-thirty to four o'clock. Upon entering the museum they sign in at the Kids Crew desk (an attractive component of our entry area) and put on a special identification badge, which is turned in at the end of the day. The desk is always staffed, ensuring that children receive personal contact and program direction each time they visit. Recordkeeping includes notes on attendance, problems, successes, etc., giving us detailed information about participants and helping to evaluate museum activities for this audience.

Kids Crew participants range in age from seven to fourteen, and include some very motivated youngsters who visit on an almost daily basis. They come primarily from the immediate Crown Heights neighborhood—ninety percent live within a twenty-minute walk. Attendance varies from ten to twenty-five youngsters on an average day after school to over fifty daily on weekends and holidays. In the summer the numbers can double. A Kids Crew Council has been formed recently to advise the after-school coordinator on program interests and help develop prototype exhibitions and other activities.

Some Kids Crew kids are obvious leaders. Others have tremendous needs. We provide volunteer opportunities in the museum for those interested, and where possible we refer children who need help to appropriate social service agencies. We are very clear about the fact that we are a museum and that our training and expertise are not in counseling or health care. Yet we feel an obligation to be aware of resources that we can direct people to, though we accept that there are indeed limits to what we can be and do.

In 1989 Kids Crew kids testified on behalf of the museum at public hearings on the city's budget. We made sure they had permission from their school and from their parents, but they wrote their own speeches and delivered them. It was clearly a learning experience for them, but in addition they brought down the house. Two Kids Crew kids received full scholarships to attend a summer archaeology program in Colorado through the Crow Canyon Archaeology Center. Four others attended an environmental education camp sponsored by the New York State Department of Environmental Conservation.

The Children's Resource Library (a research library for kids) is another integral part of the museum's after-school programming, as well as a favorite place for neighborhood youngsters. Many come every day to do homework and, particularly, for the individual attention they receive from the library staff. Very young children have a cozy area where they can listen to tape-recorded stories. Library programs stress literacy and research skills and include a newspaper and video club.

Within the library, Collection Connection is an enormously successful program with Kids Crew kids and with parents. It consists of a series of discovery boxes filled with objects related to a particular

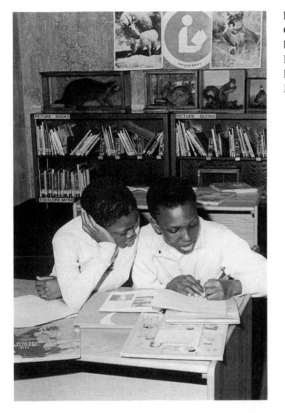

Fig. 9-7. After school in the Children's Resource Library. Photo by Rodney K. Hurley, courtesy of the Brooklyn Children's Museum.

subject, such as coins, insects, or symbols, along with accompanying worksheets. A box about African American culture and another about Jewish ritual are among those designed in response to the museum's immediate community. Children are directed to books, photos, and other library resources to research the contents of their box. We have received glowing feedback from parents who tell us that their children are performing better in school after attending the program. Computers have been also added to the library and will run software programs related to exhibitions and activities taking place in the museum.

Some grants have been received and multiyear funding is being sought to expand the Kids Crew program to include a multitiered program of training and career development. The first tier will be the Junior Curator Program, for children aged ten through seventeen. Ten to twenty Kids Crew members will be trained throughout the year to assist museum instructors working with the public, and eventually to conduct programs themselves. Participants will receive individual instruction, including emphasis on work skills such as reading schedules, punctuality, and so forth. A second tier, the Teen Intern Program, will be designed for fourteen- through eighteen-year-olds, and will give young people their first paid work experience. Interns will work seven to twenty hours a week in collections, exhibitions, education, or administration. Seminars and workshops on careers and academic training will be part of the program. We believe Kids Crew will serve as a model of institutional commitment to community needs for museums as well as for other cultural, recreational, and educational organizations.

CONCLUSIONS

In December 1989 the museum opened a retrospective exhibition entitled The Oldest Kid on the Block in celebration of our ninetieth anniversary. Sorting through the museum's archives and reviewing its history was an important exercise: it reminded us not to forget the past, and it confirmed that what we are now doing is part of a long tradition. The museum's original purpose continues to be valid, and in fact has inspired the birth of over 250 children's museums in this country and around the world. What was revolutionary in 1899 is as important today as it was then.

As part of The Oldest Kid on the Block we started an alumni project, hoping to hear from people who had spent their childhoods at the museum during past eras. Many wonderful stories unfolded, and we made some into an oral-history video installed in the exhibition. The guest of honor at the opening was a ninety-year-old woman who grew up a mile from the museum. She and her sisters used to come especially to see the museum's renowned doll collection, as they had only one doll at home. In her ninetieth year, this alumna made a ten-thousand-dollar contribution to the museum in recognition of the important role it had played in her life. When she visited she told me how thrilled she was that the contents of the museum were as important and exciting as she remembered them being over eighty years before. This is but one of many stories that illustrate the impact of the museum on individual lives. I hope I will be able to hear the reminiscences of today's Kids Crew kids when they return to the museum in years to come.

Not all museums can or should follow the direction we have

taken. It depends on location, mission, size, and audience. As we move toward a much more diverse society and museums are called upon to participate in understanding and celebrating that diversity, though, it is important for them to identify what should be done to serve visitors and potential visitors. For the Brooklyn Children's Museum, developing a social conscience has become an integral part of our mission. It has given the institution a direction and an opportunity that is at once overwhelming and inspiring.

CHAPTER 10

Compañeros and Partners:
The CARA Project

ALICIA M. GONZÁLEZ AND
EDITH A. TONELLI

Composing this essay was not easy—not that we should have expected anything connected to the CARA (Chicano Art: Resistance and Affirmation) project to be easy. We realized that to write an essay that would be the product of a true partnership—in the spirit of the project—and would also respect the complexity and richness of what was often a difficult and fragmented process of exhibition development, we would have to present a kind of case study of a work in progress. In it we would have to include our thoughts and feelings as well as those of some of our partners, or *compañeros,* in the project. The development of the CARA exhibition has been as much a process of achieving consensus as it has been an ongoing process of negotiation, beginning with the first proposal in 1983 and ending with the closing of the exhibition at its last venue in 1994.

The Wight Art Gallery at the University of California, Los Angeles, and the CARA National Advisory Council organized Chicano Art: Resistance and Affirmation, 1965–85, an interpretive exhibition of work from the Chicano art movement. The planning process represented an attempt to document and analyze, in the most inclusive manner possible, the roots and complexities of the most recent, significant, and unified development of Mexican art and culture in the United States—Chicano art. The advisory group determined that the basic assumption of the project would be that there is a distinct art that arose from the dynamic, interdependent relationship between El Movimiento (the Chicano civil rights movement of the 1960s and 1970s) and a significant segment of the expressive community of Americans of Mexican descent, and that this art was identified by its creators and participants as "Chicano."

The advisory group's mission statement for the project, written at the July 1987 national planning meeting at the University of California, Los Angeles, reads:

> Chicano art is the modern, ongoing expression of the long-term cultural, economic and political struggle of the Mexicano people within the United States. It is an affirmation of the complex identity and vitality of the Chicano people. Chicano art arises from and is shaped by our experiences in the Americas.

The language of this statement reveals that what began as an objective, third-person, outsider statement ("of the Mexicano people") very quickly became a first-person statement ("our experiences in the Americas"). Note also the recognition of the hemispheric interconnectedness among people on all sides of the United States' borders. This kind of shifting and blurring in the perception of who "we" and "they" are has been a keynote of this project.

This blurring is evident even in the first visual element that was produced for CARA: its logo (see Figure 10-1), which subtly emphasizes the shift between the observer and the observed. The acronym CARA, which means "face" in Spanish, became the symbol for the exhibition, although it was created unwittingly: it was recognized long after the title had been approved. (Because it occurred serendipitously, it was also about the only thing in the project that did not have to be negotiated.) The eyes of the CARA face suggest the visible gaze that reflects back on its viewer; we realized this would conceptually embody the reflexive nature of the entire exhibition process. From a practical perspective, it is important to note that there was no immediate agreement on whose eyes to use—those of a man? a woman? a famous Chicano or Chicana?—even though they were planned to be stylized. In the end, the CARA design team, Willie Herrón and Patrice Roberts, came up with a brilliant solution: Herrón superimposed images of the eyes of his twin sister over images of his own, and used elements of both. People had strong reactions to those eyes, but it was important to the project that in such a very early stage we were able to

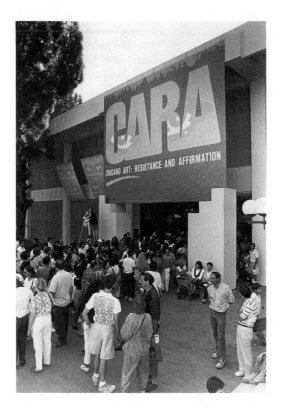

Fig. 10-1. Entrance to the CARA exhibition, Wight Art Gallery, 9 September 1990. Photo by ASUCLA Photography Department, courtesy of Wight Art Gallery, University of California, Los Angeles.

find a creative solution that reflected the inclusive spirit of the organizing process. The three colors of the logo (shades of burgundy, lavender, and yellow) were chosen deliberately, to avoid not only an obvious postmodernism but also the traditional stereotypical view of what a "Mexicano" palette is. The torn and ragged feeling of the background and the layering of the type and eyes were intended to suggest the surface of a wall in the barrio that has been painted and papered and peeled and repainted.

One reason why most final design decisions, including that about the logo, did not cause serious debate is because Willie Herrón, one of the most important mural artists of the Chicano movement in southern California, was one of the principal designers for the project. (Although the Wight Art Gallery's full-time designer on staff, Thomas Hartman, coordinated and contributed to the design process, the organizing group was committed to hiring a Chicano design firm to work with us.) Although Herrón and his partner, Patrice Roberts, were immediately made part of our organizing team and given the background on the goals and objectives of the project, very little further coaching was needed. The involvement of an outside design team is not unusual for a large-scale museum exhibition, but the criteria of community experience and sensitivity to the issues that were considered in hiring this team and the open process used to choose them reflect an important objective of this project, one that is related to the nature of the organizational process. This objective, which we will lay out shortly, is the focus of this essay and flows out of CARA's other goals and objectives.

The primary goal of the CARA exhibition was to fill the need for a national exhibition and accompanying publications and programs that present an interpretation of the Chicano art movement that is inclusive, yet coherent and of high quality; scholarly, yet accessible to a broad public. Within that goal, however, there were four important objectives. The first three were the documentation of an underrecognized American art movement; an expansion of the audience for and the understanding of Chicano art and culture; and the presentation of evidence for a reexamination and redefinition of American art and culture. The fourth objective was, in a way, an outcome of the first three, and at the same time has been a strong element in their realization and refinement: a reevaluation of the process for organizing museum presentations of artworks of living cultures (especially those cultures not represented in museums by a critical mass of professional personnel) so that the organizational process reflects the spirit and values of the culture itself. (We of course do not leave the dominant Anglo culture out of this formulation. However, it is rare for the Anglo culture, one of the multitude of cultures that make up the ethnic mix of the United States, to be underrepresented, either in values or in personnel.) It is this fourth goal—which for us meant developing a process with flexibility and with the spirit of the Chicano movement— that determined the choice of Willie Herrón as designer, and that underlay the complex organizational structure of the project.

The structural elements of the process, which were developed in a series of planning conferences and meetings conducted with the assistance of planning grants from the National Endowment for the Humanities and the Rockefeller Foundation, reflect the desire to bring an overview of national scope and direction together with the particularities required by regional representation. The heart of the project has been the large advisory council of between forty and fifty scholars, artists, and administrators, which has met in various forms at least once a year since 1986 (and which we hope will continue to meet after the exhibition closes), with a series of smaller meetings and travel to various regions in between. This council in turn formed many smaller working groups, including nine regional committees, a three-member national executive committee, a five-member national selection committee, a three-member editorial board, five task forces, and a design team, with the Wight Art Gallery serving as the host institution and facilitator.

These committees and task forces, composed primarily of Chicano arts professionals, artists, and humanities scholars, functioned as both consulting and decisionmaking bodies and actively participated in all aspects of the planning, implementation, and evaluation stages. There was a system of checks and balances, and layers of accountability at every stage. In addition, the national honorary committee, headed by Edward James Olmos, provided support from members of the public-service, education, business, and entertainment sectors of American society, and recognized those who have made substantial contributions to Chicano communities nationwide. The roster of committee members included individuals and groups as diverse as the United Farm Workers of America organizer Cesar Chavez, the musical group Los Lobos, the Congressional Hispanic Caucus, and prominent Chicano scholars.

The structure was logical and necessary when considered in relation to the fourth primary goal of the project: developing a new model for the inclusion of underrepresented groups in the process of determining how to present those groups' cultural expressions to a diverse public. The unique (if a bit cumbersome) configuration of the process we used was created by the Chicano advisors in conjunction with the Wight Art Gallery staff as a direct response to the advisors' and the staff's concerns about the Chicano community's relationship to the proposed exhibition. Our concerns reflect a growing tendency on the part of many underrepresented groups and some museum people to question the traditional museological processes that separate a group's knowledge of its own culture from the institutional means of displaying that culture. Under particular attack is the conventional designation of a single curator who ultimately determines what is to be presented.

Perhaps this need to be open to examining and altering traditional museum roles was the greatest challenge of this process. It meant that we constantly had to acknowledge and challenge our assumptions, beliefs, and values, and to struggle to build consensus. Therefore, because one of the most important results of this process for both of us was a blurring of the insider/outsider, we/they distinction, we decided that in this essay we would describe our reactions to this challenge from our individual vantage points, doing so as individuals who came to this project from different communities rather than as insiders or outsiders to a particular community. This approach was suggested by Alicia after Edith proposed a skeletal structure for this essay that alternated our participation in a typical institution-to-community fashion, that is, with Edith talking about goals and structure and Alicia discussing the community's reactions. That format set up an opposition between the "objective" neutrality of the analytical scholar and the subjective, emotive, informational role of the community representative. In contrast, the process we would be describing was quite consciously developed by the large advisory council and its executive committee, and all parties who engaged in the project—artists, scholars, gallery staff—entered into it with a spirit of camaraderie, a shared sense of history and mission, and a commitment of time and expertise.

Because of the disparate disciplines and experiences represented by the project participants, the committee recognized from the start that the notion of community had to be redefined for the specific contexts we were to discuss. It is not just that the Chicano community for this project encompassed regions throughout the United States that had their own cultural histories, which in turn defined the aesthetics from those areas. We realized that this project involved other communities as well, and that the notion of who was an outsider and who an insider shifted from one context to another. For example, Edith's role shifted from that of an outsider to the community of Chicanos to that of an insider within the institutional context of the museum at UCLA and in the community of art historians, where she is a specialist on American murals and public art. Alicia's role shifted from that of an insider to the Chicano community to that of an outsider to the UCLA institutional context and back to an insider's role in the broader museum context. What evolved during the course of the project was a *compañerismo* that flowed from an understanding of the need for different kinds of expertise to come forward when necessary and to recede into the background otherwise. The meaning of the word *compañero* may be "companion," "workmate," "associate," "friend," or "counterpart." The choice of this language for the title of this essay was meant to reinforce the bridging of the we/they gap and symbolize the opening of the possibility for true collaboration.

By using the first person to address some of the feelings that were engendered by the project, we are acknowledging and affirming that all of us bring our whole beings into each arena of discourse and that we can only attempt neutrality. The subjective "we" enters into every aspect of the negotiation over whose truth should be presented and how. The fact remains that, from the start, the CARA exhibition was fraught with challenges that sometimes brought back the intensity of emotion that was experienced during the civil rights movement and that for some of us continues as part of our personal struggle. The exhibition process has engendered strong feelings, and it is the fear or the perceived impropriety of experiencing those emotions in a professional setting that often keeps us as professionals from crossing these interpersonal borders and, therefore, from examining some of our most limiting cultural assumptions.

The only way to understand how the CARA process opened up these issues of confronting assumptions and shifting roles is to explore examples of the individual perspectives and responses that shaped this process. In this essay, because of space and logistical restraints, we can present only our two personal perspectives; however, we can also suggest the multiplicity of responses that we experienced as participants. In the following section we will describe our own role disruptions and the borders we were forced to cross. We begin with descriptions of how we defined ourselves in this special CARA context, and continue with our individual recollections.

Alicia González, a member of the three-person CARA executive committee, comes from within the bilingual Mexican American community that, from a traditional perspective, is the "subject" of this inquiry, but she is also part of the scholarly anthropological community that is traditionally the "observer" culture. Edith Tonelli, the director of the Wight Art Gallery and a member of the five-member selection committee, is part of the museum culture that is traditionally set up to do the "observing," but is also part of an art historical and American studies scholarly community that sees mainstream cultural institutions, procedures, and values as "subjects" for analysis as well; she personally comes from a bilingual Italian American community. Obviously, then, we each walked into the first official CARA planning session on 7 November 1986 with different intentions, expectations, and feelings.

ALICIA: In 1985 I received a letter and a telephone call inviting me to participate in a meeting to advise on the potential for an exhibition on

Chicano art. Up until that time I had been working for the Smithsonian in Japan on an exhibition entitled Rice in Japanese Folk Culture, which brought forty traditional artists from seven prefectures in Japan to the Festival of American Folklife. This exhibition had taken two years of planning and negotiation on many different levels, from diplomatic negotiations to fundraising to developing the design of the space on the Mall with Shun Kanda, an architect at the Massachusetts Institute of Technology. I had already started working on the Smithsonian's plans to commemorate the quincentenary of Columbus's arrival in the New World, and I was very concerned about how peoples whose histories had not been previously recognized would be represented at that institution. I did not know what to expect, but I felt that Chicano artists and Chicano art merited an exhibition that would allow people to understand how the art had emerged and how it fit into the broader contexts of American art and art in the Americas.

I was familiar with some of the developments and controversies related to the exhibition Hispanic Art in the United States: Thirty Contemporary Painters and Sculptors, which was organized by the Corcoran Gallery of Art in Washington, and I had my reservations about how that show had been conceived. I was also aware that if a show was going to be mounted at UCLA, great efforts would have to be made to bring the Chicano community into the exhibition plans. I had no knowledge about the Wight Art Gallery specifically. I did know, however, that the group that was being assembled was excellent, and I decided to wait and see how the meeting evolved.

After having done field research among Latinos and Mexican Americans in many parts of the United States, a question that I had in my mind focused on the issues of how Chicano art could be defined nationally as a phenomenon separate from the art of other Latino communities and how the integrity of those communities could be given their due. The challenge would be in also recognizing the diversity within the Chicano community itself. This would not be an easy task, and any attempt would have to consider the historical and cultural contexts. My concern with any representation of a people and its culture is how well that representation maintains the dignity and integrity of the group. Knowing full well that there is an extensive bibliography on the meaning of the word *Chicano,* I thought it would be important to leave people with an understanding about what *Chicano* meant and, more precisely, what Chicano art was.

When I first met with other members of the advisory team, I remember feeling a great sense of pride in my colleagues, who had matured to a level at which they could appreciate and accept one another's accomplishments, contributions, and points of view. It was clear from the moment that individuals began to confide in one another that we Chicanos did not want to be exploited. This was an issue because Chicano art, largely because of the visibility of murals, had become an exploitable commodity, with little credit or benefit going to the artists and with little weight given to its meaning.

As the planning meeting progressed it became clear that diverse regional representation was very important. It is easy to reinforce regional biases when a movement is concentrated in certain key locations in the United States. El Movimiento had its beginning in areas largely populated by Chicanos, where there was a constant reinforcement across time and space. Therefore, we worked quite consciously to identify key individuals, artists, and scholars who understood or were a part of the development of a self-conscious Chicano art and history throughout the United States. This allowed us to sit at the table and compare and contrast the different streams of Chicano art and history: how they had begun, how they converged, and how they differed from region to region. The advantage of having representatives from different regions was that they were able to discuss parallel histories and link together the expressive forms that evolved in different parts of the country during certain periods, such as the mid 1970s (Figures 10-2 through 10-4). Because the artists and scholars involved in the meeting also included ethnomusicologists and theater and film specialists, what was being envisioned by the group was an exhibition that was complex and vital, and that incorporated the nuances that could so easily be missed or ignored by members of the non-Chicano community. By maintaining the importance of each medium that told part of the Chicano history, scholars from the literary, music, and filmic disciplines were able to add another level of insight, each area complementing the work of the others. In this way, we were able to enhance the textural and aural appeal as well as the visual. We knew that what is in many cases perceived as trivial by people outside a group is often considered to be extremely important by the community itself. In this case, the exhibition would have to stress both the material and the performative aspects of the Chicano art movement and demonstrate the integration of those aspects into the living cultural system.

In a three-day period the group selected its executive committee and several of the other committees described earlier, and broke down into task forces that defined not only what we felt were important

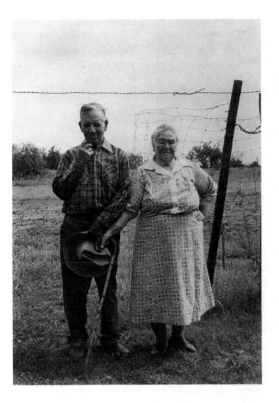

Fig. 10-2. Kathy Vargas, *Tio Gregorio y Tia Luisa* (1974). Photo by Grey Crawford. Reproduced by permission of the artist.

issues but also affiliations and characterizations that had to be avoided at all costs. For example, because the nature of the exhibition was clearly centered on the human rights issue, the group believed that the exhibition should not have funders who historically were associated with circumstances against which the Chicano community had struggled or who currently were adversely affecting the human rights cause in the world. This notion of solidarity with peoples of other nations recurred throughout the years of planning. Chicano art is a product of our experiences in this country and with our neighbors, and has influenced and been profoundly influenced by other peoples who have undertaken similar struggles.

From the beginning the CARA advisory committee's sense of identity was clear. This made the decisionmaking process easier, for the group knew what it wanted. Many, if not most, members of the committee had been a part of El Movimiento as students, artists, community activists, or workers, and were still involved in the ongoing struggles on different levels. The group was not afraid of the work

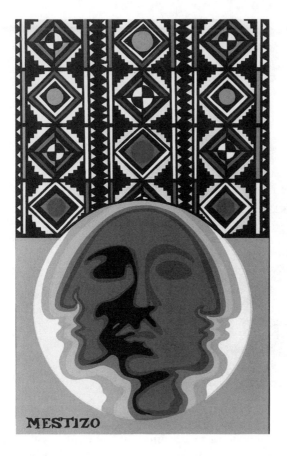

Fig. 10-3. Amado Maurilio Peña, Jr., *Mestizo* (1974). Photo by Grey Crawford. Reproduced by permission of the artist.

involved and was committed to the exhibition. This meant that the exhibition became more than any one curator's "next show," being instead the responsibility of many. The disadvantage in doing an exhibition of this nature in this way was that one could not assume that the level of understanding about how an exhibition is done was equal throughout the group. The staff at the Wight Art Gallery and others on the advisory committee had to bring to the discussion their expertise in museum culture in general along with specific information about exhibition design, publications, and storyline. It was necessary to stress that it would be impossible to present every work of art considered important by every member of the committee; the group had to be selective. But the committee did have its priorities, and often those did not converge with the staff's priorities. The process, as it

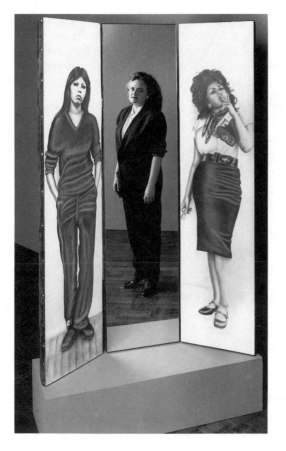

Fig. 10-4. Judith Francisca Baca, *Las Tres Marias* (1976). Photo by Grey Crawford. Reproduced by permission of the artist.

evolved for both committee and gallery staff, was constantly to determine what important issue would be the next to be negotiated.

EDITH: When I walked into the large, high-ceilinged Humanities Conference Room in the Renaissance-style Royce Hall at UCLA on 7 November 1986, I was nervous but certain that whatever happened, we were about to embark on something historically significant. I knew that despite our openness and willingness to attempt new dialogues, I and the gallery staff generally thought of ourselves as the "we" of "art museum professionals" and of any individuals outside of that museum culture as the "they" of the "community." "We" were inviting these people to our table of power, and "they" would, we hoped, "assist" us in producing an important exhibition. I had no idea at the time how

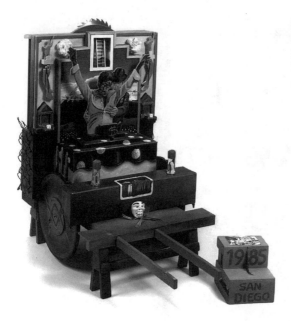

Fig. 10-5. David Avalos, *Donkey Cart Altar* (1985). Photo by Grey Crawford. Reproduced by permission of the artist.

limiting that very common museum assumption was for all of us—but I learned very quickly.

Whatever ownership of the project we felt at that time was based on the fact that at the gallery we had been working since late 1983 on an idea for an exhibition of Chicano art. At that time professors Cecilia Klein and Shifra Goldman and graduate students Maria de Herrera, Holly Barnet-Sanchez, and Marcos Sanchez-Tranquilino approached me, the new director of the Wight Art Gallery, about doing something that presented Chicano art in a context different from the conventional, modernist, art-museum presentation, where the focus is on the formal qualities of an object to the exclusion of social or cultural context.

By the spring of 1984, the gallery had written its first planning-grant proposal to the National Endowment for the Humanities, with the help of Goldman, Sanchez-Tranquilino, Barnet-Sanchez, and Victor Sorell. This proposal requested funds for the gathering together of thirty prominent, primarily Chicano, members of the scholarly and artistic communities whose interests and writings had been focused on Chicano art and culture, to discuss the propriety, feasibility, and format of some kind of presentation at UCLA. The project was denied funding in that first round because the funders were uncomfortable with the term *Chicano,* which some thought was inappropriate and even offensive to some members of the Mexican American community, and with the political resonance of the art. In our second submission to NEH, in the spring of 1985, we explained more carefully—and with additional letters of support from the Chicano community—that the group of artists, scholars, and activists we were presenting had chosen this term in the mid-1960s to identify themselves, and continued to use it as a designation of conviction and pride. We were granted the funds on the second try, in January of 1986, even though we were warned that there had been considerable debate. That debate never did cease, not least because of the political controversy that developed in 1989 and 1990 over claims of obscenity in art supported by the National Endowment for the Arts and a push to abolish the NEA altogether. Unfortunately, this public concern over use of taxpayers' money to support "inappropriate," controversial, or political art made all of the public agencies, including NEH, extremely sensitive to criticism from political conservatives. In fact, the project was later turned down twice by NEH for implementation funds, even after the Endowment's peer panel had recommended funding. We were very fortunate that the Rockefeller Foundation came to our aid in both the planning and implementation phases.

Once the planning funds became available in July of 1986, we began to research and plan the three-day November conference that would bring together almost forty scholars, artists, and administrators from all over the country to discuss what was needed and how it should be done. I was not prepared for the degree of anger, skepticism, and commitment that would come from all sides at that first meeting, but I did know that my job at that meeting was to listen and to hear.

What happened at that first meeting and the ones that followed, including the countless selection committee and task force meetings and trips, was that my understanding of management and leadership and my dual role as the financially accountable party who was also involved in conceptual development underwent radical alteration. Before we even got to lunch that first day, I was forced to face the managerial consequences of a project that emphasized self-representation and consensus. I had already accepted the unpredictability of the outcome and the risk of confrontation, conflict, and racial tension. I am, after all, not a Chicana, and my institution is white, middle-class, and mainstream, and does not have the best track record of inclusion and diversity. But self-representation and consensus were requiring me to act more often as a facilitator in service to the group, assisting them to produce the kind of exhibition, publications, and programs that they wanted. On the surface, this reversal of roles seemed to be a perfect way for this underrepresented group to have a voice in the representation of their community's art and to assert their authority over the representation.

However, it slowly and painfully became clear to all of us that the only way we could create something truly new was for us to think beyond the roles of directors and their assistants—no matter who was in each role—and truly become partners, *compañeros,* on a journey, shifting roles when and if necessary. And because it took us so long to understand what was needed, we were able to develop and maintain that *compañerismo* only in small and focused ways, rather than welding it into the more comprehensive structures and objectives of the project.

Now that we have given you some taste of how we began this process, we will discuss the issues that raised the most controversy, were the most resistant to resolution by consensus, or caused the most excitement and promise for each of us. In general, for most of the Chicano advisors who gathered for this project—when they were acting in their traditional "subject" roles—the key concepts raised were: (1) self-representation; (2) the inclusion of a multiplicity of expressive voices within the unified front of the movement and this project; and (3) the adherence to a certain Chicano spirit, aesthetic, and set of values.

From the traditional art museum professional's perspective, accepting the goals and objectives of this project raised other key concerns: (1) finding ways to make room for and accommodate new partners (the new "insiders") without abandoning the responsibility that expertise demands; (2) developing and maintaining a coherent exhibition concept that kept "art" in the forefront without diminishing the importance of the social context; and (3) finding ways to acknowledge and communicate with our culturally diverse and uninitiated American audience, many of whom would not be middle-class, educated Chicanos or Anglos, as all of us on the project were.

EDITH: The following are some of the issues that for me resulted in the most provocation, elation, and deflation.

The forced reevaluation of how I manage and lead, and of how our gallery team normally works, led me to understand how many common, unspoken assumptions and values we in museums share, and how those who work outside of museums or who were raised with different values might have difficulty understanding them or might be unwilling to accept them without question. The key project objectives of a multiplicity of voices and self-representation not only destroyed our usual way of working at the museum, but also led all of us on the gallery team to challenge the formerly sacred curatorial process. In attempting to maintain the balance of an exhibition that was focused on what we all assumed we agreed was "art" (a foolish assumption!) but that also provided multiple layers of social resonance, and in trying to reinforce the collective spirit of this project, we forced ourselves into an analysis and deconstruction of our conventional and individualistic conceptualization and curatorial processes. This, plus the "re-constructing" we eventually had to do, cost us much time and lost us a few advisors and venues. It also brought out considerable skepticism from more traditional curators and directors about the quality of the art that would end up in the exhibition and the coherence of the presentation.

This issue of quality raises red flags in the art world. In American art museums, quality has usually been judged by a set of criteria that originated in a Western European aesthetic and that is considered applicable to any object under review—that is, the criteria are assumed to be universal. Working on the CARA exhibition led me to consider whether that show truly posed a new challenge to our traditional notion of quality. Did this encounter require us to expand our criteria for judgment? Were the values that Western philosophers have debated for centuries in need of revision? Were we being required to add other aesthetic theories alongside the one we hold sacred? Even after the many hours and long debates of the selection committee meetings, we found it difficult to come to a consensus on what exactly the criteria for judgment were. I personally felt, however (and some of my partners certainly have other opinions), that having both Chicanos and non-Chicanos participating in the process forced us all to rethink and expand our criteria rather than to restrict them.

The final room of the exhibition is titled "Redefining American Art." That room and that concept were the most troublesome for all of us from the beginning. If we truly were attempting to present evidence for a reexamination and redefinition of American art and culture, then we needed to address head-on these issues of quality and the universal application of our Western aesthetic. If for David Avalos or Esther Hernández there is no art without relevant content (Figures 10-5 and 10-6), then the CARA exhibition would have limited meaning if it did not convey an understanding of the artworks' context. Iconography in Chicano art comes not so much from other art as from living, popular

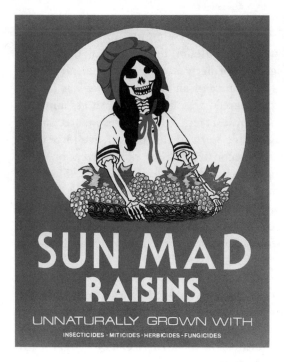

Fig. 10-6. Ester Hernández, *Sun Mad* (1982). Photo by Grey Crawford. Reproduced by permission of the artist.

forms (Figures 10-7 through 10-9). This is, of course, why in the past museums have tended to include Chicano art in exhibitions of "popular art" or "folk art." In other instances, we have created special, marginal categories, such as "socially relevant art," which of course are set up to be contrasted with "real" art. (Picasso's *Guernica* is always cited as the rare example of real art that happens to have social content—it is art precisely because we have judged that it "transcends" its content.)

We debated at great length exactly how we would present some of these questions in the last gallery. What knowledge could we expect the general public to bring with them or to absorb, and what was it that we wanted to communicate in the few minutes that most people would spend in that room? Did we want just to leave visitors with questions, or were there suggestions we wanted to make or conclusions we could draw from our study and analysis of this work, its cultural context, and its intentions?

We also asked who the audience was for this exhibition, and how we could communicate with them. With the CARA exhibition, the simultaneous challenge, cause of conflict, and stimulus to creativity

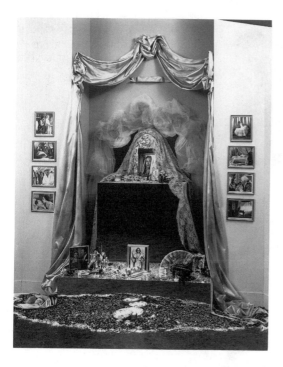

Fig. 10-7. Amalia Mesa-Bains, *An Ofrenda for Dolores del Rio* (1984). Photo by Grey Crawford. Reproduced by permission of the artist.

was the acknowledgement that our audiences are not us, whether Chicano or non-Chicano (a fact that is true of nearly every exhibition, but was particularly critical in this project). We all had to accept that there were very few who would come through the door with our eyes. Determining how our message will be received is never an easy or exciting concept for traditional scholars and artists to encounter; we are used to stopping at the level of determining what we want to say. Being concerned about who is listening and their level of visual or verbal literacy, or of interest, seems peripheral, or secondary at best. We in museums often see ourselves as the hosts, allowing guests to partake of our feast. This is a trap—for both host and guest. For the Chicano artists and scholars who saw themselves as representing their communities within the somewhat alien context of the museum, acknowledging their own distance from the experience of most Chicano visitors (another group of outsiders) was an important shift but one that was complicated to make.

The audience issues raised by CARA return us to the recurring question of what kind of balance we need between scholarship and accessibility in museums. Los Angeles, in particular, is confronting the

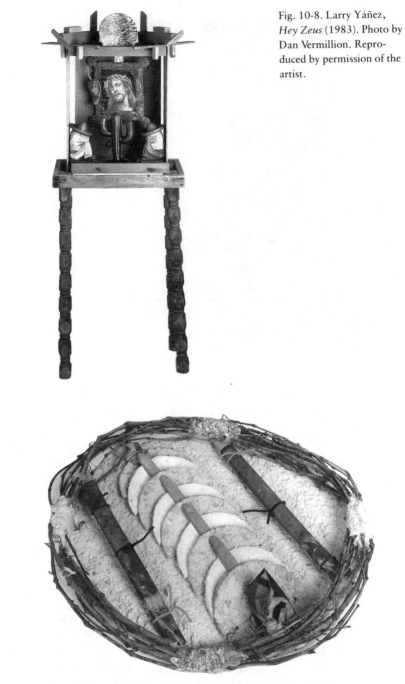

Fig. 10-8. Larry Yáñez, *Hey Zeus* (1983). Photo by Dan Vermillion. Reproduced by permission of the artist.

Fig. 10-9. Linda Vallejo, *Food of the Gods* (1984). Photo by Grey Crawford. Reproduced by permission of the artist.

challenges of being an increasingly diverse and multicultural city, and we are all finding ourselves ill-prepared to address the issue.

Finally, I would like to say that in agreeing with James Clifford, Edward Said, and many others about the unconsciousness of the West in dealing with non-Western cultures, and in acknowledging that there is both a need and a demand for change, I question the adequacy of our skills in *initiating* and *managing* the change. And this is where a project such as CARA can help us refine our theories and confront the practical world of working with groups of people. It is a common human tendency to resist the different in any form; recognizing this helps to explain what is facing all of us when we begin to cross cultural boundaries and discover our "discomfort zones." I was not, and still am not, comfortable addressing that which is emotional and value-laden; it is considered "unprofessional" and "non-neutral" in most business or scholarly communities. But I am claiming that unless we in museums, and those of us in universities as well, look at our jobs as including this kind of risk taking and confrontation, we will never accomplish the goals we often profess to have concerning the representation and participation of a diverse and multicultural citizenry, and museums and universities will fail once again to be leaders in American cultural life.

For my part, I learned a great deal about how and why communication among people breaks down and about the need to be willing to change rules and structures in midstream. I also suspect that we may always have to live with some ambiguity and unpredictability in these kinds of ventures, and let go of some of our ingrained expectations of what art exhibitions should be or look like.

ALICIA: What is to be gained by initiating a process that accommodates in realistic ways a community's notion of self-representation? In addition to the advantages mentioned already, we gained a shared sense of responsibility for what was ultimately presented, rather than succumbing to the feeling of alienation that might have resulted from an autocratically imposed and simplistic set of images based on uninformed stereotypes. The key here is that when a group of about two hundred people throughout the United States shares in the process of developing an exhibition, the group must also share the responsibility for its successes and failures.

This idea of sharing suggests another very significant expressive dimension that was brought to our attention by Ken Brecher, the director of the Boston Children's Museum: the importance of humor.

Here I want to emphasize my earlier point about nuance. We know that an object does not mean the same thing to all people. But the subtle and hidden humor that we shared in the process of developing the exhibition was also a humor that was playful and parodical. Sometimes it meant that we Chicanos were laughing at ourselves (intracultural humor). As time went by, the intracultural humor of the Chicanos was translated for our colleagues and became part of the humor of the group, including both the Wight Art Gallery staff and the Chicano artists and scholars.

Américo Paredes, one of my mentors, who is a prominent Chicano scholar and early pioneer (along with Roger Abrahams and Richard Bauman) of performance theory, equipped his students to see and value the social and historical contexts of performance, which may be captured only for a fleeting moment in a given performance (and, in a different sense, may be discernable even in a painting or other work of visual art). The performance approach that was so much a part of anthropology and folklore studies at the University of Texas at Austin in the 1970s is only now becoming popular. This is happening in part because of the demographic shift in this country. Changing population trends in the United States, particularly the increasing demands of growing minority communities, require that the museum community create a context that will help develop a better understanding of cultures, instead of relying on a fractured approach to groups. As well, the inability of the traditional museum world to interest late-twentieth-century audiences in exhibitions that continue to rely on nineteenth-century models that are now viewed as too formal or contrived is evident. As applied to exhibitions, the performance approach brings in both the tangible and intangible products of culture to illustrate how the dignity and integrity of a group can be maintained and reinforced in an exhibition that can still be presented in a formal museum setting.

This processual orientation brings to the foreground a moral imperative: the need to be conscientious and reflexive at each stage along the way. What it means to those of us who are social scientists is the reframing of what we perceive as critical distance. We must not fool ourselves into thinking that we have no stake in our roles in exhibition. Exhibition is one of the most viable ways to assert or reaffirm power, and this aspect of exhibition must be critically analyzed.

In a recent management training course that I attended, the facilitator mentioned that he was giving a course on cultural diversity in the workplace. My question to him was, did he teach managers to understand individuals from diverse backgrounds, or did he train individuals from culturally diverse backgrounds to accommodate themselves to the American mainstream? He didn't have an answer; he knew that he had to deal with cultural diversity, but he still did not know *how* to deal with it. I think many of us are in a quandary about how to deal with it. The increasing numbers and visibility of minority peoples in the United States today are forcing our society to deal with cultural diversity. But as a Chicana participating in the development of the CARA exhibition, I have been able to reinvest my energies into something that I know will help us all—not only cultural brokers but members of particular groups—to begin to deal with issues of the representation of diverse groups.

By investing a part of the self and allowing it to be viewed and (one hopes) appreciated and understood by others, there is of course the potential for criticism as well. But an environment for understanding diversity can only be created through experimentation and change, trial and error. The only way to know whether something is successful is by attempting to do it. To move a society from the nineteenth century, when museums were spaces that held objects, to the twenty-first century, when museums will be limited in what they can hold and must rely on the active participation of the people they represent, there must be an attempt to create new models. But this attempt can be made only through a partnership and a societal commitment. Museums must build a larger body of volunteers, a larger constituency, and a more active membership by looking to the obvious, rather than still believing that models of the past will continue to work with the people of the future.

The word *empower* was commonly misused (in my opinion) throughout the eighties to mean the turning-over or assigning to another some power or position of power. In many cultures power is still sacred and emanates from within. True power comes from a sense of identity, a sense of knowing, a sense of being grounded in a group. If this commitment to empower can be translated into a commitment to facilitate, then I believe that there will be less resistance on all parts and less of a feeling of having been invaded. The process created with the CARA exhibition did away with the traditional curatorial role that assumes that there is *one* person or group who is all-knowledgeable about specific phenomena. A process of facilitation reinforces the value of personal history, communal power, and personal and communal knowledge. We tend to disregard the fact that history is created by individuals. The CARA exhibition process continually reinforced this fact by identifying individuals throughout the country and incorporating their own points of view and then creating a place for them and their history in the show. The process was inclusive rather than exclusive, and encouraged a reciprocal relationship out of which future partnerships could be drawn. It dispelled the fear of the "other" and created a common ground.

The process of planning and implementating the CARA project was made logistically difficult at times by the continual interaction among the Wight Art Gallery staff, the many committees and task forces, and individual Chicano and non-Chicano consultants. Furthermore, it took place within an already demanding cultural context that called for inter- and intracultural sensitivity at all social and professional levels. However, despite the tremendous demands and inherent pitfalls, this interactive process has been followed faithfully because it has been crucial to the development of a model that encourages self-representation, inclusion, and diversity. This model provided the CARA participants—museum-based and non-museum-based alike—with a means of monitoring their contributions to the project, and of maintaining a critical approach to the subject matter as well as a self-reflective stance toward the process itself.

The power of the CARA exhibition development experience was recently summed up by the Los Angeles artist Judy Baca, a member of the national selection committee, who said during one of our planning meetings, "We made valiant efforts to think things through—every one of these sessions became a philosophical discussion. . . . In fact, I feel like I've been through an incredible course in Chicanismo."

Although the exhibition does not walk visitors through a formal academic curriculum, we do intend that the viewer will catch a glimpse of Chicano culture, hear a whisper of the language, and sense the power of humor in the Chicano community by looking at Chicano art—and maybe even get a feel for this thing called Chicanismo.

CHAPTER 11

Creating a Dialogic Museum: The Chinatown History Museum Experiment

JOHN KUO WEI TCHEN

The phrase "Falling leaves return to their roots" has been popular among Chinese immigrants in New York for a long time. It is a saying rich in multiple connotations. For many Chinese who were subject to the Chinese Exclusion Acts (1882–1943) and prohibited from becoming citizens, the phrase described the desire to return to their home villages. Despite the decades they had spent in the United States, anti-Asian racism kept them sojourners. Unwelcome here, they sought to retire back to and die in their home villages, or at the very least to have their bones sent back to their family graves. The phrase also suggests at least two other interpretations. In a more metaphorical and modern sense, falling leaves are subject to the unpredictable currents of blowing winds, implying a sense of alienation; returning to the roots can be understood as a search for origins or home. The phrase can also be interpreted in the sense that we are all subject to cycles of birth, growth, death, and rebirth; perhaps this is closer to the original naturalistic meaning. Finally, a rebellious contemporary twist on this saying, used by recent immigrants intent on settling in the United States, rephrases the saying as, "Let falling leaves root wherever they land."

These multiple connotations of such a simple phrase convey some sense of the diversity and complexity of the Chinese experience in the

United States. In order to give voice to this multivocal history, the Chinatown History Museum has been developing the theory and practice for a new type of history museum. Originally founded in 1980 as the New York Chinatown History Project, the Chinatown History Museum has experimented with a wide range of community-based approaches to historical research and public programming in our effort to document, reconstruct, and reclaim the 160-year history of what is the oldest Chinese settlement in the United States.[1] In 1990 we began the process of planning what we call a dialogue-driven museum, which will explore the previously unexamined roles of Chinese New Yorkers, non-Chinese New Yorkers, and tourists in the creation of New York's Chinatown.[2]

While the Chinatown History Museum seeks to reclaim this neglected past, we believe it must be done in tandem with the people the history is about. We want to bring together members from our various constituencies to talk, assess, and suggest. By so doing we hope to build a creative, convivial, and exciting educational space in which sustained cultural programming will facilitate the collaborative exploration of the memory and meaning of Chinatown's past. We want to fashion a learning environment in which personal memory and testimony inform and are informed by historical context and scholarship. The Memories of New York Chinatown exhibition, inaugurated during Chinese New Year 1991, is the laboratory in which this dialogic concept will be fully articulated. Out of this experimental exhibition has been emerging a plan for the full-scale development of a dialogic museum.

This essay is intended to help facilitate the discussion on how the museum community and cultural activists can reenvision museums and the communities they serve. We offer these ideas and practices to be freely copied and further developed. We ask only that you let us know what you've done and how it has worked out. We especially welcome critical comments, suggestions, and new ideas.[3]

A HISTORICAL MOMENT

As we mark the quincentenary of Columbus's arrival in the New World, countless celebrations and national debates have been probing into the very soul of *fin de siècle* America. What should this event mean for the United States of the twenty-first century? Should it be a celebration of Western civilization? Should it emphasize the nation's multicultural heritage, including the viewpoints of the indigenous peoples? Or does that put the already tattered social fabric at further risk? In the words of a *New York Times* op-ed piece, whose culture is it, anyway?[4]

It is clear that the very identity of the United States is at stake. During these contentious and very interesting times, at least three knotty, interrelated challenges face publicly oriented humanities institutions (and their staffs) and scholars. First, a great deal of concern has emerged about issues of cultural literacy and historical memory. While recent decades have witnessed a burgeoning of specialized studies of those social groups that traditionally have not been included in scholastic canons, critics have pointed out that academic scholarship seems ever more aloof from the general public. Besides the issue of insularity, one historian has termed this a crisis of "the wholes and parts": how can American history be presented as a larger synthesis without at the same time excluding most local and regional experience? No matter which side of the debate one is on, the basic form and content of historical practice are being reassessed.[5]

Second, since the elimination of racially defined immigration quotas by the Immigration Reform Act of 1965, the United States has been experiencing what many have termed "the new demographics." Asian and Latin American immigrants have been settling in our cities in unprecedented numbers, bringing with them a diverse range of cultures and a new energy. The great urban public has increasingly become majority minority. Traditional neighborhood boundaries have shifted. New conflicts have erupted—and new possibilities have surfaced.[6] Unless the humanities can more effectively provide forums to address racial antagonism, interethnic violence, the persistence of ugly stereotypes in the media, and other related thorny issues, scholars and institutions risk absenting themselves from meaningful involvement in public discourse on these issues. How can humanities institutions and scholarship respond to these "new" publics who have not traditionally been a part of "We the People"?

And third—as if the first two challenges were not enough—budget deficits have become a regular fact of life. Libraries and museums are being forced to close their doors for part of the week or curtail whole areas of programming for lack of funds. Consequently, the public venues for the burgeoning new scholarship are contracting. And the "new" audiences, which most institutions have not been able to reach, have not been actively lobbying with politicians to restore funds. A recent special issue of *Museum News* in which the challenges of this new cultural diversity for museum practice were discussed attests to the national dimensions of this issue.[7]

Many of the oldest and most established institutions are now reassessing their mission statements, board composition, programmatic commitments, and outreach activities. For example, the New-York Historical Society, which was founded in 1804, waited until quite recently to add its first Jewish member onto its largely Dutch American and Anglo-American board of directors. The N-YHS was just beginning to question its past inactivity and reach out to new audiences when in 1991 it was devastated by a huge budget deficit. A third of the staff, including the coordinator of its educational outreach programs, was laid off.

The much-criticized 1980s initiative by the New York State Council on the Arts for helping museums attract new audiences and the Common Agenda for History Museums coalition, spearheaded by the American Association of State and Local History, are but two examples of steps already taken to improve museum outreach to underserved communities and better integrate the new scholarship into museum exhibitions and programs. Unfortunately, in 1991 the arts council's budget was cut by forty-eight percent and the Common Agenda program severely cut back. At the same time, a number of studies have revealed a curious paradox: while historical scholarship has become more insular, there has been a great increase in the public's interest in historically based miniseries and films, theme parks, living history museums, and the like.[8]

Despite the insecurity and teeth-gnashing generated by these three challenges, when considered together these concerns offer a unique opportunity for creating a more resonant historical scholarship and a more engaging museum practice. Basic to all three concerns is the core question of how community experience and consciousness relate to historical discourse. It should be kept in mind that questioning the relevance of history for the public is hardly a new phenomenon. Some sixty years ago, in his presidential address before the American Historical Association, Carl Becker foresaw the potential irrelevance of increasingly professionalized historical study (and, by extension, history museums). He stated, "If we remain too long recalcitrant Mr. Everyman will ignore us, shelving our recondite works behind glass doors rarely opened." Instead, he noted that "our proper function is not to repeat the past but to make use of it." In his view, everyone is a historian, and the professional historian's goal should be to make everyone better historians.[9] This democratic and popular attitude toward the importance of history in the public's daily life has been rearticulated recently by the historian David Thelen and others, who insist that we are all involved in "rendering the past meaningful to ourselves and communicating these meanings to others." However, this activity has been "so integral to modern American life that it is largely unappreciated."[10]

This central issue of the role of history in everyday life can be recast in terms of each of the challenges mentioned above. For example, regarding the aloofness of and lack of interest in much historical scholarship, we can ask how historical research and writing can better speak to people's needs in exploring the meaning of the past. In terms of the new demographics, we can ask how new immigrants' lives as Americans are connected to established local and national cultures. And as far as museums are concerned, we can ask how new and old publics can be attracted into rejuvenated historical exhibitions and programs.

A DIALOGUE-DRIVEN APPROACH

As evidenced by the American Association of State and Local History's Common Agenda for History Museums program, there has been considerable discussion in the museum world about what Thomas Schlereth and others have called an inquiry-driven approach. Schlereth has urged that museums rethink their traditional collections orientation, so that collections can begin to reflect the needs of exhibitions, projects, and programs rather than holding the museum hostage to the limitations of an inherited artifactual base.[11] The 1988 conference at the Smithsonian Institution on the Poetics and Politics of Representation, the 1990 Smithsonian conference on Museums and Communities (of which this volume is a product), and the 1990 Chicago historical museums' conference on Venues of Inquiry into the American City: The Place of Museums, Libraries, and Archives, which was organized by the Chicago Historical Society, the AASLH Common Agenda program, and the Valentine Museum, represent notable and encouraging national movements in this direction.

In traditional museum practice, collections management and conservation have often consumed virtually all staff time. For older, established museums with large collections, an inquiry-driven approach shakes the foundations of this traditional practice, placing much greater emphasis on the assimilation by curators of insights from the voluminous new historical scholarship of recent decades and suggest-ing a coordinated planning process for exhibitions and collections development.[12] However, for many recently formed and more pub-licly oriented institutions, the inquiry-driven approach has become standard. This has certainly been true of the Chinatown History Museum. Our collections have largely been built from our various exhibitions, productions, and programs. There is no question that this makes for a much more coordinated effort between collections and public programs. Nevertheless, other problems quickly come to the foreground. If only for practical reasons, the great majority of mu-seum resources for public programs are allocated to the production of exhibitions. Once the exhibitions are installed, guards and the occa-sional museum educator are asked to take over, and often are the only points of contact between the museum staff and the public.

This lack of contact is especially troubling when the subject of scholarship and exhibition is a community that the museum is trying to attract into its membership. Even when done sensitively and well, exhibitions tend to speak in a single, authoritative voice, which pre-cludes meaningful give-and-take with visitors. For example, while an exhibition on African Americans developed for Black History Month one year may successfully bring in the local African American commu-nity, such annual efforts are all too often short-term forays, and are not usually followed up by sustained programming that can take ad-vantage of the new trust that has been developed. Many administra-tors and trustees naively hope that having one event in the museum about any given community will quickly translate into that commu-nity coming to other museum events and becoming members. Ever pressed for funds, museums often conflate the effectiveness of out-reach with the amount of membership dollars brought in, often over-looking the many nonmonetary benefits of a more sustained engage-ment with their constituencies. Tragically, such short-sighted tokenism often shuts the door more tightly against future collaboration with traditionally underserved communities.

The educational missions of many history museums tend to be implicit. A plentiful supply of exhibitions and programs is often evalu-ated only by attendance numbers, with audience interests, needs, or demands rarely incorporated into the planning or evaluation process. In this sense, exhibitions can easily become fetishes, displacing any actual engagement with those who do or do not come. It is a very effective way for museums to distance and insulate themselves from the public they claim to serve. Perhaps such an orientation can be described as talking *at* people. Nevertheless, a conversation between curator and audience is always taking place, even when it is not consciously thought through. Assumptions about the level of audience knowledge, attention span, interest, language abilities, and so forth are necessarily built into the exhibition design and content.[13]

Whether this communication between museum and audience is a lopsided and ineffective monologue or a mutually engaging dialogue has been the Chinatown History Museum's central concern. When people have "voted with their feet" and not come in, we have tried to understand what else will engage their interest. The CHM has sought to shape a museum practice that explicitly explores these dynamics, thereby regularly improving the quality of educational exchange among our scholars, production team, and constituencies. In contrast to collections-driven and inquiry-driven institutional practices, the CHM is seeking to develop a dialogue-driven exhibition and museum. In the following pages I will define what is meant by *dialogue* (which I acknowledge has become an overused term) and illustrate how the dialogic process drives our exhibitions and museum planning and practice.

WHAT PUBLIC NEEDS CAN HISTORY SERVE?

If we have learned anything since the Chinatown History Museum was founded, it has been that a community-based history organization can serve some very real and important needs felt by our constituencies. But these needs can be effectively served only by engaging in continual dialogue with people.

What, then, can a dialogue-driven museum mean? For us it has meant engaging with our audiences in mutually exploring the memory and meaning of Chinatown's past. It has meant learning how different people learn in different ways and helping to facilitate that process. And it has meant taking what we learn from these dialogues and further improving the planning and development of the organization. Ultimately, we seek to become an ever more resonant and responsible history center in which scholarship and public programs can help make a critical historical awareness a powerful factor in improving New York and the community for the future.[14]

Over the past ten years, the Chinatown History Museum has identified and tried to serve at least three needs. First, the reclamation of Chinatown's history has given recognition to individuals and groups who are normally passed over in the recounting of New York City history. Our exhibitions on laundry and garment workers, for example, have publicly validated both experiences and shown how they have constituted the lifeblood of the community. The public representation of what has usually been considered grueling and thankless work has lent a sense of the broader symbolic importance to the workers themselves and their families of what the historian Jacqueline Jones, in reference to the experiences of African Americans, has called the "labor of love, labor of sorrow." We have found that if an exhibition or public program is resonant with individuals' personal experiences, they begin to identify actively with the exhibition. And for the sons and daughters of laundry and garment workers, learning about their parents' experiences from a trusted third party augments their ability to appreciate and understand their parents' occupational and life experiences. Second, the valuation of people's past experiences better enables them to reflect upon and remember the past from the point of view of the present; that is, the past becomes a touchstone

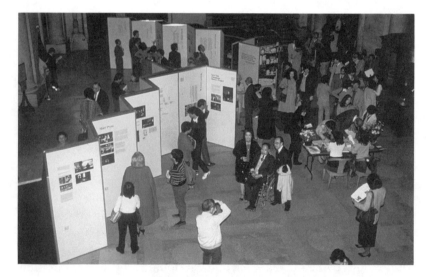

Fig. 11-1. The opening of the exhibition The Eight Pound Livelihood: A History of Chinese Laundry Workers in America at the New York Public Library in 1984 was attended by an estimated 500 people. After two years of interviews, research, and community workshops with Chinese New Yorkers, the Chinatown History Museum collaborated with the New York State Museum in producing a bilingual exhibition on one of the major occupations of Chinese in New York City. Bilingual radio programs, a video documentary, a book, and a Ph.D. dissertation were also stimulated by this effort. Photo courtesy Chinatown History Museum.

against which the present and future are interpreted and understood. The more the activities of reflecting and remembering are made public, the more individuals will become active in identifying the differences and similarities in their experiences with one another and with people who have not lived their experience. At this point more critical insights begin to challenge simple nostalgia. People can begin to bridge the differences between their experiences and others', and feelings of mutual respect begin to surface. Third, such acts of self-discovery shape and reshape individual and collective identities. People constantly reformulate their personal pasts: how people want to think of themselves in the present necessarily influences what they will remember about the past, and conversely, what they remember about themselves in the past influences how they think about themselves in the present. The need to constantly reassess this reciprocal relationship of past and present seems to be a fundamental human characteristic.[15]

A more integrative and inclusive community history can help to counter the sense of marginalization and disempowerment vis-à-vis

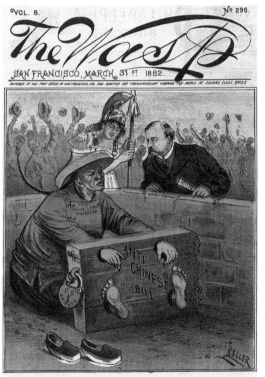

Fig. 11-2. Part of the basic dialogue to take place in the Remembering New York Chinatown exhibition is a discussion exploring why most Americans do not know that in 1882 the anti-Chinese forces in the United States were able to pass the Chinese Exclusion Act, which prohibited Chinese workers from entering the country. This law was not formally repealed until 1943, at which time a quota of 105 per year were allowed in. It was not until the civil rights–influenced Immigration Reform Act of 1965 that such racist legislation was truly ended. Illustration by Keller, *Wasp*, 1882. Wong Ching Foo Collection. Courtesy Chinatown History Museum.

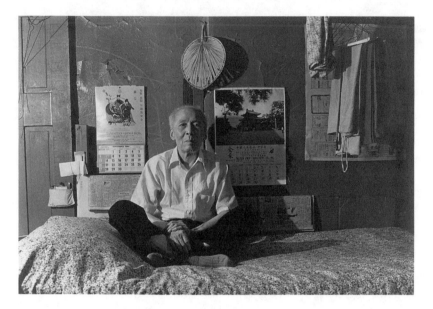

Fig. 11-3. A profile of Sin Jang Leung, a longtime laundry worker, is one of the changing individual biographies featured in Remembering New York Chinatown. Photo by Paul Calhoun, 1983, courtesy Chinatown History Museum.

the larger society that was imposed by the Chinese Exclusion Acts and decades of racism. And yet, this type of community history can also be limiting and claustrophobic. For example, the celebration of Chinatown's history can become too narrow-minded and overly culturally nationalist.[16] It can also deny other aspects of a Chinese New Yorker's experience. For example, while a person may be an "overseas Chinese" and live in Chinatown, he or she is also a Lower East Sider and a New Yorker, and may also have lived in other parts of the United States and other countries. To treat a bachelor laundry worker who spent many years in Cuba simply as a "Chinese," lumping him into the same category as a Hong Kong import-export merchant with a family, does great violence to both individuals' unique life histories. Their Chineseness can easily be overemphasized, becoming an essentialist and quasi-genetic characteristic untouchable by comparisons with other experiences.[17] The identity of a Chinese resident of New York has been formed by many layers of influences—the self is intricately tied to "others."

    In a like manner, local historical studies can become too provincial and separate from the body politic. Indeed, this has been a recurring criticism of the specialization found in much of the new social history. As was mentioned earlier, in isolation the parts cannot give us a sense of the whole—the highly nuanced social history of this or that locale inverts the sins of macro political history. Locality, region, nation, and world have all been represented as distinct entities, and their interconnectedness has tended not to be explicated. In particular, the uniqueness of the locality has tended to be either overemphasized or underrated—all-powerful to residents or all-powerless to national and international influences.

In summary, a resonant and responsible way of engaging any community in the interpretation of its own history needs to balance local, intensely private uses of history with the larger-scale understanding of why and how life has become the way it is. A variety of historical insights need to be brought together in a cultural free space for open discussion. The Memories of New York Chinatown exhibition will experiment with creating such a free space for our diverse audiences.[18]

WHO'S INVOLVED IN THE DIALOGUE?

At first glance, the target audience of a community-based history project might be assumed to be only that community. Although this may be true for some local historical organizations, it has not been true for the Chinatown History Museum. Given our recognition that the self and "others," and parts and wholes, are inextricably interconnected, we view the history of New York's Chinese community as tied to the cultural formation of the Lower East Side and New York City as a whole. Therefore, not only do Chinese have plenty to learn from this history, but so do all New Yorkers and tourists of things Chinese.

Contrary to popular assumptions, Chinatowns are not isolated "Cantons in the West."[19] They are multicultural communities that were (and are) created and recreated by the people who live in them and the people who have interacted with their residents. The history of New York's Chinatown is as much about New York and the development of an American identity as it is about Chinese Americans. The residents of Chinatown have never been all Chinese, nor has it been possible for Chinese immigrants to stay totally by themselves. Chinatown is all too often viewed as monolithic by outsiders, who also may see Chinese Americans as "clannish." Yet if one were to ask several

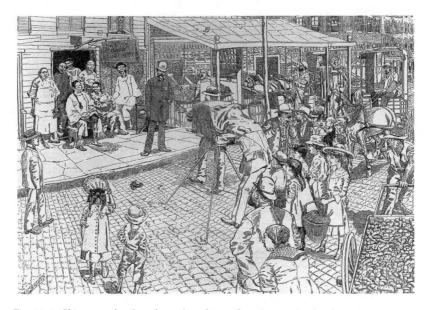

Fig. 11-4. Chinatown has long been the subject of much attention by the mainstream culture in New York City, as exemplified by this "stroller photographer" of 1883. Its representation has often been greatly exoticized, both in romantic and xenophobic ways. Negotiating between anti-Chinese discrimination and finding a means to gain a livelihood, Chinese entered the labor-intensive hand laundry business in New York sometime in the late 1860s. Drawing by A. B. Shults, *Harper's Weekly,* 1883. Wong Ching Foo Collection. Courtesy Chinatown History Museum.

Chinese—or any other "ethnic" New Yorkers—how they would describe their community, not one group identity but many group identities would quickly surface.

What roles should historians, and other professional specialists, play in the dialogue? Quite a few historians and historical organizations have tended to assume that their professional credentials and training give them greater authority to produce interpretations of the history and culture of a community than members of the community itself. Hence, exhibitions tend to be produced by curator-experts who are advised by Ph.D.'d humanities consultants and supported by funds allocated by organizations that judge these projects with panels of peer experts, all of whom are operating in a self-enclosed and self-referential world. In such an extreme and top-down approach to knowledge and standards, audiences are conceived of as more or less passive consumers, receivers of expert wisdom. The exhibition is produced so *they* can learn. As long as the institution is solvent, little attention is paid to whether people come to see the show or not. And even if they do come, little concern is given to the audience's interests or preferences. The attitude is that knowledge is there for the taking, and it is the audience's loss if they do not take advantage of it. Conversely, some historian-activists have taken an opposite (but equally extreme) approach to the relation between communities and their history. In a laudable effort to destabilize the elitist practice of top-down history, some have counterposed the voices and life histories of "the people" as a self-evident, ultrademocratic alternative history. They view their own role as only that of a facilitator and do not want to insert their voice. Historian Michael Frisch has quite rightly pointed out that neither extreme formulation of the roles of historians and the public is very fruitful. Indeed, the authorship of an exhibition, and therefore the authority associated with authorship, should be viewed as a shared and collaborative process and not as an either/or proposition.[20]

Having laid out this concern over exhibition authorship, I recognize that it is not entirely accurate, nor quite fair, to characterize all historians and museum professionals in such a stark light. Certainly many historians and curators care a great deal about the general public and would like their work to reach people effectively. Yet their good intentions are often thwarted by institutional and organizational constraints. Professors gain tenure and advancement largely by publications in the "right" historical journals and the "right" university presses. Teaching counts, but is not a major factor. And in the rather effete world of much university scholarship, publicly oriented history is considered derivative and not truly a part of scholars' work. In museums, another set of institutional practices limits effective engagement. For example, the limited amount of time and money available does not permit curators or researchers to collaborate with either the people who have lived the experience depicted in an exhibition or the people for whom the exhibition is intended—there is no opportunity to jointly interpret and debate the ideas expressed in the exhibition. And such collaborative discussions are not thought to be what brings in the grants. Although the rhetoric of interactive exhibitions has become quite popular in recent years, much of the interaction ends up being reduced to high-tech gadgetry. Computerized laser disks with preprogrammed "choices" for the museum visitor tend to predominate in even the best-intentioned efforts.[21] Like the hierarchically organized corporations of the business world, the institutional practices within which historians and curators work tend to situate these professional specialists on the supply end of the production process and place audiences on the opposite pole, the consumer end. At best, other experts are hired to evaluate a museum's programs and interview the consumers. Hence, even publicly minded historians tend to rely upon the concept of the passive general public when dealing with students and fellow academics.

Instead of such a dichotomous and segregative approach, the Chinatown History Museum has advocated a more nuanced and integrated process of producing historical knowledge. Given the complexity of the process of community identity formation, the dialogue exploring the memory and meaning of Chinatown's past necessitates the collaboration of many different people who can work with us in piecing together this huge, multidimensional spatial and temporal puzzle. We seek to bring together Chinese New Yorkers, Lower East Side residents, other New Yorkers, tourists, and scholars and other cultural producers (which includes museum professionals, journalists, designers, translators, and educators). Each group has played a major role in defining the experience and perception of Chinatown.

Four types of dialogues are being tested during the experimental, evaluative period. First, scholars and museum professionals have been working with the Chinatown History Museum planning group. Ideas and experiences have been exchanged, and plans developed, tested, evaluated, and retested. At this writing it is the end of the evaluation period, and a planning document is being produced. Second, target segments of the Chinese American community have been collaborating with the CHM planning group in documenting the history of Chinatown and reflecting upon their memories of it. Special emphasis has been placed on moving beyond exchanges of empirical information to deeper discussions of meaning. The formation of individual and community identities has been of primary concern. Staff has been soliciting ideas about how better to meet the needs and interests of Chinese Americans. Third, target segments of the non-Chinese community have been collaborating with the CHM planning group in documenting and reflecting upon their perceptions of and experiences with Chinatown. Multi- and monocultural identity formation has been of central interest; for example, how did the Italian Americans who attended P.S. 23 in Chinatown define themselves in contradistinction to their Chinese classmates? Fourth, those Chinese and non-Chinese most interested in pursuing historical exploration have been trained in historical literacy and museum work skills to help us further document and interpret community history. For example, many individuals regularly come to the Chinatown History Museum to work on papers or personal projects; volunteers often guard our exhibitions;

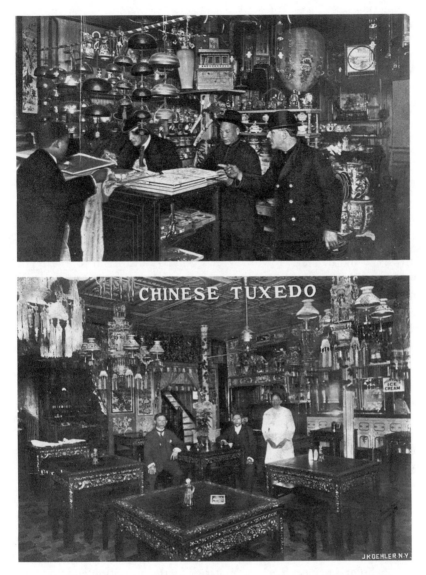

Fig. 11-5. As anti-Chinese hostility limited job options, the promotion of tourism into Chinatown became one of the few ways merchants and workers could earn a living. Postcards of New York's Chinatown began to appear in the 1890s. The postcard at top shows a tourist-oriented gift shop with Chuck Connors pointing at the right. In the 1900s, Connors was a well-known Bowery B'hoy entertainer who was dubbed by the media "the unofficial mayor of Chinatown." He gave tours of Chinatown to middle-class curiosity-seekers. The postcard at bottom shows the ornate interior of the Chinese Tuxedo Restaurant (located on Doyers Street off Chatham Square, shown sometime before 1906) as an orderly yet "exotic" place for tourists to eat while visiting Chinatown. Wong Ching Foo Collection. Courtesy Chinatown History Museum.

and members of the CHM have supported us financially and attended events. By setting up small workshops to train interested individuals, not only can we help our constituencies to appreciate the value (and difficulty) of humanities scholarship, but we can also greatly maximize limited staff time.

FORGING LINKS AND BUILDING SCHOLARSHIP

The linking of constituencies and scholarship has been the core concern of the Chinatown History Museum since its founding. This was not due to some supreme foresight or wisdom, but rather came from simple necessity. Our desire to produce historical programs for and about one of this nation's oldest ethnic enclaves was regularly thwarted by the lack of primary or secondary historical sources. The history of Asians in the United States has not been considered a part of the canon of American historical knowledge. Asian Americans have been cast as perpetual foreigners. And despite the significance of the China trade in the founding and early development of this nation, China (and Asia more generally) are seen as perpetually inscrutable and distant.

The legacy of racial marginalization and legalized exclusion (for example, the Chinese Exclusion Acts, which were in force between 1882 and 1943) left significant silences in the American historical record. So little has been known about what is now the largest concentration of Chinese outside of Asia that it has only recently been documented that Chinese have been living in New York City for at least 160 years.[22] In addition, the development of tourism in the 1890s (as a means of economic survival for Chinese American merchants) promoted a false, and oftentimes patronizing, intimacy that millions of Americans felt (and still feel) toward Chinatown and Chinese Americans.

Scholarly neglect has been matched by the alienation and low self-esteem of the New York Chinese community. In Chinatown, invaluable historical documents and personal belongings have regularly been tossed out with the trash. One embittered elderly laundry man waved us out of his store, screaming, "Laundries have no history!" This problem was made worse with the great influx of new immigrants from Hong Kong, Guangdong, Taiwan, Southeast Asia, and elsewhere. Recent estimates calculate that there are 300,000 Chinese in the New York metropolitan area. Why should these newcomers care about what happened before they arrived? What relevance does history have for their efforts to eke out a living?

Without a base of scholarship and with no archival collections to draw upon, we had to rely on those who had lived the experience to collaborate with us in reconstructing the community's history. Without the advantage of a preexisting institution, we had to build our own infrastructure and seek innovative ways of reaching Chinese New Yorkers. Consequently, we have been in a unique position to develop fresh approaches to historical research and museum craft. Instead of viewing scholarship as separate from public programming, we have found that media productions and public programs are integral to the effort to document and understand the community better. A resonant exhibition demonstrates trustworthiness and predisposes more people to contribute to our collections—people, groups, and organizations who traditionally have been closemouthed begin talking to our researchers. The responsive historical productions and programs we have created have enabled many of the residents we have worked with to look at their own lives more reflectively and comparatively.

We have discovered that reunions are an excellent beginning point for historical research and programming. Long frowned upon as simple nostalgia or distorted celebrations of the past, we have found reunions to be an excellent way to link the felt need for history directly with historical scholarship. Our cosponsorship of reunions organized in the Chinese and Lower East Side communities addresses the need people feel to reconnect with the past and find meaning in their memories. For example, since 1987 we have organized a series of reunions for those who attended P.S. 23, the grade school once located in the building our offices currently are in. The school, whose students were largely Italian and Chinese youth, represents many important memories for this largely immigrant Lower East Side population.[23] In helping to organize such gatherings, the Chinatown History Museum can document social experiences that often have left no records. Ultimately, scholarship is improved, and even more effective programming can then be planned.

Fundamental to developing an understanding of Chinatown that serves as an alternative to mainstream neglect and misperceptions has been the development of an alternative archives. The CHM archives collection has grown primarily through donations and through our staff patrolling the trash bins. It now helps scores of students, scholars, journalists, and visitors from across the United States, for whom no such resource existed a short while ago. Bilingual exhibi-

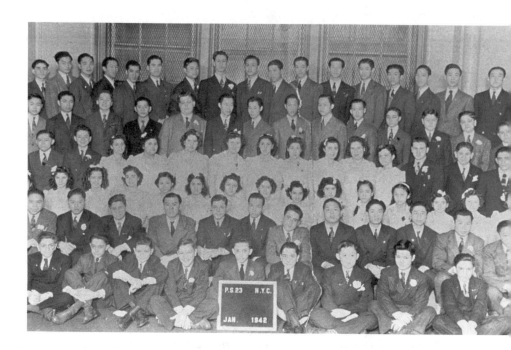

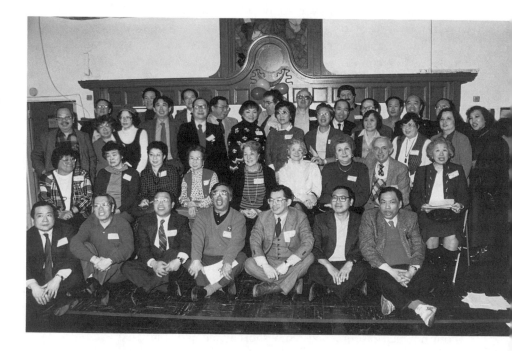

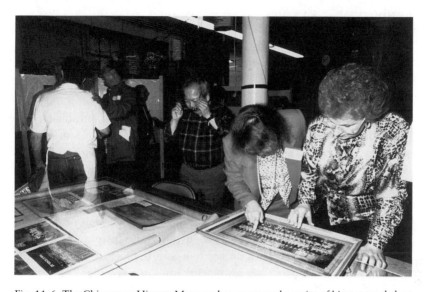

Fig. 11-6. The Chinatown History Museum has sponsored a series of history workshop get-togethers of alumni from Public School 23, the main school serving Italian and Chinese youth on Mulberry and Bayard streets. The artifacts, documents, photographs, stories, and insights gathered from these sessions have been made into an exhibition which, in turn, will be used to gather more interviews and materials. The photograph at top left, of a class from P.S. 23 in 1942, was originally shown within the Chinatown History Museum exhibition Salvaging New York Chinatown; it sparked so much interest that it prompted the organizing of a reunion for alumni of P.S. 23. The photograph at bottom left is the 1988 "class" photograph of students who graduated from P.S. 23 in the 1940s.

The program around P.S. 23 has brought together Chinese and Italians to recall and reconsider their childhood experiences with history students from New York University and staff members of the Chinatown History Museum. Although some of the attendees still live in the immediate vicinity of the school, they have not seen former classmates for decades. The photo above shows the 1989 P.S. 23 Photo Day. Photos by Michael Ramos, courtesy Chinatown History Museum.

tions, walking tours, slide shows, video documentaries, radio programs, lectures, publications, and other programs have reached hundreds of thousands of people well beyond New York's Chinatown. With over ten years of sustained work in one community, the Chinatown History Museum's efforts have begun to bridge scholarship and personal interests, and newer and older constituencies. We have also managed to attract a historically nonmuseumgoing community with engaging historical programs.

EXHIBITION AS A VEHICLE FOR DIALOGUE

The Memories of New York Chinatown exhibition has been the vehicle in which these ideas of dialogue-driven programs are being tested. We have been using this exhibition as a way to consolidate what we have learned, evaluate and improve on our successes, and build these and other insights into the plans for a new permanent exhibition and museum. In the first level of a two-tiered self-evaluation, audiences, scholars, and the CHM planning team have been collaboratively developing, evaluating, and refining this exhibition, and are reconceptualizing how it and related programs can serve as a meeting ground for diverse peoples. The exhibition itself has been engaging our collaborators in a set of humanities issues, and that engagement process has been the subject of the second level of our museum planning study. While the exhibition focuses on content and themes, the larger study focuses on museum processes and larger humanities issues.

An Exhibition in Process

Despite having been settled in lower Manhattan since the first half of the nineteenth century, Chinese Americans have been perceived as perpetual foreigners.[24] This dissonance between lived experience and perception defines the parameters of the Memories of New York Chinatown exhibition. It will explore how the cultural identity of an urban streetscape has been formed and reformed in the minds and lives of Chinese New Yorkers. And it will explore how that representation has differed from the perceptions of the larger New York public and visiting tourists. The Chinatown History Museum has chosen this seminal theme as the basis of the Memories exhibition because it is an issue relevant to the cultural identity of *all* Americans. We see a dialogic exhibition as the ideal vehicle for the public consideration of this issue.

The following humanities themes will be presented both as a set of ideas and as a framework for further documentation and discussion with visitors.

MEMORIES OF NEIGHBORHOOD   How has the space of Mott, Pell, and Doyers streets become a place of multiple and successive memories and meanings? How have people of diverse cultural experiences and national origins remembered Chinatown? How have communities interacted? How have they segregated themselves or been segregated?

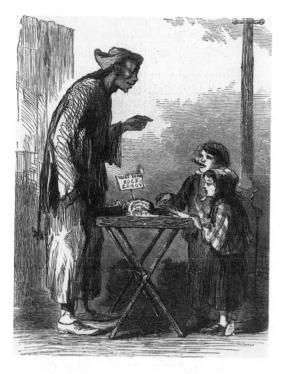

Fig. 11-7. Despite having been settled in New York City for over 160 years, Chinese are still largely viewed as "foreigners" in the United States. This paradox will be one of the issues discussed in the dialogic exhibition Remembering New York Chinatown. Chinese itinerant peddlers, such as this candy seller, could be seen in New York as early as the 1830s. Illustration from *Harper's Weekly,* 1868. Wong Ching Foo Collection. Courtesy Chinatown History Museum.

New York's Chinatown has become a fixture of the American urban landscape as much as Coney Island, the Statue of Liberty, and the Bronx Zoo. It is a place where literally millions of Americans and international tourists eat, shop, and wander. Although Chinese have been living in New York City since the 1830s, it was not until the 1890s that this Chinese settlement became a tourist destination. When asked about the whys and wherefores of its origins, most non-Chinese tend to assume that Chinatown is an enclave formed largely by immigrants to protect their own interests. Clannishness, language, new immigration, and unassimilability are often given as the reasons it continues to exist.

Unfortunately, these common impressions gloss over a much more complex reality. The streetscape we now think of as Chinatown has been the locus of a succession of ethnically or racially defined groups. Each group tied its own memories, meanings, and sense of self to the locale. Never populated only by Chinese, the area became a home base for hundreds of thousands in the metropolitan New York region.

The streetscape, housing, schools, and other shared spaces have been the subject of exhibition panels and discussion. The study of cultural geography, the history of the built environment, ethnic/racial relations, and individual and group memory have informed this theme.[25]

CULTURAL REPRESENTATIONS   How has Chinatown been represented and remembered in the mainstream culture? How has New York's Chinatown been represented and remembered in China? How has the representation jibed with direct experience?

Sensationalist films and television programs—ranging from news reports about Chinatown youth gangs and drugs to Michael Cimino's film *Year of the Dragon* to episodes of the *Kojak* television series— have regularly played upon firmly established popular stereotypes of downtown danger, mystery, and exoticism. Contemporary media have simply continued a longstanding orientalism traceable back to nineteenth-century American theater, Tin Pan Alley, and silent films.[26] Hatchetmen, gang wars, opium trafficking, white slavery, restaurants

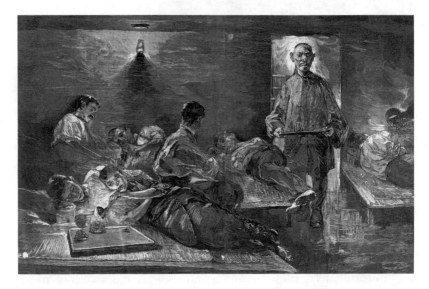

Fig. 11-8. Opium "dens" have been a stubborn, long-standing image of what goes on in Chinatowns. Indeed, filmmaker and comedian Woody Allen depicted a layout in his 1991 film *Alice* as if it were still a common practice today. Opium and its uses by Chinese and non-Chinese New Yorkers will be one of the more sensitive subjects discussed as part of the Remembering New York Chinatown exhibition. Illustration by J. W. Alexander, captioned "American opium-smokers—interior of a New York opium den," *Harper's Weekly*, 1881. Wong Ching Foo Collection. Courtesy Chinatown History Museum.

serving rat, cat, or dog meat, and laundries or stores with secret underground rooms have been recurrent, larger-than-life images in New York City's fervid cultural imagination. In recent decades other, more favorable images have come to the fore—yet the 1980s were marked by a precipitous rise in the number of acts of anti-Asian violence across the nation.[27]

How have New York and Chinatown been portrayed in the areas from which Chinese have emigrated? What have been the perceptions and expectations of would-be émigrés in China? What versions of the story of *gaam shaan,* or the golden mountain, have been accepted? How have Chinese New Yorkers colluded in spreading these stories? What happens when expectations confront realities?[28]

Popular films, photographs, and stories offer means through which these contrasting impressions and recollections are being explored. Studies of tourism, mass culture and entertainment, and racial representation have informed this aspect of the exhibition.[29]

STRATEGIES OF SURVIVAL   For individuals caught between the community's own sense of self and outsiders' portrayals of Chinatown, what has been the range of adaptive responses? How have Chinese New Yorkers defined themselves in relation to the larger American culture? To Chinese culture? How have they become New Yorkers? How have they become sojourners? How have perceived cultural differences been exacerbated, bridged, or accommodated?

Historically, Chinese in the United States have been defined in racial terms. Charlie Chan's Americanized Number One Son could be presented as entertaining comic relief for the very same reason that his trademark "Gee whiz, Pop" seemed silly tumbling off Asian lips. As long as racial categories are used to define identities rigidly, Chinese will forever be cast as "inscrutable" and "yellow" and Americans as "normal" and "white."

Once racial identities become understood as changing cultural phenomena, then bicultural heritages can be understood as much more nuanced and variegated experiences.[30] Michael Fischer, for example, has made the point that the writer Maxine Hong Kingston, when faced with a world of literature that did not reflect her Chinese American sensibility, had to reclaim her own history and find a voice within that history that would embody a freer, more multidimensional concept of self.[31]

What happened, however, to Chinese in more everyday circumstances—such as laundry workers? Did they think of themselves as temporary visitors, or sojourners, saving to retire back in China? Who decided to stay and settle? How were their lives different from merchants who could bring their wives and families?[32]

In addition to the traditional offering of historical information and interpretation developed by humanities scholars, the Memories of New York Chinatown exhibition is an experimental exhibition with various stations in which different types of dialogues can take place. Building on a concept pioneered by the Corning Glass Museum, layers of information and involvement are offered to visitors to accommodate their varying amounts of time and interest. The harried visitor with only fifteen minutes to spend in the exhibition is able to gain a basic understanding of its ideas and content. For those with more time and interest, a series of options are available so that they can increase their level of involvement with the exhibition. Ultimately, we seek to make it possible for anyone who comes to visit the exhibition to choose to collaborate with us in documenting and discussing his or her memories and reflections.

The CHM staff has been developing modules, staffed by Chinatown History Museum personnel and trained volunteers, including timelines that can be added to, a genealogy/biography database, and programs evoking group memories. The staff has been supplied with questions, various historical databases, and collections of photographs to further engage visitors in an exploration of what can be remembered of New York's Chinatown. We continually seek to create stations that will be able to both present and assimilate empirical information, such as the names of students who are in a class photograph. But we especially want to design stations that draw visitors into exploring deeper and more difficult recollections. The nature of memory and identity has been the subject of much recent interest among humanities scholars, and we have been consulting with some of these scholars, attempting to incorporate their insights into the design of the exhibition.

This unorthodox approach allows visitors to discuss themes and details of the exhibition; add their memories, photographs, documents, and personal memorabilia to the exhibition and the CHM archive collection; help the CHM staff locate collections and people to speak to; and help the staff listen to and learn from the visitors' perspectives, interests, and needs so that the organization can more effectively engage future visitors.

Perhaps two examples of interactive modules, one planned and

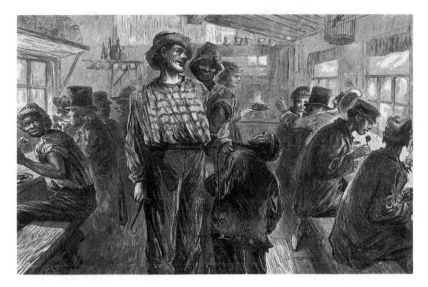

Fig. 11-9. The history of Chinese in New York City can only be understood multi-culturally, in relation to other New Yorkers. Chinese were part of the crews of U.S. merchant ships as early as 1785. Nineteenth-century artists often followed the conventions of "physiognomy," representing people as "racial types" that were purported to help viewers to understand the true character of anonymous individuals among the urban masses. The accompanying article for this illustration claimed, "Every Fig. and face in the picture is drawn from life, and each character tells its own story so well that to enlarge upon it would be superfluous." Drawing by Sol Eytinge, Jr., *Harper's Weekly,* 1871. Wong Ching Foo Collection. Courtesy Chinatown History Museum.

one installed, will make some of these ideas more concrete. One planned interactive module will be an exhibition and database on representations of Chinatown by both Chinese and non-Chinese. Panels and displays could provide some illustrations of how American popular culture has referred to Chinatown over the decades. Opposite them, more panels would document Chinese representations. Myths of *gaam shaan,* or the golden mountain, would be contrasted to the complex semiotics of Borrah Minevitch and His Harmonica Rascals performing "Chinatown, My Chinatown." At the station a filing cabinet, or a computer, would contain many more examples of stories, graphics, anecdotes, jokes, or whatever relates to this issue. Visitors would be invited to explore the database with a Chinatown History Museum staff person. Ideally, the exhibit would jog their own memories, and they could share something that might be added to the database. The staff person would also be prepared with a set of ques-

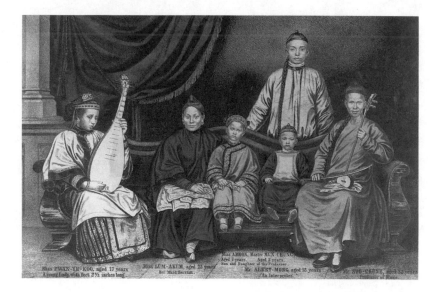

Fig. 11-10. In 1850, P. T. Barnum took advantage of the arrival of seventeen-year-old Pwan Ye Koo. He put her on display with what was represented as her retinue. Thousands of New Yorkers paid twenty-five cents to see "The Living Chinese Family" at his Chinese Museum on Broadway off Prince Street. Illustration by N. Currier, 1850. Wong Ching Foo Collection. Courtesy Chinatown History Museum.

tions that would engage the visitor in deeper levels of discussion. The staff person would be responsible for sharing information and listening for what visitors are telling him or her. (The staff would also be prepared to document what has been told to them and—if it is deemed desirable—would make an appointment for a follow-up session.) This listening would be on at least two levels. Staff would naturally be listening for explicit comments, such as "Oh, I used to cross the street when I saw a Chinese man. I was afraid he'd have a hatchet under his coat."[33] They would also be listening for implicit statements that will give us clues about which parts of the exhibition work better than others. Laundry workers, for example, asked why our Eight Pound Livelihood exhibition had more photographs showing laundrymen than photographs showing the work process. We learned from their comments that they would have represented laundry life in an exhibition very differently than the CHM staff had. This helped us refine our understanding of points of view in our expanded version of the exhibition. Different audience evaluation techniques will also be tried and their results compared.[34]

One operating module that we installed for the opening of the show evokes and documents spatial memories. We have found that many of our informants have strong recollections of the stores, public spaces, and homes they frequented many decades before. In fact, many "old-timers" enjoy recalling their old haunts with people eager to learn about them. The module will have a grid of old Chinatown streets and their buildings, and will also have overlays that show the changes in the built environment over time. We will invite Chinese and non-Chinese residents of the area to share with us their mental maps of the space. We have already collected the contrasting memories of Mott Street of Sydney Silberman, as told to his grandson, and 1914 arrival Lung Chin, as told to Dorothy Rony of the Chinatown History Museum staff;[35] their spatial references overlap but represent very different associational patterns and meanings. Staff will seek to engage visitors in discussion, comparing different maps displayed in the exhibition and inviting the more interested to add their mental maps to our database.[36] Documentation will have been created where none existed before. Scholars will be able to interpret and pursue these findings. Visitors who were or are part of Chinatown will be drawn into a meaningful encounter with their recollections, and those who have not been a part of the Lower East Side experience can easily make associations and comparisons with their own spatial memories of other places. And the exhibition will have served as a tool for a dialogue among parties who normally would not be communicating with one another, even if they were in the same room at the same time.

In a very real sense, the exhibition gallery will serve as a stage on which different activities will occur at different times. Of course, it will be open to the general public for viewing. At other times, it will be a place for group discussions about different aspects of the exhibition. These discussions will be part of the documentation process. At still other times, the CHM staff will be doing their work, such as copying documents or identifying photographs. We want the seams of historical research to be made apparent: we want to show it as a process with many steps. By so doing, we hope to move past the surface definitiveness of exhibitions and show the dynamic inner workings.

No doubt some modules will work very well. Others will need adjustments. Still others will need to be tossed out and replaced. This flexible, experimental approach will enable the planning team to do this, and to develop explicitly the theory and practice of a dialogic museum. Collections, programs, exhibitions, staff roles and time allocations, space usage, and many other aspects of museum work will be redefined by this dialogic approach. These more formal issues of museum-building and work process will constitute a second level of planning and study.

Exhibition Programs

A series of programs will bring in specific groups from both the Chinese and the non-Chinese communities to participate in discussions and special sessions at various modules. All programs will be designed to coordinate with the exhibition's themes and the overall dialogue-driven approaches. The formats of programs will vary according to the kind and size of the group; for example, groups of older people will be asked to come first because their experiences will need to be documented first.

Historical reunions will continue to be one type of program we encourage. Social, political, and cultural groups significant to the history of the community will be encouraged to cosponsor reunions with the Chinatown History Museum. Attendees at past reunions have been asked to bring photographs and talk with trained oral historians. Follow-up sessions were organized when they were mutually deemed desirable. Groups will also be asked to donate (or preserve and allow us to copy) documents, photographs, artifacts, costumes, etc. that document their experience. Selected individuals from these groups have been asked to work with us, either sharing more of their recollections or being trained to document their group. The owners of stores and restaurants, as well as the members of opera clubs, social clubs, sports groups, youth groups, and school graduating classes, are among the groupings we have asked to work with us.

The Chinatown History Museum will also organize family history and genealogy workshops, four-session series in which interested youths and adults will be trained in the techniques of tracing family genealogies and conducting family oral history projects. In exchange for the sessions, participants will be asked to place a duplicate of their work in the CHM archives. These workshops will also serve as a training ground for volunteers who will help out in CHM research projects.

We also plan to invite target constituent groups to view films, videos, and slide shows dealing with aspects of the exhibition themes. The media viewing is intended to stimulate conversation over issues of mutual concern and interest. For example, European immigrants who

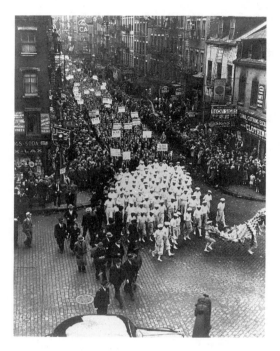

Fig. 11-11. "I remember it was drizzly that day. The Chinese papers said don't wear no hats. Those days if you step out the door people go for the hat, everyone wear hats. That's the first time I see Chinese don't wear hats. All twenty thousand of them." Gene Eng, retired welder.

As a means to fathom the collective memories of community residents, such photographs as this will be used as a starting point for individual and group discussion sessions.

Anti-Japanese-aggression demonstration, Mott and Canal streets, circa 1930s. Photo courtesy Chinatown History Museum.

passed through Ellis Island could be shown Felicia Lowe's hour-long documentary on Angel Island, *Carved in Silence,* which documents the major detention center Chinese were ferried to during the period of the Chinese Exclusion Acts. Comparative discussions can then follow.

RESHAPING THE ORGANIZATION

Over the past ten years, numerous Chinatown History Museum exhibitions and programs have allowed us to test aspects of dialogic approaches. Some efforts were more successful than others, but we learned from each instance that merely opening channels of communication is not enough; a great deal of follow-up is needed. For example, when the staff took our 1983 exhibition on Chinese laundry workers to a large senior citizens' center, many individuals who had been reticent when being interviewed by the staff began to come up to us and offer their stories. However, funding was limited, so we could not spend staff time on follow-up—everyone had to be mobilized for the next exhibition project.

A similar problem occurred in 1987, with our Salvaging New York Chinatown exhibition. The show drew great interest. One photograph in particular, that of a fourth-grade class from P.S. 23, stirred an unexpected response. Many individuals came forth to identify people in the photograph and began to tell us about their memories of the school. We quickly decided to organize a reunion of those Chinese who had attended the school. Word spread, and soon Italian residents began calling us in large numbers. We had some four hundred people come to the event, including teachers from as far back as 1917. We attempted to follow up on this enormous opportunity by applying for grants to plan and then implement an exhibition and associated programming on the public school. This was done; however, we found that our small staff was stretched too far for us to do this as well as we would have liked. Once interviews were completed, for example, we did not have the capability to process the interviews and make them accessible. People who had donated photographs wanted to see them on display. Names of other individuals were given to us by people we interviewed, but we could not get in contact with these other people quickly enough.

These experiences have taught us that the concept of a dialogic museum needs to be thought through with the entire organization in mind, for the archives, staff roles, the allocation of organizational resources, and so much more are all affected. These lessons are the reason for the two-tiered approach to our self-evaluation study. Not only does the dialogic exhibition warrant careful planning, but the overall museum structure demands consideration as well. We have been using and will continue to use an ethnographic approach to evaluating our exhibition and organizational practices: What do our audiences bring to the exhibition? How can we help improve the intergenerational teaching that goes on among grandparents, parents, and children in our space? What happens to individuals and groups after they go through our space? These questions and many more are being asked and discussed by staff. We have learned that the various levels of dialogue produce critical insights that, when taken to heart, reshape all museum productions and the museum itself.

The Memories exhibition, for example, will be refined in the following ways by insights we have already garnered from collaborators and visitors:

The form and packaging of the exhibition. How can the exhibition design be improved to better suit the cultural styles of our audiences?

How can we improve the effectiveness of the written and aesthetic languages of the exhibition (and museum) space?

The documentation of the historical experience. The interactive approach has an immediate impact, involving visitors in the documentation process and turning them into collaborators. We will seek to discover means whereby what visitors contribute will be immediately noticeable in the exhibition or collection. Their contributions should not simply be acknowledged, as most historical organizations do, in newsletter mentions, but instead put into the context of other contributions in the collection, where the contribution's significance can be made evident.

A better understanding of what is remembered, and why. How have collective memory and individual memory operated across generations? What has become a part of commonly remembered community history? The anti-Japanese-aggression demonstrations during World War II are an example of this. What aspects of life have become silences in the collective memory, as the laundry experience did? What stories or myths are retold to help understand the past?

What is more interesting to whom? More explicit interaction with our visitors and collaborators will enable us to gain a much keener understanding of who is interested in what. We can use that knowledge to improve the effectiveness of the communicative and interactive parts of the exhibition.

Short-term planning. What exhibitions should we plan next? What modifications should be made to our existing exhibitions? What programs should be planned?

At the level of the museum itself, we have become aware of how the dialogue-driven approach will have profound influences on reshaping the traditional structures and operations of museums. For example, even the way an interior space is designed will be affected. We anticipate that some of the following issues will have implications for the Chinatown History Museum's practice:

Collection practices. What constitutes our collection? How can it be organized to respond to the dialogic approach? How does this affect the roles of archivist and registrar? How can we use new technologies to facilitate quicker processing and accessibility?

Museums traditionally have been defined by their collections. Recent historical scholarship and new technologies have increasingly destabilized the primacy of artifacts and archives in museums. We need to think through what constitutes a dialogue-driven history museum collection.

New technologies of object reproduction have greatly challenged the uniqueness of museum collections. Perhaps photographs, of which multiple copies can be printed, first posed this problem for history museums. Is not a good-quality copy of an original print almost as valuable to the historian as the original? Microfilm, photoduplication, audio and video recording, computerization, and other technologies have made it possible to abstract representations from the original. This issue strikes at the very heart of what is considered historical evidence. Paul Thompson has argued that tape-recorded oral-history interviews should be considered as reliable, or unreliable, as diaries or autobiographies. And Ron Grele has pointed out that oral interviews provide qualitatively different historical information than text-based historical sources. Increasingly, oral-history collections have become a part of what museums collect.

Perhaps more important, the behavioral scientist Mihaly Csikszentmihalyi has insisted that the importance of objects lies not so much in their material value but in the value of the meaning people invest in them.[37] Should collections be formulated based on the rarity of the originals in them, or instead by the body of precious information they contain? Although no one contests the unequaled eloquence of a Remington bronze sculpture or the special feel of an original manuscript, the boundaries defining what constitutes museum collections have become increasingly blurred.

Memories and thoughts—captured by videotape, pen on paper, or whatever means—have become a fundamental element of historical scrutiny and collection. What happens when museum collections shift from being primarily object-based to being information-based? Our past experience with dialogic databases suggests that computers with graphic interface capabilities could become the backbone of our information and artifact collections. Will this be feasible?

Types of dialogues. What are the different types of dialogues that go on within our space and programs, among both Chinese Americans and non-Chinese Americans? Why should non-Chinese Americans care about the history of Chinese Americans? Can perceptions of cultural difference be bridged by new, multicultural approaches? What are the various roles that scholars could play?

Linkages beyond the CHM. What are the different types of dialogues that extend beyond our space and programs? How can the Chinatown History Museum link up with other cultural and educational institutions to combine resources and enhance effectiveness?

The CHM has regularly sought to link up with other cultural and educational institutions in New York City and elsewhere. The gradual but growing interest in Asian American studies in universities has made it easier to recruit staff members who have some background and training in scholarly work. However, the Chinatown History Museum's work with these institutions has been episodic. We want to think through the possibilities for establishing formal institutional linkages with primary and secondary schools, with local community colleges, with research units such as the newly established Asian/American Center at Queens College, and with graduate programs such as the newly established Ph.D. program in American studies at the State University of New York at Buffalo. A comparable set of relationships could be established with cultural institutions and museums.

Such linkages could have substantial implications for staffing and fundraising. They could provide interns at various levels, from high school students to doctoral candidates. It would mean that the CHM could really function as a research organization connected to broader projects and a wider range of scholarship, thus increasing its visibility and significance. And it could offer ways for museum scholars, interns, staff, programmers, and volunteers to connect their work with that of the CHM. Linkages like these have become fairly common between established museums and the world of scholarship. But rarely represented is the community whose experience is the stuff of the history being studied and exhibited, and whose capacities to deal with the present could be enhanced by direct involvement in that history's preservation and presentation in community-based museums such as the Chinatown History Museum.

The dialogic approach and museum structure. How does a dialogue-driven approach redefine organizational structure? How should the staff work together? How should our facilities be reorganized? How can greater community participation be linked to membership drives, docents, and other structural features of the museum?

Traditionally, museum staff have been segregated into distinct departments that have little interaction in their daily work. This model of organization has presented some serious problems for the Chinatown History Museum staff: for example, work becomes fragmented and uncoordinated, and the effectiveness of public engagement suffers. During our planning period attention has been paid to redefining staff roles and reallocating staff time in order to facilitate a more integrated and coordinated work process. Much more time has been devoted to joint planning and communication among our archivist, curator, and public programs coordinator so that specialty areas of work will not be fragmented from overall organization objectives. Newly created staff roles will ideally be responsible for coordinating volunteer and member participation so as to maximize the effectiveness of our limited organizational resources.

The effects of restructuring on historical interpretation. How is the interpretation of Chinese American history affected by such collaboration? Not only will this dialogic documentation process fill in many gaps in historical memory, but it will necessitate the engagement of the community in jointly exploring with us the meaning of Chinese New Yorker history. This is the most challenging, yet overdue, aspect of the dialogue-driven approach. The exploration of memory and meaning of community experience should be a shared venture that enriches both individual and community life *and* scholarship.

LIVING WITH GHOSTS

One of the ironies of our nation's fervent faith in "progress" and "being modern" is that it has also created a simultaneous fear of and longing for roots. Every time I see filmmaker George Romero's (or anyone else's) "living dead" emerging from their graveyards to eat suburbanites regardless of race, gender, religion, or age, I cannot but view it as the distinctly American compulsion to escape the past. In this world, memories of our ancestors are best kept buried. And when they pop up from the recesses of our psyches, we have to actively repress them.

In an aggressive commercial culture that constantly markets new-

ness, we are told that we are being old-fashioned and sentimental—
both negative things—if we refuse to toss away past attachments and
buy the latest. At the same time, Americans' search for identity, roots,
and "authenticity" appears to be becoming more of a preoccupation.
The huge interest in tracing one's genealogy, exploring the concept of
Afrocentrism, visiting living history museums, visiting the land of
one's ancestors, going to high school reunions, and consuming popu-
larized forms of history such as Ken Burns's Civil War miniseries
attests to the apparently opposite desire to make the past come alive—
to somehow connect.

While the ideology of Euro-American modernism is used to counter localism and "old world" habits and superstitions, the countervail-
ing grassroots search for meaning and steadying values seems all the
stronger. Even if the economic pie of "progress" continues to expand,
we are no longer so confident about the values it embodies. In our
separate living spaces we worry about Alar, environmental collapse,
AIDS, homelessness and the "new" poor, sugar and other addictions,
and the vacuousness of a technological materialism gone berserk.

In his 1944 visit to the United States, the Chinese sociologist Fei
Xiaotong noted that the major problem he saw with the United States
was that it was a "land without ghosts." Although he greatly treasured
the Western education he had received, he mused, "Our lives do not
just pass through time in such a way that a moment in time or a station
in life once past is lost. Life in its creativity changes the absolute nature
of time: it makes past into present—no, it melds past, present, and
future into one inextinguishable, multilayered scene, a three-dimensional body. This is what ghosts are." And in the United States, "a
world without ghosts, life is free and easy. American eyes can gaze
straight ahead. But still I think they lack something and I do not envy
their lives."[38] Perhaps the Iroquois have had it right all along: in their
culture, tribal leaders are empowered to make judgments on behalf of
their people as long as their decisions take into account the seventh
generation to come. We sorely need these kinds of values and
spirituality.

Plenty of academics are writing important books about these
subjects, but too often only some three thousand other academics read
them. Occasionally these concerns come out in private discussions
with trusted friends, but in such contexts challenging points of view
are rarely raised. And we know all too well how the commercial
electronic media manage to package these issues into quick doses of
"news" or scandal. There are precious few spaces for people to come

together who don't normally come together and collaboratively explore these issues by talking face to face with one another.

Many of us feel alienated in society; we feel we have no impact on social or cultural policies. While tens of millions of dollars have been spent by candidates for political office here and elsewhere, pittances have been devoted to public discussion about real issues. We must make local and regional, suburban and urban humanities forums a fundamental social priority. To do this we need locally and regionally accessible venues for these forums. Yes, community-oriented museums, libraries, and universities have to varying degrees served this purpose, and they need to do more—but what about senior citizens' centers, town halls, community recreation rooms, church basements, community organizations, shopping malls, schools, and maybe even computer bulletin boards? We need to have programs in places where people already gather, and these programs need to be participatory and inclusive.

At their best, public humanities programs should be creating expansive, convivial places in which social problems are pried open for critical examination. Such programs should make a special effort to include those who have not been a part of the traditional groupings of our public culture. In my experience, the humanities can help to fundamentally question and reenvision who we are and what we should be doing. It can be a magnificent tool for what the Brazilian educator Paulo Freire terms empowering people in "naming," and thereby changing, their worlds. Democracy, it seems to me, must be understood as a work in progress. We need to improve on it constantly, expand it, but never feel that it has been perfected.[39]

In the spirit of a dialogic approach, the Chinatown History Museum welcomes readers' responses to these ideas. We know that our experiences and goals are not unique and that we can learn from what others have done. Please write, call, or visit us.

NOTES

This essay was originally written in 1989 as a planning document to raise funds for the Memories of New York Chinatown exhibition. A version of it was then presented at the Museums and Communities conference organized by the Smithsonian Institution in 1990. Since that time, funds were raised and the exhibition has opened.

The proposal and this essay were penned by John Kuo Wei Tchen, and represent a collective effort among Fay Chew (the Chinatown History Museum's executive director), Michael Frisch, Charles Lai, and Dorothy Rony of the Chinatown History Museum. The dialogue-driven exhibition and museum concept has been developed over the past ten years by members of the Chinatown History Museum staff and community. They include Judy Austermiller, Paul Calhoun, Fay Chew, William David Chin, Adrienne Cooper, Rachael Cowan, James Dao, Toby D'Oench, Michael Frisch, Robert Glick, Yuet-fung Ho, Maria Hong, Charles Lai, Edward C. H. Lai, Lamgen Leon, Mei-Li Lin, Mary T. Lui, Judith Wing-Siu Luk, Michael Mak, Stanley Mark, Katie Quan, Dorothy Rony, Judy Susman, Joyce Yu, and Wang Yung. The Memories of New York Chinatown exhibition curators are Mary Lui, Dorothy Rony, and John Kuo Wei Tchen. Advisors for the exhibition were Hope Alswang, Rina Benmayor, Elizabeth Blackmar, Sucheng Chan, Ronald J. Grele, Keith Hefner, Marlon K. Hom, Mary E. Janzen, Ivan Karp, Barbara Kirshenblatt-Gimblett, Edward C. H. Lai, Him Mark Lai, Raymond Lum, Joan Maynard, Barbara Melosh, David Ment, Roy Rosenzweig, Jessica Siegel, Robert W. Snyder, Bell Yung, and Judy Yung. I would also like to thank Roger Sanjek for the support he has provided me at the Asian/American Center, Queens College. Special appreciation goes to James Early, Timothy Meagher, Marsha Semmel, Lynn Szwaja, and Tomas Ybarra-Frausto for their warm support and most helpful suggestions. And finally, editor Sue Warga has greatly improved this essay.

As of 1 January 1991 the New York Chinatown History Project was renamed the Chinatown History Museum. This change is part of a larger effort to consolidate and further advance the achievements of the first ten years of the New York Chinatown History Project. We now seek to create a museum ready for the twenty-first century.

1. For background about the Chinatown History Museum, see Marvine Howe, "Hard Lives of Garment Workers on Display," *New York Times,* 3 Dec. 1989; J. Tevere Macfadyen, "Recording Chinatown's Past While It's Still There," *Smithsonian Magazine* 10, no. 13 (1983), 70–79; and Candace Floyd, "Chinatown: A History Project in Manhattan's Lower East Side Documents the History and Contemporary Life of Chinese-Americans," *History News* (June 1984).

2. This planning process was made possible by grants from the Arts and Humanities Program of the Rockefeller Foundation, the Museums and His-

torical Organizations Program of the National Endowment for the Humanities, and the New York State Council for the Arts.

3. All comments, ideas, and suggestions should be addressed to the author at the Chinatown History Museum, 70 Mulberry Street, second floor, New York, NY 10013.

4. For a sampling of some of the debates, see Karen J. Winkler, "Humanities Agency Caught in Controversy Over Columbus Grants," *Chronicle of Higher Education,* 13 Mar. 1991, A5, A8–9; Henry Louis Gates, Jr., and Donald Kagan, "Dialogue: The Curriculum Wars—Whose Culture Is It, Anyway?" *New York Times,* 4 May 1991; and Sam Allis, Jordan Bonfante, and Cathy Booth, "Whose America?" *Time,* 8 July 1991, 12–17.

5. Thomas Bender, "Wholes and Parts: The Need for Synthesis in American History," *Journal of American History* 73 (1986), 120–36. For a sampling of a range of critiques, see Lynne V. Cheney, "Humanities in America: A Report to the President, the Congress, and the American People" (Washington, D.C.: National Endowment for the Humanities, 1988); Allan Bloom, *The Closing of the American Mind* (New York: Simon and Schuster, 1987); Arthur Schlesinger, Jr., "When Ethnic Studies Are Un-American," *Wall Street Journal,* 23 Apr. 1990; Russell Jacoby, *The Last Intellectuals* (New York: Basic Books, 1987); and Catherine R. Stimpson, "The Necessities of Aunt Chloe" (Washington, D.C.: Federation of State Humanities Councils, 1988).

6. For examples of media coverage of these developments, see William A. Henry III, "The Browning of America," *Time,* 9 Apr. 1990, 28–31. For a much more in-depth examination, see Nancy Foner, ed., *New Immigrants in New York* (New York: Columbia University Press, 1987).

7. Steven D. Lavine, "Museums and Multiculturalism: Who Is in Control?" *Museum News* 68, no. 2 (1989), and Donald Garfield, "Dimensions of Diversity," *Museum News* 68, no. 2 (1989), 36–42.

8. The New-York Historical Society's Why History? program series in 1990 and the Race and Class program series in 1991 are examples of this significant new outreach. See C. Gerald Fraser, "Aid to New Audiences Challenged," *New York Times,* 4 Mar. 1989; and Warren Leon and Roy Rosenzweig, "Introduction," in *History Museums in the United States: A Critical Assessment* (Urbana: University of Illinois Press, 1989); Susan Porter Benson, Steven Brier, and Roy Rosenzweig, eds., *Presenting the Past: Critical Perspectives on History and the Public* (Philadelphia: Temple University Press, 1986); Jo Blatti, ed., *Past Meets Present: Essays About Historic Interpretation and Public Audiences* (Washington, D.C.: Smithsonian Institution Press, 1987); Michael Frisch, *Shared Authority: Essays on the Craft and Meaning of Oral and Public History* (Albany: State University of New York Press, 1990); and "Common Agenda for History Museums," a special issue of *History News* (44, no. 3 [1989]).

9. Carl Becker, "Everyman His Own Historian" (the American Historical Association President's Address, 29 Dec. 1931), in *Everyman His Own Historian* (Chicago: University of Chicago Press, 1966), 253.

10. David Thelen, "History Making in America: A Populist Perspective" (Laramie: Wyoming Council for the Humanities, 1989), 1. For further exploration of this issue, see John Kuo Wei Tchen, "Notes on U.S. History Museums: Institution Practices, Collective Memory, and Racial Identity Formation" (New York: Chinatown History Museum, 1990).

11. Thomas J. Schlereth, "Defining Collecting Missions: National and Regional Models," *History News* 44, no. 3 (1987).

12. For examples of some of the institutional cleavages this issue has sparked, see William Honan, "Say Goodbye to the Stuffed Elephants," *New York Times Magazine,* 14 Jan. 1990.

13. Barbara Melosh and Christina Simmons, "Exhibiting Women's History," in Susan Porter Benson, Steven Brier, and Roy Rosenzweig, eds., *Presenting the Past: Critical Perspectives on History and the Public* (Philadelphia: Temple University Press, 1986).

14. The dialogic learning process has been most fully articulated by Paulo Freire in *The Pedagogy of the Oppressed* (New York: Herder and Herder, 1970). Also, see the problem-solving approach pioneered by John Dewey, discussed in Robert B. Westbrook, *John Dewey and American Democracy* (Ithaca: Cornell University Press, 1991). Since the original formulation of our ideas, we have learned of parallel discussions about refashioning museums and other learning environments. For example, see Georges Henri Rivière, "The Ecomuseum—An Evolution Definition," *Museum* 148 (1985) and David Carr, "Cultural Institutions as Structures of Cognitive Change," in Lorraine Cavaliere and Angela Sgrol, eds., *New Directions in Adult and Continuing Education* (San Francisco: Jossey-Bass, 1992).

15. Maurice Halbwachs, *The Collective Memory,* trans. Francis J. Ditter, Jr., and Vida Yazdi Ditter (New York: Harper and Row, 1950).

16. It should be noted here that the cultural nationalism of Chinese in the United States has often developed in direct response to the far more encompassing and racially exclusionary Eurocentric cultural nationalism of the dominant culture.

17. For more on the formation of nationalist identifications, see Homi K. Bhabha, ed., *Nation and Narration* (New York: Routledge, 1990).

18. For a discussion of the concept of a cultural free space, see Sara M. Evans and Harry C. Boyte, *Free Spaces: The Sources of Democratic Change in America* (New York: Harper and Row, 1986). Also see John Kuo Wei Tchen, "'Race' and Cultural Difference: Historical Challenges and Future Possibilities" (Washington, D.C.: Cultural Education Committee, Smithsonian Institution, 1989).

19. This is a term used by German American photographer Arnold Genthe, who began his career by photographing San Francisco's Chinese community before the 1906 earthquake and fire. See John Kuo Wei Tchen, *Genthe's Photographs of San Francisco's Old Chinatown* (New York: Dover, 1984).

20. Frisch, *Shared Authority,* xxi. Gayatri Chakravorty Spivak has an apposite response to such a self-negating reaction; see her *The Post-Colonial Critic: Interviews, Strategies, Dialogues,* ed. Sarah Harasym (New York: Routledge, 1990), 62.

21. For example, the very well intentioned Children's Bridge exhibition, which dealt with stereotyping and prejudice, at the Boston Children's Museum in 1990 relied a great deal on interactive computers while docent-guards stood by showing visitors how to operate the computers. An excellent chance for discussions between them and visitors about the issues of the exhibition was missed.

22. John Kuo Wei Tchen, "New York Chinese: The Nineteenth-Century Pre-Chinatown Settlement," in *Chinese America: History and Perspectives* (San Francisco: Chinese Historical Society of America, 1990), 157–92.

23. Joyce Young, "P.S. 23 Reunion in Chinatown," *New York Daily News,* 6 Jan. 1988; Bill Bell, "Last Ethnic Wave Rekindles P.S. 23," *New York Daily News,* 11 Jan. 1988; Dennis Duggan, "Shut School Is Still Teaching History," *New York Newsday,* 11 Jan. 1988; Jerry Talmer, "A Chinatown Picture Show," *New York Post,* 11 May 1990.

24. Ronald Takaki, *Strangers from a Different Shore: A History of Asian Americans* (Boston: Little, Brown, 1989), and Tchen, " 'Race' and Cultural Difference."

25. Elizabeth Blackmar, *Manhattan for Rent, 1785–1850* (Ithaca: Cornell University Press, 1989); Anthony Jackson, *A Place Called Home: A History of Low-Cost Housing in Manhattan* (Cambridge, Mass.: MIT Press, 1976); Kevin Lynch, *What Time Is This Place?* (Cambridge, Mass.: MIT Press, 1972); Yi-Fu Tuan, *Space and Place: The Perspective of Experience* (Minneapolis: University of Minnesota Press, 1977); Steven Steinberg, *The Ethnic Myth: Race, Ethnicity, and Class in America* (New York: Atheneum, 1981); Alexander Saxton, *The Indispensable Enemy: Labor and the Anti-Chinese Movement in California* (Berkeley: University of California Press, 1971); Elizabeth Fox-Genovese, *Within the Plantation Household* (Chapel Hill: University of North Carolina Press, 1988); Mechal Sobel, *The World They Made Together* (Princeton: Princeton University Press, 1987); Jacquelyn Hall et al., *Like a Family: The Making of a Southern Cotton Mill World* (Chapel Hill: University of North Carolina Press, 1987); Maurice Halbwachs, *The Collective Memory;* Natalie Zemon Davis and Randolph Starn, eds., "Introduction," in "Memory and Counter-Memory," *Representations* 26 (1989), 1–6; and David Thelen, "Memory and American History," *The Journal of American History 75,* no. 4 (1989), 1117–29.

26. Edward Said, *Orientalism* (New York: Pantheon, 1978) and John Kuo Wei Tchen, "Barnum's Chinese Museum," paper presented at the conference on The Politics of Portraiture: Icons, Stereotypes, and Other Approaches to Multicultural Images, National Portrait Gallery, Washington, D.C., 1990.

27. The representation of Chinese and other Asian Americans as a "model minority" has been extremely problematic in recent years. This portrayal has been linked to the rise of anti-Asian violence in the 1980s. See John Kuo Wei Tchen, " 'Whiz Kids' and American Race Relations: Some Thoughts on the 'Model Minority' Phenomenon," in Mina Choi, "Race, Gender, and Eyeglasses: Teacher Perceptions of Asian, Black, and White Students" (Flushing, N.Y.: Asian/American Center, Queens College, 1989).

28. For more on this point of view, see R. David Arkush and Leo O. Lee, eds., *Land Without Ghosts: Chinese Impressions of America from the Mid-Nineteenth Century to the Present* (Berkeley: University of California Press, 1989). This volume is one of the few published works discussing the point of view of the Chinese gentry. On the other hand, the CHM has many stories in its oral-history collection that document the perspectives of farmers, laborers, schoolteachers, and others.

29. Dean MacCannell, *The Tourist: A New Theory of the Leisure Class* (New York: Schocken, 1976); John A. Jakle, *The Tourist: Travel in Twentieth-Century North America* (Lincoln: University of Nebraska Press, 1985); Valene L. Smith, ed., *Hosts and Guests: The Anthropology of Tourism* (Philadelphia: University of Pennsylvania Press, 1989); Michael Denning, *Mechanic Accents: Dime Novels and Working-Class Culture in America* (New York: Verso, 1987); Alan Dundes, *Cracking Jokes: Studies of Sick Humor Cycles and Stereotypes* (Berkeley: Ten Speed Press, 1987); Robert Jay, *The Trade Card in Nineteenth-Century America* (Columbia: University of Missouri Press, 1987); William F. Wu, *The Yellow Peril: Chinese Americans in American Fiction, 1850–1940* (Hamden, Conn.: Archon, 1982); Pierre Bourdieu, *Distinction: A Social Critique of the Judgement of Taste* (Cambridge, Mass.: Harvard University Press, 1984); Isaac Julien and Kobena Mercer, eds., "The Last 'Special Issue' on Race?" *Screen* 29, no. 4 (1988).

30. Recent cultural studies on gender and multiculturalism have demonstrated how the seemingly rigid categories of race, gender, class, and ethnicity have changed over time and from culture to culture. Indeed, the apparently immutable boundaries between "us" and "them" have proven to be in actuality quite permeable and ambiguous. See Martin Bernal, *Black Athena: The Afroasiatic Roots of Classical Civilization* (New Brunswick, N.J.: Rutgers University Press, 1987); James Clifford, *The Predicament of Culture* (Cambridge, Mass.: Harvard University Press, 1988); Joan Scott, *Gender and the Politics of History* (New York: Columbia University Press, 1988); and Rick Simonson and Scott Walker, eds., *Multi-Cultural Literacy* (Minneapolis: Greywolf, 1988).

31. Michael Fischer, "Ethnicity and the Arts of Memory," in James Clifford

and George E. Marcus, eds., *Writing Culture: The Poetics and Politics of Ethnography* (Berkeley: University of California Press, 1986).

32. For the concept of the sojourner, see Paul C. P. Siu, *The Chinese Laundryman: A Study of Social Isolation,* ed. John Kuo Wei Tchen (New York: New York University Press, 1987) and Clarence Glick, *Sojourners and Settlers: Chinese Migrants in Hawaii* (Honolulu: University of Hawaii Press, 1980).

33. This was a story told by a participant in a CHM historical walking tour led by the author in 1986.

34. For more on audience reception and evaluation, see Constance Perin's essay in this volume.

35. "Chinatown Memories," a 1987 interview by Bennett Weinstock of Sydney Silberman, CHM archives; and a 1989 interview by Dorothy Rony of Lung Chin, CHM archives.

36. Peter Gould and Rodney White, *Mental Maps* (London: Unwin Hyman, 1974).

37. Paul Thompson, *The Voice of the Past: Oral History* (Oxford: Oxford University Press, 1978); Ronald J. Grele, *Envelopes of Sound: The Art of Oral History* (Chicago: Precedent, 1985); and Mihaly Csikszentmihalyi and Eugene Rochberg-Halton, *The Meaning of Things: Domestic Symbols and the Self* (Chicago: University of Chicago Press, 1981).

38. Arkush and Lee, *Land Without Ghosts,* 178.

39. A version of this section of the essay appeared in John Kuo Wei Tchen, "Chair's Statement," *New York Council for the Humanities Annual Report, 1989–90* (New York: New York Council for the Humanities, 1991), 6–8.

CHAPTER 12

The Museum as a Vehicle for Community Empowerment: The Ak-Chin Indian Community Ecomuseum Project

NANCY J. FULLER

T his report is about the process of implementing a community-based education model as the initial phase of establishing a community museum. First I provide a philosophical and historical framework for understanding the ecomuseum approach. Then I discuss the application of the approach in a specific setting. I open by presenting the context that led the Ak-Chin Indian Community to seek a new institution, describe a communitywide education process for learning about the nature and structure of museums and archives, and discuss the staff training program. Then I identify the results to date and highlight some elements that seemed to make the project successful.[1] The photo essay that accompanies this text consists of photographs of the Ak-Chin ecomuseum and its activities along with edited excerpts taken from statements made by ecomuseum staff members and the tribal chairperson during the Smithsonian Institution's conference Museums and Communities and at the ecomuseum's opening celebration.

In a twenty-five-year period, the Ak-Chin Indian Community, a group of five hundred people who live on 21,840 acres in the Arizona desert, have transformed their lives, achieving economic independence and in the process creating a new tool for their continued growth and development.[2] Once impoverished and dependent tenants on their own lands, the community has become a group of prosperous farmers who make use of state-of-the-art methods to compete effectively in world agricultural markets. Yet the cultural traditions that sustained the Ak-Chin for thousands of years and defined them as a community are presently in jeopardy. To meet the challenges brought about by economic development, the Ak-Chin selected an ecomuseum as the best vehicle to help the community to understand and manage everyday life as it changes.

THE ECOMUSEUM CONCEPT

An ecomuseum is an agent for managing change that links education, culture, and power. It is sometimes called a neighborhood museum or a street museum. The approach is both a framework for examining the nature and structure of cultural institutions and a process for democratizing them. It extends the mission of a museum to include responsibility for human dignity. The methodology, based on educational and psychological concepts of lifelong learning and life-stage development, seeks to put in place those conditions that enable communities to learn about themselves and their needs, and to act upon that knowledge. The ecomuseum concept establishes a role for the museum as a mediator in the process of cultural transition.[3]

Ecomuseums are based on the belief that museums and communities should be related to the whole of life. They are concerned with integrating the family home with other aspects of the community, such as the natural environment, economics, and social relationships. Ecomuseums are community learning centers that link the past with the present as a strategy to deal with the future needs of that particular society. Their activities and collections reflect what is important to the community, not necessarily conforming to mainstream values and interpretations. René Rivard, a proponent of the approach, says that an ecomuseum is a "process [that] begins with what is known by the people—the collective memory—and sees what events and objects are linked to these ideas."[4] The mission is to develop community autonomy and identity. Rather than serving as a storehouse or a temple, both of which isolate objects from ordinary people and require professional assistance for access and understanding, an ecomuseum recognizes the importance of culture in the development of self-identity and its role in helping a community adjust to rapid change. The ecomuseum thus becomes a tool for the economic, social, and political growth and development of the society from which it springs.

About twenty-five years ago, practitioners in many parts of the world began investigating the human dimension of museums. Fueled by principles of equality and autonomy, and focused on public education, they questioned the attitudes, assumptions, and principles that underlie museums. Often conventional-style museums were found not to have worked as models for community museums, because their social and cultural character was not appropriate to the needs of the audience. While some observers felt that increased public awareness of a museum's essential services would lead to expanded community use, others looked at the issue differently. They argued that it is better to change the museum into an institution that serves the needs of the public, rather than try to change public perceptions of what museums are about.

Sparked by the intellectual fervor of the 1968 Paris riots, the French established a series of decentralized museums in historically and environmentally unique regions such as Normandy, Brittany, and the Camargue. The museums were designed to preserve economic viability and included facilities to document the areas' histories and for community meetings. The father of the movement was Georges Henri Rivière (1897–1985), a French museologist and pioneer in the development of international museum cooperation. He created and defined the interdisciplinary museological approach that emphasizes the importance of place. In 1972 participants at the International Council of Museums (ICOM) roundtable conference in Santiago, Chile, claimed—for the first time, officially—that a museum should be integrated with the society around it. In 1974, the ICOM definition of a museum was revised according to the new spirit, stating that the museum should be an institution in the service of society and its development.[5]

Out of this growing ethic arose institutions (which usually had no knowledge of parallel efforts elsewhere) that attempted to respond to the need for cultural relevancy. In the mid-1960s the Smithsonian Institution created the Anacostia Neighborhood Museum in Washington, D.C. In the next decade, several Scandinavian countries, Spain, Portugal, and Brazil all developed nontraditional museums in red-light districts, psychiatric clinics, blue-collar neighborhoods undergoing gentrification, urban barrios, and rural districts. All shared a participatory approach and the goal of being a catalyst for change.

The work conducted in Mexico provides an illustration. In 1973, the Museo Nacional de Antropología closed for extensive renovation. The staff took this opportunity to experiment and develop a museum format appropriate for the city's poorest residents. The seven-year project, called La Casa del Museo, produced a participatory community leadership methodology that integrated local museums with educational institutions. The work served as the foundation for the establishment of fifty-two new community museums in five states since then.[6]

Driven by the growing emphasis on community autonomy and identity and linked by common language and customs, the ecomuseum idea spread across the Atlantic from its origins in France to French-speaking museologists in Quebec, Canada. In the middle 1970s, a private collection of objects gathered from the southern Beauce region of Quebec came on the market. This presented a unique opportunity to explore the application of the ecomuseum concept in a local setting. Residents of this rural, economically depressed area agreed that the items were valuable and that the collection should be kept intact, but no one was able to raise the purchase price. Suddenly, a potential buyer from the United States appeared on the scene, and it looked as if the collection might leave the area. Those who wanted to keep it in the region quickly formed a committee and arranged for the thirteen small villages whose heritage was represented in the collection to buy it cooperatively. The community started a dialogue about ways to care for and display the new collection. From that came a new awareness of the southern Beauce region as a place with distinctive characteristics and of the meaning of the objects in the residents' daily lives. In 1982, the thirteen communities officially designated themselves as a group by renaming their area Haute-Beauce. Simultaneously, in a second action that reflected changed attitudes, the communities defined the process in which they were engaged—identifying their culture and caring for their heritage—as the Ecomusée de Haute-Beauce.[7]

Significant differences exist between ecomuseums and traditional museums in their physical forms and collection philosophies. An ecomuseum is defined by the geographic area or audience it serves, and is not confined to a single building. Collections are viewed from much broader perspectives. They are organized around the community's interrelationship with its culture and physical environment. In addition to objects, collections can consist of audiovisual materials, paper documentation, physical sites, traditional ceremonies, oral histories, and social relationships. Inventories are taken of holdings in the community, but people are not asked to turn over valued items for storage in a repository. As a result, training community members to care for items that are kept at home is a critical function of ecomuseum staff work.

To promote the goal of autonomy, ecomuseums focus on activities in which individuals learn the skills necessary to work successfully in daily life rather than on the creation of an end product. Ecomuseum projects are tailored to community needs. Suppose, for example, the police department wants an orientation program for new recruits. The department might decide to create a slide program as one teaching tool. Ecomuseum staff could assist police officers by researching early records of the department's history in the ecomuseum archives center. They might suggest investigating other repositories or contacting families that have photographic collections. Also, they could take new pictures with the community-owned camera, or help prepare inexpensive captions and title slides to organize and focus the program. In this setting, new and diverse demands are placed on ecomuseum employees. Work such as researching a police department's history requires staff to have a broad knowledge of their community, the ability to communicate effectively, and the confidence to take risks.

In order to build group identity, ecomuseum activities examine individuals' relationships to the community as a whole. Exhibitions often address the political and economic implications of an issue from the perspective of their effects on individual community members' lives. Ecomuseum exhibitions can be staged in one central place or coordinated throughout several locations at the same time. Sometimes families will build exhibits at their homes, perhaps on the lawn or porch. In a way similar to house and garden tours in exclusive urban neighborhoods, visitors go from house to house, appreciating one another's creativity, remembering something forgotten, reconfirming values, and renewing a spirit of community cohesiveness.

To nurture the collective memory, the community needs archival and museological knowledge and skills to identify, preserve, and communicate parts of that memory. The key principle of training is that those who participate in the process grow as individuals and develop their capabilities and expertise as a result of their experiences. Therefore, staff members' roles differ from those in most museums. Instead of taking sole responsibility for content and interpretation, they help the community fulfill its own agenda. The Ecomusée de Haute-Beauce is especially noted for its methods of teaching museology to community members. In this capacity, it has strongly influenced the development of other ecomuseums throughout the world, which is a role the farmers, housewives, merchants, and stonecutters of the area had never envisioned for themselves prior to the establishment of the ecomuseum. In Haute-Beauce, the concept of community cohesiveness has been extended beyond cultural projects to help address economic needs. The new identity gave town leaders added political leverage, and as a result the provincial government has been willing to respond to funding requests submitted by this group of communities that previously had been rejected when submitted by individual municipalities.

A distinguishing feature of an ecomuseum is its role in community problem solving. The outcome of such problem solving is potentially different in each community because it originates in a specific local issue. Some examples might be a drought, an urban renewal project, or a factory closing. Inherent in the operation of an ecomuseum is a process that teaches people how to investigate an issue and speak out. An ecomuseum not only provides a place in which to hold discussions and create exhibitions about issues of common concern, but also gives community members actual practice in asking new questions, researching facts, communicating ideas, defending positions, and coming to new understandings in ways that are culturally appropriate. Established centers such as union halls, churches, or men's clubs, where groups used to meet and talk through political matters informally, now are disappearing. Yet the need to hear about the concerns of newly emerging groups—women who work outside the home, migrant laborers, latchkey children, elderly people isolated from their extended families—must be met if a community is to make the transition to a better life.

La Maison des Cultures Frontières, a documentation center in the Saar region on the French-German border, uses a combination of archives, audiovisual materials, theater productions, language retention programs, genealogy tracing, and basic education classes to clarify and resolve community problems. The region was once a thriving industrial center, but the obsolete coal mines and factories are now closed, creating severe unemployment. The nationality of the area's inhabitants had changed seven times since 1870 as a consequence of wars. This, combined with an influx of new nationalities—Poles, Turks, Italians—created a culture different from that of the governing authority. Workers and their families were not allowed to use the street language that evolved in the region nor to relate their experiences in schools and other public institutions; as a result, the residents did not know their cultural identity. La Maison does not produce stationary exhibitions, but rather tries to give value to oral traditions and community relationships. It attempts to help people who live there look at and understand the real impact of economic decline and political separation on their lives. In the early 1980s, the center's staff began going door to door, talking to people in their kitchens. Despite the millions of miners who had lived there and the importance of their labor for the industrial factories of Europe, the center's staff could find no traces of these people's past—no museum, no theater, no written literature. Slowly, community people acquired trust in the center's staff, and began to bring out photographs that had been stored in shoeboxes and other places hidden from public view. More than eight thousand photographs were collected, transferred to video-tape, and returned to their owners. The process of reflection and dialogue that accompanied this caused participants to confront their feelings and to examine their relationships with one another and with other communities. The director of La Maison des Cultures Fron-tières, Jean Hurstel, says that over time members stopped lamenting past difficulties such as the closing of the mines and shifted to discuss-ing present-day problems, for instance the stresses on family life caused by unemployment.[8] From the experience has evolved a system of co-productions. La Maison collected narratives along with the pho-tographs and assisted community members in writing short vignettes for presentation in street-theater productions. One center production dramatizes the pain experienced by grandparents who were unable to visit their daughter and her new child because they lived on opposite sides of the closed border.

Models such as these served as the foundation for planning and organizing the Ak-Chin Indian Community ecomuseum project.

THE AK-CHIN INDIAN COMMUNITY

> Our location between the Tohono O'odham [Papago] and the Akimel O'odham [Pima] reservations has caused us to become sepa-rate, although still related. . . . We never realized what our culture was until the [archaeological] mitigation study revealed the ancient objects. We found out [our culture] is more than a location, [it's] a way of life.
>
> —Charles Carlyle, ecomuseum project director

The Ak-Chin live at the northern edge of the Sonoran Desert in south-ern Arizona, about forty miles south of Phoenix. They are descen-dants of Akimel O'odham (Pima) and Tohono O'odham (Papago)

Indians who settled on the Vekol Wash of the Santa Cruz River (a wash is a seasonal floodplain created when a river overflows its banks). In both tribal-group languages, the word *ak-chin* means a place where water spreads out, and has come to describe a method of irrigation in which plants are grown in depressions created by the strong force of the water. Historians say that the Ak-Chin group acquired their name because they used this system of irrigation to produce crops of melons, beans, and squash.

Spanish explorers came to the region in 1512 and established a colonial government that endured until the Mexican revolution in the first quarter of the nineteenth century. The area was ceded to the United States by treaty in 1848, following the end of the Mexican War. Afterward, two important changes occurred—the cessation of the Apache wars, and the laying of the Southern Pacific railroad tracks across the edge of the Vekol Wash—that opened the Arizona territory to settlement. The Ak-Chin believe that they have always been farmers who lived in permanent settlements. But because of the seasonal fluctuations in the water source, historians contended that before the 1880s the Ak-Chin were hunters and gatherers, stopping at the wash for spring and fall harvests. They also say that the establishment of a railroad junction at Maricopa, three miles north of the present-day Ak-Chin reservation, encouraged permanent settlement by providing the Ak-Chin with a reliable marketplace to sell their basketry and other products. By 1911, federal records show that about 120 Indians were farming approximately two hundred acres at the wash.[9]

In the mid-1970s, archaeologists began excavating at the Ak-Chin reservation. Findings from the investigation of thirty-one prehistoric and historic sites suggest that the area was first inhabited in the Hohokam period (300–1450).[10] The Hohokam were farmers who irrigated by an intricate system of canals. Archaeologists found the Ak-Chin site intriguing. It appears that the Vekol Wash environment, where the *ak-chin* type of floodwater farming was practiced, was the site of nearly 15,000 years of uninterrupted habitation.[11] Excavations in 1989 revealed a hand-dug well on the reservation, suggesting that permanent settlement was possible by reliance on ground water. Archaeologist Richard Effland, who works with the tribe, says that the well is similar to ones documented in the historic period.

The Ak-Chin are a young and growing population. In 1991, only thirty people over fifty-five years of age were recorded on tribal enrollment rolls. More than half of the members were born since 1960. The population has increased also because more community members are choosing to return to the reservation after living elsewhere for a period of time. The community is governed by a five-person elected council, whose chief goals are full employment and education. A high-school diploma or its equivalent for each community member is one of the council's highest priorities. Despite having a small population and living between two larger tribes, the Ak-Chin have survived and prospered by cultivating good relations with their neighbors and associates. They are admired for their self-reliance and cooperation among themselves. The intricate mix that is their cultural heritage continues to be evident: local celebrations feature "chicken scratch" music, a combination of Native American, Hispanic, and Anglo-country styles. Church activities play a vital role in daily life. In addition to traditional religious practices, most community members belong to either the St. Francis Catholic Church, which was built on the reservation in 1925, or the Ak-Chin Bible Church, which was established in the early 1960s.

Like all desert success stories, this one started with water. In the 1940s and 1950s, the Ak-Chin leased their land to non-Indians and were hired back as farm laborers by the lessee. The practice returned a yearly income to the entire tribe of only $10,000. They lived without running water or electricity. In 1961, against the advice of the Bureau of Indian Affairs, the council discontinued leasing tribal land. Banking on their members' modern farming skills and personal attributes, the Ak-Chin embarked on a cooperative agricultural operation unprecedented in Indian history. They hired a non-Indian manager, and by 1964 the farm reported profits of more than $21,000. The operation rapidly increased in scale and diversity. In 1976, Ak-Chin Farms Enterprises netted over $1 million.[12]

Then in the mid-1970s, crop yields began to decrease significantly because of a lack of water, despite stringent conservation measures. As it turned out, extensive pumping by surrounding communities was rapidly lowering the subterranean water table.

When the federal government created the Ak-Chin reservation in 1912, it promised a regular and dependable water supply. That promise had never been fulfilled. Once the well water levels began dropping, the community considered legal action, but decided to negotiate with the federal government for a permanent supply of water. The final agreement, Public Law 98-530, signed in 1984, was the first water settlement negotiated among an Indian tribe, the Department of the Interior, and Congress. It called for 75,000 acre-feet of water to be diverted by canal via the Central Arizona Project aqueduct from the

Colorado River. With a reliable source of water assured, the farm began to expand once again. By 1986, the cultivated acreage had grown from less than 5,000 acres to 16,000 acres.

During the years between the creation of the farm and the water settlement, the overall pace of village life changed slowly. Farm profits were reinvested in the community. Electricity and water and sewer lines were installed, the tribal construction firm started building homes for each family, a state-of-the-art fire-and-rescue department was established, and a community center was constructed to offer programs for preschool children and the elderly. These initiatives and other tribally owned businesses, such as a lumber company, commissary, and cotton gin, provided employment for all members and funds for community services.

Yet the water settlement, paradoxically, threatened the survival of the Ak-Chin's traditions and values. While it brought about economic self-sufficiency, there were unanticipated effects. Negotiations were protracted and risky, diverting the attention and energies of the group at a time when farm production was declining because of a reduction in the water supply. At many stages during the nearly ten years of negotiations, the outlook did not seem favorable. However, strong emotions united the community. They were willing to endure sacrifices with the expectation that a favorable conclusion would allow them to maintain the status quo. But in reality, the community was moving into a world that was infinitely more complex than their old one. Strong forces were bringing about irreversible changes that were to affect every aspect of Ak-Chin life. The delicate balance of physical isolation and talent for adaptability by which the Ak-Chin had maintained their cultural identity and autonomy was no longer possible.

The first of these forces threatening community cohesiveness was the impact of sophisticated technology on tribal lifestyles. While the technology was intended to allow the farm to prosper and provide a means to maintain the Ak-Chin's autonomy, it could not easily accommodate the community's culture. Members began to question whether the new farm system placed enough value on their traditional roles and activities. The basket weavers are one example. The rituals of gathering native plant materials are rich in ceremony and meaning to the Ak-Chin. The basketmaking activities provide time for companionship with peers, mentoring younger people, reflecting on past activities, and discussing present-day situations. The special knowledge weavers possess gives them stature. When the new farm operation began all vegetation was cleared. While new sites for gathering basketmaking materials were found, they tended to be in remote areas, requiring transportation assistance and upsetting long-established social routines. Previously weavers had handled their gathering expeditions independently. These new conditions had the effect of reducing the weavers' control over their own affairs.

Changing conditions outside the reservation were a second force causing internal disruption. Increasingly, council decisions were linked to state, regional, and even global concerns. Because of the farm, members found that factors such as world cotton markets, population expansion in the Sun Belt, air quality, and state and federal legislation affected their lives profoundly. Other seeds of development began to transform the tranquil landscape near the Ak-Chin reservation. For a while, land nearby was in serious contention as a site for the new federal superconducting supercollider facility. The project went to another state, but changes in land use and the attendant problems loomed on the horizon.

The Ak-Chin native language also suffered. The Ak-Chin's distinctive dialect, which is derived from both Tohono O'odham and Akimel O'odham, is an important mark of their separate identity as well as a means of transmitting the community's knowledge about itself. As recently as the mid-1960s, tribal council affairs were conducted in the Ak-Chin language. But the practice declined as English became the primary language in which business was transacted. Today about fifteen percent of those who are over forty years of age understand the language, and fewer still speak it.

The emergence of a nationwide American Indian identity movement was a third force that influenced Ak-Chin life. Educational opportunities arising from the civil rights movement of the 1960s and 1970s expanded the perspective of a new generation of Indian people. National legislation such as the Indian Self-Determination Act (1972) and the Native American Religious Freedom Act (1978) established legal foundations for redefining relationships between Indians and non-Indians and promoted common bonds among Indian groups. In Arizona, thirteen tribal groups formed the Indian Intertribal Council. High on the council's agenda were topics related to sovereignty and cultural identity. Ak-Chin of all ages participated in the deliberations. From those discussions grew an awareness of the value of traditional practices. Young adults began to align themselves with elders to bring about a new mood of cultural renaissance among the Ak-Chin.

The confluence of these forces—technology, economic development, and the civil-rights movement—profoundly altered the community. Ak-Chin leaders traveled more often, to keep informed and to influence decisions affecting them. Their circle of advisors grew to include many who were less familiar with community norms. This led to gaps in communication with members, disrupting traditional patterns of consensus building. Most important, the conflicts crystallized profound differences in the worldview of modern lifestyles and that of traditional Ak-Chin culture.

In accordance with federal law, an archaeological study of the land was conducted in 1984 prior to installation of an intricate irrigation canal system. Excavations revealed more than three hundred pit houses, enough implements of daily life to fill seven hundred boxes, and the skeletal remains of twenty-one Indians.[13] The Ak-Chin's relationship with the land is a core element of their culture, so the transferral of these materials to a repository in Tucson aroused deeply held convictions, especially among the elderly, that sacred ground should not be disturbed. Although the human remains were returned and reburied with proper ceremonies on tribal grounds, the actions mobilized community resistance to further upheaval in their lives. The Ak-Chin began to voice concerns that their culture was gradually being undermined by outside forces. Matters came to a head over the issue of widening the two-lane road through the reservation. The road was used by drivers seeking a shortcut to the interstate highway that connects Phoenix and San Diego. The possibility of greatly increased truck traffic aroused concern about the safety of children and free-ranging animals. It also brought to the forefront the issue of declining privacy. Members were divided about ways to deal with these matters. Although the referendum on widening the road finally passed by a very narrow margin, it sent a strong political message to tribal leaders about community frustrations.

The conflicts were more than just tensions of the moment. Established roles and relationships in all spheres—political, social, economic, religious, generational, and racial—were creating an unpleasant environment. The situation called for major adjustments. The fundamental issue facing the Ak-Chin was whether they would acknowledge the implications for the future of the changes they were undergoing and deal with them. To do so required a consensus that the community could manage the economic transition while remaining a society bound together by a unique culture.

Leona Kakar, then the chair of the council, began to seek ways to defuse these tensions and reweave the community together. She reasoned that if younger generations knew about the tribe's early struggles and achievements, they would be proud to be Ak-Chin, and the community would survive. She thought a museum and archives would be the ideal means.

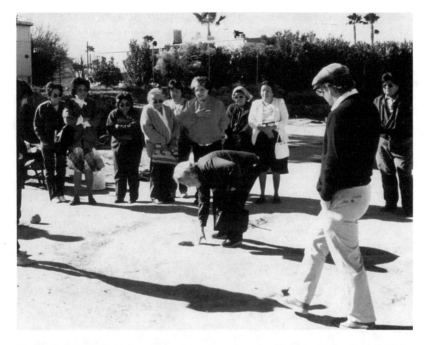

Fig. 12-1. Archaeological excavations conducted on the Ak-Chin reservation revealed evidence of human habitation dating from the Hohokam period. The findings renewed the members' interest in their past and were the impetus for establishing a community museum. Activities have been organized by the museum staff to inform members about the contributions of archaeology to tribal knowledge. Since the excavation sites on the reservation had been backfilled at the conclusion of the digs to protect the sites from deterioration, the program shown here was conducted at a newly excavated Hohokam site near the Phoenix airport that exhibited characteristics similar to those found at the Ak-Chin sites. Photo courtesy Richard Effland and Archaeological Consulting Services.

Thousands of clues to ancient human activity in the southwestern United States have survived to the present time because of a combination of factors. Often left in localities uninviting to modern development, covered by soil and rocks in a dry climate, the remains have had nature itself as the prime preserver. With that in mind, we are able to learn about those who came before, our ancestors.

Archaeology classes were first started in 1976 at the Ak-Chin Indian Community. At that time nobody in the community knew anything about archaeology. Nobody was even aware of the archaeological artifacts or the sites on the reservation. From the classes, I realized the important impact that archaeology has on learning more about our heritage and culture.

I think the museum staff can be the spark that will help the community broaden its in-depth understanding of the lifeways of our ancestors. We will be role models and educators to our community and to other tribes as well. From our archaeological training, we are becoming cultural interpreters that will allow us to preserve and celebrate our identity.

—JOHNNY LOPEZ

One very important hands-on training experience that the staff had is the archaeological test excavation on the site of the future museum. We learned the basics, such as laying out a grid system.

—TERESA VALISTO

Maybe it was the archaeology program that made us want to tell where we came from and who we are related to. But when you think about it, it is the language. I tell my kids not to believe everything they see on TV or read. It is important that they call something what it is named in the Ak-Chin language.

—ELAINE BOEHM

The land development and clearance for the farm enabled us to realize the significance of our past through artifacts and archaeological sites. These new insights awakened the curiosity of the community about where they came from, who they are, and where they are going. It made them realize and recognize the need for a cultural preservation program.

—CHARLES CARLYLE

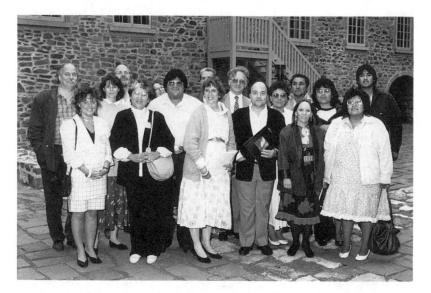

Fig. 12-2. The Ak-Chin began the yearlong process of planning and organizing their community museum by visiting more than a hundred museums and archives facilities in the United States and Canada. Members of the ecomuseum project board, staff of native-operated museums and cultural centers in Quebec, the director of the Nordic Sami Institute in Norway, and members of the staff of the Gouvernement du Québec, Ministère des Affaires Culturelles, traveled together for ten days in May 1988 to learn about models in French-speaking regions of Quebec. Here they pause for a group photograph with officials of the Musée de la Civilisation during a tour of that building prior to its public opening. This initial visit led to an ongoing series of international cultural exchange programs between groups in Quebec and the Ak-Chin. Recently, the exchange program was expanded to include people from community museums in Mexico. Photo by Pierre Souland, courtesy of the Musée de la Civilisation.

The staff has gone through various training classes and school programs to help establish themselves as qualified technicians, historians, or records managers. Along with this have come various problems and difficulties that are aggravating, such as finding enough time for classes, work, personal needs, family duties, and other obligations.

To determine if this ecomuseum concept is right or wrong for our community is also an issue we faced. At the beginning it all seemed to be an idea we felt would be good for our community, but as we continued, various issues were raised by the local community and staff as well as by nonmembers. They asked, "Why are you calling it a museum?"

In our Indian community, our view of a museum is an idea of a closed culture in a box. This is a problem for us as museum technicians and we try to eliminate this type of conflict. So we say, "Yes, we say the word museum, but it has a totally different function." An ecomuseum can be interpreted the way we want to and we can change it anytime.

This is a start to help our community in preserving today's information for tomorrow's generation and along with this, our culture. Though a museum might not be our traditional way of preserving and passing on our culture, our beliefs will always remain the same. The ecomuseum-type concept is a different, modern method that can be used with our traditional way of life, which has been escaping our community slowly.

Although planning and organizing an ecomuseum may be a difficult process, the dedication and pride that go into it will be rewarding. To know that our community as a whole will be responsible for taking care of our museum, for designing and interpreting the meaning of our culture, instills pride within the community.

—ELAINE BOEHM

You get ideas from visits to other museums. Then you go back home and apply the ideas in your culture in ways that involve the whole community. You really don't have to get your ideas from just an ecomuseum. You can get them from just about anybody. You do almost the same things but differently.

—WENDY AVILES

The visits helped us to get the concept.

—JOHNNY LOPEZ

We're developing our own ecomuseum even though we started from what we saw in Canada. That's what it is—someone giving you the opportunity to express your ideas. You use the guidelines to branch out, to try to use the museum concept in the simplest way and form.

—CHARLES CARLYLE

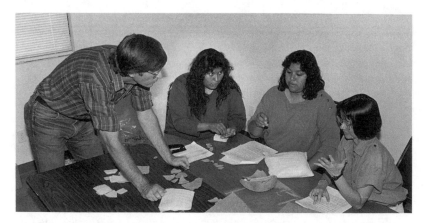

Fig. 12-3. More than seven hundred boxes of artifacts were excavated from archaeological sites on the Ak-Chin reservation and stored in a federal repository for safekeeping. Here in the artifact storage room of the ecomuseum, staff members are
accepting delivery and registering the first shipment of objects returned to the community. Photo by Eric Long, courtesy of the Smithsonian Institution.

*Much history has been recorded from only one point of view. Generating records by
tribal governments, although a relatively new process, is a way to add more interpretation to the historical perspective. Two years ago, we started to look into ways to preserve our written history, because we were losing part of our culture as we lost our oral
traditions. In the process, we created a tribal records management program.*

*We started by taking an inventory of all records held in each department, such as the
police department, the human resources center, the fire department, the tribal office,
and the farms office. When we first started, we had a hard time trying to figure out
which document goes into which file, but we learned. Before setting up our records
management and archives program, we visited several museums to get an idea of how
they document their records. In the state of Arizona we went to different places that
have worked with the community in some way. By doing this, now we know, more or
less, where we can go to retrieve information about Ak-Chin. Lately, we have started to
work with each department to set up their own filing system so that it will correspond
with our archives system.*

*In the near future, our goal is to teach our people what is involved in using the archi-
val section of the ecomuseum and encourage them to donate old documents that they
might have.*

—CAROLE LOPEZ

*The staff has started a photographic collection that will be placed in the photo archives
of the ecomuseum. To date, we have about five thousand photographs. Most of these
pictures are of events that have taken place in our community. Also, we have copied old
photographs that were given to us by community members.*

*Another archives project that the staff has been doing is going to the local library in
Casa Grande and viewing all the newspapers from 1914 to the present in order to find
all the information printed in the newspaper about the community. We will make copies
of the articles and any accompanying photographs and place them in the archives.*

—VICTORIA SMITH

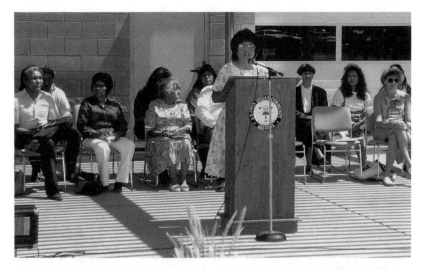

Fig. 12-4. The staff decided to name the ecomuseum the Ak-Chin Him Dak, which means "our way of life." The new building opened on 29 June 1991 with a gala celebration that began with speeches by tribal leaders, congratulatory messages and gifts from national and international friends and colleagues, and a ribbon-cutting ceremony. The festivities included a traditional feast, entertainment by Native American dancers and musicians in the afternoon, and a community dance that lasted until seven o'clock the following morning. Photo by Eric Long, courtesy of the Smithsonian Institution.

When I think about my history and culture I think of the way things were done in the old days. When you were born, you were taken to the medicine man. Now they don't do even that. Some of us try to keep the traditional practices going, but there is no medicine man.

Being more aware of the feelings of others in the community is important. I have to admit that we've just gone away from the past ways. The elders maybe don't think they are important to us. Yet they are. But we're so busy, we don't spend time with them. Once they are gone, it's gone forever. The museum has made me aware of that.

In order to help the Ak-Chin people keep in touch with each other, the community council, which is the governing body of the community, decided to establish an ecomuseum for the preservation and celebration of their culture. The opening of the ecomuseum was a day long planned for. The community is proud of the seven-member Him Dak staff for taking on the challenge and learning to take care of our precious past.

—DELIA CARLYLE

The staff has worked very hard to get to where we are today. We have had to learn so many things about ourselves, our community, about museums, about archives, about buildings, and about budgets.

—TERESA VALISTO

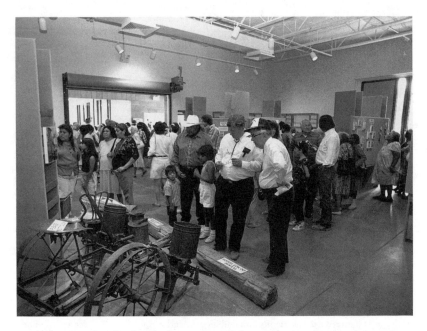

Fig. 12-5. More than five hundred guests toured the newly constructed ecomuseum on opening day. The exhibitions included historical objects contributed by the Ak-Chin, artifacts excavated from the archaeological digs on the farm's land, and displays created by tribal organizations showing the people who work there now and those who had preceded them, and telling how these efforts contribute to the functioning of the community. Photo by Eric Long, courtesy of the Smithsonian Institution.

The purpose of our education is to learn to be responsible for the operation of the building, and for the design and production of exhibits and community programs, and to gain a better understanding of museum practices and archives management.

Our ecomuseum is intended to be a place of exchange between generations, each teaching and learning from one another's special perspectives. Our culture, ever evolving, will continue to be rich and international, crossing borders geographically and through time.

The most important part of having our own ecomuseum is that we will be in charge.

—WENDY AVILES

Now that I've been through the museum development process, I want to know more about myself and to pass the language on to my children. The Makah saw they were losing their language and their dances. I went with the museum project board to the Makah museum, and that's what woke me up.

An ecomuseum is a reflection of its community. It not only connects with the past, present, and future, but also incorporates the social and psychological changes within the community. It helps bridge the gap between generations, not only with the Indians but with non-Indians in the surrounding areas. It is a vehicle and it is a tool used by the community to inform the general public, non-Indians, and other cultures and nations about the spirit and evolution of the community.

—CHARLES CARLYLE

Now I am much more aware of the importance of my past. I grew up differently from Elaine and Carole. Vicky and Teresa and I are alike because our moms and dads come from different backgrounds. I regret that my lifestyle is different, but I have learned from them. It's never too late. Being part of the staff has let me know about this life-style. I spent half my time on the reservation. I heard about it, but it didn't seem that important. Now I want my kids to have what I didn't have.

Because I don't speak the language, I feel bad when I hear others in the community speaking the language. I don't know what they are saying and yet I don't want them to say it in English.

—WENDY AVILES

I grew up at a time when the Ak-Chin didn't have all we have now. Then we still be-lieved in the spiritual stuff. In the three years since we started the training program, we have become more aware of the importance of our traditional beliefs. Now, we have the strength to take responsibility for educating those who do not know the beliefs.

—ELAINE BOEHM

Going through this museum development process has made me more aware of my cul-ture and especially my language. My kids understand the language but they are afraid to use it. They are embarrassed because other kids don't use it. Getting the elders in-volved to tell the stories or to sing is important. Now, I regret that I didn't listen to this elderly man. Going through this process has taught me that we're the ones who are re-sponsible for passing on the traditions.

—CAROLE LOPEZ

THE IDEA FOR A COMMUNITY MUSEUM

> It'll be something for the whole community to be proud of because it'll be community people running it. We don't have to hire people from the outside. . . . Plus, as Native Americans, we understand how we want to present [ourselves].
>
> —Elaine Boehm, ecomuseum exhibition technician

The archaeological excavations conducted prior to the installation of the irrigation system were the catalyst for awakening the community's interest in its heritage. As artifacts were recovered from the digs ar-chaeologists transferred them to an environmentally controlled, secure storage facility near Tucson. The community objected to their removal from Ak-Chin land because the artifacts represented ideas—the idea of a society that once existed and the idea of a culture that was still viable. The council heeded the community's feelings and withdrew approximately 190 acres of land from use as farm acreage, reserving it permanently for archaeological sites.[14] Government officials agreed to return the artifacts to the community when they had proper facilities to house the collections and a trained staff to curate them. With that, talk about building a museum began in earnest.

Archaeological experts had emphasized scientific and historical perspectives when interpreting the artifacts of the Ak-Chin's past. In direct contrast, members of the community found that, for them, the core meaning actually resided in the objects themselves. The experience of appreciating the present's continuity with the past and recognizing the objects' connection with their self-identity is what gave value to the objects for the Ak-Chin. Those who had worked on the field crew wanted to share the feelings they had had upon seeing the objects in the ground with those Ak-Chin who had not participated in the digs. They hoped to reconstruct a model of an ancient pit house at one of the excavation sites.[15] Evidence that ancient cultures had flourished on reservation land added credence to the community's sense of history. For example, the discovery of pieces of shell jewelry seemed to confirm that the Ak-Chin's ancestors had taken part in commercial exchanges with distant places. Such findings bolstered tribal oral histories that described long treks to Baja California to get salt. For some, the existence of these artifacts introduced new attitudes. While acknowledging the community's negative feelings about "archaeologists as bone diggers," Johnny Lopez says he came "to realize [archaeology] is something by which I can analyze and understand the past."[16]

In August 1986 a room in the community center was set aside as a temporary museum. Carol Antone and Eloise Pedro, two residents of the Ak-Chin reservation who had participated in the excavations, began attending museum training classes and organizing activities for the community. They were helped by the Museum Studies Program at Arizona State University and by the Pueblo Grande Museum. Their most popular exhibitions showed aspects of the changing landscape on the reservation. For one, Antone and Pedro gathered soil and pieces of vegetation from the fields. On a large table with side rails, they arranged the natural materials, along with children's toy farm implements and earth-moving vehicles, to illustrate the work occurring in the fields. Another exhibition consisted of grinding stones, pottery shards, and other artifacts found at the excavation sites. To enhance understanding, the museum staff drew illustrations showing the items' original functions. They made miniature pottery and effigy figures copied from artifacts that were in storage. The accompanying label identified the items as reproductions and linked their significance to the Ak-Chin's past, stating, "Actual clay used by our ancestors of long ago." Also available for viewing was a portable panel display created by the Central Arizona Project. It explained the statewide water delivery system, of which the Ak-Chin community was a recipient.

Antone and Pedro coordinated a variety of programs. They enlisted assistance from Joseph Smith, a community artist, to help with a presentation about Native American artists. Students with artistic talent were invited to sketch artifacts found at the archaeological sites. It was hoped that the experience would motivate students to further their education and perhaps seek careers as artists.[17] A spring program featured an outing to pick buds from cholla plants. The buds were considered a delicacy in traditional diets, but rarely have been gathered in recent times. On the tour, Leona Kakar demonstrated harvesting methods and ways of preparation for eating. Audience research was another staff job. At the museum open house, Antone and Pedro observed members responding more enthusiastically to activities requiring participation than to panel displays. Also, the two women developed a written questionnaire asking each family about their expectations and desires for the museum. In oral interviews, they asked people what should be transmitted to future generations; members of the community identified language fluency, knowledge of traditional ceremonies and oral history, native plant preservation, and arts and crafts instruction as among the most important.[18] These issues pointed toward an institution that would serve the needs of the Ak-Chin rather than a facility whose purpose would be to inform tourists (a common mission of tribal museums). Also implicit in the members' list of objectives was a call for the entire community to be active in the process.

A PLAN TO LEARN ABOUT MUSEUMS AND ARCHIVES

After listening to all the schoolchildren ask questions that I couldn't answer, I realized how important saving our culture is.

—Joseph Smith, Ak-Chin tribal council member

Initially, the tribal council had relied on advisors from the Phoenix area to shape the museum. But as members of the Ak-Chin community stated their desires, the scope of the project grew. The need for a development plan became clear.

The council started by asking their Washington-based consultant to identify a source of funds to help support architectural design costs and a team of advisors. When he sought technical assistance from the Smithsonian Institution, I suggested an ecomuseum. To me, the community seemed to have strong potential for successful implementation of the approach. By their decision to negotiate with the federal government over the water settlement, the Ak-Chin had demonstrated a willingness to attempt bold steps, and they had group experience taking risks. Their capabilities had been tested, and in the process the Ak-Chin gained a vision of themselves as a successful community. Most important was the community's agreement on the goal of continued self-sufficiency. These attitudes and skills could be transferred to new challenges.

The ecomuseum idea was presented to the council as a way to link the Ak-Chin's cultural and educational needs with the community's long-term goal to expand internal management capabilities.[19] The council was willing to explore the notion. It seemed to serve the Ak-Chin's collective interests, and they liked the idea of being first in the nation to attempt the model.

With funds from the Administration for Native Americans of the U.S. Department of Health and Human Services, the council established an ecomuseum project board consisting of Ak-Chin leaders, the staff of the temporary museum, and technical and professional experts. The board brought various perspectives to the process: council members were concerned about long-term fiscal and legal implications; the museum staff, representing community viewpoints, were most interested in learning about audience services; and the advisors, selected from across the nation, contributed resources and knowledge about architecture, archives and records management, community development, education, museology, history, and exhibition design and production. The key issue facing the museum project board was whether the community could perceive a museum as integral to its well-being. Inherent in that perception would be the community's acceptance of the idea that preservation of culture is a legitimate tribal government responsibility.

The board's initial meeting was held in October 1987. The two-year time limit on the grant shaped the planning and organizing phase. Three objectives were to be accomplished: the creation of a community awareness of the role and function of museums and archives, the establishment of a management capability within the community, and the design of a culturally appropriate facility.[20] Achieving these goals within the specified time period required the advisors to present information quickly and effectively, but also in a meaningful fashion. The board began by adopting a two-pronged community education plan that would help the community figure out ways to meet their needs through a museum and archives program, determine how the Ak-Chin culture could be reflected in an institutional setting, decide what functions should be performed and what knowledge and skills the staff would need to carry out those functions, and determine the relationship of the museum to both Ak-Chin and non-Ak-Chin people.

THE PROCESS OF COMMUNITY DISCOVERY

> I see the ecomuseum as the center of information.
>
> —Terry Enos, tribal council member

The first part of the community education plan was designed to promote an awareness of the multiple roles and functions a museum could have in tribal life, and to build cooperation and consensus for the project throughout the community. The plan called for a series of visits to museums and archives to see existing models firsthand, and to get a sense of the problems (and potential solutions) that accompany the operation of such facilities. Next, the information was to be disseminated to the community through scheduled meetings and informal discussions. The plan exposed participants to a broad spectrum of expertise and required active involvement. Implementation depended heavily upon group dynamics, with the museum project board being the motivating force. The goal of this phase of training was to convey a vision of a community museum as a place to serve community needs, and to establish a community image of the Ak-Chin people actively performing museum and archives work.

More than thirty Ak-Chin visited a total of over a hundred museums, historical societies, archives, and related cultural organizations of all sizes and forms of governance. The first trip was in November 1987 to the Colorado River Tribes Museum in nearby Parker, Arizona. After that, participants went to tribal and mainstream facilities that were geographically farther away and less similar ethnically or administratively but that provided important professional and technical lessons. In December 1987 they visited five museums in Washington state. In 1988 groups went to Wisconsin for five days, and to Washington, D.C., and Quebec for ten days each.

Museum board members and Ak-Chin community members involved with the ecomuseum project were plunged into emotionally and intellectually demanding situations. While some of the Ak-Chin had previously visited museum exhibitions, none had seen administrative offices, storage areas, and production facilities, which are normally out of public view. Many of the Ak-Chin were unfamiliar with cold, wet weather, and some were taking their first trip in an airplane. On the other hand, most project advisors were technically oriented and had little understanding of the implications of cultural diversity for community-based education and museums. Several advisors had never been in a tribal museum and had little knowledge of museum operations or nontraditional models.

The small-group orientation and the short-visit format of these study trips offered multiple opportunities for learning and reinforcement. As participants became more comfortable in their new roles as learners, they began to ask their hosts practical questions: how well the building worked for their needs, what strategies were used to attract visitors, what the operating costs were, what the sources of funds were, what they would do differently if they could start over. The method of investigation depended heavily on experiences that produced comfortable emotional responses. In the beginning, emphasis was placed on visits to institutions operated by Native Americans. These tended to be more immediately useful to the Ak-Chin because most Indian-run museums are relatively new and memories of start-up are still fresh. For example, a spirit of camaraderie developed during the visit to the Makah Cultural and Research Center in Neah Bay, Washington, where the Ak-Chin visitors attended an elders' luncheon. Charles Carlyle, the ecomuseum project director, described his feeling about being there as "a sense of belonging to an extended family."[21]

Through the visits, members of the project team were able to compare their expectations with real results. They received advice on successful strategies and pointers on pitfalls to avoid. The Oneida Nation, for example, has operated a tribal museum for over ten years. In a philosophical discussion one morning, Oneida museum staff and tribal administrators cautioned the Ak-Chin to involve all segments of the community from the earliest stages of planning and to respect different points of view. They noted that Oneida tribal elders did not visit their museum because it exhibited reproductions of religious masks, contrary to traditional mores.

Each training experience was slightly different from previous activities. Slowly, team members began to identify with what they were observing and discussing, fitting it in with their previous experiences. For example, Carole Lopez was council secretary before joining the museum staff as the archives technician. In that earlier job, she had learned the value of records when trying to establish linkages with the past. So when staff members from the Suquamish Museum and the Yakima Cultural Heritage Complex explained their records-management and oral-history programs, Lopez already had an image of herself performing aspects of that task. From that sense of familiarity emerged a greater confidence in her own abilities to take on more complex tasks.

In May 1988 the museum project board went to Quebec. There, for the first time, they saw both urban and rural ecomuseums. By this stage in the learning process, participants had numerous previous museum references on which to base their understanding of the new approach. They were able to move beyond the barriers that the vast differences in ethnic heritage, language, climate, and terrain would have presented earlier. Now the team was receptive to learning, able to recognize similarities and contrasts, and capable of raising skeptical questions.

The educational strategy employed in these training visits connected what learners knew from personal experience to new information they garnered from direct observation and from discussion with their hosts and among themselves. The content was structured to build from familiar settings to unknown ideas, and from specific experiences to general concepts. Underlying the process is a linkage in participants' consciousness between prior experiences and new perceptions. Participants began to gain insights into how issues such as changing land use, the loss of native language skills, changing community roles, and the increasing influence of outside factors had affected them personally. Ideas took shape as participants' reactions to the people and situations they encountered were creatively integrated with their own thoughts. Gradually participants began to connect the Ak-Chin's situation with similar experiences in other communities. At that point—which came at a different time for each person—participants began to envision, in their own terms, a rationale for a community museum.

Information was transferred to the community through an extended mentor strategy. At the outset, the board's technical and professional advisors were responsible for making information available to members of the community. The advisors' job was to diagnose problems and identify resources, not actually to produce the work. This required a judicious touch at appropriate times and always the ability to accommodate and adjust. The mentor relationship was different from a traditional academic one, in which a student works under the tutelage of an experienced person for an extended period of time. The plan linked each Ak-Chin participant to several experts and was fluid in design. Personal interactions were the basis for establishing trust. Advisors stepped back from close involvement when a particular segment of the project was completed, but were ready to contribute again in the future as needed. The strategy created a broad network of people who understood project goals. In turn, Ak-Chin board members were mediators, conveying information between the broader community and the advisors. They reported about questions raised and reactions observed at communitywide meetings and in family discussions. In board meetings, they presented community concerns and helped assess the implications of those concerns for the museum project.

The larger goal of the museum project board, however, was to extend the information they had garnered about museums and archives to others in the community. A critical feature of the educational plan called for the transferral of management decisions from advisors to the museum staff. As the staff's competence grew they were given increasing responsibility for sharing information with the community and infusing others with their newly acquired attitudes of enthusiasm and hopefulness. This obligation occasionally generated problems. Some community members did not come to scheduled meetings or would not discuss past events. Staff would ask advisors how they could get the community to participate and how they should explain an ecomuseum to people who had never seen one. These questions marked an important turning point in the learning process—the staff was identifying for itself a new level of need.

The staff's multiple learning experiences started to become integrated when museum workers from Quebec accepted the Ak-Chin's invitation to visit Arizona in November 1988. For the first time, the staff had to provide useful knowledge to those who were not members of the community. It forced them to reflect on the qualities of a good museum visit and to consider the Ak-Chin community from a visitor's perspective. To help the Canadians understand the intricate irrigation system, for example, the staff decided to produce portable exhibitions for placement at the reservoir and the point where the main irrigation canal divides. This cultural exchange became an opportunity to initiate meaningful linkages on the state level. Ak-Chin asked ATLATL, a Native American arts organization based in Phoenix, to organize a statewide tribal museums meeting to let other Native Americans in the state know about new museum models and to introduce the Canadians to a wider array of Arizona Indians. The meeting improved the Ak-Chin's understanding of how local efforts fit into the broader scope of cultural preservation. From these trial experiences conveying information and building relationships, Ak-Chin staff learned that they had useful information to contribute to others and that they had the ability to manage the process of passing along that information.

The on-site visits had underscored the importance of having an ecomuseum staff with the technical knowledge and skills to carry out a variety of functions. These insights prepared the way for a second stage of training.

THE STAFF TRAINING PROGRAM

> When I get a degree, I can go to other tribes and help them to do their records and preserve their history.
>
> —Carole Lopez, ecomuseum archives technician

The second phase of the education plan was a staff training program for six community members. Its goal was to put in place those conditions for learning that would enable community members to carry out public programs, research, and documentation services, and to produce exhibitions in a manner consistent with the Ak-Chin's lifestyles. The notion of lifelong learning provided the conceptual basis for the training methodology.[22] Because of a compatible educational orientation and their focus on client services, Central Arizona College was selected as the institution to administer the educational program, which was designed by Dr. Shayne Del Cohen (the records management and archives advisor) with advice from tribal leaders and museum board members. The college agreed to offer an associate's degree program in general studies with an emphasis on museum and archives management tailored for the Ak-Chin. It began in January 1989.

The college program was very demanding. As adults, each student had family responsibilities and financial obligations. None had previous museum or archives experience. In addition to working full-time in the temporary museum and archives rooms and attending school at night, four of the women had to care for young children. But, as Elaine Boehm explained, "When we make our own decisions, the difficulties tend to be way at the back."[23]

The curriculum was drawn up based on the community's expressed goals, individual talents and aspirations, professional standards, and state educational requirements. Numerous disciplines were covered in the degree program, among them archaeology, anthropology, linguistics, history, and natural science. The curriculum also included specific task training, such as oral-history techniques, exhibition design and production, and photography. In order to create a staff that could work together effectively, the curriculum was structured so that each student received a general understanding of all museum and archives functions in addition to specializing in a particular aspect of ecomuseum work. The format was nontraditional and flexible. The kind of information that members of an ecomuseum staff would need was provided. Students completed internships at the Heard Museum and the Arizona State Archives. Field experiences included conducting inventories of historical records at St. John's Catholic Mission (located about ten miles away), at tribal lawyers' offices in Tucson, and at engineering consultants' firms in Phoenix. Staff spent a week at the National Archives regional branch in Laguna Niguel, California. They observed photographic registration methods at the Arizona State Museum and gathered ideas for mounting outdoor exhibitions while visiting the Smithsonian Institution's Festival of American Folklife.

Recognition of a learner's past experiences was an important component of the Ak-Chin training program. Peer teaching helped to establish conditions in which members' special talents could be utilized. The structure of the archaeology course provides an example of this strategy. Since Johnny Lopez had had previous classwork in archaeology and excavation experience, he served as the instructor's field assistant. One staff assignment involved excavating the proposed museum site prior to construction. Teresa Valisto, the museum's oral-history technician, said Lopez was helpful and that she found the "experience of actually getting in the trenches and excavating" to be an effective way of learning.[24]

The pace at which needed information was offered, and the sequence in which it was presented, depended upon participants' readiness. Museum visits and project meetings were loosely structured to respond to new learning opportunities that arose. For instance, the Ak-Chin hosted a session of their Central Arizona College course on the native plants of Arizona at the temporary museum room. Because this class was composed mainly of visitors from northern states who wintered in Arizona and were unfamiliar with the customs of Southwestern Indians, the staff especially tailored their presentations to reflect tribal perspectives. To illustrate their points, they created a new exhibition titled What the Desert Has Given Our People. Learning strategies called for genuine participation. For example, in order to pass communication class successfully, each staff person had to speak as part of a panel presentation for the Western Museums Conference annual meeting held in Phoenix in October 1989.

This educational approach also served to strengthen relationships between the museum and its neighbors. Employees of the tribal newspaper, fire department, and lumber company joined with museum staff to attend a weeklong photographic-methods workshop taught by a Smithsonian Institution photographer. Maricopa High School provided darkroom space. The instructor helped identify vendors in the region who could supply photographic materials and be a local source of technical assistance. Through the establishment of local networks such as these, commercial concerns began to take an interest in the museum.

Through on-the-job experiences, staff developed specific skills. With two other women, Victoria Smith was responsible for taking inventory of the administrative records produced since 1961 by the farm operation and the police department. In order to create a records retention schedule and establish a procedure for the systematic transfer of materials to the archives, she had to talk with department employees, explain how this new scheme would affect their efforts, inquire about their flow of work, respond to their concerns, and organize a workable plan. In addition, the practical experiences helped develop each student's own rationale for learning. As Smith performed those tasks, she saw records documenting events that had happened when she was young. The process connected her with past experiences. She noted that as her personal stake became clearer, the tedium became more bearable.[25]

Evaluation of the students' progress was linked to meaningful work rather than being limited to formal tests. For example, the ecomuseum staff offered to teach a series of workshops in the summer youth program offered by the Ak-Chin Parks and Recreation Department. The purpose of the workshops was to heighten children's awareness of their culture and ancestry. For a ceramics class, Johnny Lopez provided examples of historic design motifs for students to use as an inspiration in decorating their own pottery. Elaine Boehm and Wendy Aviles helped children build model-size adobe houses from dry grass, twigs, and soil, and told stories about Ak-Chin people who had once lived in houses of that style. The workshops tested the staff's ability to communicate and their coordination skills. During the course of the summer's work, their motivation for learning changed from acquiring information in order to pass a test to a personal desire to transmit knowledge to Ak-Chin children because of its value to the community's future.

The physical isolation of tribal reservations often creates barriers to learning. To make courses available to the entire community and ease travel logistics, English 101, Introduction to Algebra, and Communication Skills were held at the Ak-Chin community center rather than at the college campus sixty miles away. The mathematics course attracted eighteen community members in addition to the museum staff. The training plan also addressed the long-term educational needs of individuals and the community. Despite the fact that many Native Americans have learned specialized tasks through short-term coursework, the lack of a degree tends to relegate them to low-level jobs. The plan recognized the need for certification. By meeting recognized standards, students qualify for further education or job promotions.

DEVELOPING THE BUILDING PLAN

> The building itself [will] be a gathering place—a place where all our people can come to visit, reminisce about the past, and enjoy one another's company. We want to bring the most important part of our culture to our people: the language. . . . [The building] is not a place to just keep things.
>
> —Wendy Aviles, ecomuseum education technician

Over a span of two and a half years, the project board met quarterly for several days at a time to design a new museum building. Conceptualizing an ecomuseum building was a challenging design problem. Not only were many on the team inexperienced in the design process, but the ecomuseum approach itself does not provide a standard architectural model to follow.

The project team grappled with ways to design a building that was compatible with traditional community architectural styles. Team members were attentive to the needs of their potential audience. In particular, they wanted to make the place one elders would use. As well, there were families who hoped to preserve old photographs, tribal departments with communication responsibilities that needed to produce exhibitions, and international visitors who wanted to know about the technical aspects of the solar-powered, computer-operated irrigation system. Nevertheless, a consensus existed that Ak-Chin children were the primary audience. They needed to understand the significance of the land at many different levels.

By the end of the first year of planning, members were linked by common understandings. Everyone came with valuable information to contribute. Collectively, they envisioned a place that would help make connections within the community, and that was of a scale appropriate to their budget and lifestyle. Most important, the board wanted a building that would portray symbolically the importance of Ak-Chin culture.

The second year was spent translating objectives into a practical facility for conducting program activities. Some decisions were related to technical issues, such as security versus accessibility, the amount of office space relative to community-service areas, and the problem of balancing environmental-control requirements with flexible use of outdoor areas. Other concerns involved building costs, parking for cars or school buses, and the composition and color of the building materials. The council wondered about the merits of hiring the tribal construction crew to do basic framing and foundation preparation. Advisors wanted the structure to make a visual statement about the community's relationship with land and water. Staff looked carefully at space assignments, assessing them on the basis of practical experiences—for example, they insisted on plenty of windows to see outside as they worked. Space was designated for specific purposes based on the functions that would be performed in an area and on the physical interactions that would occur there. At various stages, the architect presented scale models to help the team and community members visualize the proposed floor plan and the museum's placement in the village. Slowly, through a series of false starts that generated new discoveries, a building plan emerged with which everyone could identify.

In the spring of 1990 the project board recommended to the council an 8,000-square-foot building. Among its features were space for archives and artifact storage, an area for exhibition and activities, a community workshop, a darkroom, a soundproof recording room, a classroom, and a kitchen. So that visitors could view the farm, the design included an activity area on the roof, an elevator to give elderly and disabled visitors access to it, and a louvered structure to shade the roof during the day. A shallow canal and water fountain were proposed for the front entrance.

WHAT ARE THE RESULTS?

> The museum makes our people the cultural interpreters for our people. Tribes are no longer the objects of information but the translators of information. When I have visitors, I always drag them to the museum. . . . It is doing so much to bring back what we've almost lost.
>
> —Delia Carlyle, Ak-Chin tribal council chair

In the spring of 1990, the museum staff went door to door with the architectural model and illustrations of the proposed facility. They asked each family for their opinions. Results of the poll overwhelmingly demonstrated the community's approval, yet the council did not vote at that time to approve the plan and begin construction. In fact, the project was still facing scrutiny. Early in 1988, key personnel changes had occurred. Leona Kakar, who had been the force behind the museum idea, had not been reelected to the council. The two most experienced museum employees, Carol Antone and Eloise Pedro, had resigned their positions for personal reasons—Antone had decided to go to college full time to pursue a teaching degree, and Pedro had joined an archaeological firm. In addition, funding became an issue. The council had committed almost a million dollars to build a museum, but at an early project meeting, the council's prior promise to construct housing for the elderly was raised. A request for a gymnasium for teenagers was also heard. Some council members felt the money should be used for these purposes. The council decided to meet the need for senior citizens' housing first, and while they eventually found another source of funds to pay for the construction of that housing, the diversion slowed the projected ecomuseum schedule and revealed a lack of consensus about the project. Other stumbling blocks appeared. From nearby tribes, the council heard that maintaining a museum was a continuing drain on tribal resources. In addition, some questioned the necessity of the trips museum project board members were making.

The challenges that the project experienced are normal. Often, however, they do not surface until a facility is constructed and its management attempts to initiate programs. The Ak-Chin plan anticipated such problems. For just such reasons, it was designed not to depend upon the energies of a single person or a small contingent of dedicated people. Furthermore, community differences were not seen as obstacles. Rather, the planning and development process made community issues the starting point for creating a broad base of support.

By the fall of 1990, the leadership of the project had shifted from the advisors to the museum staff. They were motivated to act. In private meetings with the council, the staff documented the Ak-Chin's commitment to the museum project and pointed out its social, political, and educational implications for the community as a whole. In subtle ways, the museum staff had become a new power in tribal decisions. They were recognized as representatives of the community, willing to be spokespersons for them, and knowledgeable about the means needed to carry out their goals. Eventually the council and the museum staff reached agreement: the council became convinced that the ecomuseum was in the best interests of the Ak-Chin, and when they objected to having an elevator in a one-story building and to the louvered shade structure on the roof, the staff agreed to modifications. With that, the council gave final approval for the building.

A groundbreaking ceremony to start construction of the Ak-Chin Indian Community ecomuseum took place on 17 November 1990, about three years after the initial planning meeting. Soon after, the community began to offer items for the ecomuseum. The farm manager gave ten years' worth of photographs depicting various stages of the farm's development. Two account managers donated their collections of tribally made baskets. The new building opened on 29 June 1991 with a gala twenty-one-hour celebration to which all involved in the planning and organizing process were invited. They named their ecomuseum the Ak-Chin Him Dak. *Him dak* means "a way of life."[26]

The planning and organizing process worked because it concentrated on what was good for the community as a whole. The impact of the community education plan is demonstrated in the growth and development of staff capabilities and in the support the community gave the museum. The staff now think of themselves as talented and speak with assurance about their knowledge. None has dropped out of the academic program. Completion of requirements for graduation is projected for the fall of 1991. The staff are willing and prepared to take on new responsibilities. Independent of outside advice or assistance, they decided to attend a recent archaeology workshop in Alberta that brought together senior government officials, archaeologists, Indians, and non-Indians responsible for cultural resource management to discuss issues related to the disposition of human remains. The ecomuseum staff approached this meeting with a collegial attitude. In their previous roles, the notion of attending a professional meeting had never been viewed as desirable by the staff, nor would tribal officials have agreed to pay expenses for seven people.

Linking the proposed ecomuseum to the Ak-Chin community's critical needs produced broad support. Each person was challenged to rise above his or her self-interest and consider the needs of others. The tribal council's financial commitment to fund college tuitions, staff positions, and travel initiatives increased the project's chances for success. The work-study orientation gave the project high visibility from the earliest stages. The existence of temporary museum and archives rooms gave form to the idea and provided opportunities to respond to the needs of various factions in the community. Rather than merely hearing about future plans, members of the community were active participants. Activities organized by the staff affirmed common values. As community members began to perceive the museum as enhancing the general welfare, feelings of ownership of the museum began to spread throughout the community.

The problem-solving aspects inherent in the ecomuseum process provided the means for the reestablishment of harmonious relationships on the reservation. The planning and organizing activities allowed the Ak-Chin to sort out the real issues facing them and provided a process for resolving them.

The approach described here is not a formula that will produce results in a predictable sequence. The concept of an ecomuseum is difficult to grasp, and the benefits hard to quantify. When roles and relationships have been established over extended periods of time, the introduction of new attitudes and methods can produce unexpected tensions and alter alliances. In the Ak-Chin case, difficulties were certainly encountered. The multiple perspectives supplied by the advisors sometimes confused students. Advisors were inexperienced as facilitators, and sometimes questioned the validity of the process. Often, they resorted to traditional teaching methods for expediency or out of frustration. The process of stimulating students to think in new ways without distorting their form and style was not easy. Advisors had to be alert to the creation of unrealistic expectations before staff competencies were well established. For their part, the staff said they needed more time to assimilate the volume of new information presented and simultaneously to make informed decisions about the building design.

The establishment of the ecomuseum was a sign of pride and self-respect in a community whose image has changed rapidly. Opening the new building brought to a close the first phase of the ecomuseum process—the identification of a community need for a new system to transmit cultural knowledge, and the community's assumption of responsibility for the process. A new process—the operation of the Ak-Chin Him Dak—was about to begin.

CONCLUSIONS

> The farm changed our expectations. . . . The museum visits introduced us to new ways to remember [the past].
>
> —Leona Kakar, Ak-Chin Farms executive director

The case history of the Ak-Chin Indian Community's ecomuseum describes the process of planning and developing a participatory, multidisciplinary, community-operated educational institution organized around an integrated concept of culture, territory, and human creativity. The goals of the process are community identity and development. The model offers a new role for community museums: that of an instrument of self-knowledge and a place to learn and regularly practice the skills and attitudes needed for community problem solving. In this model, the museum functions as a mediator in the transition from control of a community by those who are not members of the community to control by those who are.

This case tells about the implementation of an action-learning program based on the theories and practices of lifelong learning. Its aim was to establish nurturing, supportive conditions that would foster community growth and development. The concept assumes that there is an overwhelming difference between the way those who advise or fund projects perceive a community's needs and the way those who are charged with operations perceive them. The methodology is predicated on the notion that responsible choices are made by those who have clear understandings of their needs and strengths, and who must live with the consequences of the decisions. The model provides a way to replace traditional hierarchical patterns of decisionmaking with a framework for developing shared motivation and parity among members of a group. The strategy links generations, professions, and cultures through policies of inclusion.

The plan focuses on the creation of community leadership to present new attitudes and model new behavior. Visits to other communities to learn about their experiences open the way for participants to consider alternative solutions to local problems. Applied learning experiences are combined with academic instruction to stimulate participants to question their personal decisions in terms of public values. These opportunities for exploration free the imaginations of participants, releasing unrealized potential and revealing inherent talents. Community members are trained to function as facilitators of learning and as resource consultants in their community. They are taught skills of coordination and communication. This leads to fundamental changes in participants' self-esteem. Learning becomes more satisfying as students become increasingly confident. This condition brings to consciousness a sense that individual actions can make a difference in the future of their community, and helps instill the courage to speak out because of common need.

The achievements realized by the Ak-Chin project can be initiated by people of any ethnic group, gender, class, or age and in multiple settings. Among the features that seem to be most positive are: (1) the coalition building that provides broad-based, ongoing support. These strengths stem from the team process, the mentor strategy, the interdisciplinary approach, and the collaborative use of existing resources; (2) the direct personal experiences (including the recognition of past expertise) that form the basis for meaningful learning; and (3) the provision for time to reflect and communicate with one another so that collaboration, consensus, and dialogue can be established.

It is through the learning that occurs as a result of dealing with community problems that the ecomuseum becomes a vehicle for transforming lives. The power that emerges from the resulting partnerships leads to broadened participation by members of the community and to the meeting of their human needs.

NOTES

1. The Ak-Chin Indian Community ecomuseum project was the first attempt in the United States to establish a new kind of institution for a particular cultural group by that community itself. Since 1987, I have contributed to the project by introducing the ecomuseum concept to the community and, as a

member of the ecomuseum project board, guiding their research and development process. The work was conducted as part of the broad mission of the Smithsonian Institution to share its resources and to be a catalyst for stimulating original thinking and innovative practices in the museum profession. Under that rubric, it established in the Office of Museums in 1977 a strategic program of museological study and research services to assist Native Americans to start or upgrade tribal museums. From 1981 to 1989, as coordinator of the Native American Museums Program, I learned that direct participation by the target audience in all aspects of cultural management was central to the issues facing community museums. The Ak-Chin project represents that search for a workable methodology.

2. In this essay I use the terms "the Ak-Chin," "the community," and "the members" interchangeably to identify those who are members of the Ak-Chin Indian Community. Membership in the Ak-Chin Indian Community is conferred by birth. Only members have voting privileges.

3. For further information about ecomuseums, see the entire issue of *Museum* 148 (1985); Andrea Hauenschild, *Neue Museologie* (Bremen: Ubersee-Museum Bremen, 1988), especially pages 486–89; and René Rivard, *Opening Up the Museum* (Quebec City: n.p., 1984).

4. René Rivard, "Museums as Concept," presentation at the annual meeting of the American Association of Museums, Chicago, 11 May 1990.

5. International Council of Museums, *Statutes: Code of Professional Ethics* (Paris: ICOM, 1987), 3.

6. For additional information, see Departamento de Servicios Educativos Museos Escolares y Comunitarios, Coordinacion National de Museos y Exposiciones, *In Memoria 1983–1988* (Mexico City: Instituto de Antropología e Historia, n.d.).

7. Rivard, *Opening Up the Museum*, 40–42.

8. Discussions with J. Hurstel on 2 Sept. 1989 in Freyming-Merlebach, France.

9. Leona Kakar, "The Ak-Chin Eco-Museum Design Project," proposal submitted to Administration for Native Americans, U.S. Department of Health and Human Services, Program Announcement 13612-871, 2 June 1987.

10. Dudley Meade, "Ethnohistorical and Archaeological Evaluation of the Cultural Resources to be Affected by the Ak-Chin Farm Improvement Project" (Tucson: University of Arizona, 1977).

11. Robert Gasser, Christine Robinson, and Corey Breternitz, comps., *Archaeology of the Ak-Chin Indian Community West Side Farms Project: The Land and the People* (Tempe, Ariz.: Soil Systems, 1990), 2: chap. 1, page 7.

12. *Ak-Chin Indian Community Water Settlement Celebration* (Maricopa, Ariz.: Ak-Chin Indian Community, 1988).

13. Gasser, Robinson, and Breternitz, *Archaeology of the Ak-Chin Indian Community West Side Farms Project,* 2: chap. 27, page 1.

14. Ak-Chin Indian Community tribal council resolution no. A-36-85, 31 July 1985.

15. Richard W. Effland, "Work Plan for a Museum Exhibit for the Ak-Chin Indian Community" (Tempe, Ariz.: 1986).

16. Shayne Del Cohen et al., "The Ak-Chin Indian Community's EcoMuseum Technician Education Program," oral presentation at the annual meeting of the Western Museums Association, Phoenix, 26 Oct. 1989.

17. Caroline Antone, "Ak-Chin Museum is Progressing," *Ak-Chin O'odham Runner* 1, no. 4 (1987), 1.

18. Caroline Antone, "Museum Reports to Dr. Richard Effland" (Tempe, Ariz.: July 1987).

19. Prior to 1970, most Ak-Chin students went to Indian boarding schools for their formal education. A teacher-directed model of instruction was employed. The curriculum was designed to support national goals, such as cultural assimilation, rather than to value cultural differences. Classes were taught in English and the use of native language was not allowed. Little emphasis was placed on initiative, self-expression, or the development of cognitive skills. Few opportunities were provided for students to test their capabilities in new situations or to learn to trust non-Indians.

The curriculum of the boarding schools prepared the Ak-Chin to operate small family farms, and the extended family networks and community rituals taught children about their cultural heritage. However, the Ak-Chin now own a large-scale agribusiness, and the traditional family communication systems are disappearing. No longer can they rely on past educational methods to learn needed knowledge and skills. The farm brought about a new economic order that has opened up new possibilities for jobs and community roles while obviating others. Boarding schools have been phased out of existence. Today Ak-Chin students go to public schools in nearby Maricopa and maintain very positive relationships there. Yet the community lives with dual self-images that often inhibit their expectations. On one hand, the negative attitudes and outmoded skills instilled by the previous educational system still underlie community perspectives. On the other hand, within the community there is positive group-esteem and pride. And it is this that accounts for the Ak-Chin's achievements. Unlike peoples who lack strong economic or emotional bonds, the Ak-Chin have been sustained by a common commitment to the group. Each member believes that the welfare of the community is crucial to his or her survival.

Strong barriers to interaction with other cultures long enabled the Ak-Chin to maintain their traditional roles and relationships. The Ak-Chin view was that as long as the status quo existed, their autonomy was secure. But their isolation became threatened, and outside forces were overwhelming established patterns, creating stresses with which the Ak-Chin were not educationally prepared, either academically or culturally, to deal. The gaps in members' education were placing severe restraints on the community's ability to direct its future. To manage the broad problem of change, the Ak-Chin had to develop within their own membership professional knowledge about topics such as accounting, economics, computerization, and legislation. As well, each member had to have a clear understanding of the community's goals and beliefs. They needed a new curriculum.

Some Indian groups deal with this situation by operating their own schools. However, it would not be economical or educationally sound for the Ak-Chin to develop a separate school system with offerings parallel to those of surrounding jurisdictions. In fact, one of the benefits of integrated schools is meaningful socialization between cultural groups, a skill necessary in their new economic system. Another method through which groups have addressed their needs for professional training is to support advanced education for one or two members at universities or colleges. In return, these people are obligated to commit time to the community and share the information. This plan has encountered several problems, though: student dropout rates are quite high; participants often fail to gain support for new ideas upon return to the community; and a "brain drain" occurs when participants who go to college or technical school choose not to return to the community.

20. "Proposal for the Ak-Chin Eco-Museum Design Project," 2.

21. Conversation with author, Ak-Chin Farms Center, January 1988.

22. For a comprehensive discussion of the methodology, see Malcolm Knowles, *The Adult Learner: A Neglected Species* (Houston: Gulf Publishing, 1990).

23. Cohen et al., "Ak-Chin Indian Community's EcoMuseum Technician Education Program."

24. Ibid.

25. Ibid.

26. Justine R. Jimmie, "Ak-Chins' Way of Life Preserved," *Phoenix Gazette,* 24 June 1991.

PART 3

Defining Communities Through Exhibiting and Collecting

CHRISTINE MULLEN KREAMER

The essays in this part of the volume address questions of history, identity, and ideology, the significant media through which communities are defined in exhibiting and collecting. The history of museum representations of communities and museum activities with or about communities is an important element in current relations between museums and communities. History is not just something that happened; it is a living part of people's sense of who they are and how they relate to other elements of civil society. Potter and Leone point out in their essay in this section that history goes beyond the mere recounting of events; it is understood and experienced by actors and observers in cultural frameworks that have an ideological dimension. The histories of specific collections and exhibitions and of individual museums reveal the ways in which social groups and the objects that can be made to stand for them are presented by museums and perceived by communities.

Until fairly recently, museums have often been elitist, authoritarian institutions in which the public voice was almost entirely absent and decisions about what to collect and what (and how) to exhibit rested with a small group of museum professionals, private collectors, and patrons. Although the private and privileged collections of objects from "other" cultures found in seventeenth-century cabinets of curiosities underwent change in the eighteenth and nineteenth centuries, becoming more public, the implicit and explicit intentions of museum collections have not changed much: from the seventeenth century through the twentieth, collections have helped establish positions of authority, dominion, and social imperialism over the "collected 'other' " in the service of individual or state sovereignty.[1] While the history of museums demonstrates a gradual movement toward greater awareness of "the public" and concern with community issues, progress has been slow, and it is only recently that self-conscious reflection about the political implications of exhibitions—and what exhibitions imply about the cultures on display—has been seriously undertaken. Annie Coombes points out that as early as 1902, England's museums acknowledged their educational potential and their mandate to serve diverse audiences. While audiences at that time were usually viewed in a paternalistic manner and were believed to be in general need of social and moral uplift (something museums were thought to provide), exhibition strategies were clearly intended to control the educational process and to guide the public to desired conclusions that served political ends.[2] In the nineteenth century, these associations generally reinforced colonial policies; this was achieved through representation of the "other" as being in a state of "arrested development" (see Mary Jo Arnoldi's essay in this section), both intellectually and culturally. These associations were reinforced in the more informal atmosphere of the enormously popular "colonial exhibits" at the turn of the century, which provided visitors with a sense of active participation at an event and an experience of "vicarious tourism" that generated considerable public acceptance and support of a national policy of domination. By constructing mock villages that preserved the "cultural divide" through "constructed spectacle," colonial subjects were reproduced as safe and contained and the messages of superiority and dominance over the colonized "other" were fostered.[3] Nineteenth-century exhibition strategies that utilized scientific classification and typological and geographic arrangements of material culture (and which carried over well into the twentieth century) presented decidedly generalized views of culture that denied them their own histories of change.

The general outlines of the history of displaying other cultures are clear, yet we should not paint a picture of unrelieved infamy. Some exhibitors and collectors moved from paternalistic and colonialist positions to attitudes of sympathy and engagement. Museums and exhibitions can do more than the people who run them often imagine. The objects in them may be organized in ways that demonstrate cultural inferiority, but the exhibitions can have different effects for the people whose cultures they represent. Even the organizers of a massive exhibition of what was deemed decadent art in Nazi Germany had problems controlling audience response. Instead of being instructed about the negative features of the works on display, visitors actively enjoyed the great art that they saw.

Mary Jo Arnoldi's essay provides an interesting case of how personal and historical factors can shape a collection and the exhibition of it. She describes the Herbert Ward collection of Africana and its exhibition history before and after its acquisition by the United States National Museum at the Smithsonian Institution. Arnoldi shows how the collection and its initial installation at the Smithsonian articulated nineteenth-century beliefs and attitudes about Africa and Africans. These served to support "an already popular discourse of misunderstanding about the continent and its people." Looking at Ward's written records and his own sculptures depicting Africans, as well as at the intellectual climate of Victorian England, reveals the personal history of the collector and his milieu. This history is clearly related to what Tony Bennett calls the "exhibitionary complex," a process whereby lower- and middle-class Britons came to imagine themselves as a homogeneous entity counterposed to a racially different and exotic "other."[4] Much of Victorian popular culture involved a comparison between Britons and the peoples of less-developed countries for nationalistic and imperial purposes.

The historical record shows that Ward saw his collection of African objects and zoological specimens as intimately tied to his bronze statues, sculpted in the nineteenth-century European academic tradition, which depicted anonymous Africans "in a state of arrested development." While the National Museum displayed the natural-history specimens, material culture, and sculptures of the collection all together, as Ward's bequest required, and while the documentary evidence of its initial installation at the Smithsonian suggests that museum professionals at the institution shared Ward's belief in the superiority of nineteenth-century Victorian society, it is clear that the curators did not share Ward's unique perspective on Africa and its peoples. For the curators, acquisition by the National Museum of the entire Ward collection fulfilled the Smithsonian Institution's interest in utilizing collections in scientific research. By locating in history a particular personality, the collection he assembled, and its subsequent installation at a public museum, Arnoldi reveals multiple attitudes about the "other" that existed at a particular point in time—the late-nineteenth-century Victorian era, a time when some of the major museums in the United States were being formed.

Arnoldi examines the life history of a collection to address "the issue of the politics of representation, the relations of power, and the historical practices that underlie the appropriation of these objects into Western collections, and their subsequent recontextualization and interpretation in public displays." As Peirson Jones points out in her essay in part 2 of this volume, museum audiences are keenly interested in how objects have come to be lodged in museums; their interest extends to information about the personalities who have shaped particular collections. While most exhibitions continue to remain anonymous, especially with regard to the curatorial voice, or authorship, of particular exhibitions, both Arnoldi's and Peirson Jones's essays illuminate the benefits of enhanced audience interest, which can be achieved through the presentation of the histories of specific collections and exhibitions, as well as those of the institutions in which the collections are housed.

Yet there are nuances here that cannot be accommodated by simply examining the ideological thrust of the collection and its installation. Arnoldi describes changes in Ward's own opinions during the course of his career. The international outcry about the atrocities in King Leopold's private fiefdom of the Congo Free State profoundly changed Ward's African portraits. By the end of his career the sentimentality of his early work had given way to the anger and resistance to domination portrayed in his sculpture *Defiance*. At this point in his career, rather than portray Africans as Europeans saw them, he sought to portray an African experience of a rapacious European colonial regime.

In a postscript to her discussion of the Ward Africana material, Arnoldi provides another glimpse into the multiplicity of meanings any collection can have. She cites a conversation she had with a Washington-area African American man who drew from the *Defiance* sculpture a positive sense of identity, and notes that in the early 1960s the museum's curators, by contrast, had been embarrassed by the negative stereotypes they felt were displayed in the Ward bronzes. It is clear from Arnoldi's examples, and from those in other parts of this volume as well, that people define their identities through a variety of means, including objects of material culture. Objects can be touchstones for the resonances of memory, past history, present circumstance, and future aspirations.

Communities often look to museums as places in which identity is articulated. As a result, museums have the responsibility of ensuring that exhibitions embody dynamic, not static, depictions of history and culture. Museums are increasingly asked to ensure that their exhibitions resonate with contemporary issues and present-day realities. This is a central theme for Jack Kugelmass, who in his essay on Jewish tourism in Poland concludes that in attempting to retain something of the past, American Jewish tourists have tended in their own minds to freeze Poland in a cultural past, the result being a failure to see the ways in which present-day Jewish communities struggle to maintain their culture in contemporary Poland. Kugelmass examines how the past can overdetermine views of the present; his example is the particular cultural visions of Jewish tourists to Poland as they embark on a ritual of return. He argues that the technological sophistication of communication and travel give us all the capacity to become tourists in the "global village." However, he distinguishes between what could be called armchair travelers, who "explore" via books, films, and even "exotic" clothing, and those who actually choose to roam. By using tourist culture as a metaphor for the museum experience, Kugelmass provides important insights into the ways visitors enter a situation equipped with experiences and preconceptions that tend to block other messages there. His case study shows how important it is for museums to anticipate the preconceptions of "processed experiences" audiences might arrive with and for museums to challenge these notions, to call them into question.

To a greater degree than any other study of which I am aware, Kugelmass's essay shows how people's sense of their history enters into their engagement with others, with exhibitions, and with their own notions of identity. What could be more pregnant with meaning than a Jewish tour of a concentration camp? In a sense this activity relives a painful history, and the tourists' behavior clearly indicates that they are not seeing remains of events distant from them in time and space but are in a sense reexperiencing their community's history. This inevitably makes other participants in the exhibiting encounter—tour guides, members of the Polish Jewish community, other Poles—actors in the historical drama the American Jews are reliving. This is not an objective and dispassionate history, something read about in books. It is a moral and emotional story of identity and survival. In order to reconstruct a Jewish history of the Holocaust, though, the contemporary history of Jews in Poland, as well as the history and situation of Poles in Poland, must be made irrelevant. The members of the Polish communities surrounding the concentration camps adapt; a tourist industry grows up around the interaction, and a modus vivendi of sorts is worked out.

Kugelmass's study presents elements of an encounter that may be less concentrated and dramatic within the museum but which will be increasingly common. Communities seek from museums a confirmation of their sense of history. Sometimes they find parts of their identities in museum exhibitions, but the history they seek may be missing. The actions and strategies of these museum visitors may not be significantly different from those of Jewish tourists to Poland, and the issues and dilemmas are essentially the same for them as well. Museum officials will be held responsible for past actions of their institutions and for those of the society they live in, just as contemporary Poles are held responsible for the Holocaust.

Expressive events such as tourist encounters and museum exhibitions are stages, as Ivan Karp argues in the introduction to this volume. The drama enacted in these events is the drama of civil society, reduced and concentrated on the exhibition stage. Official history, social justice, appropriate norms for behavior, definitions of identity—these are all contested and negotiated in exhibiting contexts. The drama metaphor is appropriate, but this is not a playful drama. It is more like a realistic soap opera, in which the stakes appear to be very high. The emotional investment is not small, and Kugelmass's account shows us that what is at stake is very important. Exhibitions can be, and are often taken to be, certifications of self and identity. These are no small matters.

As Adrienne Kaeppler points out in her essay on the representation of Hawai'i both at home and abroad, the capacity for museums to influence public perceptions—and, hence, notions of identity—rests in part on the fact that museums are regarded as "historical treasure houses" in which material culture and its links with history are enshrined. A lesson that can be learned from the histories of particular collections is that different perspectives about the very nature of acquisition influence the way such objects are interpreted in museum exhibitions. Kaeppler's discussion of Hawaiian feather cloaks shows how they can be interpreted as objects of art, cultural icons, family mementos, material residues of colonial relations, and artifacts of culture contact. Feather cloaks were distributed in a particular way because they were simultaneously gifts and ritually polluted (hence dangerous) objects that could be given to unsuspecting outsiders. Their history reveals Hawaiian notions of status as well as fundamental cultural categories. Kaeppler's account elegantly demonstrates the multiple perspectives embodied within the history of a single set of objects.

If the history of the collection of Hawaiian feather cloaks provides us with insights into the culture and history of earlier times, the history of their exhibition provides insights into multiple perceptions of Hawai'i itself. Kaeppler's distinction between exhibiting and collecting for local purposes and exhibiting and collecting for ethnographic purposes highlights the differences between insider and outsider perspectives on the same objects (a point noted also by Fath Davis Ruffins in her essay on African American preservation history). Kaeppler notes a distinction between the ways European and mainland United States institutions represent Hawaiian cultural achievements, presenting Hawaiian culture through the displays of objects considered as curiosities and expressions of an unknown "other," and local Hawaiian institutions' ways of presenting those achievements, utilizing a more matter-of-fact approach to exhibiting material culture. Yet the choice of objects exhibited in museums in Hawai'i generally refers to Hawaiian royalty, the "monarchical historical 'other' "— these same kinds of objects in museums abroad "emphasize a pre-European 'other.' " Interestingly, Kaeppler notes that both in Hawai'i and elsewhere, museums persist in presenting romantic views of Hawaiians and their culture. These views are locked in by the use of nineteenth-century materials and romanticized images of the exotic "other" or the idealized predecessors from whom contemporary Hawaiians draw part of their sense of identity. The point to note here is that community and outsider perspectives usually overlap. The differences may be more in terms of emphasis than content.

Parker B. Potter, Jr., and Mark Leone are also concerned with how setting affects the subtext, the implicit message of an exhibition. They examine exhibitions as manifestations of political and economic structures. Using this guiding principle, Potter and Leone show how archaeology can "illuminate the historical roots of contemporary ideological structure." They describe the theoretical bases and interpretive strategies of the Archaeology in Public in Annapolis project, which focuses on the history of capitalism and how it has shaped past and present interpretations of Annapolis history. Strategies developed by Potter and Leone to present the archaeology and history of Annapolis rest on the assumption that everyone, not just some groups, has been excluded from meaningful roles in the construction of the city's history. Thus the Archaeology in Public project seeks to provide a more inclusive view of historic Annapolis and to make the history of the city relevant to the contemporary social concerns of diverse audiences.

The process begins with their critique of outdoor history museums. They assert that the public has more often than not been perceived as passive recipients of information, rather than active agents with a desire to question and engage in dialogue. Potter and Leone maintain that interpretations at outdoor historical sites often fail to hold the attention of their audiences because they do not present the past as embodying issues and concerns related to the present. Because there is no active intellectual engagement between past and present attitudes and events, Potter and Leone argue that visitors to outdoor history museums risk retaining many of the preconceived notions with which they arrived. Not the least of these attitudes is the assumption that the past has little or no relation to the present—something that easily leads to a feeling of boredom and detachment that can spill over into other spheres of visitors' lives.

Although particular agendas always play a role in shaping a project or an exhibition, one of Potter and Leone's overriding concerns was to "experiment with the idea of museum programming as social action." They attempted to design interpretive activities in which visitors would have the chance "to ask questions, to discuss interpretations with interpreters on a more or less equal footing, to challenge the authorial voice inside any interpretation, and ultimately, to take some control over their own consumption of historical information."

Potter and Leone are also convinced that presentations of history are frequently unsuccessful and prevent active audience engagement in part because history is so often seen as a series of discrete events rather than as the interrelationships over time of individuals and groups. However, in the interpretation of these relationships and, thus, of history, insider and outsider perspectives need to be considered—for it is often those outside a community or a culture who assert that they have the authority to speak for or represent that culture or community. A number of essays touch on this issue. Potter and Leone, for example, note the tensions implicit in claims to insider status by recently arrived Annapolis residents, who seek to make their claim on Annapolis's heritage by joining historical preservation groups that shape the presentation of Annapolis history to "outsider" tourists. In fact, the history of Annapolis consists in large part of a succession of outsider groups who have been invited into the city and been prominent in it before being supplanted by yet another outsider group. Kaeppler's essay presents insider (local Hawaiian) and outsider (European and mainland United States) representations of Hawai'i, both of which persist in representing romantic views of Hawaiians and their cultural achievements that have little relevance to present-day realities. In Arnoldi's essay, the insiders (Africans) never get the chance to counter representations of their cultures by museums and private collectors (outsiders) or articulate their own perceptions of them. Kugelmass presents an interesting twist to the insider/outsider dichotomy in which Polish people, and especially Polish Jews, are perceived as outsiders by the American Jewish tourists who visit Poland; the latter group, the tourists, are formally the outsiders, but in this case their preconceptions and expectations about Poland and what it means to be a Jew in Poland provide them with a perception of insider status.

Implicit in the discussion of insider/outsider perspectives is the importance of documenting the cultural contributions of any group of people and formulating policy to ensure responsible collecting practices. Who has the right to speak for any particular group? How do groups incorporate both personal visions and group perspectives into representations of their cultural history? In her essay on the history of preservation of African American culture, Fath Davis Ruffins asserts that in this preservation history interior (African American) and exterior (non–African American) narratives or interpretations are simultaneously operative and that both kinds of narratives reflect prevailing preservation interests—and their historical, political, and economic referents—at particular points in time. Ruffins notes that personal memory and narrative are important components in the recorded and collected histories of African Americans. She describes three types of narratives concerning the past—memory, mythos, and history—that deal with personal and collective experiences and interpretations of past events that are now preserved in the historical record. Ruffins's account of these preservation efforts notes that the exclusion that African Americans have experienced for much of their history has resulted in a parallel exclusion of African American materials in mainstream museums. It has also influenced African Americans' perceptions about what it is important to preserve. These perceptions were and are intimately linked with changing notions of identity. Nineteenth-century preservation strategies sought to reinforce the heroic aspects of that era's African American historical mythos; consequently what was preserved was not the vernacular objects of ordinary rural folk, who were the majority of the African American community, but those items that extolled the African American elite's vision of what they wanted to be. In historically white institutions, preservation of African American materials was impeded by racist nineteenth-century social Darwinist theories that supported notions of black inferiority—something noted also in the essays by Arnoldi and Peirson Jones, in reference to the exhibition of African material culture.

Changes in preservation strategies over time reflected changes in the ways African Americans perceived themselves and their relation to history. For example, the sense that African Americans had a special destiny and a unique role in the history of the United States underwent a change in the early part of the twentieth century, coming to reflect a point of view that locates the beginnings of African American history not in the place to which they came as slaves but rather in Africa. The theme was continued during the Black Consciousness Era in the latter part of the twentieth century, in which cultural activists embraced the African past and encouraged unity with contemporary Africans in their struggle to eliminate colonialism.

It is significant that during the Black Consciousness Era the vast majority of African American museums and cultural institutions were founded. Most of them began with a mandate for "positive education" from the communities they served, and operated on the principle that museums can be vehicles for social change. Museum professionals were seen as facilitators working within, rather than standing apart from, the community. Conscious decisions were made to eliminate the authoritative voice commonly associated with museums and to ensure that these new museums would serve the needs of the community. Because of the political, social, and economic climate of the 1960s, discussion, debate, and open communication were seen as the most effective means for incorporating a multiplicity of voices in the museum process and for ensuring that the diversity and complexity of the African American experience would be represented in ways that met community expectations and needs. Continuing local efforts to support African American cultural institutions and the increasing power of the black electorate along with recognition by legislators and predominantly white cultural institutions have led to increased funding and the realization that it is not just African Americans' job to ensure that the unique position of African Americans in the history of the United States is understood, appreciated, and critically examined.

Most accounts of museum-community relations focus on ethnic communities, and this volume is no exception. Yet this presents us with a real imbalance. Museums will have to expand their concept of what a community is to include not only ethnic groups but also other kinds of communities whose voices need to be heard. Zolberg's essay in part 1 provides an excellent discussion of communities of living artists. Their individual and communal voices frequently are overlooked in the process of creating exhibitions and defining exhibiting policy, and analyses of museum policy and history that are concerned with issues of representation, authority, and voice frequently ignore them as well.

Although there are numerous other examples of forgotten or unrecognized communities that could be discussed within the scope of this essay, I want to describe some work that museums have done with communities of individuals with physical or mental impairments. It is only recently that their perspectives have started to be incorporated into museum practice. In many museums minimal (but still inadequate) physical access has been provided for individuals with certain physical impairments. In the United States the construction of facilities for the physically challenged is a condition for the receipt of federal and state funding. Yet exhibitions geared to individuals with sight, hearing, or mental impairments remain definitely in the minority. There are notable exceptions. A 1989 exhibition at the American Museum of Folk Art in New York, entitled Access to Art: Bringing Folk Art Closer, was the first exhibition created by that museum's Access to Art program, which was designed to make the arts accessible to all museum visitors, including the sight-impaired. The organizers of the exhibition and the program director, Irma J. Shore, were clearly aware of the risks inherent in allowing the objects to be touched, yet tactile experience is a crucial element in making these works accessible to the sight-impaired community. By acknowledging the needs of this community and making the works accessible to touch, the Museum of American Folk Art relinquished a measure of authority but gained a new audience.

Museums can draw on the resources and skills of a variety of public and private organizations and cultural institutions who have already demonstrated an awareness of such issues and a commitment to accessibility for individuals with physical impairments. For example, a Philadelphia-based project called National Exhibits by Blind Artists has been very active in promoting not only an awareness of sight-impaired individuals as a community to which museums should be responsive but also exhibitions of works by sight-impaired artists.

At the Wadsworth Atheneum in Hartford, Connecticut, the Lions Gallery of the Senses has a twenty-year tradition of accessibility for the visually impaired. Opened in 1972 as the Tactile Gallery and designed to serve the general public, this gallery has sponsored a series of experimental exhibitions that have consistently challenged the audience to utilize more than the sense of sight in experiencing works of art. Early exhibitions, such as Chair, Fiber, and The Shape of Sound, were designed to encourage sensory experiences among all members of the audience. While they were not geared exclusively to the sight-impaired, exhibitions in this gallery were very popular among individuals with sight impairments, since participation and interaction with the exhibition did not depend on vision and touching was encouraged. Their 1976 exhibition I Am Not Blind, conceived by media artist Les Levine, marked a move by the Lions Gallery to address directly issues concerning the sight-impaired; the exhibition contained personal statements by sight-impaired people in order to foster an awareness of and commitment to this community. This commitment continued throughout the 1970s and 1980s at the Wadsworth Atheneum; in 1981 they sponsored a conference about museum accessibility for sight-impaired visitors, and developed a gallery policy that would secure input into exhibitions from the community of individuals with physical impairments.

In addition to select individual activists, cultural institutions, and public and private special-interest groups, certain contemporary artists also are concerned with the accessibility of art. The New York–based artist Robin Winters actively embraces the philosophy of making his work accessible to diverse and often neglected audiences. In addition to workshops and lectures with sight- and hearing-impaired individuals conducted by Winters himself, exhibitions of Winters's own work have encouraged interaction with audiences with special needs, including those with physical or mental impairments. Most recently, his site-specific exhibition Train of Thought/Objects of Influence (1989) at the Wadsworth Atheneum's Lions and Matrix galleries granted access by touch and audio cassette to a body of his work in the Lions Gallery; these works were linked directly with other works (drawings and mixed-media works on canvas and paper, which were not available to touch) on display in the neighboring Matrix Gallery. The works on display in the Lions Gallery included an eclectic selection of found and created objects made out of a variety of materials and textures, including fragile glass and ceramic works. The exhibition sought to provide a glimpse into the creative process of a particularly eclectic and energetic contemporary artist with a decided commitment to and interest in audience response. Winters's work was directly influenced by his prior knowledge of the audience: in preparation for the exhibition, he produced, among other things, a series of braillelike monotypes of ordinary objects. As Winters's entertaining and whimsical narrative audio cassette for the exhibition noted, these were all objects imbued with personal memories that were important to him and thus should be treated with care. Winters acknowledged not only the risk involved in such an exhibition but also the very personal concerns he had in allowing his works of art to be touched; however, he realized as well that with risks come new insights into how works of art are perceived by individuals who are normally denied access to them.[5] This underscores the point that accessibility of an artist's work to diverse audiences can lead to enriching, creative experiences for both artist and public, and that artistic creativity need not be compromised by striving to reach particular audiences with special needs.

These examples illustrate that exhibition strategies can and should be innovative enough to grant accessibility for individuals with physical impairments or other special needs. For individuals who use wheelchairs, for example, lower display furniture and wide aisles and ramps will provide greater accessibility to display materials. Of course, such modifications would also facilitate traffic flow, especially when large tour groups visit, and would directly benefit children, who are often not tall enough to see into display cases of more standard height. For the sight-impaired, exhibition strategies that should be implemented include (but by no means should be limited to) large-print and braille label copy and exhibition brochures; oversized and high-contrast photographs, or pictures of display objects that can be picked up and scrutinized by visitors with reduced sight capacity; wooden floor markers as guides for individuals using canes to move through the exhibition, so that they know where to stop to pick up or use interpretive materials; and some access by touch to exhibited objects. While certain works, such as paintings, prints, extremely fragile and rare objects, and the like, are largely inappropriate candidates for exhibitions of touchable objects, special collections could be established to encourage tactile experience. In addition, free guided tours on audio cassette that are tailored to provide clear descriptive, historical, technical, and aesthetic information as well as impressions about colors, shapes, textures, materials, qualities of light, and movement would grant additional access to exhibitions and would acknowledge that "to be unsighted is not necessarily to be without vision of any kind."[6]

The capacity of museum displays to shape public interpretations of diverse communities is fast becoming a major issue in museum-community relations. This is in part because it is often a particular community or portion of a community that is represented in displays as the "other." But there is no one scheme that museums should adopt in the presentation of culture. Different museums operate on different aesthetic, ideological, programmatic, and financial principles in selecting and displaying materials and in developing interpretive strategies designed to guide (and, one hopes, to interest and challenge) the public.

Kaeppler rightly suggests, as have others in this volume, that museums (both at home and abroad) can assist in forging ethnic and national identities. Museums need to consider carefully and critically their roles in such identity formation, for issues of identity are crucial for constructing notions of community and for self-conscious reflection about collection strategies and techniques of exhibiting culture. Indeed, identity may be a matter of perspective, as individuals and communities have multiple identities that shift according to context and point of view (see Ivan Karp's introduction to part 1). Culture should not be treated as a fixed and static entity, and as Guillermo Gómez-Peña points out in his essay in part 1 of this volume, museums must learn to understand the nature and flexibility of individual and group identities, as well as the permeability of borders and boundaries. This is the first step that museums must take in order for them to be able to address the multivocal nature of communities and to develop exhibitions that seek to tell stories about individuals, societies, and the products of cultures and to place them in a particular time and space. Notions about identity imply difference as well as sameness. Therefore, effective exhibitions do not necessarily have to present ideal stories of cohesiveness. Instead they can tackle the realities of diversity, controversy, and the negotiation of identities and cultural forms that imply concepts of power-sharing.

Exhibition makers may choose any of a number of approaches. They may wish to forge a sense of national identity, to celebrate diverse identities, to consolidate a community, or to create a sense of commonality through a shared museum experience. Whatever approach they take, good intentions must be met with careful planning and well-developed exhibition development strategies that seek to include community voices and bear community interests in mind.

NOTES

1. Jo-Anne Berelowitz, "From the Body of the Prince to Mickey Mouse," *Oxford Art Journal* 13, no. 2 (1990), 70–84.

2. Annie Coombes, "Museums and the Formation of National and Cultural Identities," *Oxford Art Journal* 11, no. 2 (1988), 57–68.

3. Ibid., 59

4. Tony Bennett, "The Exhibitionary Complex," *New Formations* 4 (1988), 73–102.

5. Robin Winters, personal communications, 1989 and 1990.

6. Les Levine, *Les Levine's I Am Not Blind: An Information Environment about Unsighted People* (Hartford, Conn.: Wadsworth Atheneum, 1976).

CHAPTER 13

The Rites of the Tribe: American Jewish Tourism in Poland

JACK KUGELMASS

Frankfort airport, summer 1987: When I enter the plane to Poland I find myself seated beside a Jewish family from Brooklyn. The father, an old Hasid with a black suit and a long white beard, seems like a relic from an age gone by, which is how he must appear to the other passengers in the plane. But the children look a little better placed in this century. The son, who is wearing a blue blazer, gray pants, tie, and a homburg, is in his late twenties and is clean-shaven. He is in business. The daughter, who is in her thirties, is stylishly dressed in white and pink. She is a professor of Jewish studies and is fluent in Polish. The father is very proud of his children's secular education. For him, that is a link to the past: before the war, his sister was a professor in Cracow. The father is a survivor of Bergen-Belsen and he is taking his son and daughter to visit the graves of their ancestors. They have brought with them enough kosher food for the eight-day trip. The son assures me that his sister is a gourmet cook and has prepared everything they will need.

Once the plane is in the air and the passengers can move about, the father becomes quite a hit, especially among the older passengers, who are unaccustomed to seeing Hasidim on or even heading to Polish soil. While the father converses with other passengers in Polish, the daughter passes a note to him in English. He looks at it, laughs, then shows it to me. The note reads: "What did the Polack say when his wife gave birth to twins? 'Who's the father of the other one?' "

As we approach Warsaw the son looks out the window and comments to his father and sister, "Look how beautiful it is. Poland's a beautiful country!" They both laugh. Looking at the greenery below, I'm a little bewildered by the comment. I ask what he sees that's so special. "Oh," he replies, "I'm just referring to a family joke. We have an uncle who went to Poland with his son, and the first day in the hotel room he looked behind a picture on the wall and spotted a microphone. He's a very paranoid person, so throughout the trip he kept saying to his son, 'Look how beautiful Poland is. It's such a beautiful country!' Finally, on the last day of the trip, they were running out of kosher food and the son was hungry and exhausted because there was very little he would eat and he yells, 'I can't stand this place!' The father got so upset. He started shouting at the son, '*A gantse vokh hob ikh gemakht vi ikh glaykh dos plats itst afn letstn tog du makhst af mir a kholere* [All week I've pretended that I like this place and now on the last day you're making a plague on me].'" In a few moments the plane touches down. As it does the father murmurs, "*Borukh ha-Shem* [blessed be God]." The son does the same, and I do, too. I ask if it's appropriate to say Shekhiyanu, a prayer thanking God upon experiencing something for the first time. "No," the son replies. "I don't think so. Not for this."

From Yehudit Hendel's "Near Quiet Places: Twelve Days in Poland":

> I tried to get out of it on some pretext. I was scared and my first impulse was to refuse. Why? I thought. How? What? But suddenly it all began to move and soon I couldn't think about anything except going to Poland. Suddenly I felt I had to go to Poland and yet, at the same time, I felt a tremendous hesitation about going to Poland. All the baggage we drag around with us from Poland . . .
>
> And suddenly I was plunged into a vortex of dread and regret and memory and longing to forget and hatred and streets and house numbers and will you get to Lodz, will you be in Czestochowa and maybe you'll go to the cemetery in Lublin maybe you'll find my father, maybe you'll go to the cemetery in Krakow maybe you'll find my mother. Heavy sacks we all drag on our back and big stories and small stories, a thousand rocks pour down all at once from that volcano extinguished long ago that died and wasn't buried. Why do you have to go to Kaluszyn, the stranger from Jaffa repeated. Ten thousand Jews there were in Kaluszyn, one remained. Right after the

War, he went back to Kaluszyn and started running along the railroad tracks, he went crazy running along the railroad tracks and a
Pole passing by shot him and he was the last corpse of Kaluszyn after
the War, on the railroad tracks.[1]

Several years ago, two Warsawian Jews arrived in New York and paid
a visit to the YIVO Institute for Jewish Research. They stopped in
front of my office and read the Gary Larson cartoon one of my students had posted on the door. The drawing depicts a dark-skinned
"native" peering out the window of a hut. Having just spotted two
approaching white people wearing pith helmets and bush jackets, he
shouts frantically, "Anthropologists! Anthropologists!" Other natives
then begin scrambling to hide their television, stereo, and various
other modern appliances. My visitors commented that with the increasing flow of Jewish tourists to Poland they have begun to feel just
like those natives, constantly being scrutinized by others on their performance of Jewish rituals.

The cartoon is similar in mood, it seems to me, to a recent documentary titled *Cannibal Tours,* which spares no effort to mock the
pretentious and sometimes callous behavior of European and American tourists in New Guinea. What irks me about this film is its complete lack of reflexivity, as if the filmmaker is ever free of an objectify-
ing gaze. Moreover, I do not believe that individual tourists should
bear the full brunt of scorn for the colonization of non-Western peoples. Given the increasing incorporation of the world into a global
village through nightly newscasts and other media events, we have all
become tourists. But some of us are content to be so through the print
and electronic media or by going to exotic restaurants or commodity
emporiums such as Banana Republic or Pier One, while others choose
to actually roam the globe. Why they do so, what they see, what they
bring back with them, how they designate certain experiences as
meaningful—indeed, how they represent and appropriate otherness—
these are all topics for study in the ethnography of tourism.[2] In this
essay I examine the meaning of tourism with special reference to the
current American Jewish fascination with Poland. The thesis I shall
argue is that tourism is not necessarily the activity of buffoons, nor is
it only an act of cultural colonization. Not only is mass tourism part
and parcel of the secular rites of modern society, its public culture;[3]
sometimes it has significant cultural and religious implications for
those who participate in it, particularly for ethnic groups.[4]

Ample evidence exists that tourism was quite prevalent long before the invention of the postcard.[5] Romans were every bit as intrigued by the pyramids as we are, and travels throughout the classical, medieval, Renaissance, and early modern worlds frequently took place without any concomitant incentive of financial gain[6] other than in a Bourdieuian sense, that is, an increase in symbolic capital.[7] But whereas earlier travelers were cognizant of their own exceptionalness, modern tourists, aside from a relatively small proportion of adventure travelers, go in order to do what others have already done, afraid, perhaps, that not to do so would be a sign of lower social status.[8] Moreover, modern tourism's mass appeal speaks to the fragmented nature of contemporary culture. "Sightseeing," writes Dean MacCannell, "is a kind of collective striving for a transcendence of the modern totality, a way of attempting to overcome the discontinuity of modernity, of incorporating its fragments into unified experience."[9]

Mass tourism is a happy marriage of postwar developments in travel technology and consumer culture. But in the case of travel to Eastern Europe, not long after the end of World War I American (or, better stated, Americanizing) Jews were already heading there in significant numbers; there were American travel agents and European steamship lines advertising regularly in the pages of the mass-circulation Yiddish-language daily, the *Forverts*, and, according to the newspaper accounts, during the 1920s transatlantic liners were filled during the summer months with Jews heading to Poland or the Soviet Union.[10] It is true, of course, that many who made this journey did so for motives quite different from those that guide the leisure-oriented tourist today. Quite a few travelers were sent as delegates of various *landsmanshaftn* (hometown mutual aid societies) to bring vital relief money to fellow townspeople in Eastern Europe; others went to see families they had left behind, or to start new ones by finding a spouse; some went as artists and scholars to perform, paint, or study.[11]

Motivations had little impact on end products, and many who made the journey took with them pen and ink, still and even movie cameras: they had come not just to see, but to capture something of the old, to freeze action in time, to give voice (so to speak) to memory. World War II brought such travel to an end. And when it could resume again, what was left to see was chilling. Eastern European Jewry had been virtually wiped out by the Nazis, and the scant traces of Jewish life that remained were scattered among various localities. Warsaw, the great capital of prewar European Jewish culture, had been emptied first of its Jewish and then later of its non-Jewish population; the city itself had almost ceased to exist. Those who journeyed to Eastern Europe were few in number, mostly representatives of Jewish communal agencies or left-wing political organizations. Although some of the latter were sympathetic to the new Communist regimes, most visitors were simply overwhelmed by the enormity of the destruction,[12] the near-total absence of Jews in the countryside, and the physical obliteration of Jewish Warsaw.[13] When the capital was rebuilt and surviving Polish Jews were repatriated from the Soviet Union, ethnic neighborhoods did not figure in the social planning of the People's Republic of Poland. Jewish Warsaw was rebuilt but as a symbol only, a monument.[14]

After the war the urge to visit was still great, and considerable travel did take place—but in a vicarious form. The *yizker-bikher* (memorial books), those great compilations of folk ethnography, contained stories, anecdotes, and brief biographies of people and towns, providing their mostly American Jewish creators with their only remaining link to the world they had left behind.[15] The kind of travel offered by the *yizker-bikher* was, however, very constricted, less on account of the medium—for words are indeed very powerful—than in regard to the small number of those who participated via these books. Published in tiny editions, generally of several hundred copies, the *yizker-bikher* served the needs of émigrés and survivors; their children and certainly their grandchildren had little interest in the books' contents, and even if they did, the languages in which they were published, Yiddish and in later decades Hebrew, presented further obstacles. For the vast majority of American Jews, the thousand-year history of Jewish settlement in Eastern Europe had been transformed into an indecipherable nightmare.

Despite its decimation, the Jewish community in Poland did recover to some extent during the early postwar years. But it was difficult for American Jews to travel to and within Poland, and so the concrete ties between the two communities were broken. In the years following liberation, Jews who attempted to travel outside of major cities were often subject to assassination by right-wing antigovernment guerrillas.[16] Or, if their lives were not in danger, visitors frequently experienced the hostility of those who feared that the Jews had come to reclaim family property.[17] Even securing visas could be a problem, particularly during government-sponsored "anti-Zionist" campaigns in the late 1950s, 1960s, and even 1970s.[18] In the early years, only individuals made the trip back, and many who did so were living not in America but in the Soviet Union, or even in Poland itself but far from their native towns.[19]

When postwar American Jews thought about an "old country," they had in mind either the various cultural productions they had established in the United States—restaurants, theater, music groups, and even the old neighborhoods of first settlement—or the newly established state of Israel. Indeed, determined to appropriate for itself the legitimacy of an "old country," the Jewish state set to work digging up the past and reconnecting Jewish memory via archaeology to its earliest roots.[20] For their part American Jews, having abandoned Yiddish and adopted Hebrew as the privileged language of ethnic discourse, could use the Hebrew language as a way of journeying, in a sense, to a place untainted by such recent and bitter memories.

Tourism is a commodified pleasure; much like the annual need to refashion automobiles, there is a constant need to find new and exciting places to visit. Despite the need for the new, tourists rarely discover anything on their own. Long before they actually go anyplace they are presented with processed newness through travel accounts in the Sunday *New York Times,* articles in magazines (some of which exist solely for the purpose of promoting travel), or the travel supplements of local newspapers. Jews, perhaps more than other ethnic groups, have additional means for preprocessing the exotic.[21] Aviva Weintraub's recent bibliography on the photoethnography of Jewish communities clearly documents the emergence of a new and very productive genre in Jewish literature, the photo essay.[22] The phrase "the last Jews of . . ." invariably precedes the name of the country in the titles of these publications, cluing prospective readers in to the theme of the encounter: a chance to catch a glimpse of an almost-extinct species. A good indication of the extent to which the Jews of Eastern Europe currently occupy the primary place of interest among American, Western European, and Israeli Jewry is the increasing number of personal accounts documenting individual journeys to that part of the world. Besides what seems like an endless stream of newspaper articles there are books and photographic exhibitions, while a number of documentary films either have been made or are currently in production.[23]

Although some of this work is the output of professional journalists, travel and reporting on travel to Eastern Europe are largely amateur matters. Many Jews make the trip for reasons stemming entirely from their personal or family histories. They come either on a tour or, if they are more adventuresome, alone to Warsaw, where they rent a car and head to the town, village, or city that they, their parents, or their grandparents came from. A certain proportion of these people, perhaps the majority (including a large number of Israeli as well as American Jewish visitors) are not tourists in the strict sense. They are rather visitors returning to repay a debt and to see old friends. They are the survivors and their children, who retain some connection to the non-Jewish individuals and families that helped them during the war. Some return frequently, but more commonly individuals make the trip no more than a few times, although they may have stayed in regular contact throughout the postwar period and may even consider the Polish families as relatives. Rarely do the survivors themselves join larger groups, except perhaps as guides. And unlike adventure travelers, they do not bring back esoteric knowledge or attempt to rescue valuable objects. For them the journey is entirely personal rather than communal, an affront, really, to both Jewish and Polish perceptions of each other and the antipathetic nature of their relations before, during, and after the war.

The vast majority of Jews who travel to Poland do so not as individuals but in organized tour groups. The group that is probably the smallest in number yet the most striking by way of appearance is the Hasidim, who now flock to the burial sites of famous rabbis, particularly in southeastern Poland.[24] (I once listened to a non-Jewish Pole tell of seeing "an authentic *foreign* Jew with black hat and side curls!") The tombs that are the sites of these visits are littered with photocopied *kvitlekh* (hand-written petitions) on behalf of a sick relative, an unmarried daughter, an unemployed child, and so forth. Pilgrims to the tomb of Rebbe Elimelech in Leżajk come away believing that the visit, as the rebbe had prophesied, guarantees that they will repent before their death. The Hasidim's tours to Poland are extremely short—sometimes no more than forty-eight hours—and very insular: in Cracow they have appropriated a synagogue for themselves and restored a ritual bath; in Warsaw, the only group that ventured to the Nożyk synagogue in the six weeks I was in the city organized their own *minyan* (ritual quorum) in a separate room, purposely avoiding an existing service.

A much larger number of group travelers come with synagogue or communal organization group tours. These visitors are chiefly interested in visiting concentration camps or the sites of Jewish resistance during the Holocaust. Unlike the survivors and their children, who always return to the site of their or their parents' youth, institutional tours rarely make any attempt to see the physical remains of *shtetlakh*

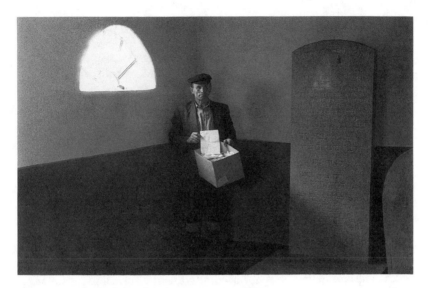

Fig. 13-1. Polish peasant with box of *kvitlekh* (petitions) inside *ohal* of Bobow ceme-
tary, summer 1989. Photo by the author.

(market towns that once characterized the Jewish settlement pattern in
Poland) that still dot the Polish landscape.[25]

Although I do not have precise figures on the current number of
Jewish tourists to Eastern Europe (my guess is that we are speaking of
a figure somewhere in the tens of thousands), the numbers are clearly
on the increase, and the fact is that no visitor to the area can look
through a camera viewfinder and be assured that another American or
Israeli will not suddenly appear to mar the "pristine" view. Major
Jewish institutions in both America and Israel now sponsor guided
tours for their members to various parts of Eastern Europe, particularly Poland, Czechoslovakia, and Hungary. The tour groups represent organizations that run the gamut of Jewish institutional life, from
the most secular and academic to the ultraorthodox. Their origins lie,
however, in Jewish communal fundraising and the special efforts made
after the war to raise money in order to relieve the plight of survivors.[26] But the displaced-persons camps that Jewish groups used to
visit are a thing of the past, and with the resurgence of fundraising
tours the focus within Eastern Europe is now primarily the death
camps.[27] Indeed, it is during the visits to them that appeals are made
directly to individual participants to increase their annual donations.
The symbolism remains the same, though: the tours are structured
around the themes of destruction and redemption, with almost all

groups concluding their travel to Eastern Europe with a longer tour of Israel. It is little wonder, then, that even a Jewish singles' tour follows the usual itinerary—although because in their case redemption is through the implicit possibility of marriage and reproduction, the trip concludes in Eastern Europe.

Various designated historical sites existed in Poland long before the current wave of Jewish tourism: the Ghetto Heroes monument, the Anielewicz bunker, and Treblinka. In recent years Poland has made concerted efforts to woo Jewish visitors, in particular by giving special training to Orbis (the Polish national tourist agency) guides and setting up Jewish desks with special brochures at tourist offices. Efforts have been made to renovate historically significant buildings and to erect monuments and markers at various sites. Tykocin, in northeastern Poland, has a reconstructed seventeenth-century synagogue that is now a museum; the Great Synagogue in Cracow has been renovated and turned into a museum, while the surrounding square is undergoing renovation and reconstruction; the Nożyk synagogue in Warsaw was renovated in the early 1980s. More recently, stone monuments have been erected in the Warsaw ghetto to form the so-called memory route, and a large monument has been constructed at the Umschlagplatz (where Jews assembled for deportation to Treblinka)—both projects were part of the commemoration of the forty-fifth anniversary of the Warsaw ghetto uprising; and the seventeenth-century synagogue in Lancut, with its magnificent polychrome walls, is undergoing extensive, if slow, renovation. In addition, the restorations of Kazimierz Dolny and Sandomierz, two sixteenth-century towns, continue to add important sites for Jewish visitors.[28]

The state's awareness of Jewish tourism is also evident in the objects available for sale in Cepelia, the government-owned folk-art outlet. In Cracow in the summer of 1987, one store had in its window a wooden figurine holding an actual piece of Torah. Although such figures (usually holding texts clipped from the *Folks-sztyme,* the official—that is, Communist—Polish Yiddish press) have their roots in peasant culture, at 5,000 zlotys (five dollars at the black-market rate)—the equivalent of a week's salary for the average Pole—the sculpture is clearly intended for the tourist market. A Cepelia branch in the nearby covered market had in stock enormous quantities of mass-produced carvings of Jewish peddlers. Two years later, the private stalls in the market had begun to cash in on the fad: one shop had about two dozen figurines of Hasidim holding Hebrew texts clipped out of prayer books; other shops had much poorer carvings of ped-

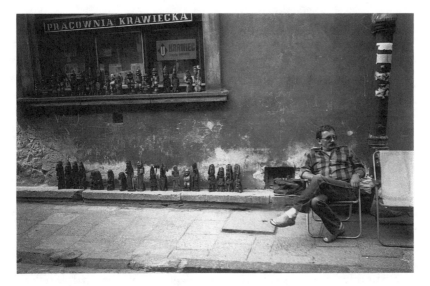

Fig. 13-2. Vendor of wooden carvings, including Jewish musicians. Old City, Warsaw, summer 1989. Photo by the author.

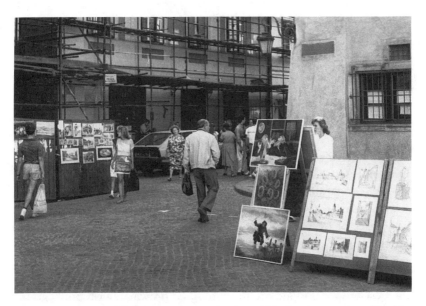

Fig. 13-3. Street scene in Old City, Warsaw, summer 1989, showing painting of Jewish moneylenders. Photo by the author.

dlers and other Jewish types. In the summer of 1989, the store that earlier had sold the peddler-and-Torah-scroll figurine had mass-manufactured miniature Jews on springs that with a little push rocked back and forth in the manner of Orthodox Jews praying. In Warsaw's Old Town Jewish figurines are now as common as in Cracow. In Warsaw, however, they are not to be found in Cepelia, but rather in the market square, where certified artists sell directly to the public. In 1987 I bought a hand-carved figure of a Jew with his arms extended, palms outward, and shrugging his shoulders. The price was one dollar, and it was the only carving of its kind that I could find in Warsaw. Today one sees "lines" rather than unique works of art, and the prices start at ten dollars. Wares in the market square include groups of hand-carved *klezmorim* (Jewish folk musicians), generally arranged next to figures of other non-Jewish musicians and Christ figures. Some are representational, while others are caricatures or even abstract. In evidence also are paintings on Jewish themes such as ghetto rebbes, match sellers, and of course *klezmorim;* one stall carries a line of caricatures including a blatantly Shylockian moneylender counting his gold coins. These are all made by non-Jewish artists. Most of the vendors are young men in their twenties and thirties: when asked about the objects they make, they are likely to refer to family stories and the memory of Jews, particularly Jews in hiding during the war—a very common theme in contemporary Polish discourse. The artist who makes the ghetto rebbes paintings, however, is in his eighties, and his work is based on what he himself has seen. He refers to himself as a "philo-Semite" and has a portfolio of Jewish subjects that he can reproduce on demand. The market also has various Jewish books for sale, all recently published translations of Sholem Aleichem, Itsek Manger, Isaac Bashevis Singer, the Talmud, and various Holocaust memoirs. Some of these books are still available in bookstores, and the market is a more direct way for private entrepreneurs—who are increasingly evident as Poland moves toward a free-market economy—to reach foreign Jewish consumers. Besides the objects in the market of the Old City, the only Jewish items for sale in Warsaw in the summer of 1989 were large quantities of brass Hanukkah menorahs copied from antique Polish models. These could be seen in jewelry shops and Cepelias near Western-style hotels.[29]

Not all tourists rely on the market to acquire things. For scholars, the best buys in Poland are microfilms of prewar Jewish publications that can be ordered from the National Library and other archives. The more daring visitors keep their eyes open for prewar ritual objects.

Although these can be bought at the government-owned art store, Desa, because they date from before the war they cannot be removed from the country legally. Their value is less monetary than sentimental: for American Jews they are metonymic representations of Polish Jewry, and buyers are convinced that through their acquisitions they are rescuing the last traces of a destroyed people.[30] For example, the following account is from a 1980 article published in a popular Jewish magazine. While visiting Przemyśl, the town of his great-grandfather, Arthur Kurzweil, a young genealogist, meets a Pole who has acquired a substantial collection of Judaica:

> Then the old man showed me something which stunned me—a little necklace with an amulet hanging from it. On one side of the amulet was a miniature painting of Moses holding the Tablets. On the other was tiny Hebrew writing, almost all of which was either too small or too unclear to read. Through the son, the old man told me that he had found this in the ghetto after the war.
>
> I had to have that necklace. I kept imagining it hanging around the neck of a young Jewish woman, and that on her way to the death camp she'd discovered it was missing. Here it was now, just another curio; another item in an antique collection.
>
> I had to have that necklace. It needed a new home, perhaps around the neck of a free Jewish woman in America, perhaps on my shelf.[31]

The narrative reaches its climax when the Pole shows him a Torah, then takes it away, only to return with a small piece of it that he had cut out. Horrified by the desecration, the author leaves with the amulet and Torah fragment, convinced that the text of the fragment contained a message that he, a descendant of one of the town's former inhabitants, was fated to receive.

The desire to salvage vestiges of prewar Jewry may even go beyond artifacts to the remains of actual people. At Treblinka, one synagogue youth-group tour leader collected pieces of bone from the surrounding fields. These he placed in a plastic container with the intention of burying them in Israel at the next stage of the tour.

Whereas some entrepreneurial non-Jewish Poles profit from the influx of Jewish tourists, the advent of the tour buses has also proven to be a boon for many members of the Polish Jewish community. Tourists are an opportunity to do business—to rent an apartment, change money, or ask for donations—and those visitors who show a lack of interest in such dealings are quickly ignored by the formerly solicitous coreligionists. Of course, the success of such solicitations depends a good deal upon the solicitor's presentation of himself or herself as destitute. Consequently, there is much in the interaction of American tourists and Polish residents that resembles the interaction of the "natives" and anthropologists in the cartoon mentioned above. In Cracow I was told of one congregant who kept an extra set of poor-looking clothes near the synagogue in order to double his money from each tour group. In Warsaw's Nożyk synagogue, rumors abound that not all who relate their tales of woe are even Jewish. Indeed, one sees an occasional congregant "reading" from an upside-down prayer book. It is not surprising that these encounters are often rather distressing for American tourists, particularly for younger people, who are accustomed to the American system of rigid spatial separation by class and age and who are therefore inclined to interpret what they see as peculiar to Poland. In one case, a United Synagogue Youth group had arranged for members of the group to be called to read from the Torah during the Sabbath services. Following these *aliyes,* the young women from the group, who occupied the second-level balconies (the synagogue is Orthodox and enforces, therefore, a separation of men and women during prayer), showered the young men with candies—a traditional Eastern European Jewish custom. The candies were chocolate, which is rationed in Poland, and a number of congregants wandered around the synagogue scavenging the scattered chocolates from the floor. The service itself proved to be rather contentious, with the synagogue's officials reluctant to allow the group the full participation its leader had requested and even prearranged. Disgusted with the congregation's behavior, the group leader was determined to have future groups spend the Sabbath in Cracow, where the congregation is much smaller, less knowledgeable in Jewish tradition, and thus less likely to interfere.

Although some groups prefer to keep such encounters to a minimum, others carefully orchestrate them by arranging meetings with select members of the Jewish community, particularly with young members of the intelligentsia, who are invariably asked by the visitors to justify why they remain in Poland. The older members of the community are less offended by the question. They are more openly cynical about Poland and the country's treatment of Jews, so their answers are straightforward, usually related to family obligations and age. The younger members find their ties to the land and their very identity as Polish Jews challenged. They are proud of their country, even though they acknowledge its darker side. A young mathematician uses the encounter to explain the positive features of contemporary life in Poland and the close connections he and others feel with members of the Catholic intelligentsia. The message is not an easy one for American Jews to accept, and it requires frequent repetition. One man, who runs a Jewish travel agency in Warsaw, is particularly offended by the question despite his ready acknowledgement that Poland remains, at least in his view, an extremely anti-Semitic country. He turns the question around and asks the visitors, "Why do you stay in America? Why don't you move to Israel?" When asked the typical tourist question by a group of young Orthodox Jews from England, a man who runs the Jewish cultural club in Cracow explained that in Poland he can decide for himself how he should act as a Jew. When asked whether he would be happier if there were more Jews around, he was quick to respond, "No. Not if they're anything like those *schnorrers* [beggars] who hang around the synagogue!"

The *schnorrers,* a direct result of increased Jewish tourism, are a source of profound embarrassment for younger Polish Jews. These beggars haunt the synagogues and other remaining Jewish monuments, giving foreigners the sense that all Polish Jews are destitute. To counteract this image, the intelligentsia are careful to define their interaction with tourists on more equal terms. They will not solicit financial contributions for themselves, although they are quite happy to receive luxury goods such as tea, coffee, special foods, and even old clothes; some will accept money if it is intended to further the work of the Committee for the Preservation of Jewish Monuments in Poland, a group of Jewish and non-Jewish intellectuals who have been active in the restoration of tombstones in the cemeteries of Warsaw and other cities and towns throughout the country. And they are always glad to receive Jewish books and published material unavailable in Poland. For them, the presence of foreign Jews is vital to their often only recently acquired Jewish identity, and because of it they are ready to forgive numerous indiscretions committed by naive or insensitive visitors.[32]

In describing relations between Iranian-born Jews and Jewish visitors to that country, Laurence Loeb notes that while traveling abroad Jews will "actively seek contact with local coreligionists and their institutions, especially the synagogue. It is a noteworthy pattern of Western Jewish tourist culture that Jews, who are totally disinterested in Jewish life at home, become avid anthropologists abroad."[33] If Loeb's statement is correct for Poland, it is so only in regard to visiting synagogues. But to think of American Jewish tourists in Poland as anthropologists goes beyond even the most critical interpretation of the nature of anthropological inquiry.

Jewish visitors go to Poland to see the past; that category applies not only to the relics of the place but, by way of contagion, to all who live nearby. Whereas tourists generally engage in a form of popular ethnography (a concept John MacAloon has been developing in regard to the festival component of the Olympic games),[34] there is something quite unique about Jewish tourism in Poland. Jewish tourists see nothing quaint about the local culture, either Jewish or non-Jewish; their interest is the dead rather than the living. They go as antiquarians rather than ethnographers; consequently, they bring back with them no experiences that deepen their knowledge of the local culture. Because of the intensity of prewar anti-Semitism in Poland, the extent of the destruction during the war—a time when Jews faced a murderous German occupying army and a local population that was largely unsympathetic to their plight—and officially sponsored "anti-Zionist" campaigns followed by mass departures of most of the remaining Polish Jews in the 1950s and again in the late 1960s, Poland is not well thought of by most American Jews. It is no wonder that the experiences the visitors remember are likely to be those that enhance an already existing negative opinion. Indeed, they are the experiences these visitors expect to have in Poland, and because they confirm deeply held convictions, they are almost a desired part of the trip.[35]

Most tourists go places to have a good time. While others go on so-called adventure travel tours to see the more remote corners of the globe, in those trips there is still a balance between leisure and learning, though leisure very much has the upper hand. But when Jews go to Poland, leisure does not figure in their trip planning. One Jewish Pole, who had recently established a tourist company to deal with foreign Jewish travelers to Poland, was considering including stays at the mountain resort town of Zakopane and other scenic locales in his package tours, but soon abandoned the idea for lack of interest. A sophisticated non-Jewish Pole familiar with the usual itinerary of Jewish tour groups was actually convinced that their frightful pace was intentionally designed to instill a negative sense of place. Since American Jews are known to have very strong biases against Poland long before they go on such excursions, the question one must ask is, why do they go? There are various reasons at work here, and I shall now attempt to outline what they are.

Even the most innocent of journeys lays claim to space. "[T]he very carrying out of a tourist itinerary," writes Donald Horne, "is a form of appropriation,"[36] transforming the unfamiliar into home turf. But the case of Jewish tourism to Poland is not one of an innocent journey but of actively contested history. I recall, for example, standing at the site of the crematorium in Birkenau. The Polish guide, an educated man in his late fifties who was rather sympathetic to the subject of Jewish history, was lecturing to a Jewish group. At a pause in his talk, a woman began to question him about the Jewish population of Oświęcim before and after the war. The guide maintained that relations between Jews and Poles were generally good: the victimization of Jews had been a German rather than a Polish problem. Other visitors prodded further, determined to extract from him some admission of what they already knew: that anti-Semitism was indeed a Polish problem both before and after the war. The imminent departure of the buses for Cracow rescued the guide from a conversation he preferred not to engage in. The same anger these visitors felt upon discovering firsthand the obliteration of Jewish memory and the blatant rewriting of history appears in almost any account of travel to Eastern Europe.[37] Arthur Kurzweil writes that in Przemyśl,

> I learned about the town museum devoted to the history of the area. I went there eagerly, to learn what I could about the place my family had lived in so long. In the entire four-story building though I should have expected it I was shocked to find only two tiny showcases of Jewish items. A skullcap, a menorah, candlesticks, a megillah. Here, where several thousand Jews had lived, where Jews from the area were kept in a ghetto before being taken to a death camp, the Jewish presence was recognized only by a few relics in a dusty corner.[38]

Jews have long felt that Polish public culture was reluctant to give proper recognition to the degree of Jewish suffering during the war. This reluctance was particularly evident in the Auschwitz museum, which was established as a Polish national shrine: exhibitions at the site downplay the Jewish presence at the camp. Jews are present collectively through exhibitions about torture and the display of confiscated prayer shawls. But a display of individual biographies in a pavilion that features the portraits of scores of individuals and highlights the martyrdom of Polish political prisoners makes no reference to Jews. The one individual who stands out in that pavilion is Father Kolbe, who volunteered to die at Auschwitz in place of another. Kolbe, however, was the editor of a virulently anti-Jewish publication before the war. Although there is a Jewish pavilion at Auschwitz, it was only recently constructed—long after others had been established for various occupied countries, including East Germany. The latter's presence reflects the official Soviet line, namely, that the German Democratic Republic had been occupied by the Nazis and then liberated by the Red Army. The notion is Orwellian, and it adds to the feeling among Jewish visitors that the site has been cynically usurped. Many Jews respond to this by visiting the nearby death camp Birkenau, an unreconstructed site generally ignored by other tourists. Birkenau's starkness and decay suggest a closer approximation of historical truth. But others are determined to make their presence felt at Auschwitz. A subtle protest is evident in the large numbers of *yortsayt* (memorial) candles placed by visitors at the wall of execution, along with bouquets of flowers with Hebrew-lettered banners. The wall is like a sacred space, an *axis mundi,* of the People's Republic of Poland, legitimating the Communist state by tying it to the martyrdom of Polish political prisoners. The candles are a reminder that Jews died here also.

Often the protests are less subtle. A historian I know who was leading a Smithsonian-sponsored tour of mostly Polish Americans arranged a visit to the Great Synagogue in Cracow. A Polish guide was giving what my friend considered a highly informed and sympathetic survey of the history of the synagogue when suddenly an Israeli tourist jumped in front of her and began to harangue the visitors: "Don't believe a word she is saying. Had these people helped them during the war, this place wouldn't now be a museum. Instead there would be living Jews to pray here!" Such obtrusiveness is hardly unique. Visitors to Auschwitz and other concentration camps are likely to spot groups of young Israelis carrying their national flag as they head from pavilion to pavilion; in the summer of 1989, specially organized groups of European and American Jews protested at the Carmelite convent that had been established just outside the wall of the camp, eventually causing an international furor after an aborted attempt to breach the convent wall prompted a viciously anti-Semitic statement by Poland's Jozef Cardinal Glemp. Although most Jews do not intend to cause a violent confrontation, they do intend to provoke. Young observant Jews march through the streets on the way from synagogue to their hotels wearing yarmulkes rather than less marked headgear and singing Hebrew or religious songs. Their intention is to be as visible as possible, to reclaim—even if only symbolically—territory that had once belonged to their parents and grandparents, or if not to their own, then at least to other people's.[39]

Much of this seems to be a Jewish meditation on power and powerlessness. These demonstrations are a way of reflecting on the past, and perhaps a way of rectifying history. Little wonder, then, that tourists are hyperconscious of the gaze of Poles. In describing her experiences as a participant in the 1988 Jewish students' March of the Living from Auschwitz to Birkenau (the march is held on Israel's official day of commemoration for the Holocaust), Leah Oko describes the group's arrival in Warsaw:

> We then were flown to Warsaw by the Polish airline. It was an extremely shaky flight, but we made it in one piece. Outside the Warsaw airport, the Orthodox boys prayed the Mincha service. Polish soldiers, young and old, stood around laughing and pointing during the service. They said, *Zhid, Zhid* ("Jews, Jews") [*sic*]. That would be the first of many hostile acts directed toward our group during the tour of Poland.

And then later,

> On Yom Ha'Shoah, every one of us who marched from Auschwitz to the crematoria at Birkenau saw the hatred in the eyes of the Polish people.[40]

Another example: A young woman from Montreal, the child of survivors, was horrified to hear a Polish woman comment while watching a group of Orthodox American Jews protesting the Carmelite convent, "Look at all the noise they make now. But during the war all they could do was shiver and be quiet!" The comment confirmed everything her parents had told her about what to expect in Poland.[41] Indeed, for some people such encounters constitute a direct way of linking the self to a collective past. Concluding a description of his recent journey tracing Hasidic landmarks in Poland, Paul Fenton writes that in Płock,

> I had hoped to find the tombs of my ancestors in the cemetery, to kneel and pray for those of our family who had perished violently among the first victims of Nazi barbarity. Instead my hopes were met with the spectacle of the football field, which now occupies the spot of the age-old cemetery. As we walked along the side of the field I

discovered the debris of a tombstone with some Hebrew lettering.
What desecration! Even the memorial monument which had been
erected in a corner of the sports field by a handful of survivors of the
Shoah had been severely vandalized. As we stood there, plunged in
tearful thought, a book of Psalms in our palms, a group of youngsters jeered while passing *Zhid, Zhidka* (Jew-boy, Jew-girl). Though
I had never ever heard that cry before, the blood froze in my veins as
if I had perceived some horrific echo resounding from the depths of
time through the collective memories of generations of cowering
ancestors.[42]

This sense of experiencing "collective memories" suggests that contested history is not the only factor bringing American Jews to Poland.
An underlying dilemma of modern culture is that despite the increasing prevalence of a two-dimensional universe, made possible through
the growth of the electronic media, humans remain sensual beings,
and they are ill at ease with information that can be experienced only
via simulacra. This is the thrill, it seems to me, of seeing personalities
in the flesh: the mythic becomes tangible, and skepticism dissolves.
Most American Jews are of Eastern European descent: their sentiments about their ancestral homes, if a sense of these places is conveyed at all to them through the narratives of their parents and grandparents, lack the clarity of place that only direct experience can
provide, and even names are often obscured, either because they were
not passed down to succeeding generations or were done so in their
Yiddish form only.[43] In the words of the French Jewish historian
Rachel Ertel:

> Pendant des années la Pologne est restée terre interdite pour moi. Il
> serait peut-être plus juste de dire qu'elle n'existait tout simplement
> pas, du moins pas de façon matérielle. Celle que je portais en moi,
> comme un poids de mort, parlait yiddish. Les noms de ses villes, de
> ses bourgs, de ses bourgades, de ses rues, de ses fleuves, étaient des
> noms yiddish, on ne pouvait les trouver sur aucune carte. Un pays
> tissé de mots, de souvenirs vrais et faux, même pas les miens—je n'en
> avais aucun—, meme pas ceux de mes proches, qui ne parlaient
> jamais d'eux: des souvenirs impersonnels, collectifs qui oblitéraient
> toute realité—une Pologne fantasmatique. Une Pologne fantôme.
> Une Pologne dont je ne remettais pas d'avoir été delivrée par
> l'Extermination.[44]

Divorced from place through migration, and determined to put the
past far behind, Americanized Jews long ago put forth an image of the

shtetl as primitive and rural, and the trope has wide currency in the popular imagination. Its source is partly the negative stereotyping of the "old country" in the rotogravure section of the *Forverts* as well as in the romanticized images of paintings by Chagall, the drawings of Yudovin, and of course the Broadway musical *Fiddler on the Roof.* Such images speak to the post-Holocaust resurrection of the *shtetl* as an idyllic Jewish enclave.[45] The romanticization allows for a sense that through such journeys one may enter cosmogonic space, a place inscribed within tribal memory.

But Eastern Europe has become so remote in the memory culture of many American Jews that a precise knowledge of the locality of residence of one's grandparents or great-grandparents is quite uncommon. Moreover, not all areas have been or are readily accessible, particularly those towns that since the war have been part of the Soviet Union. So most Jews going to Poland are going for reasons having less to do with memory culture that is specific to a particular family than with memory culture that pertains to a much larger collectivity. And this memory culture has typically conflated time into the few short years of the Holocaust and place into a few of its principal camps of extermination—Auschwitz, Treblinka, and Majdanek.[46]

Of course, all people have a need to experience mythic time and space; pilgrimages sensualize history both sacred and secular. For visitors, the ability to experience narrative or image in the flesh is part of the thrill of being in a place. Sense of place, as Yi-Fu Tuan suggests, "achieves concrete reality when our experience of it is total, that is, through all the senses as well as with the active and reflective mind."[47] The continuing appeal of pilgrimages stems from the need to peer behind surface representations to reexperience culture as fully three-dimensional, as real. Ironically, it is rarely reality that pilgrims see.

Tourism and the transformations it produces within the host society have a peculiar tendency to constitute the world tourism seeks to present.[48] The tourist is increasingly presented with theme-park reenactments of local cultures, both domestically, through commodity culture in shopping malls, theme-park stores, and restaurants, and abroad, through places such as Club Med. This may sometimes suit the needs for privacy of the host community, but it also provides processed and therefore easily digestible experiences for their guests.[49] Warsaw's Nożyk synagogue is an excellent case in point. An example of what Richard Schechner refers to as the "restoration of behavior,"[50] a piece of reality extrapolated and reformulated through subsequent performances, the synagogue is undoubtedly much more lavish now, with its polished marble floors, wooden pews, and Oriental rugs, than it had ever been before. Next to it is the community's canteen and theater—both offering clean, new, almost elegant venues for contacts between Polish Jews and American Jews.

Of course, there is something in such travel to recreated places and moments in history that seeks a reality more real than the real.[51] Events witnessed on television, for example, are much easier to accept than are those we witness firsthand: unprocessed experience generally lacks a dramatic structure to make it meaningful. Without the authoritative voice of the narrator, experience seems to lack legitimacy. Hence the endless barrage of statistics in televised sports;[52] a similar phenomenon is apparent in weather reporting. The problem of the authoritative voice is particularly acute for minority cultures, and particularly so for minority cultures that, having experienced considerable social mobility, are now successfully integrated economically into the social mainstream. To some degree, marginal groups fend off the authoritative voice and create an oppositional culture with its own system of meaning. Uncertain of who they are and where they stand vis-à-vis both oppositional and hegemonic cultures, American Jews keep seeking a mirror through which to know the self. Perhaps this is why Jews have become one of the great tourist peoples of the modern world,[53] typically (although, as I've indicated, not in this case) playing anthropologist to their more primitive coreligionists across the globe.

But why go to Poland? Why has there been such an increase in Jewish travel there? What is the appeal of staying in Warsaw's Intercontinental or its Holiday Inn, "tourist bubbles" enabling visitors to be "physically 'in' a place but socially 'outside' the culture"?[54] Why would visitors desire to see the past representationally, that is, through recently constructed monuments and museums? Moreover, why go somewhere with the intention of not having a good time? For Jews, visiting Poland and the death camps has become obligatory: it is ritualistic rather than ludic, a form of religious service rather than leisure.[55] Indeed, it is the very seriousness of such visits that ultimately distinguishes Jewish travel to Poland from tourism, that tells us we are dealing not just with a matter of rite rather than festival,[56] but with something completely devoid of any trace of festival. I believe that those who go, particularly those who travel in tour groups—the majority of Jewish travelers to Poland—do so to participate in a secular ritual[57] that confirms who they are as Jews, and perhaps even more so as American Jews. I use the concept of secular ritual here for several reasons. First, it helps to make a clear distinction between these pil-

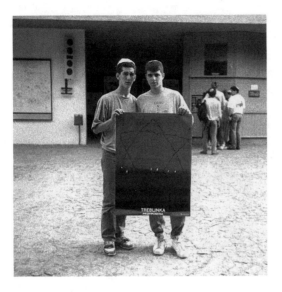

Fig. 13-4. United Synagogue Youth Group at souvenir stand, Treblinka, summer 1989. Photo by the author.

grimages and the traditional ritual of pilgrimage, which has a long-standing place within Eastern European Jewish culture, including appropriate prayers and prescribed modes of behavior. These secular rituals do not comply with traditional forms but rather appropriate them and in part invent wholly new meanings. Participants in a United Synagogue Youth tour at Treblinka, for example, are handed small index cards and told to scatter throughout the site and write notes to someone who died in the camp—an act clearly copied from the Hasidic custom of writing *kvitlekh*. Second, the concept helps to demonstrate the relative shallowness of these acts. Traditional ritual's sense of efficacy derives from an elaborate cosmology. Secular ritual is much narrower in scope, and the movement away from traditional cosmology in general among Jews is something I will discuss further below. Third, these acts are not totally idiosyncratic, and the concept of secular ritual is used here to distinguish the strictly personal from the collective.

Despite substantial evidence of the acculturation of ethnic groups within the modern world, there is equally compelling data to suggest that a considerable amount of group distinctiveness persists. One strategy for survival is the invention of new traditions, even the fabrication of new cultures. Jews have been active in this endeavor since the emergence of a secular Yiddish and Hebrew culture in Eastern Europe more than one hundred years ago. They have continued to reinvent traditions even after the near-demise of language-based Judaism in America. These traditions, which I call the "rites of the tribe" because of their largely ethnic rather than religious basis, not only serve to situate actors within some social-political framework (as opposed to a cosmological one), but they contain within them rhetorical strategies that both represent the traditional and inform participants how they should experience it. Ironically, the very inventedness of these traditions may lend them an aura of authenticity, particularly in an iconoclastic age. To a much greater extent than traditional religious rituals, the rites of the tribe tend toward the spectacular: the transcendent and the contemplation of divinity, although present in part, are of secondary importance. The eye of Man has replaced the eye of God, and the lens of the camera has becomes the means of entering the "Great Time." It is little wonder, then, that a tour group to Birkenau would pause just outside the gate for a group video portrait before entering the camp.

What is particularly striking about these rites is their appeal to large segments of American Jewry. I include among these rites dining at kosher-style restaurants, visiting Israel, buying books on Jewish subjects, and going to Jewish museums. And there is an iconic dimension to the rites, which include the purchase and display of kitsch paintings of Israeli soldiers praying or Hasidim dancing at the Western Wall in Jerusalem. There is, then, a continuing and perhaps growing tension within American Judaism between the Great Tradition and popular practice. The study of Hebrew and Aramaic holy texts, for example, is well beyond the intellectual reach or patience of people accustomed to a world in which their nonethnic native tongue, English, is dominant. But even a vernacular liturgy is problematic. Contemplative or petitionary, prayer lends itself to poetry; technical and instrumental, modern culture is most at home in prose. Increasingly prose, too, is giving way to other forms of discourse. Although American Jews are the largest consumers of books among American ethnic groups, like all Americans they spend the bulk of their leisure time watching television, not reading; the spectacle is paramount not only because of the power of the reproduced image over the reproduced word, but also because of television's very lack of poetry, which is what gives it instant accessibility.[58] Rites must fit the cultures that perform them; the rites that American Jews have preferred over the past few decades—family feasts and marches on behalf of Israel or Soviet Jewry—are nonpoetic and therefore unambiguous. They borrow their mode of discourse from television, not only because it lends itself to pageantry, but also because, like all successful American media productions, rites based on this mode of discourse are condensed, entertaining, and highly charged emotionally.[59] Rather than television replicating culture, it is culture that replicates the world of television.[60]

Although feasts, whether in delicatessens or through family-centered holiday celebrations, provide a major way for American Jews to practice Judaism, their very festiveness mitigates their potential for catharsis. Marches, whether in the United States on behalf of Soviet Jewry or in Eastern Europe and Israel, have a more serious, even self-sacrificing quality to them.[61] Participants on organized journeys to Eastern Europe are frequently required to engage in practices that they avoid in their everyday lives: attending religious services three times daily, eating strictly kosher food prepackaged in Western Europe, attending lectures and evening discussions, and enduring sometimes arduous travel schedules. Such practices contribute to the journeys' time-out-of-time quality. Their very liminality suggests to participants that what they are experiencing is charged with meaning. Indeed, the journeys themselves are called "missions" by both organizers and participants. At the same time, the shared nature of the experience has tremendous potential for generating catharsis. Participants are encouraged to talk about their feelings and to discuss what they have seen, either during the travel time between the site and the hotel or later in the evening, during group discussions. There is a tendency here to push participants away from disengagement and to pull them toward putting themselves in the place of Holocaust victims. At Auschwitz and Birkenau, a member of a Montreal synagogue group who straggled behind the others watched her fellow participants march toward the destroyed crematoria. A barbed-wire fence was in her line of vision as she looked at the distant men of her group, and she commented to others near her that for a moment she had imagined the men actually imprisoned in the camp. Such catharsis is far more likely through these rites than through the traditional liturgy. Even a lone traveler can experience such catharsis. Reflecting on the previous day's tour of Cracow and Kazimierz, Jeffrey Dekro writes,

Last night I was transported from 1987 to earlier times: before the war and even back to the eighteenth and nineteenth centuries. In that way I have become part of Polish ḥasidic life, and I also enter the world of my grandparents Dora and Josef.

Today we go to Auschwitz. By the time we enter, I have changed

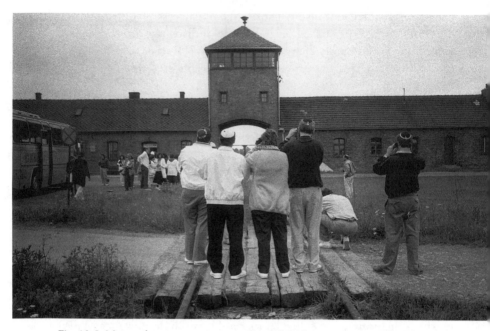

Fig. 13-5. Montreal synagogue tour group outside Birkenau, summer 1989. Photo by
the author.

from being a "surviving grandson" to being an equal, arriving at the
gates from the past in the past. Only now can I finally die with Josef,
Dora, and my father Hans. Later, as I walk back through the camp
entrance at Birkenau, I am reborn, in my present life. As witness, not
as survivor.[62]

But if Eastern Europe is able to provide such a meaningful backdrop
for staging Jewish rites, why was its value only recently discovered?
Here, I think, we need to consider a number of issues. An important
factor must certainly be the genealogical craze that began in the 1970s
with the airing of the television series *Roots* and which continues
unabated among various ethnic groups in the United States. This
should come as no surprise, given the general tendency of postmodern
culture toward pastiche and nostalgia.[63] Another factor is the recent
responsiveness, if not the very solicitousness, of Eastern European
countries themselves. Floundering economically and pressed for hard
currency, for them Western tourism represents a relatively simple way
to generate income. Here, then, lies an obvious if not entirely happy
marriage: the Eastern European thirst for cash and the Jewish search

for roots. And finally, the recent emergence of the Holocaust as a subject of popular Jewish discourse—indeed, as one of the tenets of American Jewish civil religion—certainly plays a role.[64]

Although discussions of the Holocaust have long found their place in Jewish educational activities and even in liturgical innovations, the subject itself has emerged from the confines of synagogue adult-education programs to university lecture halls and even television. The 1978 airing of the made-for-television film *Holocaust* and the annual showing of Holocaust-related documentaries on PBS has undoubtedly made the subject less parochial and more an acceptable subject of popular and even ecumenical discourse. And the response to the nine-and-one-half-hour documentary *Shoah,* a film released in 1985 that was composed entirely of recent footage, did two things simultaneously: it contemporized the Holocaust by bringing victims and witnesses together in Poland, thereby demonstrating to millions of viewers that mythical time could be experienced even now, and it also did what Joshua Meyrowitz suggests has become symptomatic of the impact of the media on social behavior generally since the 1960s: it realigned viewers' sense of place. Through repeated airings on PBS of this and other films in which Poland is a backdrop, Poland ceased to be remote, becoming instead a familiar place encapsulated and contained both literally and metaphorically within a living-room box.[65]

The reason for the earlier neglect of the Holocaust stems in part from the lack of a literature of destruction, which could transform family trauma into history, in the years immediately after the war[66] and in part from the Jewish identification with the hegemonic American culture in the years during and immediately after the war. The recent emergence of the Holocaust as a cornerstone of American Jewish civil religion is generally connected to the rise in Jewish nationalism that occurred immediately before and after Israel's Six-Day War in 1967.[67] However, the media's interest in the subject in part reflects, I think, the postwar emergence of American Jewry as a central rather than a marginal group within American society and culture, a transformation subtly apparent in the increasing prominence of Jewish characters in American television and cinema, but even more blatantly visible in the construction of a Holocaust memorial on the Mall in Washington.[68] And in part it reflects the emergence of an ironic, postmodern sensibility in which the mythic underpinnings of society are open for scrutiny. If there is anything that seems paradigmatic of this sensibility, it is the spectacle of extermination that characterized World War II. Visits to the sites of mass death are for all people a way to

experience the mythic birthplace of the postmodern, to witness cosmogonic time: Auschwitz, after all, is Poland's major tourist
attraction.

Still, Auschwitz has special meaning for American Jews, and its
current appeal may have as much to do with contemporary issues as it
does with the past. Herbert Gans argues that the Holocaust has come
to serve as a "symbol of the threat of group destruction," and that this
need stems from increasing intermarriage, a decline in religious obser-
vance, and the fear that lack of overt anti-Semitism has made the
boundaries between Jew and non-Jew too permeable.[69] Charles Silberman argues that American Jews are extremely nervous about the
degree of success they have achieved in America, and that they are
particularly afraid that the very security of their lives in the United
States poses a threat to group survival—that without anti-Semitism,
Jews will lose their group solidarity. In the words of Jacob Neusner,
"The central issue facing Judaism in our day is whether a long-be-
leaguered faith can endure the conclusion of its perilous age."[70] Seen
within this context, it remains rather clear that the attraction of the
Holocaust in general (and because of it the attraction of Poland in
particular as a place of pilgrimage) is that it represents a journey to a
much simpler past.

Although pilgrimages to Poland began as inducements for securing donations from a wealthy and often nonobservant elite within the
Jewish community, it is striking how common they have become. So
much are they part of the lives of American Jews that, increasingly,
Jewish children are sent on them as part of their religious or ethnic
education,[71] and even United Jewish Appeal fundraising tours now
promote multigenerational participation. Several years ago, an American Jewish family arranged to have their son's bar mitzvah in Cracow;
the event was captured in a documentary film titled *A Spark Among
the Ashes*. In the summer of 1989, an American Jew married a Polish-
born convert to Judaism at the Nożyk synagogue, and the event was
covered by NBC and CNN. These examples point to two interrelated
aspects of what Herbert Gans refers to as the emergence of "symbolic
ethnicity": one is the heightened value placed on rites of passage in
Jewish ritual, since they are generally less demanding than calendrical
rites; the other is the tendency for ethnics in general to express their
identity by trips to the "old country."[72] But Gans's model lacks any
underlying sociopolitical or economic explanation. Cultural symbols,
as Abner Cohen suggests, are often intricately tied to political and
economic conflict.[73]

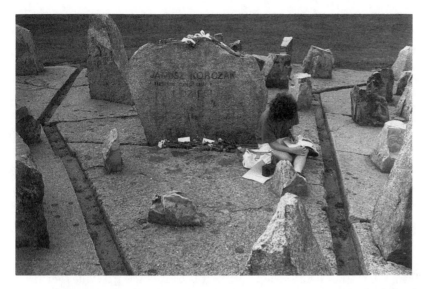

Fig. 13-6. Participant in United Synagogue Youth Group writing note to the dead, Treblinka, summer 1989. Photo by the author.

The case I would like to make is that the expansion of rites connected to the Holocaust, in particular the rite of pilgrimage to the death camps, emerged simultaneously with and probably at least to some degree in response to two conflicts with profoundly disquieting implications for American Jews. One of these conflicts has to do with the international situation, particularly the Arab-Israeli conflict. Indeed, the association of the other side with Nazis is a rhetorical strategy exploited rather shamelessly by both sides. But the evocation of the past has more concrete value in the Israeli case, since Nazism conjures up much more than political loathing on the part of Jews. For Arabs the term is a referential symbol, a type of name-calling; for Jews it is a condensation symbol, conjuring up deep emotion and tribal memory.[74] One cannot help but think that the popularity of events such as the March of the Living, a pilgrimage to the death camps involving thousands of North American Jewish schoolchildren, is growing in direct proportion to the ambiguousness of the Middle East situation: as long as Israel was perceived as a David against a Goliath, there was no need for a ritual to convince participants and spectators of the vulnerability of the Jewish people. But with the increasing perception of Israel as Goliath—the use of stones by Palestinians is also a rhetorical strategy—there is an increasing need for Jews to formulate a counter-rhetoric. Certainly the Holocaust's attraction is its very lack of ambiguity.

The other impetus to the expansion of rites connected with the Holocaust is the increasing sense of social tension within the United States, in particular the fear of rising anti-Semitism. But here the cause for pilgrimage is not anti-Semitism in general, since invoking the Holocaust, if it does anything, might only give a sense of succor to those who would do Jews harm and would certainly highlight how different Jews are from other Americans. The Holocaust has much more meaning when evoked as a rhetorical strategy to counter accusations of Jewish powerfulness only when such accusations are leveled against Jews by a group that is staking its own claim on powerlessness. In recent years, such accusations have come from African Americans, particularly as the once very close alliance between the groups grows increasingly fragile. Black nationalists argue that Jews are no different from any other white group, and that because they are white they have gained acceptance within American society. Seen within this context, the purpose of the pilgrimage to Poland is not just a reminder of the past for contemporary Jews but an attempt to make it actual, to use it rhetorically as a statement that despite current success Jews do not have, nor did they ever have, political power and are in fact a vulnerable and discriminated-against minority.

The contrast between the ways in which American and European Jews commemorate the Holocaust suggests the influence of domestic politics on Jewish secular ritual. To the best of my knowledge, at least until recently there were no regularly organized pilgrimages from Western Europe to Poland despite the fact that many Western European Jews are, like American Jews, descendants of Eastern European Jews. Of course, most Western European Jews have their own Holocaust experience to commemorate, and they do so in a manner that fits their respective national cultures. Western European Holocaust memorials are typically devoted to Jewish members of the Resistance, as are Polish Jewish memorials. Unlike its European counterpart, American public discourse on history (probably since the Vietnam War) has legitimated the victim and increasingly recognized and celebrated various modes of opposition. Indeed, the Vietnam Veterans Memorial in Washington, D.C., designed by Maya Lin, is a case in point. As "an abstract image of sacrifice," the monument's very ambiguity leaves open the possibility of a multiplicity of readings.[75] The recent construction of a memorial at the site of the Umschlagplatz, a spot just outside the Warsaw ghetto where Jews were assembled prior to deportation, speaks to the fact that over the past few years Polish Jewry has increasingly fallen into the cultural orbit of American Jewry. Not only was the memorial's commission by the Polish government an indication of the government's desire to court American Jews, but its style of commemoration, particularly the listings of representative Jewish first names to commemorate the ordinary rather than the extraordinary, is distinctly non-Polish and to a degree evokes Maya Lin's memorial.[76] Another example of superb public art is a memorial at Treblinka, among whose tens of thousands of stones representing the Jewish populations of towns and cities destroyed by the Nazis there is one stone upon which a name is inscribed, that of Janusz Korczak, the Polish Jewish educator who volunteered to accompany a group of orphaned children to Treblinka. In a sense, there are two possible readings of this monument's iconography: the Jewish reading is of mass extermination, while the Polish reading is of the lone hero in the face of countless nonheroic deaths.

By evoking the Holocaust dramaturgically, that is, by going to the site of the event and reconstituting the reality of the time and place, American Jews are not only invoking the spirits of the tribe and laying claim to their martyrdom, but they are also making past time present. And in doing so they are symbolically reversing reality: they are attempting to change current perceptions of themselves as highly privileged (in the American case) or oppressive (in the Israeli case) and to present their position as the diametric opposite of being privileged, to present themselves as what they in fact were. And it is this image of the self that remains central to the Jewish worldview.

In an essay highly critical of Jewish understandings of anti-Semitism, John Murray Cuddihy argues that underneath the contemporary Jewish worldview is a kind of Manichean radical separation of good and evil.[77] Unlike Biblical theology, which connected punishment with Jewish sin, contemporary theology, or what one might call post-Holocaust theology, sees evil as completely exterior and unrelated to the behavior of Jews. The vector of blame has shifted from Jews themselves to the instruments of God's wrath—the nations of the world. The result is an ideology of "angelism," a sense of being morally superior to others, evident in various domains of culture, including popular fiction and film.[78] Cuddihy is entirely wrong in seeing this as something unique to Jews. Angelism is really just a manifestation of ethnonarcissism, the belief that all groups have that they are the center of the universe.[79] The weak lay claim to a moral superiority; this claim is not only an underlying trope in Jewish culture since Biblical times, but it also has particular tenacity now, when acculturation has done its work. Indeed, even the moral dimension becomes confused with a more general sense of superiority, which may then serve the purpose of retarding assimilation.[80] If weakness is considered a sign of strength and persecution a sign of moral superiority, then reality often has a strange way of confirming group beliefs. As long as there is continual evidence to support such a worldview, there is little need to prop up cherished tenets. But when reality shows things to be otherwise, the task of ritual is to convince people that the group's basic tenets still hold.

In stressing the political component of the rite of pilgrimage, I do not mean to suggest that there is anything cynical at work here. On the contrary, those who perform these rites do so out of conviction, because they offer a way out of a difficult moral dilemma and allow Jews to steer a course somewhere between hegemonic and oppositional culture. Indeed, the increasing introduction of African American spirituals into the text of the Passover Haggadah is a similar case in point.[81] Moreover, the political nature of these rites is only one dimension of their meaning. These rites are performed primarily for fellow Jews: they are intra- rather than intertribal. And they have the same agenda as all ritual, namely to bridge fundamental discontinuities in life: those between American and Eastern European Jewry, postwar and prewar Jewry, the living and the dead, power and powerlessness. They are an attempt to counteract the fragmentation and loss of belief that modernity itself has brought on and the possibility that this loss of belief will cause the complete demise of the tribe. These rites are also about memory: participants are attempting to retain some connection to the past, as though even the memory of what was lost could have a salutary effect upon contemporary culture.[82]

Paul Connerton makes a persuasive argument for the performative nature of social memory, arguing that without bodily practices tribal memory cannot be maintained.[83] Because of their bodily nature, marches to the camps constitute the surest way for American Jews to remember the fate of European Jewry. Perhaps, then, we ought to consider the emergence of these pilgrimages in the context of a growing discontinuity between actual memory—that of both the survivors themselves and American Jews who lived through the years during and immediately after World War II—and social memory, which is the meaning of these events for the Jewish collectivity. As the distance between the present and the war grows, there is an increasing sense of a potential crisis of historical continuity. How are those who themselves did not witness the war to pass the memory of those events and their consequences to succeeding generations? This crisis of memory is all the more acute given the general disregard for history within contemporary society. Pierre Nora writes that *lieux de mémoire,* or sites of memory—museums, archives, festivals and the like—

> are fundamentally remains, the ultimate embodiments of a memorial consciousness that has barely survived in a historical age that calls out for memory because it has abandoned it. They make their appearance by virtue of the deritualization of our world—producing, manifesting, establishing, constructing, decreeing, and maintaining by artifice and by will a society deeply absorbed in its own transformation and renewal, one that inherently values the new over the ancient, the young over the old, the future over the past.[84]

As Nora argues, there are *lieux de mémoire* because there are no longer *milieux de mémoire,* or real environments of memory.[85] Although it is true that the transformation from one to the other is not a choice but a process of civil and social development, there is something terribly disconcerting about the change. Sites of memory are not subtle: indeed, their popular appeal is based on the fact that narrative tropes replaced the nuanced realness of social and cultural life. There is a tendency quite evident during the pilgrimages to place Poland and its people, both Jews and non-Jews, into a master narrative in which Poles are all victimizers (on a par with the S.S.) and Jews are eternal victims. It is very disconcerting, for example, that these rites pay homage to the martyrdom of prewar Polish Jewry at the expense of attempting to retrieve what the culture had achieved, not to mention expressing any curiosity in the vitality of postwar Polish Jewry and the struggle to maintain Jewish culture in contemporary Poland. All this is cast aside. American Jewish memory culture has frozen Poland in time and turned its inhabitants into a vast *tableau vivant.* Perhaps this is the only way that things could be, given the plague of anti-Semitism in interwar, occupied, post–World War II, and even contemporary Poland.[86] And if we object to the misuse of Poland's history and culture, perhaps we simply ask too much of American Jews, given the very nature of collective memory. If Nora is correct, and I believe that he is, how can we expect any group, whether Jewish or not, to maintain the past with any of its nuances intact? The answer is that we cannot. Memory, as Maurice Halbwachs argues, is socially constructed. Its base is much more in the present than in the past.[87]

Of course, these pilgrimages alone are not to blame for the dismissal of present-day Polish Jewry. Judaism's Great Tradition weighs against too much local variation, particularly when these variations begin to veer away from rabbinic precepts. Jews also have a transnational Little Tradition made possible through continuing migration, intermarriage among Jewish subgroups, and various cultural productions, including how-to books on conducting bar mitzvahs and weddings and celebrating holy days. One might also speak of the folk categories of the American Jewish worldview, particularly the great chain of being through which national and even denominational subgroups are located in terms of past, present, and future: for example, Eastern Europe is the past, America is the present, and Israel is the future. Given such a ranking, the increasing incorporation of Polish Jewry into American Jewish or Israeli cultural hegemony is likely to lead to the demise of a uniquely Polish Jewish culture. Increasing pressure is placed upon young Polish Jews in general and the intelligentsia in particular to migrate—to either Israel or the United States—in order to acquire greater Jewish knowledge and "to live as Jews." And so the trope of the past threatens this community with ultimate extinction.[88] Rather than Poland inscribing itself on its pilgrims, the reverse is the case. Here we have a museum very much invented by its public.

The case presented here indicates the need for various metaphors to help classify a museum's relationship with its community. *Shrine* and *academy* suggest a role as repository of sacred objects and ultimate Truth. Such institutions require a resident priesthood to formulate the canon, place the icons in the appropriate settings for adulation, and formulate an appropriate liturgy. The public is privileged to enter such institutions; they are expected to show sufficient awe, and unless they are recognized experts they are not expected to have any input on the canon and its presentation. But some museums are as much theater as shrine. Their objects are like props, silent evocations of powerful sensations. The text, however, is not scripted, like liturgy, nor is the public expected to behave with awe. Indeed, lacking a resident priesthood, the text is performance-oriented rather than scripted, in some ways unique for each group of visitors. Perhaps, then, *stage* rather than *shrine* is the correct metaphor for looking at Poland and its Jewish public. Indeed, the very fact that Polish Jewry is nearly extinct weighs heavily in favor of the stage metaphor, for shrines need a priesthood. For American Jews, Poland is filled with ready-made props—ruined synagogues, doorposts carrying the impressions of long-removed mezuzahs, crumbling cemeteries, and death camps. These objects are deafening in their silence, and they are scriptless; almost no one within Poland is capable of writing texts and labels for the country's Jewish monuments.[89] Moreover, the country's viability as a stage is enhanced by the fact that it is nearly devoid of actors who might contest the presence of these foreign visitors or attempt to wrest control of the performance. And what American Jews are performing is, if not their actual identity, then at least an attempt to piece together the icons of the past—to retrieve or reclaim them and then to reassemble them, albeit within a framework that inscribes their meaning in the present rather than the past. Moreover, given the dimensions of the Holocaust and the challenge it poses to Jewish thinking (particularly nonrabbinic thinking) to explain it, these rites have very special meaning, since they do what endless study and discussion cannot do: they create meaning. This is possible in part because performance itself is meaningful, and in part because the rites do attempt to shape and systematize otherwise abstract and diffuse cultural orientations.[90] Since these rituals have a clear orientation toward the future, they suggest Richard Schechner's concept of rehearsal: their work "is to 'represent' a past for the future (performance-to-be)."[91] In part a meditation on the past, and in part a scripted play about the present, the rites I have described are also very much rehearsals of what American Jews are intent on becoming, or—perhaps more accurately stated—intent on *not* becoming. How ironic it is that Poland, relegated to the past by American Jews, has suddenly emerged as a stage upon which they act out their future.

NOTES

Research on this project was made possible by grants from the Memorial Foundation for Jewish Culture, the Lucius N. Littauer Foundation, Inc., and the Wisconsin Alumni Research Foundation. I would like to thank the following people who read and commented on drafts of this essay: Michael Fischer, Kostek Gebert, Harvey Goldberg, Marc Kaminsky, and Herb Lewis.

1. Yehudit Hendel, "Near Quiet Places: Twelve Days in Poland," *Lilith* (spring 1990), 17.

2. Barbara Kirshenblatt-Gimblett, "Authenticity and Authority in the Representation of Culture: The Poetics and Politics of Tourist Production," in Ina-

Maria Greverus, Konrad Köstlin, and Heinz Schilling, eds., "Kulturkontakt/ Kulturkonflikt: Zur Erfahrung des Fremden," *Notizen* 28, no. 1 (1988).

3. Donald Horne, *The Public Culture: The Triumph of Industrialism* (London: Pluto, 1986).

4. Indeed, so pervasive is the religious motivation for travel even now that Victor Turner has argued that "many so-called 'tourists' [are] really closet pilgrims" ("Carnaval in Rio: Dionysian Drama in an Industrializing Society," in Frank Manning, ed., *The Celebration of Society: Perspectives on Contemporary Cultural Performance* [Bowling Green, Ky.: Bowling Green University Popular Press, 1983], 104). In a very insightful essay ("A Phenomenology of Tourist Experience," *Sociology* 13, no. 2 [1979]), Erik Cohen has argued for a reconciliation of the opposing views of tourism put forward by Dean MacCannell (*The Tourist: A New Theory of the Leisure Class* [New York: Schocken, 1976]) and Daniel Boorstin (*The Image: A Guide to Pseudo-Events in America* [New York: Harper and Row, 1964]). Cohen argues that the touristic experience is not necessarily either deep or spurious; there are a variety of experiences ranging from the purely recreational vacation to the search for what Mircea Eliade refers to as the center—the point where the *axis mundi* penetrates the earthly sphere. Cohen outlines five modes of touristic experience: recreational, diversionary, experiential, experimental, and existential. "These modes are ranked here," Cohen argues, "so that they span the spectrum between the experience of the tourist as the traveller in pursuit of 'mere' pleasure in the strange and the novel, to that of the modern pilgrim in quest of meaning at somebody else's centre" (183).

5. Maxine Feifer, *Tourism in History: From Imperial Rome to the Present* (New York: Stein and Day, 1985).

6. Mary Helms, *Ulysses Sail* (Princeton: Princeton University Press, 1988).

7. Pierre Bourdieu, *Distinction: A Social Critique of the Judgement of Taste,* trans. Richard Nice (Cambridge, Mass.: Harvard University Press, 1984).

8. Nelson H. H. Graburn, "Tourism: The Sacred Journey," in Valene L. Smith, ed., *Hosts and Guests: The Anthropology of Tourism* (Philadelphia: University of Pennsylvania Press, 1977), 19.

9. MacCannell, *The Tourist,* 13.

10. L. Malkes's article "Af di shifen vos firn vakeyshonikes ken Yurop, zet men un hert men dos zelbe vi in di zumer-hoteln" (*Forverts,* 14 July 1929, section 2) is an extended description of life on board an ocean liner, the kinds of people who travel, their behavior and social life, and the types of presents they brought to their relatives.

11. Jack Kugelmass and Jeffrey Shandler, *Going Home: How American Jews Invent the Old World* (New York: YIVO Institute for Jewish Research, 1989).

12. See, for example, Yoysef Sandatsh, "Vos ikh hob gezen in Folks-Poylen,"

in P. Katz et al., eds., *Pinkes Varshe* (Buenos Aires: Landsleyt fareyn fun Varshe un umgegnt in Argentina, 1955). Based on a journey to Poland in the early 1950s, the article gives a glowing account of life in the People's Republic of Poland, the remarkable pace of reconstruction, the absence of anti-Semitism, the existence of freedom and democracy, and the blossoming of Jewish culture.

13. See, for example, S. L. Shneiderman, *The River Remembers* (New York: Horizon, 1978).

14. For a history and analysis of the Warsaw Ghetto Heroes monument, see James E. Young, "The Biography of a Memorial Icon: Nathan Rapoport's Warsaw Ghetto Monument," *Representations* 26 (1989), 69–106.

15. See, for example, Jack Kugelmass and Jonathan Boyarin, eds., *From A Ruined Garden: The Memorial Books of Polish Jewry* (New York: Schocken, 1983).

16. See, for example, Khanke Ashlak, "My Tragic Night in Zhelekhov," in Kugelmass and Boyarin, eds., *From A Ruined Garden,* 218–20.

17. See, for example, Yeshaye Filer, "Mayn bazukh in mayn heym shtetl un in Oyshvits: A Memorial to the Brzozow Community," in Avraham Levite, ed., *Survivors of Brzozow* (Israel: Survivors of Brzozow, 1984), 288. Accounts of these journeys are frequently found in *yizker-bikher* (memorial books). Filer describes a visit he made to Brzozów in 1976 from Israel, during which his former neighbors inquired whether he had come to sell his parents' house! He also indicates that he was warned before leaving Israel not to go to Brzozów, his hometown, because two Jews who had returned shortly after the war to claim their possessions had been killed.

18. See, for example, Shneiderman, *The River Remembers,* 171. In an example from my own research, one informant, a survivor returning to Poland for the first time, used the same technique she had used to survive the war in Poland: she assumed a non-Jewish identity, this time traveling as part of a Polish American church group.

19. See, for example, Shneiderman's description of the editor of the Polish Yiddish newspaper *Folks-sztyme* visiting Kazimierz Dolny, in *The River Remembers,* 167–68.

20. As Amos Elon notes in *The Israelis: Founders and Sons* (New York: Holt, Rinehart and Winston, 1971), 280, "It is intriguing in this context to observe the extraordinary appeal of archeology as a popular pastime and science in Israel. The millenia-spanning mixture of ancient and modern history, coupled with notions of 'controversial' legitimacy, combine to produce this peculiarly Israeli syndrome. Archeological finds have inspired nearly all Israeli national symbols, from the State Seal, to emblems, coins, medals, and postage stamps. For the disquieted Israeli, the moral comforts of archeology are considerable. In the political culture of Israel, the symbolic role of archeology is immediately

evident. Israeli archeologists, professionals and amateurs, are not merely digging for knowledge and *objects,* but for reassurance of roots, which they find in the ancient Israelite remains scattered throughout the country."

21. The magazine *Present Tense,* for example, which began publication in 1973, frequently ran features on Jewish communities in various parts of the world.

22. Aviva Weintraub, "The Photoethnography of Jewish Communities: Related Books, Articles, and Museum Catalogues," *Jewish Folklore and Ethnology Review* 10, no. 1 (1988), 3–10.

23. Perhaps the most relevant to this subject is Oren Rudavsky's *A Spark Among the Ashes,* a 1986 film that documents an American bar mitzvah held in Cracow; the same director is currently working on a film retracing the five-month visit of a young *klezmer* (Jewish folk musician) to Eastern Europe. A photo book on the same subject appeared in 1986 along with a photo calendar. A far more serious attempt to encounter East European Jewry is *Remnants: The Last Jews of Poland* (New York: Friendly Press, 1986) by Malgorzata Niezabitowska and Tomasz Tomaszewski, a husband-and-wife writer-and-photographer team. In the course of five years the couple interviewed and photographed some of the remaining 5,000 Jews of Poland. Their work has led to an article in *National Geographic,* exhibits in Poland, the United States, and Israel, and a book of text and color photographs that has already sold over 11,000 copies in hardcover. Their work has become well known among American Jews—in part, I suspect, because they are both non-Jews and are therefore somewhat of a curiosity—and may be somewhat responsible for the current boom in Jewish interest in Poland.

24. Shifra Epstein, "Photographing a Contemporary Hasidic Pilgrimage to Poland," *Jewish Folklore and Ethnology Review* 10, no. 1 (1988), 21–22.

25. Individuals do sometimes leave the tours for half a day in order to visit their family's home village, town, or city. Also, not all the tours are ideologically motivated in quite the same way. Some are sponsored by cultural institutions: Hebrew University recently planned a tour of the Lublin area with special reference to the world of Isaac Bashevis Singer; Yad Vashem organizes tours of Holocaust sites for historians; and the Jewish Museum of New York organized a tour in conjunction with its photographic exhibition on Russian Jewry, led by the historian Zvi Gittelman.

26. In 1948 Henry Montor of the United Jewish Federation chartered a TWA airplane and took thirty-five communal leaders on a four-week mission to the displaced-persons camps in Europe and then to Israel to see the process of absorption then underway. These leaders subsequently spearheaded local fundraising drives upon their return (Charles Silberman, *A Certain People: American Jews and Their Lives Today* [New York: Summit, 1985], 197). In recent years, the UJA has begun to send an increasing number of groups to Poland, while some American synagogue groups and literally scores of nation-

ally organized synagogue youth groups, such as the Conservative movement's United Synagogue Youth and the Orthodox movement's B'nai Akiva, are doing likewise.

27. The United Jewish Appeal and other Israel-oriented groups are almost exclusively devoted to touring death camps. The Joint Distribution Committee, which sponsors relief efforts in Poland, focuses its tours more on contemporary Polish Jewish life.

28. This is despite the fact that the primary motivation for reconstruction was probably historical and architectural rather than to attract Jewish tourists. Besides the creation of physical monuments, a number of academic activities exist in Poland that are of specific interest to Jews. Various international conferences have been organized dealing with the Holocaust; the National Museum in Cracow recently mounted an enormous art exhibition dealing with the Jew in Polish painting; Warsaw's Jewish Historical Institute (ZIH) has a long and important history in postwar Polish academic efforts, and includes a permanent exhibition space devoted to the Holocaust; more recently, the Jagiellonian University has established a Center for Jewish Research. During a period of major financial crisis within Poland generally and the university in particular, the institution procured and renovated a building for the center in the hope that additional help for the purchase of books and office equipment will come from private sources, particularly foreign Jews.

29. These came about through the entrepreneurship of an American Jew who commissioned the work from Polish craftsmen.

30. Beverly Gordon, "The Souvenir: Messenger of the Extraordinary," *Journal of Popular Culture* 20, no. 3 (1986), 141. Of course, in the case of artwork, the objects take on special meaning, no matter how humble once inside its new owner's living room. As Gordon notes, the object "becomes transformed into a significant icon. It becomes sacralized in the new context, and is imbued with all the power of the association made with its original environment" (ibid.).

31. Arthur Kurzweil, "Report from Przemysl: No More Jews," *Present Tense* 8, no. 3 (1981), 15.

32. Most members of the intelligentsia are young, and they are able to gain access to hard currency by working abroad for periods of time. Consequently, tourism for them is not a business but a way to maintain contact with friends. Since the war and the destruction of Eastern European Jewish life, there arose two centers of Jewish cultural life: New York and Jerusalem. Poland is now at the border of both. Since the liberalization of travel restrictions and the wooing of Jewish tourists, the country has become a convenient stopover for both American and Israeli academics traveling between the two centers. Despite the prohibitive cost of Western books, the homes of Jewish intellectuals are virtual public libraries; their address books are a who's who of world Jewish intellectuals. A Polish ethnographer who works on Jewish subjects and

is closely tied to the network of visiting Americans and Israelis described her social calendar over the summer as a constant series of invitations to dine with foreign visitors in expensive restaurants. When I mentioned to her that I had some uncertainty as to whether I would see a mutual friend in Cracow since I hadn't been able to reach him by telephone and I was uncertain of his where-abouts, the ethnographer assured me that he never leaves the city during the summer months: "After all, it's the season!"

33. Laurence Loeb, "Creating Antiques for Fun and Profit: Encounters Be-tween Iranian Jewish Merchants and Touring Coreligionists," in Valene L. Smith, ed., *Hosts and Guests: The Anthropology of Tourism* (Philadelphia: University of Pennsylvania Press, 1977), 187.

34. John MacAloon, "Sociation and Sociability in Political Celebrations," in Victor Turner, ed., *Celebration: Studies in Festivity and Ritual* (Washington, D.C.: Smithsonian Institution Press, 1982), 269.

35. This is very much in contrast to Steven Mullaney's analysis of rehearsals in Renaissance England and France. Describing a remarkably thorough repre-sentation of Brazilian culture performed in 1551 for Henri II on the occasion of the royal entry into the city of Rouen, Mullaney concludes that the object of such a representation "was not to understand Brazilian culture but to perform it, in a paradoxically self-consuming fashion. Knowledge of another culture in such an instance is directed toward ritual rather than ethnological ends, and the rite involved is one ultimately organized around the elimination of its own pretext: the spectacle of the Other that is thus celebrated and observed, in passing. To speak of Renaissance curiosity or fascination with other cultures hardly begins to address what is odd in such an anthropology, geared not toward the interpretation of strange cultures but toward their consummate performance. What we glimpse in the field outside Rouen is not a version of the modern discipline of anthropology, but something preliminary to it; not the interpretation, but what I would call the rehearsal of cultures" (Steven Mullaney, "Strange Things, Gross Terms, Curious Customs: The Rehearsal of Cultures in the Late Renaissance," *Representations* 1, no. 3 [1983], 69).

Rehearsal is a period of license for the staging of alternatives. Renaissance rehearsals were concerned with the incorporation of other cultures. Whereas Jewish tourists visiting synagogues in various parts of the world may indeed be engaging in a form of rehearsal, experimenting albeit superficially with "oth-erness," Jewish pilgrimages to Poland do no such thing. "Otherness" here is rejected. Identification is purely with the past.

36. Horne, *The Public Culture,* 249.

37. Sigmund Diamond describes his reactions to the Archaeological and Eth-nographic Museum in Vilnius: "At the door was a guidebook in which we were requested to write our comments. I saw names from India, Laos, Egypt, Iraq and the republics of the U.S.S.R.—and of two Lithuanians from Chi-cago. I wrote: 'A lovely museum, but in an ethnographic museum why is there

no mention of the work of *all* the ethnic and religious groups in Lithuania? Professor Sigmund Diamond, Columbia University, New York, USA.' A petty thing, but I felt better" ("Journey to the East: Different Communists—Different Jews," *Present Tense* 3, no. 3 [1976], 65).

38. Arthur Kurzweil, "Report from Przemysl," 15.

39. Nor are provocative encounters limited to the unsophisticated. The following account is from the French Jewish historian Rachel Ertel: "Le soir, première rencontre avec des Polonais, à l'Institut français de Cracovie. Deux cents personnes environ, toutes francophones. Exposé sur mon livre *le Shtetl*. Certains l'avaient lu. Ulcérés par ma presentation de l'antisemitisme de l'entre-deux-guerres, par mon allusion à la passivité, parfois à la complicité des Polonais pendant le genocide. Discussion courtoise, à fleurets mouchetés.

"Je viens mettre en cause leurs deux articles de foi essentiels. Je jette une ombre sur leur âge d'or: les seules années d'indépendance que la Pologne ait connues en deux siecles, les années 1919 à 1939. J'accuse l'Eglise catholique d'avoir été le pourvoyeur principal de l'antijudaïsme. Imbrication inextricable que celle du nationalisme et du catholicisme polonais. Ils ne peuvent pas m'entendre. J'ai mal pour eux. Ont-ils mal pour moi?" ("Voyages en Pologne," in *Politiques de l'oublie,* a 1988 issue of the journal *Le Genre humain,* 59).

40. Leah Oko, "'The March of the Living': A Trip to the Edge, and Back Again," *Lifestyles* 97 (1988), 30.

41. And it brought to life her mother's story about her decision to leave the country when, in postwar Lodz, a woman who thought her to be a non-Jew commented that the Germans should have executed all Poles who hid Jews.

42. Paul B. Fenton, "Hasidic Landmarks in Present-Day Poland," *European Judaism* 23, no. 2 (1990), 29.

43. An article entitled "Tenacious Pursuit of Lithuanian Roots Is Richly Rewarded" in the *Dallas Morning News* of 10 June 1990 describes some of the problems encountered in trying to decipher an aging parent's memory of a town's name and location. As Deborah Dash Moore argues, "when World War Two destroyed the remnants of home, the world that had been abandoned, modern Jews were left bereft of the foil of an imagined past they could reject" ("The Construction of Community: Jewish Migration and Ethnicity in the United States," in Moses Rischin, ed., *The Jews of North America* [Detroit: Wayne State University Press, 1987], 108).

44. Ertel, "Voyages en Pologne," 55.

45. For a discussion of Yiddish literary reformulations of the past in response to catastrophe, see David Roskies, *Against the Apocalypse: Responses to Catastrophe in Modern Jewish Culture* (Cambridge, Mass.: Harvard University Press, 1986), 258–310.

46. Indeed, in an attempt to counteract that, one youth group decided to include the rarely visited camp Sobibor in its itinerary. When participants

learn that they alone visit this camp, they are very pleased. A camp should not be neglected.

47. Yi-Fu Tuan, *Space and Place* (Minneapolis: University of Minnesota Press, 1977), 18.

48. Kirshenblatt-Gimblett, "Authenticity and Authority." The very logic of tourism, as an encounter with the exotic, imposes upon its subjects a quality that may not be—indeed, could not be—in keeping with their (that is, the natives') reality. Moreover, because of the economic asymmetry between the tourist and the subject, the latter has a vested interest in presenting his or her world in a manner in keeping with the tourist's expectations. This is particularly true for marginal members of the host culture, sometimes elderly people divorced from the more dynamic sectors of the economy or entrepreneurial types who recognize the profit to be made by acting as cultural brokers between the host culture and tourists. (Valene Smith, "Eskimo Tourism: Micro-Models and Marginal Men," in Valene Smith, ed., *Hosts and Guests: The Anthropology of Tourism* [Philadelphia: University of Pennsylvania Press, 1977], 69).

49. Valene Smith (ibid.) discusses a case in which Eskimos in Alaska represent a Siberian house type with artifacts, draft a traditional story, and rehearse a dance. The author also mentions the discomfort of tourists when locals frequent the hotel bar.

50. Richard Schechner, *Between Theater and Anthropology* (Philadelphia: University of Pennsylvania Press, 1985).

51. Umberto Eco, *Travels in Hyperreality,* trans. William Weaver (New York: Harcourt Brace Jovanovich, 1986).

52. Todd Gitlin, "Prime Time Ideology," in *Television: A Critical Approach* (New York: Oxford University Press, 1987), 518.

53. According to Charles Silberman, American Jews travel abroad more than any other ethnic group. Two in five adult Jews have been to Israel at least once and the same proportion have been to Italy. Almost one Jew in five has been to Israel two or more times (*A Certain People,* 199).

54. Valene Smith, "Introduction," in Valene Smith, ed., *Hosts and Guests: The Anthropology of Tourism* (Philadelphia: University of Pennsylvania Press, 1977), 6.

55. Unlike Victor Turner's observation of pilgrimages among other cultures, (*From Ritual to Theater: The Human Seriousness of Play* [New York: Drama Review Press, 1982]), Jewish tours of Poland are liminal rather than liminoid.

56. As Roger Abrahams notes, "Festivals and rites still seem part of the same human impulse to intensify time and space within the community and to reveal mysteries while being engaged in revels. Cultural objects and actions become the foci of community actions carried out in common, when the deepest values of the group are simultaneously revealed and made serious. But

in our secularized world there is a felt need to distinguish between holy work and revelry. While rites in contemporary culture are still often accompanied by festivities, and a festival often has a designating rite at its core, surely we have progressively associated rituals with being 'for real' and festivals with 'fun' " ("An American Vocabulary of Celebrations," in Alessandro Falassi, ed., *Time Out of Time: Essays on the Festival* [Albuquerque: University of New Mexico Press, 1977], 177).

57. According to Sally Falk Moore and Barbara Myerhoff, *Secular Ritual* (Amsterdam: Van Gorcum, 1977), 7, "In the repetition and order, ritual imitates the rhythmic imperatives of the biological and physical universe, thus suggesting a link with the perpetual processes of the cosmos. It thereby implies permanence and legitimacy of what are actually evanescent cultural constructs. In the acting, stylization and presentational staging, ritual is attention-commanding and deflects questioning at the time. All these formal properties make it an ideal vehicle for the conveying of messages in an authenticating and arresting manner." For the most part, the ultraorthodox do not participate: delicatessen Judaism is not their culture. Although they do make pilgrimages to Eastern Europe, theirs are not for the purpose of appropriating history but to resume a prewar tradition of petitionary visits to the graves of famous sages. Even Yom Ha-Shoah, which is for other Jews the annual commemoration of the Holocaust, is ignored. Their day of commemoration is Tisha B'Av, the annual day of commemorating all great catastrophes in Jewish history.

58. In *Amusing Ourselves to Death: Public Discourse in the Age of Show Business* (New York: Penguin, 1985), Neil Postman discusses the impact of television on American culture, particularly the movement away from serious discourse—something he associates with a typographical culture—to entertainment, the slick depthlessness that characterizes the electronic medium of images. Although his chapter on religion focuses on the televangelists, the point he makes has broader application to how religion in America has both adjusted to the cultural hegemony of television and, in doing so, has degraded itself: "The spectacle we find in true religions has as its purpose enchantment, not entertainment. The distinction is critical. By endowing things with magic, enchantment is the means through which we may gain access to sacredness. Entertainment is the means through which we distance ourselves from it" (122).

59. In discussing television's syntax, Robert P. Snow points out that "television news emphasizes moments in time, particularly emotional moments, rather than stressing historical sequence. The idea is that given the importance of news film or tape, emphasis is placed on involving the viewer in the emotion of the moment rather than interpreting events as part of a chronological sequence with historical significance. While the emphasis on emotional moment is an inflection device, the impact has implications for the syntax of news over the long run. The notion that some news is old and not worth reporting

stems in part from the position that if the event is connected to some prior event and now lacks emotional punch, it is irrelevant. Over time viewers may lose a sense of history as they orient primarily to what's happening now, just as they do when viewing an entertainment program" (*Creating Media Culture* [Beverly Hills: Sage, 1983], 130).

60. This, of course, is the gist of Postman's argument in *Amusing Ourselves to Death* that in succeeding typography, the invention of television has created a cultural revolution, and that given the special character of the medium and its preoccupation with entertainment, it is a revolution with very negative consequences for serious cultural discourse. Although I agree with much of Postman's argument, I believe that he gives too much weight to the characteristics of the medium and does not provide enough analysis of the special character that the medium assumes under the conditions of late capitalism. Less negative about television's possibilities than Postman, Robert Snow in his monograph *Creating Media Culture* nevertheless argues the following: "Television format has become a form of communication that is gradually being adopted by other media, by people in their interpersonal encounters, and in the major institutions of society. Gradually the reality presented by television is becoming the paramount reality in society" (166).

61. Barbara Myerhoff and Stephen Mongulla, "The Los Angeles Jews' 'Walk for Solidarity': Parade, Festival, Pilgrimage," in Herve Varenne, ed., *Symbolizing America* (Lincoln: University of Nebraska Press, 1986).

62. Jeffrey Dekro, "First Time Home: Poland Leaves Its Mark on a Visitor," *Reconstructionist* 54, no. 2 (1988), 11.

63. Fredric Jameson, "Postmodernism and Consumer Society," in E. Ann Kaplan, ed., *Postmodernism and Its Discontents* (New York: Verso, 1988).

64. Jonathan Woocher, "Sacred Survival: American Jewry's Civil Religion," *Judaism* 34 (1985), 151–62.

65. The same thing happened to Poles. *Shoah* was aired on Polish national television and sparked a broad national debate on the Jewish view of Polish behavior during World War II. For the first time in more than forty years, Poles and Jews sparred with each other almost face to face, and yet they were really thousands of miles apart. The controversy seems also to have increased Polish curiosity about the place of Jews in the country's past: the American film *Fiddler on the Roof* was twice aired on national television, while a traveling theater troupe presenting the stage version has been receiving rave reviews throughout the country. For a discussion of television's impact on sense of place, see Joshua Meyrowitz, *No Sense of Place: The Impact of the Electronic Media on Social Behavior* (New York: Oxford University Press, 1985).

66. Nathan Glazer's argument as cited in Herbert J. Gans, "Symbolic Ethnicity: The Future of Ethnic Groups and Cultures in America," in Herbert J.

Gans et al., eds., *On the Making of Americans: Essays in Honor of David Riesman* (Philadelphia: University of Pennsylvania Press, 1979), 207.

67. Silberman, *A Certain People.*

68. Judith Miller, *One, by One, by One* (New York: Simon and Schuster, 1990), 234.

69. Somewhat the same process appears to be taking place among some young Armenians sixty years after the Turkish slaughter (Gans, "Symbolic Ethnicity," 207–8).

70. Silberman, *A Certain People,* 24.

71. In the spring of 1988, the March of the Living was organized to include thousands of Jewish schoolchildren from across North America. So successful was the event that rabbis who participated as group leaders have begun to take their congregations on a similar pilgrimage, and the event is about to be repeated for other schoolchildren.

72. Gans, "Symbolic Ethnicity," 204–5.

73. Abner Cohen, *Urban Ethnicity* (London: Tavistock, 1974).

74. See Edward Sapir's distinction between the two types of symbols, as cited in Murray Edelman, *The Symbolic Uses of Politics* (Urbana: University of Illinois Press, 1985), 6.

75. Harry W. Haines, "'What Kind of War?': An Analysis of the Vietnam Veterans Memorial," *Critical Studies in Mass Communication* 3, no. 1 (1986), 17.

76. What I mean by this is that as abstract design, it lends itself to multiple readings. Polish public culture until recently was very much imbued with state social symbolism, a symbolism that eschewed multiple readings and relied upon representational art.

77. John Murray Cuddihy, "The Elephant and the Angels; or, the Incivil Irritatingness of Jewish Theodicy," in Robert N. Bellah and Frederick E. Greenspahn, eds., *Uncivil Religion: Interreligious Hostility in America* (New York: Crossroad, 1987). 25.

78. "As David Denby writes, Woody Allen's *'Broadway Danny Rose,* conceals a good deal of Jewish self-regard—indeed, the Jews-are-more-moral-than-other-people sentiments get a little sticky here, especially as all the Italians apart from Tina [played by Mia Farrow] are pictured as outright slobs.' In *Danny Rose,* Denby continues, Woody Allen plays 'a small-time Jewish entertainment figure so insistently moral that he lingers in a restaurant to lay down a tip even as Mafia hit men are coming in the door to bump him off'" (ibid., 26). Paul Breines makes a similar point in his recent book *Tough Jews: Political Fantasies and the Moral Dilemma of American Jewry* (New York: Basic Books, 1990), 73: "The more brutal Israeli policies become . . . the more American Jews discuss, the more they need, the Holocaust.

"What vindicates power is that the unparalleled genocide against the Jews is being discussed, debated, and reconsidered. For the more the Nazi Final Solution to the Jewish question is discussed, the more the discussants (Jewish and not) can attach a moral sheen to the actions of Israel's tough Jews. This function of the Holocaust discussion is rooted in a deep, historically formed Jewish need: the need to be ethical."

79. This kind of thinking sometimes takes an ironic twist, for example, when some African Americans protested on behalf of the defendants during the recent trial of a group of African American boys who were accused of brutally beating and raping a European American woman who had been jogging in New York's Central Park.

80. Cuddihy citing Marshall Sklare's argument ("The Elephant and the Angels," 33). Cuddihy also cites a lecture to an Israeli audience by the American Jewish writer Philip Roth, in which he related that a Jewish child growing up in midcentury America inherited "no body of law, no body of learning and no language, and finally, no Lord—which seems to me a significant thing to be missing. [But what he did receive] was a psychology, not a culture and not a culture in its totality. What one received whole, however, what one feels whole, is a kind of psychology; and the psychology can be translated into three words—'Jews are better.' This is what I knew from the beginning: somehow Jews were better. I'm saying this as a point of psychology; I'm not saying it as a fact" (ibid.).

81. Anita Schwartz, "The Secular Seder," in Jack Kugelmass, ed., *Between Two Worlds: Ethnographic Essays on American Jewry* (Ithaca, N.Y.: Cornell University Press, 1988).

82. I am reminded here of a Hasidic story that is very popular among American Jews, a story that combines place, memory, and rescue. In the story the eighteenth-century founder of Hasidism, the Baal Shem Tov, would fend off danger to his fellow Jews by going to a place in the forest, lighting a fire, and reciting a prayer. In each succeeding generation memory has dissipated, so that when Israel of Rizhin tried to overcome misfortune he could no longer perform any of these rites: all he knew was the story about the place, the fire, and the prayer. According to the Hasidic tale, that knowledge was sufficient. Indeed, it is this very premise that enables American Jews to make such an easy bridge to their past (Elie Wiesel, *Souls on Fire: Portraits and Legends of Hasidic Masters* [New York: Random House, 1972], 167–68).

83. Paul Connerton, *How Societies Remember* (New York: Cambridge University Press, 1989).

84. Pierre Nora, "Between Memory and History: *Les Lieux de Mémoire*," *Representations* 26 (1989), 12.

85. Ibid., 7.

86. On 11 Nov. 1990 the English-language *Warsaw Voice* devoted consider-

able space to the issue of Polish anti-Semitism. Included were some rather shocking man-on-the-street interviews covering the spectrum of Polish society. These left little doubt that anti-Semitism in Poland even now has considerable tenacity.

87. Maurice Halbwachs, *The Collective Memory* (New York: Harper and Row, 1980).

88. Given how small the Jewish community is in Poland and its near-total intermarriage with non-Jews, the alternative may in fact be assimilation into Polish culture and society.

89. In Tarnow, for example, the surviving *bima* (elevated platform upon which the Torah is read) from the destroyed main synagogue recently received a commemorative plaque. Donated by Jews living abroad, the plaque included Polish and Hebrew inscriptions. The Polish, clearly a translation, was grammatically incorrect.

90. Sherry Ortner, *Sherpas Through Their Rituals* (New York: Cambridge University Press, 1978), 5.

91. Schechner, *Between Theater and Anthropology,* 51.

CHAPTER 14

A Distorted Mirror: The Exhibition of the Herbert Ward Collection of Africana

MARY JO ARNOLDI

Primitive life is mirrored in a remarkably interesting collection of African weapons and original sculptures left to the Smithsonian Institution in Washington by the sculptor, Herbert Ward. . . . The collection includes a splendid assembly of relics. . . . More important, however, are bronzes that Herbert Ward made when he returned from the Congo. Theodore Roosevelt, who visited his studio in Paris, said: "In his figures the Negro of the Congo is seen on his native soil, child-like and cruel, friendly and brutal, age-old man who lived in Europe several thousand years ago, and yet a man with eternal youth in his soul that has preserved him in his stalwart strength to the present."[1]

One of the major collections of African material culture currently at the Smithsonian Institution is the Herbert Ward collection, which was officially given to the Smithsonian by Ward's widow, Sarita Ward, in 1921. The quotation above is from a 1922 review of the public exhibition of the collection, which opened in that year and remained on public view until 1961, continuing as an institutional voice about Africa for nearly forty years.

The Herbert Ward collection is striking when compared with many other collections of African material culture that ultimately found homes in public museums in the nineteenth and early twentieth centuries. The collection consists of 2,714 objects, of which the majority are items of African material culture amassed between 1884 and

1889 in the former Congo Free State, now the Republic of Zaire. Included in the collection as well are zoological specimens, consisting primarily of hunting trophies (an elephant head, feet, trunks, and tails; several antelope heads; a python; gorilla skeletons, etc.). In addition, the Ward collection includes seventeen bronze sculptures by Ward himself that depict Africans (five heroic-size statues, four life-size, and nine half-size or fragments). Ward envisioned this group of objects as a single entity, and the conditions set out in the bequest to the Smithsonian required that it always be displayed in its entirety. In 1922 the collection was installed according to his wishes in the newly reopened National Museum Building (now the National Museum of Natural History).

In the past decade, the history of Western museums' displays of the "other" has received a surge of attention from scholars in a variety of disciplines. A renewed scholarly interest in material culture, along with the increasing attention being paid to the capacity of museum displays to shape public interpretations of the "other," has spawned several recent national and international conferences as well as a variety of professional panels and symposia devoted to aspects of this topic, and there is now a significant body of literature concerned specifically with Western colonial-era and contemporary representations of the "other" in museum displays, world's fairs, festivals, and expositions.[2] A number of these studies have specifically focused on the life histories of African objects in public collections, addressing the politics of representation, the relations of power, and the historical practices that underlie the appropriation of these objects into Western collections and their subsequent recontextualization and interpretation in public displays.[3] This case study of the Herbert Ward collection of Africana (in the term *Africana* I am including not only the African material culture but also the zoological specimens and Ward's bronze sculptures) examines the transformations in the various installations of this collection, first in Ward's studio/museum in Paris and later at the Smithsonian. What is compelling about both the original arrangement of the collection in Ward's Paris studio and its later installation at the Smithsonian is the clear visual tension created among the African material culture, the zoological specimens, and the Ward bronzes. Unlike many current standard presentations of African art in museums, where the museum visitor directly confronts the objects, in the Ward installation the collector's bronze sculptures mediated between the African objects and the viewer. In this case a body of Western sculpture assumed the role of a critical commentator about Africa, and the installation resulted in a complex narrative that conjoined the collector's personal artistic voice with the prevailing point of view of the museum's professional staff. The exhibition articulated and reflected the principal late-nineteenth-century beliefs and attitudes about Africa and Africans, and it contributed publicly and dramatically to supporting an already popular discourse of misunderstanding about the continent and its peoples.

Herbert Ward was born in London in 1863 and left home at age fifteen, traveling first to New Zealand and Australia, later to Borneo, and finally to Africa in 1884. In Africa Ward first worked in the manual-transport service, initially for the Congo Free State and later for the Sanford Exploring Company, an American trading interest. His duties included securing African laborers to carry goods overland to trading stations in the interior. He was initially stationed on the lower Congo River and later was made station chief of the Bangala station on the upper Congo River, in the forest region. In 1887 he joined Stanley's expedition for the relief of the Emin Pacha at Wadelai; following this ill-fated venture, he returned to England in May 1889.

During his five-year sojourn in Africa, Ward filled sketchbooks with drawings of people, landscapes, and objects, and began to collect an enormous quantity of material artifacts, including knives, swords, textiles, wooden and ivory carved figures, musical instruments, hats and caps, etc. After he returned to England, he continued to add to his core collection of Central African material through gifts, purchases, or trades with fellow travelers.

Once back in England Ward began a career as a popular writer and lecturer about his African experiences, and from 1889 to 1893 he lectured widely in both Great Britain and the United States. He often used objects from his collection to illustrate his talks, and on at least one occasion he exhibited part of the collection in a London gallery. During this period Ward also wrote several journal and magazine articles and published his first book, *Five Years with the Congo Cannibals*.[4]

Ward's biography and his written commentary about Africa, drawn from his published books and newspaper interviews, reveal that he was a man firmly embedded in Victorian attitudes about the "other." By the mid-nineteenth century, in both scientific and popular quarters, aboriginal peoples in general had come to be classified as "savages," and Africans occupied the lowest rung on this social evolutionary ladder. This scientific and popular discourse about Africa and the positional superiority granted by the West to itself legitimated European economic and cultural imperialism on the continent.

Throughout the Victorian period, travel literature about Africa stirred the public's imagination and contributed to shaping popular attitudes and opinions. Livingstone's 1857 book *Missionary Travels* sold seventy thousand copies, and Stanley's *In Darkest Africa* (1890) sold one hundred and fifty thousand copies in English alone.[5] As Brantlinger notes in his analysis of the role of popular travel literature in shaping public attitudes toward Africa,

> The myth of the Dark Continent was thus a Victorian invention. As part of a larger discourse about empire, it was shaped by political and economic pressures and also by a psychology of blaming the victim through which Europeans projected many of their own darkest impulses onto Africans. The product of the transition—or transvaluation—from abolitionism to imperialism, the myth of the Dark Continent defined slavery as the offspring of tribal savagery and portrayed white explorers and missionaries as the leaders of a Christian crusade that would vanquish the forces of darkness.[6]

That Ward shared his fellow Victorians' attitudes toward Africa is apparent in his books and articles. In *Five Years with the Congo Cannibals,* published in 1890, he echoes the refrain that Africans are savages and takes the position espoused by missionaries and abolitionists that Africans must be saved from their own darkest impulses:

> Time and the influence of the white men of upright character, as missionaries, traders, and government officials, dwelling among them and identifying their sympathies with the lives and welfare of the natives, will effect great changes in the people of the Upper Congo. As civilization spreads, and the ways of the white men become known to the dwellers of the far interior, a desire to imitate the more agreeable modes of living then presented to their gaze will spring in the breasts of these poor African savages liberated by that time, let us hope, from the devastating scourge of Arab slave-raiding in their midst.[7]

In both England and America, Ward's public lectures on his experiences in the Congo reinforced the prevailing attitudes about Africa and Africans. His lectures were widely reported and sometimes syndicated under such titles as "From the Cannibal Land." Coverage of one of his public lectures in London inspired the following commentary:

> Is the negro really capable of civilization? . . . The fate of Africa, as well as that of Brazil, the West Indies, and the Southern States of the

Union depends, in fact on the capacity of the black race. . . . The more we learn of the native negroes of Africa itself, the clearer does it appear that anthropophagy is one of the vices of the race. Mr. Herbert Ward, a member of Stanley's Expedition, who has just been giving an account of the practices of the tribes in and near the Congo State, tells us that the Bangalas, a muscular race living between Stanley Falls and Stanley Pool, are "cannibals" by whom "human flesh is much more highly relished than anything else they eat."[8]

In 1893, after returning from his American lecture tour, Ward abandoned the lecture circuit and began formal art training, first in Paris and later in England. In 1900 he turned his hand to sculpture, and throughout the next decade this was his chosen medium. During the years between 1900 and 1912, he consistently chose Africans as the primary subject matter for his work. In 1902 he moved his family to Paris, where he found that his African subject matter received a greater acceptance than in England and that African models were more readily available than in London. Moreover, there were better facilities on the continent for bronze casting.

From 1900 to 1913 he worked as a sculptor in the European academic tradition, and his works were regularly accepted for the

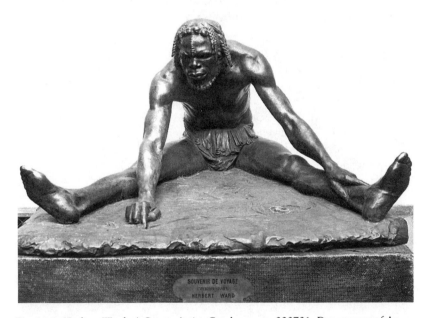

Fig. 14-1. Herbert Ward, *A Congo Artist.* Catalogue no. 323731, Department of Anthropology, Smithsonian Institution. Reproduced with permission.

annual Paris Salon. During this decade Ward received several medals from the Salon: an honorable mention in 1901 for his sculpture *An Ariumi Type,* which was the bust of an African man; a third-place gold medal in 1908 for *The Tribal Chief* (Figure 14-2); and a second-place gold medal in 1910 for *The Congo Artist* (Figure 14-1).

Ward's invention of Africa not only can be seen in his published books and lectures, but also is graphically revealed both in his sculpture and in his studio/museum. In 1906 he installed his African collection, along with his bronze sculptures, on the top floor of his Paris studio. Photographs of the studio taken in 1910 and 1911 record his personal vision of Africa. On the stairwell leading from his ground-floor atelier Ward hung a group of his field drawings, many of which

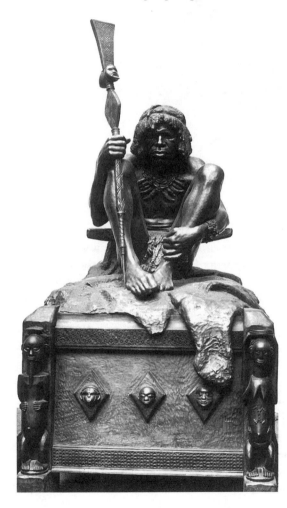

Fig. 14-2. Herbert Ward, *The Tribal Chief.* Catalogue no. 323737, Department of Anthropology, Smithsonian Institution. Reproduced with permission.

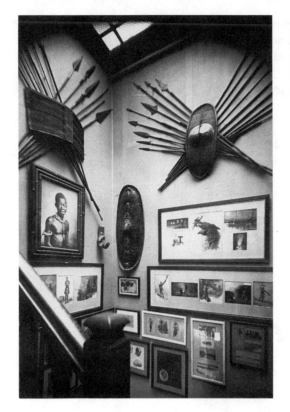

Fig. 14-3. Herbert Ward's Paris studio (stairwell view), prior to 1911. Smithsonian Institution photo no. 75–5911. Reproduced with permission.

were reproduced in his travel books. Alongside these drawings he carefully mounted an array of spears and shields, an antelope head, and a group of musical instruments (Figure 14-3). At the top of the stairs he filled the shelves lining the walls with baskets, wooden containers, small statues of wood and ivory, backrests, stools, a xylophone, and two drums.

In the main room, he covered the wall facing the door with an elaborately carved wooden screen that evoked harem quarters in North African houses. While the screen provided a point of visual interest in the room, it also effectively dappled and subdued the light flowing in from the bank of windows located behind it. In niches in the screen Ward placed his table-size bronzes *The Charm Doctor* and *The Wood Carrier*. At either end of the screen, Ward installed two tall vertical cases, which he crammed with hats, small containers, bracelets, and pendants. Atop each case he placed a Kongo figure, one representing a mother and child, the other a seated male.

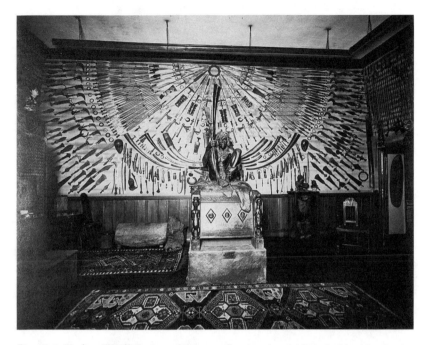

Fig. 14-4. Herbert Ward's Paris studio (upper floor), prior to 1911. Smithsonian Institution photo no. 75–5890. Reproduced with permission.

Covering the right wall, Ward arranged rows of arrows, ivory tusks, bracelets, knives, spoons, whistles, and headrests in a decorative display (Figure 14-4). In front of this wall he placed his heroic-size bronze statue *The Tribal Chief*. Flanking this statue were a number of animal trophies (including a stuffed gorilla and an elephant foot) as well as a large slit gong. In the far corner stood a bust of Ward as African adventurer, which had been sculpted by his friend, the British artist Sir William Goscombe John. The base on which the portrait bust sat was covered with several layers of embroidered raffia cloth.

In front of the opposing wall, he placed two of his life-size bronze statues, *Defiance* and *The Fugitives*. Projecting out into the center of the room was a large wooden base on which he placed an enormous python (Figure 14-5). Ward decorated the wall with an antelope head and meticulously arranged a variety of African objects in semicircular patterns. A Kota reliquary figure was at the center of the arrangement; fanning out from it were knives, spears, flywhisks, and staffs. Standing on the floor against the wall were several gorilla skeletons, and in the corner on a easel-like stand was the bleached skull of an elephant.

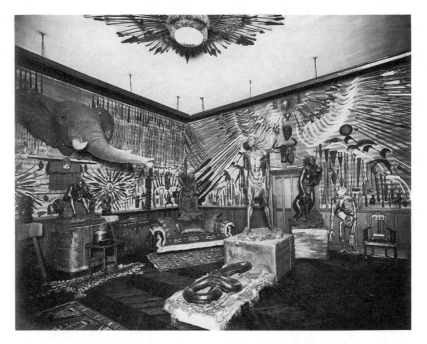

Fig. 14-5. Herbert Ward's Paris studio (upper floor), prior to 1911. Smithsonian Institution photo no. 75–5893. Reproduced with permission.

The wall opposite the harem-style screen was dominated by an elephant head, its trunk and tusks extending well into the room. Above the door Ward placed two carved African figures, and above the wainscoting he organized a dense vertical arrangement of spears. Below the elephant head he installed two circles of knives, at the centers of which were wooden camel bells. Directly underneath the elephant head he installed a Fang face mask and a raffia loom. Below the loom there were metal gongs, a wooden cup, containers of various types, a pipe, and other small objects. Standing in front of this wall were his statues *The Forest Dwellers, A Bakongo Girl,* and *Sleeping Africa,* and in the corner he placed the heroic-size statue *The Idol Maker.* A few chairs and a settee were scattered throughout the room, and the floors were covered with Oriental rugs and animal skins. Ward's wife later wrote of this installation,

> This collection to which he has added an appreciable amount from time to time as the occasion had arisen was by then [1906] a very important affair, numbering close upon three thousand objects, ri-

valling in value and interest the collection of the King of the Belgians, and the installation of it all in the studio occupied a considerable number of weeks. Every moment Herbert could spare from his "workshop" below, he would be at his task in the studio above, designing and arranging each trophy carefully and symmetrically, with an infinite amount of patience, carrying out his idea with such arresting effect that no one who had ever seen this studio, a veritable museum in itself, could forget the impression of its mystery, its subtle suggestion of the darkness of Central Africa. The sinister poison arrows, the barbaric knives and spears, glinting in a cunningly subdued light against the grey-green walls, were an appropriately descriptive background to the huge bronze figures grouped in the various phases of savage life, so fierce, so brooding, so startlingly life like, they seemed to have just emerged from the Congo swamps and forests.[9]

This self-conscious and painstakingly designed installation, with walls of weapons (recalling medieval European great halls), hunting trophies, numerous small objects, Oriental rugs, and animal skins, all bathed in a gloomy atmosphere evocative of darkest Africa, dramatically contributed to Ward's invention of an exotic Africa. The African objects in turn effectively served as a foil for Ward's own sculptural oeuvre.

Ward was never a member of the avant-garde in Paris, and his sculptures are competent representational academic works. The consistent acceptance of his sculpture by the annual Paris Salon attests to his appeal to the bourgeois. Despite working in Paris at the same time as Picasso, Braque, and other modernists, Ward's sculpture is not at all concerned with appropriating the formal properties of the African pieces. There is no evidence in either his artistic work or his writings that his large collection of African objects altered in any perceptible way his formal sensibilities. Although he had created his private vision of Africa upstairs, a photograph of his workshop below reveals that he surrounded himself with reproductions of classical Western sculpture, which served as his formal inspiration (Figure 14-6). In a 1913 newspaper interview Ward discussed his personal artistic vision. He said,

The idea was to make something symbolical—not an absolute realistic thing like wax works in an anatomical museum—but to make something which demands two different requirements: the thing must have the spirit of Africa in its broad sense, and at the same time fill the requirements of the art of sculpture.[10]

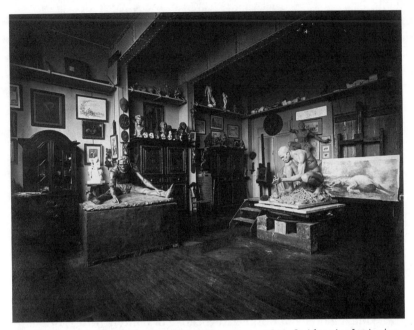

Fig. 14-6. Herbert Ward's Paris studio (atelier), prior to 1911. Smithsonian Institution photo no. 75–5888. Reproduced with permission.

Ward's sculptures of Africans are clearly not portraits of individuals; rather, they are ideas about Africa that reflect the prevailing attitudes of his time, yet were shaped by a deeply felt personal biography. In a recent book on the image of blacks in Western art, Hugh Honour notes that

> Ward's statutes are life-size, sometimes larger, and so disturbingly lifelike that they give the impression of truth to nature—though not the whole truth. His choice of subjects, the ways in which he posed the figures, and the facial expressions he gave them, reflect his belief that the Congolese were in a state of arrested development. . . . He thus chose to represent a dancing *Charm Doctor* or medicine man flourishing a fetish, a man making fire by twisting a stick into a piece of wood, the glowering *Chief of the Tribe* squatting on his throne, a *Congo Artist,* legs splayed out flat on the ground as he draws a snake with his finger in the mud, and *Idol Maker* chipping at a block of wood. They are not images of "savages" so much as of "savagery" as understood in his time—of scientific, technological, social, artistic and religious "backwardness."[11]

Although Honour's assessment of the overall impression left by Ward's sculpture rings true, there was a subtle shift in his sculpture that echoes the shift in his writings about Africa following the Congo scandals in 1904. In 1899 Roger Casement, Ward's friend from his Congo days, was appointed as the British consul to the Congo Free State in order to protect the interests of British subjects working in the area. By 1902 Casement had turned his attention to an inquiry into the misadministration of the Congo Free State.[12] During the second half of 1903 Ward facilitated a meeting and regular correspondence between Casement and E. D. Morel, who had emerged in England as a prominent spokesperson against the corrupt practices in the Congo Free State.[13] In February 1904 Casement sent Ward a copy of his consular report, which exposed the atrocities committed by the Congo Free State administrators against Africans. Ward was deeply affected by this report and he wrote to his wife,

> I found Casement's Consular Report of the "Congo question" when I got here this morning and I could not stop reading until I got to the end of it. . . . What hypocrisy it does seem this so-called civilization of savage countries. It is always the same story, but not quite so bad as in this case of the Congo.[14]

Although Ward clearly could not shake his deep-rooted, long-held attitudes and beliefs about Africans as savages, his writings after 1904 do reflect a less celebratory view of the influence of the white man on Africa. In the concluding chapters of his book *A Voice from the Congo,* published in 1910, he wrote,

> In the foregoing pages I have endeavoured to convey the spirit of something that is deep within me—a fellow feeling for the Central African natives. They are not altogether the degraded race that one might infer by reading instances of their brutality and cannibalism. They are a people whose development has been temporarily arrested by adversity. They are very human: they are often cruel, but they are often kind.[15]

As he did with these later writings, Ward invested his post–1904 sculptures (*The Fugitives, The Forest Lovers, The Tribal Chief, Defiance,* and especially his last work, *Distress*) with a degree of humanity and dignity that is absent from the more blatantly exotic and erotic early works, such as *The Charm Doctor* and *Sleeping Africa.*

In 1913, when Ward announced his promised gift to the United States National Museum, the institution was eager to acquire the collection. The American Museum of Natural History in New York had been given a comparable collection of Congo materials by King Leopold II in 1907, and this collection was opened to the public in 1910.[16] The National Museum was still driven by massive collecting efforts, and in lieu of mounting scientific expeditions to the Congo itself, the Ward collection represented the possibility of greatly increasing the museum's meager African holdings.

The museum's interest in the acquisition of such a major collection followed the general philosophy espoused by George Brown Goode, assistant secretary of the National Museum in the last decades of the nineteenth century. Goode believed that one important role of the National Museum was research, and by research he meant specifically research on collections. A second critical function of the museum was public education, in which exhibits of specimens played a primary role.[17]

The bulk of the National Museum's anthropology collections during this period were American Indian collections, although there were a number of African objects, many of which had come to the Smithsonian in the mid-nineteenth century from the defunct National Institute in Washington. However, the African collections were relatively small and the objects were for the most part poorly documented. By 1920, the museum's Africa exhibition included only one life group, representing the "Zulu-Kaffir." There were also seven individual mannequins representing "racial types" from North, West, East, and southern Africa. These figures, however, were installed alongside a variety of unrelated objects. The case displaying the "Wolof man" is a good example of this cultural hodgepodge. In an archival photograph of an early installation, the mannequin occupies one side of the case, while installed on its left is a potpourri of objects from various groups from West and Central Africa (Figure 14-7).

Thus the Ward collection of over 2,700 objects, the majority collected from one region, would appreciably increase the museum's holdings in the African area and must have been seen as a boon for the museum's scientific research as well as for its exhibitions. William Henry Holmes, Walter Hough, and most of the other members of the anthropology department were Americanists, and the Ward collection must have seemed even more valuable because of Ward's ability to provide the museum with a catalogue of the pieces that would serve the research charter of the museum. In 1912, when Ward first pro-

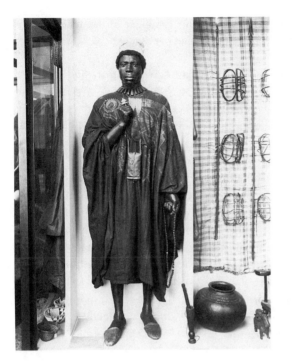

Fig. 14-7. View of Wolof mannequin in the African installation, United States National Museum. Smithsonian Institution photo no. 30299. Reproduced with permission.

posed leaving his collection to the Smithsonian Institution, Walter Hough, a curator in the Department of Anthropology, wrote in a memo to William Henry Holmes, head curator of the department,

> Since I have read Mr. Ward's letter, I have become a hundred fold more interested in his specimens for the reason that he is competent to classify and give them their origin of locality, thus making the way of the museum man smooth and adding enormously to the scientific value of the material.[18]

There followed a series of letters between the department and Ward about the type and organization of the catalogue. Later, after the collection had been installed at the Smithsonian in 1922, Hough wrote:

> More than that [Ward] had the prescience almost to gather from the Congo natives abundant examples of their weapons and other objects of their arts and industries at a time when such specimens would be of the utmost value to science. That he did not regard these

as mere bizarre trophies is shown by his catalogue of the material, preserving them in this way for the studies of ethnologists.[19]

In terms of serving the public, the name recognition and popular appeal of Herbert Ward certainly must have played a part in the museum's interest in the collection. Ward had lectured extensively about his Congo experiences in the United States and by 1913, when he announced his intention of leaving the Smithsonian his Congo collection, he had already published three books about his Congo experiences. Throughout this same period the United States had commercial aspirations in the Congo, and the Congo scandals at the turn of the century had been followed closely in the American press.

Ward's intended gift was given ample coverage in the local newspapers. The Washington headlines read: "Dark Continent Trophies Given to the Smithsonian—Herbert Ward, Famous Sculptor, Will Send Valuable Collection to Capital" (*Washington Herald,* 15 March 1913); "African Stone Age Relics Given to Smithsonian—Herbert Ward, Sculptor, Donates Complete and Valuable Collection" (*Evening Star,* 15 March 1913); "Unique Gift for the Smithsonian" (*Sunday Star,* 16 March 1913). The article in the *Sunday Star* included an extended interview with Ward and a picture of his studio/museum in Paris. When asked why Ward had chosen the Smithsonian as the benefactor of his gift, the Honorable Thomas Nelson Page, who had introduced the Wards to the museum administration, replied:

> There were several reasons, I think, for Mr. Ward deciding to give the collection to the Smithsonian Institution. In the first place, he felt that such an accumulation of relics should be kept together. He also felt a particular interest in the Smithsonian Institution because it was established by an Englishman, and *he felt that his trophies, coming from Africa, would be of especial interest to the American people, as they are thrown in intimate contact with the negroes in their daily life* [emphasis added].[20]

It is worth emphasizing here that the Smithsonian's perceived audience—the American people—really meant the middle- and upper-class Anglo-American population. African Americans were clearly marginal in the museum's conception of its community and, along with Native Americans, constituted America's "other"—albeit a domesticated "other."

During the late nineteenth century and well into the twentieth, ethnological research and exhibitions in the anthropology department were in large part shaped by the scientific philosophy of Otis T. Mason, the museum's first curator of anthropology. Mason's early training was in the natural sciences, and his subsequent approaches to ethnology were firmly rooted in these methods and theories. Intensely interested in the study of material artifacts, he held that

> by applying the methods of the natural sciences to the study of objects, the transformations of object types, like biological species, could be traced back to their sources. The scientist could "put handles on stone implements, men and women into ancient ruins, and thoughts into empty crania."[21]

Mason's system of museum classification was largely based upon one developed by Gustav Klemm at the Museum für Volkerkunde in Leipzig in the 1870s. It demanded that a subject first be analyzed in all its developmental variety; from these particulars the larger historical picture—a progression through the stages of savagery, barbarism, and enlightenment—could be drawn.[22] In Mason's version of the Leipzig model, his primary focus was on the notion of invention.

> Mason defined invention broadly: as changes in materials and processes; as modifications in structure and function of artifacts; as changes in the inventor of society. The concept referred, in fact, not merely to mechanical devices but to cultural processes. . . . All people invented, but primitive man saw dimly and thought imperfectly.
> . . . This vision produced an ambivalent judgment in which such peoples received credit as human participants, but clearly inferior ones.[23]

In collaboration with Goode, Mason developed an exhibition program for anthropology based on that of natural history. It utilized a combination of display methods: objects would be organized by geography, in synoptic series (Klemm's developmental scheme), or by material.

> Looking to Leipzig and the Pitt Rivers Museum of weaponry in Oxford Goode and Mason organized their anthropology mainly along developmental lines, stressing the unity underlying apparent diversity of human phenomena throughout the world. Significant lessons could be taught, they believed, by placing all weapons, hats, boats, fire-making apparatus or whatever, of all ages and all peoples, together in a single series in order to show the "natural history" of a particular idea from its earliest manifestations among primitive peo-

ples to its fullest flowering among the advanced industrialized nations of the world.[24]

Although Mason's strongly developmental scheme and his biologically inspired belief in the underlying unity of all objects was already being seriously challenged by Boas in 1887,[25] he nevertheless found confirmation of his methods on an 1889 visit to Europe—in the Pitt Rivers Museum in Oxford, at the Musée Guimet in Paris, and in Dresden.[26] Mason's developmental scheme continued for decades to be an important influence in the ethnology exhibitions at the Smithsonian.

However, on this same European tour, Mason began to appreciate other approaches to ethnographic display. "The British Museum's Polynesian collection, Mason reported, 'made my mouth water'; and at the India Museum he was struck with the wax figures of working groups."[27] A visit to the 1889 Exposition Universelle in Paris pricked Mason's interest in the possibility of teaching the history of human culture through ethnographic displays. The Paris exposition was attended by thirty-two million people,[28] and Mason was impressed by the popularity of the model villages, temples, and markets installed along the Seine, which featured living exhibits of peoples from Africa, Indochina, and Oceania engaged in various activities. This fair's site exhibits were based on a model for living exhibits that had been developed at the Jardin d'Acclimatation in Paris in 1877 and which had been from the beginning enthusiastically embraced by the public.[29]

Influenced by the approaches in various European museums and the site exhibits at the Paris exposition, Mason incorporated some of these ideas in the plan for the Smithsonian's American Indian exhibits at the 1893 World's Columbian Exposition in Chicago. In collaboration with William Henry Holmes, anthropologist and artist, and with advice from James Mooney, Frank Cushing, and Walter Hoffman from the Bureau of American Ethnology, the National Museum constructed a series of tableaus of American Indian groups based on "geoethnic" units. These life-size, realistic mannequins represented specific groups of American Indians engaged in various activities in daily life or ritual in the appropriate environmental setting. These life groups enjoyed a tremendous popular success at the Chicago fair; they subsequently became de rigueur for government anthropology exhibits and were quickly embraced by other American museums.[30]

The introduction of an ethnographic and environmental orientation in the life groups did not overturn Mason's original taxonomic and developmental orientation to the study of material culture. As Hinsley notes,

> What did Goode, Mason, and Holmes intend to teach the public with the new techniques? Essentially the same lessons of the earlier taxonomic exhibits: the fundamental unity beneath the diversity of human experience, a unity demonstrated in man's psychic activity—his inventions—and a unity to be achieved finally in the approaching coalescence into a single racial, linguistic, and cultural community. . . . Although Mason to some extent transcended the bald evolutionism of the Klemm model of "Kulturgeschichte," the life groups orientation that he and Holmes pioneered in Washington served rather than questioned the superiority of Victorian American culture.[31]

After Mason's death, his approach to material culture lived on for many years under the direction of William Henry Holmes, who was appointed the head curator of anthropology in 1910. A description of the exhibition program for the new National Museum Building published in the 1913 annual report makes this fact quite clear.

> The arrangement of the ethnological exhibits is geographical, the material belonging to each area being displayed as an assemblage or by classes of objects. The exhibits find their key in family lay-figure groups placed centrally in the halls, which typify the physical characteristics, the social organization, the manners and customs, and the arts and industries of selected human types. The design of the exhibit is to illustrate systematically the comparative differences in material culture and advancement of modern groups of mankind, thus giving an impression of the effects of environment and racial tendencies on the arts and industries of people.[32]

The correspondence between the anthropology department's representation of the "other" and Ward's personal vision of Africa is more complex and subtle. Indeed, Ward and the Smithsonian anthropologists shared a fundamental belief in the intellectual, moral, technological, and artistic superiority of their late-nineteenth-century society. They also subscribed to the same social evolutionary theories about the so-called primitives, yet their invention of the "other," although parallel, was not identical. Ward's "savages"—as invented in his writings, his sculpture, and in his Paris studio/museum—were more overtly romantic than were those displayed according to the museum's

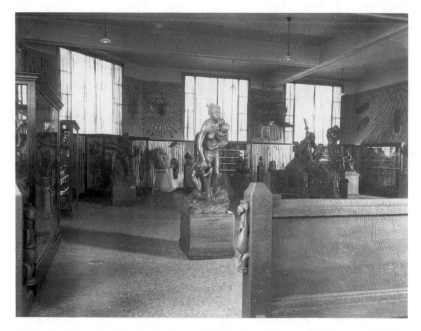

Fig. 14-8. View of the Ward collection exhibit, National Museum Building, circa 1922. Smithsonian Institution photo no. 26914–A. Reproduced with permission.

scientific attitude, and his approach to Africa was impressionistic, deeply personal, and intimate. In contrast, the "primitives" created in the Smithsonian's exhibits were consistently naturalized, depersonalized, typed, ordered, and classified in both the life groups and in the developmental series; this representation was given the imprimatur of science. The implied standard of comparison was always modern Western society, and the "primitive" was clearly defined as developmentally inferior in every category.

In 1922 the Ward collection was installed in the new National Museum Building. The style of the exhibition mirrored in several important ways Ward's studio/museum. How, then, did the museum reconcile its naturalizing and scientific posture with the autobiographical and romantic vision of the collector that is so evident in his Paris display? It is clear from archival photographs taken soon after the opening of the new collection in 1922 that the designers of the National Museum's installation consciously intended to capture the drama that Ward had achieved in his installation (Figure 14-8). Curtains were hung over the windows to recreate a somber atmosphere evocative of the jungle, and trophies of the hunt were mounted on the walls, surrounded by African weapons in decorative arrangements. The practice of mounting hunting trophies and weapons in ornate arrangements around the walls was not unique to Ward's Paris studio/museum; it was a fairly common display technique in European and American museums and expositions in the late nineteenth and early twentieth centuries. For example, the installation of the Congo collection at the American Museum of Natural History in 1910 followed a similar pattern.[33]

The integration of Western academic artworks with non-Western objects that characterizes Ward's studio/museum had many precedents in Europe as well. For instance, at the Exposition Universelle in Brussels in 1897 the section devoted to "L'Etat Indépendant du Congo" displayed African objects alongside sculptures and tapestries by Western artists. The Western artworks fell into two distinct categories: certain tapestries and sculptures depicted African themes, while another group of objects celebrated the wealth of the Congo's resources—ivory and exotic woods—and their future potential through the transformation of these resources into Western fine-art objects.[34]

Ward was only one of a number of European artists during this period who depicted African themes and whose artworks were exhibited as part of public displays about the colonial enterprise in Africa. What is perhaps unique about Ward is his singular devotion to these themes and his creation of a personalized vision of Africa in the installation of his own African collection with his bronzes in his studio/ museum.

At the Smithsonian, the Ward exhibition was further distinguished by being set off from the other ethnographic exhibits by low wooden dividers constructed by the museum. These dividers repeated designs and motifs used by Ward in his sculptures and which he had originally taken from African objects in his collection. The space that was created by physical separation and through lighting effects was made even more distinctive by the personalizing of the discourse. A brief biography of Ward was mandated by the deed of gift, and its inclusion in the installation presented an interesting departure from the anonymous voice of most exhibitions of that time (and even up to the present). The information about Ward acknowledged his role as both the collector of the artifacts and the interpreter of Africa through his bronze sculptures.

There were, however, several important deviations from Ward's original exhibition design that served the museum's philosophy and clearly asserted its voice. First, at the Smithsonian the African material

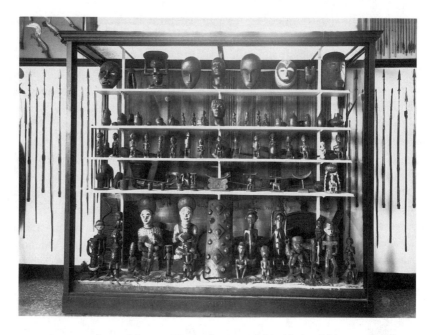

Fig. 14-9. Case of carved figures. Ward collection exhibit, National Museum Building, circa 1922. Smithsonian Institution photo no. 26819–A. Reproduced with permission.

culture and the zoological specimens were physically separated from the bronze sculptures. The former were organized by type and material in cases that ran around the perimeter of the exhibition space, bringing the exhibition more closely in line with the taxonomic interests of the museum (Figure 14-9). The bronze sculptures, rather than being integrated with the African objects, as they had been in Paris, were all positioned in the open space within the gallery, forming a secondary exhibition within the larger display. Second, the museum placed labels in each of the cases containing African material culture. The label text, designed for the edification and education of the public, reinforced the visual relationships set up in the typological developmental sequences. For example, the label for a case labeled "Costume and Ornament" (Figure 14-10) read:

> This case contains textiles native to the Congo and costumes made up in whole or part from them. This primitive industry offers instructive phases of aboriginal handicraft with filaments and some examples of the work show progress in taste and skill. Notable are

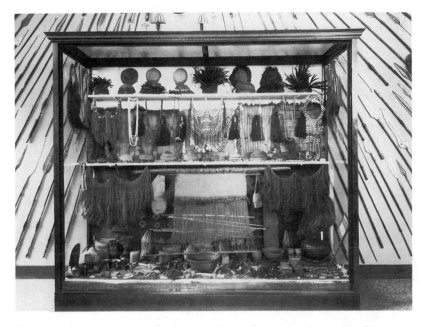

Fig. 14-10. Case of costume and ornament. Ward collection exhibit, National Museum Building, circa 1922. Smithsonian Institution photo no. 26819–B. Reproduced with permission.

the tufted and tie and dye fabrics. Personal ornaments, such as necklaces, pendants, carved combs, etc., show the striving for aesthetic effects in a savage state of culture. The primitive loom is for making raffia cloth. The basketry shows appreciation of form and decoration. On the floor of the case are neck ornaments and fetters of metal.[35]

Gone was the intimacy of the Paris installation and the relationship the arrangement had created among African objects, zoological specimens, and bronze sculptures. Ward's personal aesthetic had been compromised and the museum's scientific voice advanced, both through the physical arrangement of the collection and through text labels. Ward's Africa had become institutionalized and was now part of the official scientific discourse on the "other."

The inclusion of the Ward sculptures with the African material, as mandated by the deed of gift, would seem to have been difficult for the staff to reconcile with their exhibition philosophy for anthropology. Indeed, it was cause for some discussion among the museum's staff and administrators. In an internal memo to the administration, Walter Hough briefly outlined the installation project as follows:

> Readjustment of the East Hall of Ethnology to provide for the Ward Collection: 1. By retiring African collections covered by Ward collection. 2. By cutting down floor cases to family groups and removing synoptic series to West Hall. 3. If Ward sculptures are to be included place them in West end of East Hall to connect with art gallery. 4. Requirements as to cases and trophies on wall to be ascertained when size of Ward collection is known. (From photos collection seems to fill 5 rooms in his Paris mansion) Probably will take 1/4 to 1/2 of hall. [Initialed] W. H.[36]

During this period the National Museum Building included not only the natural-history and anthropology collections but also the national history and fine-arts collections, and so there was an internal logic to placing the Ward statues adjacent to the art gallery (Figure 14-11). The administration's reply to Hough's memo, however, precluded ex-

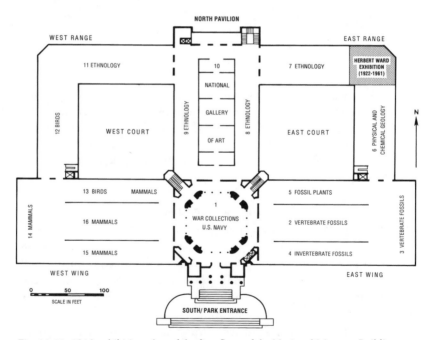

Fig. 14-11. 1919 exhibition plan of the first floor of the National Museum Building (now the National Museum of Natural History). Shaded area indicates the location of the installation of the Ward collection exhibit, opened in 1922.

tensive rearrangements of existing displays. The administration gave the age-old museum response that there was no money and no available space for extensive modification or moving of existing displays or for cutting down perfectly good cases to construct more suitable ones.[37] As a result, the Ward collection was installed in the east end of the East Range, which housed the existing African installations, rather than adjacent to the art gallery. The administrative decision seems not to have caused any particular outcry, since there were precedents in European exhibitions for placing ethnographic objects alongside Western art. From our current perspective, knowing the era's scientific and popular attitudes toward Africa and the developmental orientation of the museum's exhibitions, one wonders whether the original suggestion to place the Ward statues next to the National Gallery of Art—which celebrated Western civilization—would in the final analysis have been rejected on philosophical grounds, even if the money had been available to reconfigure the wing.

Despite the collection's physical location in the far end of the ethnology wing, however, the public still had a strong perception of the exhibition as an art exhibition, even though it was about Africa. One reviewer noted that

> African ethnology in a leading art exhibition is a novelty, not merely in Washington, but the world. . . . Guests were received in the apartment specially designed to accommodate the immense collection. . . . The walls were bedecked with the fantastic array of knives and other weapons . . . below them, in cases were exhibited other trophies—a huge elephant's head, a giant python, ivory carvings, a variety of textiles and garments, musical instruments, drums—the whole forming a setting for the magnificent sculptural compositions in bronze.[38]

Although the Ward sculptures are self-consciously art and clearly not ethnographic life groups, they do share a formal philosophical kinship with the life groups. Like the life groups, their realism is arresting. The life groups developed by Holmes (some of which have been refurbished and are still on display) generally presented lifeway scenes, which always depicted the "primitives" before contact with "civilization." Installed as a group, many of the Ward sculptures (such as *The Tribal Chief, The Idol Maker, The Forest Lovers,* and *The Congo Artist*) could have been read in much the same way as the life groups, thus supporting the museum's attitudes and beliefs about the "other."

Romantic ideas about the loss of innocence after contact would have been further reinforced in works such as *The Fugitives* and *Distress*. Holmes wrote of the bronzes,

> Thus Ward's genius has presented in an attractive, even a fascinating manner, a people whose status, according to his own story, is at the very bottom of the ladder of civilization, a people living in a manner hardly above that of the beast of prey and excelling the brute in brutality, for the lowest brute does not systematically hunt and kill and feast upon the bodies of his own kind.[39]

For the museum anthropologists, the inclusion of the Ward bronzes along with the African objects was considered a visually powerful developmental sequence. Holmes had devoted much of his research to the study of "primitive" art and he held strong opinions about the progressive evolution of art. In his view, art had evolved "from geometric, nonideographic to delineative forms; from motives of religious superstition to refined sense of beauty, from imitation to spontaneity."[40] To Holmes, no lover of modernism, the Ward sculptures must have represented examples of the highest achievement of Western art. By placing the bronzes alongside the decorated weapons and the non-naturalistically rendered African carvings, the public could see for themselves the evolution of art. Reaffirming this point of view, Walter Hough, curator of anthropology, wrote,

> The maker of an African sword and Praxiteles were one in the effort to express themselves in terms of art. The steps from the aboriginal craftsman to the sculptures of Mr. Ward are plain to those who study the development of art.[41]

The installation of the Ward collection in 1922 was certainly an anomaly for the Smithsonian when considered in terms of the exhibition style and anthropology program so carefully worked out by Mason decades before. Indeed, the dramatic style of the installation, the inclusion of a brief biography of the collector, and the fact that the Ward sculptures mediated between the viewer and the African objects and between the authoritative voice of the museum and its lay audience were all significant departures from the museum's standard practice. Yet despite its variation from the norm, through imagery and text the divergent voices in the exhibition (Ward's, on the one hand, and the curators', on the other) converged to create an interpretation of Africa that never questioned the accepted verities of Victorian categories of race and evolution, but rather intentionally and powerfully reconfirmed and supported them.

In 1961 the Africa wing was closed for modernization and was redone in line with more current anthropological thinking. This was the heady period in which many African countries achieved independence from colonial rule, and the original Ward installation was certainly an anachronism, both in the style of its representation and in its interpretation of the continent. In the reconfigured Africa Hall, the zoological specimens were removed and Ward's African objects were integrated with other African collections. This new narrative about Africa was not concerned with the evolution of forms, but instead concentrated on a synchronic analysis of the diversity of African cultural practices and social institutions through the lens of each society's material culture.

The Ward bronzes had no place in this new narrative, and most of them were moved from the hall. Since 1961 they have periodically been exhibited in various galleries throughout the museum, sometimes as individual sculptures and occasionally as a sculptural group.[42] The dismantling of the 1922 installation, the integration of the Ward collection of African material culture with other collections, and the displacement of the Ward bronzes has effectively eradicated the intimate association between the collection and the collector that once was so much a part of the collection's exhibition history. Once physically dissociated from the African objects, the bronzes no longer functioned as direct visual mediators between the African objects and the museum visitor.

Although most scholars and museum curators would probably agree that as representations of Africans, the Ward bronzes typify a particular mode of colonial discourse, the bronzes' recontextualization as independent works of art and their physical separation from the African objects did produce a radically different interpretation in at least one instance. In 1987 I had a conversation with a cabdriver who was a native Washingtonian. He said that as a young African American junior high school student in the 1960s, he had frequently visited the National Museum of Natural History. He spoke positively of the museum, and said that it had been a special place for him during his youth precisely because it was the only major public cultural institution in the area that had on display a positive image of a black man. I realized instantly from his description that the sculpture of which he spoke was Herbert Ward's statue *Defiance*.

The discussion I had with this man certainly gave me pause. While it is true that the Smithsonian's audience is now more diverse in terms of both ethnicity and social class than it was in the 1920s, when the Ward collection was first exhibited, I had just assumed that today's visitors all still react to the Ward bronzes as exotic images. Yet can we continue to generalize about our audiences and be so confident (even to the point of arrogance) that we know how each one of our visitors experiences these representations of non-Western peoples and the exhibition of non-Western objects? Unless we begin to take seriously our visitors' different attitudes and perspectives, and open up our exhibitions to allow for an explicit discussion of this diversity of experience, we run the risk of continually reproducing a distorted mirror.

NOTES

1. D. Jay Culver, "Herbert Ward—An Artist and Adventurer," *Dearborn Independent,* 27 May 1922, 2. It is noteworthy that Culver's piece on Ward was syndicated and was published in papers across the United States. Even though most of his American readers probably never had the opportunity to visit the actual exhibition, Culver's review and the accompanying photographs reinforced the commonly held stereotypes of Africa and Africans as "primitives."

2. The conferences and panels include a 1988 conference on African material culture organized by Mary Jo Arnoldi, Christraud M. Geary, and Kris Hardin at Bellagio, Italy; a 1986 conference entitled Making Exhibitions of Ourselves: The Limits of Objectivity in Representations of Other Cultures, organized by Brian Durrans at the British Museum in London; the 1988 Poetics and Politics of Representation conference, organized at the Smithsonian Institution by Ivan Karp and Steven D. Lavine; a conference entitled Depictions of the Dispossessed: Image and Self-Image of Euroamerica's Colonized Natives, organized by Celia F. Klein at the University of California, Los Angeles, in 1985; and a panel organized by Jeanne Cannizzo at the 1988 African Studies Association meeting, entitled Collecting Africa. Publications include Carol Breckenridge, "Diplomacy on Display: The Festival of India in the U.S.," in Brian Durrans, ed., *Representations at World Fairs and International Exhibitions* (London: Scholar, 1987); Carol Breckenridge, "The Aesthetics and Politics of Colonial Collecting: India at World Fairs," *Comparative Studies in Society and History* 31, no. 2 (1989), 195–216; James Clifford, "Objects and Selves—An Afterword," in George W. Stocking, Jr., ed., *Objects and Others: Essays on Museums and Material Culture,* History of Anthropology, vol. 3 (Madison: University of Wisconsin Press, 1985); James Clifford, *The Predicament of Culture: Twentieth-Century Ethnography, Literature, and Art* (Cambridge, Mass.: Harvard University Press, 1988); Brian Durrans, ed., *Representations at World Fairs and International Exhibitions* (London: Scholar,

1987); Curtis M. Hinsley, *Savages and Scientists: The Smithsonian Institution and the Development of American Anthropology, 1846–1910* (Washington, D.C.: Smithsonian Institution Press, 1981); Curtis M. Hinsley, "The World as Marketplace: Commodification of the Exotic at the World's Columbian Exposition, Chicago, 1893," in Ivan Karp and Steven D. Lavine, eds., *Exhibiting Cultures: The Poetics and Politics of Museum Display* (Washington, D.C.: Smithsonian Institution Press, 1991); Ira Jacknis, "Franz Boas and Exhibits," in George W. Stocking, Jr., ed., *Objects and Others: Essays on Museums and Material Culture,* History of Anthropology, vol. 3 (Madison: University of Wisconsin Press, 1985); Ivan Karp and Steven D. Lavine, eds., *Exhibiting Cultures: The Poetics and Politics of Museum Display* (Washington, D.C.: Smithsonian Institution Press, 1991); Cecelia Klein, ed., "Depictions of the Dispossessed," *Art Journal* 49, no. 2 (1990); George W. Stocking, Jr., "Essays on Museums and Material Culture," in George W. Stocking, Jr., ed., *Objects and Others: Essays on Museums and Material Culture,* History of Anthropology, vol. 3 (Madison: University of Wisconsin Press, 1985); and Elizabeth Williams, "Art and Artifact at the Trocadero," in George W. Stocking, Jr., ed., *Objects and Others: Essays on Museums and Material Culture,* History of Anthropology, vol. 3 (Madison: University of Wisconsin Press, 1985).

3. Mary Jo Arnoldi, "Re-presenting Africa: The History and Exhibition of the Smithsonian's Herbert Ward Collection," paper presented at the annual meeting of the African Studies Association, Chicago, October 1988; Jeanne Cannizzo, *Into the Heart of Africa* (Toronto: Royal Ontario Museum, 1989); Christraud Geary, "Art, Politics, and the Transformation of Meaning: On the History of Bamun Thrones," paper presented at the Conference on African Material Culture, Bellagio, Italy, May 1988; Christraud Geary, *Images from Bamun: German Colonial Photography at the Court of King Njoya, Cameroon, West Africa, 1902–1915* (Washington, D.C.: Smithsonian Institution Press for the National Museum of African Art, 1988); Christraud Geary, "On the Savannah: Marie Pauline Thorbecke's Images from Cameroon, West Africa (1911–12)," *Art Journal* 49, no. 2 (1990), 150–58; Enid Schildkrout, Curtis Keim, and contributors, *African Reflections: Art from Northeastern Zaire* (Seattle: University of Washington Press, 1990); William Schneider, *An Empire for the Masses: The French Popular Image of Africa, 1870–1900* (Westport, Conn.: Greenwood, 1982); Susan Mullin Vogel, "Dislocations: Baule Men's Masks, 1890–1980," paper presented at the Conference on African Material Culture, Bellagio, Italy, May 1988; Susan Mullin Vogel, ed., *Art/artifact: African Art in Anthropology Collections* (New York: Center for African Art, 1988).

4. Herbert Ward, *Five Years with the Congo Cannibals* (London: Chatto and Windus, 1890).

5. Patrick Brantlinger, "Victorians and Africans: The Genealogy of the Myth of the Dark Continent," in Henry Louis Gates, Jr., ed., *Race, Writing and Difference* (Chicago: University of Chicago Press, 1986), 195.

6. Brantlinger, "Victorians and Africans," 217.

7. Ward, *Five Years with the Congo Cannibals,* 163.

8. *Evening Standard* (London), 28 Sept. 1889, 4.

9. Sarita Ward, *A Valiant Gentleman* (London: Chapman and Hall, 1927), 165.

10. Sterling Helig, "Unique Gift for the Smithsonian," *Washington Sunday Star,* 16 Mar. 1913, 2–3.

11. Hugh Honour, *Image of Blacks in Western Civilization,* volume 4, *From the American Revolution to World War I,* part 2, *Black Models and White Myths* (Houston: Menil Foundation, 1989), 220–22.

12. S.J.S. Cockey, *Britain and the Congo Question, 1885–1913* (London: Longmans, Green, 1968), 66, 91.

13. Ibid., 107.

14. Ward, *A Valiant Gentleman,* 163.

15. Herbert S. Ward, *A Voice from the Congo* (New York: Charles Scribner's Sons, 1910), 319.

16. Schildkrout and Keim, *African Reflections,* 50.

17. Ellis L. Yochelson, *The National Museum of Natural History: 75 Years in the Natural History Building* (Washington, D.C.: Smithsonian Institution Press, 1985).

18. Walter Hough Papers, National Anthropological Archives, Smithsonian Institution.

19. Walter Hough, "An Appreciation of the Scientific Value of the Herbert Ward African Collection," *The Herbert Ward African Collection* (Washington, D.C.: United States National Museum, 1924), 37–38.

20. "African Stone Age Relics Given to the Smithsonian—Herbert Ward, Sculptor, Donates Complete and Valuable Collection," *Washington Evening Star,* 15 Mar. 1913.

21. Otis T. Mason as quoted in Hinsley, *Savages and Scientists,* 89.

22. Ibid., 87–88.

23. Ibid., 88–89.

24. Ibid., 94.

25. Jacknis, "Franz Boas and Exhibits," 77–80.

26. Hinsley, *Savages and Scientists,* 109.

27. Ibid.

28. John M. MacKenzie, *Propaganda and Empire: The Manipulation of British Public Opinion, 1880–1960* (Manchester: Manchester University Press, 1984).

29. Schneider, *An Empire for the Masses,* 127–36.

30. Hinsley, *Savages and Scientists,* 108–9; Jacknis, "Franz Boas and Exhibits," 81–82.

31. Hinsley, *Savages and Scientists,* 112.

32. United States National Museum, *Annual Report for the Year Ending June 30, 1913* (Washington, D.C.: Government Printing Office, 1914), 15. In 1913 the present Natural History Building at the Smithsonian housed the national collections and was known as the United States National Museum. It included the natural history, anthropology, American history, and fine-arts collections. Today these various collections are housed and exhibited in the following museums: the National Museum of Natural History (natural history and anthropology); the National Museum of American History (Americana collections, including the history of science and technology collections); and the National Museum of American Art and the National Portrait Gallery (the fine-arts collections). The Smithsonian Institution presently includes also the following museums: the National Air and Space Museum, the Anacostia Museum, the Cooper-Hewitt Museum (New York City), the Freer Gallery of Art and the Arthur M. Sackler Gallery, the Hirshhorn Museum and Sculpture Garden, the National Museum of African Art, the National Museum of the American Indian, and the National Zoological Park.

33. Schildkrout and Keim, *African Reflections,* 50, illus. 3.3.

34. Frances Susan Connelly, "The Origins and Development of Primitivism in Eighteenth and Nineteenth Century European Art and Aesthetics," Ph.D. dissertation, University of Pittsburgh, 1987, 161–62.

35. Exhibition case label, records of the Anthropology Department, National Anthropological Archives, Smithsonian Institution.

36. Walter Hough Papers, National Anthropological Archives, Smithsonian Institution.

37. Walter Hough Papers, National Anthropological Archives, Smithsonian Institution.

38. Gertrude Brigham, "Smithsonian Institution Receives Herbert Ward Statues of African Jungle People," *Christian Science Monitor,* 15 Mar. 1922, 8.

39. William H. Holmes, "Herbert Ward's Achievements in the Field of Art," *Art and Archaeology* 18, no. 3 (1924), 113–25.

40. Hinsley, *Scientists and Savages,* 105.

41. Hough, "An Appreciation of the Scientific Value of the Herbert Ward African Collection," 41.

42. In the early 1960s the Smithsonian Institution petitioned the Attorney General of the United States, and with the consent of Ward's heirs the original gift agreement was changed to exclude the clause requiring that the entire collection be exhibited together.

CHAPTER 15

Ali'i and Maka'āinana: The Representation of Hawaiians in Museums at Home and Abroad

ADRIENNE L. KAEPPLER

L
ike the Greek sculpture of Nike of Samothrace, the image of the Hawaiian god Kūkā'ilimoku was meant to be seen from below, and like Winged Victory (as Nike has become known), who now stands in a prominent position on a stairway landing at the Louvre in Paris (Figure 15-1), the image of the Hawaiian war god now stands in a comparable position on a stairway landing at the Museum of Mankind in London (Figure 15-2). From this juxtaposition one might wonder if this means that Winged Victory and Kūkā'ilimoku are now given equal regard by the museumgoing public and that the non-Western heritage of museumgoing audiences is being presented in a meaningful way. As seductive as this possibility might sound, we all know that museums are not equal and that the placement of objects in them probably tells us more about the curators of the collections than it does about what the museumgoing public wants to see.

The Louvre is one of the world's great art museums, and no trip to Paris is complete without a visit there. The Museum of Mankind is a small ethnographic museum, the public face of the Department of Ethnography of the British Museum, and is essentially hidden away in Mayfair, an area where most people go to shop for new and stylish clothing and decorative objects. At the Louvre there are certain things that one "must" see, including Winged Victory; at the Museum of

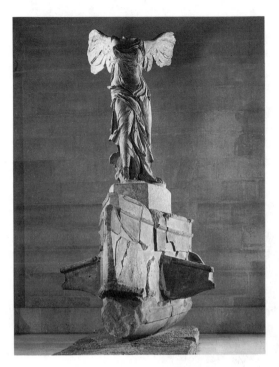

Fig. 15-1. *Nike of Samothrace,* Greek sculpture displayed on a stairway landing at the Louvre. Photo courtesy Musée National du Louvre.

Mankind the visitor sees whatever the current exhibition happens to be. Kūkā'ilimoku, however, stands permanently at attention on the landing, but with little explanation of who he is and why he is given such a prominent (and in my view, well-deserved) place. Whereas Winged Victory is immediately recognizable to most museum visitors, few of the museumgoing public recognize Kūkā'ilimoku or could say where he is from—although this prominent placement may contribute to a more widespread recognition of Kūkā'ilimoku and other important non-Western sculptures.

Who is this museumgoing public, and how do they learn to recognize what they see? What individuals make up the communities that support museums and presumably go to them to see if their support is justified? And how do these communities and their philosophies differ in museums in the places in which the objects originated and in museums to which they were brought, essentially as exotic curiosities?

This essay will explore these questions in relation to the representations of Hawaiians in museums in Hawai'i, the mainland United States, and Europe. The points on which I focus are, first, whether the

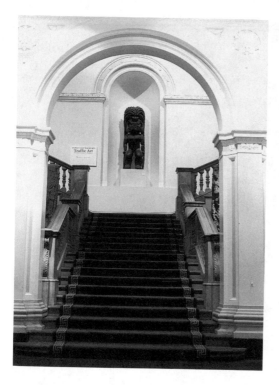

Fig. 15-2. *Kūkā'ilimoku,* Hawaiian sculpture displayed on a stairway landing at the Museum of Mankind, London. Photo courtesy Trustees of the British Museum.

representation of Hawaiians in museums in Europe or the mainland United States is significantly different from the representation of Hawaiians in museums in Hawai'i, and second, why the romantic notion of an uncontaminated "other" persists in museum contexts in Hawai'i and elsewhere when we know from walking down the street in Waikīkī that this is not reality.

Museums are collections of objects that have been amassed over time. *Ethnographic collections* consist of objects that explorers, missionaries, merchants, anthropologists, or other curious individuals happened to have obtained through gift, barter, seizure, or purchase because they were beautiful, odd, difficult to get, or available, and which were taken back to the home countries of their collectors. *Local history-museum collections* in places such as Hawai'i consist mostly of objects that were not given to, bartered to, seized by, or purchased by explorers, missionaries, merchants, anthropologists, or the curious before they were worn out or became obsolete, and were for some reason saved rather than discarded, and so have remained in their countries of origin. Thus, what is an ethnographic collection in one context (abroad) is often considered a historical collection in another context (at home).

This basic difference between ethnography and history—and their representation in museum exhibitions—is the first step in our exploration. Hawaiian collections abroad consist primarily of two types of objects: ceremonial objects given to early explorers and ship captains by Hawaiian chiefs in exchange or as tokens of esteem, and objects that became obsolete because of the introduction of Christianity or new technologies. Objects that were used every day, such as tools, objects for preparing and containing food, and objects used in the manufacture and decoration of cloth, were not readily given or traded away. Thus many ordinary, everyday objects used by commoners (*maka'āinana*) stayed in Hawai'i. Ceremonial objects worn and used by chiefs (*ali'i*) were traded and given away—after all, new ones could be made, and they weren't needed every day. Indeed, because many such objects carried the *mana* of the ancestors and were dangerous to wear or even touch, they were of little immediate use to their owners and could be given away.

Feathered cloaks are the supreme example here.[1] Made for individual chiefs, they were worn in sacred and dangerous situations as protective devices and to separate visually the *ali'i* from the *maka'āinana*. If a chief was killed in battle, the cloak would be taken as a battle prize by the conquering chief; in the case of a chief's natural death, the cloak might be kept by his son as a symbol of his legitimate acquisition of power. Liholiho (Kamehameha II), for example, had three sacred cloaks: one he inherited along with the sacred *mana* or power of his father, Kamehameha the Great; a second cloak embodied the power of Kamehameha's paternal line, in that it was the cloak of Kekuaokalani, the son of Kamehameha's full brother, and had been taken in battle by Liholiho; and a third embodied the power of Liholiho's mother's line, in that it had belonged to Kiwala'ō, Liholiho's mother's father, who had been killed in a battle with Kamehameha I, who acquired it as a battle prize. Liholiho also had several other cloaks that he took with him on his trip to England in 1823 and gave away to important people he visited along the way.

It is unlikely, however, that Liholiho (or any other Hawaiian, for that matter) ever wore these cloaks because of the important prohibition (*kapu*) against wearing clothing that had touched the body of someone else, especially the body of a high chief. Clothing carried one's personal *kapu,* and individuals who did not respect this *kapu* were considered careless and were vulnerable to sorcery. One of the important clothing *kapu* was that a son could not wear the clothing of his father, and a daughter could not wear the clothing of her mother. A father, on the other hand, could wear the clothing of his son (and the mother the clothing of her daughter), but apparently only if the child was not of higher rank through his mother.[2] In short, it was best not to wear clothing that had belonged to someone else if one did not want to make one's body vulnerable.[3] This was especially important for the *ali'i.*

What did one do with extra, potentially harmful feathered cloaks that one had inherited from one's ancestors or that had been taken as battle prizes? One gave them away to unsuspecting Europeans—who would probably not be harmed anyway because they were obviously subject to a different *kapu* system. Even today tradition-minded Hawaiians might give clothes away to persons unknown (through Salvation Army thrift shops, for example), but it is necessary to retain the *kapu* willfully so that neither the giver nor the recipient will be harmed. Although Liholiho gave away a number of feathered cloaks in Rio de Janeiro and England, he never gave away the cloak of his father, the cloak of Kiwala'ō, or the cloak of Kekuaokalani—all of which legitimated his right to rule and embodied his genealogy. Which cloak was Liholiho's own is unknown. Presumably he took it with him to England, but as he died there, it probably remained in England without its specific ownership being recorded by the European who received it. I suspect that it is the cloak now in Edinburgh, said to have been worn by Liholiho's "favorite medicine man." It is unlikely that Liholiho actually wore the cloak in England himself, as he usually appeared in European dress (see Figure 15-5). It could have been carried or worn, however, by one of Liholiho's *kapu* attendants, who would not have been harmed. After Liholiho's death, the chief Boki—the ranking member of Liholiho's entourage (see Figure 15-6)—probably gave it away in England, since he knew that no one in Hawai'i could wear it anyway.

The legitimating cloaks of the Kamehameha dynasty had been left safely at home and were inherited by Liholiho's full brother. The cloaks of Kamehameha I and Kiwala'ō were never given away, as they contained the *mana* of the male and female lines of the Kamehameha lineages. The cloak of Kekuaokalani, however, was given away in 1840 by Liholiho's brother Kauikeaouli (Kamehameha III). This cloak would not have the same significance to Kamehameha III, as he inherited his brother's kingdom legitimately and without warfare, whereas

Liholiho had had to battle Kekuaokalani, the keeper of the war god at the time, in order to consolidate his power and take his kingdom into the modern world.

This ethnographic digression not only tells us about the importance of feathered cloaks and the life they contain, but also suggests why the cloaks—as *kapu* ceremonial objects—were given away. There was, after all, no good place to keep historical objects, which could, in addition, be dangerous to those who handled them. Even after the adoption of Christianity these clothing *kapu* continued, and even today Hawaiians who work in the Bishop Museum in Honolulu do not like to touch certain objects—including feathered cloaks and capes, and especially feathered standards (*kāhili*) with human bone handles. These human bone handles incorporate the bones of historic chiefs, either enemies who were killed in battle or beloved ancestors. The bone handles carried the individual's personal *kapu* and served as memorials of people and events.

The sculptured images of the pre-Christian gods are, interestingly enough, not so dangerous. Most Hawaiians now are Christian, and the power of the new god serves as a protection from the power of the old ones. Most of these sculptures were taken away by missionaries and have found their separate ways to museums. Many of these images, as well as the feathered cloaks, have been returned to Hawai'i, where they are considered important parts of Hawaiian history. They contain, however, not just history, but the power and *mana* of the ancestors and the gods. How does one exhibit sacred power and make sense of clothing *kapu* in the modern world, especially when such considerations are relegated to ceremonial occasions when powerless replicas are used to enhance ethnic identity (Figure 15-3)? I will return to this subject shortly, but first I want to look at ethnographic museums abroad, where many of these objects have now come to rest.

The first Hawaiian ethnographic objects—or "artificial curiosities," as they were called during the eighteenth century—were acquired by Captain Cook, his officers and men, and supernumeraries such as the expedition's official artist John Webber during Cook's third Pacific voyage. The objects obtained on this voyage were for the most part spectacular ones, such as feathered cloaks and capes, helmets, and god images. They were eagerly sought after in England and Europe as beautiful and curious manufactures of people far removed in time and space from the European Enlightenment and as relics of the noble savage as conceptualized by Rousseau and other philosophers. The objects had been acquired in Hawai'i through gift or trade. Trade

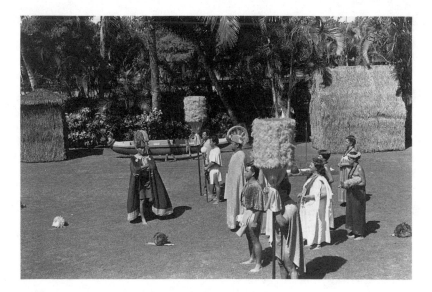

Fig. 15-3. The Aloha Week Royal Court, appearing at the Kodak Hula Show in Waikīkī, 1990. Photo by the author.

for provisions was the main concern of the ships' officers, and official gifts from Cook to the *ali'i* were often reciprocated with food and appropriate ceremonial gifts congruent with the view that Cook was somehow associated with the Hawaiian god Lono (the god of the *makahiki* [harvest] season in progress when Cook arrived in Kea-lakekua Bay).

The acquisition of objects was selective and depended not only on opportunity and occasion but also on the difference between the categories of trade and gift, gender interaction and the prestige of women, as well as the appropriateness of specific objects for specific recipients. The appropriate time for giving certain objects also had to be found, such as the official ceremony in which Cook was given eight feathered capes, as well as the cloak that the high chief Kalani'ōpu'u took off his own shoulders and placed on Captain Cook's, along with giving him his feathered helmet and *kāhili* (perhaps an indication that Cook, as Lono, was considered to be ancestral to Kalani'ōpu'u, and therefore could wear his clothing without harm). The appropriateness of objects and the time of exchange were also a consideration on the European side: firearms were not usually traded or given, and it was only just before leaving that Cook gave to the Hawaiian chief Kalani'ōpu'u "a complete Tool Chest."[4] Elsewhere I have noted the selectivity of the

Hawaiian objects collected during Cook's voyage:[5] of the some four hundred Hawaiian objects acquired during the voyage, there are numerous pieces of featherwork but no stone food pounders; many pieces of bark cloth but only one bark-cloth beater; numerous weapons but few tools; a large number of ornaments but few baskets or mats. Acquisition was probably related to where interactions took place as well as to the fact that Hawaiians were probably loath to trade objects they needed every day. Household objects are rare, and the objects acquired in Hawai'i are principally those that were carried or worn, or were objects considered to be appropriate to Cook's status as a chief or possibly a god. These Hawaiian objects were coveted by European collectors, not only because they were associated with an almost mythical Pacific island paradise but also because they were associated with Captain Cook, who after being murdered in Hawai'i in 1779 became a culture hero in England and, by extension, all of Europe.

By 1819 Hawaiian ceremonial objects were found in most important museum and private collections. From London to St. Petersburg, Edinburgh to Dublin, Göttingen to Berlin, Florence to Vienna, every collection had to have a memento of the dead hero Cook, whether it actually had come from his voyage or not. The objects were exhibited as curious works of art, remnants of a savage people, mementos of an English culture hero, expressions of an unknown "other." And so it has continued until today. Hawaiian objects are occasionally exhibited according to the theoretical notions of the curators or the strictures of the museum. For example, the collection of the Pitt Rivers Museum in Oxford, England, is arranged according to artifact type to illustrate its founder's interest in the comparative method;[6] thus Hawaiian images of gods and ancestors are exhibited with religious images from various parts of the world, and feathered cloaks are exhibited with ceremonial clothing.

In most European museums, Hawaiian objects are exhibited as "curious objects we happen to have." Little or no attempt is made to present Hawaiian culture as a whole or to educate viewers about cultural or social change. American museums are similar, except that the exhibit cases are usually a bit cleaner. And why should we expect anything else? In England and continental Europe there are no curators who specialize in Polynesia, let alone Hawai'i. There are curators for Oceania in Basel, Vienna, London, and a few other places, but their specialties are Australia and Melanesia. Nonetheless, an excellent temporary exhibition on Hawai'i was held during the early 1980s

at the Museum of Mankind in London, which houses the most important collection of Hawaiian objects outside of Hawai'i. Although that
exhibition stressed chiefly regalia, some objects of the *maka'āinana*
were also included.[7] On the United States mainland there are curators
of Oceania in only a half-dozen natural-history or art museums, and I
am the only one who specializes in Polynesia. Indeed, besides myself,
the only mainland curator knowledgeable about Hawai'i is William
Davenport at the University Museum in Philadelphia. The exhibits at
the Smithsonian Institution were done by my predecessor, a specialist
in Micronesia. They are not bad. Done in the exhibition style of the
1960s, they at least impart information about the socially stratified
society that was Hawai'i.

Shortly after I came to the Smithsonian, I was looking forward to
installing the traveling exhibition that I had helped to organize while
still at the Bishop Museum—Hawai'i: The Royal Isles. The Smithsonian exhibition designer Richard Molinaroli and I even had a tentative design worked out that would have enhanced the exhibition in a
culturally sensitive way. Unfortunately, the exhibition was canceled
because, allegedly, the people who were supposed to raise money for
its installation were unable to do so. Consequently, the exhibition
traveled primarily to art museums, where the objects were exhibited
with little context—therefore little cultural understanding was impar-
ted to the viewers.

The only other opportunities I have had to use my knowledge
about Hawai'i for exhibition purposes in Washington were as the
curator of the Polynesian section of the Art of the Pacific Islands
exhibition at the National Gallery of Art in 1979, before I came to the
Smithsonian, and as the anthropology curator for the 1985 exhibition
Magnificent Voyagers. In the latter, Hawaiian objects acquired during
the voyage of the U.S. Exploring Expedition of 1838–1842 were
exhibited as part of the natural and cultural history of Hawaii as it
was some fifty years after first contact with Europeans. One of the
interesting discoveries made during the research for this exhibition
was that as late as 1840 the artist Titian Ramsay Peale, in his oil
painting of the magnificent volcanic eruption, represented Hawaiians
watching the eruption in their cloaks and helmets; but according to
the expedition's journals, no feathered cloaks or helmets were observed and none were acquired during the voyage. It transpired that
Titian Peale illustrated the Hawaiian featherwork in his father's museum in Philadelphia! Curious Hawaiian objects had become impor-

tant for European and American artists, who had their own artistic programs and conventions.

To return to the representation of Hawaiians at home in Hawai'i, it should be noted that a wide variety of museums exhibit Hawaiian objects, ranging from large natural-history or ethnological museums (such as the Bishop Museum in Honolulu, the Kaua'i Museum in Lihue, and the Lyman Museum in Hilo) to missionary-associated museums (such as the Mission Houses Museum in Honolulu and Bailey House in Kahului) to tiny local museums (such as the Hāna Cultural Center in Hāna, Maui) to those focused on a specific person or chiefly lineage (such as the Queen Emma Museum in Honolulu, Hulihe'e Palace in Kona, and 'Iolani Palace in Honolulu). In most of these museums, objects are exhibited essentially as things associated with the chiefs and gods of old. There are a few food pounders and other tools, but little information is conveyed about the wearisome life of the commoner. An exception is the Hāna Cultural Center, which exhibits objects associated with the Hāna area and its people.

The audiences and communities served by these museums include tourists, schoolchildren, artists, and Hawaiian descendants of the makers of these objects. The descendants, however, are not *ali'i,* for most of the chiefly lines have died out and few living people can trace any association to them. The last of the Kamehameha line was Bernice Pauahi Bishop, whose heirlooms became the founding collection of the Bishop Museum—hence the Hawaiian name of the Bishop Museum: Hale Hō'ike'ike o Kamehameha (treasure house of the Kamehamehas). Another important treasure house is 'Iolani Palace, the treasure house of the Kalākaua lineage, which has also died out.

Exhibitions in Hawai'i are more culturally sensitive than those across the oceans, and objects are generally placed in historical or cultural perspective. Nevertheless, artifacts are exhibited as objects of the past and more or less as representations of a historical "other." But then, why shouldn't they be? Are not the magnificent pieces of armor from sixteenth- or eighteenth-century Europe simply another kind of "other" to the Europeans who view these objects in their museums today? Are not Hawaiian cloaks and helmets comparable to obsolete armor?

I have not yet seen a museum exhibition in which the usable past is shown to be usable in any way other than historically. Hawaiian exhibitions celebrate the history of Hawaiians and are only beginning to celebrate their present. Indeed, most current selections of objects and the manner in which they are exhibited emphasize the romantic notion of an uncontaminated "other"—a Hawai'i that does not exist today and probably never did. This false image, perpetuated by museums that present an essentially timeless past, does not address the concept of change nor the reasons for it. The confrontation of two very different worldviews—the Hawaiian one with the one brought by European and American "monarchs, mariners, missionaries, and merchants"—which resulted in "conflict and consonance" (as one Bishop Museum exhibition is aptly titled) is not pursued. Nor do exhibitions address the profound changes in values that occurred during the nineteenth century and the resulting negotiation of tradition. What is today emphasized as traditional is the system of values associated with the Hawaiian monarchy, a system that is essentially a combination of European aristocratic ideas grafted onto a Polynesian hierarchical social structure—celebrating chiefs rather than commoners, praising status over work, and encouraging emulation of royalty and events associated with it. The Bishop Museum's traveling exhibition Hawai'i: The Royal Isles, although originally planned to address change and the traditions that were selectively retained as guideposts for life in the modern world,[8] was so heavily weighted with monarchy regalia[9] that this message was not understood or even successfully conveyed. The remnants of this exhibition still dominate the lower floor of the great hall of the Bishop Museum, giving a late-nineteenth-century view of Hawaiian tradition (Figure 15-4).

Nineteenth-century Hawaiians, like most people, wanted to be up-to-date. The difference between how Liholiho and his entourage wanted to be represented (that is, in European dress) during their visit to London in 1823–24 (Figure 15-5) can be contrasted with how the English artist John Hayter wanted to represent them (that is, romantically portrayed in traditional dress [Figure 15-6]). And the illustrations of Kamehameha in a red vest—showing him in European clothes, as he wanted to be depicted[10]—is quite different from how the artist Choris wanted to depict Hawaiians in 1816, in traditional dress. How Hawaiians represent their past today, and how they use this representation as one component of their ethnic identity, is largely based on late-nineteenth-century traditions concerned with clothing, feasting, regalia, and values that incorporate Christian ideals. The extended family ('ohana) and the values associated with it are more prominent in present-day Hawaiians' representation of their pasts than the values associated with warring chiefs of the eighteenth cen-

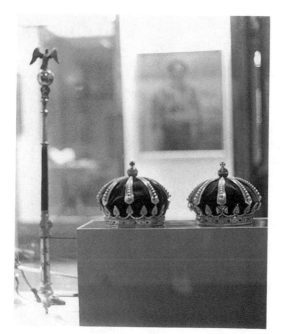

Fig. 15-4. The crowns of King Kalākaua and Queen Kapi'olani with the royal scepter. Part of the exhibition Hawai'i: The Royal Isles, at the Bishop Museum, Honolulu. Photo by the author. Reproduced with permission from the Bishop Museum.

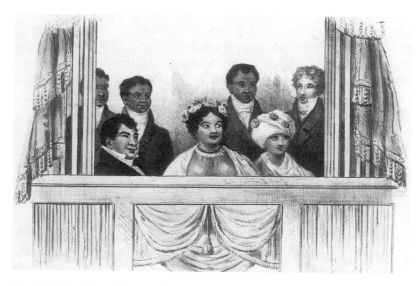

Fig. 15-5. Liholiho and his entourage in London, 1824. Lithograph by William Gear, courtesy Bishop Museum.

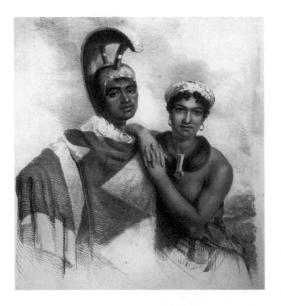

Fig. 15-6. Boki and Liliha in London, 1824. Lithograph by John Hayter, courtesy Bishop Museum.

tury. Although both eighteenth- and nineteenth-century chiefs might have worn feathered cloaks, they did so for different reasons. During the eighteenth century feathered cloaks were protective devices worn during sacred and dangerous situations, such as warfare. During the nineteenth century, Hawaiian chiefs wore feathered cloaks on ceremonial occasions and for such events as funerals of other chiefs as visual expressions of status and prestige. All of those events can be considered "traditional," but the traditions refer to different points in time. Tradition has been negotiated continuously and reinterpreted in order to make it appropriate in the modern world. The desire of modern-day Hawaiians to use religious sites of the past in rites that admittedly combine elements of the past (as they are understood today) with yoga and the teachings of Jesus Christ, Freud, Marx, and Max Freedom Long are little different philosophically from the combination of pagan and Christian rites that contemporary Christians celebrate on the holy days of the Christian calendar.

    In short, exhibitions of Hawaiians in museums in Hawai'i are little different from exhibitions in museums elsewhere; there is simply a different emphasis. Museums in Hawai'i emphasize a nineteenth-century monarchical historical "other" (Figure 15-7) while museums overseas emphasize a pre-European "other" (Figures 15-8 and 15-9), but museums in both places often use similar artifacts, primarily from the nineteenth century. As most traditional Hawaiian objects are ei-

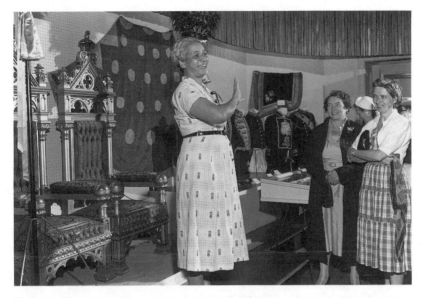

Fig. 15-7. Hawaiian guide to exhibitions, Martha Hohu, conducts a guided tour in the Bishop Museum, 1958. Photo courtesy Bishop Museum.

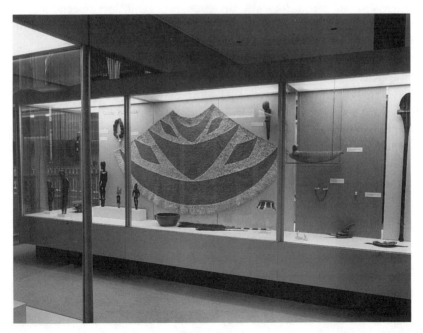

Fig. 15-8. Hawaiian exhibit, National Museums of Scotland. Photo courtesy National Museums of Scotland.

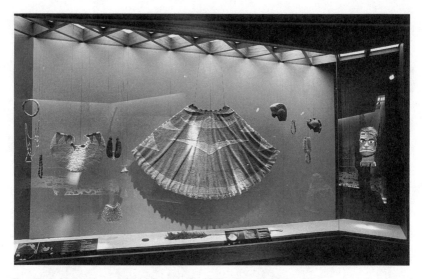

Fig. 15-9. Hawaiian exhibit, Museum für Völkerkunde, Berlin. Photo courtesy
Staatliche Museen Preussischer Kulturbesitz, Berlin.

ther obsolete technologically or *kapu* to present-day descendants of
their original owners, their safekeeping and access to them is of concern to Hawaiians.

Perhaps a potentially significant use of Hawaiian objects today,
for Hawaiians as well as others, would be to explore the history of
civilization through Hawai'i's past. An exhibition of the evolution of
Hawaiian society from a stratified social system that separated chiefs
from commoners on the basis of birth to a society based on democratic
principles might be relevant. Also important, however, is the use of
museums as storehouses for treasures in the present-day search for
ethnic identity and the renaissance of Hawaiian art and values.

Like the Austrian song "Eine Insel aus Traumen Geboren" ("An
Island Born of Dreams") suggests, we all seem to long for the uncontaminated "other"—whether it is our own past or the known or imagined past of a culture far removed from our own, such as that of
Hawai'i. While knowing that such pristine "others" do not really exist,
museums seem to project a kind of academic escapism—Disneylands
on an elevated scale. Museums continue to delude their visitors of the
separateness of objects, culture, history, and politics by focusing on
outmoded ideas of the primacy of the uncontaminated "other." Instead
museums should be exposing their visitors to the notion of the equality

of all cultures and negotiating how to integrate the usable past into modern life. In today's world we want to democratize the past and make it gender-free. But in many societies of the world, this spells the end of "tradition." When objects become artifacts or art and thus suitable to be enshrined in museums, this may mean that the descendants of their makers have recognized their past and its differences from present-day life in terms of things like gender and social stratification, and could be educating museumgoers about such controversial subjects.

It is useful to have treasure houses in which to keep important artifacts that have become technologically obsolete, important *kapu* clothing that cannot be worn and no longer has traditional keepers, objects that are embedded in hierarchical social structure when democracy has evolved, or important religious icons when Christianity has changed the way one views the world. Museums at home, as historical treasure houses, can assist in the forging of cultural, ethnic, or national identity, and can serve as a link to a future that recognizes its roots in the past. The Western concept of a museum can be reinterpreted to accommodate other social realities. In Hawai'i there were concepts about the appropriate uses of heirlooms and inherited valuables. Even if they were not worn or used, it was appropriate to keep them (which was not the case for the Melanesians, for example, who usually let objects made for specific occasions disintegrate). Hawaiians of today want to identify with and base their cultural identity on their ancestral objects, which are in museum collections at home and abroad, but for the most part they do not want to return to the old stratified society in which authority, prestige, and power were ascribed by birth or achieved in warfare.

Finally, we arrive at the question of whether we should be conserving and displaying objects or culture. In Hawai'i, as in many Pacific societies, objects were given a different kind of importance than they have now in Western society. Objects were not just inanimate things—life was embedded in them. They were part of social categories and a socially constructed reality. The motifs and forms of specific objects were part of an aesthetic system that was based on layered meaning (*kaona*) and skill (*no'eau*) and that embodied artistic memory and philosophy. Old objects should be preserved and displayed, but perhaps more crucial is the preservation of the knowledge by which objects can be reproduced. Although all museums can preserve objects and display them, it is up to local museums to preserve the knowledge about them. Conserving culture is the task of the local museum, as much of its community is the living descendants of the makers of the objects there enshrined. The tasks of the overseas ethnological museum and its curators, in contrast, are to make knowledge about objects relevant to the understanding of different worldviews, and to instruct the viewer about the equal importance of all cultures in the history of civilization and their contributions to this multicultural world.

In Hawai'i, museum communities include not only Hawaiians who want to understand their past better but also non-Hawaiians, both visitors and residents, who want to understand something about Hawai'i. In museums of the United States mainland, the audience is the multicultural nation of Native Americans and immigrants, who all coexist yet who have distinct value systems that need to be understood and appreciated, as well as visitors from all over the world. In Europe, Hawai'i is still an exotic place to be visited for sand, sea, sun, and perhaps a bit of history. Few Hawaiians have emigrated to Europe, and those who travel there do so mainly as visitors to learn about the European part of their heritage or as cultural ambassadors. Hawaiian objects in museums, no matter how they are exhibited, are a tie with home. At home or abroad, Hawaiians relate to objects of their past as a living past through which they view the present with hope for the future.

NOTES

1. The following paragraphs are essentially a reconstruction of why so many cloaks and capes were given away by the early Hawaiian chiefs, and are based on the concepts of clothing *kapu* as presented in E.S.C. Handy and Mary Kawena Pukui, *The Polynesian Family System in Kau, Hawaii* (Wellington: Polynesian Society, 1958), 181–82, and personal communications with Mary Kawena Pukui and her *hanai* (sister/daughter) Patience Namakauahoao-kawena Bacon.

2. Handy and Pukui, *The Polynesian Family System,* 181–82.

3. It is possible that these rules could be broken if the person who owned the featherwork piece was living and willfully withdrew his *mana* while another person wore it with his permission. For example, for the oil painting Robert Dampier made of her in 1825, Nāhi'ena'ena wore a feather cape that, according to Lucy Peabody, belonged to her brother Kauikeaouli (John Charlot, "The Feather Skirt of Nāhi'ena'ena: An Innovation in Postcontact Hawaiian Art," *Journal of the Polynesian Society* 100, no. 2 [1991], 147).

4. J. C. Beaglehole, ed., *The Voyage of the Resolution and Discovery, 1776–1780* (Cambridge: Cambridge University Press, 1967), 1170.

5. Adrienne L. Kaeppler, *"Artificial Curiosities": An Exposition of Native Manufactures Collected on the Three Pacific Voyages of Captain James Cook, R.N.* (Honolulu: Bishop Museum Press, 1978), 51.

6. Beatrice Blackwood, *The Classification of Artefacts in the Pitt Rivers Museum, Oxford* (Oxford: Oxford University Press, 1970), 9.

7. Dorota Starzecka, *Hawai'i: Culture and People* (London: British Museum, 1975).

8. Adrienne L. Kaeppler, "The Persistence of Tradition," in Roger G. Rose, *Hawai'i: The Royal Isles* (Honolulu: Bishop Museum Press, 1980), 62.

9. Roger G. Rose, *Hawai'i: The Royal Isles* (Honolulu: Bishop Museum Press, 1980).

10. Ibid., 33.

CHAPTER 16

Establishing the Roots of Historical Consciousness in Modern Annapolis, Maryland

PARKER B. POTTER, JR., AND
MARK P. LEONE

This essay is different from most if not all of the other contributions to this volume. The volume, like the conference on which it is based, is mostly devoted to finding ways for museums to serve communities through the representation of minority experiences and points of view. To date, that kind of work has been only a small part of the strategy of Archaeology in Public in Annapolis, the project we report on here. Instead, this article is largely a study of the creation and use of history by competing elites in Annapolis, Maryland, and it is a description of the alternative interpretations that we have attempted to develop since 1981. By making this choice we are not suggesting that minorities and others who are underrepresented in histories of Annapolis are not our problem. Rather, our point is that the history-making process in Annapolis has so consistently ignored the interests of its audiences that *everyone* has been excluded. Thus, our goal is not just to turn the history-making process over to groups previously denied access to it. In this essay we describe our disassembly of that process, which we take to be a first step toward empowering the various communities that together form what we believe is an entire historically disenfranchised city.

The focal point of this essay consists of several interpretive fragments. These fragments are a portion of the script for a multiple-projector audiovisual production we have worked on since 1983, several brief synopses of archaeological site tours we developed between 1983 and 1987, and two sections from a guidebook we first published in 1984.[1] (Selections from the audiovisual production and the guidebook appear at the end of this essay as appendices.) However, these pieces of archaeological interpretation do not just exist; they exist in the midst of, and in response to, a specific set of contemporary social conditions, and they exist in the context of a broader program of archaeological interpretation. Before we present our interpretive products, we think it is important to discuss in some detail both parts of the context in which these interpretations exist.

A CRITIQUE OF OUTDOOR HISTORY MUSEUMS

The real starting point for Archaeology in Public in Annapolis is Leone's critique of outdoor history museums,[2] which has been summarized and extended by Potter.[3] One of Leone's important observations is the boredom of many outdoor history museum visitors:

> Visitors to Colonial Williamsburg are frequently bored. This is a neutral observation and not meant to be critical. People at Williamsburg begin to wear a glazed look, children tire, husbands and wives squabble, older people begin to pat their clothes, and everybody starts to pick on the workers. They argue with guides, bully the waitresses, comment on high prices to salespeople, and doubt the reality of what they are being told.[4]

There is certainly a problem here, and there are two ways to analyze it. One way is to see boredom itself as the problem, and then to treat it by using technological means to "glitz up" outdoor history exhibitions in an attempt to accommodate the limited attention spans we normally attribute to museum visitors. Another is to see visitor boredom as a symptom of a deeper problem, namely the lack of an adequately articulated tie between past and present in the interpretations whose irrelevance brings on boredom. This second argument says that these exhibitions are more than just boring; Leone argues that by failing to discuss the relationship between past and present in a direct and well-informed way, some outdoor history museum interpretations project present-day social inequalities onto the past, thus creating interpretations that, in turn, allow the present-as-past to serve as a precedent—and a justification—for the continued production of these inequalities in the present. The mechanism that allows this to happen is a failure to provide visitors with a way to distinguish just what parts of the present are being projected onto the past. The result is interpretations of the past that, rather than delivering a trip back in time, actually serve to enmesh people more deeply in the social structures of the present.

Leone's discussion of Williamsburg's reproduction of a late-twentieth-century local social order[5] is similar to and informed by the work of Michael Wallace,[6] who has made a careful study of the ways in which history-museum exhibitions are often a function of the interests of patrons and clients, the reluctance of curators to create scandal, and the whimsy of founders. Thus, Historic Deerfield suffers from the anti-Communist bias of its founding couple, Colonial Williamsburg from the Rockefellers' early sense of what America needed from eighteenth-century history, and the Smithsonian Institution from donors whose intentions had to be listened to. This all means that when studying any museum exhibition, the first thing we need to know, not the last, is the relationship between that exhibition and its political and economic setting.

There are several key points to this position. First, stories about the past are structured by contemporary relationships among the groups directly affected by those stories. Second, this structure is ideological. That is, the story often misrepresents the roots of the conditions in which these groups currently live. Third, unless the structure or ideology is seen, the story serves to perpetuate the status quo rather than to illuminate its inequalities. Fourth, it is only by making these relationships visible that awareness or consciousness can be raised to a level that would support a discussion of the politics that are the actual determinant of a museum's story about the past.

Potter's extension of Leone's analysis is an examination of the epistemology of outdoor history museums, that is, the ways of knowing that link (or fail to link) interpreters to visitors in these places. On the one hand, outdoor history museums can encourage visitors to ask questions that cannot reasonably be answered or to draw unsupportable conclusions. In the total envelopment of an outdoor history museum, visitors are prompted to ask things such as whether or not the costumed interpreters sound like eighteenth-century people, or they are tempted to conclude that a nineteenth-century museum village or a dramatic reenactment of a seventeenth-century event is "very realistic." Obviously, outdoor history museums are filled with unverifiable assumptions, things that can never be learned from the historical record, but which must be accounted for in some way. All these "answers" to questions never asked make places such as Williamsburg *seem* very real. At the same time, it is impossible for anybody to judge the realism of a place such as Williamsburg; no visitor is old enough to have an adequate frame of reference. This conundrum is actually another side of the often unwitting reproduction of the present; when people say a depiction of eighteenth-century life is realistic, they are actually saying that it matches their expectations. The more realistic an exhibition seems, the more it confirms preconceptions, and the less likely it is to teach people about the past.

A further conundrum exists in the case of first-person costumed interpretation in which visitors have no way to get useful answers to certain important questions. A costumed worker, in character, can tell visitors that he learned how to build a tobacco barn from his father, but such a worker cannot tell a visitor how to conduct research into tobacco farming—which is more or less how the interpreter knows what he knows. The interpreter is empowered, and the visitor is left with nothing to do but listen. Rather than encouraging further questioning, reflection, study, and investigation, many outdoor history museums foreclose these activities by attempting to provide visitors with all the answers. Interaction with costumed interpreters notwithstanding, these museum settings encourage visitor passivity, which makes visitors all the more susceptible to whatever biases are inadvertently built into the interpretation and the interpretive environment.

INTERESTS AND THE INCEPTION OF ARCHAEOLOGY IN PUBLIC IN ANNAPOLIS

In the previous section we criticized history museums that hide their origins and authorship. In this section we will discuss the circumstances attendant to the creation of Archaeology in Public in Annapolis, the archaeological and interpretive program that surrounds the interpretive fragments we present later on. The most effective format for this discussion is a consideration of the interests of the key principals.

There is one central relationship around which this discussion will be based. In 1981, the chair of Historic Annapolis, Inc. (now the Historic Annapolis Foundation, or HAF) approached the Department of Anthropology at the University of Maryland, College Park, with an invitation to initiate a long-term, citywide archaeological project, to be jointly sponsored by the two institutions. This invitation, offered by Mrs. J.M.P. (St. Clair) Wright, was accepted by Leone. As is the case in any agreement, each party to the founding of Archaeology in Public in Annapolis entered the partnership with a particular set of interests.

The interests of HAF in having an archaeological project were at least twofold. To begin, Wright's invitation was based on a strongly positivist understanding of archaeology. According to this view, archaeology is one technique for producing scientifically verified facts about the past. HAF was very interested in adding a collection of archaeological facts to its Preservation Data Bank, a multidisciplinary collection of maps, photographs, architectural survey data, and social history data of many kinds. In HAF's view of the world, facts gathered through research are the basis of authority, and a serious, well-funded archaeological project represented the ability to control an entire body of facts. In addition, there is the possibility that HAF anticipated some public-relations benefits from sponsoring an archaeological project. On the one hand, such a project enhances HAF's credentials as a scholarly organization, which, in the eyes of HAF, confers increased legitimacy. On the other hand, HAF takes a variety of unpopular public stands, and Wright may have seen archaeology as a way of softening or improving the organization's image, given the popularity of archaeology with the public.

Archaeological data and a positive public image were certainly products Leone was prepared to deliver, but the chance to produce them was not the reason he accepted Wright's invitation. Leone's principal interests were to undertake an archaeological study, inspired by Lukacs,[7] of the roots of modern capitalism and to create a program of archaeological interpretation that could serve as an antidote to the things he had discovered during the course of his ethnographic analyses of outdoor history museums, undertaken from a Marxist perspective.

As a political and mercantile center in the eighteenth century, Annapolis clearly held the potential to serve as the focus for a study of early capitalism, and this potential was enhanced by the city's relative intactness, stemming from a long period of commercial and industrial inactivity that spanned the entire nineteenth century and the first half of the twentieth century. In short, Leone's archaeological goal was, and is, to create the economic underpinning for James Deetz's work on the Georgian Order.[8] Stated another way, Leone sees the Georgian Order as the order of merchant capitalism.[9]

On the interpretive side, Leone was attracted by the city's history of historical interpretation, and by the large number of visitors who could be attracted to archaeological sites located in the city's historic district. To Leone, a long-term project in Annapolis represented the chance to create an alternative to the interpretive strategy used by traditional outdoor history museums. It also provided an opportunity to focus on how capitalism itself creates and uses historical interpretations. Specifically, he wanted to create an interpretation that said something about the roots of modern life, that highlighted (rather than hid) the process of creating the past, and that allowed participants to have a voice once they understood the epistemology of interpreting the past. Leone was eager to offer visitors the chance to ask questions, to discuss interpretations with interpreters on a more or less equal footing, to challenge the authorial voice inside any interpretation, and ultimately to take some control over their own consumption of historical information. In other words, Leone's goal was to experiment with the idea of museum programming as social action. At the very least, Leone reasoned, such a program would be free from the visitor boredom he had identified at places such as Colonial Williamsburg. The best possible result would be a visitor who was able to replace his or her boredom with a better understanding of his or her own interests and of the degree to which currently available presentations of the past contribute to or thwart the achievement of those interests. Such a visitor would have the ability to go to a place such as Williamsburg, take it apart, and regain some measure of control over what he or she learned there.

While these two sets of interests, Wright's and Leone's, are not identical, neither are they diametrically opposed. Rather, they have oscillated between compatibility and competition. Compatibility requires little comment, but in the sections that follow, some reference will be made to the circumstances under which the two principal partners in Archaeology in Public in Annapolis have operated with competing interests.

ETHNOGRAPHIC ANALYSIS AND "THE PROBLEM"

In the previous section, we discussed Archaeology in Public in Annapolis as a solution to a problem within outdoor history museums. As much as that is the case, the project was also created to solve a particular social and historical problem in contemporary Annapolis. That problem is the focus of this section.

The starting point for discussing contemporary Annapolis is Leone's initial reaction to the city. This set of observations was informed both by Leone's ethnographic research in outdoor history museums and by his membership in the same general social, cultural, and economic categories as both the producers and consumers of historical interpretations in Annapolis. We will follow this set of observations with the main points of Potter's ethnographic analysis of the creation and use of history in Annapolis.[10]

There are several parts to Leone's initial impression of Annapolis as it presents itself as an educational setting. He found that members of minority groups and other historically disenfranchised people are virtually unrepresented in public presentations of Annapolis history. At the same time, however, he found no particular local objection to this state of affairs. This lack of protest, in turn, pointed up a more profound flaw in the history lesson available for visitors to Annapolis. African Americans do not protest their exclusion from mainstream versions of history in Annapolis, because African American history is treated as separate from European American history. Furthermore, history, as it is presented in Annapolis, is fragmented along almost every possible temporal, cultural, or institutional line. The result of this fragmentation of history is that in a city that describes itself as historically minded, there is nowhere available a coherent version of Annapolis history. Instead of a coherent history, one is presented with the impression that history is simply something one "picks up," as if by osmosis, through close physical contact with the aesthetically pleasing material culture left behind by wealthy white social and political leaders of the Revolutionary era. From this set of materials and interpretations the most one can learn is "good taste." We argue that this is not nearly enough. In short, Leone found himself frustrated when, as a visitor to Annapolis, he was unable to locate an interpretation that put the city's various pieces together. He was also frustrated by his inability to find anything that functioned as a tie between past and present other than the good taste exercised by the city's historic-preservation movement or anything to explain what was to be learned from the past. Thus, in our opinion, people who want to learn about the past in a sophisticated way are generally unable to do so in Annapolis.

In addition, there was the issue of commercial history. When Leone began his work with Historic Annapolis in 1981, he learned that during the eighteenth century, Annapolis had been a commercial center.[11] Its business included shipping, crafts, trading, and speculation. Given this, Leone was intrigued by his discovery that there was relatively little commercial history on public display. Instead of commercial history he found that the city was portrayed principally as a political center with an administrative core and a gentry who lived in the city for political and social reasons rather than economic reasons.

In 1982 Leone invited Potter to join Archaeology in Public in Annapolis. Specifically, Leone offered Potter the chance to conduct the ethnographic and historical study of the creation and use of history in Annapolis that ultimately served as the basis for Potter's Ph.D. thesis in the Department of Anthropology at Brown University. In addition to studying modern social and political life and the performance of historical interpretations as a participant observer, Potter examined a hundred years' worth of historical monographs, guidebooks, picture books, and other historical presentations.[12]

Potter begins his analysis by examining the political fact that Annapolis today is the capital of Maryland, the seat of Anne Arundel County, and the home of the United States Naval Academy, to name three of the city's key institutions. In addition, it is a destination for over four million tourists each year, and these visitors are interested in history, yachting, and the naval academy, among other things. Annapolis history, as presented in tours, guidebooks, and other media, seems to be composed of a series of discrete events: the city was settled in about 1650; it was named capital of Maryland in 1694; Annapolis served as the capital of the United States for eight months in 1783 and 1784 (during which time Washington resigned his commission as commander of the Continental Army to the Continental Congress and the Treaty of Paris was ratified by the Congress); the city's harbor was eclipsed by Baltimore's around 1800; the United States Naval Academy was founded in 1845; John Paul Jones was buried under the academy's chapel in 1906; the Historic Annapolis Foundation was established in 1952. One of the main points of Potter's analysis is that there is a series of unacknowledged connections among these events, and between these events and contemporary Annapolis. The key concept here is identity, and in particular the processes by which identity is established by individuals and by communities.

Potter argues that Annapolis has suffered from an identity crisis for over three hundred years. The city has never had a central extractive, agricultural, or industrial pursuit that ties Annapolitans to the local area through a set of productive relationships. Rather, Annapolis has for over three hundred years made a business of inviting individuals and institutions into the city as a way of supporting itself. The capital of Maryland was moved from St. Mary's City to this area after a twenty-year campaign undertaken by local residents. A similar effort preceded the establishment of the naval academy. And today Annapolis works hard to lure pleasure boaters and other tourists. One piece of evidence suggesting that identity is at stake here, and not just economic survival, is an interesting connection among all three of these invitations: each one has attracted, seemingly by design, a set of participants who are culturally sophisticated and connected to the water. This point is self-evident with regard to yachting and the naval academy (bearing in mind the status conferred by a military career in the nineteenth century). As for state (or colonial) government, it is important to remember that for the first century of Annapolis's existence as the capital of Maryland, the main entrance to the city was its harbor rather than a roadway; many people traveling to Annapolis on state business came by water.

In addition to these successful invitations, Annapolis has tried to attract outsiders who have, in the end, decided *not* to come. After serving as one of nearly a dozen eighteenth-century capitals of the United States, Annapolis offered itself, unsuccessfully, as a permanent national capital. Similarly, local leaders attempted to attract industrial development, again unsuccessfully, at the end of the nineteenth century. The point is that a central thread in Annapolis history is a series of invitations that have been extended to various individuals and institutions.

Of course, the Annapolitans who issued these various invitations have hoped for their acceptance; periodic influxes of outsiders have clearly meant economic survival for the city. However, survival has come at a cost. There are two ways to think about this cost. In a city that depends on outsiders, and is in many ways made up of outsiders and transients of various kinds, the insider/outsider dichotomy is important to maintain but difficult to establish. More pragmatically, the problem Annapolis faces, and has faced since the 1600s, is finding ways to extract as much as it can from its visitors while relinquishing as little of its own authority as possible. Less ominously, Annapolitans have always had to be on guard to make sure that the actions of their "guests" have not impaired the city's ability to continue attracting outsiders.

The complex issue of insider identity and visitor control has been dealt with in a variety of ways over the years by Annapolis and its local institutions. A good example of this may be found in preservation-based historical interpretations. These accounts constitute a sophisticated set of ways to discuss and deal with insider identity and visitor control.

To take one case, one of the most striking cleavages in popular presentations of Annapolis history is the separation between the city and the naval academy. There are all kinds of political, economic, social, and even territorial connections between the two, but both city and academy portray themselves as historically unconnected. Of course, the principal connection is the city's initial wooing of the academy, followed by the city's subsequent acquiescence to the academy in a wide variety of matters, including several dramatic expansions of the academy into the city. The academy does not present a coherent history of its relationship with the city because it prefers to avoid portraying itself as a threatening neighbor. And the city does not present a coherent history of the relationship because it is reluctant to provide a precedent that could be used by the academy as a basis for continuing its domination over the city. So both city and academy attempt to protect their interests by contributing to the fragmentation of history in Annapolis.

We have discussed elsewhere one of the ways in which Annapolis attempts to use history to control contemporary visitor behavior.[13] Our primary case study deals with the ways in which Annapolis histories depict George Washington. For at least the last sixty years, if not longer, most versions of Annapolis history paint a very specific picture of George Washington and his more than twenty visits to the city. A focus on the social and domestic aspects of these visits makes Washington appear almost as if he were a twentieth-century tourist in Annapolis, and we have argued that these portrayals are intended to provide a model for present-day visitor behavior. Not only do these histories emphasize Washington's wealth and sophistication, they pay particular attention to one key trait: his deference to local authority, which is precisely the attitude Annapolis wants most to see in current visitors, both individuals and institutions. Thus the city's use of history is a specific wish for the resolution of today's problems, a wish that has been projected onto the past. This process of projection does not misrepresent the past; it selects a particular part of the past for contemporary political reasons.

Finally, there is the preservation movement itself. We have identified and corroborated an attitude that lies at the center of the local preservation movement. According to that attitude, history is essentially a matter of taste. Historic preservation aims to recover and display the best and the most beautiful. More importantly, the ability to discern these qualities is seen as limited to a select few. These select few conduct painstaking and arcane research, the results of which are put on display for a public that is intended to learn simply by being in the presence of accurately recaptured eighteenth-century taste. This is essentially Leone's reading. Potter's analysis adds another level of complexity.

The historic-preservation movement in Annapolis is composed, for the most part, of outsiders and/or recent arrivals. These spouses of naval officers (both active and retired) and defense-industry executives are faced with the same problem as anyone else in Annapolis: finding a way to form a connection to the local area. What makes the preservation movement so fascinating is that it represents the largely successful attempt of a modern group of transients to establish a claim to localness by curating the buildings left behind by a previous generation of transients. Of all the eighteenth-century heroes celebrated by historic house museums in Annapolis, few were really Annapolitans, and none stayed in the city for very long after the Revolution. Yet the houses (and gardens) left behind by men such as William Paca, Samuel Chase, Mathias Hammond, and even Charles Carroll of Carrollton are the crown jewels of the local preservation movement. In some cases, the interpretations attached to these buildings today ("come celebrate Christmas at Mr. Paca's house") almost seem to suggest that Mr. Paca will be singing carols along with the guests. Furthermore, the interpretive strategy of concentrating on the late eighteenth century by ignoring the nineteenth and twentieth centuries promotes the bizarre image of Annapolis's eighteenth-century worthies stopping on their way out of town to hand their front door keys to the various docents who now open those houses to the public. The culmination of this process is the occasional action or piece of interpretation that draws a subtle parallel between eighteenth-century heroes and their twentieth-century champions.

Our point here is that it is difficult for members of any ethnic group or social class to learn much about the past in Annapolis on account of the ideological business that is currently being conducted in Annapolis's presentations of the past. The city and the naval academy pretend they have no joint past in order to preserve the fiction of independence. The city tries to use stories about Washington to keep tourists at bay. And some members of the preservation movement attempt to translate a self-proclaimed special relationship with the past into legitimacy as Annapolis insiders. In the final analysis, this sophisticated fighting with history has something to do with the past and everything to do with contemporary politics and power relations. This ideologically charged swirl of historical fragments—which is in no way unique to Annapolis—is at once the backdrop for Archaeology in Public in Annapolis *and* the problem that the project was designed to address.

ARCHAEOLOGY IN PUBLIC IN ANNAPOLIS

Archaeology in Public in Annapolis consists of a three-part program for archaeological practice. The three parts are *ethnography,* intended to isolate significant aspects of late-twentieth-century ideology, *archaeological analysis,* intended to illuminate the historical roots of present-day ideological structures, and *public performance* of archaeological techniques and findings, intended to provide the local community with a new line of evidence about aspects of late-twentieth-century life that are usually left unquestioned. The basic point, drawn from critical theory,[14] is that if the structures of everyday life, also called ideology, are shown to have histories and origins, then knowing this may serve as the basis for the self-emancipation of those normally held in check, often unawares, by ideological structures. At the very least, this approach to history education attempts to inspire, and then listen to, the voices of persons normally silenced by the process of putting history on display.

In 1982, in an effort to create an effective public program, Leone enlisted the aid of Philip Arnoult, director of the Theatre Project of Baltimore and also the producer of Baltimore Voices, a widely acclaimed neighborhood history project. Working with Leone (and under the auspices of a grant to Leone from the National Endowment for the Humanities), Arnoult created a three-part archaeologically based visitor experience, known collectively as Archaeology in Public in Annapolis. The three components of this experience are a twenty-minute, twelve-projector, multiple-screen audiovisual production, a twenty-minute site tour delivered by a working archaeologist, and a twenty-four-page guidebook that contains a two-hour self-guided archaeological walking tour of Annapolis. The audiovisual production has been transferred to videotape, which reduces its impact but increases the ease with which it can be shown. Archaeological site tours have been created for seven different sites, and have been given to over fifty thousand visitors since 1982. These site tours, all designed by Arnoult, are clearly the most successful aspect of Archaeology in Public in Annapolis. Finally, the guidebook was published in late 1984, and an initial printing of two thousand copies sold out in less than two years. The book was reprinted in 1989. In the four subsections that follow, we will discuss the audience for Archaeology in Public, and then each of our three interpretive products.

The Audience

It is easy to see the importance of understanding the audience when presenting a program called Archaeology in *Public*. We have always envisioned an audience composed of both residents of and visitors to Annapolis, and this dichotomy is in fact significant. During the first several seasons of Archaeology in Public in Annapolis, our biggest concern with the audience was getting one, principally to satisfy the Maryland Humanities Council (MHC), a major financial sponsor, which did not fund our archaeological research but rather the public performance of humanistic knowledge, which we defined as archaeological method. We quickly concentrated on attracting the audience that was most readily available in large numbers, which in Annapolis was tourists.

In subsequent years, we have paid increasing attention to the local part of our audience. Our open archaeological sites have been located farther and farther away from the core tourist areas, and the content of our site tours has become less generic, more focused on the specifics of Annapolis history, and more clearly tied to present-day social and political issues. The best example of this move away from a strictly tourist audience is our first full-scale public program on an African American site, which took place in 1990.

As for the actual composition of our audience, we have some reliable data. To satisfy a requirement of the MHC, we began distributing a visitor evaluation form at our open sites in 1982. From those forms, filled out by over a thousand visitors, we have been able to construct a profile of the "typical" visitor. He or she lives more than forty miles from Annapolis (47.5 percent do), is on a day-trip (58.8 percent are), and is visiting the site with his or her family (60 percent are). While we did not ask visitors to indicate their race, the vast majority of Archaeology in Public in Annapolis visitors are European American—in a city whose population is one-third African American. 12.5 percent of the site visitors who filled out evaluation forms were Annapolitans, and given the number of "regulars" and other local people who chose not to fill out forms because they did not consider themselves tourists, it is reasonable to claim a fairly sizeable local audience even at sites in the tourist areas of the city. As we have noted, we anticipate that our audiences will contain increasing percentages of local people and fewer white middle-class tourists as we move deeper into the city and away from Main Street and the waterfront.

The Audiovisual Production

Arnoult conceived of the audiovisual production as a visitor's introduction to Archaeology in Public in Annapolis. It is entitled *Annapolis: Reflections from the Age of Reason* and was designed and produced by Telesis, Inc., of Baltimore. Telesis adapted a script by Leone and Potter, added background music, and illustrated the script with over 450 slides (shot by photograper Howard Ehrenfeld), shown by twelve projectors on a thirty-foot-wide screen. The production focuses on archaeological finds, as well as all kinds of eighteenth-century material culture that has survived in Annapolis, including museum pieces, the historic house museums in which these pieces are displayed, and the formal gardens that surround the historic houses. At one level, eighteenth-century works of art are presented in a production that is itself a work of art. But aesthetics are not the point of *Annapolis: Reflections from the Age of Reason*. Rather, the audiovisual production attempts to replace aesthetics with economics; its goal is to demonstrate one way of looking below the surface of eighteenth-century material culture to see the role it played in fostering, legitimating, naturalizing, and ultimately hiding the effects of capitalism in the eighteenth century.

At the conference for which this essay was originally written, Leone screened the videotape version of the audiovisual production. For obvious reasons it is impossible to duplicate that experience between the covers of a book. An abridged version of the script for *Annapolis: Reflections from the Age of Reason*[15] is presented as Appendix A. Here we will discuss briefly the argument of the production.

The basic tactic of the audiovisual production is to begin by showing patterns in a wide range of eighteenth-century material culture, and then to argue that these patterns both reflect *and taught* important social and economic ideas of the time. The production asserts that "more than a matter of aesthetics, the Georgian home ordered the lives of its inhabitants." Later we suggest that "facades, floor plans, place settings, gardens, [and] greenhouses . . . witness a search for order in nature and in society, but actually they reveal an age which articulated an order and placed it on nature." Then we ask, "How was this order put to use?" Our answer is that the range of material culture patterns called the Georgian Order are not just stylistic; they are also the principles used by capitalists to organize *and naturalize* the industrial workplace. We explain the need for the audiovisual production by saying that "the idea that nature, society, and individuals can be made orderly and profitable has become so deeply ingrained in us that it is hard for us to judge or challenge this concept." The production is our attempt to describe the exploitative aspect of a profit-making economy, and we hope it encourages visitors to think more deeply about aspects of daily life today that we all normally take for granted.

Site Tours

Arnoult intended the audiovisual production to be an introduction to Annapolis and its archaeology. In the ideal visitor experience, it would be followed by a visit to a working archaeological site, where a dialogue would be possible. Site tours have been the most successful part of Archaeology in Public in Annapolis, at least in terms of the number of tours that have been created and the size of their audiences. The technical aspects of these site tours as well as their specific contents have been discussed extensively elsewhere,[16] and here they will be discussed only in terms of their relationship to the other components of Archaeology in Public.

The site tours have a distinctive feeling and two main functions. On the side of function, each Archaeology in Public site tour contains a description of archaeological techniques, a topic in which visitors are quite interested. By making our techniques and our epistemology available to the public, we begin the process of enfranchisement, a process which ends—in the ideal case—with visitors taking control of their own learning about the past. This attention to teaching visitors how we know what we know is intended as an alternative to the epistemologies we have identified in outdoor history museum settings.

Also on the side of function, each tour contains an argument that links some piece of the archaeological record with some piece of late-twentieth-century life and ideology. The 1983 Victualling Warehouse site tour, presented at the location of an eighteenth-century commercial property, discussed the possibility that Annapolis's recent commercial rebirth might create an interest in commercial history, a topic largely ignored at the level of popular interpretations. The 1985 State

House Inn tour focused on archaeologically discovered alterations to Annapolis's unique street plan as a way of discussing the city's largest architectural anomaly of all, the campus of the United States Naval Academy. This discussion of landscape and architecture was then used as a way of examining the ways in which the city and the academy use history to define their relationship with each other. Finally, in 1986 at the Main Street Site, we presented a tour about tourism to tourists. As a way of demonstrating that any version of history has a purpose, we delivered our hypothesis about George Washington as a model tourist at a site that Washington is said to have visited and which, more importantly, contained artifactual evidence of the various eighteenth- and nineteenth-century capitalist restructurings of daily life that eventually gave rise to the ideas of vacationing and tourism. These three brief descriptions of themes are clearly oversimplifications, but they give a good idea of what we have attempted to do in our site tours.

In terms of feeling, the site tours are all delivered by working archaeologists who are in the midst of recovering the data they are discussing. This gives Archaeology in Public guides somewhat more authority over their subject matter than most traditional guides have, but at the same time it allows visitors to ask a much wider variety of questions than they are normally able to. On a site tour, visitors are witnesses to *and participants in* the creation of historical knowledge. Importantly, all guides present their conclusions as tentative, and invite comments and questions from site visitors. Furthermore, the technical archaeological parts of the tour were designed explicitly to provide visitors with the necessary concepts and vocabulary to enter into a moderately sophisticated dialogue with their guides, if they choose to do so. Unlike the audiovisual production, to which one cannot respond, the site tours are intended to encourage a dialogue between visitors and archaeologists. A further hope is that our visitors will be able to use the concepts we teach them to take apart, question, and challenge other presentations of the past.

Of course, we have no way of knowing whether or not we have achieved this goal; we cannot tag along with our site visitors next summer when they visit Colonial Williamsburg or Old Sturbridge Village. However, we do sample visitor response to each of our tours by means of a one-page evaluation form.[17] The form is designed to collect data on audience demographics, impressions of the quality of the tour's presentation, interest in other interpretive venues and media, and our success in communicating the main point of each tour.

Visitor evaluations of tour quality, and in particular of the clarity with which information and interpretations are presented, have been uniformly positive. More important, however, is the issue of our success at showing people how to think of archaeological data as meaningful to contemporary life. To measure the success of our tours at achieving this goal we have used a series of short-answer questions such as "What did you learn about archaeology that you did not know before you visited the site?" and "What connection do you see between this site and everyday life today?" Evaluation forms had between one and three of these short-answer questions, and each question was answered by between seventy and eighty percent of the people filling out forms. The willingness of visitors to spend five or ten minutes to comment on a fifteen- or twenty-minute site tour and the responsiveness they show in their answers suggests that we have encouraged them to think seriously about historical interpretation and to enter into a dialogue with us.

Analyzing the responses to short-answer questions is a complicated enterprise, but several patterns have emerged. Some visitors learned only what they came to the site expecting to learn, namely specific details about archaeological techniques and findings. Other visitors seem to have expanded their understanding of archaeology, learning, for example, that archaeologists dig to answer questions, not just to find artifacts. Yet another category of responses includes those that show visitors gaining an understanding that archaeology produces results that directly discuss late-twentieth-century society. Some paradoxical responses come from people who take our data and use it to support some of the very ideas we are trying to challenge with our interpretive program. For example, some visitors have learned—though we have never tried to teach—that the present is an inevitable, evolutionary improvement over life in the past. Visitors learned this despite our intention to argue that historical change did not, and social change today does not, lie beyond human interests and human agency.[18] In sum, we are prepared to claim some success in our overall educational goals while acknowledging the tenacity and embeddedness of the ideologies we seek to explore, discuss, and challenge.

The Guidebook

Entitled *Archaeological Annapolis,* the guidebook was designed to be the third and final component in the two-hour Archaeology in Public in Annapolis experience. The book guides a reader around the city to eight spots, each of which is given a five-hundred-word essay and a selection of photographs showing how the appearance of that spot has changed over the last hundred years. Two of the eight guidebook essays appear as Appendices B and C. Each essay is a mild deconstruction that attempts to show that as one peels back the layers, either archaeological or architectural, one can uncover a sequence of different attitudes about how to construct the past and how to use it. In short, the essays attempt to examine the history of historical thinking in Annapolis while encouraging readers to do the same in Annapolis and elsewhere. On the one hand, we hope to inspire in our readers some degree of relativism when it comes to presentations of the past, while on the other hand, we attempt to teach people how to take apart complex historical presentations for themselves. With this tool, people can begin to take some control over their own education.

The book was sold in local bookstores, in various museum shops, and at one of our open archaeological sites. It seems to have been popular; its first printing sold out in a little more than a year. However, we have no good way of knowing what the book meant to its readers. We enclosed a one-page evaluation form, complete with postage, with the first several hundred copies that were sold, but we received fewer than a dozen responses. Thus, we do not know whether or not *Archaeological Annapolis* has achieved its goal of enfranchising or empowering the consumers of historical interpretations.

HAVE WE MADE A DIFFERENCE?

So far we have discussed the ideas that lie behind Archaeology in Public in Annapolis, and we have described several of the project's interpretive pieces. The obvious and necessary question is: Have we made a difference?

To restate a point we made at the outset of this essay, the difference we hope to make in Annapolis sets our program apart from most of the others described in this volume. Most of the programs reported on here assume two things: an effectively operating local history-making process, and a community or a segment of a community that has been denied access to that process. In Annapolis we have backed up a step to question not just differential access to the history-making process, but the effectiveness of the process itself. We hope to open up a distinctly multivocal discourse in which the discussion, creation, and use of history may help people to identify, define, and understand the

communities in which they live, all of which are situated in and constituted by modern capitalism. This is the difference we hope to make.

This goal may be thought of in terms of what Habermas calls
"discursive will formation."[19] There are two parts to this concept, as
Habermas defines it. First, for discursive will formation to take place,
there must be an ideal speech situation, that is, the possibility of
speech or discourse that is unconstrained by political preconditions.
Second, the discourse that takes place in such situations is a process
from which truth can emerge. For Habermas, truth is equated with
rationality, as long as rationality remains untainted by misidentified
interests, for example the economic interests of a small segment of
society presented as the patriotic interests of society at large.

What we have challenged in Annapolis is a series of seemingly
neutral historical interpretations that are actually discourses on power
and authority, discourses that are sometimes aimed directly at the
consumers of these interpretations. The careful avoidance of a joint
history by the city and the United States Naval Academy is one example of this, but the most striking examples are the historic-preservation
movement in general and the city's various interpretations of George
Washington in particular. Both of these interpretations tend to empower the interpreters at the expense of the audience. Given this, the
question becomes, does Archaeology in Public in Annapolis serve to
replace this unequal dialogue with the ideal speech situation discussed
by Habermas? Or, asked slightly more pejoratively, does Archaeology
in Public simply replace one overempowered interpretation with
another?

These questions, which turn on the issue of authoritarianism,
have a complex and ultimately inconclusive answer. The first part of
the answer is that our intention is to offer our interpretations as
hypotheses or hunches. And, happily, few members of our various
audiences take our interpretations as certainties, which we have
learned both through direct experience and from visitor evaluations.
However, no matter what our texts may say, the provisional quality of
our interpretations is difficult to translate into our several interpretive
media.

This stance is easier to adopt and maintain in our site tours,
which have always been understood as meetings rather than performances. In fact, some visitors have told us that we are flat-out wrong
in our interpretations; this clearly demonstrates to us a degree of
enfranchisement.[20] In addition to talking to us by filling out evaluation forms, visitors frequently interact on site with Archaeology in

Public interpreters. Many want more information. Some want to share their own archaeological knowledge or experience with us. A few will challenge an interpreter and push an idea back and forth. Never has a site tour even come close to generating controversy. Perhaps this is because our predominantly European American, middle-class audience does not feel particularly disadvantaged by the history-making process. There are, however, segments of society who *do* feel that history is often a weapon used against them. In particular, we began extending Archaeology in Public in Annapolis into the African American community with a field season that ran from May through September 1990.[21] On several occasions, African Americans have become very upset with aspects of our interpretations of their histories. We see this not as a failure on our part but rather as important data on the local community *and* as a vindication of our use of critical theory. With African American audiences we have been successful at encouraging a multivocal discourse over the meanings of history. Of course, we want this discourse to continue, and we are committed to listening to this dialogue as carefully as we look at the layers of soil we excavate. In turn, now that we have successfully initiated a serious and often emotionally charged historical dialogue, we can look again at our previous work and attempt to understand the meaning of the silence and politeness that were the usual responses to our site tours.

Clearly, it is easier to initiate and sustain discourse in a face-to-face site tour or public talk than it is to encourage dialogue by means of most other interpretive media. Both the audiovisual production and the guidebook were designed by media professionals, including editors, whose reputations depend on delivering products that appear polished and authoritative. This polish may well inhibit discourse.

In addition to the media used to present our messages, we need to acknowledge the categories used to present the material, particularly in the audiovisual presentation. The nouns, the passive voice, the technical wording, the order of the categories may, like ordinary history or ordinary prehistoric archaeology, impose an order that is not actually there "in" the data. The separations among material domains are quite artificial: archaeology, architecture, music, landscape, and decorative arts are all reified categories that empower professional elites whose existence is guaranteed by terminology, special knowledge, and criteria for membership. While our interpretations clearly contribute to the maintenance of the professions from which they come, they also juxtapose domains of material culture and society that are normally kept separate and made noncomparable. If they inspire the same kind of deconstructive creativity on the part of our audiences, then our audiences can do the job of replacing us. Furthermore, neither the audiovisual production nor the guidebook has any native voices, though the audiovisual production does contain several minutes of native music, composed in Annapolis. Two points are important here. First, we are not raising the spurious issue of whether there can be a value-free presentation; the solution to the overempowerment of the interpreter's position is not to deny the existence of interests or a point of view. And second, we readily acknowledge the problem of our (or any) authorial voice and the possibility that such voices may work against the creation of an ideal speech situation.

Assuming that our interpretive media, taken in sum, are somehow able to restructure the typical outdoor history museum experience as an arena for informed and uninhibited discourse, there remains the issue of whether or not any of this makes a difference in how people think about their own society. And, if we do affect how people think, can they use their new knowledge or outlook to act differently if they want to? We have no good answers for these questions because we have no reliable way of knowing what people do after they leave one of our archaeological sites. However, we are not the only ones who think of Archaeology in Public in Annapolis in these terms. Specifically, the potential power of our interpretations, particularly the audiovisual production, helps us to understand certain reactions to it. There have been virtually incessant attempts to modify the production, led by the preservationists of HAF, some of the sponsors, and some of the professional but nonacademic historians who have seen it and who have various rights to offer comments and effect changes. At one level, the issue is academic freedom and censorship, but what makes the situation difficult to understand, and therefore quite interesting, is the disproportionate amount of critical attention directed toward the audiovisual production as opposed to our print pieces and site tours. When possible we have responded to most of the objections to the production, but we have yet to identify with any precision the agendas that lie behind these objections. The audiovisual production is a commentary on the roots of capitalism, but a mild one. We suspect that it is not so much the content of the commentary that our sponsors find controversial and threatening, but rather the simple existence of an open discussion of capitalism, presumably containing a call to the logical possibility of alternatives.

Our conclusion, for the moment at least, is that we cannot yet ask whether a discussion of capitalism makes a difference. While we have created an opportunity for some visitors to respond to us, we have not yet created an interpretive environment in which a real discussion of capitalism takes place. There are many possible answers to the questions posed by this silence. A powerful answer comes from Byron Rushing, the former director of the African Meeting House in Boston and now a state representative from Roxbury, Massachusetts. Not long ago he told Leone that African Americans want to know how and why they are here now—they want to know why there is no change for them now. White people don't want to know these things, he said. They choose to remain blind.[22]

APPENDIX A

Annapolis: Reflections from the Age of Reason (abridged)

More than just aesthetically pleasing artifacts, these pieces of our past, when seen as different parts of a single world, provide a way to understand that world.

We can begin to see the relevance of the eighteenth century to ourselves. We can see that floor plans, building facades, dishes, silverware, furniture, gardens, ornamental details of many kinds, printers' type, scientific instruments, above- and below-ground remnants may be experienced as parts of one expression, one society. In the next few minutes we'd like to suggest some ways of seeing and thinking about these architectural, artistic, and archaeological remains. We present all this as our best idea about how and why the past was organized. . . .

Chase-Lloyd House on Maryland Avenue. A superb example of Georgian architecture. Outside, a harmonious balance of geometric units. Inside, the same order reflected in the ceilings and floor plans. More than a matter of aesthetics, the Georgian home ordered the lives of its inhabitants. The functions of daily life were segregated into specific rooms.

We see order even in the place settings—with nearly identical plates, glasses, forks, chairs. People were segregated from each other both by walls and by the etiquette of each daily activity.

Is this an early manifestation of the orderly society idealized by the Age of Reason? . . .

In the 1760s, William Paca, signer of the Declaration of Independence and later governor of Maryland, designed the beautiful Paca Garden. This garden was later destroyed to make way for urban development. However, through major reclamation efforts, the garden, once described as "the most elegant in Annapolis," has been faithfully restored.

Archaeologists discovered the foundations of walls which two centuries ago surrounded the orderly geometric patterns.

Here again we ask: Is this merely design? Or was it Paca's model of the natural order, with each plant and tree in its proper place—a place assigned to it by the garden's creator? Nature subjected to reason through geometry? . . .

Facades, floor plans, place settings, gardens, greenhouses. They witness a search for order in nature and in society, but actually they reveal an age which articulated an order and placed it on nature. How was this order put to use?

The Annapolis harbor in the Golden Age. A busy port of call for hundreds of ships.

To be profitable, each voyage had to be safe—and quicker than the competition. From ancient times, segmentation of the sea's surface with celestial navigation made shipping a major source of profit, but in the 1760s, there was an advance in navigation—the invention of the chronometer, which kept Greenwich mean time at sea.

When used with nautical almanacs, the net of meridians and parallels was extended over the mariner's head, predicting the precise longitude and latitude of major stars at frequent intervals of every night of the year.

The nautical almanac greatly improved the mariner's odds for a safe, quick voyage. Is it mere coincidence that the merchants' odds of profiting from these voyages also improved?

In a town like Annapolis, where investment in city land was a speculative venture, and as great a source of wealth as slaves or farming, accurate surveying was of critical importance.

In the wilderness the need was the same—to determine precisely the size and shape of parcels to be bought, sold, farmed, developed. The end product, in both cases, was the map of segmented space—a grid of standard units of measure. This grid created an order where there had been none before, facilitating a more profitable use of land.

The second revolution, therefore, satisfies the requirements of capitalism . . . imposing order on land, the sea, and even the heavens, making land speculators, lenders, and merchant-traders successful. Conventionally, this order is thought to be discovered in nature. But it is actually imposed. . . .

In cities like Annapolis and Baltimore, businessmen and merchants were imposing their own order on the rhythms of daily life. Nothing short of a revolution was taking place—a revolution in the way time and work were calculated. In the shops and shipyards, factories and manufacturing centers where industrial America was developing, employers had discovered a new source of wealth . . . the American worker. Some were no longer paid for their skill, or for the value of the goods they produced. They were paid by the hour.

Expressing the value of a person's work by using a standard hourly wage made all work appear to be uniform. This is one major basis for our modern economy.

It is easy to see how the ideas and principles put into practice after the American Revolution continue to affect our political lives. But it is less easy to see how the parallel transformation in profit-making also continues to affect us.

The idea that nature, society, and individuals can be made orderly and profitable has become so deeply ingrained in us that it is hard for us to judge or challenge this concept.

But this was the second revolution, and the great value of a commercial city like Annapolis is not in its museumlike qualities, full of curios from a bygone age—or shadowy artifacts from an era ending—but rather as a city that preserves the roots of a modern way of life.

By studying the beginnings of our government, society, and economy, we gain for ourselves the ability to judge, to question, to choose, to plot the future.

APPENDIX B

"View up Francis Street to the State House"
(*Archaeological Annapolis,* page 5)

Photos **A, B,** and **D,** show an 18th-century streetscape—a rare scene in modern cities. Francis Street is on the right; Main Street on the left. In general, over the past 300 years, the street pattern and topography have not been altered much here or in the rest of the Historic District of Annapolis. A view like this can be especially useful if we learn how to read the many pasts visible in it. Of course, we cannot always walk around in a historic environment and pick up the lessons of the past. The buildings do not speak for themselves. Current uses and appearances of buildings control how much we can see; alterations and facades can hide history from us.

But here, despite all the changes that have taken place, you can see some features of an 18th-century city, such as streetwidth and direction, and the height of the buildings. Such streetscapes no longer exist in New York, Philadelphia, or Boston, which unlike Annapolis, grew in size by going deeper and beyond their 18th-century limits, destroying their earlier appearances.

How has this street scene changed? The State House (*center of* **A**) frequently has been visibly altered or restored.

Originally it had a smaller porch and no cellar. Its roofing has changed from copper to shingles to slate. The hilltop, graded to its present form in the late 18th century, once was the site for the city market. Later on, the site was crowded with adjoining buildings, removed in 1902 when the northwest annex was built and when the trees and statues of the present park were added. Only recently, a second retaining wall and staircases were built around the House.

Even though the scale is unchanged, the view has been subject to various tastes. Some of the individuals making the changes valued the past and others chose to ignore it. The blend of the new and the old styles gives the varied streetscape you see here. At times, the "latest fashion" in architecture meant borrowing from earlier eras. In the 1930s, and in the 1950s as well, "new" meant in the form of older models; Annapolis built public buildings in the neo-Georgian style or with false colonial fronts that often covered Victorian and Federal architecture. At other times, architects tried for a new, different look that made no pretense at restoring a previous style; this was particularly true in the 1870s and 1880s, and again in the 1950s and 1960s. Notice the Victorian chimneys on the State House (C) and the commercial buildings dressed up in Victorian taste (*right side of* A). Since 1969, the city has attempted to maintain its original periods of architecture by city ordinance.

In the small building at the base of the "V" in Main and Francis Streets (*center of* A, B, *and* D), you can see some of the continual alterations: modern-day Georgian windows with many panes, paneled woodwork, and the removal of electric signs and wires. A modern purpose sometimes determines the part of the past put on view. While in Annapolis the past remains in abundance to be read and seen, it has not always meant the same thing to each age. The reasons history is important to us are not the same reasons chosen by some past era nor will they necessarily be the ones chosen by a future one.

APPENDIX C

"Chase-Lloyd House"
(*Archaeological Annapolis,* page 17)

The Chase-Lloyd House (A) was built between 1769 and 1774 by Samuel Chase, a Maryland lawyer who signed the Declaration of Independence, and by Col. Edward Lloyd, IV, a wealthy Eastern Shore planter. (Chase sold the unfinished house to Lloyd when he couldn't afford to complete it.) These associations with well-known historical figures are only one reason why the house is of interest. The Chase-Lloyd House is also important because it became in the 1890s the first of the great Georgian mansions in Annapolis to be opened to the public.

Today the first floor of Chase-Lloyd is a museum and the top two floors are an Episcopal home for elderly women. The museum emphasizes the architecture of this house designed by William Buckland, with its ornamental plaster ceiling, and the Palladian window on the second floor landing. (The window was considered significant and was termed a "three-part window" long before guidebook writers knew to call it "Palladian.")

The Chase-Lloyd museum could have emphasized furnishings. It could have focused on 18th-century lifestyles. Or it could have been a shrine to Samuel Chase, a signer of the Declaration of the Independence. But instead it emphasizes architecture. This is the nature of all historical writing and presentation. Decisions are made about what to highlight and what to leave out. In this way history is largely a product of the circumstances in which it is written.

The opening of Chase-Lloyd in the 1890s was one of the earliest and most obvious ways that Annapolis began to present itself as a historic place. At around that same time, the city saw its first preservation movement; many guidebooks and histories, large and small, were written; and some historic celebrations took place. Buildings, institutions, and cities are not historic just because they are old; people must make a conscious decision to consider old things historically significant. Annapolis developed a sense of itself as being historic 30 years after Mt. Vernon was saved and many years before Williamsburg was rebuilt.

The 1920s and 1930s were another period of historical activity in Annapolis. Two lengthy historical guidebooks were published, the Company for the Restoration of Colonial Annapolis (which wanted to make a Williamsburg of Annapolis) was formed, and the Hammond-Harwood House (B) (directly across the street from Chase-Lloyd) was opened. Today Hammond-Harwood, a Georgian mansion, is a museum of 18th-century decorative arts, furniture, paintings, silver, and other objects.

In 1976, Historic Annapolis, Inc., opened the Wm. Paca House (C), the third of the great Annapolis mansions to become a museum. . . . The museum depicts the lifestyles of the wealthy colonial leaders in Annapolis. Paca House displays few objects owned by William Paca because many of his possessions were lost in a fire at his Wye Island estate late in the 1800s. Thus, a 19th-century fire has greatly influenced the 20th-century presentation of an 18th-century mansion.

Each of Annapolis's three important museum houses is different. Each museum has a point of view, shaped by the circumstances under which it was made historic.

NOTES

We would like to thank Ivan Karp, Christine Mullen Kreamer, and Steven D. Lavine for inviting Mark Leone to the conference at which this essay was first presented; their comments, along with discussions with various conference participants, especially Jack Tchen, have significantly improved the essay. In an attempt to rescue collaboration, media expertise, sponsorship, and authorship from the agate type at the very end of this essay, the institutions and individuals who have played key roles in the production of the interpretive materials of Archaeology in Public in Annapolis have been acknowledged in our main text and in the notes. Finally, and as noted in the essay itself, Archaeology in Public in Annapolis is jointly sponsored by the Historic Annapolis Foundation and the University of Maryland, College Park. We are grateful for the support of these institutions, and we assume full responsibility for the content of this essay.

1. Mark P. Leone and Parker B. Potter, Jr. (with editorial assistance from Donna Shoemaker), *Archaeological Annapolis: A Guide to Seeing and Understanding Three Centuries of Change* (Annapolis: Historic Annapolis, Inc. and the University of Maryland, 1984). In addition, the guidebook appears as Appendix A in Parker B. Potter, Jr., *Archaeology in Public in Annapolis: An Experiment in the Application of Critical Theory to Historical Archaeology* (Ann Arbor, Mich.: University Microfilms International, 1989). The initial publication of the guidebook was funded by the National Endowment for the Humanities; the 1989 reprint was sponsored by the Maryland Humanities Council.

2. Mark P. Leone's critique of outdoor history museums includes studies of Colonial Williamsburg ("Archaeology's Relationship to the Present and the Past," in Richard A. Gould and Michael B. Schiffer, eds., *Modern Material Culture* [New York: Academic Press, 1981]); Shakertown at Pleasant Hill ("The Relationship Between Artifacts and the Public in Outdoor History Museums," in A. M. Cantwell, J. B. Griffin, and Nan Rothschild, eds., *The Research Potential of Anthropological Museum Collections* [New York: New York Academy of Sciences, 1981]); and Sleepy Hollow Restorations ("Establishing the Meaning of Objects in Context," in Ann L. Hedlund, ed., *Perspectives on Anthropological Collections from the American Southwest,* Anthropological Research Papers, no. 40 [Tempe: Arizona State University, 1989]). See also Mark P. Leone, "Keynote Address: Sketch of a Theory for Outdoor History Museums," in *Proceedings of the 1987 Annual Meeting,* vol. 10 (Ann Arbor and Dearborn, Mich.: Association for Living Historical Farms and Agricultural Museums, 1988).

3. Potter, *Archaeology in Public in Annapolis,* 272–95.

4. Leone, "Archaeology's Relationship to the Present and the Past," 11–12.

5. Ibid., 8–9.

6. Michael Wallace, "Visiting the Past: History Museums in the United States," *Radical History Review* 25 (1981), 63–96; "Mickey Mouse History," *Radical History Review* 32 (1984), 33–57; "Reflections on the History of Historic Preservation," in Susan Porter Benson, Stephen Brier, and Roy Rosenzweig, eds., *Presenting the Past: Essays on History and the Public* (Philadelphia: Temple University Press, 1986); "The Politics of Public History," in Jo Blatti, ed., *Past Meets Present* (Washington, D.C.: Smithsonian Institution Press, 1987).

7. Georg Lukacs, "Reification and the Consciousness of the Proletariat," in *History and Class Consciousness,* trans. Rodney Livingstone (Cambridge, Mass.: MIT Press, 1971).

8. See James F. Deetz's works, including *In Small Things Forgotten* (Garden City, N.Y.: Anchor Doubleday, 1977); "Scientific Humanism and Humanistic Science: A Plea for Paradigmatic Pluralism in Historical Archaeology," in

Robert W. Neuman, ed., *Historical Archaeology of the Eastern United States: Papers from the R. J. Russell Symposium* (Baton Rouge: Louisiana State University, School of Geoscience, 1983); and "Material Culture and Worldview in Colonial Anglo-America," in Mark P. Leone and Parker B. Potter, Jr., eds., *The Recovery of Meaning: Historical Archaeology in the Eastern United States* (Washington, D.C.: Smithsonian Institution Press, 1988).

9. Mark P. Leone, "The Georgian Order as the Order of Merchant Capitalism in Annapolis, Maryland," in Mark P. Leone and Parker B. Potter, Jr., eds., *The Recovery of Meaning: Historical Archaeology in the Eastern United States* (Washington, D.C.: Smithsonian Institution Press, 1988).

10. Potter, *Archaeology in Public in Annapolis,* 82–269.

11. Edward C. Papenfuse, *In Pursuit of Profit: Annapolis Merchants in the Era of the American Revolution, 1763–1805* (Baltimore: Johns Hopkins University Press, 1976).

12. Some of the key sources include Elihu Riley, *"The Ancient City": A History of Annapolis in Maryland, 1649–1887* (Annapolis: Record Printing Office, 1887 [reprinted by the Anne Arundel–Annapolis Bicentennial Committee, 1976]); Walter B. Norris, *Annapolis: Its Colonial and Naval Story* (New York: Thomas Y. Crowell, 1925); and William O. Stevens, *Annapolis: Anne Arundel's Town* (New York: Dodd, Mead, 1937).

13. Mark P. Leone, Parker B. Potter, Jr., and Paul A. Shackel, "Toward a Critical Archaeology," *Current Anthropology* 28, no. 3 (1987), 283–302.

14. See Leone, Potter, and Shackel, "Toward a Critical Archaeology"; Raymond Geuss, *The Idea of a Critical Theory* (Cambridge: Cambridge University Press, 1981); and David Held, *Introduction to Critical Theory: Horkheimer to Habermas* (Berkeley: University of California Press, 1980).

15. The audiovisual script represents a collaborative effort among Leone, Potter, and Gary Aten of Telesis, Inc. The entire script is available as Appendix B of Potter, *Archaeology in Public in Annapolis.* The audiovisual production was funded by the National Endowment for the Humanities; the videotape transfer was funded by the Maryland Humanities Council and the Office of Tourism Development of the Maryland Department of Economic and Employment Development.

16. Parts of the 1983 Victualling Warehouse site tour are described in Mark P. Leone, "Method as Message: Interpreting the Past with the Public," *Museum News* 62, no. 1 (1983), 35–42, and also in Leone, "Establishing the Meaning of Objects in Context." The 1985 State House Inn site tour is discussed in Parker B. Potter, Jr., and Mark P. Leone, "Liberation Not Replication: Archaeology in Annapolis Analyzed," *Journal of the Washington Academy of Sciences* 76, no. 2 (1986), 97–105. The Main Street site tour is discussed in Leone, Potter, and Shackel, "Toward a Critical Archaeology," and also in Christine Hoepfner, Mark P. Leone, and Parker B. Potter, Jr., "The Preserved

Is Political: A Critical Theory Agenda for Historical Interpretations of Monuments and Sites," *ICOMOS Information* 3 (1987), 10–16. For more general discussions of the content and evaluation of Archaeology in Public in Annapolis site tours, see Potter, *Archaeology in Public in Annapolis,* 311–412; and also Parker B. Potter, Jr., and Mark P. Leone, "Archaeology in Public in Annapolis: Four Seasons, Six Sites, Seven Tours, and 32,000 Visitors," *American Archaeology* 6, no. 1 (1987), 51–61.

17. Archaeology in Public visitor evaluation is discussed extensively in Potter, *Archaeology in Public in Annapolis,* 358–412.

18. Sam Bass Warner, Jr., makes a similar observation in " 'The Ideal of Objectivity' and the Profession of History," *The Public Historian* 13, no. 2 (1991), 9–24.

19. Jürgen Habermas, *Legitimation Crisis* (London: Heinemann, 1976). See also Mark P. Leone and Parker B. Potter, Jr., "Legitimation and the Classification of Archaeological Sites," *American Antiquity* 57, no. 1 (1992).

20. In response to a tour about an eighteenth-century formal garden and the use of landscape architecture to demonstrate and justify political authority (see Mark P. Leone et al., "Power Gardens of Annapolis," *Archaeology* 42, no. 2 [1989], 34–37, for the contents of this tour) one visitor went so far as to say, "You've read too much Foucault and Girouard and not enough on eighteenth-century garden design. I recommend Maynard Mack, *The Garden and the City,* and the numerous books by John Dixon Hunt." It is obvious that this visitor knew the literature before he or she ever took our tour, but what is most important to us is that we have created an interpretation that can be challenged by the well-read person *or* by the person who wrote, "Interesting (but as far as I can tell unfounded) theorizing and rather pretentious intellectually." The author(ity) in each of us would probably not mind applause for every tour and rave reviews for every print piece and media production, but in the end, such responses privilege us and our positions, often at the expense of the education of our audiences. Generally we try to teach visitors our method first, and then the content of our interpretations. Armed with some basic tools, visitors are better equipped to accept *or reject* the conclusions we draw by using those tools. We hope that by teaching some epistemology—which can be used to argue against us—we are, in fact, able to counter some of the unequal power relations that are built into our positions as authorities and interpreters.

21. For a discussion of our first attempts at interpreting the archaeology of African American life in Annapolis, see Mark P. Leone et al., "The Constituencies for an Archaeology of African Americans in Annapolis, Maryland," in Theresa Singleton, ed., *Studies in African American Archaeology* (Charlottesville: University Press of Virginia, in press). The issue of audiences for the archaeology of African Americans is also discussed in Parker B. Potter, Jr.,

"What Is the Use of Plantation Archaeology?" *Historical Archaeology* 25, no. 3 (1991).

22. That "blindness" is expressed in the substantial number of visitor evaluation forms that show visitors using our interpretations to reinforce the exact piece of contemporary ideology we are trying to challenge. A discussion of this phenomenon may be found in Potter, *Archaeology in Public in Annapolis*, 392–93.

CHAPTER 17

Mythos, Memory, and History: African American Preservation Efforts, 1820–1990

FATH DAVIS RUFFINS

I n 1968 a major television network aired an extraordinarily popular documentary entitled *Black History: Lost, Stolen, or Strayed?* Narrated by Bill Cosby, this program sought to show the public the state of historical research and thought on African Americans. Although the documentary was already somewhat outdated at the time of its airing, the title captures the feelings that many people, Black and white, shared in the late 1960s: that the history of African Americans was simply absent—whether out of willful action on the part of some or benign neglect on the part of others.

Since the 1960s there has been a revolution in the study of African American life, history, and culture. Over the last twenty years, scholars in a variety of disciplines have enlarged and in some cases radically changed our view of the American social landscape and the fundamental role of African Americans within it. Black people were once thought to be marginal to the main story of the American past, but now we know that they are central to it. African Americans were once thought only to be reactive victims of the American experiment; we now know them to have been catalysts for change since the republic's earliest days.[1]

While the experience of every ethnic group is distinctive and deserves celebration and analysis, African Americans have a unique history within the United States. There were both Native American and occasional European slaves at some points in American history, but slavery was an overwhelmingly African American experience.[2] That enslavement has fueled a powerful debate over the fundamental civil rights and appropriate governmental relationships laid out in documents such as the Declaration of Independence, the United States Constitution, and the Constitution's Bill of Rights, to name only the most important. While conflict among ethnic groups and classes may characterize many aspects of American history, the Civil War had to be fought to resolve the issues relevant to Afro-Americans. Moreover, no other ethnic group has been victimized by state constitutional amendments denying them the right to vote and to share public facilities, as were African American people in the late-nineteenth-century South. While discrimination existed within many areas of American life against certain religious groups and people of foreign origins, at the same time segregation laws were formally enacted in many states for the specific purpose of controlling the social and political access and economic opportunities of one ethnic group: African Americans. Furthermore, the modern civil rights movement, which changed American life and has proven inspirational to activists around the world, was initiated and led by African Americans. In these ways (and in others too detailed to mention) the history of Black people is deeply intertwined with the more general history of this country. African Americans have a unique history, connected at the root with virtually all aspects of the American experience. This uniqueness should be remembered as we separate the historical experience itself from the record of its preservation.

Since the 1890s, academically trained African American historians such as W.E.B. Du Bois, Carter G. Woodson, Lorenzo Greene, and others have published works detailing this history. But because of segregation in the professions, the work of these pioneering historians was not read widely outside Black universities.[3] Since 1965, however, there has been an explosion of scholarly interest in African American topics. As evidence has mounted of the enormous complexity of that American culture, scholars in various fields have debated and worked to determine the precise elements of African American life, history, and culture. In musicology, archaeology, folklore, anthropology, literature, history and other disciplines, extraordinary volumes have been published that document the rich cultural life, complex political and social traditions, and convoluted history of African Americans. Before 1965, many academically trained historians did not believe that there were enough primary sources even to study African Americans, but since then both Black and white scholars have mined the national and university libraries and state and local history archives and unearthed new information. In other cases, scholars have developed new sources, often by eliciting oral histories and doing fieldwork.[4]

Such research has identified (or in some cases rediscovered) publications, manuscripts, letters, and other documents that for years had resided in both public and private collections. Some institutions, such as the Library of Congress and the National Archives, turned out to have important holdings. Historically Black institutions had preserved a wealth of information for decades. Scholars have recently begun to utilize Black church archives and college and university libraries, as well as family and private collections. Few of the scholars who began to tap these rich resources questioned how and why these particular materials had come to be saved.

At first glance, research materials appear to be spotty in all preservation locations. But a deeper look reveals a complex pattern of preservation. In general, historically Black colleges have some very important archival and library collections that date from the 1850s and earlier; a good example is the Moorland-Spingarn Research Center at Howard University. Some institutions, such as Hampton University, have well-known museums, and others, such as Fisk University, have important art collections. However, historically white museums—whether art museums, cultural-history museums, or natural-history museums—have either no relevant material or relatively small collections, most acquired within the past ten or fifteen years.[5] The only exceptions are a few early historical societies, such as the Pennsylvania Historical Society in Philadelphia.[6] Black museums hold by far the greatest wealth of African American material culture. Although some of these institutions are more than one hundred years old, most were founded during the 1960s and later. In short, documentary and archival materials abound, and music and oral history collections have been growing over the last fifty years, but material culture collections are recent and slim.

This brief overview suggests how uneven the preservation of African American materials has been. Although the history and culture of Blacks are deeply embedded in American life, the sense that they have been lost or stolen or have strayed remains strong, especially with the general public, to whom this new scholarship has not penetrated. This sense of loss is particularly sharp among the staffs and supporters of

Black museums, who are more aware of what might have been saved from earlier times.[7]

Though uneven, these patterns of preservation are not random, but rather reflect selectivity. That which has been preserved reflects the preservers' interpretations of what was important about the African American past. These different interpretations developed over the course of decades, under different institutional structures, and at different points in the history of particular institutions; as a result, collectors preserved certain parts of Black history and culture while leaving out other elements. Informed by collective as well as idiosyncratic interpretations of the African American past, individuals and institutions have helped shape the evidence of that past by their selective preservation efforts. This essay documents some of the types and outcomes of distinct preservation strategies through the last two centuries.

MEMORY, MYTHOS, AND HISTORY

Within all cultures, various versions of the past exist simultaneously. To better investigate the ways in which views of the past shaped preservation activities, let me suggest definitions of some terms that will help me to refer consistently to visions of the past.

The Past

What most Americans colloquially refer to as "history" is probably more accurately called "the past." By this I mean the enormous body of events and movements, debates and ideas, migrations and discoveries—in short, literally everything that happened before the present. Yet not everything has become a part of recorded history; it is impossible for every single person's life and every local, regional, national, and international event to be taken account of this way. Only some portion of these events and experiences has been actively collected and preserved; this process involves the meaningful reconstruction and analysis of the past. In this sense, all history is an interpretation of the past.

One way to think about the past as being different from history is to see historical interpretation as a snapshot of the past. In a snapshot, the photographer records what he or she thinks is interesting or important about a given scene. By including certain elements and screening out others, the photographer creates a picture of a scene. But the total scene is always much larger and more complex than any photograph. So, too, the historical interpretation of the past is made out of selections of that past by people in the present in order to help them understand both the past and the present.

Many people are deeply interested in understanding the past: their individual lives at earlier moments; the lives of their older living relatives and ancestors; their ethnic, social, or political past. While most people have some general interest in times before their own, however, only some become genealogists or Civil War buffs, and even fewer become professional historians. There are different ways of remembering and interpreting the past, using different pieces of evidence and distinct methods of recovery. All interpretations contain some validity and some distortion; all have a social reality that makes them important in the present. All interpreters of the past develop their own stories or narratives that highlight the points the interpreter finds meaningful and leaves out that which he or she finds unenlightening. Each kind of narrative mode reflects a different take on past experience.

For the purpose of this essay, three distinct types of narratives are important: *memory, mythos,* and *history.* Each mode of interpreting the past emphasizes certain kinds of evidence, and often operates in different modalities. How any one of us interprets life "when we were younger," for example, will always be different from how we interpret lives during the American Revolution. We were not alive then and do not know anyone who was, so our emotional response is always far removed from actual experience. We would have to do research in available sources to find out more about what people of the Revolutionary era said about that time; in order to do research, we have to find out what has been preserved.

Preservation efforts are crucial to understanding the past, yet preservation itself has distinct modes as well. For example, to preserve the blues canon by being a professionally recognized musician is a different form of preservation from being a collector or curator of blues records. Each form of preservation adds something meaningful to our understanding of the past (and possibly the present), yet these different modalities affect what and how we expect to learn from the past. The kind of information encoded in the musical experience of a performer is different from that of a listener. Each element in that musical equation is necessary, yet each experience is qualitatively different. In this qualitative sense, *memory* emerges from personal experience, *mythos* emerges as the symbolic/spiritual/expressive elements produced by groups of people (ethnic groups, national groups, etc.), and *history* emerges from the academic experience of professional historians and other scholars.

Memory

Memory is used here to mean the individual or collective memories of people who have lived through a set of experiences. Whether internally coherent or contradictory, the memories of those who were veterans of a particular war or participants in a singular event constitute a distinctive, personally validated version of the past. For example, those who were soldiers on both sides of the Civil War left many reminiscences of their uplifting and shattering experiences. Personal and collective memories were traditionally saved in diaries, letters, and autobiographies. Today, such memories are more typically preserved as oral history or in audio or video form. Embedded in personal testimony are the different beliefs and practices that make individuals, regions, ethnic groups, and religious groups distinctive.

Mythos

Individuals, however, refract particularistic and idiosyncratic versions of those beliefs and practices. Encompassing more than individual memory is the larger narrative, or mythos, of a people. The term *mythos* is used here to mean the "pattern of meaning and valuation expressive of the basic truths and enduring apprehensions of a people's historical experience."[8] Mythos is often expressed through a medium of high symbolism, such as poetry, the visual arts, drama, political rhetoric, or the oratory of a sermon. In the African American experience, there are both oral and written full-scale narratives as well as songs, stories, and slogans that define the elements of a mythopoetic African American past.

History

There is a third version of the past, one that is produced by academically trained scholars working within the disciplinary perspectives of history, literature, anthropology, and other related fields. Unlike the two kinds of narratives mentioned previously, history as it is produced in universities is based on certain rules about what kinds of evidence constitute proof of a particular interpretation. Scholarly histories are most often recorded in books and journal articles, which are critically reviewed for their conformance to or innovation beyond these accepted rules of evidence. These rules may or may not be linked to either personal memories or a collective mythos about the past. Western scholarship values a sense of distance, which is interpreted as objectivity. This distance generally means that academic history or ethnography is formally constructed to sound different from the personal memories and collective mythos that reside in the vernacular traditions of all cultural groups.

The Past Interpreted: Interior and Exterior Viewpoints

In addition to these three modalities—history, mythos, and memory (there are probably more)—there is the added interpretive element of points of view as socially defined within a multicultural society. The concepts of mythos, memory, and history make it evident that interior and exterior interpretations of the past are always simultaneously operative. Black Americans, like all ethnic groups, have developed various narrative versions of their past. These narratives can be called interior, in the sense that they were created by African Americans about their own experience. At the same time, there are versions of the African American past that have been developed within political, educational, religious, and media circles that communicate "American" mass cultural narratives about the African American past. While these narratives may not be wholly negative, they do include racial stereotypes. These interpretations can be called exterior in the sense that they are produced by people who are not African Americans.

This difference between interior and exterior views makes manifest the biculturality of African Americans. The notion that African Americans live in not one but two American cultures was expressed most distinctively by W.E.B. Du Bois, the noted Black scholar and activist, in his essay "Of Our Spiritual Strivings" in *The Souls of Black Folk* (1903). Du Bois wrote that within every Negro chest beat two hearts: an American one and a Negro one. This sense of duality—of intimacy with and yet distance from mainstream American culture—is an important modality to consider when looking at extant collections of African American life, history, and culture. Moreover, this cultural duality reflected the extent of segregation at the time Du Bois wrote those lines.

In addition to segregation in the public aspects of American life,

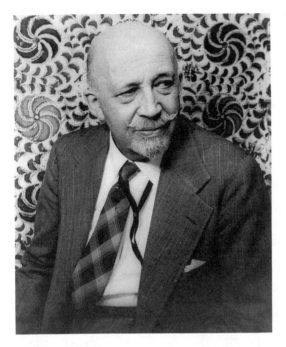

Fig. 17-1. W.E.B. Du Bois.
Photo by Carl Van Vechten,
courtesy Rose McClendon
Collection, Moorland-
Spingarn Research Center,
Howard University.

there was also a segregation of cultural mythos and history. Yet neither
the Black tradition nor the white tradition was monolithic. Over time,
generations of writers and scholars in each tradition put forth new
interpretations that in turn engendered critiques. Particularly within
African American communities, new critiques came not only from
intellectuals and scholars, but also from lay people—private collectors, self-taught historians, ministers, teachers. These groups constituted the primary audience within African American communities for
preservation activities, and they also shaped a distinctive preservation
history. Through autobiographies and biographies, through political
and religious oratory, through music and the visual arts, African
Americans have recorded their own interpretations of their past. What
all these versions share is a sense of the special destiny of African
Americans.

A SPECIAL DESTINY: INTERIOR VIEWS OF AFRICAN AMERICAN
HISTORY, 1820–1900

Collectors and curators create collections out of a complex welter of
emotions, opportunities, and resources. The life of any individual

collector helps explain the origins and inherent integrity of a personal collection. The institutional history of a museum—the interplay over time of individuals and resources within it—structures how its curators develop that museum's collections. Curators and collectors are influenced also by ideas developed by the scholars and intellectuals of their time. Through repetition, some interpretations become part of a canonical cluster of texts, stories, and songs. The individuals who organized the earliest preservation activities made their decisions within the context of specific worldviews. As private collections passed into institutions and as institutional collections passed from the hands of their creators into those of later generations, the original collecting notions may have been modified, but the broad tropes of these interpretations have remained guiding principles, influencing the formation of Black museums even to the present.

Within nineteenth-century African American communities, many internal debates were affected by the rhetoric of antislavery agitation and, in the Northern states, the quest for full civil rights. In the earliest African American newspapers (started in the 1820s) and in the Negro Convention Movement (beginning in the 1830s), publishers and political activists argued for the full emancipation of enslaved African Americans by contending that Christian charity required outlawing the fundamental inhumanity of slavery. They asserted that free African Americans deserved all the rights of other Americans because they had demonstrated their equality through their historical and literary achievements. Such an argument was a founding principle in the organization of African American literary and historical societies, the earliest of which was begun in Philadelphia in 1828.[9]

Since the free Black communities of the North and Midwest were vehemently antislavery, African American institutions there provided support for the abolitionists' work. For example, independent Black churches served as way stations on the Underground Railroad as well as centers of abolitionist argument. African American notions about the individual historical roles of Frederick Douglass and Sojourner Truth and their relationship to a wider national history coalesced into a full-scale mythos. The nineteenth-century African American mythos forged a direct expressive link between the enslaved Hebrews of the Old Testament and the enslaved Africans in America.

One of the distinctive elements of nineteenth-century African American theology was the significance of this linkage between Hebrews and African Americans. Spoken of in innumerable sermons and abolitionist campaign oratory and written about in individual "slave narratives," this special connection emphasized not only the Old Testament notion of the enslavement and deliverance of a whole people, but also contemporary Protestant millennialism. Spurred by the Great Awakenings of the eighteenth and early nineteenth centuries, African Americans connected their enslavement (and eventual freedom) with the story of Christ. Their suffering ennobled them; their history was proof that the Lord loved the humble and that the meek might yet inherit the earth. Through the sermons of great preachers such as John Jasper, the pronouncements of locally significant writers in Black newspapers, and the lectures at literary societies, many Black people heard repeated the idea that African Americans had a special destiny within the United States, and that this special destiny, so aligned with the heroism of the Hebrew children and the unforgettable sacrifice of Christ, would lead eventually to freedom.

The mythos of a special African American destiny contained within it the notion of a special social role: that of the truth-teller. In effect, African Americans would ultimately find freedom in part because they would more perfectly embody this role. Upon taking the name Sojourner Truth, Isabella van Wagener epitomized this concept.[10] She felt that her religious experiences compelled her to preach to Black and white alike about the kind of world that should exist, about the freedoms that all people, both women and men, should have. Such ideas became fundamental to African American versions of American history.

Nowhere was this sense of history, of a special destiny, more evident than in the antebellum autobiographies (formerly called slave narratives). Although there are seventeenth- and eighteenth-century narratives, after the 1830s abolitionist presses brought out dozens of these accounts each year. These narratives detailed personal memories of slavery that intersected with this larger mythos. Many of these authors recalled intense and life-shaping religious experiences. All of these writers put forward a philosophy of heroic personal striving in the face of massive violence and oppression. Many of these women and men had experienced fraud and deceit on the part of slaveholders. Most had dramatic tales of conflict, escape (perhaps after several unsuccessful attempts), and eventual freedom. Upon achieving freedom, virtually all these people tried to locate or purchase lost family members (including children borne by women while enslaved). Most had married or remarried by the end of their autobiographies; this was especially true for the men, many of whom had not married or fathered children while enslaved. Virtually all were active members of established churches. The freed people constituted a noble elite of suffering and achievement in the minds of all Black and many white Americans of a more liberal persuasion. Virtually all said that they had written their stories to help free others, to witness to the inhumanity of slavery, and to lend their hammers to strike a blow for freedom. These men and women provided the most fundamental expression of Black humanity and transcendence of earthly pain in their time. They saw themselves, and were often seen by sympathetic whites, as the ultimate truth-tellers in American society.[11]

Perhaps Frederick Douglass was the life most emblematic of this larger mythos. Born enslaved about 1817, Douglass escaped to freedom as a young man and began to lecture for abolition in the United States and England. Founder of a newspaper, *The North Star*, in 1846, Douglass wrote several versions of his autobiography. Upon his death in 1896 his Washington home, Cedar Hill, was made into the

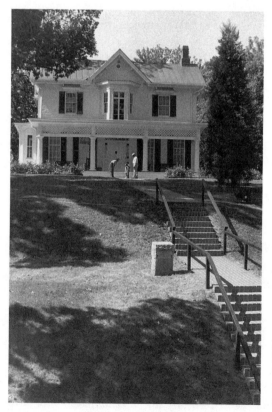

Fig. 17-2. Frederick Douglass Home, Cedar Hill, in Washington, D.C. Photo by Bill Clark, courtesy National Park Service.

first Black historic house. And in 1899 Douglass became the first African American for whom a public memorial statue was made when a monument to him was erected in Rochester, New York.[12]

Douglass was an archetype for this mythos of suffering, heroism, and eventual deliverance. Reified in his house was the image of the enslaved man who had achieved worldwide fame due to his inherent nobility and his just fight against slavery. For nearly seventy years after his death, a succession of mostly Black organizations such as the National Association of Colored Women's Clubs and the National Council of Negro Women worked hard to pay off the mortgages on the Douglass home and keep the grounds intact. In 1963 the National Park Service acquired the house as part of the celebration of the centennial of the Civil War. Douglass's home became the first African American property so acquired by the Park Service. As in life, Douglass was an archetype in death. His home was preserved for most of its history by Black institutions; however, eventually it was given national recognition and perpetual support by the federal government. Today, the Douglass home is well maintained by a dedicated, predominantly African American staff.

Douglass also embodied more prosaic notions of achievement, self-reliance, and racial pride. Afro-Americans saw themselves as embodying the notion of the heroism of everyday life. In the nineteenth century, Black people (especially men) who founded businesses, bought property, practiced professions such as law, dentistry, or medicine, taught school, or led congregations were seen not only as model citizens but as living proof that Black people could and did achieve middle-class respectability.

Perhaps the earliest written history based on this model is William C. Nell's 1854 book *Colored Patriots of the American Revolution*. This book is believed to be the earliest known example in English of African American history. In this book, Nell recounted the life histories of exemplary African Americans who were heroes in their time but whose memory he was afraid would be lost if he did not record it. A Black Brahmin from Boston, Nell was instrumental in the fight to integrate the Boston public schools in the 1850s. In writing this history, Nell was not only recounting narratives of everyday heroism and military bravery suitable for everyone's edification, but also preserving a family history of his ancestors—New Englanders since the eighteenth century. Nell was trying to ensure that as others had memorialized the lives of Washington, Adams, and Jefferson, his book would cause his ancestors, participants in America's greatest narrative, also to be remembered.[13] In a sense, Nell's work embodied the other key element in interior versions of African American history: the idea that African Americans are important, perhaps even heroic, because they can enact fully the rites and rituals of early Victorian propriety—learning, family stability, and military service.

A most intriguing aspect of the nineteenth-century Afro-American mythos was an ambivalence about Africa and African origins. In contrast to eighteenth-century African Americans, many of whom identified their connection to Africa in the titles of their organizations (such as the African Methodist Episcopal Church), the leading African Americans of the abolitionist generation rarely mentioned Africa. While some voices emerged that favored emigration to Africa, such as Alexander Crummell, Edward Wilmot Blyden, and Reverend Henry Highland Garnet, they represented a minority opinion in these years. By the 1820s, the overwhelming number of Afro-Americans were at least third- or fourth-generation Americans, most Africans having arrived in the United States before 1808.[14] Some scholars argue that the rise of the American Colonization Society (founded in 1816) also affected African Americans. The stated goals of the society were to relocate free Black people in Africa. By the 1830s, many Afro-Americans had changed their self-designation from African to Colored American, perhaps to indicate their firm belief in staying in the country of their birth. Mid- and late-nineteenth-century African Americans tended to have little direct experience of Africans and Africa. To a large extent, they were affected by European attitudes of superiority to Africans. In the 1880s and 1890s, Europeans stepped up their efforts to annex sections of the African and Asian continents. Justifications for these military episodes often hinged on the need for "civilization." For all these reasons, the African past was usually not included in mythopoetic statements about the special destiny of African Americans. While a few Black Americans emigrated to Liberia and Sierra Leone, most had contact with Africans only through their independent church missionary societies.[15]

After Reconstruction ended in 1876, a virulent racist literature developed that extolled the virtues of the Old South, idealized the moonlight-and-magnolias version of Southern history, and presented the Reconstruction era as a period of unparalleled Black violence and venality. Epitomized by Thomas Dixon's books *The Leopard's Spots: A Romance of the White Man's Burden* (1902) and *The Clansmen: An Historical Romance of the Ku Klux Klan* (1906), which was later made into the movie *Birth of a Nation* (1915), this version of American history declared that the African background of Afro-Americans was the reason they deserved enslavement. In this environment, it is perhaps easy to see why many Afro-Americans were either silent or ambivalent about their African heritage.

Consequently, the story of William H. Sheppard is particularly striking. A graduate of Hampton Institute in Virginia, Sheppard became a missionary among the Kuba in the Belgian Congo (now Zaire) in 1890. Sheppard arrived in Africa with many notions about the primitiveness of African peoples, but during his twenty years there he completely changed his mind. He became an early interpreter of the sophistication of African peoples. Schooled by the Kuba, Sheppard was eventually granted an honorary royal status, as the Kuba perceived his presence as the return of an ancestor from America. Sheppard amassed a sizeable personal collection of Kuba objects, both religious items and everyday ones. In the 1890s, he began to donate and sell objects from his collection to the museum at Hampton Institute.[16]

The museum at Hampton Institute was established in 1867 by the institute's founder, General Samuel Chapman Armstrong. Armstrong was a major figure in the white philanthropic groups committed to the freedmen. The child of American missionaries in Hawaii, Armstrong founded Hampton Institute as an educational facility for African Americans and later Native Americans. He established the museum as a way of introducing these students to natural history and world cultures. Using his sources in the Pacific, Armstrong solicited donations of material culture from the area's peoples as well as lava rock, rare species, and other natural wonders, such as petrified wood, from the American Southwest. Under its head, Cora Mae Folsom, the Hampton Museum grew over the years. Its acquisition of Sheppard's Congo artifacts gave the museum some of the earliest and finest African materials in American collections. In the twentieth century the Hampton Museum continued collecting both African and Native American materials, but also established an important collection of works by nineteenth- and twentieth-century African American artists. The Hampton library, containing important images by a number of early Black and some white photographers, is also a significant resource.[17]

Strikingly, there was only one area in which nineteenth-century Afro-Americans were slow to collect: the material culture of enslaved and rural Black people. Today we prize the comparatively few examples of antebellum Afro-American vernacular culture. Virtually no eighteenth-century examples of quilts, gourd banjos and fiddles and other instruments, distinctive dress, jewelry, ceramics, basketry, and carvings exist. Other than archaeological findings, these materials simply were not saved by postbellum Afro-Americans.

Now curators and collectors work hard to unearth quilts and other textiles, instruments, and other distinctive examples of Afro-American material culture. In most cases, these items have been preserved by families, often white families, who kept them as curiosities. Much more work needs to be done in the Southern plantations, especially those that are public or private museums. There may be a wealth of Afro-American materials contained therein that have not been identified or reinterpreted as such. However, the presently known items in public collections are few and far between. Most are preserved by Black museums established in the last thirty years.

Why were nineteenth-century Afro-Americans not much interested in this material we find so precious today? Perhaps because the African-influenced, often illiterate, considerably oppressed rural Black communities of that and earlier times simply did not fit easily into the heroic mode of nineteenth-century Afro-American historical mythos. Perhaps the people these vernacular objects represented seemed to stand for both a past the Afro-American elite of that era was proud of escaping from and a contemporary reality of ignorance and oppression. While these same Black Victorians were often active in civil rights organizations, anti-lynching campaigns, and other progressivist activities, they often saw rural Black people as a group much in need of "improvement."[18] Since, for reasons I will discuss later, no predominantly white institutions of the same era preserved these objects either, this material culture and these elements of oral traditions, once so very common, are now quite rare.

In summary, nineteenth-century Afro-Americans preserved the literary achievements of the time, the artifacts of great men, the histories of independent Black churches, and, to a much lesser extent, the histories of Africa and of Black Americans in Africa. These books and documents were preserved because they reflected Christian millennialism and the perceived special destiny of African Americans: a mythos about the African American past originated by the abolitionist generation of activists. Emphasizing a special role as truth-tellers, African American historians and collectors prided themselves on a story of achievement, self-reliance, and racial pride. While ambivalent about Africa, a small group certainly took the lead in preserving African materials in the United States. Yet they were unable to see the value of the distinctive material culture of rural Black Americans. Reflecting a Yankee, urban, and bourgeois cluster of values, these men and women selectively preserved a history that extolled their vision of what they wanted Afro-Americans to be.

BOOKS AND NOT OBJECTS: NINETEENTH-CENTURY HISTORICALLY WHITE INSTITUTIONS

As George Frederickson's and Winthrop Jordan's works have shown, the development of racist ideologies is nearly synonymous with the birth of the United States.[19] During the Revolutionary War and with the first generation of presidents, Americans created a new mythos for themselves as a nation. In literature, art, and politics, Americans were striving to define their distinctive characteristics. During this same nation-building period, theoretical racism emerged to define African Americans as being outside the American polity and national character.

Racist theories utilized Biblical exegesis, scientific arguments, and economic rationales for Black inferiority. First, and perhaps most important, to many Europeans and European Americans, Africans represented the most extreme version of the primordial "other," the absolute antithesis of civilized humanity. For many of these same people, African Americans were but a slight step up. Christianized and operating under the control of a white slaveowning and/or capitalist class, African Americans were moving toward civilization. There was, of course, some distance between them and the white folks at the top, but they were on their way.

These attitudes contained specific stereotypes of African Americans, who were seen variously as primitive, childlike, violent, musical, sexually voracious, and superstitious. Specifically, many European Americans did not believe that African Americans had developed a distinctive culture. Rather, they labeled as deviant any African American cultural forms that differed from mainstream European American forms. Africa was seen as having no meaningful relationship to Black American culture except as evidence that confirmed an inferior or primitive past.

Scientists of the nineteenth century formalized this viewpoint into several different theories of Black inferiority. Before about 1830, the dominant theory was monogenesis: the idea that all humans were part of the same species, but that Black people were at a lower level of civilization largely because of environmental factors and cultural deprivation. By midcentury, pioneers of American science, including Louis Agassiz of Harvard University, had developed a new theory: polygenesis, the notion that different human races were actually different species. Polygeneticists held that because of the inherent biological inferiority of the African race, no amelioration of circumstances would change Black character or allow African Americans to become fully civilized. People who were more favorable to the notion of racial progress tended to maintain monogeneticist views, searching for ways to change American social conditions (such as the abolition of slavery). These comparative liberals hoped that Black people, at that time certainly inferior, would actually approach equality with whites under favorable conditions that promoted the assimilation of Anglo-American middle-class views.[20]

After 1870 and the diffusion of Charles Darwin's ideas among American intellectuals, a new theory, called Social Darwinism, largely replaced polygenesis. Social Darwinists included not only American biological scientists and naturalists but a wide range of policymakers, intellectuals, and scholars in other disciplines. This ideology held that all people were of the same species, but that Africans (and others, such as Asians) inhabited a lower rung on the ladder of evolution. Not only were they less evolved and so less civilized, but these inferior, darker peoples might need generations to approach northern European superiority (and might always remain somewhat behind).[21]

During these years of scientific racism, many of the great museums of the United States were founded. The Smithsonian Institution is the earliest example.[22] Funded in 1829 by the bequest of a British doctor, James Smithson, the Smithsonian actually opened as a research center in 1846. The American Museum of Natural History in New York was announced in 1869 and opened to the public in 1877. The Metropolitan Museum of Art in New York was founded in 1870 and opened in 1880. The Field Museum of Natural History in Chicago was established in 1893. These were among the earliest publicly accessible, large-scale museums in the United States. Each in its own way is an American version of earlier European universal museums such as the British Museum, the Musée d'Histoire Naturelle, and the Louvre.[23]

Significantly, three of these museums were natural-history museums: the American Museum of Natural History, the nineteenth-century Smithsonian, and the Field Museum. Their purpose was to conduct scientific research and present this research to the public.

These museums incorporated the new science of anthropology along with the basic disciplines of natural history: botany, geology, and biology. As such, these museums became the primary scholarly means by which the public came into contact with the "primitive"—that is, people of color. These museums became the primary purveyors of scientific racism and provided scholarly support for Social Darwinist attitudes.

Elite museums became the preserve of scholars and curators who in general were trained to see African Americans as unimportant to or even invisible in American history and culture. Many of the same people believed that the documentation of vanishing Native American cultures was extremely important. The identical scientific-historical attitude of racial superiority resulted in opposite preservation outcomes for the histories of Native Americans and African Americans. American Indians were seen as "authentic," as the original Americans, but they were also seen as an outmoded race whose way of life was declining. This perception of incipient loss propelled a tremendous burst in American archaeology and anthropology, and resulted in hundreds of thousands of objects being removed from Native American communities and stored in museums. Sacred and everyday objects were purchased and stolen; graves were ransacked for treasure and human skeletons; enormous numbers of picture postcards, portraits, and Western allegorical illustrations were created. Native American images and objects filled the treasure houses of many American museums, though the values, philosophy, and traditions of the peoples themselves often did not inform the museums' records or dioramic representations. The United States National Museum at the Smithsonian (now known as the National Museum of Natural History) became a primary repository for American Indian objects, and it vied with other large museums as well as private collectors such as George Heye to acquire the largest, most diverse collection of North and South American Indian artifacts.[24]

By contrast, antebellum African American objects are few and far between in major American museums. The natural-history museums did not collect from any people of color other than American Indians, nor did they collect the objects of poor, ordinary, or immigrant European Americans. The major American museums were as segregated as other aspects of American society. In local historical societies as well as local museums, no object was collected specifically because it reflected African American culture; however, African American–related materials can be found in some of these collections. Noted abolitionist families with origins in the bluebloods of New England often have papers related to Black people. A number of Southern plantations, such as Mount Vernon and Monticello, have archaeological, artifactual, and documentary materials in which African Americans are deeply involved. Governmental papers relating to constitutional debates, legislation, and executive actions regarding slavery, abolition, citizenship, and segregation all contain information about African Americans. The records of government agencies, now stored in the National Archives, reflect how deeply intertwined the history of the United States generally is with African Americans. So there are resources that do demonstrate many aspects of African American life and history. However, all these items were inadvertently collected, and consequently reflect comparatively less about the past of African Americans, especially artifactually, than do the richly documented collections that focus on Native Americans.

Perhaps the only systematic collection of specimens and information about nineteenth-century African Americans was the group of skeletal remains and body measurements (especially of the cranium) that several naturalists collected for the Smithsonian and some universities. The most famous of these naturalists was Louis Agassiz, who created a sizeable collection of skeletal remains for Harvard University. The Swiss-born son of a Protestant minister, Agassiz first became a noted scientific figure in Europe. He came to the United States in 1846 and became a star lecturer and Harvard University faculty member. A naturalist who became a polygeneticist, Agassiz spent years trying to prove certain aspects of this theory—such as that Africans, Asians, and a variety of Europeans were all different species. In the process, he collected thousands of comparative measurements of racial types and a number of skeletal remains. European and Asian populations were represented in natural-history museums' collections of skeletal remains, but the largest collections were of American Indian specimens; African or African American examples were usually less than half the number of the American Indian examples.[25]

If African Americans were visible only as skeletons in major natural-history museums, they were completely absent from major art museums. The Metropolitan Museum of Art was founded to bring European and classical art to the unwashed in America. Finding that all Americans were in dire need of civilization, yet realizing that not all could afford the Grand Tour, the founders of the Metropolitan wanted to bring a little of that culture home. Believing that everything in American culture was imitative of purer and better traditions, this museum collected virtually nothing American and certainly nothing produced by African American artists.[26]

In preserving little related to African Americans, major nineteenth-century American museums were echoing scholarly versions of American history and a popular sense of American culture in which African Americans were invisible. The African American materials that some of these institutions inadvertently acquired usually documented the history of interactions between Blacks and whites instead of the distinctive memories and traditions of African Americans. The structure of these collections communicated the sense that Africans and most other peoples of color were absent from world culture except as the occasional subject of European artists. Hence such museums showcased American stereotypes about Africans and African Americans.

The collections of important American libraries contrast strongly with museums' preservation history. The Library of Congress was founded in 1800. In 1814, the personal library of Thomas Jefferson was purchased and added to the small existing collection. For many years, the library was a small set of rooms in the Capitol building itself, functioning almost as a lending library for members of Congress. In 1866 the books of the Smithsonian collection were added to the Library of Congress. During the 1870s, a move to establish the library on a more professional footing began to gain ground. In 1864 Ainsworth R. Spofford became the Librarian of Congress. He devoted his career to putting the library on a more solid professional footing, lobbying for a building and professional staff. Spofford succeeded in convincing Congress to make the Library of Congress "the foremost library in the world."[27] In 1893 the Library of Congress moved into the newly completed Jefferson Building and began its modern history as an omnium-gatherum of world knowledge.

Within this notion of collecting books and manuscripts related to all the world's knowledge, there was room for everyone, even for African Americans. In 1871 a young Black man, Daniel Alexander Payne Murray, was hired to serve as a clerk and personal servant to Spofford, the new Librarian of Congress. Over the next decade, as Spofford sought to professionalize the library, Murray was gathering experience and expertise. In 1881 Murray became an assistant librarian. From then until his death in 1925, Murray built up the Library of Congress collections on African Americans, collecting books, documents, published articles, manuscripts, and letters from educated African Americans.[28] In addition to collecting for the library,

Murray spent many years working on an encyclopedia that would document African and African American contributions to world history and culture. Intending to sell it by subscription, Murray could never sell enough subscriptions; his notes for the encyclopedia now reside in the Wisconsin Historical Society's archives.

Murray established a collection of African American manuscript materials as soon as a manuscript section of the library opened in 1898. With some gaps, the Library of Congress continued to employ or contract with Black librarians and/or scholars, so that there has been nearly continuous input from Black professionals since then on acquiring African American manuscripts. (In fact, there has always been a sizeable minority of Black librarians, especially those active at Black college libraries and church archives.)[29] From about 1942 until about 1964, the noted Black sociologist E. Franklin Frazier was consulted in this capacity. He was responsible for the library's acquisition of the Booker T. Washington papers, and he set the stage for the acquisitions of the papers of the NAACP, National Urban League, and American Colonization Society as well. He continued to build the African American manuscript collection, adding the papers of many well-known Black Americans. Frazier's work in the manuscript division was ably continued by Sylvia Render from the 1970s through the early 1980s.[30] As a result of their efforts and those of many others, the manuscript division and the general collections of the Library of Congress are a major source of documentary and published materials on African American life and history.

By contrast, the Smithsonian had a similar opportunity to empower an African American longtime employee and establish an important collection, but it never did so. In 1857 Solomon Brown was hired as a clerk for the first secretary of the Smithsonian, Joseph Henry. Brown worked for the Smithsonian for over fifty years, overlapping Murray's tenure at the Library of Congress by thirty years. Brown became a leading preservationist in the Black community of Washington, D.C., especially in the Anacostia section of the city, where he lived. He was active in Afro-American literary and historical societies and was renowned in the 1880s and 1890s for organizing annual trips to Harpers Ferry on the anniversary of John Brown's 1859 raid. However, Solomon Brown was never appointed to a professional position at the Smithsonian and so could not function as the founder of a significant collection, as did Murray at the Library of Congress.[31]

The Library of Congress was not the only institution collecting

African American letters, books, and documents, though it was the largest. Some white Americans, often New Englanders, also became involved in the collecting of African American materials or supported that effort financially. White abolitionists before the Civil War, Northern missionaries to the freedmen during Reconstruction, and certain capitalist philanthropists, such as Andrew Carnegie and John D. Rockefeller, were active in the Colored educational world.

While popular and scientific racism dominated white Americans' discourse about African Americans in the nineteenth century, there did exist another body of thought about Black Americans. In this alternative history, African Americans were surely in need of education, civilization, and uplift, but they were also a people who had been wronged and deserved help. This version of African American life and history was somewhat softer. For example, some believed that slavery had been a tragic and oppressive situation with unanticipated negative outcomes for all, especially for the white people involved. For these people, slavery was bad mainly because it besmirched the American Eden with sin. As such, many white abolitionists—such as William Lloyd Garrison—and some Black abolitionists saw themselves on a holy crusade. They expressed their moral outrage at slavery and identified themselves with the prophets of the Old Testament. For others, Christian principles inspired a kind of Christian guilt for complicity with slavery (and a sense of the necessity to resist, as one resists temptation and sin). Harriet Beecher Stowe's *Uncle Tom's Cabin* (1858) might be read in this manner.[32]

After the Civil War, philanthropy and the missionary spirit in education became as important as antislavery efforts had been in the antebellum years. In tandem with this push toward education, Christianity was seen as a necessary and positive force, essential for depaganizing Africans and making them into more worthwhile Americans. This same missionary zeal inspired some young men and women to migrate south after the Civil War to teach the freedmen, and resulted in the founding of schools and colleges by numerous white religious sects. In some ways, supporters of colleges "for the Colored people," church members who contributed to educational funds, and former antislavery activists all shared views about Black inferiority with mainstream American society. However, in a time of growing popular and scientific racism, people who supported schools and colleges for the freedmen constituted a white minority voice and a support system of some significance for emerging Colored institutions.

For example, as mentioned earlier, in 1868 the former Union

general Samuel Chapman Armstrong founded Hampton Institute,
from which Booker T. Washington received his degree. General O. O.
Howard, the former director of the Freedmen's Bureau, established
Howard University in 1867. The Congregational Church founded
Fisk University in 1867, and the United Church of Christ instituted
Tougaloo College in Jackson, Mississippi, in 1869. In Atlanta,
Spelman College, the elite women's college, was founded in memory
of Laura Spelman Rockefeller in 1880, and Morehouse College was
established by the Methodist Church. One of the most prolific philanthropists was Andrew Carnegie, whose foundation built libraries in
dozens of Black colleges as well as in numerous American cities. While
the philanthropically oriented whites who financially supported these
institutions may have agreed with some of the then-current notions of
Black inferiority, many of them had values similar (though not identical) to those of the Black Victorians mentioned earlier. Wealthy whites
were more likely to see Black people as victims in need of general
uplift, while Black Victorians were more likely to see progress and
diversity within the Black community. In the view of most Black Victorians, only some Black people were in need of uplift; they saw
themselves as having already achieved Anglo-American middle-class
goals on a considerably smaller income.[33]

Black schools and colleges such as those mentioned above became
the primary repositories for African American books, documents, and
art in the years before 1950. While funded by white Americans, Black
colleges were institutions in which Black scholars and other professionals could wield an extraordinary degree of social and intellectual
control. Academically trained African American intellectuals generally
could not find employment in white institutions, so the Black college
system sheltered and supported their work, helping to sustain a tradition of African American historiography. In addition, the works of
African American artists were first collected by Black institutions of
higher learning, which also provided commissions to artists and architects. Black college libraries became primary preservation entities,
saving letters documenting personal memories as well as books and
articles demonstrating a scholarly African American tradition. The
existence of these educational institutions helped foster all sorts of
religious, social, and artistic traditions within Black society and
helped sustain scholarly interpretations of the Black experience. Black
people within these institutions preserved elements of African American life, history, and culture that were important to them personally.
Yet the diversity of viewpoints found within these institutions resulted

in the preservation of a wide range of African American documents, published works, and symbols of educational or "high" cultural achievement.

In summary, by 1880 scientific racism and the increasing power of Social Darwinist ideologies dictated that few African American objects, documents, or vernacular traditions were preserved in major American museums. The only sizeable collections that existed consisted of cranial measurements of African Americans; these were used, along with the results of other detailed examinations of living people and human remains, to determine the exact evolutionary distance between pure African types, in-between African American types, and superior European types.

This was only part of the story, however. The Library of Congress actively collected published materials, manuscripts, and documents written by African Americans as part of its mission to gather together knowledge of the world. With far different purposes in mind, Black bibliophiles and librarians in the emerging libraries and archives at Black colleges saved published materials, manuscripts, and other similar documents. These Black librarians and book collectors were most often "race men" and women, who were active in Black religious, political, and social organizations. They sought ways to document the achievements of African Americans who had been forgotten but whose contributions deserved celebration. In the case of university library collections, such as those at Fisk and Howard, these efforts were supported by the philanthropy of white Americans who believed in the improvement and uplift of Black people, often as part of their Christian duty. Believing that African American materials were most deserving of preservation when they reflected the education and Christian mores of bourgeois Victorian society generally, books, documents, and fine arts were most actively collected, whereas distinctive material culture and folk art were not.

A NEW NEGRO FOR A NEW ERA: 1895–1930

Between 1895 and 1930 a number of demographic and political changes began to alter many aspects of race relations. Perhaps the Great Migration north by thousands of rural Black people was the most dramatic development. These people were drawn northward to cities such as Chicago, New York, and Pittsburgh by the possibilities of greater personal freedom, greater access to public education for their children, widening economic opportunities (especially in industrial jobs), and relief from the brutal activities of the Ku Klux Klan and other state-supported violence in the South. Although the North proved not to be the promised land many had sought, the increased presence of Black people changed the structure of Northern African American communities and enlarged the audience for African American public history.[34]

In these thirty-five years a number of new institutions and organizations were established to collect, preserve, and educate the public about the African American past. A new generation, born after Reconstruction and augmented by rural migrants, changed the mix in urban Black neighborhoods. New styles of music were heard; new organizations were founded; and a different set of mythic interpretations, personal memories, and academic histories emerged about the African American past.

The new organizations are perhaps the best gauge of this new sense of movement and progress. In 1909 the National Urban League was founded, and the National Association for the Advancement of Colored People (NAACP) was begun in 1910. Organized as interracial groups and headed by wealthy white men, these organizations epitomized a new spirit of racial concern among some white progressives. Both organizations eventually published important journals, which served as forums for discussion of racial issues as well as outlets for the expressions of Negro writers, artists, and scholars. In November 1910 the NAACP started *The Crisis: A Record of the Darker Races,* which was edited for more than thirty years by the noted Black intellectual and activist W.E.B. Du Bois. In January 1923 the Urban League founded *Opportunity: A Journal of Negro Life,* which was initially edited by Charles Johnson, another Black scholar, who later became president of Fisk University. These organizations and journals involved an interracial membership in working together to solve the race problem of the United States. The Urban League was oriented toward social-work solutions, and the NAACP focused on political and legal efforts to attack segregation and lynching. The editorial staffs of both journals helped market the artists and intellectuals of the new African American cultural movement to a much wider interracial audience than had ever existed before.

These links between activist organizations and cultural preservation were most evident during the Harlem Renaissance. Though not strictly a rebirth, nor limited to Harlem, this artistic movement was an extraordinary moment in African American culture in which the ideas, memories, hopes, and cultural strategies of a younger generation began to be articulated. Perhaps the single most famous publication of this period was a book edited by the Harvard-trained philosopher Alain Locke entitled *The New Negro*. Published in 1925 as an edition of *Survey Graphic,* a social-reform journal of the progressive era, *The New Negro* displayed the new spirit felt by younger artists, writers, and intellectuals. In producing the book and subsequent art exhibitions, poetry readings, and other literary events, Locke and the people he promoted gained prominence in New York art circles. As a result, some of these young Negro artists were able to claim private white patronage. While the writers Langston Hughes and Zora Neale Hurston eventually had some difficulties with their white patron, Locke was certainly important in ushering in a new era of appreciation for the work of Negro artists.[35]

In terms of collecting, the Harlem Renaissance in general and Alain Locke in particular can be credited with building up the first real market for African American art. Well connected with a number of wealthy and influential white patrons, Locke was instrumental in securing private and foundation support for a number of working artists and in establishing a market for their output, especially for older African American artists such as Henry O. Tanner. In 1926 the Harmon Foundation began giving prizes to young African American artists. Counseled through the years by Alain Locke, the Harmon Foundation also acquired probably the largest collection of art produced by professional Negro artists such as Archibald Motley, Jr., and William H. Johnson. The foundation did not collect only newly produced art; it also began to collect some of the works of nineteenth- and early-twentieth-century African American artists whose work had not found an audience in the United States, such as Edmonia Lewis and Robert Duncanson. When the foundation was dismantled in the 1960s, these works were distributed among Fisk University, the Howard University Fine Arts Department Collection, and the National Collection of Fine Arts (now the National Museum of American Art, Smithsonian Institution).

In supporting and promoting Negro art and artists, Alain Locke became the primary philosopher of the Harlem Renaissance. Through his writings, public lectures, and personal sponsorship of exhibitions, Locke developed a notion of Negro culture that might be called romanticist. Locke promoted the idea that Negro artists had something special to communicate. He felt that African American culture contained a distinctive set of aesthetic and spiritual values that could be

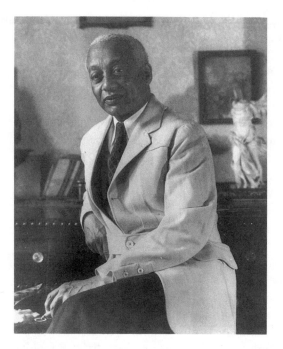

Fig. 17-3. Alain L. Locke. Photo courtesy the Locke Collection, Moorland-Spingarn Research Center, Howard University.

expressed through art. While it should be on a par technically with European art, Negro art was at the same time different. In Locke's view, that difference reflected a closer connection of the art to the Negro folk, who through their spirituals, blues, autobiographies, and life experiences expressed a more honest, perhaps even purer world-view than others could. Locke also emphasized that this purity and spiritual content were in some important way linked to the African past, to an Africa of the imagination. Expressed most clearly in Countee Cullen's poem "Heritage," published in *The New Negro* ("What is Africa to me? / Sunlit sky and star-lit sea"), this view of Africa contrasted sharply with nineteenth-century African Americans' sense that Africa was a place largely in need of missionary work. Going beyond the ambivalences of an earlier generation, Africa began to be incorporated into a new mythos of the African American past.[36]

Locke visited only one country in Africa: Egypt. During these same years a number of Egyptian tombs were first discovered and opened up to the public. The image of Egypt had been orientalized, and most Europeans considered Egypt to be part of the East rather than Africa.[37] Locke's visit there can be seen at least as much as being part of the grandest of Grand Tours than as an affirmation on Locke's part of an African heritage. The Africa imagined by most Harlem Renaissance figures was more akin to the Caribbean islands, with which some were very familiar, having migrated to New York from Jamaica, the Virgin Islands, and other locations. While uninformed about contemporary African life, many Harlem Renaissance artists and writers were able to conjure up a positive image of African artistic impulses that they could draw upon to produce new expressive forms. Their sense of the specialness and spirituality of the African part of African Americans contrasts sharply with the predominant nineteenth-century view, the view of their parents' generations.

Further, Locke's beliefs and those of other Harlem Renaissance artists paired quite well with complementary views held by certain white bohemians and avant-gardists. The novelist, photographer, and man-about-town Carl Van Vechten was a good example of white supporters of the Harlem Renaissance whose views of Negro Americans might best be described as celebrationist. These people saw Negro Americans as a distinctive source of cultural innovation, vibrancy, and creativity in American life. For Van Vechten and his café society friends, "primitive" and "exotic" meant many things. They felt that African Americans were spiritually purer, yet more able to indulge in the profane aspects of life such as sexual expression because they were socially removed from the mores of bourgeois society, and more artistic (though perhaps unconsciously so) than whites. While elements of these same beliefs may have motivated some conservatives to ban jazz as "jungle music" and the Charleston as a "nigger dance," people such as Van Vechten and his friends saw all these cultural forms as enormously positive and worthy of celebration. This celebrationist sensibility constituted a radically new mythos about African Americans. For the first time, a group of white Americans was inspired by the alternative aesthetic embodied in African American culture.

In his controversial 1926 book *Nigger Heaven*, Van Vechten celebrated the Harlem lifestyle in precisely this way. Many Negro intellectuals and writers, such as W.E.B. Du Bois and Alain Locke, roundly criticized this book for elevating to a high status the Harlem ladies and men of the "sporting life," as well as for using a fair bit of profane dialogue allegedly taken from life. However, this book in fact reflected the white romanticist's view of what was important about Harlem. Though Van Vechten was a financial supporter of the Harlem Renaissance, collecting the work of Negro artists, helping to sponsor exhibitions, and assisting Negro writers in getting published, the Harlem of his imagination was not filled with these intellectual and aesthetic types. Rather, his vision of Harlem was one that celebrated jazz musicians, singers, numbers runners, ladies of the night, and other members of a Negro cabaret society who seemed to him "primitive" in a spiritual yet profane way. In this enthusiasm, Van Vechten was typical of the white purchasers of "race records," recordings of Negro music, especially the blues and hot jazz. These people proved that there was a white market for musical recordings and concerts by other than elite Black artists. These white celebrationists of Negro life were few in the 1920s, though influential. They prefigured the collecting of African American folklore in the 1930s and 1940s. As the field of professional folklorists grew larger, a growing number of white people became interested in recording the stories, jokes, songs, and speech of rural and urban low-income Negroes.[38]

Van Vechten, Mabel Dodge Luhan, and other enthusiasts of the Jazz Age saw African American artists as America's primitives. Influenced by bohemian circles in Europe, these celebrationists of primitivism saw Negro jazz musicians and blues singers as the creators of a more authentic culture. The celebrationists often saw American society as overly civilized, as having lost some kind of primordial "juice," and consequently in danger of decay or calcification. Negro artists could tap into a premodern, more sexually explicit, more directly critical set of vernacular traditions. In these popular traditions the celebrationists saw the future of modern art.[39]

Both the African American romanticists, such as Locke, and the European American celebrationists, such as Van Vechten, shared in the emergence of a radically new mythos about African Americans. In the nineteenth century, many Blacks and some whites considered the positive aspect of African American culture to be its emphasis on suffering and salvation, which was modeled after the life of Christ. In this new generation, there was much less concern for religious example and much more of a sense that African Americans had created a unique and highly expressive culture. Langston Hughes, Zora Neale Hurston, Jacob Lawrence, and other Harlem Renaissance artists believed that their art could tap into this rich African American vernacular tradition. The art itself would have to transcend vernacular styles in form to achieve artistic respectability, but these popular traditions in music, dance, and folklore formed a deep wellspring from which to create new art.[40]

This positive sense of the importance of African American vernacular traditions was completely new. The nineteenth-century Black abolitionists and Reconstructionists had been absorbed by a set of issues involving slavery, freedom, and civil rights. The mythos they had created out of their personal memories emphasized the religious, political, and literary traditions of African Americans. This new generation of Negro artists and critics was excited by work in the expressive realm of culture. The mythos they created out of their individual desires to function as artists in American society placed a high value on the unique aspects of African American culture. For the first time, African American vernacular traditions began to be seen positively, at least within certain Northern artistic circles.

Yet this aesthetic enthusiasm for Negro folk culture was not shared by all educated African Americans of the time. In virtually complete contradiction to the interior romanticist and exterior celebrationist versions of Negro American life was the work of Carter G. Woodson. Born in the rural South, Woodson was educated in the North, eventually receiving a Ph.D. from Harvard University. Woodson made the preservation and celebration of Negro history his life's work, in 1915 founding the Association for the Study of Negro Life and History and in 1916 the *Journal of Negro History*. Woodson saw the association as the cultural analogue of the NAACP and the Urban

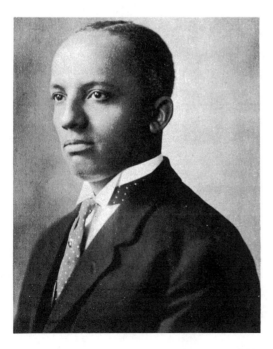

Fig. 17-4. Carter G. Woodson. Photo from *The Crisis* magazine, August 1926, Moorland-Spingarn Research Center, Howard University. Reprinted courtesy *The Crisis* magazine, NAACP.

League. In his view, racial prejudice was in large measure the result of ignorance; therefore, education must be part of the solution. Woodson wrote *The MisEducation of the Negro* (1933) to argue that internal feelings of racial inferiority could be addressed by having greater knowledge of a positive African American and African past. Woodson stated that since Negro Americans did not know enough about their "true history," they were susceptible to the negative stereotypes pervading American society. Quite directly, Woodson became the twentieth-century inheritor of the nineteenth-century sentiment that history was about truth and that African American history constituted a special form of truth-telling. Woodson followed in these ideological footsteps, building on this most deeply held mythos about the special role of African Americans and the unique voice of critical truth they embodied.

Woodson, however, introduced significant innovations to the earlier tradition as a result of the fact that he worked on several levels simultaneously. As an academically trained historian, Woodson researched and published works meant to challenge prevailing interpretations of African American history; the journal he published was an effort to appeal to professional historians. At the same time, he wanted to create a preservation institution that would stand apart from traditional African American institutions such as churches and colleges. Woodson was enormously sensitive to the question of who his audience was, and he successfully identified and organized a wider range of African Americans who supported preservationist goals.[41]

The Association for the Study of Negro Life and History was the first national-scale African American preservation organization. Woodson established it in Chicago but soon moved it to Washington, D.C., where the national headquarters remains to this day. The members of the association were self-trained historians, elementary and secondary school teachers, collectors, ministers and their congregations. This wide array of people formed local chapters of a national organization devoted solely to the preservation, analysis, and celebration of African American "life, history, and culture," as the association's motto proclaimed. The members of the association have been responsible nationally for the placing of markers at historic sites and for assisting people with the preservation of church records and objects. Through the association's conferences and publishing efforts, they have encouraged the building of private libraries on African American topics. Well into the 1960s, the association served as a primary arena for Negro cultural affairs, in addition to being one of the few large scholarly organizations that encouraged, welcomed, and supported the participation of African American scholars such as Lorenzo Greene, Rayford Logan, and Benjamin Quarles.

Woodson also continued the nineteenth-century tradition of emphasizing the contributions of educated and heroic African Americans. Free Negro property owners, educated African Americans who became lawyers, doctors, and teachers, others who established successful businesses—these people became the general focus of his historical concerns. Woodson believed that if, for example, European Americans were aware of all the contributions African American men had made in American wars, then prejudice would begin to erode. Furthermore, Woodson believed that Negro Americans needed to have a true sense of their own history to counteract the stereotypes about them that abounded in white America. This dual sense represented a more modern view of the same issues articulated by nineteenth-century preservationists.

Woodson went beyond nineteenth-century mainstream African American thinking in one very important way: he argued for the importance of understanding the true history of Africa as well. To him, one of the greatest lies put forth was that Africans were uncivilized. In fact, Woodson was a leader in making African Americans aware of the numerous West and Central African societies, some complex, from which unfortunate people had been kidnapped or coerced into slavery. Though Woodson himself primarily published on American topics, through the association he provided support for articles and books that linked Negro Americans to a more glorious African past.[42] Woodson's concern with locating the beginning of African American history in Africa, rather than at the moment of enslavement, has become a key rhetorical point for many Black preservationists and is a cornerstone of contemporary arguments for Afrocentric curricula and historical interpretations. In this sense, Woodson made a key contribution to African American scholarly historical thought as well as to a wider public understanding of Africa.

Woodson was sometimes referred to as the "Father of Black History" because his efforts to preserve many aspects of African American culture reverberated throughout Negro communities and later into wider American society in the form of Black History Month celebrations. His scholarly publications prefigured the social-history revolution of the 1960s in terms of his reinterpretation of traditional literary sources and his use of census and other publicly available data. By creating the Association for the Study of Negro Life and History,

Woodson provided support for the wide diversity of interior (that is, developed by African Americans) interpretations of their past. Academically trained African American historians could publish papers and debate each other during association meetings, expanding the horizons of formal scholarship on the African American past. The local and regional work of the association's chapters helped reinforce and preserve personal memories and local histories. The association's Negro History Week celebrations and other activities provided a platform for the reinvigoration of the mythos about the special role and destiny of African Americans. Appeals to that mythos were part of the organizing techniques of the association and helped Negro schoolteachers, librarians, and ministers in their crusade against ignorance of self in Negro society. Woodson's association, his published work, and the programs he sponsored were absolutely pivotal in the history of African American preservation.

Woodson was not himself interested in building a collection. He did develop an extensive personal library, which was given to Howard University upon his death, but beyond that he was not oriented toward acquiring objects. Working at the same time as Woodson, however, was a small group of Black bibliophiles who were deeply committed to collection building. Throughout the 1910s and 1920s, a growing number of these Black Victorians were motivated to establish private libraries and societies such as the American Negro Academy (founded in 1897 in Washington, D.C.) and the Negro Society for Historical Research (founded in 1902 in New York). These Black bibliophiles collected both American and, where possible, European editions of works by African Americans, especially autobiographies. In addition, they often had collections of the signatures and letters of famous persons. These bibliophiles were among the elite of Northern Negro communities. Their involvement in fraternal organizations, churches, and professional life gave them a distinct perspective on the African American past. In a sense, these bibliophiles were doing the same work as Daniel Alexander Payne Murray at the Library of Congress, but with their own resources. A generation later than Murray, men such as Arthur Alonso Schomburg and Jesse B. Moorland began amassing the private libraries that later became the bases of the two most important public archives on African American culture.

Moorland was a minister and an early graduate of Howard University. He became very actively involved in the YMCA as a source of strength and uplift for African American men and boys. Moorland came from a light-skinned, middle-class family and was able through real estate speculation and other activities to increase his wealth. From the 1890s on, Moorland amassed a private collection of books, letters, and manuscripts that documented the history of literary achievement among African Americans and Africans, especially in Europe. In 1914, Moorland donated his private collection of over three thousand books, manuscripts, engravings, paintings, and other objects to the library and archives of Howard University; he also provided the university with funds from the Moorland Foundation. With a proper Victorian upbringing and lifestyle, Moorland was the perfect image of the active "race man." He epitomized the bibliophilic collecting common to the members of the American Negro Academy, an elite group of forty men in Washington, D.C.[43]

Howard University already had an important archive in the papers of the abolitionist Louis Tappan. A New England blueblood, Tappan's antislavery efforts involved correspondence with many of the important African Americans and radical European Americans of his day. The donation of his papers constituted a significant resource for understanding the antislavery crusade and contained a number of African American autobiographies. Thirty years after the Moorland donation, Howard University also acquired the collections of Arthur and Joel Spingarn, who were wealthy New Yorkers of a progressivist bent and founding members of the NAACP. Arthur was the first vice president of the NAACP and later became president, and Joel was the original treasurer of the organization. Arthur was a lawyer who successfully argued several early civil rights cases before the Supreme Court. Joel established the prestigious Spingarn Medal for the NAACP. Over time, both became collectors of African American–related material; Arthur specialized in literature, amassing an important collection of African American writers of both the nineteenth and twentieth centuries. In 1947, the Howard library acquired the Spingarns' collections.[44]

Taken together, Tappan's papers, Moorland's library, and the Spingarns' collections made Howard a tremendous resource for the study of African American history. Now known as the Moorland-Spingarn Research Center, the collection was supervised from the 1930s through the early 1970s by Dorothy Porter (now Dorothy Porter Wesley). With a degree in library science from Columbia University, Porter greatly expanded upon the original collections of the institution. She widened the collecting areas to include more literature, early manuscripts, and documents, including publications relating to the history of Africans and African Americans in Europe; family docu-

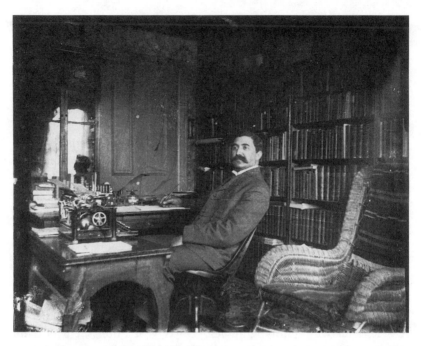

Fig. 17-5. Jesse Moorland in his library. Photo courtesy the Moorland Papers, Moorland-Spingarn Research Center, Howard University.

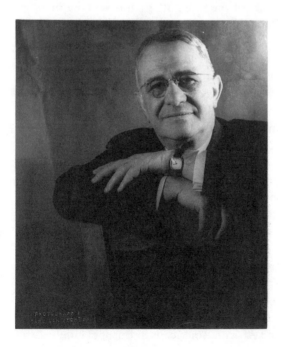

Fig. 17-6. Arthur Spingarn, first president of the NAACP. Photo by Carl Van Vechten, courtesy Moorland-Spingarn Research Center, Howard University.

ments and archives; archives on African American artists, writers, and persons of note; and early publications on Africa.[45] Today, the Moorland-Spingarn Research Center is a major center for research on African American life and culture. It includes a rare-book library, a manuscript division, and a small material culture collection.

Starting in about 1896, a somewhat younger man, Arthur Alonso Schomburg, collected roughly the same sorts of published works and unpublished letters and manuscripts as Jesse Moorland. A native of Puerto Rico who migrated to New York City as a young adult, Schomburg worked as a bank clerk for most of his life. With de facto segregation in full force in Northern cities, Colored men could rarely get these sorts of office jobs. To acquire and maintain such a job, a Negro person was expected to embody propriety, stable family life, and other elements of Victorian morality. Schomburg did so and also was an archetype of the Black bibliophile.[46] In part because Schomburg spoke Spanish and came from a Caribbean heritage, he was more interested in what is now called the African diaspora than were Moorland and virtually all of the other collectors of his acquaintance. His collection contained the works of many Caribbean writers, and he had an early interest in African history and the history of Africans in Europe,

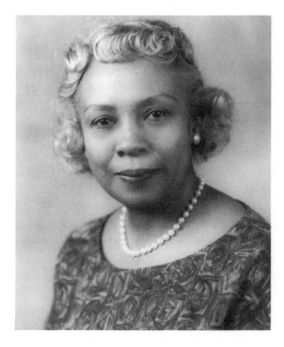

Fig. 17-7. Dorothy Porter. Photo by Addison Scurlock, courtesy Moorland-Spingarn Research Center, Howard University.

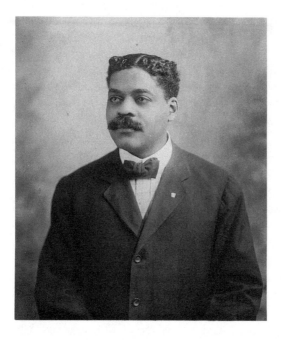

Fig. 17-8. Arthur A. Schomburg. Photo courtesy the Locke Collection, Moorland-Spingarn Research Center, Howard University.

especially diasporic communities in Spain prior to the Renaissance. In 1926, his collection was purchased by the Carnegie Corporation for the New York Public Library. Housed in a sizeable building called the Harlem Public Library, this institution became a center of cultural activity from the 1920s onward.[47] Today, the Schomburg Center for Research in Black Culture stands as a primary public institution within the New York community and as an internationally known center for research.

After selling the bulk of his private collection and struggling to stay on as curator of his own collection (he eventually succeeded), Schomburg began working with Fisk University. Invited by Charles Johnson, formerly of the Urban League and at that time head of the Research Department of Fisk, Schomburg was affiliated with Fisk for less than three years, during which time he built their collection from some five hundred or fewer volumes to over 4,500 volumes. Since then Fisk has continuously employed a number of professionally trained librarians, who have augmented Schomburg's work with additional manuscripts, books related to the history of African Americans in the southeastern United States, and important collections of African American art.[48] Schomburg's and Moorland's contributions stand as extraordinary personal efforts to preserve a distinctive vision of the African American past, a vision that was rooted in the nineteenth-century sense that civilized contributions to society were of the utmost importance. Neither Moorland nor Schomburg articulated a new mythos or historical interpretation, but their preservation efforts were extremely important in that they created organic collections that stand today as the finest sources for the study of African American history, particularly the published and painted record of the culture.

During the 1920s, perhaps the most vital movement with myth-opoetic overtones was the Universal Negro Improvement Association (UNIA), whose charismatic founder and leader was Marcus Garvey. Born in Jamaica, later migrating to England and then the United States, Garvey was the first important African American nationalist figure in the twentieth century. Arriving in the United States in 1916, within a few years Garvey had built possibly the largest international Negro organization that had ever existed. Garvey's Pan-Africanist vision was of a collective unconscious, a race pride, that could connect all African peoples, whether in the diaspora or in Africa. Garvey saw the enslavement of Black people in America and the rising tide of European imperialism in Africa as two halves of the same oppressive whole. Viewing European and American society as rotten to the core, Garvey encouraged Negroes to think of "Africa first" and to consider seriously emigration to Africa, which he saw as the solution to the race problems of the Americas.[49] Interestingly, Garvey's location of choice was Ethiopia. As the only truly independent sub-Saharan African country in the 1920s (Liberia was technically independent but was completely tied economically to the United States), and as the inheritor of a long Judeo-Christian tradition, Ethiopia was considered by Garvey to be the essential or true home of African Americans. Even though Garvey's hope that sizeable numbers of people would emigrate was never fulfilled, he succeeded in shifting African American cultural discourse away from its nineteenth-century concentration on America as a kind of holy land in which the Old Testament prophecies would be fulfilled and toward the distinctive African history of Ethiopia, thereby making an indelible impact on the symbols and rhetoric of African American cultural discourse. Garveyites and later a wide range of Blacks in the United States and the Caribbean came to see Ethiopia as their true homeland.

In speaking of African peoples in the plural, in linking the conditions of oppression of all people of African descent, in articulating a vision of a glorious African past, and in treating the retaking of Africa by Africans as a millennialist vision, Garvey and the Universal Negro Improvement Association restructured the discourse of African American nationalism. Unlike the ambivalence with which it was viewed by nineteenth-century intellectuals and activists, Africa was absolutely central to Garvey. Further, he emphasized an explicitly African version of the Judeo-Christian tradition, focusing on Ethiopia's Jews and the Ethiopian church. Although Garvey himself was not actively involved in preservation efforts, his vision of the African past and the African future was emotionally transforming for many people, especially the newer rural migrants to urban areas. Building on millennialism, the mythos of truth-telling, and the sense of special destiny that many African Americans felt, Garvey added to this a fervor about Africa's past and present. Appropriately, Garvey's main contribution was to enlarge the interior mythos of African Americans.

Garvey transformed Black nationalism in the African diaspora and created some of its enduring symbols. Perhaps the most important of these symbols was the red, black, and green UNIA flag. To paraphrase Garvey, red was for the blood of African people, shed under oppressive conditions; black was the unifying symbolic skin color; and green was for the African land, to which they would one day return. Later, gold was added to stand for the wealth in Africa that all would inherit. This flag remains an important symbol of cultural unity and consciousness. Displayed in many forms—on bumper stickers, hats, and T-shirts—during the 1960s and 1970s, this flag continues in use. Present-day T-shirts worn by African American young people include many versions of this flag, sometimes shaped like the African continent. Sometimes these colors are subtly used as the color scheme in the fabric of a dress, shirt, or background image on music videos. While Garvey's vision has been amended and updated by succeeding nationalist movements, his notion of an African-based unity and consciousness reverberates through to the present. Garvey became a legendary figure and the UNIA a legendary movement. Garvey's flag, his slogans, his international goals, and even his imprisonment and suffering at the hands of the American government—all these elements entered the mythopoetic interpretation of the African American past.

In summary, the New Negro era was a period of enormous vitality in the collection and preservation of elements of African American life, history, and culture. Within Negro communities, important national organizations were formed, such as the Association for the Study of Negro Life and History as well as the National Association for the Advancement of Colored People and the Urban League. The migration north and the resulting diversity of Negro communities provided new audiences for a wide range of political opinions and cultural activities. Many artists, writers, and musicians orchestrated a major outpouring of exhibitions, publications, and performances. Harlem Renaissance artists not only articulated a new discourse on aesthetic values but also pioneered access to a previously unavailable level of white philanthropic support from wealthy Americans of bohemian or progressivist bent. These people agreed on many elements of a romanticist and celebrationist view of African American culture and history. For many of the white enthusiasts, this celebration of the "exotic" provided an aesthetic aphrodisiac. To many of the Negroes involved, this romanticism provided a positive feeling about the African past and the African American present, which began to encompass elements of vernacular culture in addition to elite traditions.

Marcus Garvey was seen by some as a charismatic rabble-rouser, but he viewed himself as the general in a righteous nationalistic army. Garvey may have been the personal opposite of Alain Locke, the Philadelphia Black Victorian who evoked all of the dandyism of an Edwardian patrician. However, these two men shared a dramatically similar sense of the importance and primacy of an African American aesthetic. While Locke was a romanticist who emphasized the essentialist aesthetics of African American life, Garvey's nationalism likewise invoked the spiritual and innate qualities of being African. Garvey's sense of the importance of the African past, his vision of African peoples around the world united in struggle, and his prediction that emigration and landholding would result in the ultimate liberation from racial oppression—all of these elements reflected dramatic new additions to the African American mythos. Garvey's style of organization and his rhetoric changed the landscape of African American cultural discourse. After Garvey, Black nationalism—that is, a full-scale rejection of American society—seemed possible on a pragmatic level. Some of Garvey's slogans, such as "Africa First," and his red, black, green, and gold flag have come to symbolize Black liberation, not only in the United States but around the world. Today Garvey's flag can be seen on the streets of Washington, D.C.; Kingston, Jamaica; and Soweto, South Africa.

African Americans carrying on in the general tradition of nineteenth-century preservationism made significant contributions during this era. Carter G. Woodson founded the first national African American cultural organization and published works of scholarly importance as well as numerous books and pamphlets directed toward a general audience. Woodson was also critical in developing a well-documented, academic approach to the inclusion of African history in African American studies. Woodson believed that cultural preservation functioned to reinforce positive images of self and community inside Negro communities and to combat ignorant prejudice in white America.

In 1926, Woodson celebrated the first Negro History Week. This annual event, held between Frederick Douglass's birthday and Abraham Lincoln's birthday in February, was an opportunity for people to celebrate formally African American life, history, and culture. This kind of public celebration was based on church-related social functions with deep roots in Negro communities. Negro History Week become Black History Week in the late 1960s, and is now celebrated as Black History Month throughout most of the United States, especially in schools and museums. At present, Black History Month may be the largest public ritual celebrating African American culture in the United States. Months of effort at all Black and many historically white museums and schools precede this yearly celebration. Some Black museums on shoestring budgets even obtain the bulk of their annual income from the tours they book during this month, gift-shop sales during this period, and funding they receive for Black History Month programming. Incorporating and probably outstripping Woodson's dream of an integrated American history celebration, contemporary Black History Month programming reflects a major infusion of new historical information and provides the occasion for rhetoric about the preservation of the Black past. Woodson's founding of this event and his ability to develop and maintain a completely African American–based national organization devoted to preservation was perhaps the single most significant achievement of these years.

Collections built by Arthur Schomburg, Jesse B. Moorland, and others are the third major achievement of this era. All of the major research collections that are publicly available today are based on the private collections of a small group who saved materials circulating during the pivotal turn-of-the-century years. Schomburg, among others, struggled along on funds far smaller than those of comparable white collectors of the era; he believed in saving books and magazines, searching for documents, records, and letters, and in other ways helping to preserve the written evidence of African American life, history, and culture. Schomburg in particular was a visionary in seeing the Americas as part of an African diaspora.

Taken together, the efforts of Garvey, Locke, Woodson, Schomburg, Moorland, and others of their generation constituted a critical moment in the history of African American preservation. Many of the collections that remain today were shaped by their particular concerns, goals, and values. And much of the language we use to argue today about issues of African American cultural preservation derive from debates and differences among the members of this seminal generation.

GOVERNMENT SUPPORT AND ORAL HISTORY, 1930–1950

Before 1930 African American efforts at preservation far exceeded those of people outside Negro communities, even including the impressive holdings of the Library of Congress. But during the Depression and World War II, key collections were established in federally funded repositories. These new collections represented a new group of white collectors who had a set of priorities different from the African American mainstream's concern for documents and books. These new collectors tended to come with more populist or radical notions of the importance of understanding history from the bottom up. In the emerging discipline of folklore, general interest was growing in the oral testimony and musical traditions of rural people as the exemplars of an original, authentic American culture.

During the 1930s two major governmental efforts began to record the memories, folklore, and folklife of rural Afro-Americans: the Archive of American Folk Song at the Library of Congress and the Federal Writers' Project. These were the first attempts to record the oral history of African Americans, especially that of poor and rural Black folk, on a large scale and in a systematic manner. By focusing on vernacular African American culture, these folklore collections made central what had previously been preserved only marginally. In the 1920s and 1930s a number of Americans perceived that certain styles of life were either dying out or being completely transformed; as more and more people were forced off the land due to the financial and natural disasters that occurred after World War I, their community life and folkways were disrupted. Some Americans were nostalgic for the antebellum era and the "Lost Cause" (the name former Confederates used to describe the Civil War and Reconstruction); others saw the last generation of formerly enslaved African Americans passing into history. Finally, some Americans of a populist or radical bent perceived that poor people and rural people had critiques of American mainstream culture and distinctive traditions that were not being heard in intellectual or academic circles.

In 1928 the Archive of American Folk Song was established as part of the music division of the Library of Congress. The concern of the archive was to collect, duplicate, and preserve data or evidence of American culture gained through field expeditions. The director of the music division, Carl Engel, had already established connections with collectors such as Phillips Barry, Paul Bowles, and Charles Seeger. However, his most important connection was with John Lomax.[50] Lomax, a white Texan, had spent years traveling through the West and recording songs of the vanishing frontier, which were first published in 1910 as *Cowboy Songs and Other Frontier Ballads*. Over the next fifty years, Lomax traveled around the country, recording songs, stories, and jokes, publishing books, staging performances in urban centers, and aiding people in getting their music released commercially. Lomax was one of the most important of the early collectors of American folklore and folk music generally, and African American materials in particular. The discoverer of Huddie Ledbetter, better known as Lead-belly, and other rural blues and gospel singers, John Lomax essentially founded the collection of the Archive of American Folk Song (now known as the Archive of Folk Culture). Although never actually in residence as a staff member, Lomax formed a special relationship to the Library of Congress, which paid him one dollar a month as an honorary curator, loaned him expensive, state-of-the-art recording equipment, served as the repository for materials he brought in, and in some cases partly financed his travels. Something of an impresario, Lomax made his money from selling his songbooks, setting up con-certs, and in some cases working as an agent for artists, including Ledbetter, who recorded commercially. Lomax also was a leading figure in the Modern Language Association, which supported his work and gave him a scholarly audience for his findings as well.

Alan Lomax, John Lomax's son, began traveling with his father at an early age. As the younger Lomax grew up, he too became an active folklorist and received academic training as well. By 1936, the two Lomaxes had contributed about seven hundred disks with two to twelve songs each. Upon becoming the first full-time staff person of the archive in 1938, Alan, both independently and in conjunction with his father, greatly expanded the collection of the archive. Although the Lomaxes were interested in a wide variety of cultures and forms, including the songs of Mexicans in Texas, the songs and stories of the Okies in California, and various Native American materials, three-quarters of the recordings they made were of African American material.[51]

John Lomax pioneered, and Alan Lomax extended, the notion that recording the viewpoints of rural, working-class, and poor people is essential for understanding American history and culture. They elaborated on this basically populist view by making field recordings in a variety of unconventional settings, such as prisons, bars, and work camps. Earlier American folklorists had mostly been concerned with the origins of Anglo-American songs, then mostly present in revival meetings and among seamen and rural New England folk. The Lomaxes' focus was on recording the cultural forms of segments of American society in which musical and oral traditions remained strongly linked to earlier styles and concerns. Early on, the Lomaxes concentrated on African Americans and others who were downtrodden or at the margins of American life, such as hillbillies, prostitutes, and criminals.

The notion that folklore and folk songs were the central cultural contributions that African Americans had made to American culture was markedly different from the attitudes of most Harlem Renaissance artists and their European American celebrators. Some Negro scholars, artists, and writers, such as Sterling Brown, Paul Robeson, Zora Neale Hurston, and Langston Hughes, were interested in this material. For example, Hurston, who today is better known as a novelist, studied with the anthropologist Franz Boas at Columbia University and was an active collector of folklore materials for more than twenty years.[52] Hurston took Alan Lomax on several collecting trips to parts of Florida and the Sea Islands of South Carolina, Georgia, and north Florida. Still, Hurston was a maverick during the Harlem Renaissance and lampooned the "niggerati," whom she saw as uninterested in the expressive forms of Afro-American vernacular culture.

Other notable figures include Sterling Brown and Paul Robeson. Brown served as editor of *Negro Affairs* for the Federal Writers' Project in the 1930s and taught English at Howard University for many years; nevertheless, he is probably better remembered as a poet and literary critic who incorporated African Amercan folk tales, legends, and figures of speech into his works (such as the 1942 book *Negro Caravan,* which he coedited). Robeson was an international star and probably the most prominent Negro actor and concert artist of the 1930s and 1940s. Robeson was the first person to perform Negro spirituals on the concert stages of Europe and America, mixing them with German lieder, classical arias, and folk songs. Robeson's proud performances of this music, both live and for a number of record labels, including Folkways, helped fuel wider public interest in it and created a larger market for other recordings of it. Through his lifelong involvement with pacifist and other progressive causes, Robeson forged an expressive link between the Negro music of the Americas and the music of other social and political movements around the world. Although Robeson was persecuted by the American government in the 1950s and denied a passport for some years because of his leftist political beliefs, he held firm as a beacon of courage for many younger African American cultural activists.[53]

While the work of people such as Brown and Robeson was widely popular, many of the Harlem Renaissance intellectuals were embarrassed by more vernacular forms of culture and their performers. Frankly, John and Alan Lomax were recording people who might appear in a folk music program and in jail within the same week. Many of these rural Colored people told stories about ghosts and supernatural events and sang frank songs about sex, love, and crime. Though blues songs about these subjects are the most familiar, there were also working songs, religious blues, and blues that carefully and poignantly critiqued the Southern social oppression under which these rural Colored people struggled. Although W.E.B. Du Bois lamented the passing of a Black folk culture in 1903 in his essay entitled "Sorrow Songs" (in *The Souls of Black Folk*), one cannot imagine him inviting Huddie Ledbetter to his home. Twice imprisoned on murder charges and twice released because of his extraordinary musicianship and singing, Ledbetter became John Lomax's driver and traveling companion in the early and mid-1930s.[54] Ledbetter was the sort of person the Urban League had been set up to lift up, clean off, and get a regular job. Only a few Negro scholars, such as Hurston, Harold Courlander, and those in Charles Johnson's Research Department at Fisk University, were involved in making field recordings, and they were hard-pressed to find sufficient financing to continue their work, in part because they themselves had little money and in part because it was more difficult for them to obtain sponsorship and funding than it was for white individuals.[55] It was in fact the Lomaxes (and a few other white collectors) who were most instrumental in preserving this material. The equipment they required was expensive: at first they used bulky cylinders, then 315-pound "portable" disk machines, and eventually magnetic tape. For the most part financing was provided by either foundation or government sources.

Admittedly, the commercial market among whites for such talent was limited, but a highly politicized, radicalized, avant-garde market did exist. Moses Asch noted this and in 1947 founded Folkways Records. Asch was the Polish-born son of a famous playwright in the Yiddish theater. After immigrating to the United States, he returned to Germany in the 1920s to study sound-engineering technologies. Although his two previous record labels failed (perhaps because their catalogues did not cover as wide a range of recordings), Folkways Records lasted as a private label for forty years, until Asch's death in 1987. This commercial outlet for the kinds of singers and storytellers the Lomaxes recorded was also an extraordinary archive of world sound and American culture.[56]

Asch had enormous ambitions; he wanted to record as much as possible of the "world in sound." Furthermore, a progressive, secular Jewish background gave him an interest in recording the points of view of oppressed people, of political radicals, and of musical and vocal experimenters whose music critiqued the prevailing social order or musical mainstream.

Although his children's catalogue was Asch's best-selling division, he recorded ethnic songs and stories from around the world, jazz artists such as Mary Lou Williams, the early work of the experimental composer John Cage, and a wide range of sounds such as the album New York Streets in Summer. Folkways contributed to the financial and commercial survival of folk music (of all sorts) throughout the McCarthy era, during which the music industry blackballed well-known people such as Paul Robeson, Pete Seeger, and Woody Guthrie. Continuing to record during the era of the modern civil rights movement, Asch recorded the speeches of Martin Luther King, Jr., Huey Newton (a founding member of the Black Panther Party), the radical activist Angela Davis, and others, and included them in the Folkways catalogue. After years of complex negotiation, Asch's collection was purchased by the Smithsonian Institution in 1987 and is now open to researchers.[57] Asch's work stands as a private collection of commercial recordings parallel to the scope of what the Archive of American Folk Song at the Library of Congress amassed during the years Asch was active.

Music was not the only cultural form preserved during the 1930s. After 1933, government money became available to record the oral testimony of former slaves. Through the Works Progress Administration (WPA) and the National Relief Administration, a number of programs emerged that focused on recording oral testimony and other

aspects of American vernacular culture: the Index of American Design; the Folksong and Folklore Department of the National Service
Bureau; the Federal Music Project, under Charles Seeger; and the
Folklore Studies of the Federal Writers' Project, under Benjamin Botkin. The WPA used many amateur (that is, self-trained) collectors of
material. While this produced some unevenness in the recordings, it
did allow for the participation of Negro scholars without graduate
degrees, such as Zora Neale Hurston, who would have been excluded
if an emphasis on purely professional credentials had determined participation. Readings of the oral testimonies strongly give the sense that
the race of the interviewer made a critical difference in many cases, so
greater use of African Americans might have resulted in a somewhat
different record. Still, the unparalleled achievement of these programs
was the recording of the testimony of elderly African Americans, some
of them the last living generation of former slaves.[58]

Not all of the people whose stories were collected were poor, of
course. Some were property owners or tradespeople, and some had
successful businesses. The interviews were mostly conducted in the
South and the border states, and most of those interviewed did live in
rural areas or small towns. Although later criticized by professional
folklorists as too random and uneven a sample, the thirty-plus volumes of material collected during the 1930s are absolutely priceless.
With this material, Benjamin Botkin was able to publish *Lay My
Burden Down: A Folk History of Slavery* in 1945. Because of these
collections, in the 1960s and 1970s Eugene Genovese, Lawrence Levine, and others were able to begin discovering and reinterpreting
elements of slave culture.[59] These pioneering histories of slavery
would not have been possible without this collection. Together, the
Archive of American Folk Song and the Works Progress Administration collection (now also housed at the Library of Congress) constituted the earliest systematic group of recordings of late-nineteenth- and
early-twentieth-century African American vernacular culture.

While the most innovative collecting may have been of oral testimony, important new collections of traditional documents were also
created during this period. In 1935, the National Archives opened to
the public. The archives were established to preserve "documents of
American Formation," such as the Constitution, and all the noncur-
rent records of permanent value produced by the federal government.[60] In gathering together the records of the American government, the archivists included African American materials wherever
they appeared. From the debates about slavery during the Constitu-

tional era, to abolitionist agitation, to the Civil War and Reconstruction with its Freedmen's Bureau, to legislation and court rulings regarding segregation, to labor regulation and social service directives, there were numerous government agencies with records of special pertinence to the history of Black people. Records of a more personal nature, such as census forms and military pension folders, contained volumes of fairly detailed information, some statistical, about Black people. Since World War I, government surveillance of African American activists and their movements has also created fascinating and disturbing records, some of which are now available under the Freedom of Information Act.

In preserving the records of the federal government, the National Archives maintained a unique mass of materials documenting the history of African Americans. This collecting, however, did not reflect social progress on the part of the administration. Even though such a rich collection of African American materials existed, the archives were well known as a difficult place for a Black professional to get a job. Unlike the Smithsonian Institution, however, the National Archives did employ a few African American men and women in professional and paraprofessional capacities. Roland McConnell, Sara Jackson, James Dent Walker, and Harold Pinkett all worked there at various times after World War II. They developed extensive expertise in the records that related to Afro-American history, helping to make accessible much information lying buried in federal records. These archivists and historians were also active in national organizations such as the Association for the Study of Negro Life and History, and a couple of them later became founding members of the Afro-American Historical and Genealogical Society (established in 1978).[61]

At the same time, most major American museums continued their informal policy of exclusion of African American materials. Several important museums were established during these years: Colonial Williamsburg, the Henry Ford Museum and Greenfield Village, and Mystic Seaport. The restoration of Williamsburg, initiated by members of the Rockefeller family, was intended to give contemporary Americans a holistic view of the lifestyles and values of the founding fathers. Although the city of Williamsburg was more than fifty percent African American in the 1770s, no hint of slavery nor of African American culture entered into the restoration's collections or interpretive programming until the 1980s.[62] The Ford Museum and Mystic Seaport each had technological rationales. Ford wanted to show the history of European and American progress; from that record, African

Americans were routinely presumed to be absent. The seafaring enthusiasts in Connecticut wanted to preserve the history of technological change in boats and ships. Although nearly a third of American seamen in the nineteenth century were Black, and some African Americans invented new devices improving upon older techniques such as the harpoon, this participation was not directly preserved in this museum.[63] None of the major museums of the era directly acted to preserve African American culture; however, one private collector did. In 1935 Miriam Bellangee Wilson, a member of the Charleston, South Carolina, elite, began traveling to the plantations of friends and relatives to collect slave-made artifacts. Wilson's collection later became the basis of the Old Slave Mart Museum, founded by Judith Wragg Chase and her sister in the early 1960s.[64] The objects collected by Wilson remain one of the very few Southern-based African American material culture collections.

In the academic world, Melville Herskovits and his wife, Frances, emerged as the only major white collectors of African and diasporic materials. Herskovits was an anthropologist who began writing on questions of Black ethnicity and culture in the 1920s. In fact, Herskovits was one of the few white contributors to the 1925 issue of *Survey Graphic* that was published in book form as *The New Negro*. In his essay there, Herskovits argued that African Americans had achieved a high degree of cultural assimilation to Anglo-Saxon social mores and behavior. However, over the course of his long and distinguished career, Herskovits would move away from those ideas to become the primary American scholar researching American cultural survivals of African elements. For example, Herskovits was the first American scholar to discover the maroon communities of the present-day countries of Surinam and Colombia. Still intact, these "Bush Negro" communities had been established in the 1770s, after their founders successfully defeated Dutch forces. Herskovits was certainly the first professional scholar to conduct research in West Africa, the Caribbean, and South America, searching for connections among diasporic communities.[65]

The Herskovitses were also avid collectors. When Melville Herskovits began teaching at Northwestern University in 1927 and found that there were few references in the university libraries touching on subjects of interest to him, he began collecting books, photographs, documents, and unpublished manuscripts as well as art and artifacts to support his teaching and to assist the research of his graduate students. Over a period of thirty-five years, Herskovits built one of the most important collections of African and diasporic materials in the United States. The Herskovitses' Africana collection is still at Northwestern University, where it is a major resource for students and scholars of Africa. After Melville Herskovits's death, the art and artifact collections were transferred to the Schomburg Center for Research in Black Culture in New York City.

In summary, during the 1930s and 1940s, key collections were established that documented African American vernacular culture. At the same time, important records from the federal government began to be organized and systematically made available to researchers. Though the fruit of this work did not begin to affect mainstream historical work until the 1960s, these collections formed the basis for the reinterpretation of American history. Although a few African American scholars were involved with each collection, in large measure, populist or otherwise radicalized white Americans helped create publicly available collections, especially of oral testimony. The Archive of American Folk Song and the Works Progress Administration collected material that had never before been collected in such large amounts or with the same level of integrity regarding the social and cultural contexts of the material. The National Archives organized materials that had languished for years in the file cabinets and storerooms of government offices. Taken together, these agencies preserved massive amounts of new material that provided the evidentiary basis for the social-history revolution of the 1960s and 1970s.

THE BLACK MUSEUM MOVEMENT, 1950–1980

During the years following World War II, a dramatic modern civil rights movement erupted from Negro communities across America, but especially in the South. Though initially focused on citizenship rights in Southern cities, movement activism eventually addressed political, economic, social, and cultural questions. While full desegregation may not have been accomplished even today, the movement profoundly changed American life. The Brown vs. Board of Education decision in 1954 was the result of two generations of activism by the NAACP and others concerned with the legal questions of segregation. Yet the direct-action strategy of demonstrations, sit-ins, and marches galvanized people across class, race, and generational divisions. While "Freedom Now" may not yet have come, the United States in 1992 is a profoundly different place in which to live than it was in 1950.

The modern civil rights movement affected many aspects of cultural process, both within Black communities and in the wider society. It is impossible to overstate the importance of the movement in the sociocultural arena; it affected the terms of cultural discourse and modes of social process, and helped generate an outpouring of artistic expression far larger and more diverse than the Harlem Renaissance.

Within the movement, debates about goals, strategies, and resources were constant. Every leader, including Martin Luther King, Jr., was subject to intense criticism, either from within civil rights organizations or from others not associated with major civil rights organizations. Just the list of the "Big Six" national organizations of the era—the NAACP, the Urban League, the National Council of Negro Women (NCNW), the Southern Christian Leadership Conference (SCLC), the Congress of Racial Equality (CORE), the Student Nonviolent Coordinating Committee (SNCC)—gives some sense of the complexity of the activist landscape. This intense cauldron of debate and (sometimes life-threatening) direct action was the crucible in which a critical generation of Americans was formed. Within Black communities, young critics emerged to challenge the integrationist ideology and goals articulated by the majority of the early supporters of the movement. People such as Stokely Carmichael (now Kwame Touré) and H. Rap Brown inside SNCC questioned the interpretations and the power of more integrationist figures such as John Lewis and Martin Luther King, Jr. This critique, perhaps most easily summarized by the slogan "Black Power," was the battle cry in the rebirth of a younger Black nationalism.[66] Yet among the younger members of the civil rights movement, criticism itself was an important new value. Learning from the practices of numerous progressive leftist organizations and African socialist parties then emerging, these younger activists came to see intraorganizational criticism and personal self-criticism as one of the crucial elements of the struggle toward freedom and justice. Within many traditional Black institutions, such as churches and colleges, criticism was taken as a form of deep-seated rebellion, a challenge to patriarchal authority that could not be borne. Yet younger people did resist in different ways: through student rebellions at Black colleges in the 1920s, and by leaving college in the 1960s to work full-time for SNCC. In the early 1960s, a new and ultimately successful direct-action movement emerged from college NAACP groups and church junior choir meetings but evolved beyond those institutions into the activist groups listed above. Ultimately that critical quality, so crucial for the early phase of sit-ins, demonstrations, and marches, helped blow these organizations apart. By 1966 and 1967, movement activists began wrestling with questions of gender equality and vehement ideological argument within the context of rising political violence, often government-induced. Between 1969 and the early 1970s, government suppression, burnout on the part of longtime activists, and ideological divisions within the movement itself worked to cripple and ultimately to kill SNCC and most of the other groups that had emerged in the early 1960s.

Still, one legacy of this cultural shift from an integrationist ideology to a Black Power ideology was the sense that criticism had a value, that it could help both organizations and individuals grow. Criticism was to be encouraged, not feared. As former political activists moved into cultural centers and museums in the 1970s and 1980s, they brought these values of criticism to their new world. Together with all their inherent differences, the years of the modern civil rights movement (1950–1965) and the years of the Black Power movement (1965–1975) might be called the Black Consciousness Era.

The Black museum movement was born out of this enormously complex welter of cultural expression, debate, and critique. The number of Black museums formed during this thirty-year period is absolutely extraordinary. Between 1950 and 1980, well over ninety African American museums were founded in the United States and Canada. By contrast, between 1885 and 1930, though there were scores of Negro cultural societies and a few private collections, the number of Negro museums was relatively small, probably thirty or fewer. Most of these museums or cultural centers were part of the Negro college system and tended to focus either on library or fine-arts collections. Yet after 1950 scores of museums were founded in urban Black communities, mostly as freestanding entities not part of a church, school, or any preexisting Black institution. Often these new museums were founded by community activists who had worked in the civil rights movement at some level and now wanted to use that expertise for a cultural agenda. This volume of museum building was unprecedented within the Black community.[67]

Understanding the complexity of cultural influences is essential for interpreting the meaning and function of these newly established Black museums. During the Black Consciousness Era, many African American artists, political and religious leaders, and everyday people struggled with questions of personal and ethnic identity, which were informed by a new language of cultural and political discourse.[68] Activists within all wings of the movement were influenced by thinking, writing, and activism in other parts of the world. CORE was organized by an interracial group of pacifists in 1941. King began reading Gandhi in graduate school in the late 1940s.[69] Early in the history of SNCC, pacifists who believed in nonviolent practice reigned. But by 1964 some within the organization had begun reading African anticolonialist writers such as Frantz Fanon, Kwame Nkrumah, and Léopold Senghor. Through these writers, they discovered the theories of Marx, Lenin, and Mao. Soon these young people had begun to create a literature of their own: James Baldwin, *The Fire Next Time* (1964); Stokely Carmichael and Charles Hamilton, *Black Power* (1965); Eldridge Cleaver, *Soul on Ice* (1968); and George Jackson, *Soledad Brother* (1970) and *Blood in My Eye* (1972).[70] These are only a few of hundreds of works published after 1960 that take up questions of personal and cultural identity. One example of an individual who mixed cultural expression and personal identity with political and social concerns was Harry Belafonte, who was among the most popular Negro singers and movie stars of the 1950s and 1960s. Born in New York City of Caribbean parents, Belafonte lived in Jamaica from 1935 to 1940 and brought back African-Jamaican songs, singing them in a manner accessible to many Americans. Belafonte was an active supporter of and fundraiser for various progressive African American organizations of the 1960s, especially SNCC. Belafonte served as a crucial link between younger African American activists and a wider world of sociopolitical struggle; through his efforts, SNCC leaders were able to travel to Africa to meet activists such as Miriam Makeba of South Africa and Sekou Touré of Guinea.

In duration, social impact, and the vitality of cultural expression, the Black Consciousness Era is roughly parallel to the Harlem Renaissance. In fact, in virtually every way, the Black Consciousness Era *was* a true renaissance, stimulating nearly every area of African American life. New Black theater companies and dance troupes explored the African American sensibility in performance. Black jazz musicians invented bebop; Black popular singers created rhythm and blues, rock and roll, and soul music. New literary schools of poets, essayists, and critics established new magazines, created anthologies, discovered forgotten classics, and worked at defining a Black aesthetic.[71] New Black visual artists began to paint definitions of the African in African American life. Between 1950 and 1980 more Black cultural institutions were founded than at any other time in American history. During the Black Consciousness Era, many people were literally at work creating a new mythos.

This new mythos of Black consciousness contained a number of earlier elements and had no single contemporary interpretation. There were various versions of what Black consciousness meant, but they all shared a sense of the special destiny of African American people and the idea that they were the truth-tellers of American society. As in the abolitionist generation, this mythopoetic notion was borne out in the lives of many people engaged in direct action. Putting one's life on the line for justice and equality aligned personal memory and local history with that mythic destiny, as it had for Frederick Douglass and Sojourner Truth in the 1850s.

During the 1960s, some people called the movement a "second Reconstruction."[72] For some, the word *reconstruction* provided a sense of the crusading spirit and the power of morally redemptive action. For others, mostly white Southerners, the term conjured up images of federal intervention, Negroes wild in the streets, and violence. Taken together, these mutually constructed metaphors give some insight into the language of crusade or holy war that movement people used to describe their experiences. The African American millennialist rhetoric of antislavery agitation was updated and reinvigorated. During the early years of the movement, the widely used slogan "Freedom Now!" appeared on handwritten signs at demonstrations and in big bold letters at large marches. This slogan was an updated version of the same cries for freedom and justice made by abolitionists more than a century earlier.

The nonviolent approach enjoyed great legislative victories, yet suffered great losses through the violent deaths of rank-and-file members as well as leaders. The disappointments of political compromise, inner-city riots, and escalating government surveillance and violence supported the position of people within the movement who favored the concept of Black Power over the concept of an integrated society. Eventually separatism became a convincing option, in part because this option echoed the independence struggles of nations in Africa and the Caribbean.[73] In those conflicts, colonized peoples worked to separate themselves from the European colonial powers.

Separatism was a rather new element in African American political thought. Before 1930 emigrationists had journeyed to Liberia and Garvey had planned to go to Ethiopia, but no significant leader before World War II had suggested a separate Black nation within the United States. Between 1968 and 1975 Black nationalism strongly resurfaced. This nationalism had many roots, but the most culturally symbolic organization was the Nation of Islam, whose founder was Elijah Muhammed and whose chief spokesperson was Malcolm X.

Begun in the 1930s as one of a number of Islamic-inspired African

American religious sects, the Nation of Islam had survived into the 1950s. Though not a fiery orator, Elijah Muhammed was a brilliant organizer. A pacifist during World War II, he served time in prison as a draft resister. There he discovered a pool of people waiting to be converted. Muhammed was not the only religious-political organizer of the Negro masses in the 1930s. Father Divine of New York City, Prophet Jones of Detroit, and Daddy Grace of Washington, D.C., were all active in this era. However large some of these organizations became during the 1930s, though, only the Nation of Islam appealed to Black nationalists of the 1950s and 1960s.

In the early 1950s a charismatic former convict, Malcolm Little (who later changed his name to Malcolm X), became a minister in the Nation of Islam. Malcolm X was an extraordinary example of the criminal who discovered salvation in this movement. Malcolm X's life of crime and his later renunciation of it was as emblematic for Black nationalists, converts to Islam, and other alternative groups as Frederick Douglass's life as the archetypal freed slave was for an abolitionist audience. In 1959 Malcolm X became the official spokesperson for the Nation of Islam. He was roundly vilified by the white American media, the integration-oriented African American press, and—needless to say—conservative political leaders and scholars. People in most of these areas of American life condemned his rejection of nonviolence as a strategy and his embrace of separatism as a goal. In 1964 he made a mind-bending pilgrimage to Mecca that changed his views on many issues, especially race; he discovered a new world of interracial brotherhood inside a more orthodox Islam. Killed in 1965, Malcolm X may have had more influence in death than in life. For many people, his writings and the stories of his life have come to symbolize African American resistance during the 1960s. Malcolm X's birthday is celebrated in cities in the United States that have a significant African American population. In some places, Black History Month extends from King's birthday, 17 January, to Malcolm X's birthday, usually celebrated on or around 19 May. These national African American events span the sociopolitical spectrum that emerged from the activism and ideological combat of the sixties.[74]

Malcolm X and "The Nation" changed the landscape of African American cultural discourse. Dramatically shifting the interest in the ancient past from the Israelites and even Ethiopia to Egypt, the Nation of Islam helped stimulate a wide range of Black Americans already hungry for positive information about Africa. Symbols such as pyramids, all-seeing eyes, busts of Nefertiti, and other Egyptiana pervaded the growing number of African clothing shops, bookstores, and head shops of the time. Servicing a new market for Garvey flags, slogans, and literature, these shops made African and African-influenced artifacts quite saleable for the first time in African American history. This embrace of things African was the antithesis of the nineteenth-century ambivalence about African origins.

Muhammed's version of world history was based on the writings of J. A. Rogers, Drusilla Houston, and several other self-taught historians of the 1930s, who saw all world civilization as emanating from Africa, especially Ethiopia and Egypt.[75] Muhammed enlarged this notion with his white-man-as-beast theory of African racial superiority. Turning nineteenth-century physical anthropology completely on its head, Muhammed described a separate genesis for Black people, who then created all the other peoples of the world. Because of this primordial role as world-creators, the melanin content of their skin, and other physico-spiritual attributes, Africans were considered the only truly civilized and spiritual people.

While many Black intellectuals and collectors may not have accepted all of Muhammed's tenets, his focus on Egypt and early African civilization spawned a generation of both academically trained and lay historians and archaeologists. These crosscurrents of popular and scholarly thought made Egypt the central symbol of Black self-respect. Again turning nineteenth-century mythopoetic narratives on their heads, many twentieth-century nationalists saw the Egyptians, the slaveholders of the Old Testament, as the archetype for Africa and, beyond that, the genitors of human knowledge, both spiritual and scientific.

Movement activists and intellectuals also read historical and contemporary Pan-Africanist thought. The writings of Marcus Garvey and W.E.B. Du Bois, as well as contemporary African political thinking, reinforced a sense of the connection among all African peoples. Africa and Africans had moved from being an ambivalent concern to being a central element in the African American mythos. Dashikis, Afro hairstyles, jewelry, poster art, and many other cultural forms became infused with color schemes, design motifs, and symbolic elements loosely inspired by Africa. This new mythos embraced the African past and portrayed Africans around the world as linked in a united destiny. Though articulated in elaborate and often contradictory ways, this African destiny involved struggling against the forces of colonialism and white racism as well as honoring traditional values seen as under attack in the West, such as respect for the elderly, family stability, and achievements within the arts. Increasingly, in the late 1970s and 1980s, such values have come to be called African or Afrocentric.

The Afrocentricity movement is the newest significantly different cultural analysis emerging from an interior view of the African American past. This new view incorporates not only African American history within a diasporic context, both American and Asian in scope, but also scientific interpretations of human evolution in Africa and archaeological, Biblical, and linguistic analyses focusing on the African origins of civilization. As such, the Afrocentricity movement is the heir to previous Black constructions of the special role of African Americans.

Originally articulated within the context of Biblical history by nineteenth-century African American emigrationists, the present-day Afrocentricity movement takes that view to a world-historical level. Claiming that all humans were originally Black and that all culture originated in Africa, especially Kemet (Egypt) and Nubia (Ethiopia), leading Afrocentrists also see Malcolm X as a principal modern-day spokesperson for an Afrocentric praxis (though the term *Afrocentric* was not in use during his lifetime).

What can now be grouped together as a spectrum of Afrocentric organizations, institutions, and intellectuals emerged from the various threads of the movement toward Black consciousness during the late 1960s and early 1970s. After the disintegration of important radical organizations such as SNCC and the Black Panther Party, and the breakup of the Nation of Islam into various splinter groups, many on the Black left who had moved in cultural nationalist or separatist circles began a reassessment of cultural and religious life that built on yet critiqued earlier nationalist organizations.

In the introduction to *African Culture: The Rhythms of Unity,* Molefi Kete Asante and Kariamu Welsh Asante defined the concept of Afrocentricity as "an ideological statement of the unity of African culture and the need for a new consciousness. *Afrocentricity* contends that there are two types of consciousness, a consciousness of oppression and a consciousness of victory to create liberating motifs and messages." More briefly, Molefi Kete Asante has defined Afrocentricity as "the belief in the centrality of Africans in postmodern history."[76]

The Afrocentricity movement represents a new phase in African American cultural discourse. Turning Black abolitionist imagery on its head, Afrocentrists identify not with the enslaved Hebrews of the Old

Testament but with the Egyptians, who were the slaveowners. In seeing both Nubia and Kemet as the foundation of all human culture, Afrocentrists have incorporated the thinking of Rastafarianism and that of Marcus Garvey, Elijah Muhammed, and other lesser-known Black nationalist leaders. Still, in important ways, Afrocentricity has gone beyond these earlier movements. By citing new Afrocentric translations of Kemetic texts, referring to anthropological evidence of early humans in Africa, and pointing to cultural evidence of African contacts around the world, the Afrocentrists have created a new cultural discourse in which Africans (and by extension, African Americans) are unique within the context of world culture and were the spiritual leaders in all early human social life. In many Black museums and cultural organizations, Afrocentricity has become the predominant ideology. Especially in current debates about how to reform public-school curricula, Afrocentrist scholars and activists have maintained highly vocal and visible positions. Many African Americans believe that the works of Cheikh Anta Diop, Ivan Van Sertima, and others contain claims that are proven and uncontestable. In fact, many of these works are not generally accepted by academically based scholars within their respective disciplines. However, such difference between cultural mythos and historical scholarship has always energized American debates about the African American past. In terms of preservation, the Afrocentricity movement has already produced an enormous number of books, stores that sell African and Afrocentric clothing, jewelry, T-shirts with slogans, and other ephemera suggesting the power of this new view of the African American past. In the early 1990s, most Black museums are in the process of coming to terms with the implications of this new ideology for their collections, research, and outreach programs.

Though *Afrocentric* is a relatively new term for these sentiments, the founders of the new Black museums were motivated by similar feelings, even though they represented different segments of a broad ideological spectrum of political strategies and goals. In the 1950s and early 1960s, most of the individuals who founded museums were artists and/or teachers, such as Elma Lewis, who founded a dance school in Roxbury, Massachusetts, in 1950 and eighteen years later the National Center of Afro-American Artists, or Margaret Burroughs, who organized the Ebony Museum of Negro Culture in Chicago in 1961 (now the Du Sable Museum). Some of these new museums were founded by people involved in progressive politics, such as the group of trade unionists who established the San Francisco Afro-

American Historical Society in 1956. Other founders emerged from the politically active wings of liberal Christian churches, such as Sue Bailey Thurman (wife of the noted Afro-American theologist Howard Thurman), who in 1959 founded the Afro-American Historical Society of Boston (now the Museum of Afro-American History in the African Meeting House on Beacon Hill). Their concern was often to create settings where people could gather and debate issues deriving from the Afro-American experience. For example, the San Francisco society's main activities in the early years were focused around discussion groups, which studied a topic for a year and then presented their findings to the larger group during Negro History Week. Only in the mid-1960s did the San Francisco group begin to collect objects. As another example, Elma Lewis was concerned that Black children should have the early opportunities for training in dance, music, and other performance arts that can be so critical to a successful professional career; she did not establish her museum until many years later. These founders were influenced by the political rhetoric and cultural concerns of the 1930s and 1940s, often expressed in the labor movement and in leftist organizations. Many of them had had prior experience of African American preservationist activities through their work with Carter G. Woodson's Association for the Study of Negro Life and History. As artists, their focus was more on the process of positive cultural identification. They energized their students' artistic talents or expressed their own views in art. During the oppressive years of the McCarthy era, the politics of culture may have become a haven for radicals of an earlier generation.[77]

After 1964, the founders of Black museums tended to be younger people whose political rhetoric and cultural goals were informed by the demonstrations, sit-ins, and freedom schools of the Southern civil rights movement. These younger people, such as Charles Wright, who established the Museum of Afro-American History in Detroit in 1965, Edmund Barry Gaither, brought in by Elma Lewis in 1968 to be the director of the National Center of Afro-American Artists in Boston, Byron Rushing, the first director of the Museum of Afro-American History (founded in 1969), and John Kinard, first director of the Anacostia Museum (established in 1967), tended to share the older founders' sense of the absolute importance of preserving African American life, history, and culture.

In the freedom schools and within SNCC and CORE themselves, the dominant ideology hinged on the notion that people with more-than-average amounts of education and training should become facili-

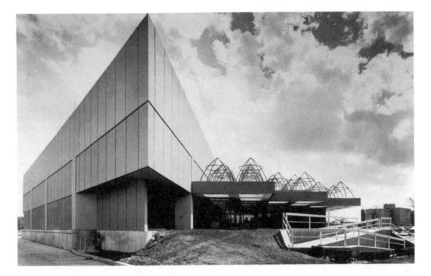

Fig. 17-9. Museum of African American History, Detroit. Photo courtesy the Museum of African American History.

tators for the community. Influenced by a number of Third World revolutionaries, this idea was more democratic than the older Marxist idea of an elite revolutionary vanguard. Rather than standing "objectively" apart from the community and making analyses, as had been true of an earlier generation of leftist intellectuals and activists, the SNCC generation saw themselves as standing inside the community and helping to give voice to community desires. These people felt that museums could be instruments of empowerment for the Black community. This idea of empowerment through cultural institutions also originated with the movement. Early on, Martin Luther King, Jr., had articulated the notion that Black people needed to develop a sense of their own entitlement as citizens and as human beings, and that direct positive action was a path toward this. The younger generation of museum founders saw museums as cultural centers that supported a constructive pathway toward the development of ethnic and personal pride.

Influenced by the SNCC and CORE emphasis on students (and teachers) as facilitators in their communities, as people who would get the news of freedom out to their communities, this group of museum founders emphasized communication. The most successful of these museums, in terms of size and longevity, became centers for alterna-

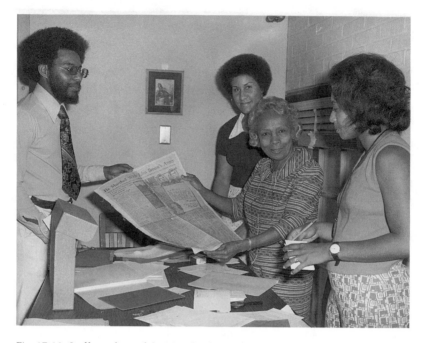

Fig. 17-10. Staff members of the Moorland-Spingarn Research Center in the early 1970s. From left to right: Thomas Battle, curator of manuscripts; Evelyn Brooks; Dorothy Porter Wesley, chief librarian; unidentified staff person. Photo courtesy Moorland-Spingarn Research Center, Howard University.

tive culture within their local and regional Black communities. One little-studied aspect of the civil rights movement was the way in which people within it helped create a new civil religion of sorts within the African American community. Though based originally on coalitions inside churches and historically Black schools, the movement went beyond those institutions: conferences, meetings, and debates were held in hotel rooms, offices, and private homes, which became new locations for social and political activity for this younger generation. New, hybrid political-cultural forms emerged: demonstrations, sit-ins, and marches always had singing and dancing along with political talk. The people who founded museums did so in part to make some of this political debate, progressive performance style, and Pan-Africanist rhetoric available to the community at a grass-roots level. Their museums were vehicles for social change, often speaking to the wider African American community through well-established expressive cultural forms such as performances of song cycles. Black museums founded in the last thirty years are places where alternative versions of the African American and African past can be debated and disseminated to a wider public.

Black museums functioned as the keepers of the African American mythos in all its diversity and complexity. For example, across the country today, Black museums generally sponsor Kwanzaa festivals during the December holiday season. Originated by Ron Karenga in 1966, Kwanzaa is an amalgamation of numerous harvest festivals held in various West African societies. Characterized by the celebration of seven principles of unity, the Kwanzaa festival has become the most widely celebrated holiday with a Black nationalist or separatist origin.[78] Another example of the singular agreement among these museums about their shared mission is the fact that most of the new Black museums have similar names, quite often incorporating along with a city or state name the phrase "Museum of African American History and Art" or perhaps "History and Culture."

The collections of these newer museums reflected the diversity of Black views of the African American past. In the early days, many of these newer museums functioned as cultural centers and were housed in old schools, churches, and theaters that had some performance spaces. The Minneapolis Afro-American History and Art Museum was a typical example. Founded by a group of artists in the early 1970s, the museum originally held exhibitions of contemporary art and gave art classes to elementary and secondary school students. Eventually the museum added a community-based board of directors and a collection of some miscellaneous African artifacts, several hundred pieces of contemporary art, a sizeable number of books, and a few documents and photographs. Such a history is rather different from the typical story of museum development in elite European American communities. Most historically white local societies and museums began with a collection and usually some resources, such as a building or a group of donors willing to raise the money to erect a building. Within African American communities, these newer museums usually began with a mandate from the community for positive education, a group of politically linked activists, and a desire to communicate. Performances, art exhibitions, tours, and classes for students, rather than financially valuable art or material culture collections, have been their focus. Resources have typically been quite slim, and not produced by a wealthy board of trustees. Often support from private foundations and the government have kept these museums afloat, albeit on a shoestring budget.

The growth of Black political power in both the electorates of major urban areas and in state legislatures and other elective offices has finally given African Americans significant control of governmental resources, which could then be made available to African American communities. The growth of Black museums was fueled in part by new sources of governmental funds being made available to cultural institutions as a result of the Great Society initiatives of the late 1960s and early 1970s. During the Nixon presidency, more federal funds became available to be dispensed on the local level. Preparations for the bicentennial of the Declaration of Independence in 1976 boosted spending for historical projects to an unprecedented level. The development of political environments newly favorable to African Americans and increased levels of governmental support made it possible, for example, for groups of politicians in Philadelphia to found the Afro-American Historical and Cultural Museum, and helped Rowena Stewart, a former social worker and teacher, to establish the Rhode Island Black Heritage Society in 1975. These are but two examples of a trend that was seen in areas with significant Black political power at the local or state level. Black museums were authorized and funded in Los Angeles, Chicago, Philadelphia, and Washington, D.C., at a rate never before seen. These particular circumstances—of comparatively large-scale government support of African American and other community programming, and African American political clout—significantly affected the structure of these new Black museums. For example, many of these museums had large boards of trustees—boards of thirty to fifty members were not uncommon. As numerous and diverse as these board members were, they rarely had much experience at raising funds and often contributed only small sums themselves, commensurate with their middle-class salaries. The staff of the museum was expected to raise funds for the operation of the museum, while the board members were expected to serve the community as cultural leaders. In successful museums, the staff was often able to raise funds from a variety of state, local, and sometimes federal agencies. As these funds shrank during the Reagan years and now threaten to dry up altogether or enmesh their recipients in public controversy, the significant role these governmental funds had in the growth of Black museums (and community museums more generally) has been made considerably more apparent.

By 1969, there were enough Black museums in existence for some of their leaders to begin to think about forming an organization. Meetings were held throughout the 1970s at several of the newer Black museums. In 1978, the African American Museums Association (AAMA) was established. Operating initially out of the National Center of Afro-American Artists in Boston and later out of the Bethune Archives of the National Council of Negro Women in Washington, D.C., AAMA has become the only direct collective voice of the Black museum movement. AAMA has functioned as a lobby on behalf of Black museums within the all-important government funding community; it has sponsored various training sessions and workshops for the often isolated and small staffs of their member museums; and its annual meetings have served as reunions or assemblies of the Black museum movement.[79]

There are other organizations with a history of African American preservationist activities, such as Carter G. Woodson's Association for the Study of Negro Life and History, founded in 1915 and still headquartered in Washington, D.C., and the National Conference of Artists, a Black arts organization founded in the late 1950s by Elma Lewis and other cultural activists. Also, newer preservationist groups exist, such as the Afro-American Historical and Genealogical Society and the Black Museum Educators Roundtable. Each of these organizations has annual meetings and a national network of members who work in both historically white and Black museums.

Throughout this entire period, but especially after the 1976 broadcast of the *Roots* miniseries, African American preservationists concentrating on particular locales and regions appeared throughout the country. As well, a number of Black people were moved to begin tracing their families' histories, erect a local memorial or monument, or become active in a national preservationist organization. For some, this has included involvement in historically white groups such as the Daughters and Sons of the American Revolution. In any event, the surge of interest in understanding the past through family memory or ethnic history is often mentioned anecdotally in relation to the *Roots* series by people in these new preservationist groups (and sometimes those in older ones). The last fifteen years have witnessed a surge of interest, both nationally and at the community level, in defining ethnicity.[80]

The creation of Black museums was one of the most important institution-building outcomes of the Black Consciousness Era. These museums sheltered alternative Black cultural activists as well as serving as repositories for more confrontational art and cultural expressions. Their influence was not limited to African Americans. One of the culturally significant outcomes of the civil rights movement was the way in which radicalism within segregated Negro communities widened into a critique of American society more generally during the Vietnam War and its aftermath. As in other areas of American life, Black people have innovated in ways that have inspired other groups dedicated to empowerment. Many succeeding movements, such as the antiwar effort, modern feminism, and rising ethnic pride and civil rights movements among Chicanos, Puerto Ricans, Native Americans, and other groups, arose directly from or within the discursive context of the political rhetoric, strategies, tactics, and social aims of the civil rights movement.

These new Black museums were in the early vanguard of the community museum movement. Many issues currently being discussed in large mainstream cultural institutions in the 1990s—audiences, communication, documenting oral histories, involving the community in cultural institutions—were dealt with by Black museums in the 1960s and 1970s. With few resources, initially small collections, and tiny staffs, Black museums generally have had deep-rooted ties to their local communities, producing exhibitions, performances, and training activities that have had great meaning for their neighborhoods and cities. Supported by an enviable network of volunteers and supporters, they served as repositories for various kinds of personal and family memory. Today, the collections of these museums are filled with objects, photographs, books, and documents that were saved by Black families over generations.[81]

Black museums have inherited all of the complex ideologies, cultural symbols, and practices that have characterized all parts of African American cultural discourse over the last 170 years. As central cultural institutions within their respective communities, these museums include people of all generations as well as radical, moderate, and conservative African Americans with a wide range of opinions, goals, and ideas about how best to preserve the African American past and reinvigorate the culture in the present. Yet they are also affected by contemporary debates among African Americans about the "correct" interpretations of Black history. They have served as the principal repositories of the memory of individuals, families, and communities. Black museums continue to be an outlet for the mythopoetic narratives of the special destiny of African Americans.

HISTORICALLY WHITE INSTITUTIONS IN THE BLACK
CONSCIOUSNESS ERA, 1965–1985

Before 1950 the Library of Congress and the National Archives contained the largest collections of African American materials. Most of the major public and private museums, including the Smithsonian Institution, made no effort to collect, preserve, or analyze any aspect of the culture of African Americans. While desegregation may not yet have been fully accomplished (and in many museums is only beginning at the present time), the civil rights movement and the Black Consciousness Era had a profound effect on historically white museums.

In 1984 the American Association of Museums issued its report on the status of museums in America, *Museums for a New Century*. Included in the report was a chapter on multiculturalism and diversifying the audiences, staffs, and exhibitions of American museums. The report clearly indicated that diversity within the museums had not yet been achieved, but the report was a clarion call for change.

Greater pluralism in historically white cultural institutions has been slow to come and hard to assess. Several studies have recently been published that survey some part of the universe of American museums: James Horton and Spencer Crew have examined history museums; Howardena Pindall sampled minority art museum professionals on the East Coast; Joan Sandler interviewed minority history and art professionals east of the Mississippi. Horton and Crew found that it was hard to measure just how much of an impact the new scholarship on African American history has had on historically white cultural institutions. They cited several examples, such as Monticello and Ash Lawn, where the changes had been uneven—new exhibitions had been installed but the docents continued to hand out the same old information. Pindall and Sandler each documented the difficult environment minority museum professionals find themselves in—few opportunities to conduct research or pursue advanced degrees, the lack of mentors, and great obstacles to the collecting and exhibiting of African American art and artifacts.[82]

While change may have been slow to come and unevenly achieved, there have been significant changes at many American museums. Perhaps the most important change to date in historically white museums has been the increasing diversity of audiences served. Horton and Crew found that nearly seventy-five percent of the museums in their survey reported that they had been influenced by recent interpretations of African American history. As well, most museums reported that minorities constituted a substantial portion (on average, about thirty percent) of their audiences. Almost half of those minority visitors were African American.[83] These newer audiences have often come to participate in public programs or sometimes to see exhibitions related to the history and culture of their own ethnic group. But a few historically white museums have also made crucial changes in the hiring of professional staff, interpretation, and collections that may have a lasting impact.

Colonial Williamsburg is a good example of such a shift. As mentioned earlier, throughout most of its existence, this living history museum made no mention of the nearly fifty percent of the city's 1770s population that was Black. However, in the late 1970s, Dennis O'Toole and Shomer Zwelling came to Williamsburg as deputy director of museum operations and research historian, respectively. Energetically pressing for the inclusion of African Americans in a more historically accurate interpretive framework, O'Toole and Zwelling began to make changes in interpretive practices. Eventually, through their efforts, the hiring of Rex Ellis, and the securing of foundation funding to promote the inclusion of African Americans in interpretation, Williamsburg began to make visible the previously invisible Black population. Ellis was the principal architect and creator of the Program in African American Interpretation. Incorporating Black interpreters into the texture of the Williamsburg experience was not easy. Stereotypes held by visitors and some staff clouded the initial experiences; in at least one instance, visitors did not realize that the "slaves" they met were really costumed interpreters who were not actually enslaved! Yet after a complex process of experimentation with their form, historical content, social context, and dramatic elements, the various programs at Williamsburg have grown into an entire department of the Colonial Williamsburg Foundation. Special interpretive emphasis on African American culture at Carter's Grove (a plantation site a few miles from the city of Williamsburg) and an ongoing series of events and seminars, as well as the mainstreaming of Black interpreters into various phases of the Colonial Williamsburg experience, have changed the face of this venerable, previously homogeneous institution. The true heterogeneity of colonial Virginia life is now beginning to be visible.[84]

Nowhere have the conflicts and changes within historically white institutions have been more visible than at the Smithsonian Institution. The Smithsonian is the preeminent national public museum in the United States. Made up of a group of museums and other research entities, the Smithsonian was established by Congress to collect and preserve, conduct research, and interpret science and culture for Americans. Not limited to the history and cultures of the United States, the Smithsonian is perhaps the world's largest attempt to be a universal or comprehensive museum. As a most venerable cultural institution, the Smithsonian has several important functions: it validates new cultural trends and arguments; it serves as a mediator between the academy and the wider public by presenting to a broad audience exhibitions and programming informed by scholarly research; and it collects materials of presumed national historical or cultural value. Because of the scope of its concerns and the tax dollars that support it, the Smithsonian is a public institution in the widest sense of the word.

At the same time, the Smithsonian is an excellent example of a mainstream cultural institution that has been historically white—that is to say, governed and staffed by middle- and upper-class European Americans, many of Anglo-American descent. The public services and programs have been traditionally (though perhaps inadvertently) designed with a WASP, middle-class visitor in mind. Although legally a public institution, during its long history the Smithsonian (and many similar institutions) has not reflected the true diversity of the American heritage. For example, in the nineteenth century, the scholars and curators at the U.S. National Museum were among the primary purveyors of scientific racism. And before 1965 the Smithsonian had only a few random objects reflective of African American culture (or indeed any ethnic American culture) on view. Ralph Rinzler, originator of the Smithsonian's Festival of American Folklife, recalled his first visit to the then-new Museum of History and Technology in 1966: "Within the large Growth of the United States exhibit, which detailed the history of all America, the only objects there to detail the richness of Afro-American culture were a single coiled grass basket, an instrument, and Asante gold weights. I was appalled."[85]

Yet the Smithsonian and other similar institutions also experienced the tumult of the 1960s—when the cities were aflame with Black anger—and the growth of Black consciousness. Between 1963 and 1972 hundreds of thousands of Americans came to Washington to protest governmental policies or to lobby for various political goals, including civil rights and an end to the Vietnam War. In 1968 the Poor People's Campaign brought many tens of thousands of Black and activist people to the Mall. Erecting masses of tents—nicknamed Resurrection City—between the Capitol and the White House, in the shadow of five governmental museums, these people almost certainly included many who had never visited the Smithsonian. But the simple presence of masses of Black people created pressure on the institution. In the 1970s Black cultural activists, many of them involved in the Black museum movement, began to critique the Smithsonian on substantive grounds. By the mid-1980s Black elected officials with seniority in Congress (and representatives of other minority groups, such as Japanese Americans) subjected the Smithsonian's budget to greater scrutiny on the questions of cultural diversity and inclusion. In short, over the last twenty-five years, the Smithsonian specifically and the historically white cultural bureaucracy generally came under increasing criticism from Black cultural activists and their allies. As a result, the institution has made changes in some aspects, particularly in its public programming and in the exhibitions at the National Museum of American History.

Over the last twenty-five years the Smithsonian has experienced an enormous growth in the number of its museums and research centers, which parallels the surge nationally of new museums and cultural institutions. The principal architect of this institutional growth was S. Dillon Ripley, secretary of the Smithsonian from 1964 through 1984. A New England blueblood and previously a professor of ornithology at Yale University and head of its natural-history museum, Ripley proved to be an innovator in Washington. While not challenging the preexisting interpretive framework at the Smithsonian, Ripley was gifted with a wider, more democratic sense of inclusion than previous secretaries. Becoming secretary in 1964, Ripley may have been influenced by the American-dream rhetoric of Martin Luther King, Jr., who was a master at combining the language of national mythos with the demand for equal justice that was a special concern of African Americans. At certain moments of potential crisis, this wider vision of the museum aided Ripley in asserting a statesmanlike leadership.

For example, as mentioned above, the Poor People's Campaign arrived in Washington in the summer of 1968. With folks walking and riding from the Deep South to the capital, the Smithsonian had time to prepare for the arrival of these new visitors to the Mall. A crisis-management meeting was called so that the Smithsonian's administrators could determine the appropriate response to this challenge to the security of the collections. Ripley took a completely different view. Rather than battening down the hatches, he suggested that the doors be flung wide open to this new and quite visible part of the American public. Vividly recalled by many participants in that meeting, this was a triumphal moment in Ripley's stewardship of the Smithsonian.[86]

Not simply concerned with grand gestures, Ripley also offered a new kind of activity inside the venerable Smithsonian. In his book *Beyond the Sacred Grove,* Ripley wrote of a desire to make museums more inclusive, to encourage all Americans to visit and enjoy the nation's museums, and his wish that museums should be lively places.[87] These ideas appear to have been the theoretical foundation for two new programs that emerged in the early years of Ripley's secretaryship; the Festival of American Folklife and the Anacostia Museum. Ripley appointed two extraordinary individuals to be the founding directors of these enterprises: Ralph Rinzler and John Kinard.

Ralph Rinzler, who was involved in the Newport Folk Festival for some years, was first brought to Washington in 1966 to discuss whether something similar to Newport could be produced at the Smithsonian. While the Newport festival had been very influential by introducing traditional folk musicians and newer folk-style groups (such as the Freedom Singers of SNCC) to a wider audience, from Rinzler's perspective the festival had some important flaws. A cultural radical at heart, Rinzler wanted the Smithsonian festival to be quite different in process and content from the Newport festival. He wanted this new festival to be a place where the performers could have meaningful interactions with one another, and he wanted their empowering critiques of the American power structures to be shared by the audience. While criticized by some university-based folklorists for creating a festival abstracted from any specific locale and context, Rinzler's exciting, distinctive, diverse festivals were praised in the *Washington Post,* on Capitol Hill, and by the general public.[88]

The Festival of American Folklife is typically held each year during the two weeks prior to July fourth. Under Rinzler the festival often went to great lengths to provide context for the participants' performances and activities; for example, traditional house-builders could actually build houses, and rice paddies could be created to demonstrate the work of a traditional farmer. Rinzler also brought in singers from the civil rights movement, labor movements, and various ethnic groups (some of which were newly emergent, such as Chicanos). However, the American components of the program in its earliest years featured different aspects of the African American and Native American experiences. The festival provided a stage for many different kinds of African American music and dance, including gospel,

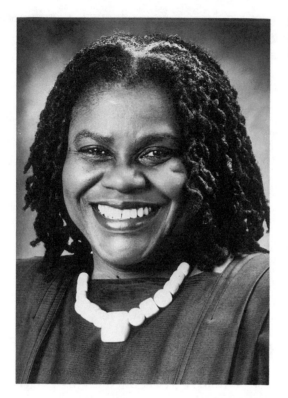

Fig. 17-11. Bernice Johnson Reagon. Photo courtesy Smithsonian Institution.

jazz, blues, rhythm and blues, spirituals, and freedom songs. In addition, the festival presented music and dance from the African diaspora, such as reggae and steel-drum music from Jamaica, calypso music from Trinidad, and capoeira and various drumming traditions from Brazil. Over the years, the Festival of American Folklife brought together performances with demonstrations of material culture and living history. For example, they brought basketmakers from the Sea Islands and wrought-iron artisans such as Philip Simmons (who later won a Living Heritage Award from the National Endowment for the Arts).

The activists, scholars, and artists whom Rinzler hired to coordinate these programs helped create the first critical mass of minority professionals at the Smithsonian. Early on, Rinzler brought in Bernice Johnson Reagon, one of the earliest members of SNCC and one of the four original Freedom Singers. While finishing a B.A. at Spelman College that had been interrupted by the activities of the civil rights movement and after working on a master's degree and doctorate from

Howard University, Reagon originally was a consultant, suggesting how to incorporate community people into the presentation of African American music or a new interpretive voice; she sometimes produced one of the festival's programs. But in 1973 Rinzler hired her to produce an African diaspora program for the three-month-long bicentennial-year festival.

After contracting with a talented group of young people to do fieldwork in the United States, the Caribbean, South America, and West Africa, Reagon produced an absolutely incandescent summerlong program.[89] The innovation of this festival may not seem extraordinary today, but it was groundbreaking at the time. Reagon invited musicians, weavers, dancers, instrument makers, master chefs, painters, and others from Africa and all over the diasporic world, including Ghana, Nigeria, Senegal, Brazil, Jamaica, Trinidad, Haiti, and the southern United States. Alex Haley's book *Roots* had just been published, and many Black Americans were deeply interested in learning more about Africa and their African roots. Scholars of history and culture were just beginning to use the term *diaspora* to describe the experience of Black people in the Americas. While many people were curious about the notion of a connection among all African peoples, Reagon made those connections manifest by juxtaposing Africans and Americans (in the widest sense). People could then judge for themselves how jollof rice from West Africa was like rice pilau from Barbados, and how the sounds of drumming in Haiti and Brazil were related to the sound of drumming from Nigeria. These were new—and for some people, heady—ideas.

The 1976 African Diaspora Festival (the title of which is believed to be the first government use of the term *diaspora* to name this version of Pan-African connection) deeply affected the Black people who attended it. By some accounts, lives were changed—careers revised, plans for travel to Africa put in place—by some of the experiences that Black people had during that summer. Pan-Africanist writers have long posited a direct relationship among peoples of African descent; however, this perspective was generally unfamiliar to the public. The Smithsonian festival provided an American audience with firsthand experience of some of those powerful diasporic links, especially in music and other performance traditions. Perhaps for the first time ever in American public history, a Black American mythos—the notion of the unity of African peoples across time and space—was presented by a preeminent cultural institution.

During the production of the African Diaspora Festival, conflicts arose from the interaction of young, radical American activists with a conservative, hoary institution. One original theme for the summerlong 1976 festival was Old Ways in the New World, and the programming would detail the connections between Americans of European descent and their origins in Europe. Initially, not much thought was given to how Black Americans would fit into such a conceptual scheme.

An interdisciplinary advisory panel, the African Diaspora Advisory Group, was organized to help determine what the relevant programming should be. From almost the first meeting, the panel agreed that the scholarly literature had not adequately dealt with the cultural aspects of the African diaspora, and it recommended an extensive program of fieldwork on three continents and in the Caribbean. Bernice Reagon and James Early (who each later became acting director of the project) implemented the advisory panel's suggestions. The outcome of several years of fieldwork and research was the spectacular festival, in which musicians and artists from Brazil, Jamaica, Senegal, Louisiana, and many other places met for the first time and vividly demonstrated the links among different parts of the African diaspora, which were then only beginning to be widely investigated by scholars.

Those involved in the planning process for the festival remember some heady moments at the thought that even a small portion of the extensive resources of the Smithsonian were to be put to such a culturally radical use. At the same time, participants remember the number of pitched battles they had to fight with the Smithsonian bureaucracy to put on the African Diaspora Festival in the manner they thought appropriate. There were arguments about the name of the festival and its placement on the Mall, problems with the fire regulations in the African-village section, and a thousand other large and small details. The festival staff felt that many people resisted this effort to make the Smithsonian more truly diverse. Let one example suffice. The artists and performers in that year's festival were housed in inexpensive lodgings in Georgetown. Many musicians wanted to have jam sessions in the evenings, sometimes culminating in drumming by African and Native American musicians. When the word came down from higher up that the drumming had to stop, a confrontation occurred. For the Black people involved, this seemed to be a crucial moment of resistance and resolve. When someone said, "This isn't the first time someone has tried to prevent us from talking with our drums," or words to that effect, the high symbolism ended the confrontation and the bureaucrats capitulated.[90] While such moments of high drama were rare, the experience of struggling within an institution to make a new place for minority peoples was long remembered. Bernice Reagon, James Early, and others involved saw in the African Diaspora Festival project yet another way to fulfill the SNCC ideal of using resources and scholarship to facilitate community empowerment.

Ultimately, Ralph Rinzler's innovations in the Smithsonian's Festival of American Folklife were twofold: first, he presented a wide range of American and world folk cultures to a diverse audience of Americans; second, he continually hired extraordinary groups of mostly younger, activist people to produce these distinctive programs. In the first instance, Rinzler succeeded in going beyond the traditional activities of university-based folklorists in a variety of ways. By presenting a wide range of musicians, storytellers, and other performers, he widened the scope of what was defined as folk culture. By bringing performers, instrument makers, and house builders to the Mall, he went beyond previous folk festivals in including material culture and the socio-material context in which folk music or other folk arts flourished. Furthermore, Rinzler's Mall audience was far larger and more diverse than those at previous festivals because he presented programs that spoke to the concerns, history, and traditions of diverse American ethnic groups. Finally, by providing transportation, equipment, contracts, and other resources, Rinzler was able to help support artists whose contributions to American culture had often been relatively financially unrewarding. To be a participant in the Smithsonian's festival gave an individual or group some funds and potentially a great deal of recognition. Rinzler's success spawned other governmental programs (such as those run by the National Endowment for the Arts and the National Endowment for the Humanities) of support for American folk artists.[91]

Rinzler's second contribution—bringing in people of color to run these programs—had an impact on the Smithsonian that extended beyond the Festival of American Folklife. In 1977 Bernice Reagon established the Program in Black American Culture as an independent entity within the Division of Performing Arts.[92] Though originating organizationally from the festival, this was a year-round program of research, public presentations, and performances that allowed her to delve more deeply into particular topics. Reagon's next big project was the Songs of the Civil Rights Movement project (cosponsored by Howard University), in which people gathered from around the country to record and notate their songs, to make a series of records, and to attend a conference sing-in at the Smithsonian in the fall of 1980. Eventually, the Songs of the Civil Rights Movement project produced not only the records and the conference but also a traveling photo exhibition (entitled We Won't Turn Back Again) and regional conferences in twelve states designed to collect the songs and reminiscences of veterans of the civil rights movement.

The extraordinary result of the Program in Black American Culture was that one of the nation's most conservative cultural institutions served as the host to some of the nation's most radical voices. During Reagon's years as director of the program, its multiyear efforts were supported by extensive research and produced public programs that allowed scholars and artists in various genres to reach out to a wide public audience.[93]

While radically shifting some of the public programs and thus part of the public face of the Smithsonian, the Festival of American Folklife and the Program in Black American Culture did not change the internal functioning of the Smithsonian's museums. Yet a museum experiment was evolving in Anacostia, a predominantly Black section in the southeastern part of the District of Columbia. Born out of Dillon Ripley's interest in trying out the community museum concept and the efforts of a well-organized group of community activists, the Anacostia Museum (originally called the Anacostia Neighborhood Museum) opened its doors in 1967. Renting space in the former Carver Theater, the museum looked and felt completely different from the rest of the Smithsonian. At its helm was its founding director, John Kinard, who was a young minister and a native of Washington. A community activist who had recently returned from an African sojourn, Kinard was picked by the community advisory board to head this new museum. After some pressure, Smithsonian higher-ups agreed.[94]

Along with an unusual staff that included Balcha Fellows (head of the International Affairs Program), Zora Martin Felton (head of the Education Department), and Larry Thomas and James Mayo (both designers), Kinard created a thoroughly unique Smithsonian museum. The Anacostia Museum may well have been the first federally funded African American museum to be established through a government agency. In its first ten years, it sponsored a remarkable series of exhibitions and educational programs, premiering a new or borrowed exhibition nearly every month.[95]

The museum staff pioneered and innovated in a number of ways. For example, the museum opened in September 1967 with an exhibition that had been thought out by Smithsonian staff before the hiring of John Kinard. The original exhibition included a small space capsule, an art section, a small petting zoo, a section of touchable objects, and a dance and performance area. This collection of objects reflected a central Smithsonian view that the purpose of the Anacostia Museum was to serve as a neighborhood outpost of the Smithsonian Institution. But Kinard and his staff did not intend simply to run an outpost. Their first independently produced exhibition opened on 22 November of that year. Called Doodles in Dimensions, this exhibition was a set of sculptures produced by a local Black designer, Ralph Tate, based on the well-known doodles of John F. Kennedy. The kernel of the idea for the exhibition came from a suggestion box that the staff had located prominently in the museum and which was quickly filled to overflowing with suggestions and comments. One young person had put forth the idea of an exhibition on the slain president.

Though most famous for the exhibition Rats: Man's Invited Affliction (1969), the Anacostia staff produced other imaginative efforts such as Out of Africa (1979) and the Anna J. Cooper exhibition (1981). Both of these exhibitions reflected the ways in which Black versions of the African American past were beginning to appear in national, publicly supported institutions. Out of Africa presented a diasporic view of Black Americans and the slavery experience. The exhibition Anna J. Cooper: A Voice from the South uncovered the life of a Black educator and clubwoman of national significance who had lived and worked in Washington. Curated by Louise Hutchinson, this exhibition was among the best examples of local history in which a smaller narrative is used to tell a story of national importance. As such, the Cooper exhibition fell well within the Carter G. Woodson school of African American historiography: careful research that results in the adding of another undeservedly obscure Black name to the roster of successful Americans.

The Anacostia Museum staff also pioneered new ways of involving the community in the museum. Long before most other Smithsonian museums hired education department staff, the Anacostia staff had developed unusual programs for children, teenagers, and adults. For example, Zora Martin Felton worked actively with groups of neighborhood teenagers, involving them in nearly every aspect of the museum. The teenagers helped to prepare exhibitions, developed programs, served as docents, and planned trips to countries such as Senegal. In a variety of ways these young people became an integral volunteer force for the museum. Over the years, some of these students became adult museum volunteers and others went on to college majors and professional careers that were spurred by their work at the Anacostia Museum. Serving as a training ground, the museum also provided some new Black museum professionals to the field, particularly in the area of design and production. Drawing on both older and newer versions of the African American past, the Anacostia Museum became another center of innovative activity within the Smithsonian. The Anacostia Museum's location away from the Mall, its exclusive concern with African American history and culture, and its focus on programming rather than collecting all served to set it apart from the Smithsonian mainstream. Initially the Anacostia Museum was organized as a program-producing entity, not a collection-producing one. While not expressly forbidden to collect objects, the museum was consistently hampered by a lack of adequate storage space and the complete lack of registrarial and collections-management staff. Also, like others in the Black museum movement, the Anacostia staff emphasized the communication of new perspectives about the African diaspora, slavery, and contemporary Black issues to the public in general and to students in particular.

By 1980 the Smithsonian had a range of African American activities: a thriving Program in Black American Culture, a continued presence in the Festival of American Folklife, and a prominent and innovative neighborhood museum. New audiences had been attracted to these rather unusual, if not unique, programs. But the exhibitions and staffs of the Mall museums remained remarkably unchanged even throughout the tremendous period of museum expansion that began in 1964. While quite visible changes had occurred at the Smithsonian, they occurred only at the margins of the institution. Central bureaus such as the National Museum of Natural History and the Museum of History and Technology (now the National Museum of American History) remained much the same, with ethnically homogeneous professional staffs, traditional collecting practices, and exhibitions about the American past that reflected an ideology of consensus and homogeneity. However, in the late 1960s greater public pressure emerged to include Black history in the Smithsonian's public face. Some efforts toward greater inclusion did occur in the 1970s.

In 1972 the National Portrait Gallery sponsored two exhibitions curated by Letitia Woods-Brown, a well-known African American historian of Washington, D.C. Her exhibitions were the first investigation by a Smithsonian museum into the rich local Black tradition. In 1973 the gallery sponsored an exhibition curated by Sidney Kaplan entitled The Black Presence in the Revolutionary Era. Stimulated by the upcoming bicentennial, Kaplan brought together for the exhibition numerous little-known portraits of some famous and some unknown eighteenth-century African Americans. In 1975 the exhibition We the People opened in the Museum of History and Technology. This exhibition included sections on suffrage movements and on modern-day civil rights and protest activities. In 1976 the exhibition A Nation of Nations opened at the same museum. Though it had a weak conceptual framework, this exhibition practiced the politics of inclusion by indicating the presence of both African Americans and Native Americans as part of the peoples from many parts of the world who make up the American nation. This consensus-oriented view of American history made invisible the tremendous racial conflicts in American history and completely obscured the distinctive aspects of the Black part of the American story. Still, these last two exhibitions helped stimulate the first systematic collecting at the Smithsonian on the African American experience.

Curators Keith Melder and Edith Mayo in what is now the Division of Political History began a systematic collection effort that focused on the civil rights movement and on the women's movement. The collection now includes numerous materials documenting the local and national aspects of both movements, such as printed signs, songbooks, buttons, clothes, and pamphlets. In what is now the Division of Community Life, curator Carl Scheele and his assistant, Ellen Roney Hughes, began documenting the history of African Americans in entertainment and sports. An extensive photo archive on baseball's Negro Leagues was one result of their efforts.[96]

While these large, comprehensive exhibitions broke new ground by including African Americans within the overall storylines, these perspectives on Black history came from an exterior point of view. The We the People and A Nation of Nations exhibitions explored how Black people had affected the larger polity through the civil rights movement and how Black people had contributed to wider American culture through sports and entertainment, but no sense of the interior historical dynamics nor any of the unique elements of African American life came through. The need for a history derived from voices inside the African American community was expressed not only by Black cultural activists but also by a new generation of university-based scholars of the Black experience.

It is clear that the civil rights movement and some of its successors, such as the antiwar and modern feminist movements, had also had an impact on American universities, though it is beyond the scope of this essay to detail that impact fully. Beginning in the 1960s, a new generation of historians developed a new social history. This was a history that told about the everyday lives of ordinary people in order to determine the large statistical patterns and dominant metaphors (or *mentalité*) that characterize an era. As part of this general movement, the work of Herbert Gutman, Lawrence Levine, John Blassingame, Eugene Genovese, Sidney Mintz, Nell Irwin Painter, and others began to redefine the landscape of African American history and culture. Evidence mounted of a series of complex patterns within the African diaspora of cultural survivals and transmissions, innovation and transmittal of religious beliefs, foodways, family structure, and material culture. In short, while the civil rights movement had stimulated a revolution in scholarly work on African American life, history, and culture, virtually none of this new research was reflected in Smithsonian exhibitions, opening the institution's exhibitions to questions about their historical accuracy and clarity.

In 1979, when Roger Kennedy became the director of the Museum of History and Technology, he helped set in motion a series of exhibitions that for the first time included some of the interior African American versions of history. After the Revolution: Everyday Life in America, 1780–1800 and the even more successful exhibition Field to Factory: Afro-American Migration, 1910–1940 created a new look on the Mall. Exhibitions in other museums began to contribute to the growing diversity. In 1985 the National Museum of American Art sponsored the exhibition Hidden Heritage, which presented the work of five nineteenth-century African American artists. In 1987 the National Museum of African Art moved from its original small Capitol Hill home to a large, beautifully appointed space in the new underground museum complex on the Mall. While this museum does not strictly deal with African American culture, many Black museum visitors and activists counted this as a further presence on the Mall for peoples of African descent. Within the last few years, important new collections have also been added. In 1987 the Duke Ellington collection was purchased from his son by special Congressional appropriation (it is now in the Archives Center at the National Museum of American History). Through the assiduous efforts of Ralph Rinzler, the Folkways Records collection came to the Folklife Program of the Smithsonian that same year. Together, these new exhibitions, new collections, and new members of the curatorial staff have begun to change some key aspects of the Smithsonian.

The Smithsonian is the largest museum complex in the world, and while some parts of it have diversified their staffs, exhibitions, collections, and audiences, other parts remain largely the same as they were twenty years earlier. The science museums—the National Museum of Natural History and the National Air and Space Museum—have been particularly resistant to change. In recent years, the various art museums of the Smithsonian have become a highly contested ground precisely because of these questions of the inclusion of minority artists' work in their collections, the hiring of minority professionals, the diversification of audiences and programming, and the widening of the frameworks within which art is presented. Broadly construed, there are five art museums at the Smithsonian: the Hirshhorn Museum and Sculpture Gallery, the National Museum of American Art, the National Museum of African Art, the Freer Gallery of Art and the Arthur M. Sackler Gallery (concentrating on Asian art), and the Cooper-Hewitt Museum (in New York). Of these, the National Museum of American Art has a sizeable collection of work by Black artists, including many important pieces by the small number of well-known nineteenth-century African American artists, such as Robert Duncanson and Henry O. Tanner. Early on NMAA did not actively collect African American artists. However, in the late 1980s, energetic collecting and exhibiting began under director Elizabeth Broun.[97] In the late 1980s, intense debates within the Smithsonian art community centered around the question of inclusion and the issue of multiculturalism versus universalism. Pressure on the art museums to diversify has come from centrally constituted advisory groups at the Smithsonian such as the Committee for a Wider Audience and the Cultural Education Committee.

These debates inside the Smithsonian have taken place within the wider context of discussions in the national museum community. Several sessions at the June 1990 American Association of Museums conference in Chicago were devoted to formal debates about inclusion, diversity, and multiculturalism. Overall, the large art-museum and science-museum communities have changed much less than the history-museum community.

While many areas of the Smithsonian, particularly the science and art bureaus, reflect little change in exhibitions, collections, or staffs, other parts of the institution have been near the forefront of change, addressing questions of inclusion, cultural diversity, collections policy, and staff hiring. During the late 1980s a continuing struggle for inclusion and cultural diversity was elaborated in letters to the secretary and directors from concerned scholars, in Congressional hearings, in advisory committee reports, and in the news media. While there is continuing resistance to these new ideas, at the same time there is a far greater recognition of the historical truth of American diversity and the need to represent it in our museums. Such a profound change reflects the extent to which the civil rights movement was able to shift the Smithsonian and other central American cultural institutions away from their long-held ethnocentric views of history.

CONCLUSIONS: THE MARTIN LUTHER KING, JR., HOLIDAY AND BEYOND

Perhaps the most symbolically significant preservation effort of the 1980s was the adoption of the holiday honoring Martin Luther King, Jr. After fifteen years of campaigning in support of the holiday by his widow, Coretta Scott King, singer-songwriter Stevie Wonder, Congressman John Conyers, and others, the bill was signed into law by President Ronald Reagan in November 1983. Reagan did not want to sign the bill because he shared the reactionary sentiment that King was not an American hero and did not merit a tax-supported holiday. But the bill passed with such a large majority in the House and Senate that he realized a veto would have been overridden. Americans were witness to an extraordinary event: the first formal declaration of an African American national hero.

It is clear that King led an exemplary, essentially heroic life. Much as Frederick Douglass was emblematic of the abolitionist generation, so King was emblematic of the civil rights movement and its positive goals to many, perhaps most, Americans. Though plagued with certain human failings that have surfaced publicly in recent years, King seemed uniquely able to embody and articulate a distinctive blend of African American millennialism and European American rhetoric about justice and democratic rights articulated in the Declaration of Independence, the Constitution, and other basic documents of American society. King's life, sermons, essays, and public speeches all reflected his belief in the transforming power of truth and truth-tellers. His rolling sermons and speeches illustrated his deep roots in the Black Baptist Church and confirmed African Americans' sense of their special role in American society. At the same time—and this is unusual for someone of his generation—King's oral and written works also conveyed the idea that the nation had a special destiny as well: to work out the American experiment in democratic rights for all. King's "I Have a Dream" speech is simply the best known of his numerous efforts to weave together the African American mythos with that of the American mainstream. Perhaps not even during the Civil War did these mostly separate mythopoetic traditions come together as forcefully as they did during the civil rights era, in which many people willingly risked their lives to secure freedom. King's birthday became the first federal holiday to celebrate the life of a Black person in part because King's ideals, activist life, and martyrdom for the cause of freedom evoked not only African American but wider American sensibilities and values.

The King holiday represents a unique intersection between the interior African American and the exterior European American notions of the American past. From an American historical perspective, King's role in articulating the rationale for the Civil Rights Act of 1964 and the Voting Rights Act of 1965 and in embodying the freedom movement made him a leader in several of the key issues in American democratic history. The notion that all people were created free and equal is inscribed in the Declaration of Independence, yet the reality of the Revolutionary era included slaveholding, restrictions on women, and other elements that are today considered inequities. Two hundred years later, King catalyzed the struggle for freedom and justice that the founding fathers articulated but did not fully resolve. By referring to the founding fathers frequently in his sermons and speeches, King clearly aligned the modern civil rights movement with a wider notion of the American creed. Eventually King became a saint in the American civil religion; the holiday in his honor fully demonstrates that.

While King's life was meaningful for many European Americans, King and the freedom movement in general also had a galvanizing effect on other nonwhite Americans. Before the Black Consciousness Era, *ethnicity* as a term was considered colloquially to refer only to European immigrant groups. Nonwhite minority groups were defined only by their color or race, not by their distinctive cultural processes and products. But the movements of the Black Consciousness Era enlarged the understanding of the cultural significance of Black Americans. By the early 1970s, ethnic-heritage movements had emerged in Native American, Puerto Rican, Chicano, Chinese, and Japanese communities in the United States, among others. After the 1976 airing of the *Roots* miniseries, genealogical groups sprang up across America: many Americans had become more interested in learning about their family histories. King posited the concept of "somebodiness"—

the idea that people everywhere, whoever they are, can stand tall and be proud of their community. The Black Consciousness Era energized similar movements in other American communities. The culturally diverse universe we perceive today is a direct outcome of the force of that movement toward Black consciousness. Scholar-activists such as Frank Bonilla (the longtime head of Aspira, a national Puerto Rican organization) and John Kuo Wei Tchen (the co-founder of the Chinatown History Museum in New York) have written of the influence of Black activists on their own work.

King was also a major contributor to the African American mythos of a special role and destiny in America. King believed that truth and truth-telling supplied the force behind a nonviolent revolution that could change all societies. King often said: "The arc of the universe is long, but it bends towards justice."[98] King's statements reflect a mature African American millennialism in its assertion that freedom may be a long time coming, but eventually it will come, and that Black Americans will play a key role as catalysts toward that new and better future. In a sense the King holiday could be seen as the fulfillment of Carter G. Woodson's dream that, if rightly educated, Americans could come to see individual African Americans for the heroes and heroines they were.

All in all, the King holiday reflects how much the United States has changed in terms of symbolic race relations since 1955. In a fitting tribute to King's heroic life, his holiday represents a philosophy of American life that recognizes diversity but demands equal rights for all; it brings together a wide range of Americans who can unite under this symbolic umbrella to affirm progressive and positive values within American society. But while King's holiday evokes overlapping interior and exterior views about African Americans, it also brings out evidence of the continuing existence of separate views about the past. For example, celebrations of the King holiday in African American cultural institutions and those in state or federally funded public institutions are rather different. In Black schools and museums, the specific details of the modern civil rights movement and of King's participation in it are remembered. Civil rights activists often participate by talking about their memories of King as a man and a leader. Other activists may talk about the contributions of other leaders and foot soldiers, some of whom also paid the ultimate price. Among Black audiences, the fact of King's martyrdom is an important element in what makes his life heroic. For churchgoing Black audiences, King's death forms an explicit parallel with the sacrifice of Christ on the cross. Even Black separatists who might disagree with King's goals view him as a heroic Black man who died resisting.

During the 1980s a critique of King's life has also come to play a role in Black cultural institutions. As King's memory has come to be celebrated by many non-Black Americans, some Black Americans have needed to continue to have a hero who is fully appreciated only by African Americans. Although Malcolm X was not seen as a leader of King's stature during his lifetime, in death he has loomed increasingly large as an interior hero of the civil rights era. By advocating self-defense, racial pride, and resistance as forms of manhood, Malcolm X symbolizes a continuing interior critique of American commitments to social justice. Black college students now wear T-shirts with Malcolm X's photo and quotes screen-printed on them. In many colleges and independent Black schools, Malcolm X celebrations are the culmination of extended Black History Month programming. However, the King holiday is celebrated in a wider range of Black institutions. For example, few Black churches have specific programming for Malcolm X's birthday, in part because he was not a Christian. Although Malcolm X is increasingly a hero to the young, the King holiday remains the most inclusive banner for the widest range of Black institutions.

In public institutions such as the Smithsonian, the celebration of the King holiday takes on an appropriately different tone. James Early, assistant secretary for public service, explained that the Smithsonian celebration sought "to utilize King's ecumenical and social-change philosophy to shed light on contemporary issues." Language such as this speaks directly to the wide array of Americans who felt themselves and their communities to have been influenced by the strategies and goals of the African American movement for civil rights and integration.[99] In the years since the holiday was instituted, the Smithsonian's celebrations have brought in speakers such as Smithsonian regent Jeannine Smith Clark, who spoke in 1987 (that year's celebration also featured a performance by Sweet Honey in the Rock), Frank Bonilla from the New York City Center for Puerto Rican Studies (1988), John Kuo Wei Tchen from the Chinatown History Museum (1989), Vine Deloria, author of various books on Native American history (1990), and Johnetta Cole, president of Spelman College (1991).[100] The views these speakers offered of King's importance emphasized an active sense of struggle and a sense that King's mission can be fulfilled today in encountering the problems of our present. The variety of speakers underscores the cultural diversity beyond the Black-white dichotomy that many African Americans see as primary.

Such public celebrations accentuate the universal aspects of King's life and his dedication to the larger ideals of truth and justice.

This kind of ecumenical public response is rather different from celebrations in Black-controlled institutions. There King's distinctiveness as an African American is decisively important, especially as a role model to hard-pressed Black youth. Some African Americans attending the Smithsonian celebrations have expressed dismay that this distinctively Black King was missing from such culturally diverse presentations. In a sense, the variations on the King holiday embody the issues facing historically Black private cultural institutions, historically white private ones, and all public cultural institutions in the 1990s. How to be culturally diverse while recognizing the uniqueness of distinctive sociocultural experiences is the issue. Can the African American mythos of a unique role and special destiny be praised appropriately at the same time as a wider group of Americans observes only those aspects of the African American story that intertwine with the history of the larger society?

In 1989 Representatives John Lewis and Mickey Leland introduced separate bills to found a national African American museum at the Smithsonian. This was not the first time a congressionally approved national institution for African Americans had been proposed. Through the efforts of Louis Stokes in the House and Howard Metzenbaum in the Senate, the National Afro-American Museum and Cultural Center in Wilberforce, Ohio, was authorized and opened in 1987. Built on the old campus of Wilberforce College, a historically Black Methodist institution, and near Central State University, also a historically Black college, this museum was at the heart of a key, longstanding Northern Black community. The Lewis and Leland bills touched off a spirited and ongoing debate about the rationale for such a museum, the role of the Smithsonian in such an institution, and the relationship of such a museum to the older Black preservationist institutions. Such questions are primary in the ongoing debate about the placement of a federally funded African American museum on the Mall. As the King holiday demonstrates, there are overlapping interior and exterior views of the African American past, yet these viewpoints contain a number of somewhat contradictory interpretations. Questions about a new museum's governance, funding, location, collections, and relations to preexisting Black cultural organizations devolve back to these central differences between interior and exterior views of the African American past. There is little agreement about how best to preserve, analyze, and interpret the mythos, memory, and history of

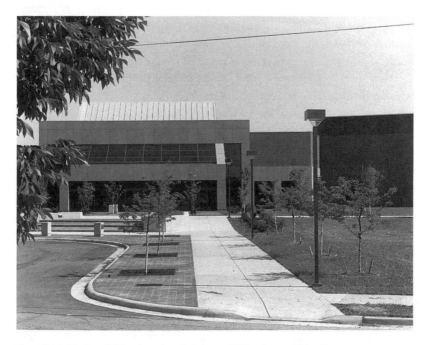

Fig. 17-12. National Afro-American Museum, Wilberforce, Ohio. Photo courtesy National Afro-American Museum.

African Americans and the distinctive historical role they have played in American society.[101]

As this essay demonstrates, various interpretations of the African American past have resulted in numerous kinds of collections and a complex preservation history. Some preservationists focused on collecting documents, books, fine arts, and artifacts. Others concentrated on preserving a record of performance styles, musical traditions, and oral forms. While African Americans have been at the forefront of most preservation activities, European Americans have also contributed important points of view and amassed significant collections. Those who have contributed to the development of these interpretations or who have controlled certain institutions have played decisive roles in the documentation of that past. Our generation inherits the large collections of documents and books, small collections of fine arts, a sizeable number of recordings from the past one hundred years, and a smaller number of material culture artifacts. In every sense, these collections are the resources upon which we build our own interpretations of the past. This long and tangled history of preservation has resulted in the foregrounding of certain views and made other views much more difficult to reconstruct. While there are significant collections, important gaps may always remain in our understanding of African American life in the nineteenth and earlier centuries because of selective preservation strategies and limited financial means of some of the primary collectors.

Our task is to take this history into account as we plan the preservation strategies of our time. While the history of African American preservation efforts is quite long, and while there are important collections of nineteenth-century origin in both large and small institutions, we have a strong mandate to preserve twentieth-century African American culture. As we prepare to move into the twenty-first century, now is the time to build the great collections of oral and musical culture, art, and artifacts that future generations of scholars will use to understand our own era. While we should save all that we can now identify as being from before 1900, we have a special responsibility to create collections about twentieth-century African American life. These materials are still abundant, and numerous earlier generations are still alive to be interviewed about their experiences and their particular visions of what being Black meant in their time. We cannot but lament what was not saved earlier. Knowing that history, we are accountable to future generations for what we do today. Learning from the strategies of the past, it is critical to see that varying and sometimes conflicting strategies of interpretation and collection are necessary in order to preserve as wide a range of cultural memory as possible. Being unable to predict the interpretations future scholars will develop does not relieve us of the responsibility of collecting in our present anything that has resonance for us. In this way, the lives, history, and culture of African Americans of our own era will be richly documented, while our collections will still be reflective of our generation's notions of the African American past.

NOTES

The author wishes to thank Paul Ruffins for his commentary and his unfailing support.

1. Over time, people of African descent within the United States have changed how they wished to be referred to. In the 1700s and earlier, *sons and daughters of Africa* was a common appellation. Consequently, independent churches formed during that era often have a name such as the African Meth-

odist Episcopal Church. By the 1830s, another designation became common: *Colored Americans* and *People of Color*. For example, Frederick Douglass often referred to "peoples of color" in his speeches. However, during these same years, *Afro-American* was often used in newspapers and other published work. By the late 1800s, *Colored* was the most frequent name used, in both oral and written language. In the early 1900s, a younger generation of people felt that *Negro* was a term that connoted a new sense of dignity and pride. For years, African American activists campaigned for white publishers to capitalize the word *Negro*. This was symbolically achieved in the 1940s, when the *New York Times* officially changed its style sheet. During the 1960s, another younger generation felt that *Black* or *Black Americans* was a term that connoted greater racial pride and identification. In the 1990s, *African American* has become more popular, coming almost full circle to the 1700s.

Because these name changes reflect significant shifts in the cultural discourse among African Americans, in this article I have used all ethnic self-designations, all capitalized, at the appropriate historical period.

2. For more information about the enslavement of American Indians and the use of slavery as punishment for whites in the seventeenth and early eighteenth centuries, see Peter Wood, *Black Majority: Negroes in Colonial South Carolina from 1670 Through the Stono Rebellion* (New York: Knopf, 1974), and Winthrop D. Jordan, *White Over Black: American Attitudes Toward the Negro, 1550–1812* (Chapel Hill: University of North Carolina Press, 1968).

3. For the work of earlier African American scholars, see the many works of W.E.B. Du Bois, including *Black Reconstruction in America* (New York: Harcourt, Brace, 1935); *The Philadelphia Negro: A Social Study, Together with a Special Report on Domestic Service,* by Isabel Eaton (Philadelphia: Publications of the University of Pennsylvania, Series in Political Economy and Public Law no. 14, 1899); *The Suppression of the African Slave-Trade to the United States of America, 1638–1870,* Harvard Historical Series, vol. 1 (New York: Longmans, Green, 1896); *The World and Africa: An Inquiry into the Part Which Africa Has Played in World History* (New York: Viking, 1947). Other works include Lorenzo Greene, *The Negro in Colonial New England* (New York: Columbia University Press, 1942); Rayford W. Logan, *The Negro in American Life and Thought: The Nadir, 1877–1901* (New York: Dial, 1954); Roland McConnell, *The Negro in North Carolina Since Reconstruction* (New York: New York University Press, 1949); Roland McConnell, *Negro Troops in Antebellum Louisiana: A History of the Battalion of Free Men of Color* (Baton Rouge: Louisiana State University Press, 1968); Benjamin Quarles, *The Negro in the American Revolution* (Chapel Hill: University of North Carolina Press, 1961); Letitia Woods-Brown, *Free Negroes in the District of Columbia, 1790–1846* (New York: Oxford University Press, 1972); Letitia Woods-Brown and Elsie M. Lewis, *Washington from Banneker to Douglass, 1791–1970* (Washington, D.C.: National Portrait Gallery, 1971); Letitia Woods-Brown and Elsie M. Lewis, *Washington in the New Era,*

1870–1970 (Washington, D.C.: National Portrait Gallery, 1972); George Washington Williams, *History of the Negro Race, 1619–1880,* 2 vols. (New York: Arno Press, 1968 [1883]); George Washington Williams, *A History of Negro Troops in the War of the Rebellion, 1861–1865, Preceded by a Review of the Military Service of Negroes in Ancient and Modern Times* (New York: Harper, 1888). See also the many works of Carter G. Woodson, including *A Century of Negro Migration* (Washington, D.C.: Association for the Study of Negro Life and History, 1918); *The Education of the Negro Prior to 1861* (New York: G. P. Putnam's Sons, 1915); *Free Negro Heads of Families in the United States in 1830* (Washington, D.C.: Association for the Study of Negro Life and History, 1925); *The MisEducation of the Negro,* ed. Charles H. Wesley and Thelma D. Perry (Washington, D.C.: Associated Publishers, 1969); and *The Negro in Our History,* 4th ed. (Washington, D.C.: Associated Publishers, 1927).

4. For bibliographies of more recent research on Afro-American history, see Janet Woods, *Research Facilities and Afro-American Documents* (Washington, D.C.: AHGGS, 1987); Janet Simms, comp., *The Progress of Afro-American Women: A Selected Bibliography and Resource Guide* (Westport, Conn.: Greenwood, 1980); and National Museum of American History, *Race and Revolution: African-Americans, 1770-1830* (Washington, D.C.: Smithsonian Institution, 1987).

5. In this article, the phrase "historically white" is used to refer to institutions or organizations that have throughout their history been largely or wholly staffed by, funded by, and/or provided services to Americans of European descent. Such usage is patterned on the designation of colleges and universities as "historically Black."

6. Institutions that have important collections of African American materials include the Pennsylvania Historical Society (Philadelphia), the New York Historical Society, the Massachusetts Historical Society (Boston), the New Haven (Conn.) Historical Society, the Society for the Preservation of New England Antiquities (Boston), Colonial Williamsburg, the Houghton Collection and Widener Library of Harvard University, the John Brown Library of Brown University (Providence), and the Beinecke Library of Yale University.

7. John Kinard, "Preserving the Black Patrimony," speech delivered at the African American Museums Association conference, Boston, Massachusetts, September 1988. Kinard was a leading spokesperson of the Black museum movement. His statements in Boston directly related to the notion of an African American museum on the Mall in Washington, D.C. Though his position later shifted on the question of a new museum, in September 1988 Kinard was opposed to such an idea and proposed in this speech that a $50 million trust fund be set up to support the "Black patrimony."

8. *Webster's Third New International Dictionary* (Chicago: Merriam, 1966). For more on the distinction between the past and interpretations of it, see Fath

Davis Ruffins, "The Exhibition as Form," *Museum News* 64, no. 1 (1985), 54–59.

9. Dorothy Porter, "Organized Educational Activities of Negro Literary Societies, 1828–1846," *Journal of Negro Education* 5 (1936), 555–76; Dorothy Porter, comp., *Early Negro Writing, 1760–1837* (Boston: Beacon Press, 1971).

10. See Jeffrey C. Stewart, "Introduction," in *Narrative of Sojourner Truth* (New York: Oxford University Press, 1991), and Deborah Gray White, *Ar'n't I a Woman? Female Slaves in the Plantation South* (New York: Norton, 1985).

11. New work analyzing Black autobiographies includes William L. Andrews, *To Tell a Free Story: The First Century of Afro-American Autobiography, 1769–1865* (Urbana: University of Illinois Press, 1986); *Sisters of the Spirit: Three Black Women's Autobiographies of the Nineteenth Century,* ed. William L. Andrews (Bloomington: Indiana University Press, 1986); Houston A. Baker, Jr., *Blues, Ideology, and Afro-American Literature: A Vernacular Theory* (Chicago: University of Chicago Press, 1984); *The Slave's Narrative,* ed. Charles T. Davis and Henry Louis Gates, Jr. (New York: Oxford University Press, 1985); the multivolume *Schomburg Library of Nineteenth Century Black Women Writers* (New York: Oxford University Press); and Henry Louis Gates, Jr., *The Signifying Monkey: A Theory of Afro-American Literary Criticism* (New York: Oxford University Press, 1988).

12. See Andrew L. Williams, "A Monumental Effort," *Upstate Magazine, Rochester Sunday Democrat and Chronicle,* 3 June 1990. For more information on the preservation of the Douglass home, see Jacqueline A. Goggin, *Carter G. Woodson and the Movement to Promote Black History* (Ph.D. diss., University of Rochester, 1983). Additional information was collected in the author's 1984 interviews in Washington with staff of the National Park Service, including Tyra Walker, curator of the Frederick Douglass Home, and Marilyn Nickels, historian for Capitol Parks East. See also Fath Davis Ruffins, "The Historic House Museum as History Text: The Frederick Douglass Home at Cedar Hill," paper delivered to the Museum Education Program, George Washington University, Washington, D.C., 9 Oct. 1984. For general works on Frederick Douglass, see Frederick Douglass, *Life and Times of Frederick Douglass* (Boston: De Wolfe Fiske, 1892), and his *My Bondage and My Freedom* (New York: Miller, Orton, and Mulligan, 1855). See also Nathan Irvin Huggins, *Slave and Citizen: The Life of Frederick Douglass* (Boston: Little, Brown, 1980); Dickson J. Preston, *Young Frederick Douglass: The Maryland Years* (Baltimore: Johns Hopkins University Press, 1985); and Waldo E. Martin, Jr., *The Mind of Frederick Douglass* (Chapel Hill: University of North Carolina Press, 1984).

13. Byron Rushing, "Black Schools in White Boston, 1800–1860," in James W. Fraser, Henry L. Allen, and Nancy Barnes, eds., *From Common School to*

Magnet School: Selected Essays in the History of Boston Schools (Boston: Trustees of the Public Library of the City of Boston, 1979). For more information on William C. Nell, see his works: "Colored American Patriots," *The Anglo-African* 1 (1860), 30–31; *The Colored Patriots of the American Revolution, with Sketches of Several Distinguished Colored Persons* (Boston: R. F. Wallcut, 1855); and "Triumph of the Equal School Rights in Boston" (Boston: R. F. Wallcut, 1856). This last is a pamphlet containing the proceedings of the Presentation Meeting held in Boston on 17 December 1855, and is available at the Moorland-Spingarn Research Center, Howard University.

14. The international slave trade was banned in the United States in 1808, by an act of Congress. While a number of Africans continued to be brought into the United States illegally until the eve of the Civil War, the vast majority of Africans were brought to the United States before 1808. For more information on the importation of Africans, see Robert Anstey, "The Volume of the North American Slave Carrying Trade from Africa, 1761–1810," *Revue française d'histoire d'outre-mer* 12, nos. 226–27 (1975), 47–66; Philip Curtin, *The Atlantic Slave Trade* (Madison: University of Wisconsin Press, 1969); J. E. Inikori, "Measuring the Atlantic Slave Trade: An Assessment of Curtin and Anstey," *Journal of African History* 17, no. 4 (1976), 607–27; James Rawley, *The Transatlantic Slave Trade: A History* (New York: Norton, 1981).

15. Sylvia M. Jacobs, *The African Nexus: Black American Perspectives on the European Partitioning of Africa, 1880–1920* (Westport, Conn.: Greenwood, 1981); Lillie M. Johnson, "Black American Missionaries in Colonial Africa, 1900–1940" (Ph.D. diss., University of Chicago, 1981).

16. For more information on William Sheppard, see Harold G. Cureau, "William H. Sheppard, Missionary to the Congo and Collector of African Art," *Journal of Negro History* 67, no. 4 (1982), 340–52; Larryetta L. Schall, "William H. Sheppard: Fighter for African Rights," in Keith L. Schall, ed., *Stony the Road: Chapters in the History of Hampton Institute* (Charlottesville: University Press of Virginia, 1977); and William H. Sheppard, *Presbyterian Pioneers in Congo* (Richmond: Presbyterian Committee of Publication, 1917).

17. Jeanne Zeidler, director of the University Museum, Hampton University, Hampton, Virginia, telephone interview with author, 14 Dec. 1984.

18. The term "Black Victorians" was originated by Jeffrey Stewart. For more information on this group, see Jeffrey C. Stewart, "Alain Locke and Georgia Douglas Johnson: Washington Patrons of Afro-American Modernism," in David McAleavey, ed., *Washington and Washington Writing* (Washington, D.C.: Center for Washington Area Studies, George Washington University, 1986).

19. George M. Frederickson, *The Black Image in the White Mind: The Debate on Afro-American Character and Destiny, 1817–1914* (New York: Harper and Row, 1971); Jordan, *White Over Black;* Guy C. McElroy, *Facing*

History: The Black Image in American Art, 1710–1940 (San Francisco: Bedford Arts, 1990).

20. For more on theories of race, see Thomas F. Gossett, *Race: The History of an Idea in America* (Dallas: Southern Methodist University Press, 1963); George W. Stocking, *Race, Culture, and Evolution: Essays in the History of Anthropology* (New York: Free Press, 1968); and George W. Stocking, *Victorian Anthropology* (New York: Free Press, 1987).

21. For more on Social Darwinism, see John Higham, *Strangers in the Land: Patterns of American Nativism, 1860–1925* (New York: Atheneum, 1973), and his *Send These to Me: Jews and Other Immigrants in Urban America* (New York: Atheneum, 1975).

22. The Smithsonian is the earliest American museum still in operation. Charles Willson Peale's museum was founded somewhat earlier, but eventually failed; his son Raphaelle Peale founded a successor museum in Baltimore.

23. In recent years, the study of re-presentation in museums has been energized by a number of new analyses, especially from scholars trained in anthropology, archaeology, folklore, art, and history. Some relevant works on this subject include: Susan Porter Benson, Steven Brier, and Roy Rosenzweig, eds., *Presenting the Past: Critical Perspectives on History and the Public* (Philadelphia: Temple University Press, 1986); James Clifford, "On Ethnographic Surrealism," *Comparative Studies in Society and History* 23, no. 4 (1981), 539–64; Daniel Defert, "The Collection of the World: Accounts of Voyages from the Sixteenth to the Eighteenth Centuries," *Dialectical Anthropology* 7, no. 1 (1982), 11–20; Peter Gathercole and David Lowenthal, eds., *The Politics of the Past* (London: Unwin Hyman, 1990); Donna Haraway, "Teddy Bear Patriarchy: Taxidermy in the Garden of Eden, New York City, 1908–1936," *Social Text* 11 (1984–85); Neil Harris, "Museums, Merchandising, and Popular Taste: The Struggle for Influence," in Ian M. G. Quimby, ed., *Material Culture and the Study of American Life* (New York: Norton, 1978); Curtis T. Hinsley, "The World as Marketplace: Commodification of the Exotic at the World's Columbian Exposition, Chicago, 1893," in Ivan Karp and Steven D. Lavine, eds., *Exhibiting Cultures* (Washington, D.C.: Smithsonian Institution Press, 1991); Warren Leon and Roy Rosenzweig, eds., *History Museums in the United States: A Critical Assessment* (Urbana: University of Illinois Press, 1989); André Malraux, *Museum Without Walls,* trans. Stuart Gilbert and Francis Price (Garden City, N.Y.: Doubleday, 1967); Roderick Nash, "The Exporting and Importing of Nature: Nature-Appreciation as a Commodity, 1850–1980," *Perspectives in American History* 12 (1979), 517–60; Roderick Nash, *Wilderness and the American Mind,* 3d ed. (New Haven: Yale University Press, 1982); and Ruffins, "The Exhibition as Form."

24. The Bureau of American Ethnology tilted against the general activities of the United States National Museum, but ultimately was unsuccessful in changing the collecting trends of the Smithsonian.

25. The collection of Louis Agassiz eventually became part of the Peabody Museum at Harvard University. The National Museum's collections are now part of the Department of Anthropology in the National Museum of Natural History, Smithsonian Institution. For more information on this, see Michael L. Blakely, "American Nationality and Ethnicity in the Depicted Past," in Peter Gathercole and David Lowenthal, eds., *The Politics of the Past* (London: Unwin Hyman, 1990), and Michael L. Blakely, "Skull Doctors: Intrinsic Social and Political Bias in the History of American Physical Anthropology," *Critique of Anthropology* 7, no. 2 (1987), 7–35.

26. Carol Duncan and Alan Wallach, "The Universal Survey Museum," *Art History* 3, no. 4 (1980).

27. This phrase is used by the Library of Congress in most of its official guides. For more information on Ainsworth C. Spofford, see *Librarians of Congress, 1802–1974* (Washington, D.C.: Government Printing Office, 1977).

28. For more information on Daniel Alexander Payne Murray and other early African American librarians, see E. J. Josey and Ann Allen Shockley, eds., *Handbook of Black Librarianship* (Littleton, Co.: Libraries Unlimited, 1977). See also E. J. Josey, ed., *The Black Librarian in America* (Metuchen, N.J.: Scarecrow, 1970).

29. Deborah Newman Ham, curator of the Afro-American Collection, Manuscripts Division, Library of Congress, interview with author, 7 Mar. 1990.

30. Annette L. Phinazee, ed., *The Black Librarian in the Southeast* (Durham: School of Library Science, North Carolina Central University, 1980).

31. Brown served under the first three secretaries of the Smithsonian: Joseph Henry, 1846–1878; Spencer F. Baird, 1878–1887; and Samuel P. Langley, 1887–1906. There is material concerning Brown in the Smithsonian Archives and in the Washingtonia section of the Martin Luther King Library, Washington, D.C. For more information on Solomon Brown, see *"Kind Regards of S. G. Brown": Selected Poems of Solomon G. Brown,* comp. Louise Daniel Hutchinson and Gail Sylvia Lowe (Washington, D.C.: Smithsonian Institution Press, 1983). Other material came from Louise Daniel Hutchinson, head of the Research Dept., Anacostia Neighborhood Museum, in an interview with Jeffrey Stewart and the author, 13 Nov. 1984.

32. For more information on the ideas that white abolitionists held about African Americans, see George Fredrickson, *The Inner Civil War: Northern Intellectuals and the Crisis of the Union* (New York: Harper and Row, 1965).

33. For more on the Black Victorians and examples of their lives, see Irving Bartlett, *From Slave to Citizen: The Story of the Negro in Rhode Island* (Providence: Urban League of Greater Providence, 1984); Stephen Birmingham, *Certain People: A Black Elite* (New York: Little, Brown, 1977); Du

Bois, *The Philadelphia Negro;* James Oliver Horton and Lois E. Horton, *Black Bostonians: Family Life and Community Struggle in the Antebellum North* (New York: Holmes and Meier, 1979); Louise Daniel Hutchinson, *Anna J. Cooper: A Voice from the South* (Washington, D.C.: Smithsonian Institution Press, 1981); Gail Lumet Buckley, *The Hornes: An American Family* (New York: Knopf, 1986); Kenneth R. Manning, *Black Apollo of Science: The Life of Ernest Everett Just* (New York: Oxford University Press, 1983); and Gilbert Ware, *William Hastie: Grace Under Pressure* (New York: Oxford University Press, 1984). For more on the origins of Black Victorians, see William D. Piersen, *Black Yankees: The Development of an Afro-American Subculture in Eighteenth-Century New England* (Amherst: University of Massachusetts Press, 1988).

34. For more information on the Great Migration, see St. Clair Drake and Horace Cayton, *Black Metropolis: A Study of Life in a Northern City* (New York: Harcourt, Brace, 1945); Florette Henry, *Black Migration: Movement North, 1900–1920* (Garden City, N.Y.: Anchor, 1975); Claude McKay, *Harlem: Negro Metropolis* (New York: Harcourt Brace Jovanovich, 1968); Gilbert Osofsky, *Harlem: The Making of a Ghetto: Negro New York, 1890–1930* (New York: Harper and Row, 1966); Roi Ottley and William J. Weatherby, eds., *The Negro in New York: An Informal Social History, 1626–1940* (New York: Praeger, 1969); Allan H. Spear, *Black Chicago: The Making of a Negro Ghetto, 1890–1920* (Chicago: University of Chicago Press, 1967); William M. Tuttle, Jr., *Race Riot: Chicago in the Red Summer of 1919* (New York: Atheneum, 1970).

35. I am indebted to Jeffrey Stewart for many conversations over a number of years about Alain Locke and the circle of Black intellectuals, artists, and activists of the Harlem Renaissance. See Jeffrey C. Stewart, *A Biography of Alain Locke: Philosopher of the Harlem Renaissance* (Ph.D. dissertation, Yale University, 1979).

36. *The Critical Temper of Alain Locke: A Selection of His Essays on Art and Culture,* ed. Jeffrey C. Stewart (New York: Garland, 1983); Jeffrey C. Stewart, ed., *Race Context: A Study of the Theory and Practice of Race in Five Lectures* (Washington, D.C.: Howard University Press, 1992).

37. Edward Said, *Orientalism* (New York: Pantheon, 1978).

38. For more information on the Harlem Renaissance, see Jervis Anderson, *This Was Harlem: A Cultural Portrait, 1900–1950* (New York: Farrar, Straus, Giroux, 1981); Arna Bontemps, ed., *The Harlem Renaissance Remembered* (New York: Dodd, Mead, 1972); Harold Cruse, *The Crisis of the Negro Intellectual* (New York: William Morrow, 1967); David Levering Lewis, *When Harlem Was in Vogue* (New York: Knopf, 1981); Nathan Irvin Huggins, *Harlem Renaissance* (New York: Oxford University Press, 1971); and Nathan Irvin Huggins, ed., *Voices from the Harlem Renaissance* (New York:

Oxford University Press, 1976). On cultural strategies, see Houston A. Baker, Jr., *Modernism and the Harlem Renaissance* (Chicago: University of Chicago Press, 1987); David Levering Lewis, "Parallels and Divergences: Assimilationist Strategies of Black American and Jewish Elites, 1910–1930," *Journal of American History* 71, no. 3 (1984), 543–64; and Arnold Rampersad, *The Life of Langston Hughes,* 2 vols. (New York: Oxford University Press, 1988). Histories touching on the recording of "race records" in the 1920s are numerous. A great introduction to this literature appears in Eileen Southern, *The Music of Black Americans* (New York: Norton, 1971).

39. The discussion of the relationship of modern art in Europe and America to art forms created in Asia, Africa, and Oceania has a long and tangled history. For a detailed discussion of this, see William Rubin, ed., *"Primitivism" in 20th-Century Art: Affinity of the Tribal and the Modern* (New York: Museum of Modern Art, 1984).

40. The Studio Museum in Harlem, *Harlem Renaissance: Art of Black America* (New York: Studio Museum in Harlem, 1987); Gary A. Reynolds and Beryl J. Wright, *Against the Odds: African American Artists and the Harmon Foundation* (Newark, N.J.: Newark Museum, 1989).

41. Goggin, *Carter G. Woodson and the Movement to Promote Black History;* Jacqueline Goggin, "Banquet Address," Afro-American Historical and Genealogical Society conference, Washington, D.C., May 1990. I am indebted to Jacqueline Goggin for numerous conversations about Woodson and his work.

42. See the works of Carter G. Woodson, including *The African Background Outlined* (Washington, D.C.: Association for the Study of Negro Life and History, 1936); *African Heroes and Heroines* (Washington, D.C.: Associated, 1939); and *African Myths Together with Proverbs* (Washington, D.C.: Associated, 1928).

43. Thomas Battle, director, Moorland-Spingarn Research Center, Washington, D.C., interview with author, 19 Dec. 1984; Thomas Battle, "Research Centers Document the Black Experience," *History News* 36, no. 2 (Feb. 1981), 10–11; Dorothy Burnett Porter, "A Library on the Negro," *American Scholar* 7 (1938), 115–16; Dorothy Burnett Porter, "Library Sources for the Study of Negro Life and History," *Journal of Negro Education* 5 (1936), 232–44; Michael Winston, "Moorland-Spingarn Research Center: A Past Revisited, A Present Reclaimed," *New Directions* (newsletter published by the Moorland-Spingarn Research Center, Howard University), summer 1974. For more information on Jesse B. Moorland, see Jesse B. Moorland, *The Demand and the Supply of Increased Efficiency in the Negro Ministry* (New York: Arno, 1969). See also "The J. E. Moorland Foundation of the University Library," *Howard University Record* 10, no. 1 (1916), and Joseph H. Reason, "University Libraries," *Howard University Bulletin* 36 (15 Nov. 1957), 10–17.

44. Thomas Battle, director, Moorland-Spingarn Research Center, Washington, D.C., interview with author, 19 Dec. 1984

45. Harriet Jackson Scarupa, "The Energy-Charged Life of Dorothy Porter Wesley," *New Directions* 7, no. 1 (1990); Thomas Battle, director, Moorland-Spingarn Research Center, Washington, D.C., interview with author, 19 Dec. 1984.

46. Elinor Des Verney Sinnette, W. Paul Coates, and Thomas C. Battle, eds., *Black Bibliophiles and Collectors: Preservers of Black History* (Washington, D.C.: Howard University Press, 1990); Elinor Des Verney Sinnette, *Arthur Alfonso Schomburg, Black Bibliophile and Collector: A Biography* (Detroit: Wayne State University Press, 1989). Sinnette's book on Schomburg contains a great deal of information about the circle of collectors, bibliophiles, and Masons who made up the nucleus of Black collectors in the late nineteenth and early twentieth centuries and about the various cultural institutions they founded. Another work focused on a single individual but with a wide range of general information is Goggin, *Carter G. Woodson and the Movement to Promote Black History.*

47. Sinnette, *Arthur Alfonso Schomburg*; Howard Dodson, chief of the Schomburg Center for Research in Black Culture, New York Public Library, Astor, Lenox, and Tilden Foundations, telephone interview with author, 21 Dec. 1984.

48. Edmund Barry Gaither, "Survey of Afro-American Works in the Holdings of Historically Black Colleges and Universities" (Boston: National Center of Afro-American Artists, 1990).

49. For more information on Marcus Garvey, see Randall K. Burkett, *Garveyism as a Religious Movement: The Institutionalization of a Black Civil Religion* (Metuchen, N.J.: Scarecrow, 1978); Randall K. Burkett, *Black Redemption: Churchmen Speak for the Garvey Movement* (Philadelphia: Temple University Press, 1978); E. David Cronon, *Black Moses: The Story of Marcus Garvey and the Universal Negro Improvement Association* (Madison: University of Wisconsin Press, 1955); Robert A. Hill, ed., *The Marcus Garvey and Universal Negro Improvement Association Papers,* 7 vols. (Berkeley: University of California Press, 1983–); Tony Martin, *Race First: The Ideological and Organizational Struggles of Marcus Garvey and the Universal Negro Improvement Association* (Westport, Conn.: Greenwood, 1976); Wilson J. Moses, *The Golden Age of Black Nationalism, 1850–1925* (Hamden, Conn.: Archon, 1978); and Judith Stein, *The World of Marcus Garvey: Race and Class in Modern Society* (Baton Rouge: Louisiana State University Press, 1986). For connections between Garvey and succeeding movements, see Horace Campbell, *Rasta and Resistance from Marcus Garvey to Walter Rodney* (Trenton: Africa World Press, 1987); and Edwin S. Redkey, *Black Exodus: Black Nationalist and Back-to-Africa Movements, 1890–1910* (New Haven: Yale University Press, 1969).

50. Peter Thomas Bartis, *A History of the Archive of Folk Song at the Library of Congress: The First Fifty Years* (Ph.D. diss., University of Pennsylvania, 1982). All information about the history of the Archive at the Library of Congress and the work of the Lomaxes was gleaned from this dissertation.

51. Bartis, *A History of the Archive of Folk Song at the Library of Congress.*

52. See also Zora Neale Hurston, *I Love Myself When I Am Laughing,* ed. Alice Walker (Old Westbury, N.Y.: Feminist Press, 1979), and Zora Neale Hurston, *Mules and Men* (New York: Harper and Row, 1970).

53. On "niggerati," see Robert Hemenway, *Zora Neale Hurston: A Literary Biography* (Urbana: University of Illinois Press, 1977), 43–44, 56, 70, 121. On Sterling Brown, see Sterling A. Brown, Arthur P. Davis, and Ulysses Lee, *The Negro Caravan: Writings by American Negroes* (New York: Dryden, 1941), and Sterling A. Brown, *Southern Road* (Boston: Beacon, 1974 [1932]). For more information on Paul Robeson, see Rebecca Larsen, *Paul Robeson: Hero Before His Time* (New York: Franklin Watts, 1989); Martin Duberman, *Paul Robeson* (New York: Knopf, 1988); Paul Robeson, *Here I Stand* (Boston: Beacon, 1971); and Susan Robeson, *The Whole World in His Hands: A Pictorial Biography of Paul Robeson* (Secaucus, N.J.: Citadel, 1981).

54. Huddie Ledbetter, a.k.a. Leadbelly, is a legendary figure in the history of the blues in America. For more information on Ledbetter's place in American musical history, see Southern, *Music of Black Americans.* See also Samuel B. Charters, *The Country Blues* (New York: Rinehart, 1959); David Evans, *Big Road Blues: Tradition and Creativity in Folk Blues* (Berkeley: University of California Press, 1982); William Ferris, *Blues from the Delta* (Garden City, N.Y.: Anchor/Doubleday, 1978); Albert Murray, *Stomping the Blues* (New York: McGraw-Hill, 1976); and Robert Palmer, *Deep Blues* (New York: Penguin, 1986).

55. Harold Courlander, *Negro Folk Music, U.S.A.* (New York: Columbia University Press, 1963); Harold Courlander, *Negro Songs from Alabama,* 2d ed. (New York: Oak Publications, 1963).

56. Anthony Seeger, director, Folkways Records Archives, Smithsonian Institution, interview with author, May 1990; Ralph Rinzler, assistant secretary for public service emeritus, Smithsonian Institution, interview with author, 14 Sept. 1990. Rinzler, who had known Asch for years, was instrumental in securing the collection for the Smithsonian Institution.

57. Ralph Rinzler, assistant secretary for public service emeritus, Smithsonian Institution, interviews with author, 26 June 1990 and 14 Sept. 1990.

58. For more information on the Federal Writers' Project, see Bartis, *A History of the Archive of Folk Song at the Library of Congress; Lay My Burden Down: A Folk History of Slavery,* ed. B. A. Botkin (Chicago: University of Chicago Press, 1945); George P. Rawick, ed., *The American Slave: A*

Composite Autobiography, 19 vols. (Westport, Conn.: Greenwood, 1972) and later supplements published under the same title in 1977 and 1979.

59. Historians who have used the Federal Writers' Project works include Eugene Genovese, *Roll, Jordan, Roll: The World the Slaves Made* (New York: Pantheon, 1974); Herbert Gutman, *The Black Family in Slavery and Freedom, 1750–1925* (New York: Vintage, 1976); and Lawrence W. Levine, *Black Culture and Black Consciousness: Afro-American Folk Thought from Slavery to Freedom* (New York: Oxford University Press, 1977).

60. National Archives of the United States, *General Information Leaflet,* no. 1 (Washington, D.C.: National Archives and Records Administration, 1986); Deborah Newman Ham, curator of the Afro-American Collection, Manuscripts Division, Library of Congress, interview with author, 7 Mar. 1990.

61. Deborah Newman Ham, curator of the Afro-American Collection, Manuscripts Division, Library of Congress, telephone interview with author, 22 June 1990. Newman Ham was formerly an archivist at the National Archives, working on Afro-American materials. She produced several important published collections guides, and was particularly interested in the history of Black participation in the federal government in the twentieth century.

62. Michael Wallace, "Visiting the Past: History Museums in the United States" and "Reflections on the History of Historic Preservation," in Susan Porter Benson, Steven Brier, and Roy Rosenzweig, eds., *Presenting the Past: Critical Perspectives on History and the Public* (Philadelphia: Temple University Press, 1986); Rex Ellis, vice president for African American interpretation, Colonial Williamsburg Foundation, telephone interview with author, 12 Oct. 1990.

63. Portia James, *The Real McCoy: African-American Invention and Innovation, 1619–1930* (Washington, D.C.: Smithsonian Institution Press, 1989).

64. Judith Wragg Chase, *Afro-American Art and Craft* (New York: Van Nostrand Reinhold, 1971). I am also indebted to Chase for a number of detailed conversations we had about the history of her collection when I was in the process of negotiating loans from the Old Slave Mart Museum to the National Museum of American History, Smithsonian Institution, for the exhibition After the Revolution: Everyday Life in America, 1780–1800. These conversations took place at the museum and in her home in Charleston and by phone during 1984 and 1985.

65. There is an extensive literature on what is African in African American life; it has grown dramatically in the last fifteen years. However, an early scholar interested in these questions was Melville Herskovits. For more information, see Walter Jackson, "Melville Herskovits and the Search for Afro-American Culture," in George W. Stocking, Jr., ed., *Malinowski, Rivers, Benedict and Others: Essays on Culture and Personality,* History of Anthropology, vol. 4 (Madison: University of Wisconsin Press, 1986), and James W.

Fernandez, "Tolerance in a Repugnant World and Other Dilemmas in the Cultural Relativism of Melville J. Herskovits," *Ethos* 18, no. 2 (1990). Herskovits's books include *Acculturation: A Study of Culture Contact* (Gloucester, Mass.: P. Smith, 1958); *The American Negro: A Study of Racial Crossing* (Bloomington: Indiana University Press, 1964 [1928]); *Dahomey: An Ancient West African Kingdom,* 2 vols. (Evanston: Northwestern University Press, 1967 [1938]); *Life in a Haitian Valley* (New York: Knopf, 1937); *The Myth of the Negro Past* (New York: Harper, 1941); with Frances S. Herskovits, *Rebel Destiny: Among the Bush Negroes of Dutch Guiana* (New York: McGraw-Hill, 1934); and with Frances S. Herskovits, *Suriname Folk-lore* (New York: AMS, 1969 [1936]). Important articles include his contribution to Alain Locke's special issue of *Survey Graphic* on "The New Negro" in 1925, and "What Has Africa Given America?" *New Republic* 84, no. 1083 (1935).

66. The history of the civil rights movement is voluminous. Some important volumes include: Taylor Branch, *Parting the Waters: America in the King Years, 1954–1963* (New York: Simon and Schuster, 1988); Clayborne Carson, *In Struggle: SNCC and the Black Awakening of the 1960s* (Cambridge, Mass.: Harvard University Press, 1981); Septima Poinsette Clark with Le Gette Blythe, *Echo in My Soul* (Boston: E. P. Dutton, 1962); James Farmer, *Lay Bare the Heart: An Autobiography of the Civil Rights Movement* (New York: Arbor House, 1985); James Forman, *The Making of Black Revolutionaries: A Personal Account* (New York: Macmillan, 1972); David J. Garrow, *Bearing the Cross: Martin Luther King, Jr., and the Southern Christian Leadership Conference* (New York: William Morrow, 1986); Martin Luther King, Jr., *Stride Towards Freedom: A Leader of His People Tells the Montgomery Story* (New York: Harper, 1958); Martin Luther King, Jr., *Why We Can't Wait* (New York: Harper and Row, 1964); Mary King, *Freedom Song: A Personal Story of the 1960s Civil Rights Movement* (New York: William Morrow, 1987); Richard Kluger, *Simple Justice: The History of Brown vs. Board of Education and Black America's Struggle for Equality* (New York: Knopf, 1976); Genna Rae MacNeil, *Groundwork: Charles Hamilton Houston and the Struggle for Civil Rights* (Philadelphia: University of Pennsylvania Press, 1983); James Meredith, *Three Years in Mississippi* (Bloomington: Indiana University Press, 1966); Aldon D. Morris, *The Origins of the Civil Rights Movement: Black Communities Organizing for Change* (New York: Free Press, 1984); Howell Raines, *My Soul is Rested: Movement Days in the Deep South Remembered* (New York: Putnam, 1977); Wyatt Tee Walker, *"Somebody's Calling My Name": Black Sacred Music and Social Change* (Valley Forge, Penn.: Judson, 1979); and Juan Williams, *Eyes on the Prize: America's Civil Rights Years, 1954–1965* (New York: Viking, 1987). See also the 1987 six-part video series *Eyes on the Prize,* produced by Henry Hampton and distributed by Blackside.

67. *Profile of Black Museums* (Washington, D.C.: African American Museums Association, 1988).

68. For more information, see Bob Blauner, *Black Lives, White Lives: Three Decades of Race Relations in America* (Berkeley: University of California Press, 1990).

69. Garrow, *Bearing the Cross*; see also David Garrow, "Martin Luther King, Jr., and the Spirit of Leadership" and Cornel West, "The Religious Foundations of the Thought of Martin Luther King," both in Peter J. Albert and Ronald Hoffman, eds., *We Shall Overcome: Martin Luther King, Jr., and the Black Freedom Struggle* (New York: Pantheon, 1990).

70. During the 1970s and 1980s, feminist and womanist critiques of the civil rights movement and the Black Power movement emerged. Key texts in this debate include Toni Cade Bambara, comp., *The Black Woman* (New York: New American Library, 1970); Toni Cade Bambara, *Gorilla, My Love* (New York: Random House, 1972); Toni Cade Bambara, *The Seabirds Are Still Alive* (New York: Random House, 1977); Toni Cade Bambara, *The Salt Eaters* (New York: Random House, 1980); Lorraine Bethel and Barbara Smith, "The Black Women's Issue," *Conditions* 5 (1978); Angela Y. Davis, *Women, Race, and Class* (New York: Random House, 1981); Bell Hooks, *Ain't I a Woman: Black Women and Feminism* (Boston: South End Press, 1981); Gloria T. Hall, Patricia Bell Scott, and Barbara Smith, eds., *All the Women Are White, All the Blacks are Men, But Some of Us Are Brave* (Boston: Kitchen Table Press, 1982); Barbara Smith, ed., *Home Girls: A Black Feminist Anthology* (New York: Kitchen Table–Women of Color Press, 1983); Barbara Smith, *Toward a Black Feminist Criticism* (New York: Out and Out, 1980); Michele Wallace, *Black Macho and the Myth of the Superwoman* (New York: Dial, 1979).

71. For more on the Black aesthetic, see Conference of Negro Writers, *The American Negro Writer and His Roots, Selected Papers* (New York: American Society of African Culture, 1960); Baker, *Blues, Ideology and Afro-American Literature;* Houston A. Baker, Jr., *The Journey Back: Issues in Black Literature and Criticism* (Chicago: University of Chicago Press, 1980); Dexter Fisher and Robert B. Stepto, eds., *Afro-American Literature: The Reconstruction of Instruction* (New York: Modern Language Association of America, 1979); Addison Gayle, Jr., comp., *The Black Aesthetic* (Garden City, N.Y.: Doubleday, 1971); Stephen Henderson, *Understanding the New Black Poetry: Black Speech and Black Music as Poetic References* (New York: William Morrow, 1973); Stephen Henderson, "Saturation: Progress Report on a Theory of Black Poetry," *Black World* (Oct. 1972); LeRoi Jones, *Blues People: Negro Music in White America* (New York: William Morrow, 1963); LeRoi Jones and Larry Neal, eds., *Black Fire: An Anthology of Afro-American Writing* (New York: William Morrow, 1968); Houston A. Baker, Jr., *Reading Black: Essays in the Criticism of African, Caribbean, and Black American Literature* (Ithaca, N.Y.: Africana Studies and Research Center, Cornell University, 1976); and National Conference of Afro-American Writers, *Theme:*

The Image of Black Folk in American Literature (Washington, D.C.: Howard University, 1974).

72. For more on Reconstruction and its rhetorical relationship to the modern civil rights movement, see Vincent Harding, *The Other American Revolution* (Los Angeles: Center for Afro-American Studies, University of California), and Eric Foner, *Reconstruction: America's Unfinished Revolution, 1863–1877* (New York: Harper and Row, 1988).

73. Though there is not space in this article to detail it, the slogan "Black Power" had multiple expressions and meanings, particularly in relationship to the concepts of freedom and integration. In some instances, it may have meant absolute separation; in others, it spanned the spectrum from community-based control of schools to Black capitalism. Those who wanted to emigrate to Africa represented yet another interpretation. Another interpretation motivated a group of Yoruba-influenced African Americans to establish a village in Sheldon, South Carolina. Somewhat similar in rhetoric to other counter-cultural communes founded in the rural South in the 1960s and 1970s such as The Farm, the Oyotunji Village community is meant to be a separate Black nation in which there is strict adherence to an interpretation of a West African culture in the twentieth century. See Carl Monroe Hunt, *Oyotunji Village: The Yoruba Movement in America* (Washington, D.C.: University Press of America, 1979). These variations on the theme of separation and integration—each with its own literature and specific rhetoric—are critical in the history of Black cultural institutions in the Black Consciousness Era. These narratives and texts constitute the interior voices of recent African American culture. I am much indebted here to a series of discussions on these questions during 1990 with James Early, assistant secretary for public service at the Smithsonian Institution.

74. For more on Malcolm X, see *Malcolm X Speaks: Selected Speeches and Statements,* ed. George Breitman (New York: Grove, 1966); Malcolm X with the assistance of Alex Haley, *The Autobiography of Malcolm X* (New York: Doubleday, 1967); and Malcolm X, *The End of White World Supremacy: Four Speeches,* ed. Benjamin Goodman (New York: Merlin, 1971). For more on the Nation of Islam and similar groups, see Albert B. Cleage, Jr., *The Black Messiah* (New York: Sheed and Ward, 1968); C. Eric Lincoln, *The Black Muslims in America* (Boston: Beacon, 1961); Wiley H. Ward, *Prophet of the Black Nation* (Philadelphia: Pilgrim, 1969); and Joseph R. Washington, Jr., *Black Sects and Cults* (Garden City, N.Y.: Anchor, 1973). On other spiritual leaders of the 1930s, see Robert Weisbrot, *Father Divine: The Utopian Evangelist of the Depression Era Who Became an American Legend* (Boston: Beacon, 1984).

75. Drusilla Dunjee Houston, *Wonderful Ethiopians of the Ancient Cushite Empire* (Oklahoma City: Universal, 1926). Some of Joel A. Rogers's best-

known works include *The Ku Klux Spirit* (New York: Messenger, 1923); *Nature Knows No Color-Line: Research into the Negro Ancestry in the White Race* (New York: H. M. Rogers, 1952); *100 Amazing Facts about the Negro: With Complete Proof; A Short Cut to the World History of the Negro* (New York: J.A. Rogers, 1934).

76. Molefi Kete Asante and Kariamu Welsh Asante, "Bibliographic Essay," in Molefi Kete Asante and Kariamu Welsh Asante, eds., *African Culture: The Rhythms of Unity* (Westport, Conn.: Greenwood, 1985), 258; Molefi Kete Asante, *Afrocentricity* (Trenton: Africa World Press, 1989), 6. Some seminal works on the subject of Afrocentricity are by Molefi Kete Asante. See, for example, Asante and Asante, eds., *African Culture: The Rhythms of Unity;* Asante, *Afrocentricity;* Molefi Kete Asante and Abdulai S. Vandi, eds., *Contemporary Black Thought: Alternative Analyses in Social and Behavioral Science* (Beverly Hills: Sage, 1980); and Molefi Kete Asante, *Kemet, Afrocentricity, and Knowledge* (Trenton: Africa World Press, 1990). As Arthur Lee Smith, Asante also wrote *Rhetoric of Black Revolution* (Boston: Allyn and Bacon, 1969) and numerous other works. See also Cheikh Anta Diop, *The African Origin of Civilization* (New York: Lawrence Hill, 1971); Yosef Ben Jochannon, *African Origins of the Major Western Religions* (New York: Al-kebu-Lan, 1970); Martin Bernal, *Black Athena: The Afroasiatic Roots of Classical Civilization:* Volume 1, *The Fabrication of Ancient Greece, 1785–1985* (New Brunswick, N.J.: Rutgers University Press, 1987); Frances Cress Welsing, "The Cress Theory of Color-Confrontation and Racism (White Supremacy): A Psycho-Genetic Theory and World Outlook," in Frances Cress Welsing, *The Isis (Yssis) Papers* (Chicago: Third World, 1991), and Na'im Akbar, *Chains and Images of Psychological Slavery* (Jersey City, N.J.: New Mind Publications, 1984).

77. For more on the history of Black museums, see Jeffrey C. Stewart and Fath Davis Ruffins, "A Faithful Witness: Afro-American Public History in Historical Perspective, 1828-1984," in Susan Porter Benson, Steven Brier, and Roy Rosenzweig, eds., *Presenting the Past: Critical Perspectives on History and the Public* (Philadelphia: Temple University Press, 1986).

78. See Maulana Ron Karenga, *The African American Holiday of Kwanzaa: A Celebration of Family, Community, and Culture* (Los Angeles: University of Sankore Press, 1988). Kwanzaa is a mixture of a large number of African elements. Within Black nationalist communities during the 1970s Swahili became the principal African language that was studied; however, the ethnic groups that they most often learned about were West African (especially the Yoruba, the Asante, and to a lesser extent the Fon). Karenga modeled Kwanzaa on West African first-fruits festivals, though in the 1988 revised edition of his book he mentions southern African festivals as well. This mingling of elements from across the continent provides a sense of the unity of African culture that is valued by many African Americans. Some Black femi-

nists have criticized the Kwanzaa rituals, though, because they provide no formal role for adult women.

79. On the history of the African American Museums Association: Joy Ford Austin, former executive director, African American Museums Association, telephone interview with author, 22 Dec. 1984; also a letter, conference brochure, and memoranda circulated to participants in the National Black History Museums Conference, Wayne State University, 27 Sept. 1969, furnished to me by James Mayo, acting co-director of the Anacostia Neighborhood Museum, in December 1990.

80. See also the following essays in Susan Porter Benson, Steven Brier, and Roy Rosenzweig, eds., *Presenting the Past: Critical Perspectives on History and the Public* (Philadelphia: Temple University Press, 1986): Linda Shopes, "Oral History and Community Involvement: The Baltimore Neighborhood Heritage Project"; Jeremy Brecher, "A Report on Doing History from Below: The Brass Workers History Project"; Lisa Duggan, "History's Gay Ghetto: The Contradictions of Growth in Lesbian and Gay History"; Sonya Michel, "Feminism, Film and Public History"; and James Green, "Engaging in People's History: The Massachusetts History Workshop."

81. For more on the collections and circumstances of Black museums, see *Profile of Black Museums*.

82. James Oliver Horton and Spencer R. Crew, "Afro-American Museums: Toward a Policy of Inclusion," in Warren Leon and Roy Rosenzweig, eds., *History Museums in the United States: A Critical Assessment* (Urbana: University of Illinois Press, 1989), 224. For more detailed information on the history of Black professionals and museums, see *Museums for a New Century* (Washington, D.C.: American Association of Museums, 1984); Joan Sandler, "Minority Art Museum Professionals in Northeastern and Mid-Atlantic States: An Exploratory Study of Their Problems and Needs" (New York: Division of Education Services, Metropolitan Museum of Art, 1987); and Howardena Pindall's testimony delivered at the Agenda for Survival conference at Hunter College, New York, June 1987.

83. Horton and Crew, "Afro-American Museums."

84. Rex Ellis, vice president for African American interpretation, Colonial Williamsburg, telephone interview with author, 12 Oct. 1990. For more information on Colonial Williamsburg and its history of Black programming, see Rex Ellis, "A Decade of Change: Black History at Colonial Williamsburg," *Colonial Williamsburg,* spring 1990, 14–25; Harold Gill, "The Distress of Sam and Caty," *Colonial Williamsburg,* spring 1990, 26–29; Zora Martin, "Colonial Williamsburg—A Black Perspective," in Susan K. Nichols, ed., *Museum Education Roundtable, 1973–1983: Perspectives on Informal Learning—A Decade of Roundtable Reports* (Washington, D.C.: 1984); and Edgar A. Toppin, "Setting the Record Straight: African American History," *Colonial*

Williamsburg, spring 1990, 10–12. See also *On Myne Own Time,* a video produced by the Program in African American Interpretation detailing the complications of producing live interpretations at Colonial Williamsburg; this is available from the Colonial Williamsburg Foundation.

85. Ralph Rinzler, assistant secretary for public service emeritus, Smithsonian Institution, interviews with author 26 June 1990 and 14 Sept. 1990.

86. Various versions of this meeting were recounted to the author during interviews with John Kinard, Ralph Rinzler, James Mayo, James Early, Zora Martin Felton, and Bernice Johnson Reagon.

87. Dillon Ripley, *The Sacred Grove: Essays on Museums* (New York: Simon and Schuster, 1969).

88. Ralph Rinzler, interview with author.

89. As many of my informants for this essay pointed out, Reagon was actually hired by Gerald Davis, who was then the assistant director of the overall festival. In this position, he was an early example of a high-level Black staff member at the Smithsonian. He originated the idea of bringing in non-Smithsonian scholars to work on the festival. After several internal disputes, however, he resigned, and Reagon took charge of the African Diaspora Festival Project. All descriptions of the growth and development of the Festival of American Folklife and the Program in Black American Culture have emerged from the author's interviews with Bernice Johnson Reagon, curator, Division of Community Life, National Museum of American History, Smithsonian Institution, 27 Aug. 1990 and 18 Sept. 1990; James Early, assistant secretary for public service, Smithsonian Institution, 28 Nov. 1990, 6 Dec. 1990, and 20 Dec. 1990; and Ralph Rinzler, 1990.

90. This event was described by Bernice Johnson Reagon in an interview with the author in 1990.

91. Rinzler, interviews with author, 1990.

92. The program's name was originally the Program in Black American Culture (PBAC). In 1990 it became the Program in African American Culture (PAAC). The audio and video tapes, transcripts, and papers of the PBAC have now been deposited in the Archives Center of the National Museum of American History, where they have been arranged and described for research purposes.

93. Bernice Johnson Reagon, interviews with author, 1990.

94. John Kinard, founding director, Anacostia Neighborhood Museum, Smithsonian Institution, Washington, D.C., interview with author, 11 Apr. 1985.

95. James Mayo, acting co-director, Anacostia Museum, interviews with author, 20 Nov. 1990, 7 Dec. 1990, 11 Dec. 1990; Louise Hutchinson, interview with Jeffrey C. Stewart and author, 1986; Zora Martin Felton, interview

with Jeffrey C. Stewart and author, 1986. For more information on the early history of the Anacostia Museum, see Ralph Tate, *Doodles and Dimensions* (Washington, D.C.: Smithsonian Institution, 1967); *Anacostia Neighborhood Museum, Smithsonian Institution, September 15, 1972* (Washington, D.C.: Smithsonian Institution, 1972) (this includes a profile of every staff member and some volunteers over the first five years, as well as a list of exhibitions held at the museum); and *The Anacostia Neighborhood Museum, 1967/1977* (Washington, D.C.: Smithsonian Institution, 1977) (this catalogue includes an almost complete record of exhibitions, held nearly every month for the first ten years of the museum's life).

96. Aspects of the internal history of collecting at the National Museum of American History were gleaned from numerous informal conversations between the author and key participants, such as Edith Mayo (one of the curators of the We the People exhibition) and Carl Scheele (principal curator for the exhibition A Nation of Nations), during the years in which the author was a historian and program manager in the Department of Social and Cultural History, NMAH (1981–1988). Additional information was developed by the Afro-American Index Project at the Smithsonian Institution. Principally directed by Theresa Singleton (who is now curator of historical anthropology at the National Museum of Natural History), this project has begun to document for the first time materials related to African Americans in the historical and anthropological bureaus of the Smithsonian. The exhibition Field to Factory: Afro-American Migration 1910–1940 was curated by Spencer Crew, now head of the Department of Social and Cultural History at NMAH. The author had numerous informal conversations with him about changes in NMAH over the last ten years.

97. Linda Hartigan, curator, National Museum of American Art, interview with author, 1 Mar. 1990.

98. Garrow, *Bearing the Cross.*

99. For a theoretical perspective blending mythos, memory, and history, see Vincent Harding, *Hope and History: Why We Must Share the Story of the Movement* (Maryknoll, N.Y.: Orbis, 1990).

100. James Early, interviews with author, 1990. People from a wide range of ethnic backgrounds have spoken at these annual celebrations. For a list see the pamphlet "Martin Luther King, Jr., Holiday Celebration" (Washington, D.C.: Cultural Education Committee, Smithsonian Institution, 1989).

101. In April 1991, after extensive internal and external debates, the Regents of the Smithsonian approved the idea of an African American museum on the Mall. As this essay goes to press, the U.S. Congress has not yet passed a bill authorizing funds to support such a museum. However, revised legislation on the matter is pending before several Congressional committees. Information about the history of this museum came from Claudine Brown, deputy assis-

tant secretary for museums, Smithsonian Institution, interviews with author, 27 Dec. 1990 and 8 Jan. 1991, as well as numerous informal conversations since.

The author learned about the history of the National Afro-American Museum and Cultural Center when she served as guest curator for that museum's inaugural exhibition, From Victory to Freedom: Afro-American Life in the Fifties, 1945–1965. From 1986 through 1988 the author had numerous informal conversations with longtime members of the staff, including John Fleming, founding director of NAAM; Juanita Moore, then head of the Education Department; Edna Harper, then head researcher at the museum; and Barbara Andrews, registrar.

Contributors

ARJUN APPADURAI is professor of anthropology at the University of Pennsylvania. He is author of *Worship and Conflict under Colonial Rule* and the editor of *The Social Life of Things*.

MARY JO ARNOLDI is associate curator of African ethnology at the National Museum of Natural History, Smithsonian Institution. She is the author of numerous articles on the arts of West African societies and is currently completing a monograph on youth association puppet masquerade in Mali.

CAROL BRECKENRIDGE is a lecturer at the University of Pennsylvania and the author of articles on Indian history and public culture.

MINDY DUITZ has been director of the Brooklyn Children's Museum since 1984. Prior to that she served for eight years as the first director of the Staten Island Children's Museum. She has served on the Task Force on Museum Education of the American Association of Museums and chairs the Association of Youth Museums Task Force on Standards.

NANCY J. FULLER is the research program manager of the Office of Museum Programs at the Smithsonian Institution. Her interest in exploring the educational potential of museums began at the National Museum in Bangkok in 1970.

EDMUND BARRY GAITHER is the director of the Museum of the National Center of Afro-American Artists and has been a leading spokesperson for Boston-area black artists for more than twenty-five years. He is co-founder of the African American Museums Association and is a consultant to the Museum of Fine Arts, Boston.

GUILLERMO GÓMEZ-PEÑA is an interdisciplinary artist and writer whose performance work focuses on United States–Mexico relations and border issues. He is co-editor of the bilingual arts magazine *The Broken Line/La Linea Quebrada*, a founding member of the Border Arts Workshop, and a regular contributor to the national radio program *Crossroads;* his performance work has been presented in many countries and has appeared in several films.

ALICIA M. GONZÁLES is director of the Smithsonian Institution's Quincentenary Programs. A folklorist, she is currently completing her book "Edible Baroque."

JANE PEIRSON JONES is keeper of archaeology and ethnography at the Birmingham Museum and Art Gallery. She has published on pre-Columbian ceramics and museology and is writing a book on museums in a multicultural society.

ADRIENNE L. KAEPPLER is curator of Oceanic ethnology at the National Museum of Natural History, Smithsonian Institution. She has carried out field research in Tonga,

Hawaii, and other parts of the Pacific. Her research focuses on the interrelationships between social structure and the arts, especially dance, music, and the visual arts.

IVAN KARP is curator of African ethnology in the Department of Anthropology at the National Museum of Natural History, Smithsonian Institution. He is the author of books and articles on social theory and East African societies and co-editor of *Exhibiting Cultures: The Poetics and Politics of Museum Display.* He is the author of a regular column for *American Art,* "Another Perspective."

CHRISTINE MULLEN KREAMER was from 1987 to 1990 a research associate in the Department of Anthropology, National Museum of Natural History, Smithsonian Institution. She has conducted extensive field research on art, ritual, and gender among the Moba of northern Togo; her research interests include cross-cultural aesthetics, proxemics, ritual performance, and gender distinctions in visual and performance arts. She was co-curator for the traveling exhibition Wild Spirits, Strong Medicine: African Art and the Wilderness and co-authored the exhibition catalogue of the same title.

JACK KUGELMASS is assistant professor of anthropology and folklore at the University of Wisconsin, Madison. He is the author of *The Miracle of Intervale Avenue,* co-author of *From a Ruined Gárden: The Memorial Books of Polish Jewry,* and editor of *Between Two Worlds: Ethnographic Essays on American Jewry.* He is currently working on a series of essays on the culture of New York City and a book on the rites of American Jewry.

ROBERT H. LAVENDA is professor of anthropology at St. Cloud State University. He has carried out field research in Caracas, Venezuela; Otavalo, Ecuador; and, for the last decade, around Minnesota on community festivals. He is co-author of a cultural anthropology text and has written about carnivals and festivals in Caracas and Minnesota. He is particularly interested in issues of irony, intentionality, carnival, and multiple voices in festivals and their communities.

STEVEN D. LAVINE is president of the California Institute of the Arts. Formerly associate director for arts and humanities at the Rockefeller Foundation, he is co-editor of *Exhibiting Cultures: The Poetics and Politics of Museum Display.*

MARK P. LEONE is professor of anthropology at the University of Maryland, College Park. Since 1981 he has also been the director of the interpretive program Archaeology in Public in Annapolis. Leone has written or edited four books, including *Contemporary Archaeology* and (with Parker B. Potter, Jr.) *The Recovery of Meaning.*

GEORGE F. MACDONALD is director of the Canadian Museum of Civilization and associate professor at Carleton University. He began his museum career as a field archaeologist for the Royal Ontario Museum and soon after for the National Museum of Man, where he also served as chief of the archaeology division. He has published extensively on the archaeology and anthropology of Pacific Coast Native American cultures, and is the author of *A Museum for the Global Village: The Canadian Museum of Civilization.*

CONSTANCE PERIN is a cultural anthropologist specializing in contemporary American social thought and practice. She has taught at Rice University and been a research associate at the Sloan School of Management of the Massachusetts Institute of Technology. Her book *Belonging in America: Reading Between the Lines* suggests what the study of cultural systems reveals about American society in particular and human behavior in general.

PARKER B. POTTER, JR., is the principal planner and director of publications for the New Hampshire Division of Historical Resources in Concord, New Hampshire; prior to that he was assistant director of Archaeology in Public in Annapolis. Potter's work on archaeological interpretation has appeared in *Current Anthropology, American Antiquity, The Journal of the Washington Academy of Sciences, American Archaeology,* and several edited volumes.

FATH DAVIS RUFFINS has been a historian at the National Museum of American History, Smithsonian Institution, for eleven years. For the last four years, she has been the head of the Collection of Advertising History in the Archives Center of the museum. She is currently at work on an exhibition and catalogue on ethnic imagery in American advertising, 1790–1990.

JOHN KUO WEI TCHEN is the acting director of the Asian/American Center at Queens College (CUNY) and a co-founder of the Chinatown History Project; he has served as chair of the New York Council for the Humanities. He has written and spoken on museums, representation and self-representation, race relations, immigration and migration, community-based knowledge, and cultural studies. His publications include *Genthe's Photographs of San Francisco's Old Chinatown,* and he edited and introduced Paul C. P. Siu's *The Chinese Laundryman: A Study of Social Isolation.*

EDITH A. TONELLI received her Ph.D. from Boston University in American studies and was director of the Wight Art Gallery and adjunct assistant professor in art history at the University of California, Los Angeles, from 1982 to 1991. She directed the exhibition project Chicano Art: Resistance and Affirmation, 1965–1985. Currently she is an independent consultant for curatorial and arts management projects in Los Angeles.

VERA L. ZOLBERG teaches in the Department of Sociology in the Graduate Faculty and the Eugene Lang College of the New School for Social Research. She is author of *Constructing a Sociology of Art,* and has written extensively on the sociology of art museums and other cultural institutions; art criticism; American and French cultural policy; and how these structures and practices contribute to the designation of works as art.